SUEZ 1956

D1381407

SUEZ 1956

The Crisis and its Consequences

EDITED BY

WM. ROGER LOUIS

AND

ROGER OWEN

CLARENDON PRESS · OXFORD

Oxford University Press, Walton Street, Oxford OX2 6DP
Oxford New York Toronto
Delhi Bombay Calcutta Madras Karachi
Petaling Jaya Singapore Hong Kong Tokyo
Nairobi Dar es Salaam Cape Town
Melbourne Auckland
and associated companies in
Berlin Ibadan

Oxford is a trade mark of Oxford University Press

Published in the United States
by Oxford University Press, New York

British Library Cataloguing in Publication Data
Suez 1956: the crisis and its consequences
1. Suez crisis
I. Louis, William Roger   II. Owen, Roger,
1935–
956'.044
ISBN 0-19-820241-5
Library of Congress Cataloging-in-Publication Data
Suez 1956 : the crisis and its consequences / edited by Wm. Roger
Louis and Roger Owen
Bibliography: p.   Includes index.
1. Egypt—History—Intervention, 1956.   2. Egypt—History-
-Intervention, 1956—Influence.   I. Louis, William Roger, 1936–
II. Owen, Edward Roger John.
DT107.83.S79   1989
962'.053—dc19   88–26995   CIP
ISBN 0-19-820241-5

Printed and bound in
Great Britain by Biddles Ltd
Guildford and King's Lynn

Foreword

WE are pleased to present a volume resulting from a collaborative effort of St Antony's College, Oxford, and the Woodrow Wilson International Center for Scholars in Washington, DC, during 1986 and 1987. The collaboration grew from a desire to combine our institutional strengths to reassess events believed by contemporaries to be of great significance in the history of Egypt, Israel, and the Middle East generally, in British and French decolonization, and in Anglo-American relations. Suez, 1956, was an emotional moment in the lives of many in Britain, in Egypt, and in Israel. After thirty years, new perspectives and new evidence could be brought to bear on the question: How far-reaching were the consequences of the Suez crisis?

The connecting links between our institutions were forged by Roger Louis and Roger Owen, the two editors of this volume. Both have long been interested in the Middle East, the former in Britain's control and influence, the latter in the economic and social history of the region itself. St Antony's College has, since its early years, been hospitable to scholars from the Middle East and has encouraged scholarship on its history and politics. The Wilson Center has appointed as Fellows many scholars concerned with Middle Eastern affairs and has conducted a number of conferences on Middle Eastern themes. Both our institutions have devoted much scholarly attention to Britain since 1945, and the Suez crisis was clearly one of the moments of greatest tension in the 'special relationship' between Britain and the United States.

The decision by Britain, France, and Israel to invade Egypt in late October–early November 1956 brought about as one of its consequences the responses of the United States and as another the response of the non-aligned nations to which Nasser appealed. By coincidence of timing with the Hungarian revolt in Budapest and the Soviet repression of it, the events of Suez may also have affected the ability of the Western powers to pursue a coherent policy towards the Soviet reaction to ferment in Eastern Europe. Thus, for a brief period of time Suez became the focal point of much international activity both within and without the United Nations.

We have drawn into this reflective review of the tumultuous months in late 1956 authors who possess a variety of perspectives and who come from countries principally involved in these events. The book is based on two conferences. The first was held at St Antony's in June 1986 and the second at the Wilson Center in September 1987. The participants included those in government service in 1956 who were able to recall the stress, emotions, deliberations, and judgements of the time as well as younger scholars who have studied the archives from the distance of thirty years. The discussions were designed to answer the following basic questions: Did the policies hammered out under emergency conditions lead ineluctably to other decisions, intended or unintended, in the Middle East, in the Maghrib, in Africa, or within the Commonwealth, or in the French overseas community, such that Suez must be regarded as a major turning-point? Or should we say with thirty years' perspective that it really was a tempest largely in an Anglo-Egyptian teapot which affected long-term policies to a surprisingly small extent?

We wish to thank the Ford Foundation which, by means of its support of the international programmes of the Wilson Center, made these conferences possible. We also extend our thanks to the Rhodes Trust and the St Antony's Trust of North America. Janice Tuten of the Wilson Center aided immeasurably with both the conferences and the book. Robert Stookey of the Center for Middle Eastern Studies at the University of Texas translated two of the essays from French and assisted with other editorial tasks. Mary Bull has given us invaluable assistance with the manuscript and has prepared the index.

April 1988

PROSSER GIFFORD
The Wilson Center
Washington

RALF DAHRENDORF
St Antony's College
Oxford

Contents

List of Contributors

MORDECHAI BAR-ON (Ph.D., Hebrew University) is Professor of International Affairs at the Hebrew University, Jerusalem. He rose to the rank of Colonel in the Israel Defence Forces, 1948–68, and has served as head of the Youth Department, World Zionist Organization, 1969–78. From 1984 to 1986 he was a Member of the Knesset. He is the author of *The Six Days War* and *Peace Now*. In 1956 he was military assistant to the Prime Minister of Israel, David Ben-Gurion.

LORD BELOFF (D.Litt., Oxford) is Emeritus Fellow, All Souls College, Oxford, former Gladstone Professor of Government and Public Administration at Oxford, and past Principal of University College at Buckingham. His books include a two-volume study of the British Empire and Commonwealth, *Imperial Sunset*, and *The United States and the Unity of Europe*. He is a Fellow of the British Academy and the Royal Historical Society, a Knight (1980), and, since 1981, a Life Peer. In 1956 he was a Fellow of Nuffield College, Oxford.

ROBERT R. BOWIE (JD, Harvard) is Clarence Dillon Professor of International Affairs, Emeritus, Harvard University, where he was also a Professor of Law, 1945–55, and Director of the Center for International Affairs, 1957–73. His public service includes the High Commission for Germany, 1950–1, the State Department, 1953–7 and 1966–8, and the Central Intelligence Agency, 1977–9, where he was Deputy Director for Intelligence. Among his books are *Shaping the Future* and *Suez 1956*. In 1956 he was Director of Policy Planning and Assistant Secretary at the State Department.

JOHN C. CAMPBELL (Ph.D., Harvard) has been Deputy Director of Eastern European Affairs and a member of the Policy Planning Staff of the State Department as well as Senior Fellow and Director of Studies at the Council on Foreign Relations. He is the author of a three-volume study of *The United States in World Affairs 1945–48*. His other books include *Defense of the Middle East*, *Tito's Separate Road*, and (with Helen Caruso), *The West and the Middle East*. In 1956 he was at the Council on Foreign Relations. Having concluded a study trip in the Middle East, he was in Israel on 29 October, in London on 30 October, and in New York on 1 November.

ALI E. HILLAL DESSOUKI (Ph.D., McGill) is Professor of Political Science and Director of the Centre for Political Research and Studies at Cairo University. He has been visiting professor at UCLA, Princeton, and the American University in Cairo. His books include *Islam and Power, Islamic Resurgence in the Arab World,* and *Foreign Policies of the Arab States.* In 1956 he was a student in Cairo.

HOWARD DOOLEY (Ph.D., Notre Dame) wrote his PhD. dissertation on the historiography of the Suez crisis. He is Professor of History and Assistant Dean of International Education at Western Michigan University. He is co-author of *Hesburgh's Notre Dame: Triumph in Transition.* His articles and reviews have appeared in *The Nation, The Progressive, The Middle East Journal,* and *The Review of Politics.* He is presently completing a book entitled *1956: The Year of No Return.* In 1956 he was in the seventh grade in Pittsburgh, Pennsylvania, and his first clear historical memories are those of the Suez crisis and the Hungarian revolution.

HERMANN EILTS (MA, Johns Hopkins) is Distinguished Professor of International Relations and Director of the Center for International Relations at Boston University. A career Foreign Service officer, he was US Officer-in-Charge, Baghdad Pact, 1957–9, Ambassador to Saudi Arabia, 1965–70, and Ambassador to Egypt, 1973–9. He holds the Department of State's Distinguished Honor Award and the Egyptian Collar of the Nile. In 1956 he was Chief of the Political Section in the US Embassy in Baghdad.

MICHAEL G. FRY (Ph.D., London) is Professor of International Relations at the University of Southern California. He was the Director of its School of International Relations, 1981–7. His books include *Despatches from Damascus: Gilbert MacKereth and British Policy in the Levant 1933–1939,* and *Lloyd George and Foreign Policy, 1890–1916.* He has been a Scholar-in-Residence at the Annenberg School of Communication, Washington, DC. In 1956 he was completing his undergraduate degree at the London School of Economics and contemplating the unavoidable prospect of military service.

SARVEPALLI GOPAL (D.Litt., Oxford) is Emeritus Professor of Contemporary History, Jawaharlal Nehru University, New Delhi, and Fellow of St Antony's College, Oxford. He was Director of the Historical Division of the Ministry of External Affairs, New Delhi, 1954–66, and Reader in South Asian History at Oxford, 1966–71. His books include a three-volume biography of *Jawaharlal Nehru.* In 1956 he was Director of the Historical Division of the Ministry of External Affairs.

AMIN HEWEDY (Graduate of the Military Academy in Cairo, Faculty of Journalism, Cairo University, and the Staff College, Leavenworth,

Kansas) served as Political Counsellor to President Nasser, Ambassador to Morocco and to Iraq, and as Minister of Defence, Minister of National Guidance, and Head of General Intelligence. He is the author (in Arabic) of *Arab National Security and the Israeli National Security, Nasser's Wars, the 1967 War, Henry Kissinger and International Security, Ambassador to Iraq* and *The Military Industry in Israel*. In 1956 he was Lieutenant-Colonel and Vice-Director of the Planning Section, Operational Department, General Staff of the Egyptian Armed Forces.

ALBERT HOURANI (MA, Oxford) is Emeritus Fellow, St Antony's College, Oxford. He is an Honorary Fellow of Magdalen College, Oxford, and an Honorary Member of the American Historical Association. In 1958 he became Director of the Middle East Centre at St Antony's. He was Reader in the Modern History of the Middle East at Oxford until 1979. His books include *Arabic Thought in the Liberal Age* and *The Emergence of the Modern Middle East*. In 1956 he was Visiting Professor at the American University of Beirut.

J. C. HUREWITZ (Ph.D., Columbia) is Emeritus Professor of Government at Columbia and was Director of its Middle East Institute, 1971–84. He was Senior Analyst on the Near East, in the Second World War, in the Office of Strategic Services and, after the war, in the Department of State. He was a Political Affairs Officer in 1949–50 in the United Nations Secretariat. His books include *The Struggle for Palestine, Middle East Dilemmas*, and *Middle East Politics: the Military Dimension*. In 1956 he was Professor of Government at Columbia.

RASHID I. KHALIDI (D.Phil., Oxford) is Associate Professor of Modern Middle Eastern History, University of Chicago. He has been Assistant Professor at the Lebanese University, and Associate Professor at the American University of Beirut and at Columbia University. He is the author of *British Policy toward Syria and Palestine*, and *Under Seige: PLO Decision-Making during the 1982 War*. He is the co-editor of *Palestine and the Gulf*. In 1956 he was a schoolboy. His father, at that time a member of the Political and Security Council Affairs Division of the UN Secretariat, made him aware of the crisis.

DIANE B. KUNZ (Ph.D., Yale) is Assistant Professor of History at Yale University. She was a corporate lawyer, 1976–83. She is the author of *The Battle for Britain's Gold Standard in 1931*, and *The Economic Diplomacy of the Suez Crisis* (to be published by the University of North Carolina Press in 1990). In 1956 she was three years old. Her first awareness of the Suez crisis came three years later during a trip to

Israel where she heard resentful comments about the American role during the crisis.

KEITH KYLE (MA, Oxford) is Special Assistant to the Director, Royal Institute of International Affairs, London, and Senior Associate Member of St Antony's College, Oxford. From 1967 to 1968 he was a Fellow of the Institute of Politics, JFK School of Government, Harvard University. He has been correspondent for *The Economist* and the *Sunday Times* and was a television reporter and interviewer for the BBC, 1960–82. He is the author of *The Suez Conflict: Thirty Years Later*. In 1956 he was the Washington correspondent of *The Economist*.

WILLIAM ROGER LOUIS (D.Litt., Oxford) holds the Kerr Chair in English History and Culture at the University of Texas. He is a Supernumerary Fellow of St Antony's College, Oxford. His books include *Imperialism at Bay* and *The British Empire in the Middle East*. He is the co-editor of *The End of the Palestine Mandate; Musaddiq, Iranian Nationalism and Oil;* and *African Decolonization: the Transfers of Power, 1960–1980*. In 1956 he was a student in Freiburg, Germany. During his summer travels he happened to be in Cairo when Nasser nationalized the Suez Canal Company.

PETER LYON (Ph.D., London) is Reader in International Relations and Academic Secretary of the Institute of Commonwealth Studies at the University of London. He is the author of *Neutralism*, and *War and Peace in Southeast Asia*. He is the editor of *Britain and Canada*, and has been editor of *The Round Table: The Commonwealth Journal of International Affairs* since 1983. He has been a visiting Professor at UCLA, Cornell, and the University of Illinois. In the first half of 1956 he was in the Ministry of Defence in London, and later a research student at the London School of Economics.

J. D. B. MILLER (MA, Cambridge) is Emeritus Professor of International Relations at the Australian National University. His books include *The Commonwealth in the World, The Politics of the Third World, Britain and the Old Dominions, The EEC and Australia, Survey of Commonwealth Affairs, 1953–1969*, and *Norman Angell and the Futility of War*. He is a Fellow of the Academy of the Social Sciences in Australia. In 1956 he was teaching politics at the University College of Leicester, and chaired discussions on Suez on the Home and Overseas Services of the BBC.

ROGER OWEN (D.Phil., Oxford) is Director of the Middle East Centre, St Antony's College, Oxford, and a Lecturer in the Recent Economic History of the Middle East. He is the author of *Cotton and the*

Egyptian Economy, and *The Middle East in the World Economy, 1800–1914*. He is co-editor of *Studies in the Theory of Imperialism*. In October-November 1956 he was a first-year undergraduate at Oxford having just completed his National Service as a Signals Officer in the British Army in Cyprus.

SHIMON SHAMIR (Ph.D., Princeton) holds the Kaplan Chair in the History of Egypt and Israel at Tel Aviv University, where he has taught since 1966. He was Director of the Israeli Academic Center in Cairo, 1982–4. His books include *A Modern History of the Arabs in the Middle East*, and *Egypt under Sadat: The Search for a New Orientation*. He has edited *The Decline of Nasserism*, and *The Jews of Egypt*. In 1956 he was an undergraduate student of Modern Middle Eastern History at the Hebrew University of Jerusalem and a Lieutenant in a reserve infantry brigade in the Israel Defence Forces.

MAURICE VAÏSSE (Ph.D., Paris) is Professor of Contemporary History, University of Rheims. He has been Deakin Visiting Fellow at St Antony's College, Oxford. He is the author of *Sécurité d'abord: la politique française en matière de désarmement (1930–1934); Alger: le putsch;* and (with Jean Doise), *Diplomatie et outil militaire, 1871–1969*. He has edited *Victoire en Europe*. In 1956 he was in a lycée in Algiers.

J. H. ADAM WATSON (CMG, MA, Cambridge and Oxford) is Visiting Professor at the Center for Advanced Studies at the University of Virginia. He has served as British Ambassador in West Africa and Cuba, and in the Foreign Office as Assistant Under-Secretary of State. He is the author of *Emergent Africa, Diplomacy*, and *The Nature and Problems of the Third World*. With Hedley Bull he co-edited *The Expansion of International Society*. In 1956 he was head of the African Department at the Foreign Office, which covered Egypt and the Canal.

Chronology

1856
5 Jan.   Concession for the construction of the Suez Canal.

1866
22 Feb.   Convention between Viceroy of Egypt and Suez Maritime Company.

1869
17 Nov.   Opening of Suez Canal.

1882
15 Sept.   British forces occupy Cairo.

1888
29 Oct.   Constantinople Convention on Suez Canal.

1914
18 Dec.   Britain establishes Protectorate over Egypt.

1922
28 Feb.   Egypt declared independent by Britain.

1936
26 Aug.   Anglo-Egyptian Treaty.

1948
14 May   Ben-Gurion proclaims establishment of Israel.

1949
24 Feb.   Egypt–Israel armistice.

1950
25 May   United States, Britain, France sign Tripartite Declaration upholding 1949 armistice frontiers and regulating arms traffic.

1951
1 July   Egypt blockades Gulf of Aqaba.

1952
23 July   Military *coup* overthrows King Farouk.

1954
1 Aug.   Israel begins secret arms purchases from France.

19 Oct.   Britain signs Suez base evacuation agreement with Nasser.

1955
24 Feb.   Iraq and Turkey sign Baghdad Pact.

28 Feb.   Israeli raid on Gaza Strip.

5 Apr.   Britain joins Baghdad Pact.

18–24 Apr. Bandung Conference of Asian and African states condemns 'colonialism in all of its manifestations'.

18 May	Nasser initiates Czech arms deal.
27 Sept.	Czech arms deal announced.
21 Nov.	Egypt, United States, and Britain begin talks in Washington on financing of Aswan High Dam.

1956

1 Mar.	King Hussein of Jordan dismisses Sir John Glubb, Commander of the Arab Legion.
13 June	Britain completes Suez base evacuation five days early.
19 July	Dulles withdraws Aswan Dam offer.
26 July	Nasser nationalizes Suez Canal Company.
1–3 Aug.	Britain, United States, and France agree to call London Conference on Suez.
2 Aug.	Britain and France begin military planning for invasion of Egypt.
23 Aug.	Eighteen members of London Conference agree on Suez proposal and name committee of five nations under Robert Menzies, Prime Minister of Australia, to 'present and explain' the plan to Nasser.
3–9 Sept.	Nasser rejects Menzies' proposal.
12 Sept.	Eden, with United States and France, announces plan for setting up Suez Canal Users' Association (SCUA).
15 Sept.	European Canal pilots leave Egypt.
19–21 Sept.	Second London Conference of eighteen nations agrees to form SCUA.
23 Sept.	Britain and France refer Suez dispute to UN Security Council.
30 Sept.–1 Oct.	Franco-Israeli secret talks in Paris to co-ordinate military and political action against Egypt.
1 Oct.	First meeting of SCUA in London.
5 Oct.	UN Security Council considers Suez.
13 Oct.	Security Council and Egypt accept 'Six Principles'.
22–4 Oct.	Britain, France, and Israel negotiate secret accord at Sèvres.
	Revolt breaks out in Hungary.
29 Oct.	Israeli forces attack Egyptian Army in Sinai.
30 Oct.	Britain and France issue ultimatum to Israel and Egypt.
31 Oct.	Britain and France attack Egyptian airfields.
1 Nov.	Serious drain of British gold and dollar reserves begins.
2 Nov.	Israeli forces complete occupation of Gaza and Sinai.
	General Assembly calls for cease-fire and withdrawal.

3 Nov.	Britain and France give conditions for cease-fire.
	Israel accepts cease-fire, provided Egypt does the same.
4 Nov.	Egyptians sink ships in the Canal, effectively blocking it.
	Soviet invading forces take Budapest and crush Hungarian revolt.
	UN General Assembly adopts plan for Emergency Force.
	Egypt accepts cease-fire; Israeli reply is conditional.
5 Nov.	Britain and France drop paratroops at Port Said and Port Fuad.
	Soviet notes to Britain, France, and Israel threaten military action unless cease-fire is accepted.
6 Nov.	Eisenhower re-elected as President.
	Anglo-French seaborne force invades Port Said. Eden and Mollet agree to cease-fire.
	Israeli cease-fire.
7 Nov.	Anglo-French troops cease fire.
12 Nov.	Egypt accepts UN forces provided Egyptian sovereignty not infringed.
15 Nov.	UN forces arrive in Egypt.
3 Dec.	Britain and France announce withdrawal from Egypt.
4 Dec.	United Nations Emergency Force (UNEF) troops move into Sinai.
	Britain announces $279 million drop in gold and dollar reserves and the promise of American financial aid.
10 Dec.	Britain obtains $561.47 million from International Monetary Fund and stand-by commitment for $738.53 million.
21 Dec.	US Export-Import Bank announces that it has authorized $500 million line of credit for Britain.
22 Dec.	Britain and France complete withdrawal from Egypt.
31 Dec.	Canal clearance begins.
1957 5 Jan.	Eisenhower Doctrine proclaims that United States will use armed forces in the event of Soviet or International Communist aggression in the Middle East.
9 Jan.	Anthony Eden resigns as Prime Minister, succeeded by Harold Macmillan.
2 Feb.	UN General Assembly adopts resolutions on Israeli withdrawal.

11 Feb.   United States supports Israeli right of 'innocent passage'
             in Gulf of Aqaba.

20 Feb.   Eisenhower makes television speech on Israeli withdrawal.

25 Feb.   Britain obtains $500 million line of credit from US
             Export-Import Bank.

1 Mar.   Israel announces withdrawal plans in UN General
             Assembly.

7–8 Mar.   Israeli troops withdraw from Gaza Strip and Strait of
             Tiran.

10 Apr.   Suez Canal reopens.

ANGLO-FRENCH PARACHUTE LANDINGS

Nov. 5

INVASION FORCE
BOMBARDMENT AND LANDINGS
Nov. 6

34°

Hebron

Gaza

JORDAN

Port Said Port Fuad

MEDITERRANEAN SEA

Rafah

Beersheba

El Arish

Nov. 1

ISRAEL

EL CAP
LIMIT
OF
ANGLO
-FRENCH
ADVANCE
Nov. 7

El Qantara

Nov. 2

EGYPT

Abu Ageila
Oct. 30-31

El Auja

Ismailia

SUEZ CANAL

Oct. 31

Oct. 30-31

El Quseima

Oct. 29-30

SWEET

WATER

CANAL

Nov. 2

Bir Gafgafa

Bir Hasne

Oct. 30-31

EGYPT
BLOCKS
CANAL
Nov. 1

BITTER LAKES

ISRAELI PARATROOP DROP
Oct. 29

Oct. 29-30

–30°

Suez

Nov. 2

Nov. 2

MITLA PASS

El Nakhel

Oct. 30

Kuntilla

Oct. 29-30

30°

Nov. 1

SUEZ
1956

Gulf of Suez

Nov. 3

Sinai Peninsula

Ras el Naqb

Oct. 29

Eilat

Nov. 2

Oct. 29:Israeli
invasion
Nov. 7, 2:00 A.M.
Middle East Time:
Cease Fire

Gulf of Aqaba

Nov. 3

SAUDI

ARABIA

Nov. 4-5

Israeli Troop Movements

–28°

El Tor
Nov. 2

Nov. 4-5

Sharm
el-Sheikh
Nov. 5

STRAIT OF TIRAN

28°

0   75

KILOMETERS

0   75

RED SEA

MILES

32°

34°

MARCH 1989

BY DAVID WILSON

Introduction

WM. ROGER LOUIS AND ROGER OWEN

MORE than thirty years have passed since the Suez crisis of 1956. Yet only recently have the archives divulged evidence necessary for full and measured reassessment. The chapters in this book represent a combination of detailed research, analysis, and reflection by historians, some of whom, in one way or another, participated in the events of 1956. The book is thus intended to be a balanced discussion of the origins, course, and consequences of the crisis. It explores the contradictory interpretations derived from national perspectives. The events of 1956 have a special place in the collective memory of the British, Egyptians, and Israelis. Those who lived through the crisis often still perceive it as part of their immediate experience. What does the archival evidence reveal that alters or corrects the popular view of Nasser, Eden, Ben-Gurion, and Eisenhower? To what extent did their decisions represent national attitudes and perceptions of strategic and economic necessity? Regardless of perception, what of actuality? What were the immediate reasons for the decisive clash between Egypt and Britain? What of the parts played by France and Israel? With the benefit of three decades' perspective and the rich archival sources that have recently become accessible, the question should be asked, what were the underlying causes of the confrontation? Above all, what were the consequences?

Since the book has both a historical overview and a conclusion, it would be presumptuous to answer those questions here. But a word should be said about the scope and organization of the book as well as certain themes. After the preliminary chapter by J. C. Hurewitz, the point of departure is the Egyptian revolution of 1952 and the consolidation of power by Gamal Abdel Nasser. In all of the chapters Nasser's personality and the interpretation of his goals form a common theme. In the judgement of Ali Dessouki, Nasser was representative of his generation of Egyptian nationalists whose formative experience was the British occupation of their country. Foreign troops and military bases shaped the Egyptian national consciousness. This danger did not cease to exist in 1954 when British troops began to withdraw from the Canal Zone. Nasser wished to break the economic grip of the European powers in the Middle East and to neutralize or destroy the military alliance known as the Baghdad Pact consisting of Britain, Iraq, Turkey, Iran, and Pakistan. In his quest for a pan-Arab movement, Nasser made a populist appeal, over the heads of the leaders of the countries of the pact, to Arabs throughout the Middle East. Thus under Nasser's leadership Arab nationalism became a protest movement against Western dominance. His nationalization of the Suez Canal Company on 26 July 1956 becomes more comprehensible in view of his bold and resolute aims. In Dessouki's words, it was a 'stunning act of defiance'.

Roger Louis's chapter demonstrates the consistency of British aims through 1954, when 80,000 troops began the evacuation of the Canal Zone. The withdrawal was completed a month before Nasser's act of nationalization. On the British side the purpose was to indicate that Egypt would be treated on the basis of equality and that the old era of military domination had at last ended. The invasion of 1956 thus contradicted the policy of Sir Anthony Eden himself, who as Foreign Secretary and then as Prime Minister had pursued a course of reconciliation. A study of the 1954 settlement reveals not merely the irony of the reversal of course in 1956 but also the awareness of how calamitous and irreversible it would be if British forces again invaded Egypt. Looking back on the achievement of 1954, the British Ambassador in Cairo, Sir Humphrey Trevelyan, wrote on the eve of the new invasion in 1956: 'If British forces again occupied Egypt and then withdrew, as they would have to, there would be a new chapter added to the emotional anti-British history of Egypt, which would be made use of for many years to come by anti-British politicians and would become embedded in distorted form in the history books as a glorious incident in the history of the Egyptian struggle for liberation from the imperialist oppressor.' The 1954 settlement between Egypt and Britain was sound, but in itself could not prevent the drift towards confrontation. In this chapter's interpretation, the whirlpools of Palestine and the eddies of the Baghdad Pact stirred the currents that flowed into the Suez crisis.

The chapters are not designed comprehensively to encompass the origins or directions of the crisis but rather to probe in detail certain questions that have been and remain controversial. Thus Shimon Shamir's chapter investigates the peace initiatives in 1954–5 that might have prevented the Suez crisis. 'Project Alpha' was a highly secret set of discussions between the representatives of the British and American governments to solve the Palestinian refugee problem and adjust the frontiers of Israel, thus redressing Arab grievances and establishing a new order of Israeli–Egyptian relations. The planners of 'Alpha' believed that the modified borders would have marked a slight retreat for Israel, but, since they would have been guaranteed by Britain and the United States, they would have been to the advantage of all parties concerned. Shamir argues that such a settlement would not have been possible in any event. He portrays the demise of this enterprise by revealing the persistence of mutual suspicions, misconceptions, and false assumptions, especially on the part of the British. 'We must first try to frighten Nasser,' wrote one British official, 'then to bribe him, and if neither works, get rid of him.' In Shamir's view, many British experts underestimated the authenticity and intensity of the Arab national movement as well as the Arab perception of the Baghdad Pact as a system of military bases and alliances designed to perpetuate Western dominance. Nor did the Americans fully see that it was an illusion to believe that they could create a network of anti-Soviet and anti-Communist alliances while trying to remain on good terms with the pan-Arab movement championed by Nasser. Shamir demonstrates that each of the four principal powers involved at this stage—Egypt, Israel, the United States, and Britain—was motivated by consistent ideologies but faulty assumptions about the others. This fundamental conclusion is important to bear in mind in the period of the crisis itself when all of these powers as well as France and the Soviet Union remained consistent—except Britain. Britain veered off course and contradicted her own principles.

In the part of the book dealing with the crisis itself, Keith Kyle treats the immediate antecedents of the emergency: the Soviet military assistance to Egypt through the 'Czech arms deal', the British discovery of the transaction in September 1955; and Eden's growing suspicions of Nasser. The policy of the British government in the months preceding the crisis, more than that of any other party, has remained vague until the recent opening of the archives. Kyle's account is thus a key chapter in establishing the twists and turns of Eden's attitude, which was decisive. The critical period was March 1956, when Sir John Glubb, the Commander of the Arab Legion of Jordan, was dismissed by King Hussein. In this Eden saw the hand of Nasser—mistakenly, as to the actual timing. Intelligence reports led the British Cabinet to believe that Egypt was becoming 'an out-and-out Soviet instrument'. When Nasser nationalized the Canal Company, the British began planning for a military operation, *Musketeer*, which had to be revised in view of changing estimates of probable Egyptian casualties and the difficulty of co-ordination with the French. There are important new details about the combined operations with France and Israel in this chapter, but it is conspicuously instructive on two further points as well: the part played by Harold Macmillan, the Chancellor of the Exchequer, first in

taking a wholeheartedly adventurist line but, later, in abruptly changing his view when the utterly unexpected force of American opposition
threatened Britain's fragile economy; and the plans for a regime to
replace Nasser's government. The argument holds that the momentum
of military planning led, in some circles, to political optimism. It was
hoped to topple Nasser either by military and political pressure or by
air attacks alone but, if necessary, by full-scale invasion, and that the
Egyptians themselves would replace him with a leader more congenial
to the British. When the fierceness and determination of the Egyptian
resistance became clear, the false premiss of British plans became
apparent. All in all, Kyle paints a picture of British statecraft at this
juncture that was unstable, racked by contradictory impulses, and
presided over by a Prime Minister who fatally misjudged the reaction
of the United States.

The other chapters in this section can be understood on the basis of
Kyle's chronology and narrative. On the French side Maurice Vaïsse
establishes the central part played by Maurice Bourgès-Maunoury, the
Minister of Defence, in military assistance to Israel. It was Bourgès-
Maunoury who pressed for an accord first with Israel and then with
Britain. The motive was to quell the Algerian revolution. French
leaders, like the British, erroneously saw Nasser as the cause of their
troubles in northern Africa and the Middle East, and, equally erroneously, applied the 'historical lesson' of the 1930s. Nasser appeared to
be a dictator comparable to Mussolini or even Hitler, towards whom a
policy of appeasement would lead to disaster. Vaïsse refers to this as the
'Munich syndrome'. There was another historical influence. Bourgès-
Maunoury and others were former members of the Resistance. They
now conducted the Suez operation in a similar atmosphere of clandestine manœuvres and moral conviction, with a fixation on Nasser and
Algeria. There emerged, in Vaïsse's interpretation, a clear pattern of
French determination and British procrastination. In the end the
French found themselves abandoned by the British and condemned by
the Americans. In retrospect, some French leaders tended to justify
their actions as a splendid effort in the spirit of the Resistance to assist
Israel, but in reality the motive was Algerian.

Mordechai Bar-On's chapter is a post-mortem on the question of
collusion, which he witnessed at Sèvres as one of Ben-Gurion's military
assistants. Ben-Gurion's purpose is brought into clear focus. He was
certain that Nasser would attack Israel as soon as he could; he knew
that the French wished to launch an attack on Nasser to quash the
Algerian rebellion; but he harboured a deep mistrust of the British: he
believed that they would encourage Jordanian annexation of the
southern part of Israel, the Negev, to establish a British military base as

a substitute for the Suez installations. Nevertheless, Israel needed Britain as a military ally if a successful operation against Egypt were to be mounted. This chapter systematically analyses the collaborative arrangement arrived at by the three parties at Sèvres on 22–4 October 1956. Bar-On reinforces Vaïsse's interpretation of Bourgès-Maunoury and the spirit of French wartime resistance as well as Kyle's view of British uncertainty, vacillation, and lack of a clearly defined goal other than to destroy Nasser. Ben-Gurion knew that the British needed to keep the collusion with the Israelis absolutely secret in order to preserve good relations with the Arabs. From his own perspective, he knew that it would be impossible to keep the collusion secret, but secrecy, then and later, was a price he willingly paid. Ben-Gurion himself emerges as a man of singularly lucid and determined intent, the only statesman in 1956 who at first seemed to achieve his goal—only to be frustrated in the end, again by the Americans.

The chapter by Amin Hewedy is testimony to Nasser's response during the crisis. Himself a participant in the events of 1956 as a military officer, Hewedy was present at a critical meeting between Nasser and his Chiefs of Staff. He later became Minister of Defence. His assessment of Nasser's strategic aims is therefore of considerable interest. But above all this chapter establishes, from an Egyptian vantage-point, the proximate cause of the Suez crisis and Nasser's stature as a national leader during the emergency. In Hewedy's judgement, the Suez crisis was triggered by the Czech arms deal, which upset the regional balance of power. Nasser's announcement of the deal on 27 September 1955 caused 'a thundering international and regional explosion'. From this point onwards Nasser braced himself for the Western response. After the nationalization of the Suez Canal Company it is remarkable that his calculation was similar to the American speculation (notably by John Foster Dulles): the chances for armed conflict, Nasser believed, would be 'up to 80 per cent the first week after nationalization, 40 per cent during August, 20 per cent during October, and negligible after October'. Nasser also misjudged the prospect of an Anglo-French combination with the Israelis: 'Surely it is impossible that both the French and the British would degrade themselves to such an extent.' But if Nasser made mistakes of judgement they hardly compared with the faulty British estimate of him as a national leader. Here Hewedy touches on the heart of the matter: 'Nasser was a charismatic leader who commanded the full confidence of his people.... The people rallied round Nasser's leadership and established a united front against the invaders.' The result, Hewedy points out, stunted the Baghdad Pact and divided the Commonwealth.

It is useful to shift attention away from Egypt, Israel, and the

Western powers to get an Asian perspective on the crisis as it developed in the summer and autumn of 1956. Sarvepalli Gopal relates that Jawaharlal Nehru of India met Nasser in Yugoslavia shortly before the latter's nationalization of the Suez Canal Company. Nehru did not have a high regard for Nasser's intellect. He did not deny Egypt's right to nationalize; but he regretted Nasser's method as 'intemperate and even warmongering'. Conversely, Nehru respected Eden's achievement at the Geneva conference on Indo-China and generally regarded him as a judicious statesman. During the part of the Suez crisis up to the invasion, Nehru worked with the British to reduce tension and to find a peaceful solution, though to Eden it may have appeared as untoward interference. Like Nasser and Dulles, Nehru believed that the threat of war would recede with the passage of time. India would best help to achieve a non-violent solution by practising the principles of non-alignment. The Indian response came as a disappointment to Nasser, but Nehru's attitude changed immediately upon news of the invasion. India now swung wholeheartedly to the side of Egypt. The balancing act of non-alignment was no longer possible. 'I cannot imagine a worse case of aggression,' Nehru wrote. 'The whole future of the relations between Europe and Asia hangs in the balance.' The Suez crisis had become a crisis that now extended throughout the world. Gopal establishes Nehru's own sense of tragedy at the outcome: 'he did not conceal the strength of his feelings and his deep regret that Britain, with her record of liberal policies, should now have become again the symbol of colonialism'.

Robert Bowie's chapter is of central importance because it sets the record straight not merely about the reasons for the American response to the crisis but also about the relationship between the President, Dwight D. Eisenhower, and his Secretary of State, John Foster Dulles. Bowie was Assistant Secretary of State at the time. His theme is that Eisenhower was a strong President served by a strong Secretary of State. Nevertheless, Dulles in every sense was the executor of policy set by Eisenhower. Eisenhower himself took command during the Suez crisis, but Dulles's racy language and strong statements in press conferences gave the impression, especially to the British, that he rather than the President often took the lead. This chapter contains a detailed analysis of the Aswan Dam negotiations and Dulles's attempt to create an international authority to take the place of the Suez Canal Company. There are two general points that connect with other chapters. The first is the estimate of Nasser. Eisenhower and Dulles had a fairly realistic assessment of him as an Egyptian patriot and Arab nationalist attempting to combat what he perceived to be foreign domination. 'He wished to enhance the independence of Egypt and the region, and was prepared to use Soviet assistance to advance his own ends.' Thus the United States wished to reduce his influence, isolate him, perhaps undermine him (though not by military confrontation, which proved to be the main difference between the American and British responses). The second point is that Dulles, despite his celebrated statement about wishing to make Nasser 'disgorge', persistently worked for a negotiated settlement. He and Eisenhower made it clear to the British that the United States would not condone the use of force, but it is equally obvious that the British made it clear to them that they intended to use force if necessary. Dulles's mistake (like Nehru's, as described in the preceding chapter) was to believe that, by protracting the negotiation, the crisis would dissipate. When the news reached Eisenhower and Dulles of the invasion, they responded logically and consistently according to their own principles. Until the actual invasion, they had been sympathetically disposed to the British, but the collusion of Britain, France, and Israel to deceive them, as well as the actual act of force, caused them to react with the full political and economic weight of the American government against the tripartite aggression.

The chapter entitled 'The Importance of Having Money' by Diane Kunz explains how the Americans quite ruthlessly brought to bear their economic arsenal against the British. Once this decision had been made in the wake of the invasion, 'the question became not whether, but when, Britain would bow to American imperatives.' From thirty years' distance, it is difficult to recall the economic circumstances of 1956. As the author states, it was a different monetary world. There were two major Middle Eastern reasons why British sterling was vulnerable during the crisis. The largest holders of transferable sterling included Arab countries and oil companies. If either or both decided to turn against Britain, the situation would quickly become precarious, especially if oil supplies were curtailed (as of course happened). After the invasion, reserves of both petroleum and pounds began to dwindle. The Americans refused to provide assistance. So intense was the economic pressure, and so imminent did it appear that the sterling area itself might collapse, that the British almost immediately, on 6 November 1956, agreed to a cease-fire. But this was by no means the end of the pressure—or, as Diane Kunz puts it, the economic warfare. The Americans would not come to the rescue economically until the troops were actually withdrawn. 'The British attempt to place conditions on their withdrawal was totally unavailing as the double-barrelled pressure of no aid for the pound and no oil for western Europe forced them inexorably into surrender.'

John Campbell's chapter reviews the Hungarian uprising and its relation to the Suez crisis. How did the two contemporaneous crises affect each other? Did the Hungarian revolution influence decisions on Suez? The answers to those and other searching questions are cautious and generally negative. One of the striking features of the 'twin crises' is the coincidence of chronology. On 30 October 1956, the day before the Soviets decided to intervene in Hungary, the British and the French issued their ultimatum to Nasser. Each decision, made on grounds of national interest in an area deemed vital, was no more than marginally affected by the other. The two crises developed independently. Yet none of the involved powers could be certain of the intention of others. Even at this stage, as Campbell demonstrates, it is extraordinarily difficult to disentangle how much was real and how much was bluff in the Soviet threats in 1956. On the other hand, Diane Kunz does prove in the preceding chapter, and Campbell gives additional substantiation, that the British decided on a cease-fire on 6 November primarily because of American economic pressure, not because of Bulganin's threat at about the same time to destroy England by rocket attacks. This was an empty threat, identified as such by American intelligence reports which verified that the Soviets did not have the necessary missile capability or warheads. Nevertheless, the reader will gain a general chilling impression from this chapter: both American and Soviet participants believed their own rhetoric and were capable of magisterial misjudgement—so much so that Campbell has inserted his own exclamation point in square brackets in one of John Foster Dulles's resounding statements at the time: it was 'nothing less than tragic that at this very time when we are on the point of winning an immense and long-hoped-for victory over Soviet colonialism in eastern Europe [!], we should be forced to choose between following in the footsteps of Anglo-French colonialism in Asia and Africa, or splitting our course away from their course'. The United States did not in fact intervene in eastern Europe, nor did the Soviet Union become directly involved in the Suez crisis. Ending on a note of realism, Campbell points out that Nasser, though looking for help where he could get it, had no intention of exchanging one form of imperialism for another.

The next part of the book deals with the response of the Commonwealth to the crisis. India of course was a vital member of the Commonwealth at this time. But Gopal's chapter has been dealt with in the preceding section as an integral part of the crisis itself. Nehru raised fundamental questions of non-alignment and 'colonialism' that are still today controversial issues between the Western countries and the 'Third World'. Peter Lyon's chapter is directed more towards the 'old Dominions' and the significance of the crisis in the history of decolonization. Thus he points out that the British government of the day dealt with the Australians, New Zealanders, South Africans, and Canadians on a slightly different footing from the south Asians. During the summer and autumn of 1956, there were informal meetings of the 'old' members of the Commonwealth at the United Nations in New York so that issues such as Nasser's 'theft' could be candidly but confidentially discussed. There was a rather quaint attitude towards the 'new-fangled' post-1949 Commonwealth, which now included south Asians and was later to include Africans. How significant was the Commonwealth at this time? As Lyon makes clear, it was still mainly a small international club run by the British. It was intended in part to be a continuation of the British ex-imperial world by other means. It eased the pangs of decolonization. But it had no power. The Suez crisis exposed its frailties. This chapter thus makes clear the weak political actuality as contrasted with the seductive myth of the Commonwealth as a significant influence in world affairs. Seen from this vantage-point, the Suez crisis represents a moment of truth, in Lyon's phrase, a 'psychological watershed' after which the world would never again seem the same.

The residual attitudes of the colonial age found robust expression in Australia just as they did in Britain. Bruce Miller's chapter explains how anti-United Nations sentiment coloured Australian views at the time, in part because of the backlash against the unstable and legalistic leader of the opposition, H. V. Evatt, who had been President of the UN General Assembly. The Prime Minister, R. G. Menzies, did not believe that Nasser's action was legally valid. It was Menzies who was entrusted with a mission by John Foster Dulles and Anthony Eden to travel to Egypt in early September 1956 to secure Nasser's acceptance of the proposal for an international agency to manage the Canal. He found Nasser to be a man of 'immature intelligence'. Menzies himself afterwards publicly denounced the Egyptian tactics of 'smash and grab'. This description of Menzies and his attitudes leads Miller to ask the fundamental question: why did Australia support Britain so aggressively? The answer extends far beyond the fact that Menzies happened to be Prime Minister at this juncture. The Australians were anti-Egyptian because of the experience of the First World War, when troops from the antipodes had regarded the 'Gyppos' as both dirty and untrustworthy. Now the 'Gyppos' had stolen 'our' Canal. At the United Nations Australia voted along with Britain and France. Menzies was unrepentant. He was dismayed at the humiliating end of the invasion. Suez as a political issue, however, passed quickly in Australia. Indeed it seemed to fade from public memory and was discussed in retrospect mainly by intellectuals, who condemned the British and French action. The crisis itself had little impact on Australia. Post-Suez developments such as the admission of Ghana to the Commonwealth were unpalatable to Menzies and those with similar outlook. Nevertheless Suez has symbolic importance for Australia as it does for many other countries, and Miller, like Lyon, concludes that it represents 'the end of an era'.

The Canadian response in many ways was the opposite of the Australian. In Michael Fry's chapter the significance of the United Nations comes fully to light. Lester Pearson, the Canadian Minister for External Affairs, believed in Anglo-American co-operation, a functioning Commonwealth, a united NATO, and an effective United Nations. The Suez crisis shook those foundations of international society. This chapter, on the basis of detailed archival research, demonstrates the skill and ingenuity of Canadian political leadership in holding middle ground throughout the crisis and in assisting the United Nations to emerge as the keeper of the post-Suez peace. The Canadians judged Nasser to be 'one of the most enigmatic personalities of our time', and Pearson especially disliked his provocative style. But the Canadians also emphatically disagreed with Eden's overdrawn assessment of the danger of Nasser and the British insistence on the use of force (the true moment of Canadian disillusion appears to have come with the discovery that the British had no clear ideas about Nasser's replacement). After the invasion the Canadians worked tenaciously through the United Nations to salvage the situation. Fry's evidence throws favourable light on Dag Hammarskjöld, the UN Secretary-General. According to Pearson, 'Thank God we have Dag Hammarskjöld . . . He has really done magnificent work under conditions of almost unbelievable pressure.' It was Pearson, guided by the State Department, who on 2 November 1956 proposed 'a truly international peace and police force', which in turn helped to bring about a cease-fire, withdrawal of troops, armistice lines, and the clearing of the Canal. This chapter thus establishes the central importance of the United Nations in ending the crisis. It also serves as a reminder of the bitter sentiment in the Western alliance. Britain had been frustrated in marrying the woman she loved, according to a British Foreign Office official, and had therefore visited a whore-house. 'The United States was the woman she loved and France the brothel.'

In the next part of the book, Lord Beloff critically evokes the turbulent emotions aroused by the Suez crisis. In Harold Macmillan's words, the British controversy over intervention caused rifts in friendships, divisions in families, and stresses in political parties. Part of the purpose of this chapter is to test the accuracy of Macmillan's analysis, and to assess Anthony Eden's historical reputation. Beloff, like Louis and Kyle, emphasizes Eden's long and distinguished record before

Suez. During the early part of the crisis, Eden drew support across the political spectrum and was admired throughout the country. On the resort to arms, public sentiment was divided, and by no means strictly along Labour and Tory lines. This was not a new phenomenon. To understand the consequences of the crisis, especially for the Conservative party, it is instructive to study comparable historic controversies, especially Churchill's campaign against the transfer of power in India and Britain's pre-1956 security arrangements in the Canal Zone. In the crisis itself, Hugh Gaitskell, the leader of the Labour party, responded ambivalently and inconsistently. His reputation was damaged by Suez, though only momentarily. R. A. Butler's standing was much more seriously affected: had it not been for the Suez crisis, Beloff explains, Butler might have succeeded Eden as Prime Minister. Eden emerges as the last statesman of his generation to believe that Britain could remain a world power along with the Soviet Union and the United States. In the brutal economic finale of the crisis, Beloff points out, there developed in Britain the suspicion, shared by those of all political parties, that the United States was attempting to become the successor to the British Empire. This suspicion was by no means new, but it now more than ever coloured British perceptions of American motives. As Eden's successor, Macmillan decided that Britain must align herself decisively with the United States. The Conservative party, in a major transformation, now presided over the dissolution rather than the preservation of the British Empire. Suez thus helped to remove some of the barriers to Britain's entry into the European Common Market.

Maurice Vaïsse's comments on France after Suez bears many similarities to Beloff's analysis of Britain. After 1956 it was as difficult for France as it was for Britain to sustain a claim to be a 'world power'. In some ways the French responded more successfully than the British. 'Europe will be your revenge', Konrad Adenauer commented to Guy Mollet on the day the Suez operation halted. In March of the next year, 1957, the Treaty of Rome established the basis for a Franco-German axis. Mollet, in contrast to Eden, remained in power. French public sentiment did not disapprove of intervention at Suez, but, in Vaïsse's interpretation, the sense of humiliation and resentful nationalism led France ever deeper into the Algerian war. De Gaulle's supreme achievement was to provide the leadership necessary to extricate France from Algeria. And his accomplishment in liquidating the colonial empire was comparable to Macmillan's. But de Gaulle reassessed the alliance with the United States in a radically different way, asserting French independence and autonomy in defence, and pursuing the 'European option' versus the American. The immediate conclusion to be drawn in relation to Suez, in Vaïsse's words, is that

'The seeds of General de Gaulle's return were sown in the failure of the Suez operation.'

Adam Watson, who was head of the African Department at the Foreign Office during the Suez crisis, later became Ambassador to independent Francophone countries in West Africa. His chapter assesses the impact of the Suez crisis on French decolonization. De Gaulle, like Macmillan, came to the conclusion that the value of the colonies was less than their cost. His solution was also similar: if the management of the colonies could be handed over to élites who had been educated and trained by the French, then the prospect would be good that French economic and military influence could be sustained. De Gaulle here moved more rapidly than Macmillan, who proceeded in more piecemeal fashion. The British moved more slowly, but they granted fuller independence. In 1960 eleven former French colonies became independent and joined the United Nations. De Gaulle's speed helped to keep the 'independent' countries dependent on France. At the same time he drew a radically different lesson from the British about Suez. Here Watson's interpretation interlocks with Vaïsse's. De Gaulle shared the French army's distrust of military integration under British command, the disastrous results of which, in his view, were apparent from Suez. The aftermath of the crisis confirmed his suspicion of 'Anglo-Saxon' motives when Macmillan and Eisenhower moved quickly to restore the 'special relationship' between Britain and the United States. With the 'Paris–Bonn axis', de Gaulle sought in Europe to exclude the British, who had proved themselves, again in his view, untrustworthy at Suez. As for the United States, Watson judges that the anti-colonial principles of Eisenhower and Dulles succeeded, on the whole, in winning the 'grudging respect' of the Afro-Asian countries while the United States also restored good relations, if not with France, at least with Britain and Israel.

Hermann Eilts was a United States Foreign Service officer in Washington during the Suez crisis and later became Ambassador to Egypt. The formative years of his career coincided with Nasser's rise to power and influence as the champion of Arab nationalism. Here we have a harsh judgement of Nasser, who in Eilts's view was a man of still limited political experience and given to rhetorical extravagance. This was Eilts's assessment at the time, and it remains unchanged after thirty years' reflection. The theme of this chapter is security arrangements, past and present, and the legacy of the Suez crisis to the present day. Eilts argues that the Baghdad Pact, despite Nasser's rhetoric, was hardly a threat to Egypt's quest for political hegemony and might have provided security in the Middle East. Nasser's pan-Arab ambitions were regarded in some official circles in Washington as legitimate nationalist aims. Some Americans optimistically believed that Nasser as a political realist might find a peaceful solution to the Arab–Israeli conflict. 'These were major American delusions.' The faulty assessment of Nasser contributed to the rebuff of Israeli efforts to obtain American security guarantees. Even though a partial security guarantee was offered in 1957 in return for Israeli withdrawal from Sinai, the United States failed to honour the commitment in 1967 because of involvement in Vietnam. As Eilts points out, these are controversial issues, no less now than at the time. In his view it was the disastrous Arab military defeat of June 1967, for which Nasser must be held in large part responsible, that brought about the emergence of 'a full-blown Palestinian national mystique'. On one further issue Eilts establishes a remarkable point of consensus between American and Russian officials. After John Foster Dulles withdrew the offer for assistance to build the High Dam at Aswan in July 1956, he was widely criticized for precipitating the Suez crisis. But today even the Russians agree that their involvement in the Aswan High Dam project produced but transitory political benefits.

Roger Owen's chapter makes clear that, despite American and Soviet views about Nasser's Aswan decisions, the High Dam eventually stored enough water to save Egypt's agriculture from disaster after the decline of the Blue Nile water supply in the mid-1960s. The short-term economic arrangements with the Soviet Union and China also proved to be beneficial to the Egyptian economy: by 1958 Egypt sent half her exports to the Soviet bloc and China and received, on the basis of barter agreements, one-third of her imports; and eastern Europe opened up as a market for Egypt's expanding exports of manufactured goods. By 1960—described by Owen as Nasser's *annus mirabilis*—not only had work on the High Dam begun but also a comprehensive five-year plan for economic development had been introduced with both the United States and the Soviet Union supporting the Egyptian effort to modernize the management of the economy, to broaden the infrastructure, and to determine industrial priorities. In the direct context of the Suez crisis, this chapter analyses chronologically the economic results of Nasser's nationalization of the Suez Canal Company. After July 1956 there followed the take-over of British shares in Egyptian banks and industrial and commercial companies as well as the economic dislocation caused by the blocking of the Canal. The Canal was reopened on 10 April 1957; operation resumed in quick time; it was efficient; and British and French shareholders were compensated. The short-term balance sheet was to Egypt's advantage. It is in the longer term, however, that the lasting influence of Nasser's policies have to be judged. Here Owen believes that the 'exuberant' phase of Egyptian development in the 1950s and 1960s resulted in a huge and badly managed public sector. Nevertheless, most of the country's major companies were brought under state ownership. Nasser presided over a period of trial and error in the management of the Egyptian economy, but he directed investment towards the expansion of the manufacturing industry, which he saw as the heart of Egypt's independent, modern economy. And despite all Western doubts to the contrary, he achieved a well-managed, efficient, and profitable *Egyptian* Suez Canal Company.

Nasser emerged from the Suez crisis as the pre-eminent leader of Arab nationalism. 'Nasserism' was elevated to the status of an ideology throughout the Arab world. As Rashid Khalidi points out in the penultimate chapter, the confrontation at Suez had the opposite effect to that intended by the planners of the invasion. The intervention stimulated radical nationalism. Existing trends were magnified and strengthened. He traces the antecedents of these developments from the time of the Egyptian revolution of 1952 and calls attention to Nasser's 'extraordinary feat' in 1954 of securing British military withdrawal from Egypt after seventy-two years of occupation. 'Such an achievement had a powerful resonance in an Arab world still dotted with French bases in Morocco, Algeria, and Tunisia, British bases in Libya, Jordan, Iraq, Aden, and the Gulf, and American bases in Morocco, Libya, and Saudi Arabia.' The outcome of the Suez crisis to the Arabs held out hope for the demise of the Western military presence in the Middle East. The Arab leaders who had co-operated with the British and the French were now fatally tarred as collaborators with the Israelis. Suez ultimately proved to be the kiss of death for Nuri Pasha. The crisis also had a profound effect on Palestinian nationalism. 'Suez 1956' was one of the historic events that shaped the political consciousness of the future leaders of the Palestine Liberation Organization. Nasser's influence thus continues to the present day.

The concluding chapter by Albert Hourani, like the one on the 'historical context' by J. C. Hurewitz, should be allowed to speak for itself. But a brief word needs to be said about the scope and purpose of these two chapters since they are companion pieces at the beginning and end. Hurewitz focuses on the enduring British occupation of Egypt since 1882 as the heart of the historical substance of the book. 'The Anglo-Egyptian dispute', he writes, 'was the center-piece. . . . If that is understood, the wider repercussions will fall into place.' Thus Hourani's chapter also deals with the relations of Britain with Egypt, and—the repercussions—with France, Israel, the United States, and the Soviet Union. His analysis offers a corrective to national stereotypes and the tendency to view Nasser, Eden, Ben-Gurion, and others 'simply as actors in a drama'. The concluding chapter assesses the irrational dimension of the crisis as well as the 'inner logic' of the events. It attempts to answer a wide range of questions raised throughout the book.

BACKGROUND

I

The Historical Context

J. C. HUREWITZ

THE British occupation of Egypt in 1882 embittered relations with France and stimulated the development of the nationalist movement that reached its zenith some seventy years later with Gamal Abdel Nasser. Six years after the invasion the maritime powers of Europe in 1888 signed a convention securing the conditions for free transit through the Suez Canal in peace and war. Seventeen years elapsed before the convention of 1888 was ratified: only in 1904 did Britain and France resolve their Egyptian difficulties by concluding the *Entente Cordiale*. The delay in French, and thus European, acceptance of Britain in Egypt institutionalized the lack of legal clarity in the imperial status—a military occupation without fixed term until 1914, a Protectorate for a little more than seven years, and a period of further indirect control that lasted until the conclusion of the 1936 Anglo-Egyptian alliance.

Britain's mode of subordinating Egypt conditioned the unfolding relations with Europe over Egypt as well as with Egypt itself. In 1920 the nationalist leader Saad Zaghlul proposed that Britain transfer its peacetime garrison from the Delta to the thinly populated 'bank of the canal, and preferably on its eastern side'. The chief Egyptian negotiator argued that it would remove the stigma of an occupation army, that is, 'a force intended to "keep order" in Egypt, which was merely another way of saying to keep Egypt in subjection'. This Lord Milner, head of the British mission, rejected out of hand. He held that 'the presence of British troops in the neutral "canal zone" would be calculated to raise trouble with other Powers interested in the international waterway' and 'the permanent occupation of the canal zone by troops of any single Power might be challenged as a breach' of the Canal's neutrality that the 1888 convention had guaranteed.[1]

For the first time the signatories of the 1936 treaty removed the confusion of the imperial status by agreeing in an annexe to Article 8 that British troops might be deployed 'in the vicinity of the Canal' but

---

[1] From the text of the 1920 Milner report in Lord Lloyd, *Egypt Since Cromer* (London, 1934), vol. ii, appendix A, pp. 381–2.

'shall not exceed, of the land forces, 10,000, and of the air forces, 400 pilots, together with the necessary ancillary personnel for administrative and technical duties. These numbers do not include civilian personnel, e.g., clerks, artisans, labourers.'[2] This clause, flexibly interpreted, provided the legal foundation for Britain's construction of the gigantic multi-purpose Canal base in World War II.

The Anglo-Egyptian dispute over the continued British military presence was the centre-piece in all later developments. If that is understood, the wider repercussions will fall into place. The present chapter examines the origins and execution of Whitehall's strategy for safeguarding British interests in post-war Egypt and the Middle East. Its architects had shaped a frame of reference that was designed to promote a regional perspective, little, if at all, related to evolving reality. These guide-lines set the British diplomatic service to work on an impossible assignment. Instead of changing course and cutting losses, Whitehall persisted in the attempt to execute its strategy, breeding confusion and frustration.

In the crisis of 1956, Britain had the most to lose and Egypt, as the unwilling symbiotic partner, the most to gain. Since Britain still sat at the wheel in 1945, it is fair to ask what went wrong. After all, at the end of World War II, the Middle East still was largely in the British sphere with only an expiring French presence in Syria and Lebanon under the League of Nations mandate. Labour's surprising succession to the coalition War Cabinet occurred in July 1945, when Britain was just turning from six years of preoccupation with the uncertainties of war to the baffling problems of establishing a stable peace. Yet it led to fewer changes in overall strategy towards the Middle East than many might have thought likely, and these were mostly nominal. Continuity could be ascribed to the inexperience and the divided attentions of the new Foreign Secretary and, because of that, to the influence of the bureaucratic experts in the relevant ministries at home or on duty abroad, including some recruited by the wartime agencies and the armed forces.

From the outset as Labour's Foreign Secretary (1945–51), Ernest Bevin seemed determined to allay the worst effects of Britain's imperial decay by devising means to retain Britain's leadership wherever its power was receding. As one method, former dependent territories of the Empire were invited to join the British Commonwealth on a status of equality with the metropole. This occurred in the Indian subcontinent, Burma and Ceylon included, once the decision on the early

---

[2] From the text in J. C. Hurewitz, *The Middle East and North Africa in World Politics* (New Haven, 1979), vol. ii, pp. 487–8.

transfer of sovereignty was taken in 1947. Three successor states (India, Pakistan, and Ceylon) accepted the new relationship. Burma opted for a mutual defence accord. Britain, however, did not offer the Commonwealth option anywhere in its Middle East empire. Apart from the Crown Colonies of Cyprus and Aden, Whitehall claimed only restricted sovereignty. In principle, Britain managed foreign, fiscal, and military affairs only, leaving residual rights to variably supervised local rulers.

Bevin came to the Foreign Office with no experience in the conduct of external affairs. None the less, as Minister of Labour and National Service in Churchill's wartime coalition, Bevin had learned the art of directing a complex bureaucracy and drawing upon its expertise. Less than six weeks after taking office, he summoned the heads of British missions in the field, among them spokesmen of the nascent British Middle East Office (BMEO). Joining them were experts from the Foreign, Colonial, Commonwealth, and India Offices, the Defence Ministry, and the Treasury, who gave the untried Foreign Secretary a crash course on the Middle East during such moments in September 1945 as he could spare from preparations for the first session of the Council of Foreign Ministers. Among these seasoned career Civil Servants was Lord Altrincham, who had served as a Minister Resident in the Middle East during the war. Altrincham's post-mortem on lessons learned from his ministerial residency seems to have served as a Bevin text, or at least as a prominent source for the Foreign Secretary's recommendations to the Cabinet.[3] And these recommendations in turn became Bevin's 1945 'guide-lines'.

In home departments and in the field, the Middle East imperial establishment tended to become indoctrinated with a set of standard views. For the most part, these had been pulled together into a coherent set of beliefs and updated at intervals in the second half of World War II by the Resident Ministers either in meetings of the Middle East War Council in Cairo or at special conferences, such as that in April 1945 at Fayyum (Upper Egypt) to assess the regional implications of a Palestine partition project framed by a War Cabinet committee.[4] Indeed, many of those who had gone to Fayyum took part, five months later, in the new Foreign Secretary's conference in Whitehall. The civilian and military bureaucrats became, in effect, the custodians of the evolving Middle East imperial ethos and the carriers of the message from the War Cabinet to the Labour Government.

[3] 'British Policy and Organisation in the Middle East', 2 Sept. 1945, FO 371/45252 (Public Record Office, London).

[4] The Fayyum Report, 4 Apr. 1945, CAB 66/64, WP(45)214, reproduced in Hurewitz, *The Middle East and North Africa*, ii. 761–79.

Once Bevin had adopted many of the assumptions as his own, giving them a socialist veneer, he personally became the custodian of this ethos within the Labour Government.

To remain a world power, Bevin's advisers persuaded him, Britain would have to continue to exercise 'political predominance' in the Middle East and 'overriding responsibility' for its defence. The imperial interests that such hegemony would uphold formed part of the bureaucratic mentality in 1945. No official posted to the Middle East for a reasonable time had to be reminded that access to regional communications, oil, and export markets, and to bases for their protection, were the paramount imperial interests. '[A]s an area in which, without desiring to dominate ourselves, we cannot allow any other Power to dominate and must preserve for ourselves the maximum of friendship and goodwill,' ran Altrincham's farewell, 'the Middle East is no less vital to Britain than Central and South America to the United States, or than the eastern and western glacis of the Russian landmass to the Soviet Union.'[5]

When officials and ministers spoke freely of the Middle East, what more often than not they seemed to keep uppermost in mind was the Arab East—Egypt, Sudan, and Libya in North Africa plus adjacent Arab Asia. The Suez Canal was 'the jugular vein' of the British Empire, as Bevin later described it. Indeed, from the opening of the waterway in 1869, British-flagged vessels passing through accounted on average for 70 per cent or more of the total, tying the metropole to India, East Africa, and Australia. In the inter-war years, Britain had also opened air routes (adapted to the short plane range of the day) approaching the Persian Gulf and points east via Egypt or via Palestine and Iraq. Civilian air traffic on the trunk routes could hardly fail to become brisk, and promote subsidiary routes, in a reconstructed post-war world economy. Understandably, Whitehall wanted to reserve these air routes for British nationals.

Partly, or fully, owned British oil concessions were located chiefly in the countries that rimmed the Persian Gulf. The leading producer in 1945 with more than 360,000 barrels per day, or nearly two-thirds of the region's total, was the British-owned Anglo-Iranian Oil Company (AIOC), which operated an exclusive concession in Khuzistan province (south-west Iran). AIOC had also built at its terminal on the island of Abadan in the Shatt al-Arab (the confluence of the Tigris and Euphrates rivers at the head of the Gulf) the world's largest refinery, which in the war had fuelled the Royal Navy east of Suez. The AIOC operations in non-Arab Iran, noted Foreign Secretary Anthony Eden in April 1945, in commenting on the high priority of British interests in

[5] 2 Sept. 1945, FO 371-45252.

the Arab states, 'are not entirely independent of the Arab sphere; in order that they shall continue to function properly free passage is required through the national waters of Iraq for oil tankers to and from the great Abadan refinery. The control of navigation and conservancy on the Shatt al-Arab, by agreement with the Iraqi Government, is thus itself an important British interest.'[6]

All the remaining British concessions lay on the Arab side of the Gulf. The Kirkuk field (north Iraq) belonged to the Iraq Petroleum Company, an international consortium in which British companies (including Royal Dutch-Shell, an Anglo-Dutch firm registered in London) were entitled to a half-share (50,000 barrels per day) of a 600-mile Anglo-French pipeline system to the Mediterranean, with a French-owned terminal at Tripoli (Lebanon) and a British-owned one at Haifa (Palestine), where a major refinery turned out products for all branches of the armed forces. AIOC and the (American) Gulf Oil Corporation jointly held a concession for the exploitation of an even richer field in Kuwait, where oil, discovered in 1938, did not come on stream until 1946. In its concessionary areas in Qatar, the Trucial States, and Oman, the Iraq Petroleum Company delayed the search for oil until after the war.

In 1945 the jurisdiction of Britain's Middle East Command, with headquarters for ground and air forces at Cairo, extended from Greece, Turkey, and Iran to Kenya and from Malta to the Indian border of Iran. In the area, however, the Royal Navy named two commands: that of the Mediterranean Fleet at Alexandria and of the East Indies Fleet at Bombay (for coverage of the Indian Ocean, the Arabian and Red Seas, and the Persian Gulf). Here again, the facilities were concentrated in the Arab area. Army units were dispersed among Egypt, Sudan, Libya, Palestine, Transjordan, and Iraq with an occupational presence in Lebanon, Syria, and southern Iran. The fleets on both sides of the Suez Canal had stations at Alexandria, Haifa, Tripoli (Libya), Aden, and Bahrain. The bases and staging posts of the Royal Air Force (RAF), within reinforcement range of one another, honeycombed the region. Outside Egypt the largest were in Habbaniya (Iraq), Lydda (Palestine), and Khartoum (Sudan). The air command stressed the base needs in peacetime to service RAF imperial trunk routes and to maintain operational and training units.

On Bevin's advice, the Labour Government followed the counsel of the bureaucratic guardians of these interests. Their geographic usage was generally vague. For them, the Middle East almost invariably meant the Arab East, especially the treaty states (Egypt and Iraq) and

---

[6] 10 Apr. 1945, CAB 66/64, WP(45)229, reproduced in Hurewitz, *The Middle East and North Africa*, ii. 781.

others that might later join the treaty network (as Jordan and Libya did). They argued that the Arab states in general should be seen and treated as a cohesive region. The bureaucrats seemed carried away by the prevailing euphoria exuded by the British military victory over Germany and the Arab political victory in creating an Arab League. The British Middle East establishment was confident that the League would gather power and prestige, as step by step, it institutionalized Arab unity. The concealed British support in 1943–5 that helped the Arab governments to overcome the obstacles to forming a regional organization doubtless reinforced the belief that comparable influence might also help shape a durable Anglo-Arab partnership. To shore up the perceived unifying process in the expectation that it might benefit the Arab states and Britain alike, the strategists chose such functions and institutions of the wartime experience as they believed could be adapted from a compulsory to a voluntary system.

These policy guide-lines, clearly, failed to take fully into account Britain's insolvency and the parochialism of the Arab regimes. Each of the latter sought neighbourly co-operation, not for political or economic merger, but for the realization of its own aims. Each gave the highest priority to the removal of European imperial control. Besides, the concepts of primacy and equality were in conflict. By definition, if Britain continued as the region's paramount power, Egypt and the Arab states had to remain subordinate. In no way could unequal allies form the equal partnership that Bevin proposed in January 1946 when he offered to revise the 1936 treaty. In the Arab East, Egypt was Britain's 'gate and key', as Altrincham had put it. The site of the Arab League headquarters, Cairo, had become the Arab world's political capital. As Egypt went, so might the others be expected to go. But it was precisely in Egypt that the Suez base had embedded Britain in concrete.

The view from London focused on the importance of the base to a global empire. Uniquely located at the juncture of Asia and Africa and close to south-east Europe, the base lay at the pivot of the Eastern Hemisphere. It occupied more than 750 square miles of desert, between the Nile Delta (Lower Egypt along the Mediterranean) and the west bank of the Canal, accessible by land and air and by the Atlantic and Indian ocean approaches. By 1945, it had grown into the world's most elaborate military complex. Built to accommodate land, air, and naval forces, the base boasted: regional communications networks; ten airfields and a facility for seaplanes; docks; a railroad system (50 engines and 900 coaches); depots (for ammunition, ordnance, railroad tracks, and thousands of cars, trucks, motorcycles, and armoured carriers, along with medical and general stores); assembly plants and factories (for jerrycans and clothing, among other commodities); repair shops for everything from vehicles to surgical equipment; power stations, water filtration plants and distribution outlets for water, coal, and oil (including storage tanks, pipelines, and filling stations); to say nothing of barracks, hospitals, and recreational facilities. For the Ministry of Defence, the base's primary asset was its very existence, needing little, if any, infrastructural outlay; but for the Treasury, that benefit was offset by the steep costs of deploying large numbers of troops for local and regional duty, as nationalist pressures spread.

In principle, the view from Cairo in 1945, and indeed among successive Egyptian governments and regimes until 1956, hardly differed from that in the Zaghlul–Milner exchanges of 1920. Egypt continued to levy the charge that the British military presence, as highlighted in World War II, constituted an occupation. Cairo's postwar preoccupation centred on Egypt's junior partner status in the 1936 alliance. As such, Egypt had served as a reluctant host to Britain and its allies. The security demands of Britain's swollen wartime presence had made too explicit its preferential rights. Egyptian complaints listed, after control over mail and communications, Britain's freedom without prior notice or approval to deploy in Egypt British and allied military units of any size, to assemble *matériel* of any quantity, to use the terrain to mount campaigns against Britain's enemy, to run the economy, and, even at gunpoint, to force the King into replacing a government with one of Britain's choice (as it had done in February 1942). In the perception of Egyptian nationalists, such a record of abuse aroused an abiding fear that any alliance that allowed Britain a future military presence could only curtail the sovereignty of their country. Britain's advantage had become Egypt's burden.

Bevin's insistence on the 1945 guide-lines to resolve the Anglo-Egyptian differences from 1946 to 1951 led to a progressive weakening of the British position. The talks on treaty revision came to nothing. Meanwhile, in 1948, Iraq followed Egypt in refusing to adjust its treaty relationship with Britain. Transjordan, however, replaced its 1946 alliance by entering two years later into an 'equal' partnership, as Bevin defined it, and in 1953 Libya became an ally. Nevertheless, it was the aborted talks with Egypt and Iraq that gave rise to British disengagement, and its flip side, national liberation, in the first post-war decade.

A series of Egyptian Cabinets rigged by the palace were the first to carry the post-war liberation standard in Egypt. Prime Minister Ismail Sidky Pasha, King Farouk's personal choice, headed a delegation that outwitted Bevin in 1946. But Sidky reneged on his commitment to defer the negotiations on a settlement in Sudan until 'after consultation with the Sudanese'. He thus left Bevin saddled with a conditional promise to evacuate the military installations in the Delta in five months and those in the Canal base in three years. As a token of good faith, Bevin kept his word on the Delta. But the Egyptians took as absolute the conditional promise of total evacuation. That is where Prime Minister Mustafa Nahas Pasha, brought to power by the Wafd party's victory in the monarchy's only free post-war election, started in 1950. After Herbert Morrison succeeded Bevin in March 1951, Nahas moved the Egyptian position forward in October by unilaterally repudiating the 1936 treaty and the 1899 Sudan agreement whereby Britain and Egypt held Sudan as a condominium. Nahas then categorically turned down a British plan for a Middle East Command, originally conceived by Bevin, a proposed regional security system, with extra-regional members, that Whitehall believed would overcome Egyptian fears by the inclusion of the United States and France as well as Turkey as joint sponsors. The military junta that overturned the monarchy in 1952 proved agreeable, with American mediation, to treating Sudan separately from the Suez base and to signing an agreement in February 1953 for ending the Sudan condominium within three years. But the Egyptian military officers could hardly have been expected to consent to anything less than the total evacuation of the base (with no more than face-saving clauses for Britain). They were unwilling to participate with Britain in a collective security system that would admit members from outside the region. These were the dynamics of evolving post-war Anglo-Egyptian relations.

Meanwhile, the 1945 guide-lines had implied the reduction of Britain's commitment to the Zionist cause in Palestine. In the context of American strategic planning, including access to oil and bases, the Department of State echoed the British inclination; but on domestic political and humanitarian grounds the White House tended to favour Zionism. To compensate for expected American opposition to the Labour Government's anti-Zionist policy, Bevin departed from the letter of his Middle East strategy, against the judgement of his staff, by trying to induce the United States to share responsibility for seeking a negotiated Zionist–Arab settlement that would assure a future British presence. This was the British intent behind the Anglo-American Committee of Inquiry on Palestine (November 1945–April 1946) and the futile attempt to find a solution. Instead of narrowing the Arab–Zionist gulf, the Committee opened on that issue an abiding Anglo-American controversy, that did not, however, harm allied relations elsewhere in the region.

A man of independent mind and powerful will, Bevin did not let go.

He persisted in courting the United States yet again, even before retreating from Palestine as a lost endeavour. He managed far beyond expectation to draw the United States into taking over the protective shield of the Middle East. In this he was helped by Stalin's rough-and-ready initiatives in 1944–7 to try to force Iran, Turkey, and (with Tito's assistance) Greece into the Soviet orbit. To London and Washington Stalin's tactics seemed to reveal a strategy to ease Britain out of the Middle East and prevent the United States from becoming a political player there. After six months of exploratory exchanges on the possibility of transferring to the United States the British military and economic aid commitments to Greece and Turkey (which were not parts of Britain's Middle East empire), Bevin, in February 1947, formally notified the new Secretary of State, General George C. Marshall, that Britain could no longer carry that burden. In less than three weeks the decisive response came in the proclamation of the Truman Doctrine, a global American pledge to contain Soviet expansion, whether this was by direct action (as in Turkey) or by local subversive, in this case Communist, groups (as in Greece).

From then on, Bevin, and Eden after him, welcomed a deepening US strategic commitment in the Arab East and its neighbourhood that either made up for Britain's diminishing influence or provided for allied partnership with joint responsibilities. Even before the Truman Doctrine, Washington had begun laying down the infrastructure in 1946 for a primary role in the Middle East by creating the Sixth Fleet on permanent Mediterranean duty. Three years later, with British assent, the American navy moored its token Middle East Force to the Bahrain archipelago on permanent station in the Persian Gulf, still viewed as a British sphere. The American Strategic Air Command procured access to bases in Libya (1949), Morocco (1950), and Saudi Arabia (1951); and in Morocco the navy received use of port facilities. With admission to membership in NATO in 1952, Greece and Turkey made air and naval bases available to the United States and its allies. Meanwhile, in the May 1950 Tripartite Declaration the United States, Britain, and France announced their plan to prevent an Arab–Israeli arms race by jointly monitoring the flow of weapons into that zone where they enjoyed a monopoly of the modern arms market. As a further stabilizing measure, the three partners declared that they would 'immediately take action, both within and outside the United Nations, to prevent . . . [the] violation' of boundaries or armistice lines.

By implying an offer of military aid to those states that volunteered 'to play their part in the defense of the area as a whole', the declaration was also designed as preparation for setting up a regional collective security system. The idea for such a regime under British leadership went back at least to the conference of the Minister Resident at Fayyum in April 1945. 'I contemplate that the new Treaty (reproducing . . . the essential features of the old)', Bevin advised the Cabinet in January 1946, when he reported that he would seek to revise the 1936 Egyptian alliance, 'should be bilateral in character, but should be drafted so as to fit into a regional defence system for the Middle East as a whole (such as I hope to bring about in due course).'[7]

By 1949 Bevin concluded that there was no way of bringing Egypt into a British-managed regional organization. He therefore modified the blueprint to provide for US and other extra-regional sponsorship, still hoping thereby to attract Egyptian co-operation. These thoughts formed the basis for the Bevin–Morrison Middle East Command proposal to which Nahas Pasha turned a deaf ear in 1951. Eden on becoming Foreign Secretary promptly revived the proposal. The plan was alive as 'a future rather than as an immediate possibility', Secretary of State John Foster Dulles reported in the spring of 1953, on his return from a first formal visit to the Middle East. He sensed among 'the northern tier of [Middle East] nations' an 'awareness of danger' from the Soviet Union and 'a vague desire to have a collective security system'.

The blending of British and American principles led finally in 1955 to the formation of a regional collective security system. A Turkish–Iraqi pact signed in Baghdad in February became the enabling instrument. Less than six weeks later, Britain acceded to the Baghdad Pact by special agreement with Iraq that simultaneously ended the Anglo-Iraqi alliance of 1932. Pakistan joined the organization in September 1955, and Iran in October. Without accepting formal membership, the United States attended its committee meetings from the outset and acted as its primary arms provider. The creation of the Baghdad Pact simultaneously alienated: the Soviet Union, because the security system was advertised as anti-Soviet; Egypt, because of the ill-concealed promotion of Iraq as a rival in Arab regional politics; France, because it was not invited to become an affiliate; and Israel, also a non-invitee, because of sharply mounting anxiety about Arab threats to its national security. As an early consequence, the pact stimulated an alignment of Egypt with the Soviet Union, and Israel with France, each Middle East state making its own arms deal.

The unsettling effects of such an abrupt realignment of the Middle East states and the extra-regional powers concerned led speedily to the 1956 crisis, which the chapters that follow amply document.

One final word on the 1945 guide-lines. With a till that simply could not replenish itself in the first post-war decade, the British Treasury

[7] 18 Jan. 1946, CAB 129/6, CP(46)17.

placed severe curbs on experimental outlays. On the other hand, there is little evidence to suggest that it tried to hem in the staggering annual outlays of the Foreign Office for telegraphic exchanges between departments and the diplomatic missions in the Middle East and in Washington as well as the copies shared with one another. The taxpayer's loss is the researcher's gain, for the record discloses in minute detail how the privileged communicators were putting their collective skills to work on a slippery errand. But the statesmen and diplomats carried on with an unshakeable dedication as they marched from embarrassment to greater embarrassment. It was not only the indomitable Ernest Bevin, who had become Whitehall's manager of external affairs without prior grooming; it was also Anthony Eden, the very personification of an experienced and masterly diplomat, who had been exposed to Islamic culture at Oxford: both were entrapped in the coils of a strategy more imaginary than imaginative, from which neither could find an escape. In consequence, Britain slid into deepening entanglement, compounding confusion, and finally explosion.

2

Nasser and the Struggle for Independence

ALI E. HILLAL DESSOUKI

F EW events in contemporary history have had as great an impact upon the Middle East and its significance in world affairs as the Suez crisis. During the fatal months from July to November 1956, major international figures were involved in dangerous, close, and intensive interactions that brought a new political–strategic balance with changing roles for the different regional and global actors. Thus, the importance of the crisis lies not in what happened, but mainly in what it heralded.

From this perspective, the real significance of the Suez crisis lies not in its immediate precipitating cause, the nationalization and management of the Canal, but rather in its larger impact on relations between the Western powers and the newly independent states in Africa and Asia. Putting it differently, the Suez crisis reflected a conflict between two systems and their underlying concept: one of the pre-World War II order, in which colonial domination and international political inequality were predominant, and the other of the aspirant ex-colonies that demanded full equality and sovereignty. The Anglo-American rift during the crisis indicated another conflict within the Western camp over ways of handling problems in Third World countries. Eisenhower and Dulles sought to achieve the same objectives as Eden, but by different means.

In sum, the Suez crisis mirrored the contradictions and confrontations of the changing international scene in the mid-1950s. The crisis brought to an end the system of military–political–economic control of the Arab world by European powers. In this chapter I shall examine Nasser's decisions on the road to the Suez crisis: how did he understand it at the time, and in what terms did he perceive it as a turning-point in Egypt's long search for dignity?

As early as 1953 Nasser reflected:

Existence cannot come out of nothing. We cannot look stupidly at a map of the world not realizing our place therein and the role determined to us by that place. Neither can we ignore that there is an Arab circle surrounding us and that this circle is as much a part of us as we are a part of it, that our history has been mixed with it and that its interests are linked with ours. These are actual facts and not mere words. . . . Can we ignore that there is a continent of Africa in which fate has placed us and which is destined today to witness a terrible struggle in its future? This struggle will affect us whether we want or not. . . . Can we ignore that there is a Muslim world with which we are tied by bonds which are not only forged by religious faith but also tightened by the facts of history?

Nasser considered this central position of Egypt and its potential role as one of the necessary conditions for assuming Arab leadership. He maintained:

I do not know why I always imagine that in this region in which we live there is a role wandering aimlessly about seeking an actor to play it. I do not know why this role, tired of roaming about in this vast region which extends to every place around us, should at last settle down, weary and worn out, on our frontiers beckoning us to move, to dress up for it and to perform it since there is nobody else who can do so.[1]

Egypt's suitability for Arab leadership, however, was by no means sufficient for it to play that role. Needed was an understanding of the crisis that the region faced, and a development of credible policies and symbols. Nasser perceived a situation which required a dynamic foreign policy not only within the region but also in the international arena. Thus, Egypt under Nasser entered the mainstream of international politics as a factor to be dealt with. The Suez war was the turning-point.

The essence of Nasser's policy was the restoration of 'dignity',[2] which triggered an outpouring of emotional mass support inside Egypt and throughout the Arab world. The concept of 'dignity' was rather vague, but the vagueness itself corresponded to the *mélange* of amorphous feelings of resentment toward major powers, a yearning for past glories, and aspirations towards a brighter future. In operational terms, the concept of dignity was based on the idea of eventual Arab unity. It emphasized independence from external control as its primary objective. In carrying out the theme of independence, it opposed alignment with the major powers that might diminish the sovereignty of small nations.

The concept of dignity could have remained an empty slogan incapable of galvanizing the Arabs had not Nasser endowed it with dramatic and credible acts of defiance. Breaking the Western monopoly on arms supply, resisting Western military pacts, recognizing the

---

[1] Jamal 'Abd al-Nasir, *Falsafat al-thawra* (Cairo, 1956), pp. 91–2; trans. as Gamal Abdel Nasser, *The Philosophy of the Revolution* (Buffalo, NY, 1959), pp. 59–61.

[2] Ibid., p. 94 (Arabic edn.); p. 50 (English edn.).

People's Republic of China, and nationalizing the Suez Canal Company, these were all aspects of the search for dignity that was the basis for Egyptian foreign policy.

Notwithstanding the shifts and the rhetoric, Nasser's speeches and writings reveal that the core concept is national independence (*al-istiqlal al-watani*); a complex notion that involves state power, assertion of national sovereignty, and a search for dignity and equality for small countries. This implied the maintenance and enhancing of Egypt's independence, defined not only in terms of international law but also to mean control over the country's resources and wealth (manifested in the 1950s in the Egyptianization of the economy) and freedom of action in the external arena (manifested in the policies of positive neutrality and non-alignment).

The emphasis on national independence in Nasser's perception of the world and Egypt's role in it can be explained by reference to two factors: (1) Egypt's national experience in the 1930s and 1940s (a period of heightened anti-British and anti-colonial agitation); and (2) the independence of an increasing number of Asian and African countries, and Nasser's recognition of the role Egypt could play within them. Let us now look at his perception of the global system, particularly his views of the West.

In 1952 Nasser's image of the world was heavily conditioned by his limited experience. By his mid-thirties, he had not travelled abroad other than to the Sudan and Palestine. His first major tour in April 1955 included India, Pakistan, and Indonesia, and the first European country he visited was Yugoslavia in 1956. A turning-point in his development was the conference of Afro-Asian states at Bandung. Nasser was impressed by the size of the gathering, its potential as a force in world politics, its support of Arab causes, and most importantly by the role Egypt could perform in the movement. His talks with Nehru, and later with Tito, had a profound impact upon him. He became increasingly aware of the common bonds between Afro-Asian countries struggling to achieve their independence or to disengage themselves from bloc politics, and he went home from Bandung filled with a new confidence in himself and in the role of Egypt in the Arab and Afro-Asian movement.

Nasser had an ambivalent appreciation of the international order. It was for him a source of both threat and opportunity. On the one side, there were the major powers with their colonial legacies and machinations to control and manipulate the newly independent states. It was from these major powers, however, that the new states must endeavour to buy arms and mobilize aid and assistance. By 1955 two predominant ideas existed: (1) that the imperialist European powers, through neocolonial means, diplomatic blackmail and bullying, were attempting to maintain their privileged position in Africa and Asia; and (2) that the Afro-Asian countries must act as a third force in world affairs, as a referee and bargainer between the two conflicting power blocs.

Nasser visualized international politics as a bipolar hierarchical system in which major powers tend to control and dominate small states. The obvious form of domination was colonialism, military occupation, and the denial of political independence, and he blamed colonialism for the deteriorating state of affairs in Egypt before 1952. Almost immediately after July 1952, he launched a diplomatic campaign against the British military base in Suez and eventually signed an evacuation treaty on 18 June 1954.

Nasser's perception of colonialism during the early years of 1952–4 referred basically to the presence of military bases and the joining of military alliances with major powers. It was directed against those powers which were involved in these colonial practices, rather than Western states in general. In fact, Nasser initially thought that his anti-colonial position was no barrier to the establishment of cordial relations even with colonial powers such as Great Britain. Thus, his criticism was more of a political rather than ideological nature and was not extended to the United States during this period.

Evidence for this conclusion abounds. The June 1954 Anglo-Egyptian treaty which Nasser heralded as achieving the true independence of Egypt can indeed be viewed as a treaty of indirect alliance with Great Britain. The treaty allowed British military access to the Suez base if, for seven years, any Arab country or Turkey were attacked by an outside power. Nasser justified the inclusion of Turkey on the basis that a Soviet attack on Turkey would be a first step towards Egypt and Arab oil.[3] (Ironically a few months later he attacked Iraq for joining an alliance which included Turkey since Iraq, in his view, was then allying itself with NATO.) In a message over Radio Cairo on the Anglo-Egyptian treaty he informed his people: 'This is a turning point ... with this agreement a new era of friendly relations based on mutual trust ... opens between Egypt and Britain and Western countries.'

The weight of evidence suggests that in 1952–4 Nasser continued to appeal to the West on global issues. In fact, by linking Egypt's security to that of Turkey in the Anglo-Egyptian treaty, Egypt indirectly became involved in Western strategy. In September 1954 Nasser informed the *New York Times'* correspondent that Russia and Communism constituted a major danger to Egypt's security and that the Arabs

---

[3] Speech of 21 Aug. 1954.

would naturally turn towards the West to request arms and assistance. In the same interview he argued that 'cooperation [with the West] based on trust and friendship, even though it is not specified by any written agreement, is better than a treaty that is regarded suspiciously by the average Egyptian'.[4] Thus he was not objecting to the idea of defence co-ordination with the West; rather he had his own views on the means of achieving it and did not think that military treaties with Western countries was the way. It seemed that Nasser's idea was to develop an Arab collective security treaty with Western arms. 'The Arab collective security pact is the basis of defence of the Middle East; give us weapons and we will defend it.'

In the January 1955 issue of *Foreign Affairs* Nasser projected the image of a moderate leader bent on the constructive policy of economic development of his country. 'Israel's policy is aggressive and expansionist, and Israel will continue her attempts to prevent any strengthening of the area. However, we do not want to start any conflict. War has no place in the constructive policy which we have designed to improve the lot of our people. We have much to do in Egypt. . . . A war could cause us to lose, rather than gain, much of what we seek to achieve', he wrote.[5] On 13 September 1954 he told the United Press Agency's correspondent that he considered himself a friend of the West. He criticized Israel because it sought only its own interests without due consideration of the consequences of its policies on Western defence in the area: 'Israel is not a friend of the West. It changes its position according to its interests.'[6] Even after announcing the Soviet arms deal Nasser declared: 'We would have preferred to deal with the West, but for us it was a matter of life and death.'[7]

Against this background must be viewed two developments of January–February 1955 that had far-reaching consequences. On 12 January Turkey and Iraq, with the blessing of Britain and the United States, announced their plan to conclude a defensive alliance, known as the Baghdad Pact. Later, on 28 February, Israeli armed units crossed the armistice demarcation line east and south of Gaza and attacked an Egyptian military camp. When the Israelis withdrew, they left behind thirty-eight Egyptians dead and thirty-one wounded. The first event broke the Arab League's solidarity and threatened Egypt's leadership role; the second exposed its military vulnerability. The first

---

[4] *New York Times*, 3 Sept. 1954.

[5] Gamal Abdel Nasser, 'The Egyptian Revolution', *Foreign Affairs*, 33 (Jan. 1955), 211.

[6] *Khutub wa tasrihat al-ra'is Jamal 'Abd al-Nasir* (Collected Speeches and Declarations of President Nasser) (Cairo, 1959), vol. iii, pp. 521–5.

[7] Interview with the correspondent of the *New York Post*, 14 Oct. 1955, ibid., v. 1021–5. See also the record of Nasser's meeting with George Allen, 1 Oct. 1955, Records of the US State Department, Decimal File, 774.56/1-10-55 (National Archives, Washington, DC).

led to a major Egyptian effort against the pact; the second opened the way for a hectic arms race in the 1950s and 1960s.

Perhaps Egypt's campaign against the Baghdad Pact is a useful illustration of the complex and changing orientation of Nasser's policy. Until then, he had been willing to co-operate with the West, but insisted, for a number of reasons, that the West should not press the Arabs to join any military alliances such as the Baghdad Pact. First, whenever there was a pact between major powers and small states, the latter would be manipulated by the former. Second, the Arab countries had enough ties with the West, such as the treaties between Britain and Egypt, Iraq, and Jordan, to ensure adequate co-operation. Third, the Baghdad Pact was a blow to the prospects of Arab unity because it linked Arab with non-Arab states. Fourth, and possibly most important in Nasser's thinking, the pact challenged Egypt's regional leadership. He viewed it as a Western attempt to use Iraq as a competitor to Egypt.

This perception prompted Nasser to launch an activist regional policy which radically altered the prevailing power relationships in the area. The Egyptian leadership, through its powerful radio broadcasting the 'Voice of the Arabs', urged the Arab masses to oppose 'the stooges of imperialism' and warned the pro-Western regimes to stay away from 'imperialist devices' (meaning the Baghdad Pact). Nasser's outpouring of propaganda against the effects of the pact and his emphasis upon Arab nationalism and the importance of Arab solidarity against imperialism and Israel, soon began to affect Arab public opinion, undermining any inclination other Arab leaders might have had to join the pact.

It is unfortunate that this evidence about Nasser's initial perception of the West has been ignored and put aside, for different reasons, by Egyptian and Western scholars alike. The emphasis has been on the image of a revolutionary anti-Western Nasser. His much publicized break with the West, the Soviet arms deal, and Soviet help with the High Dam came only after the West had rejected such requests. In dealing with the West, he was faced with rebuffs and unacceptable restrictive stipulations. The example of the Soviet arms deal is a case in point. It was not an attempt by Nasser to align his country with the Soviet Union. Nor was it a reflection of ideological affinity or converging strategic views of the world. Rather, circumstances forced his hands: the Israeli raid on Gaza, French arms sales to Israel, and the inability of Egypt to secure arms from the United States.

Nasser pleaded for arms from the West for two years, but the West took as bluff his threat to turn to the Soviets. Nasser's prestige was enhanced by the arms deal which, in Arab eyes, endorsed Egypt's proclaimed independence from Western influence. The deal signified the elimination of the Western arms monopoly and the manifestation of Arab independence. As for Nasser, due to consistent Western rejection of his demands, he started to believe in a Western conspiracy to keep the Egyptian army weak and limit Egypt's freedom of action.

The experiences of 1955 brought to the fore certain strands of Nasser's thinking. In one of his early statements on the international system, on 23 July 1953, he made a revealing statement which later became a basic component of his world-view. He said, 'This is no longer the age of power politics, but one in which great powers are competing for the friendship of small states.' He later developed the notion that Afro-Asian countries could get better terms by playing off the Russians against the Americans.

He became increasingly convinced that Afro-Asian countries must avoid alignment with great powers. He thought that the most significant fact of the world situation was the Cold War between the two blocs. So the best course of action for small and Afro-Asian countries was to avoid involvement in Cold War politics because it would inevitably spell foreign influence. In the spring and summer of 1955 Nasser progressively developed his ideas on positive neutrality. In this context, the Soviet arms deal was a crucial step; it was evidence of Egypt's freedom to decide on its policy and assert its independent will; it was a symbol of the dignity Nasser had been promising Egyptians all along.

The year 1956 saw the ascendancy of Egypt in the Arab world: Syria, Saudi Arabia, and Yemen were allies, the pro-Western Lebanon and Jordan had refused to join the Baghdad Pact; and Iraq—Egypt's contender for regional leadership—was successfully isolated. The ideological weapon that helped Nasser to identify Egypt's interests with those of the Arabs was Arab nationalism. Thus, on the eve of the Suez confrontation, Nasser had effectively made Arabism a protest movement against Western dominance in the region.

It is against this background that we can appreciate Nasser's reaction to the American decision of 19 July 1956, followed the next day by Britain, to withdraw an offer to help finance the Aswan High Dam project. Without being unduly 'xenophobic', he sensed the element of conspiracy; he could not help but question the coincidentally similar manner and action of the United States and Britain in wording and announcing their decision. He perceived it as a deliberate move to embarrass him and his regime domestically and regionally. It was also an insult to the emerging neutral countries; the decision was announced to the world while Nasser was attending a meeting in Yugoslavia with Tito and Nehru. The key to Nasser's reaction was hurt dignity. From all available evidence, it seems that he took the decision of nationalization on his own and informed his colleagues and members of the Cabinet on 26 July, just a few hours before announcing it.

Analysis of Nasser's speeches and interviews reveals the existence of a number of concepts and images. At the global level, the dominant image relates to the continuous colonial policy of Western powers in relation to small countries. At the Arab regional level, we find the beliefs that the Egyptian people constitutes the vanguard of the Arab nation, and that as Nasser is the spokesman of this emerging Arab nation, his leadership largely depends on success in the foreign policy field. At the larger Afro-Asian and neutral level, Nasser's ideas include: Egypt is a leading neutralist country: an insult to Egypt is a slight to all neutral countries; and Afro-Asian nations should solidly support any move by Egypt to counter the Western challenge.

From Nasser's perspective, the nationalization had two objectives: to provide foreign exchange for Egypt to build the Dam and pursue its development plans; and to demonstrate that small countries need no longer accept public insult and degradation from great powers. Indeed, though shrouded in economics, Dulles's withdrawal of the High Dam offer was seen as a deliberate blow to Nasser's neutralism and his leadership position in the Arab world. Similarly, he saw the nationalization of the Canal as a deliberate challenge to Western dominance in the region, a step towards the completion of Egyptian independence and the acquisition of a strategic asset.[8]

From the preceding analysis it seems that Nasser's first act of defiance triggered off a chain reaction which continued for several years. The West, in a penalizing and humiliating move, withdrew an earlier offer to finance the High Dam project. Nasser counter-attacked with a more stunning act of defiance—the nationalization of the Suez Canal Company. After some diplomatic manœuvres, the British and French (in collaboration with Israel) attacked Egypt. The attack began with the Israeli invasion of Sinai on 29 October 1956, and on 5 November as prearranged, Britain and France intervened. However, the allied initiative slowly came to a halt, partly because urgently needed American support was not forthcoming, partly because of the strong reaction it generated among Arab countries and the Afro-Asian world, and partly because of continued Egyptian resistance to the invasion.

When Egypt was attacked, the entire Arab world felt and acted in unison. The support that Nasser received during the Suez crisis from the Arab world was considerable and this gave credibility to his policies

---

[8] Mohamed H. Heikal, *Milaffat al-Suways* (The Suez Files) (Cairo, 1986); trans. al-Ahram Centre for Translation and Publishing (Cairo, 1987), p. 459.

not only in his own country but throughout the Arab world. The pro-British Iraqi government was compelled through pressure of public opinion to condemn the Anglo-French attack as flagrant collusion with Israel. Iraq refused to sit with Britain in a Baghdad Pact meeting, and diplomatic relations with France were severed. Syria and Saudi Arabia broke relations with both countries, while the Jordanian Arab Legion seized some of the British army stores in Amman. Thus, at the end of the crisis designed to effect Nasser's fall from the regional scene, he emerged as the prime mover in Arab politics.

The insistent national demand for dignity and for equal status with the West was the most salient factor in that confrontation. Nasser recognized the significance of these dimensions when he reflected:

The battle of Suez which was one of the major landmarks in the Egyptian revolutionary experiment was not merely a moment in which the Egyptian people discovered themselves or the Arab nation discovered its potentialities, but was a moment of international significance and helped all oppressed people discover infinite latent power in themselves and find out that they can revolt and that revolution is the only course to take.[9]

At the end of 1956 Nasser's influence became more apparent in the Arab world. In Jordan a nationalist government headed by Suleiman al-Nabulsi was elected on 21 October 1956, and it promptly joined Syria and Egypt in a military pact which placed Jordanian and Syrian forces under Egyptian command. In January 1957 the 'Treaty of Arab solidarity' was concluded between Egypt, Saudi Arabia, Syria, and Jordan for a period of ten years.

Nevertheless, Nasser's increasing influence was soon to be opposed also by his allies, who had become suspicious of what his popularity and 'Arab nationalism' could do to their own positions within their own states. It was, however, external factors that precipitated the crisis in the Arab world, namely the Eisenhower Doctrine announced in January 1957 which pledged US assistance, including the sending of armed forces, to nations requesting American help 'against overt armed aggression from any nation controlled by international communism'. This development coincided with King Saud's visit to the United States and his subsequent shift in policies away from the Egyptian line. The shift in policy became evident when Saudi Arabia sent troops to help King Hussein of Jordan against the pro-Nasser Premier, al-Nabulsi, and on 5 March 1958 Nasser disclosed that Saud was involved in an attempt to assassinate him in order to stop the union between Egypt and Syria. The next event which signalled the further

[9] Gamal Abdel Nasser, *Speeches, Declarations, and Press Interviews, 1952–1970* (Cairo, State Information Department, n.d.), p. 11.

erosion of Nasser's influence occurred when King Hussein dismissed al-Nabulsi on 10 April 1958 and sought military help from Egypt's rivals—Iraq and Saudi Arabia. For the next few weeks, civil war broke out in Jordan, and Egypt launched a propaganda campaign against Hussein, which resulted in the breaking of diplomatic relations between the two countries.

In 1957, Egypt's only ally—Syria—was in the midst of an internal crisis, which encouraged some of the neighbouring countries to contemplate intervention in its domestic affairs. It was a challenge to Nasser's leadership, and he responded by attacking the Eisenhower Doctrine and the 'stooges of American imperialism' in the Arab world. The policy succeeded in preventing possible outside intervention in Syria, as well as in strengthening the pro-union forces within it. In response to Syrian pressure, Egypt finally agreed to a merger of the two countries under the presidency of Nasser in February 1958; and a new state called the United Arab Republic came into being.

The formation of the UAR was greeted with almost universal enthusiasm by the Arab masses who hoped that Arab unity would soon become a reality. However, this event had adversely affected other Arab leaders who perceived the union as a direct threat to their own positions. For example, the kings of Iraq and Jordan announced on 12 February 1958 the formation of the 'Arab Union', the primary purpose of which was to consolidate the Hashemite alliance against the upsurge of nationalist, anti-Western sentiment generated by the UAR. Further, within the traditional context of Egyptian–Iraqi rivalry over Syria, the creation of the UAR meant a political and strategic intrusion into Iraq's role in the configuration of forces in the Arab East.

The formation of the UAR was a catalyst in the polarization of Lebanese internal politics, which, among other factors, led to the civil war of 1958 and the landing of US marines. Despite the downfall of the monarchy in Iraq and the establishment of a nationalist revolutionary regime, conflict with Nasser continued.

The period 1955–8 was crucial in transforming Arab and Middle Eastern politics. The Suez crisis of 1956 represents a major milestone in this transformation. It was the culmination of Egyptian patriotism and a catalyst for Arab nationalism. It established Nasser as a hero of the Arab masses. It indicated the end of the British era in regional politics and accelerated the process of Britain's decline as a world power. It furthered decolonization and the independence of Afro-Asian countries. Finally, it brought the United States and the Soviet Union into direct contact in the region and provided an early instance of their collaboration.

In conclusion, one is tempted to compare the situation of the 1950s with the 1980s. The Western influence which Nasser resisted has now been requested by ruling élites for protection and safety. Bases have re-emerged under the diplomatic and more polite name of military facilities. The revolutionary zeal is no longer to be found except in the councils of Islamic fundamentalism, and a sort of cynical pragmatism prevails. The old system of dominance has reasserted itself, and its values, in new and fashionable forms. In this context, the Suez episode appears as a nostalgic memory of a distant past. But it may also refer to a realm of possibilities and potentialities. Some have suggested that Khomeini is a new Nasser in Islamic garb. Others have observed the signs of instability in many Arab countries. Thus, the Suez legacy is likely to persist in the collective memory of the Arabs, at once as a catalyst and a trigger, but also as an escape and a solace.

3

The Tragedy of the Anglo-Egyptian Settlement of 1954

WM. ROGER LOUIS

'[I]N dealing with unreliable and improvident people like Egyptians', wrote Sir Evelyn Shuckburgh (the Under-Secretary of the British Foreign Office in charge of Middle Eastern affairs), 'you do well to have short term arrangements which, if they work can be extended, and if they do not work do not become a sort of symbol of "main-morte", as the 1936 Treaty has.'[1] Part of the purpose of the 1954 agreement was to replace the old symbolism of domination with an indication that Britain would now deal with Egypt on the basis of equality. The year 1954 thus marked the achievement of the aim established by the Labour Foreign Secretary, Ernest Bevin, after the end of the Second World War. Sir Anthony Eden, Foreign Secretary from 1951 until he became Prime Minister in 1955, upheld the same principles and perceived his policy as an extension of Bevin's.[2] The Suez crisis of 1956 is ironic in relation to the preceding years because Eden's goal, like Bevin's, was to extricate Britain from Egypt.

The British in 1954 agreed, essentially, to evacuate troops from the Canal Zone in return for the right to re-enter in the event of an attack on the Arab states or Turkey. This chapter will study the reasons why the British saw it in their own interest to come to an agreement with the Egyptians, and, by discussing the history of the 1954 settlement, why it failed to avert the type of crisis it was designed in part to prevent. At the time, guarded optimists held that the end of the British occupation

[1] Minute by Shuckburgh, 17 July 1954, FO 371/108424; see also Evelyn Shuckburgh, *Descent to Suez: Diaries, 1951–56* (London, 1986), ch. 8. This book is the most illuminating guide to the official thought of the period. From late 1951 until mid-1954 Shuckburgh was Eden's Private Secretary; from then until June 1956 he was Assistant Under-Secretary at the Foreign Office. The following abbreviations are used for records at the Public Record Office, London: CAB (Cabinet Office), COS (Chiefs of Staff), DEFE (Defence Ministry), FO (Foreign Office), PREM (Prime Minister's Office), and WO (War Office).

[2] For Eden see especially David Carlton, *Anthony Eden: A Biography* (London, 1981); and Robert Rhodes James, *Anthony Eden: A Biography* (London, 1986). For Bevin's policy see Alan Bullock, *Ernest Bevin: Foreign Secretary* (London, 1983); and W. R. Louis, *The British Empire in the Middle East, 1945–1951* (Oxford, 1984).

of Egypt, which had continued in one form or another without interruption since 1882, might turn a page in the history of the two countries. Egypt, wrote Kingsley Martin of the *New Statesman*, 'may be as ready for friendship with Britain as India proved to be, once we had the sense to act as equals and withdraw our occupation'.[3]

Not merely the dead hand of 1936 but the burden of Egyptian history entered into British calculations. It was difficult for those directly concerned with the country not to be pessimistic. Sir Ralph Stevenson, the Ambassador in Cairo, wrote before the revolution in 1952:

Overlooking short-term fluctuations in the situation here ... [there] are symptoms of the progressive and rapid decline of Egypt to financial bankruptcy, administrative chaos and possible civil war. This would be entirely in accord with the rhythm of Egyptian history over the last three thousand years.[4]

This unsatisfactory state of affairs could perhaps be remedied by the restoration of a British administration, but it is significant that, in 1952, Stevenson flatly rejected the solution of the intervention merely to save the Egyptians from themselves: 'Military intervention and the reoccupation of Egypt, in order thereby to set up a sounder system of administration than the Egyptians are themselves capable of maintaining—another Cromerian régime in fact—is ruled out for many reasons, both political and practical.'[5] But what if the situation deteriorated to the extent that it might be necessary to protect British lives and property—a 1950s version of the events that had justified, or rationalized, the original occupation in 1882?[6] What were the assumptions about the necessity for intervention in the years preceding the Suez crisis?

After the revolution of July 1952 it was by no means clear that General Mohammed Neguib, and the other military officers responsible for ousting King Farouk, would be able to sustain, from the British point of view, a more satisfactory regime. The new military government might become even more virulently anti-British, though some officials held that anything would be better than Farouk, and that the military officers would not necessarily be hostile. In any event, there was the prospect of a further military *coup*, or revolution, that would endanger Britain's position in the Canal Zone. Roger Allen, the

---

[3] *New Statesman*, 1 Aug. 1953.
[4] Stevenson to Eden, 'Top Secret', 25 Feb. 1952, FO 371/96923.
[5] Ibid.
[6] For a recent reassessment of the British occupation of Egypt in 1882 which is highly relevant to the present analysis, see A. G. Hopkins, 'The Victorians and Africa: A Reconsideration of the Occupation of Egypt, 1882', *Journal of African History*, 27 (1986).

Assistant Under-Secretary supervising the Middle East, reflected on the prospect of necessary intervention:

> In general, there is no doubt that we have the physical means at our disposal of kicking out Neguib's government, but we might nonetheless have to occupy Cairo, in the first place to rescue British lives and in the second place to set up a new administration in Egypt.
>
> The latter would certainly be a heavy commitment on us, but the Canal Zone is in fact an integral part of Egypt and we should probably find it impossible to sit there and ignore a revolution taking place in Cairo (it would be rather like trying to sit in Lancashire and ignore a revolution in London and the rest of the country).[7]

Allen believed in short that the British eventually might be forced to intervene, especially if the Egyptians renewed guerrilla warfare in the Canal Zone. Nevertheless every effort should first be made to find accommodation.[8]

Allen was a principal figure in the origins of the 1954 agreement. A lawyer before entering the Foreign Office in 1940, he had also served as liaison to the Chiefs of Staff. He later became Ambassador in Greece (1957–61), Iraq (1961–5), and Turkey (1967–9). As head of the African department in 1950–1, he had presided over Libyan independence. The Libyan treaty of 1951, which secured British base rights and thus placed on a firm footing the redeployment of British troops in the Middle East, was an essential step toward the 1954 agreement with Egypt.

The 1954 agreement was the work of many hands. In mid-1953, at a critical time when both Eden and Stevenson were ill, the Prime Minister Sir Winston Churchill directed R. M. A. Hankey to take charge of Embassy affairs in Cairo. Churchill's purpose was to stiffen the Cairo end of the negotiations so that there would be no appeasement of the Egyptians. Hankey had previously served in both Egypt and Iran. He was the son of Lord Hankey, the legendary Secretary of the Committee of Imperial Defence in the inter-war years, who now played an important part in these events as one of the directors of the Suez Canal Company. Along with Lord Killearn, the former Ambassador to Egypt, now in retirement but using his influence in the House of Lords, Lord Hankey demonstrated a consistent scepticism about Egyptian good faith. On more than one occasion he tried to block the negotiations. Robin Hankey shared the pessimism of Churchill and his

---

[7] 'Apart from all this', Allen continued, 'the effects of our action would not of course be confined to Egypt but there would be wide international repercussions, e.g. in the United Nations, in the Far East, and in the other Middle East countries', minute by Allen, 28 Mar. 1953, FO 371/102764.

[8] See Louis, *British Empire in the Middle East*, pp. 728–9.

father, but he discovered that the Egyptians had their own reasons for wishing to come to terms with the British. He eventually concluded that failure to come to terms with the Eygptians would be a greater evil than consummating an agreement.

Robin Hankey had a penchant for historical reflection. An assessment written by him in September 1953 illuminates contemporary judgement on the corner-stone of the British position in Egypt, the 1936 Treaty, which had affirmed Egyptian independence and had given Britain the right to station 10,000 troops in the Canal Zone (the figures would vary, but in 1952–4 there were up to 80,000 British troops, thus far exceeding the 1936 limitation). Nahas Pasha, who had signed the 1936 treaty, denounced it in 1951 as the head of the Wafd government. In Hankey's view the Wafd party remained the principal nationalist force in Egypt, and it was difficult to see how a lasting arrangement could be made without its support. Hankey also believed that the Muslim Brethren would play an important part in any settlement with Britain because, despite their reformist purpose, their organization also represented the forces of Egyptian nationalism.[9] According to Hankey:

Egyptian politicians will, I fear, always try to outdo each other in patriotism; to misquote the old saying, it is *surtout pas d'ennemi à droite* in Egypt. When we made the 1936 Treaty, we took the wise precaution of getting virtually every political leader of importance into a coalition government and having his signature on the treaty.

This procedure is out of the question today. In the present political situation is seems really impossible to get the Wafd or even the Moslem Brotherhood to share responsibility with the present [post-Farouk] Government. In any case even the procedure we adopted in 1936 did not stop the Wafd in general or Nahas Pasha personally from attacking the agreement they had signed or even from abrogating it altogether.

This is sobering reflexion for any who are tempted to believe that we can ever place much trust in the Egyptians.[10]

Hankey's mistrust of the Egyptians characterized most British official thought of the period.

---

[9] Allen also emphasized this point: '[T]he Moslem Brotherhood *is* tied up with Egyptian nationalism,' he wrote, 'and the disagreement & dissension between it and the Egyptian Govt. certainly worry the latter & make them afraid to agree with us on anything which the Brotherhood would disapprove'; minute by Allen, 5 Sept. 1953, FO 371/102706. In the judgement of the Embassy in Cairo, the principal goal of the Muslim Brethren was to arrest 'the present corruption of public life', though the extremist wing aimed 'to establish a theocratic government in Egypt', Stevenson to Eden, 'Confidential', 1 Jan. 1952, FO 371/96870. '[W]e should be faced with a Government composed of stern fanatics and fundamentalists', Stevenson wrote at another time, Stevenson to R. J. Bowker, 'Confidential', 26 Jan. 1952, FO 371/96872.

[10] Hankey to Lord Salisbury (Acting Foreign Secretary), 'Confidential', 29 Sept. 1953, FO 371/102706.

There were two other salient aspects of Hankey's thought that were also representative. One was that if the British did not conclude an agreement with the military regime, they might face something worse:

[N]o better Government than the present one can be foreseen, and certainly none with a better understanding of basic strategic realities. The alternative is likely to be either an obscurantist Moslem Brotherhood Government or a demagogic Wafdist Government. Neither would be at all conducive to our interests.[11]

The other aspect was the recurrent theme that the Egyptians, like other Arabs, respected only force. If the British did conclude an agreement, then, in the view of Hankey and many others, 'The real question is whether we are able and willing to make it unrewarding and dangerous for any Egyptian Government to disregard the treaty . . .'[12]

In the 1952–4 period, the British gradually shifted their attention from Neguib, whom they regarded as the figure-head of the revolution, to Nasser, its moving force. 'I derived quite a good impression of Gamal Abdel Nasser', Hankey wrote in June 1953. 'My feeling is that he is trying to be reasonable though he probably has a deep emotional dislike of the British conflicting with a very considerable admiration of us.'[13] Hankey and his colleagues in Cairo believed that Nasser wished to come to an agreement with the British in order to move ahead with economic reconstruction and social reform. The dispute over troops in the Canal Zone prevented him from devoting his full concentration to domestic priorities. According to Hankey:

Nasser and his colleagues are undoubtedly anxious to secure American and for that matter British economic and military assistance. They know they cannot settle their internal problems while the instability caused by the dispute over the Canal Zone endures.

But one of their main purposes in seeking an agreement over the Canal Zone is to put an end to what they regard as the occupation of their country. They have said . . . often that the presence of any foreign soldiers in uniform is an infringement of their independence . . .'[14]

Hankey's interpretation of Nasser's aims coincided with the view held by those in London who believed that it might be possible to come to terms with the Egyptians if an acceptable formula could be found for the withdrawal of British troops. There was also a less explicit motivation on the British side. Nasser appeared to be the best chance, perhaps the last, to reach a lasting accommodation. A minute by Allen provides a clue to the underlying rationale. The British had the

---

[11] Ibid.   [12] Ibid.

[13] Hankey to Sir James Bowker, 'Confidential', 17 June 1953, FO 371/102766.

[14] Hankey to Bowker, 'Secret', 17 Aug. 1953, FO 371/102814.

opportunity, he wrote, 'to consolidate his [Nasser's] position . . . it looks as though he is our best bet'.[15]

The British aimed in part to bolster Nasser as the best bet. But the origins of the 1954 agreement also reflected military calculations. The invention of the hydrogen bomb at one stroke appeared to make the base at Suez obsolete. Two other collateral issues must also be borne in mind to understand the 1954 agreement in relation to the Suez crisis of 1956. The original goal was to create the Middle Eastern equivalent to NATO, in other words, a defence organization in the Middle East in which Egypt would nominally play a central part. This part of the plan disappeared early on because of refusal by the Egyptians to countenance what was in their view a continued British military occupation of Egyptian soil. Nevertheless the British persevered towards the establishment of a Middle Eastern defence system—the Baghdad Pact—that conflicted with Nasser's bid for the leadership of the Arab states. The other issue was Palestine. The British believed that, as long as the Palestine question remained unresolved, there could be no lasting peace in the Middle East, and therefore no satisfactory answer to their own political and military problems. In itself the 1954 agreement had sound prospects. But it resolved neither the Palestine question nor the one of regional defence, and both these issues in turn contributed to the Suez crisis.

THE REVOLUTION OF 1952 AND THE ASCENDANCY OF NASSER

In analysing the origins of the Egyptian revolution, British observers saw the Palestine war of 1948 as one of the principle causes. Sir Ralph Stevenson wrote in the aftermath of King Farouk's abdication in July 1952: 'The morale of the Egyptian Armed Forces never fully recovered from the defeat in Palestine and the accompanying evidence of inefficiency and corruption in the high ranks.'[16] This interest in the antecedents of the revolution was more than historical. Might the military take-over lead to another round with Israel? In the judgement of British officials in Cairo, the Palestine issue was too dangerous for the Egyptians to plan immediate revenge. Restraint rather than recklessness would probably characterize the new regime, especially as long as Ali Maher remained influential. Ali Maher was the statesman of long experience to whom the military officers at first turned to consolidate their political authority. He had served as Prime Minister at the time of the outbreak of the Second World War, in the aftermath

---

[15] Minute by Allen, 3 Apr. 1954, FO 371/108478.
[16] Stevenson to Eden, 'Confidential', 2 Aug. 1952, FO 371/96879.

of the Cairo riots in early 1952, and now at the beginning of the revolution. Sir Ralph Stevenson commented in the second week after Farouk's overthrow:

I should say that the Palestine debacle [in 1948–9] ... was only one of the causes of the coup. The discontent and dissatisfaction of the Army at their treatment by the King and politicians started from that time, but the coup itself probably arose more immediately from the subsequent accumulation of grievances in the Army ...

It seems to me true to say that their defeat in Israel still rankles bitterly in the minds of the Army leaders and they might well be glad of an opportunity to have a second round with Israel if they ever feel themselves strong enough. At present, however, they are too preoccupied with reorganisation of the armed forces and efforts to obtain more arms and equipment to plan any such venture, and I doubt if they would be allowed to as long as Ali Maher remains in charge of the Government.[17]

Ali Maher's reputation as a shrewd Egyptian politician—Eden described him as 'skilled and cunning'[18]—endured into the 1956 crisis. At that time there was speculation within some circles in the British government that he might be a good replacement for Nasser.

In 1952 Ali Maher's tenure of office lasted only six weeks. In early September Neguib removed him from power. Ali Maher nevertheless continued to give support to the military regime and provided it with a historical justification that was studied closely in London. In November 1952 in a public lecture in Cairo introduced by Neguib, Ali Maher developed the theme 'The New Régime and the Renaissance of Egyptian Society'. He traced the origin of the movement for Egyptian independence to the nineteenth century and the achievements of Mohammed Ali. 'There followed a line of Egyptian patriots from Urabi to Zaghlul, whose activities, in spite of differences, were the expression of one thing, namely the will of the Egyptian people.' Four decades after the occupation, Egyptian nationalism forced the British to end formal rule in 1922, but their influence continued to prevail, and the next 'unhappy' stage of Egyptian history did not come to a close 'until the army intervened on 23rd July, 1952'.[19]

To British officials pondering the aftermath of Farouk's overthrow, the point of this and other speeches and writings was that the revolution had produced no definite political philosophy other than

---

[17] Stevenson to Bowker, 'Confidential', 12 Aug. 1952, FO 371/96898.

[18] *The Memoirs of Anthony Eden: Full Circle* (Boston, 1960), p. 258.

[19] As reported in Stevenson to Eden, 'Confidential', 2 Dec. 1952, FO 371/96883. There was a remarkably similar line of interpretation about the lasting consequences of the occupation in British appraisals as well: 'A fundamental cause of anti-British feeling in Egypt, not least in the present Army Movement, is the memory of our suppression of the Egyptian Nationalist Movement of 1882', Stevenson to Eden, 'Secret and Guard', 18 Jan. 1954, PREM 11/629.

'the peculiar blend of nationalism and socialism which dominates Egypt today'.[20] This was not necessarily a negative assessment. The Egyptian leaders, like the British themselves, seemed to prefer an empirical to an ideological approach to politics.[21] These were military officers, fewer than a dozen in number, with little book learning but with great determination to put an end to an exploitative and corrupt regime. With the exception of General Neguib, they were roughly of the same rank and seniority (majors and colonels) and all had the same middle-class or lower middle-class origins. None belonged to the land-owning class that had dominated Egypt. Taking account a year later of the type of leaders the revolution had produced, Robin Hankey wrote: 'their standard of integrity is very much higher than anything that has been known in Egypt for years'.[22]

Some eighteen months after the events of July 1952, Lieutenant-Colonel Gamal Abdel Nasser published a short book entitled *The Philosophy of the Revolution*.[23] Nasser disclaimed any comprehensive analysis, but British officials on the whole responded favourably to his ideas about the regeneration of Egypt. Sir Ralph Stevenson wrote:

Despite a certain awkwardness of style . . . and a tendency to lose himself in anecdote, the book throws a not unfavourable light upon its writer's own beliefs and upon the patterns of thought and expression which are characteristic of him, and of the partly-educated younger generation of the Egyptian middle-class which is to-day in power. His shortcomings and prejudices are those of his class, his age, and his country, and it is remarkable that he should have avoided succumbing to them entirely.

His book has a certain breadth of vision, humanity and idealism which one might be excused for not expecting from a man of his background. It is encouraging to be able to record that his idealism and moral conviction appear to be standing the test of time, and that there are no signs as yet of his empiricism degenerating into unprincipled opportunism.[24]

The contemporary reaction of British officials in Cairo to Nasser's book was thus entirely different from Sir Anthony Eden's later description. In his memoirs Eden regretted that Western readers had been slower to

[20] Stevenson to Eden, 18 Jan. 1954, PREM 11/629.

[21] Roger Allen commented on this point: 'They may be empirical, but in Egypt it is all too easy for empiricism to degenerate merely into the use of old slogans, because Egyptian thinking tends to be conditioned by certain standard preconceptions', minute by Allen, 15 Dec. 1952, FO 371/96883.

[22] Hankey to Allen, 'Confidential', 24 Sept. 1953, FO 371/102706.

[23] 'It seems that the book was actually written—after detailed discussion with Colonel Nasser—very largely by Mohammed Hassanein Heikal, the journalist on the staff of *Akhbar el Yom* who has done a certain amount of ghost-writing for the Prime Minister', Stevenson to Eden, 'Confidential', 14 Sept. 1954, FO 371/108317. Of Heikal's various writings on Nasser and the Suez crisis, see especially Mohamed H. Heikal, *Cutting the Lion's Tail: Suez through Egyptian Eyes* (London, 1986).

[24] Stevenson to Eden, 'Confidential', 14 Sept. 1954, FO 371/108317.

read it than *Mein Kampf* ('with less excuse because it is shorter and not so turgid').[25] The comparison had no justification, either in content or in the suggestion that appeasement might have been prevented if more attention had been paid to Nasser's book at the time. Only later did the description of Nasser as 'another Hitler' begin to appear on British tongues.

The Egyptian revolution altered the nature of one issue that in the past had been the stumbling-block in the way of any agreement between Britain and Egypt. Farouk had regarded himself as sovereign of the Sudan as well as king of Egypt. He had upheld the traditional Egyptian attitude that the sovereignty of the Egyptian crown in the Sudan was vital to Egypt itself. The military officers of the revolution broke the symbolic unity. Neguib, who was half-Sudanese and had been educated at Gordon College in Khartoum, declared that one of the goals of the revolution was to ensure for the Sudanese self-determination without foreign influence. At one stroke he transformed the situation. Previously the British had been able to champion the principle of self-determination for the Sudan against Egyptian ambition to dominate the Nile valley under the Egyptian crown. Now the Egyptians proclaimed themselves comrades-in-arms with the Sudanese. The main prop of British rule in the Sudan was suddenly destroyed. The Sudanese and the Egyptians combined against them. The British could not now repudiate their own principle of self-determination. It is beyond the scope of this essay to discuss the events leading to the Anglo-Egyptian agreement of February 1953 on self-determination in the Sudan, except to say that it removed one of the two major sources of discord between Britain and Egypt and, by doing so, held out hope that the other issue, the Canal Zone, might also be resolved.

With words that perhaps best describe Neguib's permanent contribution to the Egyptian revolution, the official in the Foreign Office responsible for the affairs of the Sudan, Willie Morris, wrote in October 1952: 'We must give General Naguib the credit for having executed the kind of public *volte face* on the Sudan which no previous Egyptian politician has dared to make.'[26] On most other issues, however, Neguib, even from the outset, appeared to be less influential than some of the younger officers, particularly Nasser. Collectively they remained, to borrow Ali Maher's description, just as anti-British as the long line of patriots from Urabi to Zaghlul. Yet it was, according to the principal British political officer at the Embassy in Cairo, Michael Creswell, a mistake to believe that their anti-British attitude

---

[25] Eden, *Full Circle*, p. 608. [26] Minute by Morris, 31 Oct. 1952, FO 371/96883.

would prevent them from coming to an accommodation on the Canal Zone, as the agreement on the Sudan seemed to indicate: 'We ought not to write off the members of the Régime as a bunch of "totalitarian minded gangsters" ... we do not know what the real intentions of the Egyptians are, but at least they showed a greater breadth of view in reaching an agreement with us on the Sudan than any of their predecessors.'[27] Their motives were, in part, to promote economic and social reform, which an agreement on the Canal Zone would facilitate. According to Robin Hankey:

Such an agreement would not of course solve the pressing economic and social problems of Egypt, but it would create considerable confidence in the internal stability and general capability of the régime and would assist the Government to persuade Egyptians to lead the way in getting business going again and in investing money in the great economic projects which are necessary to extend industry and agriculture and provide employment for the people of Egypt.

An improvement of economic conditions would be the first step in getting more popular support. General Neguib and his followers have therefore strong motives for seeking a settlement with us.[28]

Among Neguib's 'followers', Nasser would probably emerge as the dominant figure, but not for reasons that correspond with the usual, retrospective British interpretation of him as a brigand. According to T. E. Evans, Oriental Counsellor at the Cairo Embassy in 1953: 'Colonel Nasser's determination, patience and strength of character seem most likely to prevail.'[29]

'General Neguib's record, and that of his associates,' Eden wrote, 'contains a number of disquieting features and there is a real danger that extremist anti-foreign elements in the new régime may gain the upper hand.'[30] Nevertheless Neguib and his colleagues appeared to be more willing than any previous Egyptian government to come to a settlement. By early 1953 Eden thought that an opportunity had arisen which, if seized, might lead to the creation of a Middle Eastern defence organization comparable to NATO (but with the all important difference of a British Supreme Commander). He based his assessment on the belief that the Egyptians themselves wished to resolve the problem of the Canal Zone, if only to further their own aims, and recognize their own needs for security. On the British side of the calculation, he bluntly warned his colleagues in the Cabinet about the

[27] Creswell to Bowker, 'Secret & Personal', 30 Apr. 1953, FO 371/102731.
[28] Hankey to Lord Salisbury, 'Confidential', 29 June 1953, FO 371/102705.
[29] Memorandum by T. E. Evans, 29 Sept. 1953, FO 371/102706.
[30] Memorandum by Eden, 'Egypt: Defence Negotiations', 27 Oct. 1952, C. (52) 369, CAB 129/56.

discrepancy between the 80,000 troops in the Canal Zone and the 10,000 allowed by the 1936 treaty: 'Let us not forget that we are ourselves in serious breach of it.'[31]

Even more fundamental to Eden was the necessity to come to terms with Middle Eastern nationalism. The Iranian nationalization of the Anglo-Iranian Oil Company did not provide a happy precedent:

In the second half of the 20th century we cannot hope to maintain our position in the Middle East by the methods of the last century. However little we like it, we must face that fact. Commercial concessions whose local benefit appears to redound mainly to the Shahs and Pashas no longer serve in the same way to stengthen our influence in these countries, and they come increasingly under attack by local nationalist opinion. Military occupation could be maintained by force, but in the case of Egypt the base upon which it depends is of little use if there is no local labour to man it.

We have learned the first lesson in Persia: we are learning the second in Egypt.[32]

He rejected out of hand the possibility of a continued British occupation. 'We cannot afford to keep 80,000 men indefinitely in the Canal Zone', he wrote. It was not merely a question of expense. The presence of British troops might provoke a clash with the Egyptians leading to full-scale military action and to the reoccupation of Egypt itself. Eden's analysis of the problem in 1953 makes ironic reading in relation to the course of events in 1956. Effective military operations against the Egyptians, he held, 'would compel us to re-occupy Egypt, with all the consequences which this would entail. We should be likely to have world opinion against us and would find it difficult to make a case if Egypt took us to the United Nations.'[33]

Within the British government, the principal sceptic about reconciliation with the Egyptians was the Prime Minister himself. Before, during, and after the Egyptian revolution, Churchill consistently advised Eden not to be intimidated. 'If . . . you make what looks like a surrender to violence and evacuation of forces by threats and atrocities,' Churchill wrote in a minute that revealed his concern with the Iranian oil crisis as well as Suez, 'it may cause deep resentment in that element of British public life whose regard sustains you, and also mockery from the Party that scuttled from Abadan.'[34] In the summer of 1952, he wrote: 'I am quite sure that we could not agree to be kicked

[31] Memorandum by Eden, 'Egypt: the Alternatives', 16 Feb. 1953, C. (53) 65, CAB 129/59.
[32] Ibid.
[33] Ibid.
[34] He added: 'Some of the advisers of the late Government have had more experience of getting out of British possessions and rights than I have had', minute by Churchill, 15 Feb. 1952, PREM 11/91.

out of Egypt by Nahas, Farouk or Neguib and leave our base, worth £500 millions, to be despoiled or put in their care. . . . How different would the position have been if the late Government had not flinched . . . at Abadan.'[35] In early 1953 Churchill's attitude began to shift. For reasons of economy and because he believed that the Suez base was becoming strategically obsolete, he now favoured eventual withdrawal. But he held highly ambivalent feelings about retreating from the position that he had always regarded as Britain's supreme strategic position in the world. He was contemptuous of the Egyptians. He spoke of 'appeasement', according to Shuckburgh, 'saying that he never knew before that Munich was situated on the Nile'.[36] This train of thought had a powerful logic. As Shuckburgh summed up the Prime Minister's thinking: 'If we go out of the Sudan and Egypt it will be another stage in the policy of scuttle which began in India and ended at Abadan. It will lead to the abandonment of our African colonies.'[37]

Through one of the quirks of history, the ill health of three of the British principals helped to shape the course of these Egyptian affairs. Eden was absent from the Foreign Office from April to October 1953. Stevenson was also ill and away from Cairo during most of the same period. In June Churchill had a stroke. But until then he himself presided over the Egyptian business. He read telegrams with a sharp eye, determined not to be jockeyed or rushed. '[H]e intends to run the Egyptian negotiations in his own way when A.E. is safely tucked out of the way,' Shuckburgh noted in his diary.[38] In place of Stevenson, Robin Hankey was sent to Cairo to ensure a robust outlook. 'The Prime Minister asked me to dinner this evening,' Hankey wrote shortly before his departure, 'and over a period of well over an hour explained his view about the policy we should pursue in Egypt. He was most categorical. . . . At one point he said I should be a "patient sulky pig".'[39]

Churchill believed that the Egyptians needed an agreement with the British much more than the British needed one with the Egyptians. 'If H.M. Embassy did nothing for 6 months except avoid giving things away,' Hankey wrote, 'he would be very content.' Despite his growing conviction that the Suez base would have to be given up, or at best transformed into the equivalent of a NATO base, Churchill still held a Victorian attitude towards the Egyptians. 'The Prime Minister said he was not afraid of physical trouble', Hankey wrote. 'Although we

---

[35] Minute by Churchill, 19 Aug. 1952, PREM 11/392.

[36] Shuckburgh, *Descent to Suez*, p. 75.

[37] Ibid., p. 76.

[38] Ibid., p. 86.

[39] Memorandum by Hankey, 'Secret', 22 May 1953, FO 371/102765.

should not of course say so, he would in some ways welcome it. It would do the Egyptians no sort of good.'[40] To some extent Hankey's ideas were similar. 'General Neguib and his henchmen have good reasons to want a settlement with us', he reported from Cairo.[41] But Hankey eventually demonstrated a far more liberal attitude than Churchill thought desirable, and among Neguib's 'henchmen' Hankey identified a key figure who might be able to guide the negotiations to a successful conclusion. 'Gamal Abdel Nasser', according to Hankey, 'is probably more willing to learn than some of the others.'[42] In June 1953 Nasser became Minister of the Interior. Hankey described him as a tough, intelligent, and determined military officer who, though anti-British, had the best interests of his country at heart. '[H]is ideas on internal policy are progressive or left wing,' Hankey concluded, 'and he and his colleagues are strongly "anti-imperialist".'[43]

GENERAL SIR BRIAN ROBERTSON AND THE MILITARY BASIS OF THE SETTLEMENT

In April 1953 Churchill announced to the Cabinet that General Sir Brian Robertson would relinquish his duties as Commander-in-Chief, British Middle East Land Forces, a few weeks earlier than had been intended, to become the principal military representative in the discussions with the Egyptians. Robertson had served in this tour of duty since 1950. During the war he had been a key figure in the logistical success of the Abyssinian campaign and later won distinction as Field Marshal Alexander's chief administrative officer in Italy. After the war he became Military Governor and Commander-in-Chief of the British Zone in Germany, where he acted, according to the *Dictionary of National Biography*, as 'a liberal and sympathetic "viceroy" intent on guiding the social and democratic advancement of a future ally'. Konrad Adenauer described him as a great British 'soldier statesman'.[44] Robertson brought with him to Egypt the same determined attitude that he had demonstrated towards the Soviet Union while in Germany. The son of the Field Marshal of the 1914–18 war, he had a clear intellect, a commanding presence, and considerable powers of persuasion.

'I have been watching this situation now for two and a half years', Robertson wrote in November 1952, 'and I feel that I cannot hold my

[40] Ibid.
[41] Hankey to Lord Salisbury, 'Confidential', 29 June 1953, FO 371/102705.
[42] Hankey to Bowker, 'Confidential', 17 June 1953, FO 371/102766.
[43] Hankey to Bowker, 'Secret', 17 Aug. 1953, FO 371/102814.
[44] *Dictionary of National Biography, 1971–1980*, p. 729. See also especially the obituary in *The Times*, 30 Apr. 1974.

peace when everything that has been said and done during this time seems to be in peril of being cast away.'[45] Like Churchill, Robertson feared that Britain's strategic advantage at Suez, won by skill and fortitude, might be bartered away for false promises of security. He wrote for example of Stevenson's 'constant endeavour to whittle away our position in Egypt'.[46] He suspected that the Foreign Office preferred a policy of appeasement. Roberston was by no means alone in questioning Stevenson's approach to the problem. Stevenson himself held that refusal to evacuate, virtually lock, stock, and barrel, would lead to deadlock. Sir Norman Brook, the Secretary to the Cabinet, wrote to Churchill: 'I wonder whether ... the negotiations should continue to be entrusted to our Ambassador, Sir Ralph Stevenson. He has been very sceptical ... I cannot help wondering whether we are likely to get the agreement which we want if it is negotiated by a man who believes from the outset that this attempt must fail.'[47] To prove good faith, Stevenson favoured a declaration from the outset that the British intended to withdraw. Robertson preferred to take nothing for granted, especially the assumption that the Egyptians might co-operate with British defence plans in return for withdrawal. Actually the two attitudes were not far apart and certainly not irreconcilable, but Stevenson's illness in 1953 averted an awkward discussion of whether or not his conciliatory approach made him the best person to negotiate Britain's withdrawal. Robin Hankey's tougher attitude was much closer to Robertson's and Churchill's. It is a measure of Robertson's ability that he managed to remain on good terms with Stevenson, to win the confidence of the Foreign Office, and, occasionally, to woo Churchill away from the inclination to take a die-hard stand.

'I have never advocated that we march on Cairo as a deliberate act to bring about a solution', Robertson wrote in summing up his attitude towards the question of intervention.[48] Nevertheless he had been centrally involved in drawing up contingency plans for intervention should unrest or riots endanger the lives of British subjects in Alexandria or Cairo. ('Large-scale murderous attacks on British subjects', was his description of the circumstances that might precipitate British action.) The principal plan bore the code-name Operaton *Rodeo*. Robertson's ideas in this regard help to clarify the nature and extent of pre-1956 plans for intervention. He was alarmed at the unpredictable

---

[45] Robertson to General Sir John Harding (Chief of the Imperial General Staff), 'Top Secret', 5 Nov. 1952, WO 216/842.

[46] Ibid.

[47] Minute by Brook to Churchill, 14 Feb. 1953, PREM 11/486.

[48] Robertson to Lieutenant-General Sir Nevil Brownjohn (Vice-Chief of the Imperial General Staff), 'Top Secret', 12 Feb. 1952, WO 216/754.

consequences, and he wished to limit the scope of the operation to the two major cities:

It is undoubtedly correct that, if we launch Operation RODEO we start a train of events the conclusions of which cannot be estimated with any certainty.

Such attempts as have been made to estimate the consequences of RODEO have arrived at the conclusion that we should have to occupy CAIRO and ALEXANDRIA for an appreciable period, and to control communications thence with the Canal Zone, but that we should not attempt to occupy EGYPT, which must necessarily be quite beyond our military and political resources.

By occupying these two cities it is hoped that we should have such a grip on the country as would enable us to compel the establishment of an Egyptian Government acceptable to ourselves.[49]

Robertson did not speculate whether a collaborative regime would last long. That was the Foreign Office's business. From the military vantage-point, any action to restore order, however limited in purpose, might lead to the nightmare of another indefinite reoccupation of the entire country. 'From my point of view', Robertson commented, 'RODEO is and always has been a thoroughly distasteful prospect.'[50]

Robertson had definite ideas about what realistically could and could not be achieved in a settlement with the Egyptians. He did not believe that a 'Middle East Defence Organization' (MEDO) on the model of NATO had the faintest chance of becoming an effective fighting unit. The Egyptians had no intention of becoming part of it. Instead of insisting on the illusion of a defence pact, Robertson believed that the British should put their major effort into salvaging a small but effective base. Here was his main argument:

MEDO does not yet exist and is unlikely to have any military value. ... I personally consider that it would be a grave political and military mistake to evacuate Egypt without maintaining a nucleus base there. There is no alternative base. ... Without a base in Egypt we cannot make an effective contribution to the defence of the Middle East.[51]

The question of MEDO, in Robertson's judgement, should be put forward merely as a bargaining point from which the British could retreat to secure a base under British control. It would be a mistake to think that Egypt would ever seriously consider participating in a Middle East defence organization. 'She has told us repeatedly and

[49] Robertson to Harding, 'Personal & Top Secret', 26 Nov. 1952, WO 216/842.
[50] Ibid.
[51] Robertson to Harding, 'Top Secret', 5 Nov. 1952, WO 216/842.

emphatically that she will not so agree', Robertson wrote in March 1953. 'There is not the remotest chance of her changing her mind.'[52]

As opposed to the shadow of collective defence, the principal British military aim was to retain effective control over a base that could quickly be reactivated in the event of war. At any cost Robertson wished to retain, to use one of his favourite phrases, 'a foot in the door'. There were three 'cases' ranging from good to bad whereby that goal might, or might not, be achieved. He summarized them in a memorandum circulated by Churchill to the Cabinet:

Case A—We retain control of the management of the principal installations in the Base. . . . The Base functions in peace time for the maintenance of some of our Forces in the Middle East. It is nominally available for immediate use on the outbreak of war.

Case B—We hand over control completely to the Egyptians, including control of our depots and workshops. A small British technical staff is left to assist the Egyptians, but this staff also will be under Egyptian executive control. . . .

Case C—This differs from Case B in that no British personnel are left behind other than a few Inspectors. It would not be possible to use the Base in peace, nor even to turn over the stocks. It is estimated . . . that such a Base might be re-activated within ninety days.[53]

Robertson advised Churchill to accept nothing less than the substance of 'Case A'. 'Case B', he warned, would quickly slide into 'Case C'. 'We should then no longer have any kind of "foot in the door" and we should find it very much harder to get back into our base installations when we needed them in war.'[54]

In 1946 Churchill as a leader of the opposition had criticized the Labour government for unilateraly making a declaration stating that Britain intended to withdraw from the Canal Zone. Here was a major issue of tactics. Was it best to begin with a gesture of goodwill (Stevenson's preference), or to let the Egyptians know that the British would take a resolute stand (Robertson's choice)? Churchill preferred to negotiate from a position of strength, bargaining hard and yielding only in exchange for advantage gained. It would be better to break off discussions rather than to embrace anything that might be interpreted, in his phrase, as 'dead-level scuttle'. It is therefore ironic that, to reach a settlement, the Tory government moved virtually from 'Case A' to 'Case C', ultimately using the same arguments as Sir Ralph Stevenson as well as the Labour leaders who had earlier stated that Britain should

---

[52] Robertson to Lieutenant-General H. Redman (Vice-Chief of the Imperial General Staff), 'Top Secret', 21 Mar. 1953, WO 216/848.

[53] 'Egypt: Defence Negotiations', 7 July 1953, C. (53) 192, CAB 129/61.

[54] Minute by Robertson to Churchill, 6 June 1953, PREM 11/485.

demonstrate magnanimity. The British in return received guarantees, including the right to re-enter the Canal Zone in certain circumstances of war, but they relinquished the 'foothold' so highly valued by both Churchill and Robertson.

The military officers who shaped British strategy, as well as Churchill himself, knew that the Americans would have to be brought into the discussions. Only if confronted with a unified Anglo-American stand would the Egyptians be disposed to make adequate arrangements for British security. In the conventional British view, the Egyptians respected only force. The Chief of the Imperial General Staff in early 1953, Field Marshal Sir William Slim, believed, like Churchill, that it would be better to break off negotiations than to make unnecessary concessions—either to the Egyptians or to the Americans:

We should not be afraid on a matter of importance or principle to let the negotiations fail. That would be much better than weakly yielding to either Egyptians—or Americans. It is comforting in this affair to remember that there are few countries in the world weaker than Egypt. We are for the first time negotiating from a position of strength.[55]

The uncompromising military view had support in the House of Commons. 'I feel very strongly', wrote one of the members of the 'Suez group', Julian Amery, 'that, in addition to any technicians who stay to maintain the Base, we must keep some R.A.F. Units and some "teeth" troops—even if it is only a Brigade Group—in the Canal Zone. It is not enough to have a right of re-entry to the Zone'.[56] The question of 'teeth' troops became an essential issue. The Foreign Office believed that the Egyptians would never accept them, nor would the Americans, when it came to the test, support the British insistence on them as a vital ingredient of the settlement. Roger Allen wrote about 'keeping "teeth" troops', in what proved to be an astute comment: 'This is obviously impossible. Either we have an agreement with Egypt, or we do not.'[57]

Churchill was dismayed when the President, Dwight D. Eisenhower, and the Secretary of State, John Foster Dulles, did not respond positively to the suggestion of a united front. 'My dear Friend,' Churchill wrote to Eisenhower, 'I am very sorry that you do not feel that you can do much to help us about the Canal Zone.'[58] Eisenhower stated that the United States certainly would support 'Case A', and that he hoped the Egyptians would accept it. But the United States

[55] Minute by Slim, 'Negotiations with Egypt', 10 Mar. 1953, PREM 11/486.
[56] Amery to Eden, 'Personal and Confidential', 18 Mar. 1953, FO 371/102807.
[57] Minute by Allen, 2 Apr. 1953, FO 371/102807.
[58] Churchill to Eisenhower, 19 Mar. 1953, PREM 11/486.

would not be a party to anything that smacked of 'ganging up', the phrase of the American Ambassador in Cairo, Jefferson Caffery. In May 1953 Dulles visited Cairo, where he gained the impression of such Egyptian adamancy on the subject of British troops that he began to shift his ideas away from Egypt possibly playing a central part in a Middle East defence organization. He now began to develop his scheme for a defence line drawn along the 'northern tier' of Turkey, Iraq, and Iran.[59] From the British point of view, Dulles and Caffery made the problem worse, not merely by failing to stand by the British, but because they held too optimistic a view about the Egyptian character. The Americans in Cairo, Hankey reported, could only be described as 'starry-eyed'.[60] To the British, Caffrey seemed bent on enhancing his own reputation by playing the broker between Egyptian nationalism and British imperialism.[61] The Egyptians were thus led to believe that if they sat tight they might be able to use the Americans against the British. 'Because they are the miserable fellows that they are,' Robertson wrote about the Egyptians after Dulles's visit to Cairo, 'it is my guess that they will let matters drift.'[62]

The Egyptians were not the only ones playing for time. Robertson had been instructed by Churchill to ' "sit tight" and to leave it to the Egyptians to make the first move'.[63] By mid-1953 little progress had been made other than to gain a better idea of what both sides would emphatically reject. Robertson wrote that the substance of 'Case A' might still be obtained if the Prime Minister would agree 'to pander to Egyptian conceit'.[64] Churchill had to be coaxed. In late June he suffered his stroke, which made it easier, for the time being, for others to move forward. Robertson now began to work with the minister delegated to take charge of the Egyptian business, Lord Salisbury (Lord President of the Council).[65] Robertson himself had already

---

[59] See William J. Burns, *Economic Aid and American Policy toward Egypt, 1955–1981* (Albany, 1985), p. 15.

[60] Hankey to Foreign Office, 'Confidential', 5 July 1953, PREM 11/485. Hankey's view was representative: 'The Americans', Sir Norman Brook had written a few months earlier, 'have less experience than we in negotiating with Eastern peoples', minute by Brook to Churchill, 14 Feb. 1953, PREM 11/486.

[61] 'There seemed to be people in the U.S. Embassies in the Middle East', the Permanent Under-Secretary at the Foreign Office Sir William Strang complained about Caffery, 'who were dominated by the old anti-colonial feeling to the extent that they seemed to think that the British were always wrong', minute by Strang, 30 Mar. 1953, FO 371/102803.

[62] Robertson to Churchill, 'Secret', 12 May 1953, PREM 11/485.

[63] COS (53) 72, 'Confidential Annex', 9 June 1953, DEFE 4/63.

[64] Minute by Robertson to Churchill, 'Top Secret', 12 June 1953, PREM 11/485.

[65] Salisbury resisted the pressure of the 'Suez group'. He once wrote 'extremely irritating' about one of Lord Hankey's letters. 'Lord Hankey ignores the immense strain, both military & economic, which the keeping of 70,000 men on the Canal imposes on us'; minute by Salisbury, 9 Sept. 1953, FO 371/102816.

begun to move away from 'Case A', becoming reconciled to British withdrawal and insisting that the key issue had become that of re-entry.[66] In his discussions in Cairo with the Egyptians, he had become convinced of the same point emphasized earlier by Roger Allen: if there were to be a settlement, it would be on the basis of British withdrawal. The Minister of Defence, Lord Alexander, also realistically accepted the necessity of British evacuation: 'if we are to get an agreement with the Egyptians,' he wrote, 'it is clear that our troops must leave Egypt.'[67] The convergence of British military and political thought represented a watershed. A settlement was now possible.

Churchill recovered from his stroke, but the initiative of Salisbury and Robertson had placed the negotiations on the basis of British evacuation and had reduced the outstanding issues to four principal points: (1) reactivation of the base; (2) the duration of the agreement; (3) the British technicians who would stay on, and whether or not they would wear uniforms; and (4) the time limit for withdrawal of troops.[68] All of those issues continued to be debated while the Egyptians as well as the British sorted out their priorities and calculated how much they wished to sacrifice. Churchill still played a central part, which was marked by suspicion and obstruction. 'He starts confused and wrong on almost every issue', Shuckburgh wrote in December 1953. 'Always he has wished a war with Egypt, after which we would march out and leave them.'[69] Churchill was now fully convinced that evacuation was the only course, but he still wished to teach the Egyptians a lesson. That he was not more disruptive was in part because of the influence of Robertson, but above all because of Eden, who had returned to the Foreign Office in October and demonstrated great skill in preventing the Prime Minister from going off the rails. From that time on the settlement was essentially Eden's work.

The development of British attitudes towards the Egyptians and the Canal Zone was well summed up by Robertson's analysis of the problem after he had accepted evacuation as a necessity. The Foreign Office believed it to be 'very persuasive'.[70] There were only three courses. The first was to tell the Egyptians 'to go to blazes' and to

---

[66] Robertson carried the Chiefs of Staff with him on the transition from 'Case A' to 'Case B' in a critical meeting of 9 June 1953. See COS (53) 72, 'Confidential Annex', DEFE 4/63. The Foreign Office comment was: 'General Robertson's proposals appeared to be the most practical solution'.

[67] Minute by Alexander to Churchill, 'Secret', 11 Sept. 1953, PREM 11/485.

[68] See memorandum by Salisbury, 'Egypt: Defence Negotiations', C. (53) 232, 15 Aug. 1953, CAB 129/62.

[69] Shuckburgh, *Descent to Suez*, pp. 112 and 121.

[70] Minute by Strang, 7 July 1953, FO 371/102817. 'Excellent', added Lord Salisbury. There is a copy of Robertson's memorandum, dated 6 July 1953, in PREM 11/484.

continue to occupy the Canal Zone, a tempting but dangerous and expensive solution. The second was completely to clear out of the Middle East, a course he rejected because of the strategic issues at stake and also, no less important, because of 'the effect on our prestige'. The third course was to reach an accord with Egypt. 'I believe that if we pick our way very carefully we may be able to get an agreement which can be accepted only in view of the serious consequences of having no agreement.' What guarantee would there be that the Egyptians would stick with this agreement 'any more than they have honoured others'? Robertson had no complete answer to that question, but his concluding thought represents the underlying military and political rationale of the British side of the settlement: 'The best that we can do is to persuade the Americans to underwrite the agreement, and to keep ourselves as strong a force as we can afford in the Middle East near to Egypt in the hope that this evidence of our strength will induce them to be loyal to their undertakings.'[71]

THE SETTLEMENT OF 1954

An agreement in 1954 would not have been possible without Churchill's acquiescence. He concurred only when he perceived a convergence of events and political forces that, he believed, conspired against him. The Chancellor of the Exchequer demanded prodigious cuts in defence expenditure of £180 million. The upkeep of military installations in the Canal Zone alone was £56 million a year. If reductions were not made in Europe at the expense of NATO, Britain's principal pillar of security, then they would have to be made in the Middle East. The Foreign Office favoured an agreement with the Egyptians. So also, for entirely different reasons, did the Chiefs of Staff. Churchill himself was convinced of the need to redeploy troops from the Canal Zone into other parts of the Middle East, but he did not want to give the Egyptians the impression of British weakness. His preference was to retreat at British convenience, to maintain 10,000 troops in the Canal Zone in any event, and, if provoked, to break off relations with the Egyptians. It is clear from the historical record that he would have welcomed a fight. He wished to give the Egyptians a military thump, then to redeploy British forces in Libya and Jordan.[72] In March 1954, however, a momentous development in nuclear weaponry altered his views and helped to reconcile him to the necessity of withdrawal. The American explosion of the hydrogen bomb on the first of that month

---

[71] Robertson's memorandum, 6 July 1953, PREM 11/484.
[72] 'He does not change', Shuckburgh wrote in his diary; *Descent to Suez*, p. 121.

loomed like a cloud over the discussions about Britain's evacuation from Egypt.

In these final deliberations General Sir Brian Robertson played no part. In late 1953 he had become Chairman of the British Transport Commission. Churchill had offered him this position in recognition of his 'gifts of leadership and experience'.[73] Before he assumed his new responsibilities he wrote a final appraisal of the Egyptian question. Eden circulated it to the Cabinet. It gives perhaps the best rounded assessment of the situation as seen by the British in late 1953–early 1954. Robertson was steady in his views, and his analysis reveals the coherence of British thought. Though he now commented on such matters as the possible duration of the agreement, the period of withdrawal of British troops, and whether or not British technicians staying on to maintain the base would wear uniforms, he regarded these things as secondary. The principal point was the availability of the base in event of war. 'We need assurance', Robertson wrote, 'that we shall be able to put our Base on a war footing immediately a major war breaks out.' He knew that the Egyptians also regarded access to the base as the vital point:

From the Egyptian point of view the main issue is undoubtedly availability. They are haggling on the other points, partly no doubt, for sheer love of bargaining, but mainly, it seems to me, in the false hope of weakening thereby our stand on availability.[74]

The Egyptian government, in Robertson's view, had already made as many concessions as it could politically afford. 'This is the main reason', he wrote, 'for Egyptian obduracy on the question of availability. Gamal Abdel Nasser has told me so.'[75] Would the Egyptians make this vital concession?

Everything would now turn on Nasser. Robertson regarded him as a temperamental person, but also as a man of honour. If he were to conclude an agreement, he would stick by it. In Robertson's judgement, Nasser had compelling domestic reasons for wishing to settle with the British:

He is a man of moods. . . . [But] he is no fool, and he knows that his régime depends for its continued existence on getting an agreement with us, and this for two simple reasons: first, without it the régime cannot fulfil its promises that it will get rid of our troops; second, without it neither foreign capital nor tourists will come to Egypt, and the economy of the country, upon which the stability of any Government ultimately depends, cannot be put on a sound basis.[76]

[73] Churchill to Robertson, 'Top Secret', 5 Aug. 1953, Eden Papers, FO 800/774.
[74] 'Appreciation by General Robertson, 18th November, 1953', C. (53) 328, CAB 129/64.
[75] Ibid.   [76] Ibid.

Most important of all, Robertson believed it would be in Britain's own interest to come to terms with Nasser:

> If we do get an agreement, I believe that the present Egyptian Government will do their best to honour it. No alternative Government is likely to behave better in this respect: on the contrary. Therefore it will be in our own interests to support the present régime, doing all we can to ensure that it shall retain power as long as possible.[77]

Robertson expressed a growing consensus within British official circles in late 1953–early 1954. To repeat Roger Allen's phrase that summed it up, Nasser appeared to be 'our best bet'.

Churchill was the notable exception. He preferred a course of action that would lead to 'all bets being off'. 'My thought has been moving along these lines', he explained to Eden.[78] Churchill wished to place the Egyptians in the position, in the eyes of Parliament and the United States, of having refused a good offer. These were remarkably similar tactics to those of 1942 when the Cripps negotiations had broken down and Churchill had been effectively able to argue that the Indians bore responsibility for rejecting a sensible solution to the problem of India's future. He would now do the same with the Canal, holding 10,000 'teeth troops' there and, perhaps, luring the Egyptians into an attack. 'Neg-wib's gone', he said in his inimitable lisp to Shuckburgh in February 1954 (somewhat prematurely, as it proved). When Shuckburgh pointed out that Nasser might not be an improvement, Churchill responded, 'No, no. Much worse. That's the point. Perhaps he will bring it to a head. I have been afraid they might agree.' When Shuckburgh reflected on what the Prime Minister meant by Nasser's forcing matters to a head, he concluded that Churchill 'can only mean attacking our troops, so that we have an excuse for fighting'.[79]

One of the issues at stake, which troubled Members of Parliament as well as the Prime Minister, was the possible decline of British nerve. The leader of the 'Suez group' in the House of Commons, Captain Charles Waterhouse, bitterly opposed withdrawal as evidence of sagging will and confidence. Churchill did not publicly support the extreme right-wing Tories who opposed a retreat from Egypt, but privately he encouraged them. 'You keep it up', he said to Julian Amery. 'You're on the right lines.'[80] According to the 'Waterhouse theory', as it was called, British forces could be reduced to 10,000 'teeth troops' and the Canal Zone held indefinitely. Though Churchill upheld the principle of the continued presence of an effective fighting

---

[77] 'Appreciation by General Robertson, 18 November 1953', C. (53) 328, CAB 129/64.
[78] Minute by Churchill to Eden, 'Secret and Private', 28 Dec. 1953, FO 371/108413.
[79] Shuckburgh, *Descent to Suez*, p. 136.
[80] Brian Lapping, *End of Empire* (London, 1985), p. 255.

force, he also acknowledged, as a nod to redeployment, that British troops might withdraw in their own time. Depending on the belligerency of his mood, he sometimes urged that they destroy the military installations at the time of their departure. Eden opposed the jingoistic stand of maintaining 'teeth troops' in the Canal Zone. So also, with a complementary set of reasons, did the Chiefs of Staff.

The underlying theory of retrenchment, granted to be an economic necessity, held that British forces in the Middle East might be reduced and redeployed without diminishing military effectiveness or influence. As a military exercise, the winding up of the bases in the Canal Zone might take place by the end of 1956 (to be within the legal limits of the 1936 treaty). The retreat would begin by rolling up from the south and closing down the huge supply depot at Tell-el-Kebir in the east. In the final area near Moascar/Abu Sueir, 10,000 land forces and some 3,000 Royal Air Force personnel would defend port facilities and at least one airfield. Contrary to the Prime Minister's views, the troop commanders would not welcome hostilities. Good relations with the Egyptians were necessary for successful redeployment in Libya and Jordan. The Chiefs of Staff were emphatic on this point:

If we have to wind up the Base, it is important to get Egyptian co-operation. If we have to face Egyptian non-co-operation and increased terrorist activity . . . [then] withdrawal in these conditions would be regarded as a victory for Egypt and would prejudice our chances of obtaining satisfactory agreements with the other Arab states.[81]

The Chiefs of Staff regarded a smooth withdrawal as so important 'from the general strategic point of view' that they would be willing to make concessions on such minor points as the uniforms of the technicians staying on to maintain the skeleton base.

The Chiefs of Staff did not wish indefinitely to retain 'teeth troops', 10,000 or otherwise. In seeking support for his own position, Churchill appointed a ministerial committee to review the situation. Unfortunately for him, the three lawyers on the committee, Lord Simonds (Lord Chancellor), Sir David Maxwell-Fyfe (Home Secretary), and Selwyn Lloyd (Minister of State), held that the continued presence of British troops would be justified only by reducing them to the number and area specified by the 1936 treaty, and only then with the aim of eventual withdrawal. In these discussions the Minister of Defence, Lord Alexander, introduced a phrase that summed up the military view of reduced forces. They would be no more than 'hostages of fortune'.[82] Moreover in February 1954 the Chiefs of Staff warned that,

[81] Memorandum by Chiefs of Staff, 'Middle East Defence', 9 Jan. 1954, C. (54) 9, CAB 129/65.

[82] See e.g. Minutes of Meeting of Ministers, 8 Feb. 1954, PREM 11/701.

if the Egyptians were to renew guerrilla warfare, the garrison at
Moascar might be placed 'in a position similar to our forces in Berlin'.
In this judgement, the withdrawal should be total. Otherwise British
troops, far from being a symbol of British determination, would
become, to repeat the recurrent phrase, 'a complete hostage to
fortune'.[83]

The critical period was the spring of 1954. Not only the explosion of
the hydrogen bomb but also the French defeat in Indo-China at Dien
Bien Phou conveyed a sense of a turning-point in history. The British
evacuation from Egypt seemed to hang in the balance. In March
Nasser gave the British a clear indication that he wished a settlement
and accepted the condition of availability.[84] If Turkey or an Arab state
were attacked, Britain would have the right to activate the base
(though, significantly enough, then as later, Israel was not mentioned
in any part of the formula). In April Nasser removed Neguib and
assumed full control over Egyptian affairs. During this time violence
again erupted in the Canal Zone. On the British side, five soldiers were
killed. The Chiefs of Staff became increasingly sceptical whether an
accord would be possible in the face of renewed Egyptian terrorism.
William Clark (the diplomatic correspondent of the *Observer* who in
1955 became Eden's press secretary and later resigned during the Suez
crisis) reported that Nasser intended to prosecute those responsible for
the murders in the Canal Zone, but that, in Nasser's view, it was 'only
human that magistrates would not convict Egyptians accused of theft
or assault against the British forces'.[85] That outlook may have been
realistic, but it did not reassure those working for a settlement. Roger
Allen doubted whether Nasser was capable of controlling 'thuggery in
the Canal Zone'.[86] Nasser himself appeared to be developing aims at
variance with his desire to come to terms with the British. The
perception of his imperialistic ambitions became clear at the time of his
advent to full power. William Clark, for example, gained the impression 'of a desire that Egypt should pursue an expanding, even
imperialistic, policy in the Middle East and Africa'.[87]

Despite suspicions about Nasser, and reservations by Churchill and
opposition from the Suez group in Parliament, the Foreign Office
moved ahead with the agreement. It was concluded in July 1954 and
finally signed in October. In return for access to the base in an
emergency (an attack on an Arab state or Turkey), the British yielded

---

[83] Memorandum by Chiefs of Staff, 'Egypt', 25 Feb. 1954, C. (54) 74, CAB 129/66.

[84] See Makins to Eden, 'Top Secret', 9 Mar. 1954, PREM 11/701.

[85] As related in a minute by A. A. Duff, 21 Apr. 1954, FO 371/108317.

[86] Minute by Allen, 22 Apr. 1954, FO 371/108417.

[87] Minute by A. A. Duff, 21 Apr. 1954, FO 371/108317. See William Clark, *From Three Worlds*
(London, 1986).

on almost all remaining issues of substance. Rather than 'teeth troops' remaining in the Canal Zone, the skeleton base would be maintained by civilian technicians. They would not wear British uniforms, thus removing one of the symbols of the British occupation. British troops would withdraw within twenty months, and the agreement would last for a definite period, which in the end proved to be merely seven years. So rapidly did this strategy of withdrawal develop that the Commander-in-Chief, Middle East Land Forces, General Sir Charles Keightley, described the tactics as 'political acrobatics'.[88] How did Eden manage to perform this feat of political agility?

A clue can be found in the phrase 'hostages of fortune'. The Foreign Secretary followed the lead of his staff (notably Sir Evelyn Shuckburgh, still his Private Secretary but in mid-May to become Assistant Under-Secretary supervising the Middle East). Eden now proposed that troop withdrawal be total and that the soldiers be replaced by civilian contractors.[89] British soldiers remaining in the Canal Zone in reduced numbers, he told his colleagues in the Cabinet in mid-March 1954, 'would in fact be hostages of fortune' whereas the installations could be maintained by civilian contract labour and the military danger thus averted. Lord Alexander supported this argument in the identical language of 'hostages of fortune' and emphasized that this 'new proposal' would facilitate the removal of all troops from Egypt.[90] The proposal of complete evacuation was of course disagreeable to Churchill, who professed 'great anxiety'. Other members of the Cabinet agreed with him that great care would have to be taken to avoid the impression of a 'complete surrender' to the Egyptians. Nevertheless the discussion demonstrated that an alliance had been forged. With the Foreign Secretary allied with the Minister of Defence, it was an unbreakable combination.

A further figure played a vital part in sustaining the link between the Foreign Office and the military and in carrying the day with the Egyptians. This was the Secretary of State for War, Antony Head. For reasons of economy and morale as well as the danger of reduced forces trapped in another 'Berlin', Head wished to see British troops entirely withdrawn from the Canal Zone. At the very least he hoped to begin the dismantling of archaic military installations and the redeployment

---

[88] Keightley to Sir John Harding, 'Top Secret', 13 May 1954, WO 216/867.

[89] 'He is like a sea anemone', Shuckburgh wrote when Eden put the proposal before the Cabinet, 'covered with sensitive tentacles all recording currents of opinion around him. He quivers with sensitivity to opinion in the House, the party, the newspapers', Shuckburgh, *Descent to Suez*, p. 148.

[90] CC (54) 18th Conclusions, Minute 1, 15 Mar. 1954, CAB 128/27. For Eden's Cabinet paper (drafted by Shuckburgh) that provided the basis of the discussion, 'Egypt: Defence Negotiations', 13 Mar. 1954, C. (54) 99, CAB 129/66.

of troops to better purpose. 'Where the interests of the British Army are concerned,' he wrote to Eden, 'that day cannot be too soon for us.'[91] The danger he foresaw, as did the Chiefs of Staff, was that troop withdrawal might tempt the Egyptians to attack, thus forcing the remnant to evacuate in humiliating circumstances. In any event the reduction of troop numbers would render inoperable the *Rodeo* plan to restore order in the Delta in the event of breakdown of authority or danger to British subjects. Sir John Harding, the Chief of the Imperial General Staff, pessimistically held that British commitments thus could not be fulfilled, and he, rather like Churchill, believed that the Egyptians would see British withdrawal as an opportunity to attack.[92] The Chiefs of Staff would have to be prepared to strike back. By contrast, Head, a man of robust views and vigorous intellect, held that the Egyptians would see it in their own interest to facilitate evacuation in order to achieve their overriding goal—the departure of British troops from Egyptian soil.

Although the spring of 1954 represented the breakthrough period in which the British began to see the final outlines of the settlement, not until mid-summer did the actual negotiations take place. The lull in the Egyptian question was caused in part by Eden's preoccupation with the Persian oil crisis and the emergency in Indo-China. During this time the consequences of the hydrogen bomb were also widely debated both publicly and within the government. Churchill, who saw the development in nuclear warfare as a turning-point in the history of mankind, attempted to deflect attention from Egypt. The question of troops in the Canal Zone, he wrote, had become 'less urgent' because of 'all this Hydrogen business which has swooped down on us'.[93] To the Chiefs of Staff, however, it was intolerable to let things drift without a decision to withdraw or to maintain sufficient strength to carry out the *Rodeo* plan and its commitment to protect British subjects. It was 'of tremendous importance from the military point of view', Sir John Harding stated to the Chiefs of Staff, 'to bring the present situation to a head one way or another'.[94] The main obstacles on both the Egyptian and British sides had been cleared away. The Egyptians had made the settlement acceptable to the British by including an attack on Turkey (as well as on the Arab states) in the formula for emergency reactiva-

---

[91] Head to Eden, 'Top Secret', 15 Apr. 1954, FO 371/108416.

[92] See Harding to Churchill, 17 Mar. 1954, PREM 11/701. Harding wrote that the failure to achieve a 'worthwhile' or 'workable' agreement 'may lead us into open conflict with Egypt'. Churchill responded that he was 'very much impressed'. When Eden saw this exchange of views he warned Churchill that such a conflict could not be limited and would have 'consequences in Cairo and elsewhere', Eden to Churchill, 18 Mar. 1954, PREM 11/701.

[93] Minute by Churchill, 29 Mar. 1954, PREM 11/701.

[94] COS (54), 32, 'Confidential Annex', 22 Mar. 1954, DEFE 4/69.

tion of the base. The British had yielded on the question of military uniforms (by putting forward the proposal of civilian contract labour), thus making the settlement possible on the Egyptian side. When the matter finally came before the British Cabinet in June 1954, Churchill waxed eloquent on 'the political disadvantages of abandoning the position which we had held in Egypt since 1882'. But he concurred. During this discussion the point was made, and Churchill himself agreed with it, 'that our strategic needs in the Middle East had been radically changed by the development of thermonuclear weapons'.[95]

At the initiative of the Foreign Office (again specifically Shuckburgh) it was decided to send Antony Head to Cairo. By delegating this business to the Secretary of State for War, it would be clear to the Egyptians that the British meant business. They would be forced to accept or reject a British final offer. The major remaining issues were the time allowed for evacuation, which had been narrowed down to two years, and the duration of the agreement. The latter appeared to be a breaking point, especially since the British had initially hoped for a twenty-year period. Shuckburgh emphatically believed that it would be best to concede a much more limited period of seven years. Describing the Egyptians as an 'unreliable' and 'improvident' people (quoted more fully at the beginning of this chapter), he wrote that it was better to have an agreement that would work over a short period rather than no agreement at all. 'We have waited over two years for a concatination of circumstances here and in Egypt which would make an agreement possible', he wrote, and, if the talks were now to break down, 'I doubt very much if another opportunity will occur.'[96] The essence of Shuckburgh's position was that the British should secure the best possible terms, no more and no less. When he left for Cairo with Antony Head in July 1954, their terms of reference were to proceed on that basis. 'In the last resort', Shuckburgh wrote, 'we were authorized to accept Egyptian terms.'[97]

Head's own tactics were to calculate a minimally acceptable formula to both sides and to offer it to the Egyptians as a take-it-or-leave-it proposition. He believed that the mutually agreeable terms might be twenty months for evacuation and seven years for the duration of the agreement. He did not wish to haggle. He did not intend to create an impression of piecemeal surrender. He was determined to convey the impression of an act of will on the part of the British government. He presented the British case to Nasser and other ranking Egyptian leaders on 26 July. According to Shuckburgh, the meeting was 'tense and

---

[95] CC (54), 43, 22 June 1954, CAB 128/27.
[96] Minute by Shuckburgh, 17 July 1954, FO 371/108424.
[97] Shuckburgh, *Descent to Suez*, p. 229.

suspicious' and Head 'made our position in a brief, soldierly and effective statement'. The Egyptians said that they would reply shortly; in the event, they were ready to do so after half an hour. The result is jubilantly recorded in Shuckburgh's diary, quoting words of the Egyptian Foreign Minister: 'You will not be surprised to hear that we accept seven years . . . we also accept twenty months.' 'Great relief on our side', Shuckburgh exclaimed, 'It is in the bag.'[98]

In London, Sir Ivone Kirkpatrick, the Permanent Under-Secretary at the Foreign Office, summed up the reasons why the agreement should be accepted. He related the proposed settlement to the broader themes of the 1950s. During the Suez crisis of 1956 Kirkpatrick proved himself to be an official with a will of iron who ruthlessly held the Foreign Office together and relentlessly supported Eden's goals. His minute of July 1954 is thus of historic significance. He wrote in regard to the sticking point, whether or not to accept a seven-year duration of the agreement:

I do not believe that in this atomic age we shall have either the wish or the ability to reactivate the base. We will be sufficiently occupied struggling for survival. And in seven years' time the power and the numbers of these frightful weapons will be so great that the chance of our wanting to conduct a campaign in the Middle East will be less than it is today.

But the period given to us for evacuation [20 months] is of considerable importance.

In a word, I favour nipping on to a real advantage instead of haggling for an illusory one.[99]

Kirkpatrick eventually became one of the most determined foes of the Egyptians, but it is clear that in 1954 he believed that a permanent settlement was possible and that self-interest, if not goodwill, might sustain it.

It is beyond the scope of this chapter to explain why the 1954 agreement failed to prevent the Suez crisis, but those who concluded it knew that it would only be a step along the way towards solving even greater problems. The whirlpools of Palestine and the eddies of the Baghdad Pact—and more immediately, of course, those of the Russian arms and the High Dam at Aswan together with Eden's suspicions of Nasser—were the currents that flowed into Suez, not those of the settlement of 1954. Looking back on the 1954 agreement from the perspective of the Suez crisis, Sir Humphrey Trevelyan, the British Ambassador in Cairo at that time, warned that a new invasion would reverse the British achievement:

---

[98] Shuckburgh, *Descent to Suez*, pp. 231–2.
[99] Minute by Kirkpatrick, 26 July 1954, FO 371/108424.

The mystique of the Egyptian revolution is that they gained real independence from the British and in particular ended the occupation of Egypt by
British forces. If British forces again occupied Egypt and then withdrew, as
they would have to, there would be a new chapter added to the emotional
anti-British history of Egypt, which would be made use of for many years to
come by anti-British politicians and would become embedded in distorted
form in the history books as a glorious incident in the history of the Egyptian
struggle for liberation from the imperialist oppressor.[100]

Therein lay the tragedy. To the architects of the 1954 agreement, they
had achieved what many of their opponents in both countries neither
wished nor even believed to be possible. British troops would finally
and permanently leave Egyptian soil. Sir Ralph Stevenson touched the
heart of the matter, perhaps with some exaggeration, when he wrote
about the Egyptian reaction to Antony Head's soldierly proposition in
July 1954: 'There is no doubt that the Egyptian Delegation were
moved by deep and startled delight, when, as a result of Mr. Head's
proposal, they realised that the prize of evacuation which had eluded
so many of their predecessors was at last in their grasp.'[101]

[100] Trevelyan to A. D. M. Ross, 'Top Secret and Personal', 24 Oct. 1956, FO 371/118997.
[101] Stevenson to Eden, 'Confidential', 29 July 1954, PREM 11/702.

4

The Collapse of Project Alpha

SHIMON SHAMIR

THE years 1952–6 were a period of intensive efforts to move towards a settlement of the conflict between Israel and the Arabs, particularly between Israel and Egypt. Contacts between the parties in pursuit of this goal were conducted with great reticence, and only a few trusted persons on each side were privy to their secrets. The success of policy-makers in keeping the rest of their body politic completely ignorant of these endeavours is indeed remarkable. It was a classic case of secret diplomacy, predicated on the notion that political expediency some-times requires leaders to go beyond declared positions or contradict ideological commitments. The contrast was particularly sharp in the case of the Egyptian leaders, who apparently did not feel they should—to use the expression of a keen observer of the intricacies of secret diplomacy—'allow themselves to be petrified into exaggerated reverence of something that they themselves had created'.[1]

Accordingly, Egyptian–Israeli relations in those years assumed two different forms—both of them genuine, albeit in differing ways. For public consumption Egypt considered itself to be in a state of war with Israel, abided by the rules of the Arab boycott on any diplomatic contacts with Israelis, and ruled out as illegitimate and unthinkable any quest for a settlement—not to mention peace—with the Zionist state. The covert reality was that the Egyptian leadership often exchanged messages (sometimes preceded by the customary pleasan-tries) with the Israeli government, and in its confidential communica-tions considered various arrangements for narrowing the conflict with Israel—not even recoiling from discussing the possibility of peace.

Some secret contacts between Egyptian and Israeli diplomats had of course taken place before that period, but it was only after the take-over by the Free Officers in July 1952 that the exchanges reached a meaningful level. The Suez crisis in mid-1956 marked the end of these ventures, which subsequently diminished to almost nil.

Several factors explain the proliferation of initiatives towards recon-ciliation in those particular years. They could be summed up, by way

[1] Abba Eban, *The New Diplomacy* (New York, 1983), p. 351.

of generalization, as follows. The vigorous way in which the young
leaders of Egypt's revolutionary regime coped with the major issues of
their country brought hopes that they might apply an innovative
approach to the Arab–Israeli conflict. The armistice arrangements
proved incapable of controlling the escalating crises created by a
number of thorny issues (demilitarized zones, violent infiltrations,
water resources, a divided Jerusalem, navigation in international
waterways), occasionally generating search for agreements that might
neutralize the threat of these disputes. Those years were the formative
period of the new state of Israel and the Egyptian revolution, and they
both needed a quiet period for establishing themselves and pursuing
their priority objectives. The Western powers, engaged at that time in
attempts to establish a new regional strategic system for the post-
colonial period, came to believe that an Egyptian–Israeli settlement
could serve as a corner-stone for the new order. To this end they
focused on the two major problems unsolved by the armistice agreements: permanent borders and refugees. Egypt and Israel, greatly in
need of economic and military assistance, could not afford to reject
offhand such peace initiatives, regardless of how they felt about the
various points of substance.

Some hints of the secret contacts and negotiations conducted in those
years leaked out in the course of the three subsequent decades—mostly
in the memoirs of the personalities involved in them. The full picture,
however, is emerging only now with the opening of the major archives.
The Israeli side is systematically covered by the documents in the Israel
State Archives, which also include a special file compiled by Gideon
Rafael and Pinchas Eliav summarizing the contents of these exchanges
until early 1956.[2] No such documentation is accessible on the Egyptian
side, but here too we have numerous personal accounts of that period,
some of which cite the texts of original documents. A case in point is a
recently published book on Nasser's contacts with the Israelis, written
by Muhammad al-Tawil and presenting the account of Hasan
Tuhami; it is a tendentious and quite unreliable account, but the
numerous documents from Tuhami's private collection which accompany it make the book an invaluable source. Similarly, the Arabic
version of Heikal's *Cutting the Lion's Tail* has an appendix of some 250

---

[2] G. Rafael and P. Eliav, Papers on Egyptian–Israeli Contacts, 10–19 Jan. 1956, Israel State
Archives (ISA), 2454/2 and 2460/4. I wish to thank Dr. Michael Oren of Beersheva University for
making available to me a draft paper on the secret Egyptian–Israeli peace initiatives, which is
based mostly on documents from the Israeli archives, as well as documents from the British Public
Record Office up to 1954. I should note, however, that my own research in these archives led me
in several cases to different conclusions.

documents, many of them from confidential Egyptian diplomatic correspondence.[3]

The temptation to treat the story unfolded by those sources as a separate and self-contained chapter in this region's recent history should be resisted. It must be borne in mind that the contacts in search for a settlement were always by-products and side-shows of greater dramas. Their significance varied with the changing contexts of the times. Although the behaviour of the principal actors in these contacts usually falls into clear patterns, identical positions expressed in different circumstances may represent entirely different intentions. Thus positions expressed by Nasser before and after such turning-points as the consolidation of his power, the agreement with Britain, the Gaza raid, the Bandung conference, and the Czech arms deal may have different meanings. Similarly, Israeli policies presented when Sharett was in office may signify something different from the same positions expressed by Ben-Gurion.

EGYPTIAN–ISRAELI CONTACTS

Bearing this caveat in mind, we still need to classify the numerous and diverse activities that emerge from this material. For analytical purposes we may arrange the main facts pertaining to the subject in three major categories.

First, there were direct channels of communication between Cairo and Jerusalem, mostly through their delegations in third countries. The most important link operated in Paris. According to the report from the Egyptian Embassy to the Prime Minister in Cairo, it was initiated in August 1952 when an Israeli diplomat presented himself at the residence of Ali Shawqi, the Egyptian chargé d'affaires, to deliver a message from the government of Israel.[4] This political initiative taken by Jerusalem welcomed the Egyptian revolution and its aspirations, and invited the new government to enter into peace negotiations with Israel. The officers of the ruling junta, unable to agree on the proper answer to this appeal, did not respond to the invitation, but they wished the contacts to continue. This channel remained open for over two and a half years, the two principal interlocutors being the Israeli

---

[3] Muhammad Tawil, *La'bat al-Umam wa-'Abd al-Nasir* (The Game of Nations and Abdel Nasser) (Cairo, 1986). Mohamed Hassanein Heikal, *Milaffat al-Suways* (The Suez Files) (Cairo, 1986), pp. 613–927. The other documents are mostly translations from British and American archives.

[4] Paris Embassy to PM Ali Maher, 23 Aug. 1952, document (from US sources) published in Muhsin Muhammad, 'Al-Ittisalat bayna Misr wa-Isra'il lil-Salam' (The Contacts for Peace between Egypt and Israel), *Akhbar al-Yawm*, 9 Nov. 1985. The parallel reports of the Israeli Embassy—Divon to Foreign Office, 22, 24 Aug. 1952, ISA 2453/20.

chargé d'affaires Shmuel (Ziama) Divon and the Egyptian press attaché Abdel-Rahman Sadeq.

A particularly interesting exchange through this link took place in the first half of 1953. Israel suggested secret high-level talks, offered compensation for the refugees and right of passage through the Negev, in return for which it expected to receive strict adherence to the armistice agreement, freedom of passage through the Canal and the Gulf, lifting of the economic boycott, and termination of the threats of war. The Egyptian Revolutionary Council declared that it did not harbour any belligerent intentions, but it could not afford to deviate from the Arab concensus in its public statements and from the rules of the boycott on Israel. It maintained that progress should be gradual, and at that point was ready to consider passage of Iraeli ships through the Canal. What the Egyptian leaders most wanted from Israel was to facilitate the conclusion of an evacuation agreement with the British and economic assistance from the Americans (as well as help for exporting Egypt's cotton)—requests which Jerusalem was ready to meet only *after* receiving a concrete positive response to some of its own demands. A high point of this dialogue was reached in December 1954, with the exchange of formulated messages between President Nasser and the Israeli Prime Minister Moshe Sharett, in which both expressed their desire to reach 'a peaceful solution'. Cairo rejected the basic demands of Jerusalem as untimely, in view of the recent Israeli operations that were designed to sabotage the evacuation agreement (*Bat-Galim*) and discredit Egypt (the 'affair').[5] Nasser, nevertheless, expressed his wish to keep the borders quiet and continue the dialogue through the Paris channel.[6]

[5] The *Bat-Galim* was sent by the Israeli government to test the freedom of passage through the Suez Canal. It was stopped by the Egyptians in September 1954. The ship was confiscated and its crew was held in prison for three months. The term 'the affair' refers in Israeli political vocabulary to an attempt to sabotage Egypt's relations with the United States and Britain by instructing an Egyptian-Jewish espionage ring to plant bombs in certain Western institutions. The group was caught in July 1954, stood trial in December, and two of its members were condemned to death in January 1955. The identity of the Israeli personalities who ordered this operation remains controversial up to this day.

[6] As Divon reported it to Jerusalem, Sadeq had delivered Nasser's message 'on a white sheet carrying no addresses or signatures', ISA 2453/20, 21. The text of these communications appears also in Gideon Rafael, *Destination Peace* (New York, 1981). The secret contacts between Nasser and the Israelis were also reported, based on Israeli sources, by Hart (Washington) to Caffery (Cairo) on 15 June 1953, and Russell (Tel Aviv) to the State Department on 24 Aug. 1954—United States, State Department, *The Foreign Relations of the United States, 1952–1954*, vol. ix, pp. 1240–1, 1624–5. Several Egyptian observers challenge the veracity of the reports on this dialogue, which they find incompatible with Nasser's position *vis-à-vis* Israel. This is not surprising considering the utmost secrecy in which Nasser held these contacts and the unavailability of official records to researchers in Cairo. However, the extensive and detailed reports from Paris in the Israeli Archives leave no doubt about this matter. The Egyptian side supported its communications to the Israeli government by showing official dispatches from the Revolutionary Council or written instructions to Sadeq signed by Nasser. Actually, Nasser himself revealed the existence of these

Israeli diplomats maintained contacts with the Egyptian side, at various times, through other channels as well, such as Dr. Mahmud Azmi of the Egyptian delegation at the United Nations; Abdel-Hamid Ghaleb, the military attaché in Washington; and Salah Gohar, of the Armistice Commission.[7] As late as the spring of 1956 contacts were still maintained between Israeli and Egyptian diplomats, by that period in Athens and Brussels.[8] But in fact the stress had shifted in 1955 to third-party mediation.

A second category of communications includes the cases in which third-party personalities, not officially representing their governments, attempted to make a contribution towards the resolution of the Egyptian–Israeli dispute by offering mediation, conciliation, or good offices.[9] The initiative for these undertakings came either from the Israeli side or from the Egyptians or, as has most often been the case, from the mediators' own sense of mission.

One of the most significant of such cases was that of the British MP Dr. Maurice Orbach, who between November 1954 and January 1955 made three trips to Cairo with the encouragement of the World Jewish Congress. His mission was to persuade the Egyptian leadership to show clemency to the 'affair' group, but in his talks with Nasser and Ali Sabri he took up the whole range of Israeli–Egyptian problems and submitted specific Israeli proposals. Nasser expressed his wish for peace with Israel, but he conceded that Arab pressure hindered it at the present. Orbach was authorized, however, to convey to the Israeli government Egypt's readiness to release the *Bat-Galim*, allow the passage in the Canal of Israeli non-strategic cargoes, stop hostile propaganda and political warfare, take measures to prevent border incidents and infiltrations, and begin high-level secret negotiations—preferably in Paris. The death sentence passed on two members of the 'affair' group drastically aborted these contacts.[10]

Another interesting case was that of Elmore Jackson, formerly the

---

contacts with the Israelis to the American Ambassador. Although he claimed that he had in mind 'an eventual settlement with Israel', he said he held these contacts 'for informational purposes only', Caffery to Hart, 30 June 1953, ibid., p. 1251. Divon, in a conversation with this author, maintained that Nasser's objectives were clearly to explore the possibilities of some *modus vivendi* with Israel that would prevent it from undermining its negotiations with Britain and would help him to mobilize economic and political support in the United States.

[7] ISA 2454/2.

[8] FO 371/121709 and FO 371/121710. All FO references are to Foreign Office records at the Public Record Office, London.

[9] On the distinction between these three types of intermediaries, and their characteristics in general, see Saadia Touval, *The Peace Brokers* (Princeton, 1982), pp. 3–19.

[10] The brief for Orbach, 15 Dec. 1954, and Orbach's reports to WJC and Sharett, 30 Nov. 1954, ISA 2453/21. The main reports were published in *New Outlook*, Oct. 1974, pp. 6–23, Nov.–Dec. 1974, pp. 8–21, Jan. 1975, pp. 12–20.

first American Quaker to serve at the United Nations. He was invited by the Egyptian Ambassador in Washington, Ahmad Hussein, and his Foreign Minister, Mahmoud Fawzi, to undertake a mediation mission on the basis of the two fundamental Egyptian demands: the right of refugees for repatriation, and changes in Israel's borders, including the ceding of the Negev, that would link Egypt to the Arab East. Jackson shuttled three times between Cairo and Jerusalem in July to September 1955—a stormy period both in Middle Eastern politics and in the military situation along the Israeli–Egyptian border. The Israelis proposed, on the first issue, some compensation for refugees and reunion of families; and on the second, limited boundary adjustments and right of passage through Israeli territory. They reiterated their persistent demand for a high-level meeting, as well as the usual demands for total cease-fire, exchange of prisoners, and lifting of the blockade. Nasser told Jackson that 'things must cool down before he could respond to Ben-Gurion's proposal'.[11]

Other personalities who acted, with different degrees of effectiveness, as channels of Egyptian–Israeli dialogue included Hector McNeil, a British Labour MP; Richard Crossman, Labour MP and editor of the *New Statesman and Nation*; Zafrullah Khan, the Pakistani Foreign Minister; Ralph Bunche, the former head of the UN Commission for Palestine; Jacob Blaustein, president of the American Jewish Congress; Roger Baldwin of the International Human Rights Commission; Dom Mintoff, the Maltese leader; Lester Pearson, the Foreign Minister of Canada; Ira Hirshman, an American Jewish leader; and Colonel Cyril Banks, a British MP.[12]

BRITISH AND AMERICAN QUESTS FOR SETTLEMENT

A third type of attempt at settlement were those initiated by the United States and Britain. Compared to the previous category, the number of these cases in the 1952–6 period is quite small, but their political significance is clearly higher. The mediation attempt that received the greatest exposure was that of Eric Johnston, an industrialist and businessman who was sent to the Middle East as Eisenhower's personal envoy to find a solution to the dispute over the Jordan river water resources. Dulles hoped that such a solution might also alleviate the refugee problem and lead to negotiations on a comprehensive Arab–Israeli settlement. Between October 1953 and October 1955, Johnston

[11] Elmore Jackson, *Middle East Mission* (New York, 1983): the quotation is on p. 55; Moshe Sharett, *Yoman Ishi* (Personal Diary) (Tel Aviv, 1978), vol. iv, p. 1131; ISA 2454/2, 2460/4.
[12] ISA 2593/22, 2454/2; Trevelyan (Cairo) to Foreign Office, 2 and 15 Jan. 1956, FO 371/121722; Jackson, *Middle East Mission*, p. 33; Sharett, *Yoman Ishi*, iii. 680; iv. 1114.

made four visits to the region, shuttling between Israel and its neighbours. His plan was reluctantly accepted by Israel but rejected by the Arab League.[13]

The US Embassies in Cairo and Tel Aviv showed great interest in the possibilities of some movement towards a settlement of the conflict and helped facilitate the exchange of relevant information between the two governments. In March 1953, the possibility of creating channels of communication or appointing an intermediary was explored by the Ambassador in Cairo; Nasser showed interest, but nothing was implemented. In April 1954, Francis Russell of the US government managed to arrange, through the Ambassador in Cairo, a meeting between Reuven Shiloah, the minister in Israel's Washington Embassy and an expert on Arab affairs, and Colonel Mahmud Riad, who was to become the Egyptian Foreign Minister (and who had visited Israel several times during his term in the Armistice Commission). The announcement caused great excitement in Jerusalem, but it was soon discovered that the approach was based on false assumptions and nothing more was heard of it.[14]

In Cairo—as Tuhami reveals through Tawil's narrative—the influential CIA operatives headed by Kermit (Kim) Roosevelt made several attempts to convince Nasser of the expediency of an agreement with Israel and a meeting between him and an Israeli leader, preferably Sharett. In January 1955 Nasser agreed to receive an Israeli representative secretly in Cairo. Jerusalem chose the former Chief of Staff Yigael Yadin and provided him with proposals concerning the two major Egyptian demands: Israel was ready to pay compensation to the Gaza Strip refugees and allow its Arab neighbours right of passage through its territory. Just at that point the death sentences on some of the 'affair' participants were ratified by Nasser, and Israel withdrew from the project. The Israeli raid on Gaza further aggravated matters. Later that year, in May and June, Sharett made attempts through the CIA to revive the initiative, but by that time both parties had become more suspicious, the CIA had lost much of its previous freedom of action, and the project never took off.[15]

[13] Yoram Nimrod, *Mey Meriva* (Disputed Waters) (Givat Haviva, 1966); George Saliba, *The Jordan River Dispute* (The Hague, 1968). Cf. Miles Copeland, *The Game of Nations* (London, 1969), pp. 109–10.

[14] The contacts in Cairo are described on the basis of declassified US documents in Rida Shahata's series of articles *Amirika wa-Thawrat Yulyu* (America and the July Revolution) in *al-Musawwar*, 28 Aug. 1987. The Shiloah–Riad affair is reported in Sharett, *Yoman Ishi*, ii. 459–60, 465–6.

[15] Ibid. iii. 675, 677, 682, 683, 691; iv. 1050, 1056–7; Tawil, *La'bat*, pp. 93, 126–8, 133–7, 238, docs. 399–404. A last ditch attempt was made by Roosevelt even after Nasser's arms deal with the Soviets. Roosevelt tried to persuade Nasser to balance the negative impact of the deal by a public appeal to Israel for a joint effort to establish peace in the area. Nasser said he liked the idea, but he never implemented it; Copeland, *Game of Nations*, pp. 156–66.

The most systematic attempt at Egyptian–Israeli mediation made in that period by the United States was the mission of Robert Anderson, a personal friend of Eisenhower and former Deputy Secretary of Defense. The mission, carrying the code-name Gamma, was launched in November 1955, as part of Washington's efforts to check the deterioration of the situation in the region after Nasser's arms deal with the Soviets. Anderson's purpose, as he declared at the opening of his talks with Ben-Gurion (one of the passages omitted from the published version of the minutes of the talks in Jerusalem),[16] was to 'explore the negotiability of differences' and 'to urge negotiations where negotiability will be feasible'.

Between December 1955 and March 1956, Anderson conducted three rounds of talks, shuttling between Cairo and Jerusalem in conditions of utmost secrecy. Nasser and Ben-Gurion were sceptical of Anderson's objectives, but they had their own agendas: Israel wanted the goodwill of the Americans for obtaining arms, and Egypt wanted it for guaranteeing assistance for the High Dam and other needs, as well as for weakening the Baghdad Pact.

The positions on the substantive issues taken by the parties in these talks did not differ much from those taken in previous contacts. Nasser wanted the Israelis to give the Arabs territorial contiguity by ceding the Negev and to allow the refugees free choice between repatriation and resettlement. The Israelis were ready to discuss minor border changes and contributions to the solution of the refugee problem only within the framework of direct peace negotiations. As immediate measures for reducing tension, Ben-Gurion wanted Egypt to lower the barriers of the Canal–Gulf blockade and the Arab boycott, which Nasser in turn said could be done only as part of the final settlement. An issue which became particularly acute in those weeks was that of restoring a stable cease-fire along the borders—upon which Israel and the United States insisted and on which Egypt remained evasive. There were discussions of the problems of Jerusalem and the Jordan waters, again with no results. Anderson's immediate objective of arranging a high-level meeting between the two parties, which Ben-Gurion regarded as the test for Egypt's real intentions, was eventually rejected by Nasser. As the documents in the Arabic version of Heikal show, Nasser also refused to put his signature on a paper summarizing his own position. Eisenhower concluded from Anderson's debriefing that

---

[16] That version was published in David Ben-Gurion, *My Talks with Arab Leaders* (Jerusalem, 1972), pp. 274–325; this is a re-translation from a Hebrew version that appeared in *Ma'ariv*, 2, 9, 16, 23 July 1971. I was allowed to consult the complete records taken by Jacob Herzog.

while Israel was not ready to make serious concessions, it was Nasser who had 'proved to be a complete stumbling block'.[17]

Britain initiated only one attempt to settle the Israeli–Egyptian conflict and it was done jointly with the United States. The project, known by the code-name Alpha, was a major endeavour by the two powers that dominated their policies in the Arab–Israeli arena throughout 1955 and early 1956. The plan was kept secret, and in spite of the fact that its pursuit necessitated the gradual disclosure of its main points, its full dimensions remained unknown until the opening of the archives thirty years later.[18]

An early (evidently first) British version of the plan was drafted by Evelyn Shuckburgh—who was in charge of Middle East policy in the Foreign Office—following the conclusion of the treaty with Egypt at the end of 1954. The purpose was to work out an Arab–Israeli settlement that would consolidate the position of the West in the changing Middle East and check 'the penetration of the Arab world by the Communists'. The main principles of the plan were: close co-operation with the United States; 'visible concessions' by Israel (territory and refugees); 'guarantees of security' by the major powers; an understanding worked out mainly with Egypt; and the definition of the objective as 'an over-all settlement', not 'peace'.[19]

That broad outline was endorsed by Eden and Dulles, and in January 1955 Shuckburgh started working in Washington on the details with his American counterpart Francis Russell (a former chargé d'affaires at the Embassy in Tel Aviv). The plan was completed in February and various changes were introduced in the subsequent months. A good many of the Alpha papers should not be regarded as

---

[17] Ibid.; Sharett, *Yoman Ishi*, v. 1316, 1337, 1345, 1370; Rafael, *Destination Peace*, pp. 49–50, 53–6; Touval, *Peace Brokers*, pp. 120–33. The Egyptian version, brief but accompanied by important documents, in Heikal, *Milaffat*, pp. 386–94, docs. 780–4. Eisenhower's views are in a memorandum on his conversation with Hoover and Anderson, 13 Mar. 1956, Eisenhower Papers (hereafter DDE), Abilene, Kansas: Diary, Declassified Documents, 1977, 252A. The correspondence of Dulles and Eisenhower on the Anderson mission is in microfiche 8403037 of declassified documents: 'The Anderson Mission' (I am indebted to Professor Jay C. Hurewitz for making this material available to me).

[18] The Alpha project has been mentioned in several personal accounts, such as Wilbur C. Eveland, *Ropes of Sand: America's Failure in the Middle East* (London, 1980), pp. 153–8, 164, 180; Humphrey Trevelyan, *The Middle East in Revolution* (Boston, 1970), pp. 40–7. The most important is Evelyn Shuckburgh, *Descent to Suez: Diaries, 1951–56* (London, 1986), pp. 205–356. Alpha is also discussed in several studies: Touval, *Peace Brokers*, pp. 110–20; Shahata, *al-Musawwar*, 4 Sept. 1987. The most complete discussion is included in a still unfinished Ph.D. dissertation by Mordechai Bar-On of the Hebrew University of Jerusalem (pp. 118–35 of the draft).

[19] The original Shuckburgh plan appears under the title 'Notes on the Arab–Israel Dispute' and is dated 15 Dec. 1954; FO 371/111095. Since a great number of the US documents on Alpha have not yet been declassified, I did not manage to determine exactly the contribution of Washington to the initiation of the Alpha plan.

more than staff planning and contingency schemes, but the essence of the project can be summed up as follows: linking Egypt to Jordan by ceding to them two triangles in the Negev without cutting Israel's link to Eilat; ceding to Jordan some 400 square miles of land owned by villages on the Jordanian side of the border; ceding to Jordan certain problematic areas like Mt. Scopus and the Semakh triangle; ceding to Jordan an equivalent area south and west of Hebron should the Gaza Strip be given to Israel; dividing the demilitarized zones between Israel and its neighbours; the repatriation of a considerable number of refugees, to be agreed upon between Israel and the two Western powers; compensation for the rest, financed with international help; an agreement on the distribution of the Jordan waters as well as on Jerusalem; terminating the economic boycott which was based on a state of war; and Western guarantees for the new frontiers. Economic assistance was planned to increase incentives for the acceptance of the plan.[20]

As agreed between the two sponsors of Alpha, Egypt was approached first. In late March–early April the US Ambassador in Cairo, Henry Byroade, submitted the plan, first to Fawzi and then to Nasser.[21] The first open proclamation of the essence of Alpha was made by Dulles in a speech at the Council on Foreign Relations in late August. He presented the plan in very broad lines and was particularly cautious in phrasing the territorial elements.[22] Nasser's arms deal with the Soviets did not lead the sponsors of Alpha to abandon it, but on the contrary to regard it as more urgent. In November Eden outlined Alpha in his famous Guildhall speech, using much stronger formulations of the concessions expected from Israel, and defining them as a compromise between the 1947 partition lines and the present borders. Israel was not directly presented with the plan before the Sharett–Dulles meeting later that month. Both Ben-Gurion and Sharett vehemently rejected the project as long as it was based on unilateral or substantial territorial concessions. Nasser essentially welcomed the plan, without committing himself to it in any way; but he made clear

---

[20] The detailed Alpha plan, over 50 pages dealing with the territorial and refugee issues, is in FO 371/115866. A summary prepared for Attlee is in FO 371/115867. Numerous policy papers written by Shuckburgh present the rationale of Alpha, e.g. on 15 Oct. 1955, FO 371/115480; 9 Nov. 1955, FO 371/115469.

[21] Stevenson (Cairo) to Shuckburgh, 1 Apr. 1955, FO 371/115867; Shuckburgh, *Descent to Suez*, p. 254. Actually the main ideas of Alpha were conveyed to Nasser by Eden during the latter's visit to Cairo in February.

[22] Dulles–Macmillan meeting in Geneva, 9 Nov. 1955, FO 371/115469. On the drafting of Dulles's speech and his sense of urgency with regard to its delivery: Russell's comments on Dulles's draft, 18 June 1955, Declassified Documents, 1982, 2561; Personal messages from Dulles to Macmillan, 19, 26 Aug. 1955, Declassified Documents, 1983, 1050, 1051.

that what he expected Israel to cede was the Negev 'south of Beersheba', not just corridors or triangles.[23]

In spite of all the setbacks, the occasional anger at Nasser, the mounting military tension in the Middle East, and the growing doubts about the feasibility of Alpha, in early 1956 it was still Britain's policy. In the papers prepared for the major political meetings of January and February of that year, Shuckburgh told his colleagues that the Guildhall speech 'restored our impetus'; the papers reiterated the principles of Alpha and expressed cautious optimism about the chances for progress.[24] Yet a streak of disillusionment becomes discernible in these texts and the question of alternatives begins to arise. At the end of March, when London lost all hopes of co-operation with Nasser and decided to adopt a hard line towards him, Alpha died a natural death.[25]

As the Western 'peace brokers' abandoned the quest for an Egyptian–Israeli agreement, the ball passed into the hands of the UN Secretary-General Dag Hammarskjöld, who had visited the area in January in an attempt to achieve pacification of the armistice borders. He returned in April, once again shuttling between Israel and the Arab states, gathering commitments to preserve the cease-fire.[26] In his third visit, in July, he undertook an additional assignment: to explore how much substance there was in what was called the 'Fawzi initiative'. According to reports of the British Ambassador, Sir Humphrey Trevelyan, from Cairo, what Fawzi initiated was a two-phase plan: first,

[23] Israel and Alpha: Sharett, *Yoman Ishi*, iv. 1147; v. 1251–2, 1305; Shuckburgh to Nicholls (Tel Aviv), 28 Apr. 1955, FO 371/115867; Macmillan's meeting with Sharett, 26 Oct. 1955, FO 371/115537; Dulles to Macmillan, 6 Dec. 1955, FO 371/115469; Makins (Washington) to FO, 8 Dec. 1955, FO 371/115886; Arthur to Shuckburgh, 13 Dec. 1955, FO 371/115887; Shuckburgh's paper for Middle East Ambassadors' conference, 3 Jan. 1956, FO 371/121708; Nicholls to FO, 16 Jan. 1956, FO 371/121270; Shuckburgh, *Descent to Suez*, pp. 258, 309. Egypt and Alpha: Mohamed Hassanein Heikal, *The Cairo Documents* (New York, 1973), pp. 55–7, 78; Trevelyan, *Middle East in Revolution*, p. 42; Stevenson to FO, 7 Apr. 1955, FO 371/115867; Trevelyan to FO, 31 Dec. 1955, 1 Jan. 1956 and Minutes, FO 371/121708 ('the Egyptians will take no positive or overt steps until they are assured of getting satisfaction on the Negev'); Burrows (Bahrain) to FO, 3 Mar. 1956, FO 371/121709.

[24] Paper prepared for the Middle East Ambassadors' conference, 3 Jan. 1956, FO 371/121708; papers of Shuckburgh's talks at the State Department, 7 Jan. 1956, FO 371/110409, 12, 14, 19 Jan. 1956, FO 371/110166; papers of the Eisenhower–Eden summit meeting, 29 Jan. 1956, FO 371/121270, 1 Feb. 1956, FO 371/121271. The major statesmen conducted their diplomacy along these principles: see for example Dulles to Macmillan, 6 Dec. 1955, FO 371/115469, or the meeting between Selwyn Lloyd and Ambassador of Israel, 18 Jan. 1956, FO 371/121722. Cf. Shuckburgh, *Descent to Suez*, pp. 300–1, 308, 323, 327, 341.

[25] The assertion of the new policy towards Nasser: FO spokesman, 25 Mar. 1956, FO 371/118861; Secretary of State's instructions to Trevelyan, 3 Apr. 1956, FO 371/118861; Shuckburgh to Middle East Ambassadors, 28 May 1956, FO 371/118862 ('we have therefore decided on a number of steps to reduce Nasser's influence in the rest of the Arab world'). Cf. Trevelyan, *Middle East in Revolution*, pp. 69–71, Shuckburgh, *Descent to Suez*, p. 345.

[26] Minutes by Laurence, 24 Apr. 1956, FO 371/121709 ('Since the failure of Alpha . . .').

Hammarskjöld would try to narrow the differences between Israel and Egypt; second, an international conference, with the participation of third-party states, would try to reach a settlement. Washington and London were quite sceptical, but some of the old hands at the Foreign Office eagerly visualized the revival of Alpha.[27] Hammarskjöld, for his part, found no reason for optimism; in the reports he sent after his return to Geneva he gloomily concluded that 'the gap is likely to remain considerable with very inflexible views held on points not open for compromise'.[28] Two days after the date of that report, Nasser nationalized the Suez Canal, and the international crisis was in full swing.

In the following sections we shall focus on the last phase of the search for an Egyptian–Israeli settlement, examine the role played by the two Western powers in promoting this cause, and reflect on the failure of their endeavours.

BRITISH PLANNING AND THE MISCONCEPTIONS OF ALPHA

Alpha was not meant to deal merely with the Arab–Israeli conflict. British foreign policy planners never regarded the settlement of this dispute *per se* as a major goal, unless they believed it would serve more important British objectives in the Middle East. Shuckburgh, the chief British architect of Alpha, made it crystal clear in his first blueprint and the numerous papers that followed it that the purpose of an Egyptian–Israeli settlement would be to strengthen what he called Britain's 'influence and position in the Arab World' and check Soviet penetration into the area; he expected the plan to win Egyptian co-operation and harmonize Anglo-Egyptian relations with the rest of Britain's connections and assets in the Middle East, and with the entire Western strategic system in the region.

On the face of it, the Shuckburgh project was a case of Whitehall planning at its best. Initially, it was recognized that the conclusion of the evacuation agreement with the revolutionary regime in Egypt would open a 'new era' for the British in the Middle East, and this was correctly viewed against the background of the growing involvement of the two superpowers in the region and the changing political situation in the states of the local subsystem. Then a new man, Shuckburgh, was brought in to serve as an Under-Secretary for Middle Eastern affairs; he soon set out for a six-week tour of the region, talking to the principal local leaders and the British men on the spot. Upon his return he had a plan which had some obvious merits: it would attack

---

[27] Trevelyan to FO, 6–12 July 1956; correspondence with Washington and New York, 8–11 July 1956; Rose, 8, 13 July 1956; Laurence, 20 July 1956; FO 371/121710.
[28] Hammarskjöld to Selwyn Lloyd, 24 July 1956, FO 371/121710.

the crux of the problem; it would be fully co-ordinated with the United States; it would boldly seize the initiative for Britain; it would be kept secret and unfold only with the gradual implementation of its carefully laid-out stages; and it would manipulate the local actors precisely where London wanted them. The precedent of Eden's success with the Trieste problem was encouraging. Understandably the plan was well received, and its overt optimism was echoed in numerous Foreign Office documents and statements throughout 1955, in spite of that year's cumulative disasters.

Seen in retrospect, it is difficult to understand how it could have been imagined that the project had any chance of success. From its inception, the British understanding of Alpha was predicated on four assumptions: (1) that 'it ought to be possible to persuade the Israelis to make visible concessions', particularly in the Negev, 'provided they can be given guarantees of security by the Great Powers'; (2) that should persuasion fail, the United States would apply sufficient pressure on Israel to extract the necessary concessions; (3) that a deal with Nasser could be made on that basis, because Alpha offered him what he wanted and he in turn could deliver what the West needed; and (4) that once such a settlement was achieved, regional harmony under Western patronage would prevail, because it is 'the Israeli issue ... [that] stands in the way of cooperation between the Arab countries and the West', making the West 'impotent to counter the Communist advance', and constituting the main cause of regional tensions.[29] In fact, none of these assumptions could be substantiated by the realities of that period.

With all the differences among the Israeli leaders of the time on the issue of relations with the Arabs, there was no dent in their unified front against the kind of territorial concessions demanded by Alpha. When the nature of the required concessions was made known by Eden's Guildhall speech, Ben-Gurion rose in the Knesset to declare that 'the essence of Sir Anthony Eden's proposal is the crushing of the State of Israel'.[30] Alpha's expectations were particularly unrealistic with regard to the Negev. It was not that the planners of Alpha did not know the Israelis' position on this subject, but that they definitely failed to sense the intensity of their attachment to that part of their country. For the founding fathers of the Zionist state, the Negev was the focal point of the vision of blooming deserts and vistas to the four corners of the world. In their eyes the Negev was not merely what

[29] 'Notes' (cited n. 19), pp. 5, 6.
[30] Text of speech on 15 Nov. 1955 in David Ben-Gurion, *Ma'arekhet Sinai* (The Sinai Campaign) (Tel Aviv, 1959), pp. 33–6. (Cf. Golda Meir in New York, 18 Dec. 1955: 'Not one grain of sand! Not one!' FO 371/121708.)

Dulles described in his Alpha speech, a 'barren territory' which somehow 'has acquired sentimental significance', but an embodiment of the whole difference between Israel as a normal state with a future and Israel as an unviable enclave.

The Israelis' perception of the issue was very different from that of Alpha. Since they did offer their neighbours free passage through their territory and met with little interest in the proposal, the rationale of the Arab demand in their eyes was not to restore territorial contiguity but to reduce Israel to indefensible proportions thereby tightening the siege around its populated core. The strategy of Alpha unwittingly played on these fears and nourished the Israelis' perception that they were facing a challenge to their very survival, which had to be resisted at all costs. Moreover, Alpha insisted that at that stage Israel should not be supplied with weapons to compensate, even partially, for the arms that were flowing to the Arab countries and should not be given any security guarantee, for 'such a guarantee must remain the prize for an Alpha settlement'.[31] Thus, instead of providing the Israelis with a sense of security that would allow them greater flexibility (as was eventually done with great success by Kissinger in the post-1973 peace process), it confronted them with alarming international pressures which only consolidated their determination never to exchange their strategic self-reliance for outside guarantees of any kind. The fact that the plan refrained from even mentioning the conclusion of full peace with the Arabs certainly did not facilitate Israel's readiness for territorial concessions.

The calculation that Israel's hands could be forced by pressure from the United States took the concerned party too much for granted. Although in principle Dulles saw eye to eye on this issue with Eden and the Foreign Office Middle East planners, he also frequently reminded them that domestic pressures in his country set a limit to what he could do. As the presidential elections drew near, the chances of such American action further diminished. It is true that, in the event, Eisenhower proved that he could act against Israel even at the height of his campaign; but it was one thing to stop an invasion of the sort originated by the triple collusion of 1956 and quite another to tear away territory from the young Jewish democracy, which was struggling to establish itself no more than ten years after the Holocaust.

Moreover, in order to undertake such a role in the British scenario, the Americans had to feel at least the same enthusiasm towards Alpha as that shown by their partner. This clearly was not the case. The US officials on the Alpha team, headed by an expert on Israeli affairs,

---

[31] 'Policy in the Middle East', 15 Oct. 1955, FO 371/115480.

repeatedly expressed their doubts about the realism of Shuckburgh's demands on Israel and urged him to moderate them.[32] An enlightening indication of this emerges from a comparison between the Alpha plan as formulated by the joint team (described above) and Shuckburgh's prototype model, which was much more ambitious. It had gone as far as demanding from Israel 'the surrender to Jordan of an area in Galilee', 'the internationalization or neutralization' of Jerusalem, and 'the final adjudication to Syria and Jordan of the demilitarized zones'. Shuckburgh also spoke in his original project of achieving the link between Egypt and Jordan by ceding 'part of the Negev south of Beersheba' rather than just small linking triangles (the American proposals); and even after the latter concept was adopted by Alpha he continued to press his reluctant colleagues to enlarge that area so that 'it would be based on the 1947 Resolution'.[33] Clearly, the American side did not share Shuckburgh's exhilarated feeling that a 'mention of the 1947 Resolutions' was 'something deliciously bold and dramatic'.[34]

No less problematical were Alpha's premises concerning the projected deal with Nasser. The plan took for granted a basic identity between Nasser's principal claims in the dispute with Israel (refugees, the Negev) and his operational policy-priorities. While there is no reason to doubt the sincerity of his concern for the plight of the refugees, he hardly regarded it as an urgent problem. Even a generous compromise on this issue would have been for him less attractive than was assumed in the West, knowing that in the Arab world he would always be denounced for the number of refugees resettled outside Palestine more than he would be credited for the number he managed to repatriate. Similarly, the promised boundary changes in the Negev must have been a mixed blessing for him. On this Alpha's offer was more tempting, and Nasser certainly wished the Israelis out of the Negev; but contrary to what is generally believed, the documents do not reflect a great desire on his part (at least on the tactical level) formally to annex it to Egypt.[35] From his perspective, he was invited to make a major concession on Arab rights in 'occupied Palestine' in return for a limited territorial gain in the desert. The authors of Alpha did not discover that Nasser, it may be deduced, was more interested in the benefits he could derive from the *process* of negotiations—economic

---

[32] Shuckburgh, *Descent to Suez*, pp. 245, 257.

[33] 'Notes', Annex; Shuckburgh to Kirkpatrick, 4 May 1955, FO 371/115867; Shuckburgh, *Descent to Suez*, p. 256. Cf. the memorandum of the conversation between McClintock and Salah Salem, 27 Feb. 1953, in Muhsin Muhammad, cited in n. 4.

[34] Shuckburgh, *Descent to Suez*, p. 297.

[35] See, e.g. Stevenson to FO, 14 Apr. 1955, FO 371/115867; Shuckburgh to Kirkpatrick, 14 Jan. 1956 ('Nasser ... not sincerely or profoundly interested in a land link'), FO 371/109973; see also the document in *Milaffat*, p. 782.

assistance, political support, gaining time—than in any concrete outcome from them.

Then there was the problem of reciprocity. The plan hardly explains how any quid pro quo could be secured from Nasser. It is eminently unclear what Nasser could realistically deliver as his part of this deal. Was he supposed to make an unequivocal commitment to the West and thus undermine his own credibility at home and shatter the basis of his prestige in the Arab world? Was he expected to become, in the framework of Alpha's grand design, another Nuri Said? In the course of 1955, as Nasser was marching from one international success to another and rapidly boosting his self-confidence, any expectations in this direction became absurd. Shuckburgh sometimes offered simple answers to such problems: 'We must first try to frighten Nasser, then to bribe him, and if neither works, get rid of him.'[36] In reality the sponsors of Alpha were far from being able to accomplish any of these things.

Finally, there were serious problems with the premisses of Alpha's ultimate vision. In the mid-1950s it was perhaps harder to see these as clearly as it is today, but even then facts had to be stretched considerably to support the notion that anti-British postures, local conflicts, and Soviet penetration could all be attributed to the Palestine problem, and would presumably disappear with its solution. Shuckburgh's view of the Middle East was more sophisticated than that, but he firmly believed that Arab–British relations were 'poisoned' primarily by the Israel issue and that there were no 'basic' clashes of interests between the two parties.[37] He failed to understand the intensity of Cairo's rivalry with Baghdad ('I had no idea they were quite so jealous of Iraq'),[38] and did not pause to ask himself whether giving Egypt easy access through the Negev to the Jordanian and the Saudi regimes would pacify the region or further destabilize it. Similarly, he did not manage to see the Soviet penetration as part of the broad Third World phenomenon of that time, but insisted that 'it is the Israel–Arab conflict which has weakened Western influence in the Middle East and opened the door to Russia'.[39] Supposedly, this door would be reshut once the Israel–Arab conflict was settled, according to the concepts of the planners of Alpha.

---

[36] Shuckburgh, *Descent to Suez*, p. 281. The idea that Nasser could be frightened into an agreement with the West was probably shared by Eden, who wrote in the margins of a dispatch presenting Byroade's suggestion to suspend Baghdad Pact activities for a while in order not to alienate Nasser from the Palestine settlement efforts: 'I don't agree at all. The stronger the Northern Tier the better Nasser will behave. A.E.', Trevelyan to FO, 3 Nov. 1955, FO 371/115469.

[37] Shuckburgh, 'Policy towards Nasser', 22 Feb. 1956, FO 371/118861.

[38] That was a surprised reaction to Egypt's fury on the Iraqi–Turkish pact, Shuckburgh, *Descent to Suez*, p. 249.

[39] Shuckburgh, 'The Middle East', 9 Nov. 1955, FO 371/115469. See also Shuckburgh, 'Policy in the Middle East', 14 Oct. 1955, FO 371/115480.

'Alpha seems like a beautiful dream', writes Shuckburgh in his diaries.[40] It transpires that not only was Alpha impossible to realize, but even as a dream it was highly questionable.

On a closer look it seems that most of the faults in Alpha's premises emanated from the way its British planners perceived the two parties to the conflict. These particular perceptions can easily be detected in the writings of Shuckburgh, but it can safely be assumed that they were shared, to different degrees, by most of his colleagues and superiors (Eden, Macmillan). Although Alpha was master-minded in London by Shuckburgh, it also reflected various ideas and views that were quite common in the Western foreign ministries of that time. The prompt and warm manner in which the plan was received is a reflection of the common denominator on which it was based.[41]

The outstanding feature of this British perception of the Arab side was its low awareness of the authenticity, intensity, and autonomy of the Arab anti-Western posture. It was hardly understood that if the search for dignity was the essential disposition of Nasser's nationalists, this inevitably led them to put some distance between themselves and the former masters of their countries. London was very slow in reading the state of mind of that generation, which—nourished by the residues of a long period of humiliating subjugation to Europe—was defiant and vindictive.

Oblivious to this deeply ingrained attitude, Foreign Office experts often tended to explain away eruptions of anti-British hostility throughout the Arab world as caused by Communist instigation or provoked by the West's association with Israel. Wilbur Eveland, of the CIA, describes a conversation with Shuckburgh in which the latter bluntly attributed the hostilities the British were facing at that time in the region to those factors. When it was suggested to him, relates Eveland, that the real cause might be that Britain was 'vulnerable to attacks against colonialism', Shuckburgh had rejected this point 'with considerable heat'.

Eveland puts his finger on what *did* constitute the essential component in Nasser's resistance to the West: 'If one examined Nasser's anti-Western outbursts,' he concludes, 'one saw that he struck out more often at foreign troops and bases than he did at our role in creating Israel as a Jewish state.'[42] What Nasser, as a good representative of his generation, rejected most was the perpetuation of Western regional hegemony through a system of military bases and alliances (and not

---

[40] Shuckburgh, *Descent to Suez*, pp. 211, 275.

[41] Ibid., pp. 242, 246. Wm. Roger Louis, in another chapter in this book, states that Shuckburgh's diary 'is the most illuminating guide to the official thought of the period'.

[42] Eveland, *Ropes of Sand*, p. 159.

the maintenance of correct relationships with the Western powers, whose assistance he wanted to have). In order to be faithful to the historic role of national liberator that he was willing and expected to play, he had unavoidably objected to any attempt to involve Egypt in a Western strategic system, and understandably objected even more strongly to the attempt to build such a system around a competing Arab regime. In a way, his willingness to discuss Alpha, or other projects for settling the Palestine problem, was designed to mobilize some goodwill for freezing or neutralizing the Baghdad alliance. His British interlocutors tried to achieve exactly the opposite: to use Alpha to get him to accept the reality of that Western strategic system. These cross-purposes could not be reconciled.

'We did not face up soon enough to this basic contradiction in our strategy', wrote Shuckburgh in hindsight, and in a conversation with the present author he admitted: 'We simply overlooked the absolute hostility of Nasser to the Baghdad Pact; I don't think we quite understood these jealousies.'[43] It is indeed remarkable how long the British planners persevered in their belief that Nasser's pan-Arabism could somehow be reconciled with a Western-controlled regional strategic system. Disillusionment with Nasser gradually grew,[44] but in late February 1956 Shuckburgh still argued that there was no basic contradiction between Arab interests and the British determination to defend the essential elements of their position, 'including strategic bases . . . [and] the protection of our vital oil requirements'. If Nasser saw it differently, it must be 'a misinterpretation of our actions and a misunderstanding of our policies'.[45] The image of Nasser in the British documents is that of an erratic or even opportunistic leader who, with some skill and patience, could be manipulated to a reasonably pro-Western posture. There is hardly a reflection of the inner logic of Nasser's policies which led him, step by step, to make a deal with the Soviet Union and challenge the Western position in the Middle East— not in response to some accidental circumstances or blunders committed by Western governments (or Israel), but as the ultimate consummation of the decolonization process and the newly won national freedom of action.

In October 1955, Shuckburgh was told by Ambassador Sir Ralph Stevenson that 'Egypt is fully committed to the West, but hates the idea of acknowledging it.' Like many other observers of that time,

---

[43] In his paper 'Policy in the Middle East', 15 Oct. 1955, Shuckburgh explains that the two policies must 'accompany' each other. FO 371/115480; see also Shuckburgh, *Descent to Suez*, p. 211. Shuckburgh was interviewed by this author by telephone.

[44] See e.g. Shuckburgh's papers on 15 Oct. 1955, 7 Jan. ('he now seems firmly set on a neutralist course and unlikely to swing definitely towards the West'), 19 Jan. 1956, FO 371/118861.

[45] Shuckburgh, 'Policy towards Nasser', 22 Feb. 1956, FO 371/118861.

Shuckburgh evidently confused Nasser's anti-Communism on the domestic front with a pro-Western posture on the international level. Eight months later, on the day of Shuckburgh's departure from the Foreign Office, he finally discovered the depth of anti-British feelings in Egypt; with disarming candour this architect of the Alpha project sadly concludes, 'Obviously my policy and efforts to save relations with Egypt have been all wrong.'[46]

The British perception of the Israeli side in the conflict was no less problematic. It seems that at that stage Whitehall still had difficulty in viewing Israel as a fully established sovereign state. British officials who had for many years been accustomed to seeing the Jews as a controversial community in a country under their mandate were somehow impeded from coming to grips with the realities of Israeli statehood. Shuckburgh's analysis of the situation in the Middle East, in the introduction to his original project, presents an image of Israel which is almost hopeless: its leaders are out of touch with realities across their borders, its European Jews are emigrating, contributions from the United States are declining, the damage of Arab boycott and blockade could prove fatal, and the economy as a whole is not viable.[47] In referring to Israel, Shuckburgh uses language he would not use with regard to any other state. As a condemned people, he argues, the Israelis should be grateful for any offer to guarantee their security. In a typical entry in his diary he writes: 'I ... am left with the strong conviction that the Jews are doomed if they don't change their ways.' The apocalyptic vision apparently appealed to his sense of drama, and he could not avoid being moved by the 'tragedy in which the Israelis are embroiled surely to their eventual perdition'.[48]

These were not just the idiosyncrasies of one person, as one can see, for instance, from the material that the Foreign Office was receiving from its Embassy in Tel Aviv. The dispatches of Ambassador Sir John Nicholls were strewn with gems like 'the centre of infection in the region is Israel and I believe that we must treat the Israelis as a sick people', and 'it is not reasonable to expect that a nation made up of individuals so psychologically unstable should be capable of a mature foreign policy'. To do justice to Nicholls it should be added that his

---

[46] Shuckburgh, *Descent to Suez*, pp. 291, 356–7. In a review of Shuckburgh's book, David Pryce-Jones reaches the conclusion that 'Shuckburgh's conception of the nature of Middle East politics was too shallow to have any practical application', *Commentary*, July 1987, p. 66. Yet one cannot but agree with the comment made by Shuckburgh in the interview mentioned above to the effect that it was not easy to formulate an effective policy within an outdated framework of reference which did not recognize the passing of the British Empire.

[47] Shuckburgh, 'Notes', pp. 1–2.

[48] Shuckburgh, *Descent to Suez*, pp. 259, 286. (On the influence of the experience of Evelyn Shuckburgh's father on his own feelings on the Palestine question, see pp. 212–13.)

attitude was basically benevolent: 'I am sure that ... carrots ... are more likely to be successful as a treatment than persistent flourishes of the stick.'[49]

In the context of Alpha, the most consistent theme in Shuckburgh's position is the unequivocal reiteration that Israel must pay the price of the new arrangement for the Middle East, for this is what British interests require. For him Israel is in the way, an obstruction, 'the greatest irritant of all'. There is no trace of apologetics in his assertion that 'any initiative, if it is to be realistic and to avoid damaging even more seriously our position in the Arab world, will have to be something which the Israelis will detest'. He is perfectly honest about this in his talks with Israelis: the Western powers, he tells Peres, 'must necessarily nurse their relations with the Arab world and cannot, even if they should be inclined to do so, sacrifice their major interests there for Israel'. And to the Israeli Ambassador he says bluntly: 'After all, we did not ask you to go there: we have no obligation to keep you there.'[50]

The idea of a strategic balance between Israel and the Arabs he finds to be an 'idiotic concept'. Without pausing to reflect how a basis for a settlement of the Arab–Israeli conflict could be conceived without it, he declares that it 'will have to disappear from our vocabulary'. Moreover, in October 1955, Shuckburgh warned that if his present plan were not implemented, 'some form of abandonment of Israel will become the only alternative to the loss of Middle East oil'. He had no illusions about the nature of this alternative scenario: 'The process of betraying Israel is going to be both dangerous and painful.'[51]

At one point Eden said to Shuckburgh, 'You are much more pro-Arab than you used to be', to which the latter commented drily, 'This is really incorrigible.'[52]

AMERICAN PERFORMANCE AND THE ABORTION OF ALPHA

The area where Shuckburgh turned out to be particularly effective was that of co-ordination with Washington. Working closely, he and Russell managed to produce for all the major meetings of their principals policy papers that rarely reflected any disagreements. This harmony was facilitated of course by the fact that the basic views of

[49] Nicholls to Shuckburgh, 8 Mar. 1955, FO 371/115825; also to Rose, 17 May 1956, FO 371/121709.

[50] Shuckburgh, *Descent to Suez*, pp. 210, 265–6, 297, 301. Shuckburgh's anti-Israeli bias is analysed in Pryce-Jones's review, cited n. 46.

[51] Shuckburgh, 'Policy in the Middle East', 15 Oct. 1955, FO 371/115480. An excellent quotation reflecting this position appears in Keith Kyle's chapter in this book. See also Shuckburgh, *Descent to Suez*, pp. 267, 279.

[52] Ibid., p. 297.

Eden and Dulles on these issues had been compatible even before the crystallization of the Alpha plan. Eden's search for an alternative system to preserve time-honoured British interests in the Middle East converged on Dulles's wish to include the Middle East in a new global network of anti-Communist alliances. Both of them regarded the Arab–Israeli conflict as a principal obstacle to the fulfilment of their objectives, and both believed that if Israel made the necessary concessions it would clear the way for the realization of their grand design.[53] While Shuckburgh was writing the first draft of his project, Russell was working with Dulles on similar plans, and the question of who deserves the copyrights to Alpha is thus of little importance in the light of this remarkable congruence.

The fact that the systematic co-ordination between the two powers on this matter did not leak out was one of the notable feats of the period's secret diplomacy. The Israelis, for instance, could not even have guessed that the contents of Eden's Guildhall speech was approved by the Americans, just as the essence of Dulles's speech at the Council on Foreign Relations had been approved by the British;[54] consequently, they read into them significant differences and planned their preventive campaign on the basis of this perceived gap. And yet, the Israelis were not entirely wrong. While both powers agreed on the broad principles of project Alpha and shared many of its premises (and sometimes the Americans were even more active than their British counterparts in its execution), their consent arose from different contexts and accordingly sometimes had different purports, or at least nuances.

For one thing, the American statesmen had a certain sense of commitment to the state of Israel, which was hardly prevalent among their British colleagues. Reflecting on the outcome of the Anderson mission, Eisenhower wrote in his private papers that the United States had strong interests in the Arab world, whereas 'Israel, a tiny nation, surrounded by enemies . . . has a very strong position in the heart and emotions of the Western world.'[55] Hence, the American approach to the proposed settlement was somewhat more symmetrical. The concept of 'evenhandedness', so strongly stressed by Dulles, was seen by the

[53] Like the Whitehall officials, Dulles sometimes used the 'Israel's doom' concept; Conversation with Eisenhower and Anderson, 11 Jan. 1956 ('Unless the Israelis realize this, they were doomed'), Declassified Documents, 1982, 316.

[54] Although Dulles was informed about Eden's speech only one day before delivery and he was extremely unhappy about its timing ('Dulles did approve of the passage about Palestine in the Prime Minister's speech tonight at the Mansion House.'); Shuckburgh, *Descent to Suez*, p. 298. On the Israeli perception of the US policy towards a settlement, see memorandum of Mar. 1956, ISA 2446/3.

[55] 8 Mar. 1956, DDE, Declassified Documents, 1977, 352A.

Israelis as sinister, but compared to the British approach, it did have some substance. The image of the desired settlement that emerged from the statements of the Americans was somewhat closer to a negotiated and contractual model than to the imposed arrangement projected by the British. The need to bring the Israelis into the picture was usually addressed by the American side, which also remained alone in its interest in direct meetings between the Israelis and Egyptians— not to mention in its efforts to arrange such meetings.

The official American policy adhered strictly to the commitment to suspend arms sales to Israel until Alpha was implemented, but the declassified US documents reflect a growing uneasiness with these tactics and an awareness that denying Israel a sense of security might become counter-productive. Likewise, there was more interest on the American side in the eventual inclusion of Israel in some defence system. Although Dulles was opposed to the immediate conclusion of a treaty with Israel or granting security guarantees, the principle itself was recognized, and it constituted one of the few issues on which Shuckburgh and Russell could not find a common formula and had to record their disagreement.[56]

Similarly, the US position also differed with regard to the Egyptian side. As newcomers to the region, the Americans were freer from the residues of the colonial period that so often obscured the view of their British partners. They were more attuned to the anti-colonial mood in the Arab world in general and better sensed the basic contradiction between the Baghdad Pact concept and the orientation towards a new deal with Nasser.[57] Accordingly, the Americans had no difficulty developing, at the beginning of 1956, a policy option that, in combination with Alpha, called for accepting Egypt's neutralist posture, freezing the expansion of the Baghdad Pact, and endorsing both the concept of Arab unity and Nasser's leadership. The British were quite worried by the possible implications of this position, and Anthony Nutting, Minister of State at the Foreign Office, suggested 'treat[ing] this volte face with reserve', but to their relief it remained a short-lived episode.[58]

---

[56] 'Mr. Shuckburgh said that he agreed with Mr. Russell's general approach, except that the U.K. had not reached the point of considering joint defence arrangements—as distinct from the guarantee of the boundaries—with Israel'; 'Extracts from Minutes', FO 371/115866. An example of the Americans' uneasiness about the denial of arms to Israel: Conversation Hoover–Eisenhower, 1 Mar. 1956, Declassified Documents, 1984, 2553.

[57] On the anti-colonial sentiment of the Secretary of State: Dulles Papers, 18 Oct. 1955, Declassified Documents, 1982, 312; Anthony Eden, *Full Circle* (London, 1960), pp. 133, 499; Townsend Hoopes, *The Devil and John Foster Dulles* (Boston, 1973), pp. 315–16. Carlton even argues that Dulles used Alpha to delay the movement towards the Baghdad Pact, David Carlton, *Anthony Eden* (London, 1981), p. 382.

[58] Nutting's comment on Makins (Washington) to FO, 20 Jan. 1956, FO 371/121270. On

The burden of executing Alpha fell mainly on the American diplomats, not necessarily because they were more single-minded with respect to this project but due to their greater credibility and leverage with both parties. Washington was the first, in April 1955, to propose Alpha formally to Nasser, and it was first, at the end of that year, to undertake the unpleasant task of confronting Sharett with its realities—while London sent its congratulations from a distance.[59]

Typical of Dulles's strategy was the systematic use of all the incentives and pressures Washington could muster in order to maximize the prospects for successful negotiations. Thus, for instance, in a top secret report by the Egyptian Ambassador in Washington on a meeting with Dulles in the wake of the Czech arms deal, he listed the following topics raised by the Secretary to back up his objection to the deal: economic and military aid to Egypt, the export of Egyptian cotton, the allocation of Nile waters to Egypt and the Sudan, regulating the use of Jordan waters by Israel, the possibility of a pre-emptive Israeli war, and the policy on arms sales to Israel. The financing of the Aswan High Dam developed as another incentive for a settlement.[60] In the briefing of Anderson by Dulles and Eisenhower, the following bargaining cards were suggested (in addition to the Alpha proposals of triangles in the Negev and financial aid to solve the refugee problem): financing the High Dam, constructing a parallel canal to the Suez, exporting Egyptian cotton, providing economic aid in general, and freezing the Baghdad Pact.[61] There was perhaps something crude and mercantile in these methods and their effectiveness could be called into question, but nothing the British could offer could possibly match them.

The most remarkable aspect of the US involvement in the search for a settlement was the management of political contacts in Egypt (and to a much lesser extent in Israel) through the CIA, in addition to the normal State Department channels. The prominent position of the CIA agents alongside Nasser constituted both the strength and the

Washington's new policy towards Nasser and the British reaction to it: Shuckburgh to Kirkpatrick, 14 Jan. 1956, FO 371/121708; Conversation Shuckburgh–Allen, 14 Jan. 1956, and Hadow, 24 Jan. 1956, FO 371/121270.

[59] Makins to FO, 8 Dec. 1955, FO 371/115886.

[60] Ahmad Hussein to Foreign Ministry (Cairo), 3 Nov. 1955, Heikal, *Milaffat*, pp. 774–6. Following Nasser's arms deal with the Soviets, a consultation was held between an American team headed by Dulles and a British team headed by Macmillan. Raymond Hare proposed inducing Nasser to take 'steps toward some sort of settlement with Israel'; and was followed by Russell who suggested using aid for the High Dam as an incentive. Dulles decided to make an approach to Nasser and invited Russell and Shuckburgh to 'work out the details'; 'Memorandum of Conversation', 3 Oct. 1955, Microfiche 8401145, Sect. 1, of Declassified Documents: 'U.S. Policy towards Egypt, 1955–1956', No. 9.

[61] Memorandum, 11 Jan. 1956, Declassified Documents, 1981, 552b; 1982, 316; 1984, 562.

weakness of American diplomacy in Cairo. The CIA operatives, headed by Roosevelt, had managed to establish their credentials with Nasser during the Revolution's early phase, when the inexperienced and vulnerable Free Officers needed all the advice and assistance they could get, and during the crucial negotiations on the evacuation of British troops, in which Nasser desperately sought some American backing.[62] Being aware of the CIA's role in the making and unmaking of regimes in the Middle East, and having had some conspiratorial experience himself, Nasser had a great belief in the usefulness of this link with the Washington power centres (where the CIA chief was, of course, the Secretary of State's brother).

Roosevelt and his agent in Cairo, Miles Copeland, who were on first-name terms with Nasser and had access to him at any time (including the worst periods of US–Egyptian tension), used their position to try to advance American objectives in that part of the world as they understood them. Not the least of these objectives was progress towards the settlement of the dispute with Israel. According to the accounts made available thus far, their work in Cairo included such activities as joint consultations in which solutions to the Arab–Israeli conflict were discussed, preparations for arranging meetings between Nasser and Israeli statesmen, and attempts to persuade Nasser to make public gestures of peace.[63]

All this was basically compatible with the goals of Alpha, and Nasser's insistence on strict secrecy in this matter and his relative confidence in the CIA operatives could have made them a good channel for advancing the project. Yet their *modus operandi* in Cairo had some drawbacks. They had initially taken Nasser to be a junta ringleader who could be manipulated in almost any direction if the necessary techniques were employed (their most notorious blunder in this area was the attempt to bribe him with $3 million in cash). Nasser usually saw through their machinations and used them for his own purposes—much more than Copeland's account is ready to admit. In order to strengthen their position with the Egyptian leader, they engaged in a wide range of clandestine activities whose value for US diplomacy was quite questionable. The account in Tawil's book of their liaison with Nasser and Hasan Tuhami (code-name Angrylion) presents a vivid picture of CIA involvement in 'black' propaganda and domestic political intrigues, which even after the dismissal of parts of it

---

[62] The precise role of the Americans in general and the CIA in particular in precipitating the evacuation agreement with Britain remains a matter of controversy. See Copeland, *Game of Nations*, pp. 135–46; Tawil, *La'bat* pp. 71–89 and doc. on pp. 390–1; Shahata, *al-Musawwar*, 28 Aug. 1987.

[63] Tawil, *La'bat*, pp. 92–3, 124–9 and doc. on pp. 399–400; Copeland, *Game of Nations*, pp. 157–66.

as Tuhami-style exaggerations, remains quite alarming.[64] On his visit to Egypt, Eveland was taken aback by the way 'the CIA was building an empire behind Nasser', and by the presumption of its men that they had 'invented' Nasser. He also noted (as Copeland's book extensively documents) how the authority and efficiency of the regular political channels were undermined by letting 'covert operators of the CIA conduct American diplomacy in Egypt'.[65]

The particular character of the CIA channel also affected the contents of the messages transmitted through it. In order to preserve their credibility and effectiveness with Nasser, these operators went a long way to endorse his perspectives and positions. This approach also applied to their involvement in the issues of the Egyptian–Israeli settlement. In a letter to Nasser—revealed in the Tuhami–Tawil book—Roosevelt tries to persuade the Egyptian President to approve a secret visit to Cairo by a 'fully responsible' Israeli representative. The following argument is used in the letter to induce Nasser to agree to this peace mission: 'you are in danger of walking into some well laid Israeli traps ... with the results which will handicap seriously the ability of your friends in the United States to counter Zionist pressures ... [the proposed meeting] is, I feel, the only way at hand to head off mounting tensions which are certain to endanger your position ... I am hoping through it to be able to provide our President with concrete evidence that if tensions continue to increase, it will be due to the Israelis rather than to the Egyptians.'[66] Needless to say, whatever the tactical advantages that could be gained by this approach, its merits for the long-term cause of Egyptian–Israeli settlement were questionable.

Roosevelt's correspondence with Cairo (published by Tuhami–Tawil) and the Egyptian Ambassador's reports on talks with him in Washington (published in the Arabic version of Heikal) reveal the CIA operators as eager to win Nasser's co-operation by endorsing his outlook, to the point of virtually becoming a pro-Nasser lobby in Washington. The positions presented by Roosevelt and Copeland clearly exceeded the boundaries of Washington's official policy at that time.[67] This could only nourish in Cairo expectations that could not be fulfilled and boost the kind of self-confidence that leads to a hard line.

[64] Among other things Tuhami claims that the attempt on Nasser's life was actually staged by the CIA to give him a pretext for suppressing the Muslim Brethren: see Tawil, *La'bat*, pp. 94–5 and cf. Copeland, *Game of Nations*, pp. 176 and 112–13; Eveland, *Ropes of Sand*, p. 103.

[65] Eveland, *Ropes of Sand*, pp. 92, 97, 103–4, 125, 159.

[66] Roosevelt to Copeland, 11 Mar. 1954, Tawil, *La'bat*, pp. 390–1.

[67] Correspondence between Copeland and Roosevelt, Tawil, *La'bat*, pp. 390–8; Ahmad Hussein to Foreign Ministry, Cairo, 22 Oct. 1955, Heikal, *Milaffat*, pp. 778–9; Copeland, *Game of Nations*, pp. 152–69. In an interview with the author Roosevelt recalled that Nasser used to say that he should have served as Egypt's Ambassador in Washington instead of Ahmad Hussein.

The CIA was also put in charge of the execution of Operation Gamma, the Anderson mission—the most important attempt made before the Suez–Sinai war to explore the possibility of an Egyptian–Israeli agreement. Copeland attributed to the CIA the whole concept of the mission ('masterminded by Kermit Roosevelt and executed by one Robert Anderson'),[68] but as the declassified documents show, Eisenhower and Dulles were deeply involved in the operation, briefing and debriefing Anderson at the various stages of his mission and sending supportive correspondence to the Israeli and Egyptian leaders. Although Operation Gamma thus brought together the major branches that were involved in the search for a Middle Eastern settlement, it remained basically an improvised and poorly co-ordinated affair. As both Egyptian and American participants agreed, the choice of mediator left much to be desired.[69]

In the literature on Operation Gamma it is sometimes pointed out that the frames of reference of the mission were unclear and contradictory. From the documents of Anderson's briefings, however, a basic target for the mission emerges quite clearly. It transpires that after a year of trial and error with Alpha, the American principals sought, *independently of the British*, a clear answer as to whether anything close to the concept of Alpha still had chances of success—and they wanted at least a preliminary answer before the summit meeting with Eden, scheduled for the end of January, was convened.[70]

From this point of view only, the mission can be considered a success, for it did lead to clear answers. The findings were not yet conclusive when Eden arrived, and Dulles could only say vaguely that efforts at conciliation were being made, that 'the Egyptians are dragging their feet', and that no results had yet been achieved.[71] But the following March, a clear turning-point could be perceived: the disappointment with Nasser was unequivocally expressed and at least for the time being no prospects of co-operation were seen. In his letter to Cabot Lodge at the United Nations, Dulles reported that he had 'been making the most careful exploration of the possibility of a comprehensive settlement'

[68] Miles Copeland, 'Nasser's Secret Diplomacy with Israel', *The Times*, 24 June 1971.

[69] Eveland, *Ropes of Sand*, p. 159. Heikal reported that Nasser simply could not communicate with Anderson and after his experience with him decided to eliminate the 'unofficial' channels to Washington altogether; *Milaffat*, pp. 389, 393.

[70] Briefing of Anderson, 11 Jan. 1956, Declassified Documents, 1981, 552B. There is some vagueness about the usage of the code-name of this operation. Some observers refer to it as operation Beta. Documents in the archives referring to the Anderson mission carry the code-name Alpha.

[71] Memorandum, Eisenhower–Eden, 30 Jan.–1 Feb. 1956, Declassified Documents, 1978, 283B.

and was 'convinced it is impossible at the present time unless and until Arab hopes vis-a-vis Israel are somewhat deflated'.[72]

In precisely the same week that the rift between London and Nasser came out into the open and the British began secretly planning steps to curtail Nasser's influence in the Middle East (leading eventually to plans of assassination), Washington, as the result of its own particular experience, adopted the same posture. In the last days of March, Dulles prepared a whole list of punitive measures to be taken against Nasser; it was decided to try to drive a wedge between Egypt and Saudi Arabia and to promote King Saud as an alternative Arab leader.[73] Project Alpha was no longer mentioned.

EPILOGUE

No analysis of the two Western powers' attempts to work out a settlement of the Egyptian–Israeli conflict before the 1956 war can be complete without an examination of the other two sides of this quadrangle. The scope of this paper does not permit the inclusion of a discussion of these aspects as well (which are the topic of a separate study by the present author),[74] but at least a brief note should be made here to set this critique of the two powers' engagement in arbitration in the proper perspective.

The truth of the matter is that even if the planning and execution of the British and American settlement projects had been perfect, they hardly had any chance of success. By the time Alpha took off, the governments of Egypt and Israel neither regarded a settlement between them as an immediate objective nor believed that it was a realistic proposition. Nasser, who since Bandung had been chalking up one international success after another, was now confident of his capabilities and saw no reason to accept a painful compromise with Israel. He had become committed to a messianic-type vision of pan-Arabism which generated a tremendous response in the hearts of Arabs and was predicated on a historic confrontation with Western 'Imperialism' of which Israel was deemed an integral part. This perception of

[72] Dulles to Lodge, 31 Mar. 1956, Declassified Documents, 1982, 2565. Other statements of Dulles to the same effect: 13, 28, 30 Mar. 1956, Declassified Documents, 1977, 252A; 1983, 1054; 1982, 2564.

[73] Eisenhower's notes from conversation with Dulles, 28 Mar. 1956, Declassified Documents, 1978, 447A; also Conversation Hoover–Anderson, 12 Mar. 1956, Declassified Documents, 1984, 1825. Cf. Geoffrey Aronson, *From Side Show to Center Stage: U.S. Policy toward Egypt, 1946–1956* (Boulder, 1986), pp. 165–8.

[74] 'The Peace Option in Egyptian–Israeli Relations, 1952–1956' (Hebrew), paper prepared for a conference on 'Forty Years of the State of Israel', The Institute for Zionist Research, Tel Aviv University.

the Zionist state was reinforced by his reading of Ben-Gurion's intentions, particularly after the Gaza raid, as seeking a power confrontation. The Israeli leader, for his part, was convinced that Nasser was determined to launch a 'second round' against Israel at a time and place that would suit him. His vision of security was based on possessing the capabilities to pre-empt such threats and convincingly demonstrate the power of the Jewish state.

Thus, while Western diplomats were engaged in exploring possibilities of a settlement, the two local parties had entirely different agendas. Their expectations at this stage were orientated towards the Western powers, not towards each other: Israel wanted arms, Egypt wanted economic assistance. To gain the confidence and goodwill that would facilitate the granting of these requests, they tended to respond positively to propositions which they definitely considered non-starters. They would even launch peace initiatives—such as the Sharett peace offer of December 1955 and the Fawzi plan of July 1956—which were designed to impress the West and did not rest on any belief in their feasibility. The nature of Egyptian–Israeli contacts may well have been different until early 1955, but in the year before the Suez crisis scoring points was the 'name of the game' and each player's purpose was to expose the other's intransigence.

It seems that in the end Israel somehow won this game. Given Nasser's brilliant manœuvring skills, and the many points Jerusalem had lost because of its rigidity on the territorial question and its excessively vigorous reprisal strategy, this outcome was quite remarkable. Thus, when in late March both London and Washington lost their patience with Nasser, the ground was set for Western collaboration with Israel of a kind that would have been unthinkable before the collapse of Alpha.

After the 1956 war, the secret diplomacy in quest of an Egyptian–Israeli settlement was not resumed. Political realities, ideological positions, and territorial boundaries had solidified, and the diplomatic games and exercises of the pre-Suez period lost their rationale. Whereas until 1956 the Palestine question was at the centre of the Arab–Israeli dispute, now the focus shifted to the bilateral problems between Israel and its neighbouring states. Only the cataclysm brought about by the 1967 war changed the situation radically enough to create conditions for the revival of this quest—this time through an essentially different type of diplomacy. It also reopened the Palestine question.

THE CRISIS

5

Britain and the Crisis, 1955–1956

KEITH KYLE

Sir Anthony Eden ended 1954 at the peak of his renown as a diplomatist of the first rank. In a period of British economic decline he embodied, in the opinion of his many admirers, the evidence of Britain's retained skill at the 'great game'. For Eden the battle honours for this one year were headed by the Geneva conference on Indo-China and the resolution of the political problem of German rearmament, both topics on which his judgement was demonstrated to be superior to that of the American Secretary of State, John Foster Dulles. His achievements also included the ending of the Trieste dispute between Italy and Yugoslavia and, in the Middle East, an oil agreement with Iran and a Canal Base agreement with Egypt.

It was no doubt with the confidence born of this experience that Eden told the Cabinet on 4 October 1955, when it was discussing the Soviet arms deal with Egypt:

The British should not allow themselves to be restricted overmuch by reluctance to act without full American concurrence and support. We should frame our own policy in the light of our interests and get the Americans to support it to the extent we could induce them to do so.[1]

But not all the glittering prizes had been won despite the United States. Eden was perfectly well aware that Britain needed from time to time to plug into America's highly charged batteries of economic strength. During the eighteenth century there was a phrase in use to describe England's most effective weapon in the forming of Continental coalitions—it was *la cavalerie de St Georges*, the English money-bags. The part that Britain wished in the 1950s to continue to play in the Middle East required that function to be filled, if not directly then at one remove, by the United States. Also United States backing was sometimes needed by Britain as a character reference because of her recent past as a colonial power. For both reasons Eden (as Bevin before

[1] Cabinet Minutes, 34(55)8, 4 Oct. 1955. The following abbreviations are used for records at the Public Record Office, London: ADM (Admiralty), AIR (Air Ministry), CAB (Cabinet Office), COS (Chiefs of Staff), DEFE (Defence Ministry), FO (Foreign Office), LCO (Lord Chancellor's Office), PREM (Prime Minister's Office), and WO (War Office).

him) aimed to co-opt American policy for British purposes, using anti-Communist solidarity as sufficient argument.[2] The aim, as *The Economist* once put it, was British negotiation from American strength.

Throughout 1955 under Anthony Eden's leadership (as Foreign Secretary until April and Prime Minister thereafter) Britain had been pursuing two policies towards Gamal Abdel Nasser, the ruler of Egypt, each of which could be defended but which were difficult to operate in harmony. On the one hand, in the strictest privacy and in close partnership with the United States, Britain was seeking to promote the project code-named Alpha, which aimed at a final settlement of the Arab–Israeli conflict. Since it was hoped to work through Nasser on the Arab side this required the upholding of his confidence and prestige so that he could make a peace agreement stick. On the other hand, to protect Britain's crucial oil interests and prop up her sagging presence as a regional power, Eden had endorsed the ruthless diplomatic drive of Turkey and the fecund imagination of Nuri Pasha, the veteran Prime Minister of Iraq, to develop the Baghdad Pact, which began as a grouping of the 'northern tier' of Middle East states and was threatening to move south. The Pact itself and Nuri personally had the effect of seriously antagonizing Nasser; any spread of their influence would be regarded by him as a direct challenge to his position and authority.

In mid-September, at an Anglo-American officials' meeting on Alpha, the British proposed to approach the Israelis thus: 'The first great obstacle has been overcome, Egypt is ready to negotiate. The price is high: the whole Negev. There must be something in between the whole Negev and nothing at all. What do you suggest?' The Negev was the virtually unpopulated southern 40 per cent of Israel which Count Bernadotte, the UN Mediator, had wanted to transfer to Arab rule (in exchange for western Galilee) after the second truce in 1948 and which would have provided territorial contiguity between Egypt and the rest of the Arab world. Nasser and his Foreign Minister, Mahmoud Fawzi, had indicated, though not without some ambiguity, that on other matters they were disposed to be accommodating provided that this territorial requirement was met. The Foreign Office knew where its interests lay. 'We should at each stage', runs an office brief on possible Negev negotiations, 'try to see that we are in a position where the blame for failure can be laid wholly or at least partly on Israel.'[3]

Israel had been aware for most of the year that something of the sort

---

[2] But it was not always sufficient. Bevin never persuaded the Americans to equate Zionism and Communism. Wm. Roger Louis, *The British Empire in the Middle East, 1945–1951* (Oxford, 1984), pp. 569–70.

[3] Minute by Geoffrey Arthur, 20 Sept. 1955, FO 371/115879.

was going on and was engaged in an energetic spoiling action.[4] It was David Ben-Gurion, returning to the premiership in November, who was personally devoted to the cause of the development of the Negev and of what he thought was going to be a great industrial port at Eilat on the Red Sea. But opposition to any negotiation on this basis was much wider than that—it was orchestrated by Moshe Sharett, who exploited his reputation as the leader of the dovish wing of the Israeli Cabinet to declare again and again that no conceivable Israeli government would consent to the sacrifice of even a part of the Negev. First Dulles in August (to Eden's extreme irritation) and then Eden himself in November lifted part of the veil off the Alpha exercise. Eden's speech on 9 November gave more specific pointers to a settlement which would be a compromise between the 1947 UN partition boundaries and the existing armistice lines; at the same time he offered his own services as a peacemaker. From that moment onwards Anthony Eden was Israel's least favourite British statesman.

THE 'CZECHOSLOVAK' ARMS DEAL

On 21 September 1955, the Foreign Office got the first word ('from a delicate source') of an event that altered the Middle Eastern scene radically and was the first step leading to the Suez crisis. This was the Czechoslovak arms deal, which Colonel Nasser defiantly affirmed to be a Soviet arms deal in his Alexandria speech of 26 July 1956. Hitherto the three Western powers, Britain, France, and the United States, had exercised a monopoly of arms supplies to Israel and the Arab states and had, since the Tripartite Declaration of 1950, sought to regulate that supply in a manner that would make a 'second round' of the Arab–Israeli war unlikely. By another part of the declaration, to which none of the Middle East states was a party, these three external powers undertook to take immediate action 'both within and outside the UN' to stop any threatened action to violate frontiers or armistice lines. Soviet incursion into this scene and on the scale that was being reported would distort a rationing system which, despite abuses,[5] did have the merit of imposing some measure of control over the arms race.

For Israel the deal threatened to alter the whole military balance once the MIG fighters, Ilyushin bombers, and Stalin tanks had been absorbed by the Egyptian forces. In Washington Secretary of State

[4] Jon Kimche, 'Suez, the Inside Story', *Jewish Chronicle*, 31 Oct. 1986.

[5] Notably those arising from the warm relationship developing between the French and Israeli military establishments. Nevertheless the actual deliveries of French weapons were not developing as fast as was generally supposed. The French, resentful of British-inspired criticism, were circulating exaggerated accounts of British supplies to Israel.

John Foster Dulles's immediate reaction was to worry that the Israelis would launch a pre-emptive strike in a mood of desperation before the arms were delivered.[6] In the British Foreign Office there was intellectual turmoil. The Under-Secretary dealing with the Middle East, Evelyn Shuckburgh, committed to paper his innermost thoughts; they stemmed directly from the insecure state of the British economy and its massive and still growing dependence on cheap oil paid for in sterling and shipped through the Suez Canal. Consequently,

we are faced with the disagreeable truth that we must somehow keep Egypt on our side even to the extent of paying a very high price which may well include having to abandon Israel. It has long been evident that we were retaining our position and interest in the Middle East only because the Russians were not interfering. Once they start bidding for Arab support as they are now doing we are compelled either to outbid them or to lose the main source of power on which our economy now depends. It has long been my firm belief that the continued support of Israel is incompatible with British interests and this is the occasion on which it must be stated.[7]

Shuckburgh's colleague, Harold Caccia, added a significant minute. He realized that the British had to go to great lengths to keep out Soviet influence but, he asked, was the price that had to be paid really the complete abandonment of Israel?

Before we come to a final answer on price we may have to get rid of Nasser, especially if be becomes publicly committed to the [arms] contract.

On 30 September Caccia sent a consensus of Foreign Office views to the Foreign Secretary, Harold Macmillan, who was at the United Nations. 'We do not consider that our main object should be to oust Nasser', he said. Three blows against his position were suggested, two of them typically to be carried out by the Americans: America should join the Baghdad Pact and should then pay (with American dollars) for Iraq to have 80 British Centurion tanks.[8] There was no such luck: Iraq got twelve tanks (two of them paid for by Britain); the United States did not join.

What is intriguing is to follow the traces of Britain's line towards Nasser's Egypt through the next few months. It started with Harold Macmillan's instinctive reaction to the arms deal—'This cannot be allowed to go on'—changed to 'I do not wish to reproach Nasser unduly' in a cable to Sir Humphrey Trevelyan, the new British Ambassador in Cairo, telling him to promise serious Alpha talks when

---

[6] Nutting (New York), 22 Sept. 1955, FO 371/113673.

[7] Shuckburgh to Macmillan, minute by Caccia, 23 Sept. 1955, FO 371/113674.

[8] But possible replacements for Nasser were discussed in the Foreign Office and with the State Department, FO 371/113676.

he could 'count on our seeking with Israel a settlement which could meet at least part of his major requirements', and ended up in a British drive to get American finance behind Nasser's most ambitious domestic project, the Aswan High Dam. Nasser himself took considerable trouble to disarm Western criticism: it was a once-for-all deal, there would be no Soviet technicians, he would now be in a position to negotiate from strength.[9]

INTELLIGENCE REPORTS ON ISRAEL AND ON EGYPT

During the course of November British policy-makers received two worrying sets of reports from the intelligence services. One was about Israel, indicating that she was planning a preventive war against Egypt; the other was about the extent of Soviet influence in Cairo. The Israeli report was based on plans presented by General Moshe Dayan, the Israeli Chief of Staff, and submitted to the Cabinet by Ben-Gurion. The object of the operation would have been to break the stranglehold which Egypt held (and was tightening by new regulations) on the approaches to the planned Negev port of Eilat. It was eventually to be turned down by a Cabinet majority. But Britain could have been involved in war with Israel in either of two ways: under the Tripartite Declaration, along with the United States and (theoretically) France or by herself, if Jordan were involved, under the bilateral obligations of the Anglo-Jordanian Treaty. Jordan was at that time regarded as a British client state, whose army, the Arab Legion, was paid for by Britain and led in the top ranks by British officers. The Jordanian Chief of Staff was Major-General John Bagot Glubb, who for example did not hesitate to forward to Whitehall the report from the Jordanian military attaché in Cairo on the Egyptian training programme for Palestinian commandos (the *fedayeen*).[10]

As the year came to an end, plans for war with Israel were being urgently revised in Whitehall. The Middle East commanders-in-chief felt strongly that 'if an Arab–Israeli war breaks out British prestige in the Middle East will suffer irreparable damage unless UK aid to Jordan is immediate and effective'. The Israeli Air Force would have to be 'neutralised' and the sea-coast blockaded; there would be commando raids on the Israeli coast. It was expected to take six months to bring Israel to her knees.[11] Glubb, from Jordan, proposed a scenario of intervention: Israel attacks Egypt, whereupon the Arab Legion

[9] Trevelyan (Cairo), 31 Oct. 1955, FO 371/113680.
[10] Radi Abdullah to General Glubb, 5 Sept. 1955, FO 371/115905.
[11] DEFE 4/79 Annex to JP(55)88, 16 Sept. 1955 for COS(55)78 of 29 Sept. 1955; DEFE 4/82 JP(55)100, 22 Dec. 1955 for COS(56)2.

marches into Israel and assumes a defensive position along a suitable new frontier line where it is reinforced by the British Army. This scenario reached Eden toward the end of January 1956 as he was about to leave for Washington to confer with Eisenhower.[12] He rejected the particular scheme but devoted much energy in Washington to obtaining American commitment to staff talks under the Tripartite Declaration. This would make it more likely that the Americans would be in the firing line if need be and not Britain alone.

The second critical intelligence document reaching Eden before the end of November was the first of a series of such reports—numbering some twenty-five by the end of March—provided by M.I.6 from a new and purportedly highly reliable source in Nasser's entourage who had been recruited by an agent code-named 'Lucky Break'. The information was supported by documents, starting with one entitled 'Popular Socialism', and a steady stream was supplied during the following months.[13] William Clark, Eden's press secretary, and Evelyn Shuckburgh both recorded in their diaries the impact of this development in Downing Street. 'It is clear that Nasser has gone further than I had ever supposed towards a tie-up with the communists. It is impossible to believe that we can go on supporting him in the long run', wrote Clark. Shuckburgh said: 'There is a terrible scare that the Egyptians are going to give the Aswan project to the Russians'.[14] Nuri Pasha supplied the additional information that there were three prominent associates of Nasser who were communist sympathizers. One of the three named was the regime's most prominent propagandist, Anwar Sadat.

The Russian scare over Aswan drove Eden into frenetic activity to harness American wealth behind the gigantic construction which was to take control of the flow of the Nile waters within Egyptian territory. It was to be a World Bank project but required grant money as well as the bank loans. On 26 November Eden sent Eisenhower in great haste a dramatic cable saying that from disturbing information just acquired he was convinced that if the Egyptian delegation currently in Washington left empty-handed the Russians were certain to get the contract. 'I hate to trouble you with this but I am convinced that on our joint success in excluding the Russians from this contract may depend the future of Africa.'[15] Although there was powerful opposition to the idea

---

[12] Glubb to Duke (Amman), 18 Jan. 1956, FO 371/121723; Duke to FO, 21 Jan. 1956, FO 371/121722; E. M. Rose, 'Military Planning with Jordan', 6 Feb. 1956, FO to Duke, 17 Feb. 1956, FO 371/121723.

[13] Wilbur C. Eveland, *Ropes of Sand: America's Failure in the Middle East* (New York, 1980), pp. 169–71.

[14] William Clark, unpublished Diary: entry for 29 Nov. 1955; Evelyn Shuckburgh, *Descent to Suez* (London, 1986), p. 305.

[15] Eden to Eisenhower, 26 Nov. 1955, FO 371/113739.

from the outset in Washington, Eden's drive succeeded with the active assistance of Dulles. The offer was made by Christmas but Nasser did not rush to take it up; while he queried its conditions for monitoring the whole Egyptian economy, the scheme's enemies in Washington did not rest.

THE 'NEW DOCTRINE' ON NASSER

Britain's attitude towards Nasser changed radically over the first three months of 1956 to the extent that a 'new doctrine', articulated by the Minister of State Anthony Nutting, was spoken of inside the Foreign Office—it was one of Nasser's basic animosity towards British interests and the dethronement of Alpha from its position of priority. The novelty of such thoughts should not be exaggerated. As early as June 1955 Eden was writing angry minutes about Egyptian propaganda help to the Saudis in their sharp disputes with Britain. ('This is gross impertinence by these people who are likely to be attacked and destroyed by Israel before long. I hope we give them no help. Anything in our power to hurt Egyptians without hurting ourselves?')[16] There had been the immediate reaction to the arms deal. There had been the bitter resentment in December when Egyptian influence, including Anwar Sadat operating from inside the Egyptian Embassy in Amman, and Saudi money had helped Jordan's Palestinian politicians to secure the rejection of Britain's attempt to bring Jordan into the Baghdad Pact. Finally, King Hussein's abrupt dismissal of Glubb on 1 March was treated in Britain—by the media as well as Whitehall—as a calculated Egyptian slap in the face for Britain. A bitter press war between Britain and Egypt went on for several months. At the same time the sequence of M.I.6 reports was building up a portrayal of Egypt as 'an out-and-out Soviet instrument'.

On 14 March the chairman of the British Chiefs of Staff committee, Marshal of the RAF Sir William Dickson, cabled the head of the British Joint Staffs mission in Washington to hasten the Anglo-American staff report on combating Israeli aggression against Egypt, without waiting to cover the opposite contingency. The next day he cabled a correction; after talking to ministers, he now wanted the plan to provide effectively for 'the probability that Egypt is more likely to be the aggressor'.[17] On the same day Eden cabled Eisenhower: 'Dear Friend, I send you herewith a most secret note of Egyptian intentions of whose authenticity we are entirely confident.' Comments by the British Chiefs on an Anglo-American planning paper that was then

---

[16] Macmillan Papers, PM's minute, 20 June 1955, FO 800/669.
[17] Dickson to Whiteley, 15 and 16 Mar. 1956, FO 371/121761.

drawn up indicated fears that the Americans might think it sufficient to stop Egyptian aggression by air attacks on lines of communication alone. That might be enough to save Israel but it would not stop the Egyptians from closing the Suez Canal. Because of the drastic effect that that would have on Britain, three or four divisions must be landed to keep the Canal open. The British Chiefs also thought that the plan underestimated the chances that 'volunteers' from the Soviet Union and East Germany would fly the planes and operate the weapons which Egypt had acquired.[18]

The sudden withdrawal of the offer of American grants towards the Aswan Dam did not, as was sometimes supposed, come to Britain as an unpleasant surprise. At the beginning of June the American Minister told the Foreign Office that in the altered climate of American opinion there was no chance whatever of inducing Congress to put up the money.[19] The Americans suggested that Nasser should be put off with a riparian conference of all the states and colonies involved with the Nile, to discuss its overall control. A British Treasury official on hearing of this declared that Nasser 'will undoubtedly be appalled by the apparent breach of faith by the two governments and will seek an occasion to revenge himself. There is not much he can do against the US but a lot he can do against us. Obvious examples are renewed pressure on the Suez Canal Company or stirring up trouble in the Gulf.'[20] The British press was outspoken on the issue of the Dam. 'Does anyone in his right mind really *want* to give a £5m present of British taxpayers' money to Colonel Nasser?' demanded the *Sunday Express* of 15 July. 'If the Dam does not go up he may fall down. But why should we help to maintain him in power?' Selwyn Lloyd, now the Foreign Secretary, told the Cabinet on 17 July that the American government was 'likely to share our view that the offer should now be withdrawn'.

When the deed was done with, perhaps, more publicity than Britain would have wished, a Foreign Office minute noted: 'Mr Dulles has taken the decision for us. We were not absolutely in step at the last moment but the difference between us was no more than a nuance.'[21]

NATIONALIZATION

When Nasser in revenge nationalized the Suez Canal Company, the thoroughness of his preparation demonstrated that there was obviously a well-researched contingency plan. The Americans argued this vigor-

[18] COS(56) 33rd Meeting, 20 Mar. 1956, JP(56) 78, 12 Apr. 1956, DEFE 4/85.
[19] P. F. Hancock (FO) to F. Bishop (No. 10), 4 June 1956, FO 371/119055.
[20] Michael Johnston (Treasury) to John Phillips (FO), 6 June 1956, FO 371/119055.
[21] FO 371/119056.

ously to refute the attempt by Christian Pineau, the French Foreign Minister, to throw the entire responsibility on the United States. But there seems insufficient evidence to support Lord Blake's view that basically Nasser wanted to nationalize the Company and forced the issue in the High Dam negotiation to give him an excuse.[22] But Egyptian researchers had revealed the legal weaknesses of the Company's position which sprang from the wish of Ferdinand de Lesseps, the founder, to treat the Company as alternately Egyptian and international as it suited him. Its legal status was, however, Egyptian; and it had suited Britain in the past to insist that this was so and to oppose any form of international control.[23] An Egyptian company, said Egypt, could be nationalized; the shareholders should have compensation; the 1888 Convention, providing for free passage, would be observed.

The seizure transformed the standing of France in the eyes of British policy-makers. France had been classed with Egypt, Israel, and Saudi Arabia in the mixed ranks of the enemies of the Baghdad Pact, which was becoming the core of British policy.[24] Lacking real influence anywhere in the Levant, the French were accused in the British files of going on acting as if they were Syria's patron and adopting 'irresponsible positions' in the hope of retaining their 'pockets of influence'. 'I find it impossible as between allies to accept their obstructive attitude', wrote Eden on one occasion. And again, 'The French are double-crossing.'[25] As a sponsor of the Tripartite Declaration France was entitled to a place in Western policy-making. But each occasion on which a new move was taken by Britain and the United States, a top point on the agenda would be whether to include France; and the decision was always against. They were left out of Alpha, left out of the financing of the Aswan Dam, though there was a French member of the original consortium of firms interested in building it, and even left out in early 1956 of the military talks set up in Washington on the implementation of the Tripartite Declaration. This was on the insistence of the American military who objected to French lack of security,

[22] Lord Blake, 'Anthony Eden', Lord Blake and C. S. Nicholls (eds.), *Dictionary of National Biography, 1971–1980* (Oxford, 1986), p. 270.
[23] Douglas Farnie, *East and West of Suez: The Suez Canal in History 1854–1956* (Oxford, 1969), pp. 71–2, 575; Prof. R. Y. Jennings to Gwilym Lloyd George, 13 Aug. 1956, LCO 2/5760; HMG Memorandum to Mixed Court of Appeal, Alexandria (in 'gold currency case') 12 Apr. 1939, cited in *White Paper on the Nationalisation of the Suez Maritime Canal Company* (Cairo, 1956), pp. 59–61.
[24] Memorandum by Shuckburgh 13 Dec. 1955, 'French Attitude to the Baghdad Pact'; *aide-mémoire* from French Government on Middle East, 4 Jan. 1956; minute by Ivone Kirkpatrick, FO 371/121244.
[25] Eden to Kirkpatrick, 6 Mar. 1955, FO 371/115495; Jebb (Paris) to Eden, 24 Mar. 1955, minutes by Eden, 'Cheek! ... more cheek! ... thoroughly unsatisfactory', FO 371/115502.

which meant both the supposed special tendency of the French to leak secrets and also the closeness that had been observed of the French defence establishment to the Israelis.[26]

In March the French Socialist Prime Minister, Guy Mollet, fell foul of Eden specifically on the subject of the Baghdad Pact. After a weekend visit to Chequers, Mollet told the Press that he had 'recalled our reservations' about the pact which remained undiminished. Then Eden's irritation was aggravated by an interview in an American magazine in which Mollet repeated his strictures. Gladwyn Jebb, the British Ambassador, was ordered to see him at once and 'express to him strongly my own resentment at these continued attempts to undermine the . . . only sure foundation of policy in the Middle East'.[27] Christian Pineau was causing even more offence by his habit of making unscripted speeches attacking the Cold War basis of Western foreign policy. What Jebb called 'that foolish fellow' was due in London on 29 July in any case to have out his differences with Selwyn Lloyd. The purpose was totally altered by Nasser: Pineau now came offering to place French forces and facilities under British command and to plan a policy of joint action against a man the French looked on as the flame behind the Algerian insurrection.[28]

The fact that the character of the Suez Canal Company was French, with its headquarters in Paris, while the British government was the principal shareholder, made for an Anglo-French alignment. Yet an interesting feature of the controversy was that virtually no one in either country proposed the restoration of the Company. In Britain Lord Hankey was the only public figure to do so and he was a long-time Suez director. The two governments undertook to take the high ground of internationalization, which received massive support until people began to think how it was going to be enforced. This would also solve the problem which they saw occurring in 1968 when the Company's concession expired, and the management of the Canal reverted to Egypt. The new arrangement would be permanent. The Egyptians would be offered some symbols and more money than before.

The government from the outset faced up to the problem of enforcement. Among themselves ministers were frank that their legal position was weak. The Canal Company was Egyptian, subject to Egyptian law. The Cabinet of 27 July conceded that from a strictly legal point of view Nasser's action 'amounted to no more than a decision to buy out the shareholders'. But at that meeting ministers

---

[26] Makins (Washington) to FO, 18 Mar. 1956, FO 371/121761.

[27] Jebb (Paris) to FO, 3 Mar. 1956, Jebb to Eden, 19 Mar. 1956, Eden to Jebb, 25 Mar. 1956, FO 371/124430.

[28] Conversation between Lloyd and Pineau, 29 July 1956, PREM 11/1098.

were asked by Eden 'whether they were prepared in the last resort to pursue their objective by the threat or even the use of force and whether they were ready in default of assistance from the United States and France to take military action alone'. The Cabinet decided these two questions in the affirmative; afterwards even the more dovish members such as the Minister of Defence, Sir Walter Monckton, felt themselves bound in principle by these decisions.[29] The actual conduct of the affair was handed over to a small group of ministers, originally numbering only six, called the Egypt Committee. At its first meeting this body decided that its first and most immediate objective was to bring about the downfall of the present Egyptian government. International control of the Canal might take longer, but it would be on that that their case before world opinion had to be based. The original intention was that a maritime conference should be allowed two days to ratify a scheme drawn up by Britain, France, and the United States; Britain would send it to Egypt in a note which would be 'a virtual ultimatum' and then, if Nasser refused, in two weeks military operations would commence. The only objections at this stage were that a conference might offer 'an unwelcome opportunity ... to indulge in prolonged discussion', which could lead to an equivocal policy, since some states might be reluctant to contemplate drastic measures.

But the military plans turned out to require six weeks not two, and John Foster Dulles required rather more preservation of appearances about the composition and duration of the conference. Also Eisenhower in his messages made it abundantly clear that he was opposed to the use of force in this dispute. Nevertheless Dulles's zeal for international control and the deep bias he had now adopted against Nasser personally made Eden suppose that with care American policy and pressure could be co-opted for British purposes. The American Joint Chiefs of Staff would have been happy if that had been true since they recommended that the United States give the British and French all military and political support short of actual combat action.[30] Such recommendations were ignored.

The House of Commons debate of 2 August, before Parliament disappeared for the summer recess, left the impression of a national consensus behind Eden's firm stance. Only afterwards, when the Prime Minister's press secretary and the head of the Foreign Office News Department had gone in for heavy lobby briefings of the press about

[29] PREM 11/1098.

[30] Record Group 218: Records of the Joint Chiefs of Staff, 'Joint Chiefs of Staff, History, vol. vi, Chapter X, The Suez Canal Crisis', National Archives, Washington. Discussions of the 295th Meeting of the National Security Council, 30 Aug. 1956, Eisenhower Papers, 1953–61 (Ann Whitman file), Presidential Library, Abilene, Kansas.

Britain's willingness to use force, was there a ground swell of uneasiness. The government's lawyers were divided unevenly by the talk of using force. The Legal Adviser to the Foreign Office, Sir Gerald Fitzmaurice, continually reminded anyone who would listen of

> the immense change that has taken place in the climate of world opinion on the question of the use of force ... Justification that would have been accepted without question fifty or even twenty-five years ago would by now be completely rejected.

The law in his view, which was shared by the two Law Officers of the Crown, was now governed by the Kellogg Pact of 1928, which had been enforced at Nuremberg and by the UN Charter. The grounds for using force had been drastically narrowed to self-defence, forcible denial of rights, and protection of nationals. The plea of 'vital interests' was, he said, the very one the Charter was intended to exclude.

> We are on an extremely bad wicket legally as regards using force in connection with the Suez Canal. Whatever illegalities the Egyptians may have committed ... these do not in any way ... justify forcible action on our part ... such a justification could only arise, if at all, from some further and much more drastic step on the part of the Egyptian Government amounting to a closure of the Canal or at any rate a definite refusal or impeding passage through it.[31]

Thus, if illegality were to be avoided, President Nasser must contribute to his own ruin. This he declined to do despite the expenditure of much effort during the Suez crisis to tempt or provoke him.

There was, however, another proponent of legal standards at the heart of the government, who unlike the legal advisers was a member of the Cabinet: the Lord Chancellor, Lord Kilmuir. Vigorously inside Cabinet, publicly in the House of Lords, and in long memoranda, he expounded the thesis that 'the Charter of the United Nations leaves untouched the general principal of self-defence under customary law'. Thus the whole history of precedent in the law-books remained open for citation; it was not superseded by Article 51 of the Charter.[32]

In a memorandum drawn up on 1 November when the die had been cast for military action, Fitzmaurice recorded that he and his deputy 'from the beginning and at all times strongly opposed the use of force as having no legal justification in any of the circumstances that had or have arisen hitherto'. Incensed by the claim in the telegrams sent out

---

[31] Fitzmaurice to Harold Beeley, 13 Aug. 1956, Fitzmaurice to Kirkpatrick, 31 Aug. and 4 Sept. 1956, Fitzmaurice to Coldstream, 6 Sept. 1956, FO 800/747; memorandum on 'The Use of Force' by the Law Officers of the Crown, 31 Oct. 1956, LCO 2/5760.

[32] Kilmuir, 'Suez Canal: Memorandum by the Lord Chancellor on the Use of Force', n.d., LCO 2/5760.

from the Foreign Office to defend the bombing of Egypt that 'HMG are advised on the highest legal authority that they are entitled under the Charter' to do as they were doing, the Legal Adviser, who had not been consulted any more than the two Law Officers, wrote:

The Prime Minister has, however, taken his advice on the matter from the Lord Chancellor and virtually all the legal arguments which the Government have put forward on the question of the use of force and which I have constantly queried have emanated from that quarter.[33]

THE MILITARY PLANS

There were basically three military plans, corresponding to three different layers of command. The first, drawn up by the joint planners and presented by the Chiefs of Staff on 2 August, was the product of the flurry of the immediate crisis; the second, *Musketeer*, was prepared under the supervision of the three Task Force commanders; the third, *Musketeer Revise*, was the brain-child of General Keightley who by then had become Allied Commander-in-Chief.[34] They also responded to different political assumptions and circumstances. The French were not involved in the adoption of either of the first two planning concepts.

The first argument which continually resurfaced was about the effectiveness of air power in obtaining the real (as opposed to the formally stated) objective, namely the overthrow of Nasser. There was a school of thought which held that the RAF and carrier planes could do the job alone, without requiring an assault landing. They could break the morale of the Egyptian state and Nasser would fall. The initial decision was not to count on this happening but to land troops at Port Said and occupy the line of the Canal. Because of the extreme shortage of assault craft available it was necessary to unload vessels either there or at Alexandria. When the Task Force commanders had been appointed, they expressed themselves as being much in favour of landing at Alexandria, a larger harbour, a more direct challenge to the seat of government. Also Port Said was at the end of a narrow causeway and fifty miles from the nearest jet airfield, neither circumstance ideal for the rapid buildup of forces.[35]

The second plan was to capture Alexandria harbour after an air and

[33] Fitzmaurice to Kirkpatrick, 31 Oct. 1956, FO 800/747.

[34] The original intention had been for the expedition to be commanded jointly by the three commanders without a Supreme Commander. Keightley, who was Commander-in-Chief, Middle East Land Forces, was named as Allied Commander-in-Chief on 11 August and established his headquarters in the War Office on 22 August.

[35] Operation *Musketeer* Section 1: Outline of events 30–6, WO 106/5986, ADM 116/6209.

naval bombardment which would have to be heavy because the initial assault party would be so small. Its size, as much else in this operation, would be governed by the extremely limited supply of assault craft. But the defences were weak, the number of Egyptians believed to be manning them was low, and once the harbour was secure the troopships would be able to dock alongside. There was a large airfield nearby which could be seized by the French in the first wave. Eighty thousand troops would be landed followed by an advance on Cairo by the desert road. This, General Stockwell, the Land Force Commander, wrote, 'would menace the seat of Government and the Egyptians would be forced either to capitulate or to stand and fight us to the north-west of Cairo where their army could be annihilated'.[36] The intention was not to linger in the Cairo area but, with a new government installed, to push on to the Canal Zone.

On 10 August, just as the British had switched to this second plan, the French commanders and their military planners arrived in London, causing grave misgivings about the risks involved in exchanging secrets with the French. All the old fears surfaced. French security, it was said, was notoriously bad. The Egypt Committee decided to send Patrick Dean, the chairman of the Joint Intelligence Committee, to Paris as the Prime Minister's special representative to teach the French what was meant by military security. Until this had been done the French planners were to be confused. For a week the British team, reading documents marked 'UK Eyes Only' were obliged to mislead their partners as to the probable destination of the expedition on which they were both working. It was a situation, Stockwell wrote in his report of the campaign, that was 'both distasteful and foreign to British principles'.[37]

The military had been urged by the politicians to hasten so as to permit the earliest possible D-day. The days in between were for filling out with diplomatic and political events, such as the conference of maritime powers, Nasser's anticipated rejection of its plan for international control of the Canal, and the withdrawal of the Canal pilots. But because the British wanted to involve the Americans, the Americans were able to take over the timetable, and while the Americans also had decided that they wanted to get rid of Nasser they did not want it done by force.[38] Moreover, public opinion in Britain no longer gave the

---

[36] Stockwell, 'Operation *Musketeer*', WO 288/77.

[37] 10 Aug. 1956, Stockwell, 'Operation *Musketeer*', CAB 134/1216.

[38] Makins (Washington) to Lloyd, 9 Sept. 1956: 'Mr Dulles's statement that the Administration are determined to join with us in cutting Nasser down seems to me very significant ... It is true, as the President says, that there is no support in the US for the use of force in present circumstances ... It is a matter of comment here, both private and public, that British opinion is sharply divided'; FO 800/740.

impression of being united and even the Egypt Committee was
divided. It was, ironically enough, the Minister of Defence, Walter
Monckton, who was most opposed to some of the warlike procedures
being proposed. On 24 August an exchange which is not recorded
in the Committee's official minutes led to an outburst from Monckton,
which was afterwards described by a colleague as 'both painful and
rather disturbing'. It had apparently been provoked by some ungar-
nished remarks of Harold Macmillan, the Chancellor of the Exchequer, on the lines of how a recall of Parliament (to illustrate consultation) and a debate in the UN Security Council (to illustrate
'impotence') could be briskly accommodated to a fixed military
timetable. Monckton had been holding sessions of conscience with
Lord Mountbatten, the powerful and persuasive First Sea Lord, who
had brought home to him the scale of civilian casualties that would be
caused by the attack on Alexandria. Assuring Eden in a letter
afterwards that 'I need hardly say that I am absolutely at one with
you', Lord Salisbury, the fairly hawkish Lord President of the Council,
wrote to Eden about Monckton, 'I think that you and I knew that he
had for some time had doubts about a firm policy over Suez.' Because
junior members of the Cabinet were becoming restless at not knowing
what was going on, it was decided to have a full Cabinet on 28 August
so that Eden could know where he stood. Alan Lennox-Boyd, the
Colonial Secretary, wrote to him:

I remain firmly convinced that if Nasser wins or even appears to win we might
as well as a government (and indeed as a country) go out of business . . . I was
horrified by the doubts expressed by the Minister of Defence. All these
difficulties stood out miles when we first embarked on our policy . . . If there
really is uncertainty in the Cabinet we can't be surprised if it exists in the
country.[39]

At the full Cabinet, Macmillan produced a report on the economic
implications of Suez. The cost of the military operations would not be
large in relation to the current scale of defence expenditure. But, if the
Canal were closed and the pipelines cut, Britain could not sustain for
long the burden of paying for dollar supplies in replacement. Early in
the Suez crisis the Americans had in fact started planning how to
supply replacement oil from the Western Hemisphere, but at no time
would they agree to provide the financial help with the dollar cost that
Britain would want. The Cabinet was told that this would place a
serious burden on the balance of payments and a drain on the reserves.
But Macmillan said that the experience with Musaddiq in Iran showed

[39] Lennox-Boyd to Eden, 24 Aug. 1956; Salisbury to Eden 24 Aug. 1956; Home to Eden,
24 Aug. 1956; Brook to Eden, 25 Aug. 1956; PREM 11/1152.

that these Middle East oil countries could not be relied on to be governed by commercial self-interest. And, as promised in advance, Lennox-Boyd backed Eden up with the news that the Governors of Aden, Somaliland, and Kenya had all warned that their Arabs were watching closely the outcome of the contest between Nasser and the West; if Nasser won, British influence in these colonies would be destroyed.

In what must have been an unusually schizophrenic performance, Monckton declined to discuss details of the military plans with the Cabinet but made the point that up till then they had been based on the assumption that operations should be launched at the first possible moment. The stage would soon be reached when 'the efficiency of the operation might be endangered by any long postponement of the date on which planning was being based'. If that sounded like a plea to go forward, what the Defence Minister also said sounded like a plea to go backward. British military action would be condemned by much of world and Commonwealth opinion, opinion at home would be divided, and oil installations in the Middle East would be sabotaged. 'Once Britain had sent troops into Egypt how was she going to get them out?' It is rather remarkable that Eden, knowing his views, kept Monckton at the Ministry of Defence until 18 October and that Monckton, knowing Eden's, stayed on. R. A. Butler, as Leader of the House, said that the Government would not in practice be able to act without Parliament behind it. A substantial section of the government's supporters in the House would want to be sure that all practicable steps had been taken first to ensure a settlement by peaceful means. Salisbury, starting from the point that no course now open to them was free from serious risk, thought that, if the Cabinet were satisfied that Nasser's policy would undermine Britain's economy and destroy her influence as a world power, Britain should be resolved to take whatever action was needed. But if force were needed, Britain should first go to the United Nations, since she would require all the international support she could get.[40]

The third military plan, pushed by General Keightley, who was now Allied Commander-in-Chief, was intended to meet the situation revealed by this Cabinet discussion. The second plan, being elaborately calibrated, was highly sensitive to political changes, costly, both financially and in terms of morale, to maintain on a stand-by basis, and getting more perilous as D-day was twice postponed. This was because the Egyptians were thought to be reinforcing the defences of Alexandria in ways that might break the dash of the rather small landing

[40] 28 Aug. 1956, PREM 11/1104.

parties. Also those few ministers who knew the plans, including notably the new First Lord of the Admiralty, Lord Hailsham, were shocked at the large number of predicted civilian casualties from the naval bombardment. It is evident from the personal notes which he appended to the fresh concept that Keightley was an ardent advocate of its merits, just as it is apparent from the reports of the Task Force commanders, especially General Stockwell, that they did not share his enthusiasm.[41] *Musketeer Revise*, which was finally endorsed by the Egypt Committee on 14 September, had three phases: first, three days' neutralization of the Egyptian Air Force; second, seven to eleven days of disrupting the Egyptian economy, morale, and armed forces from the air which was to be combined with a major campaign of psychological warfare; and third, and only when the task of the second phase was achieved, an unopposed military occupation of the Canal Zone or one that was exposed only to disorganized resistance. This was a virtual reversion to the argument that had been heard at the outset that the whole business should be conducted from the air.[42]

From the adoption of this plan three things followed. First, a great weight was being placed on psychological warfare, to be waged mainly by 'black radio', which had been considered to be one of Britain's great successes in World War II and which had begun operating a personal campaign against Nasser—called Gamalov and *Fashil* ('the unsuccessful one')—within 36 hours of the seizure of the Suez Canal Company.[43] Secondly, the date of the landing at Port Said was a movable one, depending on the success of Phase 2, so that the pause before it took place might be as long as fourteen days. And thirdly, as was made clear to them in advance, the British and French governments would with this strategy be exposed to much sustained criticism if military and economic targets—the armed forces, oil installations, and communications systems of Egypt—were systematically destroyed from the air. General Keightley went so far as to say that to succeed his

---

[41] Notes by General Sir Charles Keightley, 7, 10, 18 Sept. 1956, PREM 11/1104; General Stockwell's report on Operation *Musketeer*: 'The new concept was in effect a complete change of plan' (p. 23); 'Phase 2 of the operation produced considerable apprehension in the minds of the Joint Task Force commanders' (p. 25), WO 288/77. For Hailsham's reaction see William Clark, *From Three Worlds* (London, 1986), p. 191.

[42] WO 106/5986.

[43] BBC Summary of World Broadcasts, Part IV, 1956, daily series, No. 7, 31 July 1956, and succeeding dates; e.g. the broadcast of 28 July: 'This Abdul Nasser is a traitor who betrays the Arab cause and is worthy of immediate death. His hour is very near and all of you will witness it ... The tyrant Abdul Nasser is trembling from fear after committing his greatest mistake two days ago ... You must know that Britain has sent her fleet to patrol the sea before the shore of Alexandria ... Egypt will not be in a position to oppose the fleets of the Western States should they decide to occupy Egypt.' Directional checks suggested that this station was in the south of France.

operation would first require 'some enemy action which makes British and world opinion wholeheartedly behind us'.

The principal advantage Keightley claimed for the new plan was its greater flexibility, being more geared to a situation in which unpredictable deadlines were determined by political circumstances. He also claimed that there would be many fewer civilian casualties than if the Alexandria landing had been carried out—which, though no doubt true, would not be the standard of comparison critics would have in mind. If the air attack was really to work, it would need to have an impact like the German blitz. In some alarm, Admiral Grantham, the Commander-in-Chief Mediterranean, described, in a personal message to Lord Mountbatten, a conversation he had had with Keightley.

When I asked him what would happen if all the tanks, guns and transport were hidden in the towns and villages, he said they would go for them there and that the civilian population would have to take it. He added that this would form part of the breaking the will to resist . . . I understand . . . that the Chiefs of Staff or anyway you do not consider that the *Musketeer* Plan is to bomb civilians.[44]

The Directors of Plans went out of their way to stress that the new plan would 'require considerable resolution from HMG in authorising the necessary programme of air bombing in the face of adverse world opinion'.[45] This in effect was the plan in being when the British government called upon the military commanders to act as 'an international police force separating the combatants'. In extreme haste it was adapted to fit the new purpose.

Alongside the military planning there was planning for the post-war organization of Egypt and the Canal. This was done mainly by officials but was supervised by Macmillan and Salisbury.[46] It was assumed for planning purposes that, Nasser being overthrown, an 'acquiescent' government would be installed. Who would be in it and whether any of them had already been approached are matters that remain secret even after the release of documents under the thirty-year rule. The records available assume that, as the Egypt (Official) Committee, presided over by Sir Norman Brook, the Cabinet Secretary, noted, 'There are good reasons to believe that, given the defeat of the Egyptian Army and the collapse of the Nasser regime, a successor government can be formed which would be able to maintain law and order.' Trefor Evans, the Oriental Counsellor at the Cairo Embassy, is known to have flown back to London with a list of potential ministers.

    [44] Grantham to Mountbatten, 24 Sept. 1956, ADM 205/133.
    [45] 'We again voiced our anxiety lest HMG might find this pressure irresistible at some stage before Phase II had achieved its aim', DEFE 6/37.   [46] PREM 11/1098.

This was presumably the basis for the mandarins' confidence which enabled them to say that 'Allied troops would not be required to maintain law and order throughout Egypt.' There was to be no AMGOT (the civil affairs organization in Italy at the end of the war), because, it was said,

On the basis of past experience it is probable that the Egyptian administrative machine would continue to function with something approaching its normal state of efficiency despite a change of government. But it would be better to accept the risk of a breakdown in central government and to assemble a remedy at the time than to assemble a standby organisation now.[47]

The draft political directive for the Commander-in-Chief conceded that it might be necessary for him to occupy Cairo briefly to install the new 'co-operative' government and to capture the headquarters of any resistance movement that Nasser might have left behind. But British troops should rapidly fall back on the Canal Zone area; no general responsibility must be accepted under the new Geneva conventions dealing with military occupation for feeding the population. The directive managed to seem minimalist in concept while being in fact infinite in potential. Military government was to function only in the Canal Zone where a provisional Military Canal Operating Authority was to guarantee free passage until agreement was reached about international control. But the Commander-in-Chief was also to be told to support the successor government in eliminating any serious opposition it could not handle itself and in crushing any fresh attempt by Nasser to stage a come-back.[48]

The Chiefs of Staff submitted a further paper on 25 October different in tone and having reflected what state the country would be in after prolonged air bombardment. 'Under such conditions the restoration and maintenance of law and order would be no rapid or easy task.' Guerrilla activity, strikes, and other forms of civil unrest were to be expected. This was a picture very different from that of a cowed and politically indifferent population in previous documents. An occupation army of three or four divisions would be needed with administrative backing. To keep the 'friendly' government in power Cairo might need to be occupied, even Alexandria. This would mean the indefinite withdrawal of one division from Germany, the commit-

---

[47] Egypt (Official) Committee, 1st Meeting, 24 Aug. 1956, CAB 134/1225.

[48] On 21 Aug. 1956 Sir Charles Key, Deputy Under-Secretary at the War Office, said that risks of civil disorder would not be so great 'if the operations could proceed as quickly as the Foreign Secretary seems to contemplate and if in fact it were possible to confine our stay in Cairo and other urban areas such as Alexandria to "no more than a day or two"', WO 32/16709. 'The Role of Civil Affairs in the New Military Plan', 30 Aug. 1956, CAB 134/1225.

ment of most of the strategic reserve to Egypt, and the indefinite retention of conscription.[49]

IN SEARCH OF A PRETEXT

As Selwyn Lloyd remarked to Pineau on 5 September it would be hard for the British public to understand 'bombing from the blue' after an ultimatum but without any incidents to justify it. It was difficult, for instance, to bomb Egyptian airfields without Nasser having stopped a single ship. 'It would be much better to have an incident first.'[50] The main reason why Eden grasped at Dulles's SCUA (Suez Canal Users' Association) scheme, even though by requiring a second conference it would take up more time, was that the scheme itself was so untidy that it was likely to create an incident and one, moreover, in which the United States would be implicated alongside the British and the French. Dulles's aim was the opposite: to engage all concerned in the discussion of technicalities in the course of which the crisis would seep away.

The Suez Canal Company had from the moment of nationalization wanted to remove its pilots and other expatriate staff. It had been restrained by the British and French governments but, after the failure of the Menzies mission to commend international control to Nasser, the Company got from Pineau precise instructions for the staff to leave on 15 September. The British did not want to be caught giving such instructions, for fear of being accused themselves of interfering with free passage in the Canal but they approved of the result and made plans on the assumption that it would come about.[51] Harold Watkinson, the Minister of Transport, had prepared a scenario whose code-names, Operations *Pile-up* and *Convoy*, betrayed its intention. Watkinson's order provided that:

On and after 15 September sufficient ships should be routed to Suez and Port Said to cause serious congestion at the entrances of the Canal well beyond the capacity of the remaining force of pilots to clear. All offers of compromise methods of transit must be refused as unsafe. . . . [A] barrage of complaints to Nasser and to UK and France about unavailability of transit and *unsafe* conditions must be organised.

This was to be *Pile-up*. Then would come *Convoy*—British and French warships which would organize these frustrated vessels in the name of SCUA, provide them with pilots on demand, and, if necessary, assure

---

[49] Chiefs of Staff Committee Annex, 25 Oct. 1956, PREM 11/1103.
[50] Annex to Record of Meeting, Lloyd–Pineau at Quai d'Orsay, 5 Sept. 1956, FO 800/740.
[51] Record of a meeting in the Foreign Office, 8 Sept. 1956, of Lloyd, Watkinson, Nutting, Chauvel, and Georges-Picot, FO 371/119136.

by show of force free and unobstructed passage.[52] This plot resulted in the Egyptians' finest triumph. They noticed that there was an unprecedented number of ships awaiting passage—Nasser referred to them in his Bilbeis speech—but the Egyptians got them through without a hitch. The argument about Egyptian inefficiency, which most governments privately regarded as Britain's strongest, was, as far as the Canal was concerned, dramatically refuted.

Similar frustration was to follow over the Canal dues. To their bitter indignation Eden and Lloyd discovered that they had wrongly assumed that Dulles would allow SCUA to be used as an instrument for withholding from Egypt revenues from the Canal. It had been a major part of the psychological warfare against Nasser to portray him to the Egyptian people as a blundering idiot whose policies had brought them no material reward. Now, thanks to the Americans, they were without a goad to drive their enemy into interrupting normal Canal services.

When, in a telling passage addressed to Eden, Eisenhower had said that there was a danger in 'making of Nasser a much more important figure than he is', the phrase cut to the quick Eden's principal draftsman of transatlantic messages. Sir Ivone Kirkpatrick (the Permanent Undersecretary at the Foreign Office), the 'small, brisk, dapper, decisive and self-confident' Irishman described by his biographer,[53] had had a long personal exposure to Nazi Germany. As a result, so far from diluting, he fed Eden's tendency to facile historical analogies. His comment on Eisenhower's phrase, contained in a personal note to the British Ambassador in Washington, best expressed what it was that drove Britain's leaders on to try risky policies in the absence of American support.

I wish the President were right. But I am convinced that he is wrong ... [I]f we sit back while Nasser consolidates his position and gradually acquires control of the oil-bearing countries, he can, and is, according to our information, resolved to wreck us. If Middle East oil is denied to us for a year or two our gold reserves will disappear. If our gold reserves disappear the sterling area disintegrates. If the sterling area disintegrates and we have no reserves we shall not be able to maintain a force in Germany or, indeed, anywhere else. I doubt whether we shall be able to pay for the bare minimum necessary for our defence. And a country that cannot provide for its defence is finished.[54]

Since these were the stakes, some way had to be found of striking at Nasser.

[52] Ministry of Transport, 10 Sept. 1956: 'It is only fair to add that Picot and shipowners see great practical difficulties to this plan'; CAB 128/30 Pt. 2.

[53] Sir Con O'Neill, 'Sir Ivone Kirkpatrick', E. T. Williams and C. S. Nicholls (eds.), *Dictionary of National Biography, 1961–1970* (Oxford, 1981), pp. 616–17.

[54] Kirkpatrick to Makins, 10 Sept. 1956, FO 800/740.

ENTER THE ISRAELIS: FRIEND OR FOE?

As the crisis advanced, the chances seemed to be increasing of Britain having not just Egypt but also Israel as an enemy. Operation *Cordage*, which provided for air and naval units to intervene against Israel under the Anglo-Jordanian Treaty and the Tripartite Declaration, remained in being to within days of the Suez war. The Israeli reprisal raids on Jordanian police posts and school buildings were getting worse, with higher casualties, after every incident of Arab infiltration; at any moment the clashes might escalate into war. Much time was being devoted by the British Chiefs of Staff to planning operations against the Israelis. Consideration was even given to a simultaneous war[55] against Egypt and Israel (though this was found unfeasible). Some people began to feel that Britain was getting into a tangle.

When the Foreign Office had administered a sharp public rebuke to Israel after a reprisal raid, Fitzmaurice, the Legal Adviser, wrote to Kirkpatrick:

There really seems to be no end to the contradictions we involve ourselves in ... Apart from the question whether it is really quite appropriate for us to be reading people this sort of lecture at the present time, is it wise for the British official spokesman to be condemning in such round terms action of a type which we might very well be led to take ourselves, and have indeed, as all the world knows, made extensive preparations for taking?[56]

The Israelis were extremely worked up about troops from Iraq, which had never signed an armistice agreement with them, moving into Jordan with British approval in order to help stabilize the country. Sir Gladwyn Jebb, the Ambassador in Paris, wrote to Kirkpatrick that Britain was proposing to say that if Israel attacked Jordan in response to the Iraqi move Britain 'would immediately declare war on Israel and notably proceed to bomb Israeli bases from the air'. The French were developing very close relationships with the Israelis.

Such a war, which might or might not be extended, would I need hardly say affect the French very gravely for apart from anything else they would ... rightly come to the conclusion that we could hardly be at war with the Israelis and in a position to impose our will on Colonel Nasser at one and the same time.[57]

It was only the visit to Chequers on 14 October by Albert Gazier, the

[55] COS(56)310, Memo by the British Defence Co-ordination Committee, Middle East, 17 Aug. 1956, FO 371/121763.

[56] Fitzmaurice to Kirkpatrick, 27 Sept. 1956, FO 371/121780.

[57] He went on to say: 'I will not dwell on the really agonising position of Mr Dulles if he were confronted just before the election by an effort on our part to exterminate not Col Nasser ... but that hero of New York, Mr Ben-Gurion'; Jebb to Kirkpatrick, 2 Oct. 1956, FO 371/121487.

Acting French Foreign Minister, and the ingenious General Maurice Challe that cut through these contradictions at the expense of committing Britain to the policy of collusion: Israel to attack, Britain and France to appear as peace-keepers, issuing ultimata and dropping bombs on whoever (meaning Egypt) had not accepted the terms, and the Suez Canal Zone to be occupied 'to separate the combatants'.

The negotiation of the secret 'protocol' of Sèvres between the three parties—Britain, France, and Israel—is described elsewhere in this book. It does not feature in the documents released under the British thirty-year rule. Indeed, apart from Sir Ivone Kirkpatrick and a handful of other top Civil Servants, the normal government machine was shut out from what followed. The vital circuits of paper were severed. Middle East experts at the Foreign Office, even the head of the political section at M.I.6, no longer received normal circulation of key documents. No explanation was offered but there were obvious interruptions in numbered sequences. Ambassadors were not forewarned. Some like Sir John Nicholls in Tel Aviv had some idea. He cabled on the morning of 29 October, before the Israeli attack, that according to the American Embassy, a great many Israelis favoured a theory holding that Britain had agreed with Israel and France to launch a concerted attack on Egypt. This was because Israeli mobilization had taken place without the usual sharp British reaction.[58]

What is of interest in the papers is how much the Cabinet was told. During the Cabinet meeting on 18 October Eden reported on the talks he and Selwyn Lloyd had had in Paris. It had been agreed to take every possible step to stop Israel attacking Jordan. 'If Israel was going to attack it was much better from our point of view that she should attack Egypt.' If she did, the French were told (to pass on to the Israelis) that Britain would not support Egypt under the Tripartite Declaration. Eden then remarked that, in his view, Britain at all costs must prevent fighting over the Canal, and damage to the Canal itself as well as to shipping passing through. No one in the Cabinet disagreed with that sentiment.[59]

On 23 October, with Lloyd back from his encounter in the villa Bonnier de la Chapelle in the Parisian suburb of Sèvres, Eden revealed something of the nature of those talks. The Confidential Annex to the Cabinet Minutes of that date appears twice in the Public Record Office volume, once, as is usual, restored to its place in the sequence of minutes, and the second time as an appendix. Only the second copy contains the italicized clause in the passage which follows:

[58] Nicholls (Tel Aviv), 29 Oct. 1956, FO 800/741.
[59] Cabinet Meeting held 18 Oct. 1956, Selwyn Lloyd Papers, FO 800/728.

The Prime Minister recalled that when the Cabinet had last discussed the Suez situation on 18 October there had been reason to believe that the issue might be brought rapidly to a head as a result of military action by Israel against Egypt. *From secret conversations which had been held in Paris with representatives of the Israeli Government* it now appeared that the Israelis would not alone launch a full-scale attack against Egypt. The UK and French Governments were thus confronted with the choice between an early military operation or a relatively prolonged negotiation.[60]

Selwyn Lloyd then reported that the Egyptians were now ready to put forward proposals for the future control of the Suez Canal and that it was quite possible that he might be able to negotiate a settlement that 'would give us the substance of our demand for effective international supervision'. There were three objections to bear in mind: the French government would not give their full co-operation to such a policy; Britain's negotiating position would be weakened because military preparations could not be kept at the present state of readiness; and, thirdly, such a settlement as could be arrived at would not be of the kind which would diminish Nasser's influence in the Middle East. This expressed the position very candidly: the truth was that the Eden government was in favour of a peaceful settlement provided the terms were such that Nasser would ruin himself by accepting them.

The Cabinet resumed the discussion the next day, without any decision being made. Should the Egyptians be given a time limit to produce their alternative Canal regime? The trouble was, 'if such a demand were made the Egyptians were likely to comply with it'. They would produce proposals, which, though unsatisfactory, would appear to offer a basis for discussion. On this day they decided what they had to decide.

They could frame their demands in such a way as to make it impossible for the Egyptians to accept them—being resolved, on an Egyptian refusal, to take military action designed to overthrow Colonel Nasser's regime. Alternatively, they could seek the sort of settlement ... which might be reached by negotiation—recognising that by accepting such a settlement they would abandon their second objective of reducing Col Nasser's influence.[61]

Whereas, said Eden to his Cabinet on 25 October, two days ago 'it had seemed unlikely' that the Israelis would attack alone, 'it now appeared' that they 'could not afford to wait for others to curb [Nasser's] expansionary policies'. France felt strongly that intervention would be justified as a means of limiting hostilities. Eden then

---

[60] Cabinet Minutes (56) 72, Confidential Annex, CAB 128/30.
[61] 24 Oct. 1956, PREM 11/1103.

suggested the demand for a ten-mile fall-back from each side of the Canal. Israel, he said, might well accept. 'If Egypt also complied, Colonel Nasser's prestige would be fatally undermined.' If she did not, there would be 'ample justification' for military action against Egypt. Eden warned his ministers that they would be 'accused of collusion with Israel'. But, he went on,

this charge was liable to be brought against us in any event; for it could now be assumed that if an Anglo-French operation were undertaken against Egypt we should be unable to prevent the Israelis from launching a parallel attack themselves; and it was preferable that we should be seen to be holding the balance between Israel and Egypt rather than appear to be accepting Israeli co-operation in the attack on Egypt alone.[62]

Substantial objections were raised—the danger of doing lasting damage to Anglo-American relations, the failure to comply with the Tripartite Declaration that Britain had gone to such lengths to affirm and reaffirm, the usurpation of an international function without the authority of the United Nations—but they were not pressed. The Cabinet had committed itself to a policy.

When Patrick Dean and Donald Logan, the two Civil Servants who represented Britain on the day when the actual protocol was drawn up at Sèvres, brought back their copy, Eden showed himself to be very cross and sent them back to Paris to try to recover the other copies, though without success.[63] He had meant nothing to be on paper. Now there was a 'smoking gun' that would eventually be found. He attempted to make his own conduct, and that of anyone he could control, conform to the public explanation. That explains the six-day pause between the expiry of the ultimatum and the landing at Port Said. Although the Israeli invasion date was known in advance, no advantage was taken of this to sail the expedition in from Malta and hold it over the horizon from Port Said. *Musketeer Revise* was used as the basic strategy with the eleven-to-fourteen day pause compressed to six, but although the Egyptian Air Force was put out of action, bombing was not used on anything like the scale calculated to break the Egyptian will to resist. Even among the top priority 'semi-military' targets, Cairo Radio was not hit for three days, because of the fear of killing civilians, and the oil installations were not attacked at all, partly for fear of setting off reprisals in the oil states. This was a neutered *Musketeer*. Britain was, after all, on a peace-keeping expedition.

While Britain sought to be circumspect, France fought a war of

---

[62] 25 Oct. 1956, PREM 11/1103.
[63] Sir Donald Logan, interviewed in *Secrets of Suez*, transmitted BBC 2, 14 Nov. 1986.

alliance with Israel. General Keightley, the Allied Commander-in-Chief, cabled the Chiefs of Staff on 31 October:

I would welcome direction at what stage or in what degree it is visualised we fight as the Allies of the Israelis. The French are doing a lot covertly and are proposing to increase their effort.[64]

By 2 November, 'The situation regarding Franco-Israeli cooperation is getting increasingly disturbing.' Admiral Barjot, Keightley's French deputy, quoted his liaison officer with the Israelis as saying that 'an agreement was made for certain help between governments and if it is not honoured the Israelis will publicise and exaggerate the agreements made'.[65] Eden protested urgently to Mollet on 1 November, listing the incidents of French partisanship and concluding: 'Nothing could do more harm to our role as peacemakers.'[66] The Americans soon knew the whole story of collusion as Christian Pineau informed Allen Dulles of the CIA and Admiral Radford, chairman of the Joint Chiefs of Staff, in separate interviews on 16 November.[67]

When, on 29 October, President Eisenhower first heard of the Israeli invasion of Egypt he sent for the British chargé d'affaires and told him that the prestige of both countries was involved. The previous spring when the British and Americans declined to provide arms for Israel and Egypt they had said that their word was enough in the Tripartite Declaration about supporting any victim of aggression. Now, he said, the United States and Britain must stand by what they said.[68] This was gloomy news for Britain. When the American Ambassador vigorously followed it up in London the next morning, the British government felt anxious. In the morning session of the Cabinet, Selwyn Lloyd reported the American determination to have Israel condemned as an aggressor before the Security Council. He then suggested that, provided Mollet and Pineau agreed, action should be deferred for twenty-four hours—in complete default of the pledges made to the Israelis at Sèvres, which were of course unknown to most of those round the Cabinet table—while an appeal was made to the Americans to back Britain and France in their efforts to end hostilities. The Cabinet members were deeply worried by the thought of the consequences of having got so far out of

[64] Keightley to Chiefs of Staff, KEYCOS 2, 31 Oct. 1956, AIR 8/1940. Also Ralph Murray (Political Adviser to C.-in-C.) to Kirkpatrick: 'As seen from here there is little if anything covert about French close and active support of Israel'; 1 Nov. 1956, FO 800/727.

[65] Keightley to Chiefs of Staff, 2 Nov. 1956, AIR 8/1940.

[66] Eden to Mollet, FO 800/727.

[67] 'Joint Chiefs of Staff, History, Vol. VI, Chapter X', National Archives, Washington. Memcon Allen Dulles with Pineau, memcon Radford with Pineau, OCJCS File 091 Palestine (June–Dec. 56).

[68] White House Memoranda Series, Box 4. Meetings with the President, Aug.–Dec. 1956. Memcon Eisenhower, Dulles, Coulson, 29 Oct. 1956.

step with the United States. Such concerns either had precedence with Eden and Lloyd over the written terms of the Sèvres protocol or else they wanted the French to shoulder the burden of making the rest of the Cabinet swallow their doubts and conform. Moreover, at the same meeting there were clear signs from the most hawkish Minister, Macmillan, that they had good reason for taking trouble over American goodwill. He told his colleagues:

Our reserves of gold and dollars were still falling at a dangerously rapid rate; and in view of the extent to which we might have to rely on American economic assistance we could not afford to alienate the US Government more than was absolutely necessary.[69]

When the French came, they insisted on compliance with the promises made to the Israelis.

The British needed to rely on the Americans for three things during the operation—cover to prevent the intervention of the Soviet Union, backing for the currency and the mechanism of the sterling area, and benevolent neutrality of the American armed services. They assumed that in practice they would get all three. They got only the cover against the Russians. When Bulganin sent Britain, France, and Israel what Eisenhower and Dulles considered virtual ultimata, the United States immediately fell in line alongside her allies. On the other two points, her behaviour was vastly different. General Keightley, in a part of his dispatch that was not published in the *London Gazette*, goes so far as to say: 'It was the action of the US which really defeated us in attaining our object. Her move of the Sixth Fleet was a move which endangered the whole of our relations with that country. . . . This situation with the US must at all costs be prevented from arising again.' It is clear from the military and naval reports that the British were severely rattled by the Sixth Fleet's constant covering presence, which so cramped operations that it was stated that if there had been any opposition at all to the naval task force from the air (let alone by submarine) the necessary counter-action could easily have led to dangerous accidents with American aircraft or vessels.[70]

The collapse of Britain's currency reserves is a subject dealt with in another chapter. But this, plus America's refusal to spring to British defence, was the decisive factor which swung opinion in a Cabinet already caught in the coils of the logical consequences of the intervention story. The withholding of the necessary American rescue effort gave to the United States what has often been lacking in an inter-

---

[69] Cabinet Minutes, (56)75, 30 Oct. 1956, CAB 128/30.
[70] Annex to JP (57)142, 11 Dec. 1957, AIR 8/1940.

national crisis: the power of inflicting economic sanctions of immediate and devastating effect.

Keightley concluded afterwards that 'The one overriding lesson of the Suez operation is that world opinion is now an absolute principle of war and must be treated as such.' Still more to the point was the recognition, echoed in the following year in Duncan Sandys' White Paper on Defence, that 'in a limited war in the Mediterranean or the Far East the UK would only act in co-operation with the US . . .'. The habit of using the language and assumptions of a Great Power had been smothered. These mannerisms, rather than any guiding rules of conduct, had passed finally and irrevocably to the United States.

6

France and the Suez Crisis

MAURICE VAÏSSE

THE French documents on the Suez Crisis soon to be published will not bring any sensational revelations.[1] Their essence has been revealed in the works of privileged participants or well-informed journalists.[2] It is now well known that the role played by the Quai d'Orsay in the affair was by no means a central one. One cannot, therefore, expect new light to be shed on the Suez conspiracy by these diplomatic documents.

They are nevertheless not without interest.[3] Of course, they do not include any papers concerning the Franco-British military preparations or the Franco-Israeli discussions. One will not find among them memoranda of the tripartite conversations at Sèvres, and the Sèvres agreements themselves are not included. On the other hand, the French diplomatic documents do shed light in three fields:

—the question of arms sales;
—the motives for the French intervention;
—and, finally, relations between the French, British, and Americans.

Along the way, the Quai d'Orsay's role will emerge as more preoccupied with its own constituent parts, and with its own divergent analyses.

---

[1] Two volumes of the new series of French diplomatic documents, beginning July 1954, were published by the *Imprimerie Nationale* in 1987. The volume containing the 1956 documents will be published in 1989.

[2] Among the diplomatic actors: Christian Pineau, *1956: Suez* (Paris, 1976); Abel Thomas, *Comment Israël fut sauvé: Les Secrets de l'expédition de Suez* (Paris, 1978); Jean Chauvel, *Commentaire*, vol. iii (Paris, 1973); Jacques Baeyens, *Un coup d'épée dans l'eau du canal* (Paris, 1976). Journalists: Michel Bar-Zohar, *Suez: Ultra-secret* (Paris, 1964); Henri Azeau, *Le Piège de Suez (5 Novembre 1956)* (Paris, 1964). Among recent publications in French: Marc Ferro, *Suez* (Brussels, 1982) and *1956: La Crise de Suez* (Paris, 1986); Paul Gaujac, *Suez 1956* (Paris, 1986); *Revue Historique des Armées*, No. 4 (1986); special issue of *L'Histoire*, No. 38 (1981): articles by Pierre Milza, Jean-Pierre Rioux, Maurice Vaïsse.

[3] My warm thanks to Jean Batbedat, Director-General of the Diplomatic Archives, for permitting me to consult these documents, and to Maurice Degros, former chief curator of the Diplomatic Archives, for placing at my disposition the documents of the Commission for Publication of Diplomatic Documents. I have studied the chronological series of documents related to the Suez crisis from 1 Jan. to 30 Nov. 1956.

ARMS SALES

The question of arms sales to Israel dominated the entire first half of 1956. It developed against a two-fold background of mistrust: among French official agencies on the one hand, and between the French, British, and Americans, on the other. Representatives of the Ministry of Defence, favouring arms deliveries to Israel, emerged in opposition to the far more reluctant diplomats. In his book, Abel Thomas, who played a well-known and key role in the affair, criticizes the diplomats as 'true to the Quai d'Orsay tradition, vacillating, equivocating, given to an ambiguous conformity, and in the grip of a legendary inertia'.[4] The decision of the Ambassadors in the Near East Armaments Control Committee (NEACC), charged with implementing the Tripartite Declaration of 1950, to suspend all deliveries of arms until the United Nations ruled on the Syrian complaint against Israel is a convenient point of departure. France's Ambassador in Israel, Eugene Gilbert, echoed Israeli feelings and drew the government's attention to the risk of seeing Great Britain 'regain at our expense the ground lost over the past two years'.[5] Lieutenant-Colonel Livry, the military attaché, drew up a list of the arms shipments desired by the Israelis, following his conversation with Shimon Peres.[6] From the first discussions it appeared that the British and Americans, far from wanting to ship arms to Israel, were not unhappy to let France do the job. The Americans raised no objections to the delivery by France of 12 Mystère IVs produced within the offshore procurement framework.[7] Thereafter, the debate constituted a major preoccupation of the French agencies concerned with arms sales, and set one against the other. As soon as the United Nations had voted on the Syrian complaint, the Foreign Minister, Christian Pineau, requested the Permanent Secretariat-General of National Defence to lift the embargo and give a decision in favour of the export of the arms requested (500 rocket-launchers, 9,900 rockets, 25 75-mm. guns, and 30 AMX tanks).[8]

Meanwhile, the ministry's Africa–Levant Directorate obtained the Minister's signature to a note to the contrary. According to this note, the French government was anxious not to bear the *total responsibility* for Israeli rearmament, 'which would concentrate on us the hostility of the Arab countries'.[9] The Quai d'Orsay suggested that the Americans,

---

[4] On this entire affair, see the point of view of Abel Thomas, *Comment Israël fut sauvé*, esp. pp. 25 and 26.

[5] Doc. No. 130, Gilbert/Pinay, 12 Jan. 1956.

[6] Ibid.

[7] Tel. from Couve de Murville, 21 Jan. 1956.

[8] Letter Pineau–Geoffroy de Courcel, Secrétariat Général Permanent de la Défense Nationale, 2 Feb. 1956.

[9] Tel. 1286–91 Pineau–Couve de Murville, 10 Feb. 1956.

British, and Italians replace the French for the transfer of tanks and shells, and requested the French Ambassador in Washington, Couve de Murville, to intervene to this effect; he made his *démarche* on 13 February 1956.

On 5 March Christian Pineau made a renewed effort.[10] Considering that the arms balance had been upset to Egypt's advantage, he sought to rearm Israel through co-operation with western European countries. The latter, however, did not share this view, and even had misgivings respecting the French shipments.[11]

Meanwhile, at a meeting of the Interministerial Committee on arms sales, the Minister of National Defence's representative attacked the delaying action of the Foreign Ministry.[12] Africa–Levant Director Pierre Maillard requested the ministry's Secretary-General, then René Massigli, either to order the cancellation of the Israeli arms sale or refer it to the NEACC. And on 9 March the Africa–Levant Directorate reiterated this demand.[13] France was prepared to participate in a programme of Israeli rearmament, but insisted on not acting alone, for fear of incurring the hostility of the Arab states. The debate erupted again following the 16 April meeting of the Interministerial Committee.[14] The Minister of National Defence, Maurice Bourgès-Maunoury, made it known that he had obtained the formal agreement of Pineau, the Committee's chairman, for the signing of a new arms sale contract with Israel (12 Mystère IVs, 12 Mystère IIs, 10 AMX tanks). The offices of the Quai d'Orsay knew nothing about this agreement, and Henri Roux, in charge of Africa–Levant affairs at the Quai d'Orsay, demanded to be told what it was all about.

The Africa–Levant Directorate pointed out that these matters lay within the authority of the Ministry of Foreign Affairs, and reviewed the irregularities committed by the Ministry of National Defence, which might place France in a delicate position with respect to the United States, Great Britain, and Italy.[15] Abel Thomas stigmatizes this 'inquisition' and the 'dragging' of the United States and Great Britain into French affairs under cover of the NEACC.[16]

Prime Minister Ben-Gurion's assertion before the Knesset on 22 April that France was Israel's best arms source embarrassed France deeply. During the NATO Council session Christian Pineau spoke with

[10] Tel. 2174–81 Pineau–Couve de Murville, 5 Mar. 1956.
[11] Tel. Couve de Murville–Pineau, 6 Mar. 1956.
[12] Note by Pierre Maillard, Africa–Levant Director, 20 Feb. 1956.
[13] Note by Africa–Levant Directorate, 9 Mar. 1956; on this point cf. Abel Thomas, *Comment Israël*, p. 60.
[14] Note by Africa–Levant Directorate (Henri Roux), 19 Apr. 1956.
[15] Note by Africa–Levant Directorate, 11 May 1956.
[16] Abel Thomas, *Comment Israël*, p. 63.

John Foster Dulles on 2 May, and with Selwyn Lloyd on 6 May, and reaffirmed his position regarding the supply of arms to the state of Israel. Dulles replied that the United States was not a regular supplier of arms to Israel; that it did not wish to give the Arabs and Soviets a pretext for initiating an arms race; and that the United States approved the sale of aircraft by France to Israel. As for not leaving France to act alone, Dulles suggested that Canada might perhaps take part in rearming Israel by supplying a few F-86s.[17]

By contrast with Selwyn Lloyd, who did not wish to give the impression of a too conspicuous agreement among the three ministers with respect to arms sales, Pineau considered that the formation of a joint policy was desirable in order to help Israel remain capable of defending herself. The same objections of the American, British, and Italian governments were confirmed during the meeting of the NEACC Ambassadors on 28 May.[18] Dulles and Pineau agreed that the situation was becoming dangerous.[19] The American government's withdrawal of its offer to finance the Aswan Dam opened a new phase in the Suez crisis. Colonel Gamal Abdel Nasser's decision to nationalize the Suez Canal Company removed all the obstacles. The government immediately approved a new order for Mystère aircraft.[20] But the Cabinet's inner circle had in fact already decided to 'leave out the Quai d'Orsay as far as possible' in preparing the Suez operation, not to consult the NEACC any longer, and to facilitate the supply of arms to Israel.[21] Thenceforth the entire affair was conducted by the inner Cabinet, to the exclusion of the Quai d'Orsay.

MOTIVES FOR THE INTERVENTION

Although motives are rarely mentioned in the diplomatic documents, the arguments set forth in the discussions are often revealing. Two factors in the French intervention should be emphasized: the Algerian war and the Munich syndrome. The Munich complex operated effectively among legislators and journalists, who vied with one another to compare Nasser with Hitler, and the 1956 situation with that of the 1930s.[22] It was a veritable contest of collective memory in which the Frenchmen most closely involved in the preparations literally immersed themselves in the Resistance atmosphere, and even recap-

---

[17] Memoranda of conversations Pineau–Dulles 2 May 1956, and Pineau–Lloyd–Dulles, 6 May 1956.

[18] Tel. Couve de Murville–Pineau, 28 May 1956.

[19] Tel. Couve de Murville, Foreign Minister, 20 June 1956.

[20] Tel. Pineau–Chauvel, 12.45 p.m., 27 July 1956.

[21] Abel Thomas, *Comment Israël*, pp. 73–4, 76, 83, 85.

[22] Cf. article by J. P. Rioux in *L'Histoire*, No. 38, and Ferro, *1956: La Crise de Suez*.

tured the reflexes of clandestine action.[23] This amalgam provided French opinion with a moral justification and a mobilizing slogan. But in the diplomatic documents historical references to Munich are much less frequent than allusions to the Algerian problem.

At first, indeed, the perception of Egypt was a nuanced one. As a conciliatory gesture Pineau even went to Cairo, and took care to contrast his point of view with that of Guy Mollet, who equated Nasser with Hitler. Seeking to preserve good relations with the Arab world, the Africa–Levant Directorate insisted upon efforts by the French government to improve relations between Paris and Cairo. 'Nothing, therefore, must be neglected in order to hold Egypt back from the precipice which would plunge her ... toward the Afro-Asian bloc and an anti-Western policy.'[24] The confusion of the French diplomats regarding the Egyptian regime was obvious. 'Can one trust Nasser, or is he a double-dealer?' asked Henri Roux.[25] The British were not sure.

According to the British Ambassador in Cairo, Sir Humphrey Trevelyan, Nasser was not pro-Communist and sincerely desired *rapprochement* with the West. The American Ambassador, Henry A. Byroade, was of the same opinion. Evelyn Shuckburgh of the British Foreign Office had a contrary view. Nasser was by no means a passive man: he aspired to become the leader of a vast federation of Arab countries embracing the Maghrib, and to erase Israel from the map.[26] The same split existed in France.

The Africa–Levant Directorate sought above all to maintain ties with the Arab countries. 'It is thus the future of our Arab policy, patiently consolidated during the year just past, that would be jeopardized, inevitably bringing disastrous consequences in North Africa, if Francophobia were to permeate the Muslim world.'[27] Pro-Israelis were above all preoccupied with Israel's survival. The Minister of National Defence and his staff were sympathetic to the Israelis' appeals for help, and wanted to arm them.

France's Ambassador in Tel Aviv, Gilbert, presented the situation in the most contrasting colours: on one hand, 'a young state, the only stable and peaceable element in a tormented region'; on the other, 'an Arab bloc ... increasingly turbulent, backward and bellicose'.[28] Gilbert saw Dmitri Shepilov's visit to Cairo as 'a veritable resumption of

---

[23] Abel Thomas, *Comment Israël*, p. 93; conversation with Louis Mangin.
[24] Joint *aide-mémoire* in French by British Foreign Office and US State Department, 14 Jan. 1956.
[25] Conversation Roux–Shuckburgh, 23 Jan. 1956.
[26] Tel. Couve de Murville–Pineau, 3 Feb. 1956.
[27] Tel. No. 1286, Pineau–Couve de Murville, 10 Feb. 1956.
[28] Tel. No. 211–15, Gilbert–Pineau, 19 June 1956.

the Cold War'.[29] The French Ambassador in Cairo, Armand du Chayla, was far from pro-Egyptian, and did not appear to have much grasp of the situation in Egypt.[30] He did not foresee the nationalization of the Suez Canal Company. When he reported it, he added very harsh comments. 'It is time to stop Colonel Nasser in his tracks. . . . Unless there is an immediate and very energetic reaction from abroad the Egyptian leader will think that henceforth he can do anything he pleases.'[31] Nevertheless, he seems to have changed his mind between July and October. Perhaps he later wished to appear anti-interventionist.[32]

The French circular of 29 July to diplomatic posts set forth the reasons for France's dissatisfaction, particularly attacking 'Colonel Nasser's insane regime . . . capable of such follies . . . contemptuous of human liberties', etc.[33] The circular of 8 August was less brutal, but more threatening.[34] It referred to Nasser's *fait accompli*, and demanded international operation of the Canal. The portrait of Nasser drawn by Australian Prime Minister Robert Menzies upon his return from Cairo on 10 September strengthened the French conviction that against Nasser only force counted. According to Menzies, 'reason, logic, enlightened self-interest, all these considerations have no effect on Nasser. In fact, we don't speak the same language.' And Sir Anthony Eden remarked, 'It's exactly like when we tried to discuss things in the 1930s, and it is foolish to imagine that it is possible.'[35]

It is not known why the president of the French colony in Egypt, M. Guyomard, happened to visit the Africa–Levant Director on 20 October: was the visit spontaneous or in response to a telegraphic invitation? Nor do we know the Director's reaction to the peremptory assertions of his visitor who, we are told, was 'well known to M. Couve de Murville, who considers him a thoughtful and serious man'. In any case, these assertions correspond to the convictions of the anti-Nasser clan. M. Guyomard portrayed the Egyptian 'dictator' as 'a true fanatic, intransigent and spiteful'. He considered it urgent to 'deprive him very soon of the ability to do damage' by a police operation.[36] One

[29] Tel. Gilbert–Pineau, 21 June 1956.

[30] Tel. du Chayla–Pineau, 23 July 1956.

[31] Ibid.

[32] Baeyens, *Un coup d'épée*, p. 44, relates that when du Chayla was summoned to Paris for consultation at the end of October, Pineau told him that Ambassadors are agents executing orders. He retorted by saying he believed they should be intelligence agents as well. He also saw Bourgès-Maunoury and attempted to talk with him about the immense economic and cultural interests in Egypt, the contracts in progress, the traditional policy with regard to Islam: nothing made an impression.

[33] Circular tel. No. 58 by Secretary-General, 29 July 1956.

[34] Circular letter, 8 Aug. 1956.

[35] Conversation with Menzies, 10 Sept. 1956, at 10 Downing Street.

[36] Visit of the president of the French colony in Egypt to Africa–Levant Director, 20 Oct. 1956.

may conclude from this brief account that until the summer of 1956 the perception of an 'Egyptian threat' was not pre-eminent in Quai d'Orsay circles. On the contrary, these circles were endeavouring to maintain the French presence. The French motive as set forth in the diplomatic documents is clear: the Algerian war.

From the beginning of 1956 the responsibilities of power had been exercised by the Republican Front government presided over by Guy Mollet. Hostility toward Nasser was nourished mainly by considerations dictated by the Algerian war, which in 1956 became the principal focus of French politics. It is true that Christian Pineau maintains in his memoirs that the Algerian affair was not that decisive. But his pronouncements at the time contradict his recollections.[37] We have seen that Pineau had gone to Cairo to meet Colonel Nasser. The latter had promised not to assist the Algerian rebellion, and had given his 'word of honour as a soldier' that he would not train Algerian cadres in his territory. Given such flagrant lies, why not turn the nationalization weapon against Egypt and kill two birds with one stone: eliminate a budding dictator and settle the Algerian affair?

On 28 July Jean Chauvel explained to British and American representatives that 'If Egypt's act went without response it would be impossible for France to pursue the struggle in Algeria.'[38] This statement, however, did not appear in the circular letter from the Quai d'Orsay Secretary-General to the diplomatic posts.[39] The letter set forth the reasons for French anger: the expropriation of French assets, restrictions on the freedom of transit through the Canal, the fate of the Company's employees. During the tripartite meetings in London (30–1 July and 1 August) Christian Pineau explained that the French government was moved by one special preoccupation: 'If Egypt's action remained without a response, it would be useless to pursue the struggle in Algeria.'[40] In the same meeting Pineau went so far as to say that 'France considers it more important to defeat Colonel Nasser's enterprise than to win ten battles in Algeria.' In his conversation with John Foster Dulles, Pineau painted an apocalyptic picture of the situation. 'According to the most reliable intelligence sources we have only a few weeks [!] in which to save North Africa. Of course, the loss of North Africa would then be followed by that of Black Africa, and the entire territory would rapidly escape European control and influence.'[41] Even with the Soviets, Pineau evoked the Algerian motive, albeit with some adaptation. Pineau accused Nasser of lying when he

---

[37] Pineau, *1956: Suez*, p. 76.   [38] Tel. Chauvel–Pineau, 28 July 1956.
[39] Circular tel. No. 58, 29 July 1956.
[40] Memoranda of tripartite meeting in London, 30 July 1956.
[41] Dulles–Pineau conversation, 1 Aug. 1956.

stated that he had no Algerian leaders in his camp. How, in such conditions, could he be trusted with running the Canal?[42]

To their British interlocutors, the French revealed more, since Algeria appeared to be one stake in the new *entente cordiale*. On 14 August Pineau informed Gladwyn Jebb that the French government had a solution in mind. Jebb, while recognizing that Algeria was a purely French concern, considered that 'If, before the landing, a gesture could be made by the French government, such a gesture would have immense effect and repercussions in the Middle East and throughout the Arab world.'[43]

That Algeria was an important element in the Franco-British discussions emerged clearly in the 24 August meeting.[44] Selwyn Lloyd opened the conversation by asking Christian Pineau to tell him something about Algeria. The French minister explained that the plan for elections after a cease-fire was now somewhat outdated. The Prime Minister was now thinking of announcing a new plan, sometime in September, providing for a federal solution. Just before the launching of Operation *Musketeer* the French Foreign Minister took the occasion of the interception of the ship *Athos*, 'stuffed with arms and munitions loaded at Alexandria', to conclude that the Egyptian state bore direct responsibility in the Algerian rebellion.[45] Whereas the link between the Algerian war and the Suez intervention had long been known, here it appears as a subject of formal discussion: a striking confirmation.

FRENCH–BRITISH–AMERICAN RELATIONS

The important new contribution of the diplomatic documents is what we learn about relations between France, Great Britain, and the United States.

From the diplomatic documents the French government emerges as anxious for close collaboration among the three allies; but the more the crisis evolved, the more France evinced the will to take action, in contrast with American prudence and British procrastination.

At the beginning of the year, just before the Anglo-American discussions in Washington, the attitude of the French government, as formulated during Antoine Pinay's period of office (February 1955 to January 1956) was still determined by the traditional mistrust regarding British interests in the Middle East and possible Anglo-American

---

[42] Conversation on 17 Aug. between Pineau and Shepilov.

[43] Pineau–Jebb conversation, 14 Aug. 1956.

[44] Franco-British meeting, Pineau–Lloyd, 24 Aug. 1956.

[45] Instructions of Christian Pineau to the French representative at the United Nations, 30 Oct. 1956.

collusion.[46] French policy was influenced by the 1950 Tripartite Declaration, and by objections to the Baghdad Pact; in view of the rising prestige of the Egyptian regime, it was considered necessary to find a way to turn Egypt away from the Soviet camp. The Quai therefore contemplated setting up a mutual economic aid programme, and promoting collaboration by the three Western powers with a view toward mediation between Israel and the Arab countries. The British and Americans appeared to agree. But Shuckburgh explained to Henri Roux that, in the absence of adequate financial resources, the British wished to grant loans only to members of the Baghdad Pact.[47] Sir Anthony Eden went further, opining that friends must be treated a little better than neutral or hostile states.[48] Invited to attend discussions on the Middle East within the Tripartite Delaration framework, France participated in the meetings of 8 and 15 February.

A new phase of diplomatic collaboration opened on 27 July.[49] Successive meetings were held in London, some military and secret, others making no progress while waiting for Secretary of State Foster Dulles. At the first meeting at No. 10 Downing Street, Jean Chauvel noted that Colonel Nasser's decision had placed the three allies in an invidious position: 'All the members of the British government want decisive action, but don't see clearly how to take it.'[50] Certainly, both the French and the British contemplated precipitating Nasser's downfall; but the question was: with or without Israeli help? Similarly, the British were more reluctant to act without the Americans.[51] Pineau undertook to convince Lloyd and Eden to 'act bilaterally rather than do nothing trilaterally'. Selwyn Lloyd observed that 'the Americans often went along when others took the initiative'.[52]

But the gap was even wider with the Americans. Responding to Couve de Murville's arguments for joint action, the Under-Secretary of the State Department, Herbert Hoover, Jr., was very cautious. 'We must avoid ... anything that might place the Western powers in an indefensible position in the eyes of the world.'[53]

The next day George Allen of the State Department set forth this attitude even more clearly. 'There can be no question of organizing a colonial operation of the Nineteenth Century sort.'[54] In London,

[46] Tels. Chauvel–Pinay, 17 Jan. and Couve de Murville–Pinay, 21 Jan. 1956.
[47] Conversation Roux–Shuckburgh, 23 Jan. 1956.
[48] Tel. Chauvel–Pinay, 24 Jan. 1956.
[49] Tel. Chauvel–Pineau, 27 July 1956.
[50] Cf. Chauvel, *Commentaire*, iii, 184–5. In his telegrams, Chauvel says nothing of the sort.
[51] Tel. Couve de Murville–Pineau, 27 July 1956, and *Commentaire*, iii. 185–6.
[52] Memorandum of Franco-British meeting, 1 Aug. 1956.
[53] Tel. Couve de Murville–Pineau, 28 July 1956.
[54] Tel. Chauvel–Pineau, 31 July and memoranda of tripartite conversations in London 31 July–3 Aug. 1956.

Robert D. Murphy of the State Department raised the possibility of military intervention, only to assert immediately that it should be left in the background, and made his doubts clear when Christian Pineau spoke of military operations. Dulles pressed for the alternative approaches of a tripartite declaration in a tone that appeared too weak to the French, and of a conference of Canal users. For Pineau, 'This does not mean that the United States contemplates a common action with England and France, but implies tacit acceptance on their part of the consequences of a probable refusal by Nasser.' There was no question of delivering an ultimatum to Nasser. Dulles explained to Pineau that military action would be inopportune: it would be supported neither by Congress nor American public opinion. A diplomatic effort must thus be made. If Nasser accepted it, so much the better. If he refused, this would be grounds for stronger action, supported by the United States; but Dulles made clear that this would be moral support.

For Pineau the danger was so grave and the French government's conviction so strong that even if the Americans withheld their moral support, and the British their concrete co-operation, 'we would be obliged to take military action'. The French, nevertheless, agreed to try other means first to reach a 'good solution', that is, 'a solution that would make Nasser back down'. If Nasser were to refuse, 'we will intervene with the British; if the Americans do not take part in the intervention we would expect them to take a position, namely, to persuade the Russians not to intervene.' At no other moment were the respective positions so lucidly set forth: on one hand, the Americans' refusal to participate in any intervention; on the other, the French determination to intervene.[55]

The third phase of the consultations took place in the context of the Canal Users' conference, 16–23 August 1956. In corridor conversations Christian Pineau and Gladwyn Jebb agreed on the objectives for possible Franco-British action in the Canal Zone (in particular, replacing Nasser), but they also disagreed on arms sales to Israel and the Baghdad Pact.[56] The conference ended in failure, aggravated by John Foster Dulles's rejection of any sort of pressure on Nasser.[57] He explained lucidly that exertion of pressure would risk retaliation against Europe, and the Americans would be the principal beneficiaries. Pineau courageously appeared to accept all the consequences of intervention, since it was advisable to take measures against Egypt. As for Selwyn Lloyd, he advocated economic sanctions against Egypt,

[55] Memorandum by Pineau of luncheon conversation, 2 Aug. 1956, at Anthony Eden's residence.
[56] Conversation Pineau–Gladwyn Jebb 4.00 p.m., 14 Aug. 1956.
[57] Dulles–Lloyd–Pineau meeting, 23 Aug. 1956.

which Pineau thought would be ineffective, and preferred to keep military preparations secret for fear of public opinion and the United Nations.[58] Franco-British conversations on 10 and 11 September ended in confusion because of the fear that Dulles would not keep his promises.[59]

After the second London conference (19–22 September) the differences among the three allies were aggravated. Unlike Great Britain and the United States, France reserved her position at the end of the conference, being determined to preserve her freedom of action. The visit to Paris by Sir Anthony Eden and Selwyn Lloyd appears to have been an effort to reunite the fragmented *entente*, whose vitality they extolled. The French Ambassador in London commented perceptively, 'I fear that Eden and Lloyd's visit to Paris may have left in the minds of their interlocutors too strong an impression of the British government's firmness toward the Suez matter. . . . It would be difficult for the team in power to undertake and maintain a forceful policy that would place it in conflict with a determined opposition.' Jean Chauvel concluded by quoting the British Prime Minister's private remark to him: 'Make sure they understand that I completely agree on the substance, but I must take my public opinion into account.'[60]

On the American side, Foster Dulles's press conference on 2 October, and his reproaches to Selwyn Lloyd and Pineau at their 5 October meeting in New York, reveal disturbing differences among the allies.[61] We hear a veritable dialogue of the deaf between Dulles and Pineau. Once again Dulles considered that 'Recourse to force, in his opinion, would be disastrous for the Western position.' For Pineau, 'If Nasser believes that any resort to force is excluded . . . then war might become inevitable'; and he warned Dulles, 'if the negotiation with Nasser does not produce results, we shall resume our freedom of action'.[62]

The conversations organized by Dag Hammarskjöld with Mahmoud Fawzi, the Egyptian Foreign Minister, got nowhere, and were unsatisfactory from Pineau's point of view because Selwyn Lloyd let himself be drawn on to confusing terrain. Later, upon the launching of military operations, Franco-British co-ordination misfired in the United Nations. Relations with the Americans, already strained, went through a critical phase. Carried away by his emotions, Foster Dulles, receiving Ambassador Hervé Alphand, compared the Franco-British

[58] Franco-British meeting, 24 Aug. 1956.
[59] Conversations Eden and Lloyd, Mollet and Pineau, 10 and 11 Sept. 1956.
[60] Tel. No. 4246, Chauvel–Pineau, 1 Oct. 1956.
[61] Tel. by Pineau, 5 Oct.; transcript of meetings, 10 and 11 Oct. 1956.
[62] Tel. 6806, 30 Oct. 1956, Alphand–Pineau.

intervention to the Soviet intervention in Hungary.[63] The crisis of confidence was serious: the British–French–Israeli collusion, keeping the Americans in the dark, was resented by Eisenhower and Dulles as a 'personal slap in the face',[64] and France, which was believed to have led the game, was blamed more than Great Britain. The peak of the crisis was reached with the visit of Alphand to the State Department upon receipt of the threatening message from Moscow on 6 November. Whereas the French Ambassador had come to request the United States to bring NATO mechanisms into play, Acting Secretary of State Herbert C. Hoover, Jr., could see only one solution: an immediate cease-fire, withdrawal of the troops, and the establishment of an international police force.[65]

The French diplomatic documents thus permit us to refine our knowledge in two domains. First, the internal conflict between agencies holding opposing views regarding France's role in the Middle East is clarified. The stumbling-block was the question of arms sales, where the Quai d'Orsay, in particular its Africa–Levant Directorate, fought step by step to preserve a courageous and balanced position, not refusing to arm Israel, but insisting on the condition that France should not act alone. The small group of men who were in charge of planning during the Suez affair (Mollet, Maurice Bourgès-Maunoury, Max Lejeune (Minister for War), Pineau; the confidential agents Abel Thomas and Louis Mangin; Generals Paul Ely and Maurice Challe) handled everything from outside the Administration, especially excluding the Quai d'Orsay. From this point of view the archives permit us to refine our knowledge: until the summer of 1956 ministry officials and diplomats assigned to London and Washington were more involved in conversations preparing for action than they usually admitted. However, after the summer the diplomats were bypassed or even muzzled (René Massigli was replaced by Louis Joxe at the Secretariat-General; Couve de Murville was transferred from Washington to Bonn). They were left out of the top-secret Franco-Israeli negotiations.[66] The Suez intervention was thus a foreign policy operation conducted outside the Quai d'Orsay.

---

[63] Tel. 6812, Alphand–Pineau, 30 Oct. 1956.

[64] Tel. 6844, Alphand–Pineau, 31 Oct. 1956.

[65] Tel. Déjean–Pineau, and tel. 6897, Alphand–Pineau, 6 Nov. 1956.

[66] The politicians' distrust of the Quai d'Orsay is further illustrated by an incident that occurred when Abel Thomas attempted to communicate with Bourgès-Maunoury and Pineau, then in London, through the intermediary of Louis Joxe. Guy Mollet learned of it, and exploded in anger: 'You are stark, raving mad! You want all our enemies at the Quai d'Orsay to know what's going on, when we put them out of the picture six months ago!' (Abel Thomas, *Comment Israël*, pp. 226–7.)

The second incontestable contribution of the archives defines the gravity of the cleavage that appeared in the Atlantic alliance. Contrary to a persistent legend, the United States did not abandon its allies. Time after time, and forcefully, it warned that it was opposed to any military operation. Pineau's powers of persuasion made not the slightest impression.[67] He used all the arguments: Atlantic solidarity, anti-Communism, the memory of the 1930s. In this respect the French diplomats were impeccable reporters: they never allowed the American opposition to the use of force to be forgotten. In these circumstances, the Suez operation seems a major political mistake.[68] 'Blinded by an outmoded conception of the situation in the Middle East and distracted by the Algerian war, the French leaders believed their activism would sweep the British along with them. The British indeed went along, reluctantly, but abandoned them in mid-course. The Americans deserted them.'[69] The bottom line was especially grave. Not only had France failed to topple Nasser, but she became more deeply mired in the Algerian war, whereas the Egyptian President's prestige emerged from the crisis enhanced. French political, economic, and cultural positions in the Middle East and the Arab world were compromised. Solidarity among the Western allies was impaired. While the principal fault lay with France, her allies were far from innocent, Great Britain by her vacillation and lack of firmness, the United States by its refusal to face the consequences of the Aswan Dam financing episode.

Beyond these immediate results, the French diplomats became aware of two questions that were to dominate the end of the Fourth Republic and the beginning of the Fifth: how was France to have an autonomous policy apart from the United States, and how could she settle the Algerian problem, a pre-condition for France's relations with the allies? It is fascinating to observe how the Suez crisis contributed to the two major developments in French foreign policy between 1956 and 1962: the *force de frappe* as an instrument of independent national defence, and the granting of Algerian independence.[70]

[67] Pineau, *1956: Suez*, pp. 65–7.

[68] Pineau, who accuses the Americans of having feigned surprise (*1956: Suez*, p. 154) 'guarantees that they were informed through other channels'.

[69] Note by Étienne de Croüy-Chauvel, Deputy-Director of Political Affairs, 10 Nov. 1956.

[70]. On this subject, see the work of Maurice Vaïsse (in collaboration with Jean Doise), *Diplomatie et outil militaire, 1871–1969* (Paris, 1987).

7

David Ben-Gurion and the Sèvres Collusion

MORDECHAI BAR-ON

> Let us now leave the cloacked collusion that remayned in France, and return to the open dissimulation which now appeared in England.
>
> *Grafton Chronicles*, 1568

THE *Oxford English Dictionary* defines the term 'collusion' as a 'secret agreement or understanding for purposes of trickery or fraud'. Every case in which two or more parties unite to make war against another party, or another coalition, inevitably involves secret agreements or understandings which include plans for the use of tricks and disinformation. Yet only seldom do we bestow on such contracts the negative title 'collusion'. It must be the 'trickery or fraud' which was perceived to characterize the Sèvres agreement, concluded between Great Britain, France, and Israel in late October 1956, which soiled it with this title of notoriety.

Was it indeed an act of fraud and trickery and, if it was, whose interest did it serve? Who instigated it and required that it be a collusion rather than a simple military treaty? Moreover, was Sèvres conceived equally by the three participating governments, or for that matter by their national constituencies, as a moral blemish to be hidden as much as possible from the public eye?

We can learn something from the way the different participants handled the story in later years.

The French were the first to admit the facts. Christian Pineau, then French Minister for Foreign Affairs, published his memoirs of the affair only in 1976,[1] but Hugh Thomas must have received ample collaboration from French officials much earlier,[2] and Merry and Serge Bromberger were able to tell much of the story quite correctly as early as 1957.[3] It seems that the French did not feel they had too much

---

[1] Christian Pineau, *1956: Suez* (Paris, 1976).
[2] Hugh Thomas, *Suez* (New York, 1966).
[3] Merry and Serge Bromberger, *Les Secrets de l'expédition d'égypte* (Paris, 1957).

to conceal or be ashamed of, though in later years, when the futile attempt to keep 'Algerie française' became in the eyes of many Frenchmen morally and politically untenable, they tended to describe their involvement in the Suez Affair as a gallant commitment to save Israel.[4]

The first Israeli publication, which was based on the thinly veiled testimonies and memories of Shimon Peres, then Director-General of the Israeli Defence Ministry and one of the main architects of the 'collusion', appeared in 1963.[5] Ben-Gurion, however, felt deeply committed to his implied pledge to Sir Anthony Eden to cover for him by prohibiting any formal or authorized concession coming from any of the Israeli participants, until after Eden's death.[6]

Information originating from the British side started to leak out from the beginning. Yet Eden tried hard to hide the unpleasant facts, which he blatantly though misleadingly denied in Parliament. One can hardly wonder that his own autobiography is quite coherent and detailed up to 16 October 1956, only to become thereafter confused and muddled.[7]

The memoirs of Selwyn Lloyd, which describe briefly his meeting with Ben-Gurion in Paris on 22 October 1956, were published only in 1978, a few weeks after his death, and one year after the death of Lord Avon.

Of all the participants, Israel had the least to hide. Beyond normal operational requirements of military secrecy and diversionary disinformation implemented to assure tactical surprise, Israel had a keen interest to the contrary. If it had to attack Egypt at that time, and collaborate in that venture with France and Great Britain, Israel preferred to do it in the frame of as formal and internationally acknowledged an agreement as possible. By the summer of 1956, Nasser had supplied Israel amply with *casus belli*, certainly from the moral perspective as perceived by the Israelis, and even from the legal point of view.[8] The Egyptians had insisted for many years that they considered themselves to be in a 'state of war' with Israel, and

---

[4] A good example can be found in Abel Thomas, *Comment Israël fut sauvé* (Paris, 1978).

[5] Joseph Evron, *Beyom Sagrir* (in Hebrew) (Tel Aviv, 1968).

[6] General Moshe Dayan's *Story of My Life* was published in 1976. His earlier version, *The Diaries of the Sinai Campaign*, which was published in 1965, did not include any of the details of the political background. It was rather the death of Ben-Gurion, who died four years before Sir Anthony Eden, which enabled Dayan to publish his story.

[7] Sir Anthony Eden, *Full Circle: The Memoirs of Anthony Eden* (London, 1960).

[8] The legal status of Arab–Israeli relations in the 1950s and 1960s was highly controversial and gave birth to many written briefs and arguments. For the Israeli advocacy see: Julius Stone, *The*

therefore demanded the 'rights of belligerents'. Moreover, since 27 September 1955, when Nasser announced the conclusion of his arms deal with the Communists, the belligerent tone of his generals and political colleagues had become more virulent than ever, and the recurrent excursions of the *fedayeen* into Israel helped create among the Israelis a deep sense of siege and imminent war.

During the autumn of 1955, a serious debate took place in Israel on whether or not to launch a 'preventive war' against Egypt before it could absorb the dramatic amounts of armaments just acquired from Russia, and before an Egyptian 'first strike' would become possible and probable.

When the Israeli government eventually decided, at the beginning of December 1955, to refrain from such a preventive strike, to try to restore the balance of power, and to deter attack by procuring arms in the West, these decisions were not taken as a result of any moral qualms. In a speech Ben-Gurion made before the entire Israeli High Command on 16 December 1955, he chose to explain these decisions with three main arguments.

1. Wars seldom end wars. Even after a victorious campaign against Egypt, there would be another round. A 'preventive war' does not really prevent war. On the contrary, by definition it fulfils one's own fear, and materializes the very war one wanted to prevent.

2. Israeli aggression would bring on its head a total embargo on arms sales, and would leave Israel at a great disadvantage in terms of the balance of power.

3. Great Britain, coveting the Israeli Negev as an alternative military base to the Suez bases, might interfere in the war on the side of the Arabs.[9]

Ben-Gurion did not have any moral hesitation, since he was sure that Nasser would attack Israel as soon as he was ready: 'I assume that they will attack at the beginning of the summer [1956]', he told General Dayan and Shimon Peres at their weekly meeting on 1 December 1955. 'It would be wrong not to assume it.'[10] To allay the opposition of the United States, Ben-Gurion was ready to forgo many strategic advantages which a preventive strike might give, and allow the Egyptians to take the initiative. The same considerations were still valid in the

---

Middle East under Cease Fire (Sydney, 1967), and Nathan Feinberg, *The Legality of a 'State of War' after the Cessation of Hostilities under the Charter of the U.N. and the Covenant of the League of Nations* (Jerusalem, 1961).

[9] Summarized in Moshe Dayan, *Avnei Derech* (Hebrew) (Tel Aviv, 1976), pp. 174–5.

[10] 'Protocol of Weekly Meeting with the Chief of Staff and the Director-General of the Ministry of Defence', 1 Dec. 1955; Ben-Gurion Archives, Sde Boker.

autumn of 1956. Only a full and formal collaboration with two nations, Britain and France, which were still considered by 'little Israel' as major powers, could prevent the diplomatic isolation or even ostracism which might befall Israel in the wake of unprovoked aggression by her.

Early in the morning of 16 October, a lengthy cable from Joseph Nahmias, the representative of the Israeli Defence Ministry in Paris, reached Ben-Gurion's desk. The cable described the new 'scenario' which General Maurice Challe, then Deputy Chief of Staff of the French Forces, had suggested a day earlier to the British. According to this, Israel would be asked to launch an independent attack on the Egyptian army in the Sinai peninsula, and provide the British and French with the proper pretext to serve an ultimatum to both Egypt and Israel, and thereafter to launch their own Operation *Musketeer* without any complicity with Israel.[11]

Ben-Gurion's spontaneous reaction was violently negative. Though he must have been aware that the 'scenario' came off the desk of the French general, Ben-Gurion saw it as a British manipulation since it was designed primarily to satisfy British political requirements. 'He saw in this proposal the acme of British hypocrisy', writes Peres in his memoirs. 'It reflected', he said, 'the British desire to harm Israel more than their resolve to destroy the Egyptian dictatorship.'[12] Only after much effort did Peres manage to calm his wrath, and indeed to cable a reply which would leave the door open for further negotiations. The very warm relations which had developed over recent months with the French were too dear to him to let the British insult have an undermining effect.

Ben-Gurion had a number of reasons to object to the scenario. The most important was his deep mistrust of the British and his indignation at what he considered British arrogance. The scenario required that Israel expose herself to grave military and political dangers, performing a task in the service of France and England, without being recognized or even directly talked to by the British, and, even worse, running the risk of being branded by her 'allies' as the aggressor, who was endangering the Suez Canal, who had to be stopped by an ultimatum. Ben-Gurion apparently felt treated, to use the figure of speech at the time, as a concubine, not deserving of so much as a greeting 'unter den Linden'.

[11] The Files of the Bureau of the Chief of Staff, Incoming Cables, No. G.553, 15 Oct. 1956, Israeli Defence Forces (IDF) Archives.

[12] Shimon Peres, *Mivtza Suffa*; a summary of the Sèvres Conference written a few days after the event; Peres's personal papers.

Ben-Gurion's attitude towards the British can be defined as a 'love–hate' relationship. He admired the British political system and was deeply impressed by their stamina and courage during World War II. On the other hand, his long struggle against the British mandate, and what he conceived as British double-crossing during 1948, had left deep scars on him.

During 1955, Ben-Gurion did not know about 'Project Alpha', and tended to delude himself that there was a great divergence between British and US policies with regard to the Arab–Israeli conflict. But he could not fail to perceive that Whitehall had a consistent scheme to push Israel to make significant concessions to the Arabs.

Less than a year earlier, he had reacted vehemently to Eden's 'Alpha' speech at the Guildhall.[13] The British scheme to send a 'loyal' Iraqi contingent into Jordan, in October 1956, in order to forestall a probable pro-Nasserite outcome of the national elections scheduled for the end of October, was opposed by Israel, who saw in it a threat to her own security. Israel in turn threatened to invade Jordan in case of an Iraqi expedition.

Only a few days earlier, a clash between Israeli planes and British aircraft based in Cyprus was averted at the last minute. During the night of 11–12 October 1956, Israeli troops attacked Kalkilia; battle ensued, and King Hussein called on British help in accordance with their Mutual Defence Pact. 'Our help had been called for', writes Eden in his memoirs, 'and our aircraft were on the point of going up.'[14] Only the fact that the battle ended, and the Israeli troops retreated before dawn, averted the clash.

Against this backdrop, no wonder Ben-Gurion was utterly suspicious of British intentions. He wrote in his diary: 'The British plot, I imagine, is to get us involved with Nasser and bring about the occupation of Jordan by Iraq.'[15]

The one thing that Ben-Gurion coveted most, when a joint operation against Nasser was proposed, was exactly the thing Eden wanted to grant the least: that Israel be recognized by the British for what it actually was—a full partner with equal status.

When, later in the day on 16 October, information reached Jerusalem that Guy Mollet and Sir Anthony Eden were having a summit meeting at the Palais Matignon, Ben-Gurion cabled to Nahmias urgently: 'In connection with the arrival of the British representatives

---

[13] Ben-Gurion's speech at the Knesset, 15 Nov. 1955; reprinted in David Ben-Gurion, *The Sinai Campaign* (Hebrew) (Tel Aviv, 1964), pp. 33–6: '[Eden's] proposal to cut Israel's territory in favour of her neighbours is devoid of any legal or moral basis and is utterly unthinkable.'

[14] Anthony Eden, *The Suez Crisis of 1956*, a reprint from *Full Circle* (Boston, 1968), p. 150.

[15] Ben-Gurion, *Diaries*, 17 Oct. 1956; Ben-Gurion Archives, Sde Boker.

in Paris, you should contact the French immediately and ask them whether the meeting can be made tripartite. The Israeli representatives are ready to come immediately, in utmost secrecy. Their rank will equal the ranks of the British and French representatives.'[16]

The time for such a tripartite meeting was apparently not yet ripe. At this stage, Eden and Selwyn Lloyd were ready to go along only if the French were able to induce the Israelis to open full-scale hostilities in the Sinai peninsula, without any pre-condition or pre-co-ordination, and let England be 'surprised' by the Israeli action and appear on the scene as an umpire, not an accomplice. The most Eden was ready to concede at Matignon was to leave with the French two formal diplomatic notes, which the French, for their part, would deliver to the Israelis as a diplomatic assurance of compliance with the proposed scenario. These notes read as follows:

In the event of any threat of hostilities in the neighbourhood of the Canal, the French and British Governments would call the belligerents to halt and to withdraw from the immediate vicinity of the Canal. If both agreed, no action would follow. If one or both refused, Anglo-French forces would intervene to ensure the free passage of the Canal.

In the event of hostilities developing between Egypt and Israel, Her Majesty's Government would not come to the assistance of Egypt, because Egypt was in breach of a Security Council Resolution and had moreover repudiated Western aid under the Tripartite Declaration.

Different consideration would of course apply to Jordan, with whom Her Majesty's Government had, in addition to their obligation under the Tripartite Declaration, a firm treaty.[17]

At this stage, Ben-Gurion too was not yet ready. The only concern which prevented him from slamming shut the door on future negotiation outright, was the alliance with the French. The large-scale deliveries of arms from France had started to arrive in Israel shortly before the nationalization of the Suez Canal, and would redress the balance of power between Israel and Egypt that had been shattered a year earlier by the Czech arms deal.

In addition to the symbolic and emotional objections Ben-Gurion raised against the Challe scenario, there were a number of more practical problems to be solved:

1. Israel demanded that the allies' air strike be launched simultaneously with the Israeli land attack in the Sinai peninusla. Ben-Gurion,

---

[16] Outgoing Cables, No. AF/686, 16 Oct. 1956, IDF Archives.

[17] These diplomatic formulae were transmitted by Nahmias a day later to Jerusalem and are quoted in the Official Diaries of the Bureau of the Chief of Staff (Hebrew), IDF Archives.

who had spent some time in London during the Blitz in 1940, was keenly worried about exposing Israeli towns to massive Egyptian air retaliation.

2. Ben-Gurion demanded a clear British assurance against Iraqi interference in Jordan. The formulations of Eden's notes of 16 October were far from satisfactory in this respect.[18]

3. The same applied to the exact interpretation of the British–Jordanian Defence Treaty. What if Jordan were to opt to intervene in the war to help Egypt?

4. Then there was the question of what Israel might reap as her own spoils of the proposed campaign. Would England and France support her demand to occupy permanently Sharm-el-Sheikh and the Straits of Eilat?

It must have become clear to the French at this point that only a top-level meeting could sort out some of these questions, and establish a minimum level of trust between the Israelis and the British. Without such trust the 'scenario' had no chance of being complied with by the prospective 'actors'. The French were eager to attack Nasser from the very beginning. Accumulating proofs of Egyptian involvement with the National Liberation Front (FLN) in Algiers convinced them that Nasser must be ousted before the Algerian rebellion could be quashed. Of the three prospective partners, the French had the least hesitation, and could not have cared less how their war was launched, as long as it actually broke out. Their role as matchmakers was therefore natural. As soon as the Palais Matignon meeting was over, without any assurance of British participation, and before Nahmias had the opportunity to pass on Ben-Gurion's suggestion for a tripartite meeting, Guy Mollet sent Ben-Gurion an invitation to come to Paris. After consulting with a few Cabinet colleagues, Ben-Gurion cabled back: 'The British idea of an Israeli attack and of British interference as umpire is out of the question. But Ben-Gurion is ready to come to Paris if Guy Mollet considers it necessary in spite of the disqualification of the British idea.'[19]

Whether the British would participate in the scheduled Paris meeting, and on what level, remained unclear until after the arrival of Ben-Gurion in Sèvres on the afternoon of 22 October. According to Selwyn Lloyd's memoirs, he was summoned to Chequers on the afternoon of the 21 October to an informal meeting of a few Cabinet ministers, at

---

[18] 'Operation Straggle', intended to bring about a pro-Iraqi coup in Syria, was not divined by the Israelis at the time.

[19] Peres, *Mivtza Suffa*.

which it was decided to send him to meet the French and the Israelis.[20] Yet the cable announcing his arrival only mentioned 'a representative of the highest level'. The French hoped it would not be Lloyd, whom they considered antagonistic to their scheme. Ben-Gurion was completely indifferent regarding the actual identity of the British envoy.

On thing was clear: Ben-Gurion was as eager to meet any high-ranking British official representative as the British were eager to avoid such a meeting. At the same time, Eden was as eager to see Israel perform her role according to the scenario as Ben-Gurion was eager to avoid it.

If Ben-Gurion had been able to take into account only purely Israeli considerations, i.e. what was best for Israel from the narrow perspective of her military relations with Egypt, he would most probably have preferred to postpone the war for the following reasons:

1. A significant number of new armaments—effective tanks, mobile artillery, and Mystère IV aircraft—had started to arrive in Israel only three months earlier, under the highly secret agreement concluded between Israel and France at the end of June in Vermans.[21] Additional shipments, which were agreed upon during the St-Germain Conference held between Golda Meir, then Minister of Foreign Affairs, and the French leaders from 30 September to 2 November 1956,[22] were still on their way, at the end of October. It would take the Israeli army a few more months to absorb all this new equipment and bring its forces to their maximum efficiency and strength.[23]

2. In spite of their strong conviction as to their right to use military initiative in self-defence, the Israelis still felt it was necessary to base their preventive strike on clear provocation by their opponent, so that the danger they thus sought to avert would be clear to world public opinion and, more importantly, to their own public, whose energies and sacrifices they required for the essential military effort. After the nationalization of the Canal, however, the southern frontier of Israel

[20] Selwyn Lloyd, *Suez 1956: A Personal Account* (London, 1978), p. 180.

[21] Vermans is a little village south of Paris, in which a top-secret meeting between Israeli and French military officers and intelligence officials took place at the end of June 1956. At this meeting an agreement was concluded to exchange intelligence information and to supply modern French arms to Israel. For details see, Mordechai Bar-On, *Etgar ve Tigra* (Hebrew), to be published shortly.

[22] Mordechai Bar-On, 'The St-Germain Conference' (Hebrew), *Ma'ariv*, 29 Oct. 1976.

[23] During the Sinai Campaign, the Israeli Airforce was in possession of a few dozen Mystère IV fighter planes, for which it did not yet have sufficiently trained pilots. As part of the Sèvres agreement, France sent to Israel French pilots to man those Israeli planes. A third armoured brigade was in its early build-up stages and could not be used in battle properly. A small armoured detachment, commanded by the Brigade C.-in-C., was committed to the Battle of Um Kataf prematurely and failed miserably. The Commander, Col. Galinka, died in the battle.

was very quiet. Nasser had his hands full with the Suez crisis and wanted to avoid provoking Israel as far as possible.

3. In 1956 Israel was already highly dependent on the United States. Ben-Gurion would have preferred to take all the time needed to persuade the United States to back Israel in any prospective violent clash with the Egyptians.

4. Ben-Gurion, a pragmatist through and through, was not exceedingly sensitive to ideological considerations of a global nature. Yet the disadvantages which might accrue to Israel as a result of her collaboration in a colonial war *par excellence* did not escape his attention. Minister Moshe Carmel of the left-wing *Ahdut Haavodah* faction, who participated with Golda Meir in the St-Germain Conference, had already explicitly brought this to Ben-Gurion's attention,[24] and so had other left-wing partners in his coalition, before the final approval of the Sèvres agreement was given by the Israeli Cabinet.

Yet at Sèvres, Ben-Gurion faced contrary considerations:

1. Israel had already been branded by the Arabs, Communists, and some Third World nations as an agent of colonialism. There was little to lose on this score. Faced with the overwhelming numerical superiority of the Arabs, however, Ben-Gurion had been eagerly seeking an alliance with a Western power for quite some time.

2. The possibility of launching the war jointly with two of the major powers, especially the prospect that the Egyptian airforce would be handled by others, outweighed, in his opinion, the lack of full Israeli preparedness.

3. Ben-Gurion was always afraid of British interference in a prospective war between Israel and the Arabs, on the latter's side. To go to war with Britain on Israel's side was the best assurance against such a frightening contingency.

The most important consideration was, however, the vital need to preserve French friendship and ensure that France continued to supply Israel with more modern military equipment in the future.

On the morning of 24 October, after Ben-Gurion made his final decision to commit the Israel Defence Forces (IDF) to the battle, he briefly summarized his main considerations in his diary as follows: 'I think we have to undertake this operation. This is a unique opportunity that two "not so small" powers will try to topple Nasser, and we shall not remain alone against him while he becomes stronger and conquers all Arab countries.'[25]

---

[24] For his later version of the events see Moshe Carmel, 'Kah Nafla Hahachlata' (Hebrew), *Skira Hodshit*, 33, Nos. 10–11 (Dec. 1986).

[25] Ben-Gurion, *Diaries*, 24 Oct. 1956.

Beyond these general considerations, we have yet to explain a rather strange feature of the Sèvres Conference. We have seen that before starting his voyage, Ben-Gurion cabled Guy Mollet to let him know that the 'British scenario' was out of the question. When Ben-Gurion entered the luxurious DC-4 the French government had sent to fly him to Sèvres, he there met General Challe and Louis Mangin, who came to escort Ben-Gurion to Paris, in order to try to soften his objections *en route*. Ben-Gurion told Challe right away: 'If you intend to use the "British proposal", the only advantage of my trip will be to make the acquaintance of your Prime Minister.'[26] This was not tactics; it expressed deep indignation and resistance.

Yet, seventy-two hours later, Ben-Gurion agreed to what amounted essentially to the 'British scenario'. To be sure, some important changes were introduced into the original plan. The time gap between the Israeli attack and the first allied air strike was shortened from 72 hours to 48 hours.[27] To abate Ben-Gurion's fears of a massive Egyptian air strike against Israeli civilian targets, it was agreed to station two French fighter squadrons at Israeli air bases and man the Israeli Mystère IV planes with French aircrews. The undertaking of the British not to double-cross Israel by sending Iraqi and Jordanian troops to flank Israel from the East became much more explicit.[28] Some cosmetic changes were also introduced into the diplomatic formulas to be used after the Israeli attack. Yet in essence the scenario was kept and agreed upon by Ben-Gurion: Israel was to launch, at zero hour, a 'real act of war' deep in the Sinai peninsula; the British and French would send Israel and Egypt a simultaneous ultimatum; *Musketeer* would not be launched simultaneously, but after a significant delay. Most important, the whole agreement must remain secret, and Britain would remain aloof and not admit any previous knowledge of the plot.

What happened during those seventy-two hours at Sèvres that persuaded Ben-Gurion to give in to the British demands? What happened at Sèvres which caused him to retreat from his position of absolute objection to the scenario?

Reading through the detailed records,[29] it seems that during the

---

[26] Official Diaries of the Bureau of the Chief of Staff, 23 Oct. 1956, IDF Archives.

[27] Eventually the British postponed the bombing by another twelve hours.

[28] While the Sèvres Conference was in progress, news came in from Amman announcing the victory of the pro-Nasserite Suleiman al-Nabulsi in the election. This made the Iraqi intervention in Jordan obsolete.

[29] The only detailed (almost verbatim) record of the Sèvres Conference was kept by Mordechai Bar-On, then the Chef du Bureau of General Dayan, who participated in the conferences as the secretary of the Israeli delegation. This record is included in the Official Diaries of the Bureau of the Chief of Staff, and is quoted extensively in Mordechai Bar-On, *Etgar ve Tigra*, a book written in 1958 (in Hebrew), which will be published soon.

conference Ben-Gurion was made aware of three further considerations.

1. French pressure

Even before arriving in Paris, Ben-Gurion did not delude himself that future relations between Israel and France would depend to a large degree on the willingness of Israel to go along with and help the French in their hour of need, and thus enable them to encourage the British to overcome their hesitations and put *Musketeer* into action. Yet only when he sat face-to-face with Mollet, Pineau, and Bourgès-Maunoury could Ben-Gurion realize how desperately the French leaders wanted that plan executed. On the second day at the conference, Guy Mollet came under heavy fire at the Assemblée Nationale for not moving against Nasser. The capture of an arms shipment from Egypt to the Algerian rebels, the day before, and the hijacking of the FLN leader Ben Bella and his retinue heated up the political atmosphere in Paris. During all the meetings at Sèvres, the French ministers did not mince words in stressing their conviction that at this stage the Challe scenario was the only way to push the British into action, and that for France this was a vital step. During the first meeting, held on the porch of the villa Bonnier de la Chapelle in Sèvres, on the afternoon of 22 October, all three French ministers, each in his own personal style, made this very clear. Maurice Bourgès-Maunoury, the youngest and most aggressive of the three, was also the most outspoken. Short of a direct ultimatum, he used every possible pressure. During an informal, though rather crucial, lunch meeting on the second day, Bourgès-Maunoury said to Ben-Gurion:

During the last few months, in which I have had many dealings with Israel, I have always been utterly frank with you. You should take my words as expressed in the fullest sincerity; I do not believe [unless we act now] that France will be able to return in the foreseeable future to a position which will enable her to commit herself to a joint action ... I can promise you that in the future, too, France will not cease to help Israel to the best of her ability, with equipment and information, but I doubt if we shall be able to help you in the way we intend to do now, that is through this joint operation we propose today.[30]

These were strong and explicit words that could not fail to impress Ben-Gurion.

2. Dayan's operational plan

The scenario required Israel to confront the entire Egyptian army alone and be exposed to its maximum strength for 48–72 hours. This

---

[30] Official Diaries, 22 Oct. 1956.

requirement gave Ben-Gurion some serious worries, given his night-marish fear of air attacks on Tel Aviv and other Israeli cities. Ben-Gurion was also afraid of great losses the IDF might suffer during the first phase of the campaign, and especially of the danger to the forward troops, who might be cut off by the Egyptians before Israel could give them proper air and ground support. Only two weeks earlier, an Israeli paratroop company had come close to being annihilated by the Jordanians during the Kalkilia raid. Even putting aside the lack of trust in the good faith of the British, Ben-Gurion was still afraid that international or internal pressures during the first days of the campaign might coerce the British to put off their military intervention after all, and leave the Israeli forces exposed in the desert.

The British required for their *casus belli* that the Israelis commit a 'real act of war' which would look like an actual threat to the Suez Canal. A border skirmish of the kind Israel had performed a number of times since the Gaza raid in late February 1955 would not be sufficient. General Dayan provided the solution to that impasse: during consultation within the Israeli delegation at Sèvres, he proposed to drop, at zero hour, a para-battalion at the Mitla Pass, a desolate and empty spot far from any Egyptian force deployment, yet only thirty miles away from the Canal. He also suggested three additional steps to be taken at zero hour: firstly, to commit two more para-battalions to a mobile excursion along the Kuntilla–Mitla axis in order to reinforce the air-dropped battalion and, if necessary, to enable it to retreat back across the border and end the whole affair as if it were merely another Israeli 'reprisal'; secondly, to capture two more Egyptian border positions, at El Quseima and at Ras el-Naqb, in order to open two more axes leading towards the Mitla Pass, for a possible rescue operation; thirdly, to withhold any other land or air operation of the IDF, especially of the two Israeli armoured brigades, until after the Anglo-French military intervention.

Some military observers[31] have hailed the Mitla drop as a brilliant performance of a military 'indirect approach'. It was in reality nothing of the sort, yet it was a brilliant *diplomatic* idea, and, perhaps no less, a brilliant exercise in psychological manipulation. The main effect of this plan was to enable Ben-Gurion to overcome his fears and suspicions. It allowed the Israeli army to perform a 'real act of war' and create an illusion of a 'threat to the Suez Canal', thus satisfying the British requirements while minimizing the risk for the Israelis during the first two crucial days.

If we can trust the testimony of Mohamed Hassanein Heikal, the

---

[31] A good example is Robert Henriques, *100 Hours to Suez* (London, 1957).

Mitla drop indeed left Nasser puzzled and caused him to commit his army to the Sinai Front only hesitatingly and belatedly.[32]

3. Confronting the British

The main events that occurred at Sèvres and made the most important difference to Ben-Gurion were, however, the participation of Selwyn Lloyd in a face-to-face encounter with the Israeli delegation on the first evening, and the signing of the Sèvres Protocol by Sir Patrick Dean and Donald Logan on the third day.

The encounter between Selwyn Lloyd and Ben-Gurion was rather awkward. Both were obviously ill at ease. Lloyd writes in his memoirs: 'Ben-Gurion himself seemed to be in a rather aggressive mood, indicating or implying that the Israelis had no reason to believe in anything that a British Minister might say. He said in his book that I treated him like a subordinate. No doubt we were both tired.'[33]

Moshe Dayan writes in his autobiography: 'Britain's Foreign Minister may well have been a friendly man, pleasant, charming, amiable. If so, he showed near genius in concealing these virtues. His manner could not have been more antagonistic. His whole demeanour expressed distaste—for the place, the company and the topic.'[34]

In my own records, I used blunter language, giving my spontaneous impressions of the British Minister: 'His voice was shrill and saturated with an unpleasant tone of cynicism and a humour dry as a clay shard. His face gave the impression of something stinking hanging permanently under his nose. The snobbish air of his entire personality, prevents him from opening himself up to his fellow negotiators and sheds on the entire conversation a cold and formal atmosphere.'[35] Having read, many years later, Lloyd's most honest, humble, and humane memoirs, I have realized that those earlier impressions must have reflected either my Israeli prejudice or Lloyd's own utmost embarrassment.

In spite of the poor chemistry of that meeting, for Ben-Gurion it must have served as a strong vindication. Moreover, if war were to follow, it was vital for Ben-Gurion that this encounter never be undone and never be denied in the future. Too many people were around that dinner table. What was important for Ben-Gurion was not the details of the conversation, or the tone, but the sheer fact that it had taken place.

---

[32] Mohamed H. Heikal, *Cutting the Lion's Tail: Suez Through Egyptian Eyes* (London, 1986), p. 177.

[33] Selwyn Lloyd, *Suez 1956*, p. 183.

[34] Moshe Dayan, *Story of My Life* (London, 1976), p. 180.

[35] Official Diaries, 22 Oct. 1956.

This is exactly the reason why Sir Anthony Eden and Selwyn Lloyd were so eager to act as if it had never occurred. As they had justly appreciated that the entire British residual interest in the Middle East was at stake, they wanted more than just to keep it secret; they wanted it utterly erased from the annals of history. They wanted it denied, or even, if possible, 'undone', that is, completely forgotten.

The signing by two British officials of a written Protocol, incorporating quite explicitly the various undertakings of the different parties involved in the Challe scenario, only gave an added formality and a ready proof of those commitments.

At the end of the third day, Ben-Gurion received in his hand a signed copy of the Protocol of Sèvres. He folded the document with emphasized care and put it, almost with a ritualistic gesture, into his waistcoat pocket. His face was grave but shining with deep satisfaction.[36]

When Sir Anthony Eden, on the other hand, heard of the signing of the document, he fell into one of his worst rages, and sent Patrick Dean and Donald Logan immediately back to Paris to retrieve all copies of the document.[37] Alas, it was too late. Ben-Gurion was already on his way back to Israel, still holding the treasured document in his pocket.

Ben-Gurion was willing to keep the story secret for a long time, and at least not to allow any official Israeli confirmation of it. But in no way was he ready to allow anybody to deny its occurrence in history.[38]

Her Majesty's Government was confronted by a delicate, nay insoluble dilemma: should the British let Nasser get away with the nationalization of the Suez Canal and the many other anti-Western steps he had undertaken? His increasing stature as the national hero of the Arabs might undermine the entire British deployment and the important interests and influence Britain still held in the Middle East. Yet to attack Nasser without a proper pretext, or worse, to ride piggy-back on a previously agreed upon act of Israeli aggression against Egypt, would be disastrous.

The only way out, so Eden and his colleagues believed at the time, was to take action and yet not appear to do so, that is to promote the Israeli attack without apparently being involved.

The only way open to Eden was therefore to exercise 'trickery and fraud'. Ostensibly, 'collusion' was not aimed against Nasser. Yet Eden wanted Nasser ousted and he became indifferent to the moral and

---

[36] Official Diaries, 24 Oct. 1956.

[37] Robert Rhodes James, *Anthony Eden* (London, 1986), p. 532.

[38] When I presented a copy of my book *Etgar ve Tigra* to Ben-Gurion, in 1958, it included only a paraphrased version of the Protocols. Ben-Gurion had the only copy of the Protocol. When he read the book, he took the effort to order an extra copy; he pinned it personally into the proper page in his personal copy of my book.

political issues at stake. Fraud had to be used in order to trick other Arab regimes, who were still friendly to the British, so that they would believe that Britain was indeed innocent of any collaboration with the hated Israelis. From the British perspective, it was 'collusion' all right. In order to 'collude', one has to *intend* to 'collude'; one has to have the intention of misleading and acting consciously in a fraudulent manner. The secrecy required in a collusion is not aimed at military surprise but is a cover-up. Military secrecy becomes irrelevant as soon as the military act is performed. He who colludes will try to keep his secrets as long as he can.

Ben-Gurion had no intention of misleading anybody as to his motives. His efforts were directed at disinforming the Egyptians, but only as much as was necessary for tactical surprise. He needed no excuse *vis-à-vis* any of the other Arab states, or even *vis-à-vis* other nations. For Ben-Gurion the word 'collusion' had no meaning. It will remain forever a great wonder, how Eden and his colleagues could delude themselves that the collusion could be kept secret for any length of time. As soon as the Anglo-French ultimatum was announced, 12 hours after the Israeli attack, it became quite clear that it was part of a previously agreed upon plot. The details were not known until later, but London echoed with outrage right away, and the accusation of 'collusion' appeared even before the British intervention started. Such indignation and accusations were not heard in Paris, and certainly not in Tel Aviv.

The only worry Ben-Gurion had during the first 48 hours was not what kind of moral blame somebody somewhere would attach to Israel, but rather whether the British would stick to their commitments and start their air strike on time.

To be sure, the Arab world, and many in the Third World and among their European ideological sympathizers, accused Israel of serving the fading colonial powers. Yet Arabs did not need reasons to blame the Jews and Zionists beyond their erstwhile intrusion into the Middle East, and as to the second grouping, the period 1956–67 became the honeymoon of Israel's relations with the Third World.

According to Santayana, the famous Spanish philosopher, people or nations who do not learn from history will be doomed to repeat it. Sèvres may serve as an excellent example that sometimes the opposite may happen. People or nations become prisoners of their own past to such an extent that they tend to make incorrect analogies, and rush into conclusions which doom them to repeat history in the wrong place and at the wrong time, and thus make first-rate blunders.

The analogy Anthony Eden and others, French as well as British, made between Nasser and Hitler or Mussolini in the 1930s is well known. It seems that Eden felt compelled to live up to his own reputation and stand up against upstart dictators.

In France, it went much deeper. The Cabinet of Guy Mollet was a coalition of parties, differing on most of the issues besetting contemporary French politics. But beyond partisan delineations, many of the French ministers, especially the three who took part in the Sèvres Conference, cherished an overriding common sentiment: they were all *anciens combattants* of the French World War II Resistance.

Most of the meetings at Sèvres took place in the salon of the villa Bonnier de la Chapelle. Above the fireplace, an oversize bust of a young man was unavoidably apparent. This was the bust of the young son of the Bonnier de la Chapelle family, who was sent by the French Resistance to kill Admiral Darlan in Algiers during the allied invasion of North Africa in 1943. He was executed by the Vichy regime and became a martyr. This was symbolic. One could not fail to observe a warm intimacy among the French ministers who used to joke and revive memories of the 'good old days'. Their resolve to destroy Nasser was certainly imbued with their utmost inner compulsion not to repeat the mistakes of past history. They may have interpreted correctly the fallacies of the past, but certainly they misinterpreted the present, and therefore made no less fallacious judgements than their predecessors.

Ben-Gurion was no exception. He too was a prisoner of his past. His greatest glory, as the man who in 1948 successfully resisted the invasion of five Arab armies, pushed him to consider Arab enmity as irreconcilable. His memories of the German Blitz over London exaggerated his fears of Egyptian air raids on Tel Aviv. But the most important distorted image was his perception of the British. He certainly over-rated their enmity to Israel, he over-suspected their deviousness, overestimated their capabilities as a military power, and over-appreciated their wisdom.

Nevertheless, since his primary considerations had little to do with the British but were focused rather on the Nasserite danger and French friendship, even if he had known in Sèvres what became quite clear about the British only a few weeks later, I doubt if his decisions would have been much different.

8

Nasser and the Crisis of 1956

AMIN HEWEDY

A LINK IN A CHAIN OF CRISES

SOME historians write that the Suez crisis of 1956 began on 26 July 1956, the date of nationalization of the Suez Canal Company, and ended on 16 March 1957, when the last Israeli troops withdrew from Sinai. This was not the case. The crisis began several years before and probably has not yet come to an end. The crisis of 1956 was a link in a long chain, a battle in a long war fought by a whole nation and not only by one man, Gamal Abdel Nasser, even if history puts on his shoulders the responsibility for leading two generations of Egyptians.

The links in the long chain of conflict between Nasser's regime and the West were:

(a) The war of liberation against the British base in the Suez Canal Zone that was ended by the 1954 treaty.

(b) The refusal by the revolutionary regime after 1952 to enter foreign pacts except with the Arab League. When the Baghdad Pact was contracted, Nasser attacked and resisted it. At the same time the new regime backed the regional national movements especially the Algerian revolution.

(c) The rejection by Nasser of an unjust solution to the Arab–Israeli conflict.

(d) Domestic measures taken by Egypt to achieve economic and social development.

(e) The 1955 Czech arms deal.

(f) The High Dam crisis followed by the withdrawal of Western loans, including the International Bank's loan for the construction of the new project.

(g) The nationalization of the Suez Canal Company.

(h) The triple aggression by Britain, France, and Israel.

What was the high point of these interrelated and successive interactions? 'Sparks cause big fires', says one of our Arabic proverbs. In international and regional conflicts, minor incidents may precipitate direct confrontations. In spite of the importance of the nationalization of the Company, the act was a precipitant and not the direct cause of the triple aggression. The main cause of the crisis, in my judgement, was the Czech arms deal of 20 May 1955, because that agreement upset the balance of power that had been maintained since the 1950 declaration by the United States, Britain, and France. That declaration aimed at enforcing a situation favourable to Israel that undermined Arab interests, especially those of the Palestinians.

The declaration restricted the purchase of arms to the markets of the three powers, thereby making it easier for them to control the regional status quo, because their belief was that if their monopoly were broken, the region would be engulfed in an arms race, the preservation of the status quo would be made difficult, and the Soviet Union might succeed in entering the area. The change would upset the order previously existing in one of the most important zones of their global strategy.

The 1950 declaration imposed a *de facto* embargo on the transfer of arms to Egypt, notwithstanding the efforts by the new Egyptian regime to break through this restriction. The British not only resisted American initiatives to meet Egyptian requests, but also refused to deliver planes and tanks for which the Egyptians had already paid. The Israelis, the French, and even the 'Egyptian' Suez Canal Company cooperated in preventing any deliveries. At the same time, the new regime was under two main pressures: on the one hand, to enter into the defensive alliance of the Baghdad Pact, and, on the other, to resist the Israeli attacks on its borders. Unable to gain arms for his army, and facing a critical political and military situation, Nasser had no time to lose. On 27 September 1955, while opening a picture exhibition held by the Armed Forces, Nasser announced the Czech arms deal, thereby causing a thundering international and regional explosion.

The deal was the cause of the Suez crisis of 1956, and the sensitive juncture between peace and war in the region. When it became known, the aggressors waited for the opportunity. The Czech deal affected the international and regional balance of power while the nationalization of the Suez Canal Company was a matter of transferring the control of the Canal to its real owners, with reasonable and just compensation to the shareholders and a promise to respect free navigation in accordance with the Constantinople Treaty of 1888.

Since our ancient history, the main threats to Egyptian national security have come from the East. Sinai was a bridge to Egypt not only for Prophets but also for would-be conquerors of Egypt. After digging the Canal in the nineteenth century, the strategic importance of this area to global strategy increased, for understandable reasons.

Nasser inherited a critical and dangerous situation on the eastern front. This was why he fought his main battles in the Canal Zone and

Sinai. Egypt confronted three threats from that direction: the Israelis on the eastern border, the British in the Suez Canal base, and the Suez Canal Company as a state within the state. Nasser's strategy in the Red Sea was planned, executed, connected with, and based on the Canal as one of the three passages which dominate the region: the Hormuz Strait into the Gulf; Bab-el-Mandab, the southern gate to the Red Sea; and the Canal, the northern gate connecting the Red Sea with the Mediterranean.

The British base in the Canal was a real and urgent problem confronting the new regime, because it was at the top of Egyptian national aspirations to see foreign troops evacuated. It was also a real threat to the regime. The British in the Canal base held many cards in their hand—even before the revolution—to enforce certain policies upon the Egyptian government. On 18 February 1953, Egyptian intelligence obtained a document from inside the Headquarters of the British High Command of the Canal Zone about plan *Rodeo* prepared by the High Command to deal with agitation and disorder in the Canal or inside other parts of Egypt. The object of the plan was the occupation of the Delta, Cairo, and Alexandria whenever the situation required. Directly after the revolution, the British government sent a warning to the British Commander of the Canal base to prepare for implementation of plan *Rodeo* within six hours of receiving orders. Leaflets were printed inside the base to be distributed to the inhabitants in Cairo and Alexandria by the British forces. When information reached the British command and the British government that the Egyptians would launch *fedayeen* attacks after the British authorities stopped the negotiations for the evacuation of the base, General Festing, the Commander of the Base, received a message from his superiors in London to be prepared to put *Rodeo* in force.

Based on the experience of seventy years of negotiations with the British, Nasser's strategy was twofold: to draw to his side the United States (which he believed anxious to replace the British and the French in the region); and to seek agreement with the British by employing force against the occupying troops.

In the autumn of 1952, the Planning Section of the Egyptian General Staff prepared a memorandum suggesting the following:

(*a*) The Egyptian Army is confronted by two aggressors: the British in the Canal, and the Israelis on the eastern border.

(*b*) Negotiations with the British will never come to a satisfactory result unless we use force, concentrating on guerrilla warfare.

(*c*) The British threaten our communication zone to the east, making it impossible for us to confront any Israeli move encouraged by the British, if we start the guerrilla war.

(*d*) Consequently, the British are the main enemy while the Israelis are a secondary threat. Every effort must be made to freeze the frontier.

(*e*) Sinai should be evacuated by our main force (one division) to escape any British move to isolate it.

A conference was held by the General Staff, attended by Nasser, the Chief of Staff, the Director of Operations, and the author. Three decisions were taken:

(*a*) Guerrilla warfare was approved, preparations to be taken immediately with the greatest secrecy.

(*b*) Evacuation of Sinai approved. Planning and preparation including deceptive measures to start immediately.

(*c*) Execution on further orders.

There was the probability of British interference to hinder the evacuation and to keep Egyptian troops as hostage in Sinai. Plans were made by the Egyptians to confound such interference while delaying a withdrawal of the troops to the last and planning an evacuation within one night. Some of the measures planned were: prohibition of written orders, a reduction by one half of the number of troops allowed to return to the Sinai from leave, and withdrawal of materials by train at night through the British base. To be kept at El-Arish would be some locomotives and trucks commensurate with the estimates of troops and loads to be moved; some units were sent to the Sinai peninsula by day to disguise the night withdrawals to the west; and rations were sent from the main base in the Delta in ordinary quantities.

When the orders were given, they pulled back in one night without any British interference. Although the withdrawal was dangerous, it was the best decision under the circumstances. All the options confronting Nasser were unsatisfactory, but leadership carries with it the responsibility of making such hard choices. In any event, the limited forces in the Sinai could do nothing while sandwiched between the Israelis in the east and the British in the west.

Thus, to conclude:

1. The critical point in the chain of successive interactions which ended with the triple aggression was the Czech arms deal because it undermined the delicate balance of power on both international and regional levels.

2. To evaluate Nasser's decision, we must consider the pressures on sensitive issues he confronted at the time. In the little room he had for manœuvre, after calculating the risks, he opted for the dangerous action of confronting the real challenges that faced him.

NASSER AND THE CRISIS

Nasser was the central figure in the Suez crisis of 1956. His aim was to avoid war, but he never flinched from fighting should war be forced on Egypt. As with any leader, he must be judged in terms of his personal qualities and the circumstances confronting him. Nasser was a nationalist, an Egyptian patriot, and a deep believer in Arab nationalism. His bravery was more that of a bold statesman than a gambler. A gambler counts on luck. On the other hand, the bold statesman exerts qualities of leadership. He has a daring personality, not hesitating in times of danger to sacrifice himself for his country. These qualities Nasser had in abundance.

To appreciate the soundness of Nasser's actions in the Suez crisis, four elements must be considered: the rightness of his response; his elasticity without compromising his strategic aim; his correct evaluation of his enemies' intentions, and his appreciation of local, regional, and international sentiment.

THE RIGHTNESS OF RESPONSE

In Nasser's thinking, the appropriate response to a challenge was always based on the ability to keep the initiative in his own hands. Some of his critics have written that he was a master of reaction and not action during the Suez crisis. The ability to react embraces the will to act. Crucial to international stability is the ability to react correctly to threats to national security and then respond with a counterstroke. The response is correct only if it is legitimate, lawful, and credible.

Nationalization is generally an act of the sovereign state. The French government in 1946 nationalized the electrical industry, previously owned by British, Swiss, Belgian, and French shareholders. Mexico nationalized its oil industry and compensated the shareholders. The US government deemed this action to be in conformity with national sovereignty. As for the Suez Canal Company, its nationalization conformed to the national aspirations of the Egyptian people. It did not affect free international navigation, a principle that Nasser declared several times. Nasser's principles of freedom of navigation and adequate compensation legitimized the nationalization.

Nationalization also did not violate the Treaty of Constantinople. It was within Egypt's sovereign right, as it affected an Egyptian company within the terms of the treaty. When Anthony Eden asked for advice from his international lawyers, they told him that the nationalization was lawful. It did not usurp any rights but embraced the principle of compensation to shareholders, even as it benefited the Egyptians by providing support for their new schools and economic programmes. General benefit is the main source of law. After nationalization all efforts were directed towards maintaining freedom of navigation. This was recognized internationally.

In his appreciation of the situation before nationalization, Nasser observed the difference between Musaddiq's nationalization of Iranian oil and Egypt's nationalization of the Suez Canal Company. Iranian oil was a commodity; its production, transfer, and marketing were under foreign monopolies that could combat nationalization by substituting oil production from other sources, thereby causing loss to the Iranian Treasury. The Suez Canal Company was a service with no substitute at that time. Western industry depended on this waterway for transferring oil from its sources by the shortest route. No losses for the Egyptian Treasury were expected because the total income from the nationalized company was only one million Egyptian pounds.

Nasser came to the conclusion that the success of nationalization depended mainly on the efficient operation of the Canal. Accordingly, he delegated full authority to Mahmoud Younes, the man responsible for the execution of the nationalization. This included the enforcement of martial law over foreign labour in the Canal. The measure was oppressive, but it gained time for assembling alternative teams of pilots and technicians. When the foreign pilots withdrew *en masse* on 15 September 1956 to demonstrate the inability of the Egyptians to operate the Canal, the new company was able efficiently to meet the new situation.

Nasser's strategy was to escape from any direct confrontation and thereby preserve the nationalization without war. He was elastic without compromising his strategic aim. He yielded on some minor and tactical details but not on principle.

Throughout the crisis the argument behind his strategy was: Egypt's right of nationalization was not involved; the right to use his country's national resources for the benefit of his people was ensured by international law and UN resolutions; and compensation to shareholders was granted. This balanced approach was based on the assumption that the nationalized company was Egyptian. The Company had been given the concession for 99 years by the Egyptian government. Article 16 of the 22 February 1866 Agreement with the Canal Company conceded that the Company was Egyptian under the jurisdiction of Egyptian law.

From the start of the crisis, Nasser fought to gain time to mobilize international, regional, and local public opinion; to absorb the rage and fury caused by the nationalization; to avoid war; to prove his good intentions and ability to run the Canal; and, lastly, to exploit the differences between the East and West, and between the British and French on the one side and the United States on the other. Nasser thus made sacrifices on minor details as long as this did not contradict principle.

Although he refused to attend the London Conference, he did not resist it. He did not refuse to meet the Menzies delegation to Cairo, but he did not accept the conference's guidance. Even as he urged Britain and France to go to the United Nations, he employed tactical manœuvres to explain his stand internationally and to gain time to achieve a peaceful solution. When asked on the eve of the nationalization about procedures to be taken against ships refusing to pay the designated dues to the new Egyptian Company, he ordered undelayed passage while postponing the payment of dues. He thus avoided any interruption in the operation of the Canal for which his adversaries were waiting. Even after the invasion had begun, he did not declare war on the aggressors. He looked forward to an end of the fighting, saying, 'How can I declare war against a nation, half of it backing Eden, and the other half in the streets and Trafalgar Square objecting to him?' When British subjects were arrested as a security measure, the higher echelons of the detainees were lodged in the luxurious Semiramis Hotel. Others were put up in schools and hospitals.

ELASTICITY WITHOUT COMPROMISING STRATEGIC AIMS

But this tactical elasticity never concealed Nasser's strategic decisions. When the invasion started, he unhesitatingly ordered the closing of the Canal to halt the flow of oil to the aggressors. This action was strengthened by the cutting by the Arab nationalists of the oil pipelines from the Gulf to the Mediterranean through Syria. Some of the Western propaganda represented the blockage as purely punitive. It also had historical and strategic significance. Nasser had always remembered what happened on the Canal front when Ahmed Urabi resisted the British invasion of Egypt in 1882. British troops under the command of Sir Garnet Wolseley landed in Alexandria, but the Egyptian command headed by General Urabi excluded the possibility of an invasion from the east using the Canal as its main base. Urabi intended to block the Suez Canal and the Ismailia Canal to prevent British ships from concentrating at El-Ismailia. Ferdinand de Lesseps assured Urabi that the Canal would never be used by the invaders and that no British soldiers could land unaccompanied by French troops. Urabi believed the assurance. When his doubts were aroused, he gave orders for the blockade. It was too late. Using the Canal, British troops surprised Urabi and advanced swiftly to outflank his defensive positions at Tell-el-Kebir.

When collusion became clear in the 1956 invasion, Nasser acted courageously. Despite a spirited protest from his military command, he ordered a complete withdrawal of all troops east of the Canal to prevent their encirclement by the Israelis from the east and the British and the French from the rear. Again over the protests of his military advisers, he defended the main cities of the Canal Zone—Port Said, Ismailia, and Suez—to the last man and round. He fought on the Sinai front only to the extent necessary to gain time for the main body of troops to withdraw to the west of the Canal. He fought in Port Said long enough to mobilize international public opinion and intervention by other powers. More concerned for the security of his pilots than for his planes, he husbanded his air force for a probable later round. When the fighting stopped, Nasser did not give up any of his strategic objectives. A one-sided declaration by Egypt for unimpeded navigation of the Canal was all that he conceded. The Canal returned to full Egyptian sovereignty.

EVALUATION OF ENEMIES' INTENTIONS

During the days immediately preceding nationalization, Nasser anticipated different Western reactions and threats, including the use of force by Britain. But he had hoped to avoid provoking forceful action by the United States, France, and even Israel. Eden was in a weak position; and weakness can lead to violence. The Middle East was the main focus of his interest and his ambitions. He was also under psychological and political pressure from his party and from British public opinion. Eden, Nasser thought, would be confronted with three choices: (1) an immediate attack using available forces in Cyprus (three infantry brigades, one carrier, one destroyer); (2) action in collusion with the French; or (3) a peaceful solution. He estimated the probability of an armed collision would be up to 80 per cent in the first week after nationalization, 40 per cent during August, 20 per cent during October, and negligible after October.

Nasser committed a mistake when he fell captive to such conjectures, notwithstanding the information flowing to him. Indeed, with the passage of time, the probability of aggression did seem to fade, especially after the approval of a six-point plan to meet the interests of the parties directly concerned. Nevertheless, information came through regarding suspected meetings between the French and the Israelis in Paris as well as about French arms transfers to Israel. Egyptian intelligence in the late summer of 1956 estimated the arms transfers to be seventy planes, one hundred tanks, one hundred 105-mm. guns, and fifty anti-tank 75-mm. guns. The Egyptian military attaché—Colonel Zakaria Imam, a distinguished cavalry officer—sent information about the collusion that appeared to be accurate as details were revealed.

On 27 October 1956, two days before the act of aggression, the Egyptian military attaché in Paris, Colonel Tharwat Okasha, a distinguished officer and one of the liberal officers who had led the revolution—received full information about the collusion from a well-placed French friend. Okasha thought it would be more secure to send the information verbally by an envoy, who reached Cairo at 4.30 a.m. on Tuesday 29 October 1956. Nasser was in the Barrage, a safe retreat twenty miles north of Cairo, and when he returned to his office at noon he met the envoy. He listened carefully to the message but commented thoughtfully: 'Surely it is impossible that both the French and the British would degrade themselves to such an extent.' After a few hours, the Israelis dropped their paratroops at the Mitla Pass as their main troops penetrated the border. After the fighting, Nasser commented to Okasha: 'We escaped through the eye of a needle. I did not believe it at first. It seemed impossible.'

Nasser dismissed the idea of a triple collusion for the following reasons.

(*a*) Collusion with Israel would expose the Arab regimes friendly to France and Britain to outraged public opinion.

(*b*) Israel had no reason to collude with Britain and France. The balance of power was on Israel's side. A collusion with those two powers would reveal Israel to be their dependant, an entirely unsatisfactory state of affairs for the new state.

There was, however, keen fear of collusion in the Egyptian Military High Command. In its report of September 1956 on the 'Military Situation in the Eastern Mediterranean', the Command estimated as follows:

(*a*) Britain and France will enjoy a great military advantage against Egypt. It is probable that any attack will be directed first to seize Alexandria thus diverting our defences to the west of the Nile preparatory to the main counter-attack against the Canal Zone. The interval between the two successive attacks will be short.

(*b*) Air raids will be launched to paralyse our air force and as preparation for the landings.

(*c*) Land forces from Libya and Malta will seize Alexandria harbour; airborne troops from Cyprus will capture the Canal airports; and follow-up echelons will take the Canal Zone.

(*d*) An air attack to seize some of our forward bases up to El-Arish and to isolate the Gaza Strip is probable.

The High Command's directives were:

(*a*) The enemy must be prevented from seizing the Canal Zone.
(*b*) Measures to control Bir-Audib on the Red Sea must be taken to prevent enemy landings and advances on Cairo.
(*c*) Enemy troops landing in Port Said must be prevented from advancing south or seizing Ismailia.
(*d*) The Canal must be blocked by demolitions. H—hour for execution will be the start of any enemy landings in the Canal Zone.

Orders were given to reinforce the National Guard troops in the Delta, and plans to defend Cairo, Port Said, and Alexandria were prepared.

CONSIDERATION OF LOCAL, REGIONAL, AND INTERNATIONAL REACTIONS

Nasser had an exceptional feeling for his people's aspirations. He believed that those who carry responsibility for change, either revolutionary or ordinary, are merely individuals in the forefront who feel and respond to their people's demands and aspirations. The failure to fulfil this sacred obligation gives others the right to replace them. Nasser was a charismatic leader who commanded the full confidence of his people. The planners of the aggression failed to consider this important fact. When they declared that their object was not to harm the people, but to liquidate Nasser and his administration, this declaration had just the reverse of the intended effect. The people rallied round Nasser's leadership and established a united front against the invaders. When Nasser announced from the Al-Azhar Mosque— the most ancient university in the world—his rejection of the ultimatum and his determination to fight, millions of people in cities, villages, schools, and factories joined him to resist invasion. Thousands of small arms were distributed without registration throughout the country. All Egyptians followed their leader in their great battle. When the authorities ordered the return of the weapons at the end of the fighting, ninety-nine per cent were handed back without hesitation.

Public sentiment throughout the Arab world was already mobilized as a result of the successive confrontations. The campaign against the British base in the Canal Zone, the resistance to the Baghdad Pact, the Czech arms deal, the nationalization of the Suez Canal Company—all these were local confrontations that drew Arabs together in common cause. The pressure of public sentiment forced Arab leaders to back Egypt's position without hesitation, even though some may have secretly harboured second thoughts. The Baghdad Pact cracked, and the Commonwealth was nearly split. The oil pipeline from the Gulf to the Mediterranean was cut. Arab unions boycotted the aggressors in harbours and airports.

Nasser assumed that there was strategic agreement between the United States and Britain on what to do against him and his administration, but he also knew that they differed over methods. Their aim was to force him to 'disgorge' the Canal by means ranging from strangling to shooting; but he also believed that the United States aspired to replace Britain and France in the region, and he sought to exploit these rivalries.

The Russians played an important part in his planning. Would they follow their usual cautious line, or would they seize the opportunity to exploit the result of the crisis arising from the Czech arms deal? Nasser played his cards with caution because he appreciated the danger from taking a false step. He preferred to let the Russians take the initiative. This came on 6 November 1956, when Bulganin sent his ultimatum to the three capitals and a separate message to President Eisenhower. Undoubtedly the ultimatum had its positive effect, but Nasser remained silent. He encouraged the United Nations to take action while he sought support from developing countries throughout the world. Within a few days, the aggressors found themselves isolated and condemned.

CONCLUSIONS AND PERSPECTIVES

The Suez crisis of 1956 was a turning-point in global history that marked the emergence of a new international order. Britain and France, their empires in an advanced state of decline, virtually handed over leadership in the Middle East and other regions to the United States. As the position of the Soviet Union was enhanced, there thus began the competition for influence in the Third World between the two superpowers.

It was clear from an Egyptian vantage-point that a nuclear confrontation was impossible. If the Suez crisis of 1956 was the moment of this awareness, the Cuban missile crisis of 1961 demonstrated its certainty. If the 1956 experience proved anything, it was that force as a means of international policy could not be abolished. Rather, the global struggle would provide new opportunities for *coups d'état*, economic and psychological pressure, destruction from within, and regional confrontation by proxy.

On the regional level, the Suez crisis resulted in a new regional order because the nationalization of the Suez Canal Company proved an Egyptian administration capable of managing and even overseeing increasing traffic through the Canal. This was the last link in the chain that included the removal of the British base, the termination of the 1954 agreement, the confiscation of storage in the base, the beginning of the High Dam, the breaking of the monopoly of arms transfer, and the complete withdrawal of the aggressors. Rather than liquidate Nasser's regime as the aggressors had desired, these successes raised his dignity not only in the region but also throughout the Third World. The national movements in Africa, Asia, and Latin America were encouraged by the Egyptian example.

The flames of Arab unity blazed among the Arab people and brought the Syrian–Egyptian union of 1958. At the same time, however, the Arab world divided into revolutionary and conservative camps. Only Palestine remained a source of Arab unity. Israel attached itself to the rising star of the United States. With full American assistance, Israel became the proxy for the United States in the Middle East.

It is dangerous to mix terrorism with genuine nationalist movements. If terrorism is only meant to counter other terrorism, where will the escalation end? Regional stability can be achieved only if all participants can reach just and accurate answers to the following questions.

What is meant by security? Is justice based on right or might? Is there a balance of interest as well as of power? Is legitimacy established in the context of historic right or forced changes? Can self-determination be provided without people living on their own land? Nasser spent all his life, and fought all his battles, to get the right and just answers to those questions.

9

India, the Crisis, and the Non-Aligned Nations

SARVEPALLI GOPAL

THE Suez crisis was the first major international test of non-alignment. Elaborated by the leaders of the newly independent countries of Asia after the Second World War as the policy best suited to them from the viewpoints of both principle and advantage, it had worked to their satisfaction in keeping them out of the Cold War as well as making the best of it. Non-alignment had even, in the hands of its leading practitioner, Jawaharlal Nehru of India, been of some use to the world in maintaining a line of communication to the People's Republic of China and in reducing tensions in Korea and Indo-China. But Suez in 1956, involving one of themselves in collision with a Western power and bringing in the United States and the Soviet Union, raised more basic and immediate issues. This brought the non-aligned nations on to the centre stage in world affairs; but this importance brought with it dangers.

The crisis came to them without warning. While generally sympathetic to the Arab cause, Nehru had taken care not to involve India too deeply in the dispute with Israel. He agreed with reluctance to the Arab demand that no invitation to the Bandung Conference of Asian and African nations be sent to Israel,[1] and accepted that this was an illogical surrender to Arab susceptibility.[2] At Brioni, where Tito, Nehru, and Nasser met in July 1956, an informal message was received from Ben-Gurion saying that Israel had erred in leaning on the Western powers and the Israelis now realized more than ever that they belonged to Asia and must look to Asia.[3] The friendliness of this initiative suggested that there was no near prospect of war in western Asia, and the Arab–Israeli problem was discussed by the three leaders of non-alignment in passing and in very general terms. On the flight back from Brioni to Cairo Nasser showed Nehru the text as it was being

---

[1] Nehru's note, 19 Dec. 1954, Nehru Papers.
[2] Nehru's telegram to Indian missions, 4 Jan. 1955, Ministry of External Affairs, New Delhi (hereafter MEA files).   [3] Nehru's note, 9 Sept. 1958, Nehru Papers.

broadcast of Dulles's speech announcing the withdrawal of American assistance for building the Aswan Dam; and Nehru found the speech insulting in tone: 'These people, how arrogant they are.'[4] Nasser's own reaction at this stage, and during Nehru's two days in Cairo, was that he would abandon the Aswan Dam project; and Nehru approved. It seemed wiser to distribute Egypt's resources among a large number of small projects yielding quick results rather than to concentrate on one major scheme which would not begin to function for at least another ten years and would vest any country providing the bulk of assistance with a commanding control of the Egyptian economy. In the conversations Nehru had with Nasser, the Suez Canal was not even mentioned.

The announcement by Nasser of the nationalization of the Canal therefore came to Nehru as an unpleasant surprise. He liked Nasser as a person but, judging by his pamphlet *The Philosophy of Revolution*, did not think highly of his intellectual capacity; and now he felt that Nasser had acted in anger and in haste. Egypt had the right to nationalize the Canal and had done well to give an assurance that the Canal would continue as an open international waterway. But the language was intemperate and even warmongering. Nasser seemed to Nehru to be undertaking more than he could manage and allowing himself to be pushed by extremist elements. In contrast, at this time Nehru was much impressed by Eden, who was passing through a phase of what Pineau described as 'une sorte de Nehru brittanique, en plus fragile'. Nehru appreciated Eden's role at the Geneva Conference on Indo-China; they had got on well when Eden visited Delhi in the spring of 1955 on the eve of becoming Prime Minister; and the next year Krishna Menon reported after meeting Eden that there had been a real change in his views on the Soviet Union and his mind was now exercised about peace initiatives and competition in trade.[5] At the Conference of Commonwealth Prime Ministers in July, Eden spoke of changes of outlook and of direction in Soviet policy even if without any fundamental change of heart and referred to the new opportunities provided by a new element of flexibility in the internal situation in the Soviet Union.[6] The whole approach was highly acceptable to Nehru, who was confirmed in his opinion of Eden by a message from Moscow that Bulganin and Khrushchev were very appreciative of Eden after their meetings in London and had been impressed by his friendliness and readiness to listen to views different from his own.[7]

[4] M. H. Heikal, *Nasser: The Cairo Documents* (New York, 1973), pp. 67–8.

[5] Krishna Menon's telegram from London to Nehru, 8 June 1956, MEA files.

[6] Record of Eden's remarks at Conference of Commonwealth Prime Ministers, 4 July 1956, MEA files.

[7] Telegram of Indian Ambassador in Moscow to Nehru in London, 10 July 1956, Nehru Papers.

So, when the crisis broke, Nehru decided to make no public comment and to resist being swept away by blind anti-imperialist emotion. He would not support Nasser uncritically for, however legitimate the nationalization of the Canal, it had been done in a manner which would have far-reaching consequences and could add to international tensions. The non-aligned countries did not form a bloc, and mutual support could not be taken for granted. Britain and many other countries greatly resented the action; and Nehru hoped that, as in 1953, he would be able to provide an emollient influence in Anglo-Egyptian relations. He was content, therefore, for the time being with informing the major powers, Yugoslavia, and the Colombo powers[8] that he had had no previous information that Nasser had decided to nationalize the Canal. He sought Tito's views; but other non-aligned governments he intended only to keep informed. Nehru was instinctively inclined to play a lone hand, and in this crisis India's membership of the Commonwealth and close relations with Britain provided added justification for this attitude.

The deliberate silence and refusal to commit India to either side received Tito's approval. He, like Nehru, believed that Nasser's action had been precipitate, and he directed the Yugoslav press, which had supported Egypt enthusiastically, to adopt a more cautious attitude. 'In my opinion, the whole issue, although very serious, is not so dramatic as some quarters want to present. The main thing now is not to be nervous. I believe that it is possible to act towards both sides with a quietening effect.' So he advised Nasser to be moderate and conciliatory and suggested that Nehru, in like manner, try to calm down bellicose sentiments in Britain.[9] Certainly Nehru's failure to react immediately had misled official opinion in that country. Eden thought it possible that Nehru might be willing to accept action against Egypt,[10] and Lord Home (then Commonwealth Secretary) asked Vijaya-lakshmi, the Indian High Commissioner, if India would be interested in a conference to discuss international control of the Canal and whether, in case a plan emerged, India would be prepared, in the final analysis, to enforce implementation.[11] This obliged Nehru to reveal his mind. He informed Home that what was of importance was to ensure the continuance of the Canal as an open international highway, and an agreement to this effect should not be difficult as Nasser had publicly committed himself to it. Any attempt to use force to secure this was,

[8] India, Burma, Sri Lanka, Pakistan, and Indonesia were known as the Colombo powers because their Prime Ministers had first met at Colombo in 1954 and agreed to keep in regular touch.

[9] Tito to Nehru, 2 Aug. 1956, MEA files.

[10] I. McDonald, *A Man of the Times* (London, 1976), p. 144.

[11] Vijayalakshmi to Nehru, reporting conversation with Home, 1 Aug. 1956, Nehru Papers.

however, likely to defeat its own purpose and create widespread resentment in Asia.[12] The same day he wrote to Nasser in terms not brimming over with fraternal solidarity. He knew that his not giving prompt and public support to Egypt had bewildered opinion in that country as well as in the whole Arab world, where popular enthusiasm, whatever the attitudes of the governments, for Nasser's defiance of the Western powers had been general. Even now Nehru claimed to write, not as the head of a fellow anti-colonial, non-aligned country, but as the representative of a major user of the Canal and one interested in a friendly settlement. Aware that Britain was thinking of convening a conference, he suggested that Nasser himself take the initiative and call together, on the basis of Egypt's sovereignty, all those interested in the international aspects of the Canal. His own attitude he described as governed by a desire for a peaceful settlement and by due adherence to friendships and international usage.[13]

'In this letter', writes Mohamed Heikal, 'it was Nehru the lawyer, the cautious elder statesman who was speaking.' It was thought that Nehru was annoyed because he had not been given prior warning of the decision to nationalize; but if, at the time of his visit to Cairo, no decision had been made, then the speed with which the decision had been later taken showed irresponsibility.[14] But Nehru's position was not a result of pique, but was adopted in accordance with the strict canons of non-alignment, uninfluenced by emotional sympathy, having equal regard for India's friendship with Egypt and with Britain, and motivated by concern for the interests of both.

Nasser was worried by Nehru's clear warning that Egypt could not, in a crisis of her own making, take India's support for granted. It was not just that Nasser missed the comfort of India's backing; as important as was the fact that many non-aligned countries could be expected to follow India's lead. When the British government sent out invitations to sixteen countries for a conference in London of major users of the Canal, Sri Lanka and Indonesia sought India's guidance as to the reply that should be given. Nasser wrote to Nehru that Egypt would not attend a conference the result of which was a foregone conclusion. An international authority for the Canal would be sought to be imposed, making the whole effort a fresh colonial move against a 'comparatively weak and an oriental people'. So he appealed to Nehru that India should also refuse to attend and suggested as a counter-proposal the placing of all international waterways under the jurisdiction of the United Nations. Egypt would also be willing to execute a fresh treaty

---

[12] Nehru to Vijayalakshmi, with message to Home, 2 Aug. 1956, Nehru Papers.
[13] Nehru to Nasser, 2 Aug. 1956, MEA files.
[14] M. H. Heikal, *Cutting the Lion's Tail* (London, 1986), pp. 135–7.

with all concerned nations guaranteeing again the security of the Suez Canal and freedom of navigation; and such a treaty could be registered with the United Nations.[15]

Nehru was not impressed, particularly after he heard that the waterways Nasser had in mind were the Panama Canal, the Dardanelles, the Straits of Gibraltar, and the Gulf of Aden;[16] for the countries concerned with these would obviously not agree to multilateral discussions at the United Nations, and this deprived Nasser's proposal of any touch of reality. So Nehru was inclined to consider participation in the London conference. Now that Egypt had secured physical control of the Canal, attention should be given to the grievances of Britain and France, irrespective of their legitimacy. The demands of the two sides were not contradictory and the crisis could be settled by negotiation provided that rigid attitudes did not result in further unilateral decisions. There was scope for some institutional arrangements which did not violate the sovereignty of Egypt but which yet conformed to international requirements and commitments and were sufficient to create confidence. It was in India's own national interest that arrangements in regard to the Canal should be such as to secure general acceptance.

Nehru, therefore, followed his lone path. He rejected suggestions that the Colombo powers should meet along with Egypt or even on their own. He did not request, as desired by Syria, that the conference should meet somewhere other than in London; but he did point out to Eden that the list of invitees was too restricted. Burma, Yugoslavia, Saudi Arabia, and Poland should have been asked. He also advised against restricting the conference to consideration only of an international authority to manage the Canal. Attempts to impose a solution on Egypt would lead to armed conflict and powerful reactions all over Asia and large parts of Africa. If the conference was to have positive results, the whole approach would have to be different.[17] He then wrote to Nasser that if India participated it would be not in order to weaken Egypt's position but to work for conciliatory approaches and to prevent the conference from becoming a barrier to settlement. 'We wish', he added, in what was clearly a rebuke, 'to emphasize these aspects and not to support any unilateral action taken by one nation or any group of nations.' Then, in response to Nasser's request for advice, he suggested that Nasser should reply to the British government expressing surprise at the convening of a conference without reference

[15] Nasser to Nehru, 4 Aug. 1956, MEA files.

[16] Egyptian Ambassador's conversation with Indian High Commissioner in Pakistan, 4 Aug. 1956, reported in telegram of same date, MEA files.

[17] Nehru to Eden, 4 and 5 Aug. 1956, MEA files.

to Egypt but affirming Egypt's willingness to attend if there was an agreed list of invitees and no prior conditions and commitments. While Egypt could not accept any challenge to her sovereignty, she would be prepared to execute a fresh agreement which would guarantee freedom of navigation. As he himself had been disillusioned by the developments at the United Nations on the Kashmir issue, Nehru advised Nasser against any reference to that organization.[18]

Nasser rejected this advice. He was not prepared under any circumstances to participate in a conference convened by Britain. This deprived the London conference of the possibility of reaching firm decisions, for nothing could be settled in Egypt's absence. Nehru was also informed that the list of invitees could not be expanded. Yet, with an assurance from Eden that participation need not imply acceptance of the British demand for an international authority,[19] Nehru decided to send a delegation with Krishna Menon as its leader.[20] If nothing else, attendance could prove a check on the policy of intimidation and, by enabling a more balanced approach than was possible if only the Western nations discussed the issue, prepare the ground for another conference with which Egypt could be associated.[21] In this effort he hoped for assistance from the United States.[22] But he did not overestimate the prospect of success. 'This is far the most difficult and dangerous situation in international affairs we have faced since independence. I do not think we can do very much, but it is just possible that we might stop the rot. Probably we shall end by displeasing our friends on both sides.'[23]

To assure Britain that India was not Egypt's unhesitating champion and, provided that she refrained from the use or display of force, India would do her best for her, Nehru discouraged the Egyptian government from adopting the rupee as the medium of exchange for her trade with third countries and secured disallowance of discussion in the lower house of Parliament of a private member's motion advocating India's withdrawal from the Commonwealth. Eden himself seems to have been confident of Nehru's support, for he rejected Pearson's suggestion that the Suez crisis be discussed by the NATO Council before the meeting of the London conference, because this might antagonize and alienate Nehru.[24] Such friendliness to Britain made Egypt distrustful—and with some justification, for the Indian Ambassador in Cairo was

---

[18] Nehru to Nasser, 5 Aug. 1956, MEA files.
[19] Eden to Nehru, 7 Aug. 1956, ibid.
[20] Nehru's statement in the Lok Sabha (House of the People), 8 Aug. 1956.
[21] Nehru to Prime Minister of Indonesia, 6 and 7 Aug. 1956, MEA files.
[22] Message to Dulles through Indian Embassy in Washington, 8 Aug. 1956, ibid.
[23] Nehru to C. Rajagopalachari, 10 Aug. 1956, Nehru papers.
[24] L. B. Pearson, *Memoirs*, vol. ii: 1948–57 (London, 1974), p. 229.

toying with the idea of an international authority excluding the great powers and perhaps presided over by Egypt.[25] To deal with these suspicions, Nehru directed Krishna Menon to break his journey in Cairo on his way to London. But Menon was the wrong man for this. He patronized Nasser, whom he described later to Selwyn Lloyd as politically a beginner with a great deal to learn, but gaining experience,[26] and started on the course since described by Heikal which prevailed right through the crisis, of being unable to get on with Egyptian officials. To Nehru Menon reported that, while he found Nasser somewhat mellowed and appearing to realize that perhaps he had been precipitate, he was unyielding on such issues as international control.[27] Menon's stance and tone were certainly not calculated to change this position.

In London Menon and his team assured the British government that India did not approve of Nasser's manner of nationalizing the Canal and agreed fully that the Canal should be placed under some form of international control. Informed that the British government was prepared to have recourse to force in the last resort, they advised Britain not to say so much and so often that she had it in mind, for Indian public opinion was well ahead of the Indian government and took a far less balanced view.[28] At the conference Menon sought to persuade the Western powers to negotiate with Egypt on the basis of her sovereignty, and was embarrassed by the Soviet Union taking the same line.[29] His compromise formula, tabled on 20 August, provided for a review of the 1888 Convention, particularly incorporating clauses regarding just tolls and maintenance, a conference of all signatories of the 1888 Convention and all user nations, association of international user interests with the Egyptian corporation for the Canal without prejudice to Egyptian ownership, a consultative body of user interests, and transmission by Egypt to the United Nations of the annual reports of the Egyptian corporation. Minority representation on the Egyptian corporation and a consultative body of user interests appeared inadequate to Britain and France and an appeasement of Nasser; but the formula as a whole was disliked by Egypt. So far from the Indian delegation virtually functioning, as Eden and Home later alleged,[30] as

[25] See telegram from British Embassy in Cairo to Foreign Office, 7 Aug. 1956, FO 371/119091. I am grateful to Professor Roger Louis for copies of these documents. (The following abbreviations are used for records at the Public Record Office, London: FO (Foreign Office); PREM (Prime Minister's Office).)

[26] Record of Selwyn Lloyd's conversation with Menon, 15 Aug. 1956, FO 800/739.

[27] Krishna Menon's telegram to Nehru, 15 Aug. 1956, MEA files.

[28] N. R. Pillai's conversations with Sir G. Laithwaite, 14 Aug., and Sir N. Brook, 15 Aug. 1956, PREM 11/1144; Krishna Menon's conversation with Selwyn Lloyd, 15 Aug. 1956, FO 800/739.

[29] Menon's second telegram to Nehru, 15 Aug. 1956, MEA files.

[30] Anthony Eden, *Full Circle* (London, 1961), p. 444; Lord Home, *The Way the Wind Blows* (London, 1976), p. 140.

Egypt's spokesman and egging on Nasser, at the time Krishna Menon complained that the Egyptian government gave him no room for manœuvre and pressed it to counter the growing impression that India had no influence in Cairo.[31] But Nasser could not be persuaded. Nehru was not surprised, and while urging Nasser to be a little more flexible and enable a revised proposal to be put forward,[32] he also directed Menon to formulate a 'more constructive' scheme,[33] implying that the earlier formula leant further to the British side than he himself would have wished. This lack of close accord between India and Egypt made it easier for the majority at the London conference to approve the Dulles plan for an international board of control. Only Indonesia and Sri Lanka, apart from the Soviet Union, sided with India; Ethiopia, Turkey, Iran and Pakistan went along with the Western powers, although Pakistan, bearing in mind public opinion at home and in other Islamic countries, preferred to play a subdued role. Menon's suggestion that he walk out of the conference was overruled by the Prime Minister,[34] who had at no time attached much significance to a conference without Egypt. But he was unwilling to advise Nasser, as requested by Eden, to consider the Dulles plan. He told Malcolm MacDonald, the British High Commissioner, that to him it was unthinkable to impose a solution on Egypt and it was politically impossible for Nasser to undo the act of nationalization. The first step was to get Egypt to negotiate and then, in the course of negotiations, to secure a reasonable settlement. The London declaration did not make such steps possible.[35]

The London conference, however, had at least, in Nehru's view, made any resort to force very unlikely, though, with neither the declaration nor the Menon proposals being generally acceptable, the deadlock continued. India, therefore, as the leading non-aligned country on the stage, obviously had to think again. MacDonald saw this: 'I feel that he [Nehru] is doing a lot of hard thinking and perhaps some re-thinking.' But it was a thankless task. Along with the British government's efforts to recruit India's help to attain a settlement to their liking, there was suspicion of her future objectives rather than appreciation of her present goodwill. 'I am convinced that we are finished if the Middle East goes and Russia and India and China rule

---

[31] Menon's telegrams from London to Indian Ambassador in Cairo, 20 Aug. and to Nehru, 21 Aug. 1956, MEA files.

[32] Nehru's telegram to Indian Ambassador in Cairo, 21 Aug. 1956, ibid.

[33] Nehru's telegram to Menon, 21 Aug. 1956, ibid.

[34] Menon's telegram to Nehru, 22 Aug., and Nehru's reply, 23 Aug. 1956, ibid.

[35] Telegram of British High Commissioner in Delhi after meeting with Nehru, 22 Aug. 1956, FO 371/119168.

from Africa to the Pacific.'[36] As for Egypt, she too was still chary of India.[37] So Nehru decided prudently to await developments. On 6 September, as the Menzies mission moved to its predestined end and the threats by Britain and France to use force became more open, Nasser wrote that he intended to appeal to the Security Council as well as offer to negotiate regarding freedom of navigation, tolls, operations, and management; and he requested Nehru to use his influence to secure favourable responses and start immediate discussions on the basis of safeguarding the legitimate concerns of user interests without acceptance of international control.[38] Nehru was willing to help. He again dissuaded Nasser from approaching the United Nations and suggested that the offer to negotiate be drafted in very general terms, opening the door for talks but making no specific proposals.[39] This was also in line with Tito's thinking. He felt that Egypt was in a difficult and dangerous position and Nasser should move cautiously; a peaceful settlement was still possible but the intentions of Britain and France were uncertain.[40]

On 10 September the Egyptian government announced, as advised by Nehru, their keenness for a peaceful solution without detriment to their country's sovereignty and dignity and suggested as an immediate step the formation of a negotiating body representative of all views among the user nations. Nehru followed this up with a very friendly letter to Eden, arguing that the Egyptian memorandum provided a chance to establish some common ground from which a settlement on the points of difference could emerge. 'I need hardly assure you of my goodwill or of my awareness of your feelings and difficulties.'[41] He also wrote in similar terms to Eisenhower, from whom he expected much,[42] for by now the United States had rejected the possible use of force, and Nehru thought that 'a harmony of peace' had been reached between India and the United States.[43]

The buoyant hopes which Nehru conveyed to Burma, Sri Lanka, Indonesia, and Yugoslavia were dissolved by Eden's speech on 12 September, announcing the formation of a Suez Canal association which would virtually take over the operational control of the Canal and adding that other steps in assertion of British rights were being

---

[36] Home to Eden, 24 Aug. 1956, quoted by P. Hennessy, 'Reopening the wounds of the end of Empire', *The Listener*, 5 Feb. 1987.
[37] Menon's telegram to Nehru from Cairo, 31 Aug. 1956, MEA files.
[38] Nasser to Nehru, 6 Sept. 1956, ibid.
[39] Nehru's message to Nasser, 7 Sept., and Nasser to Nehru, 8 Sept. 1956, ibid.
[40] Telegram of Indian Ambassador in Belgrade after interview.
[41] Nehru to Eden, 11 Sept. 1956, MEA files.
[42] Nehru to Eisenhower, 11 Sept. 1956, ibid.
[43] Nehru to Eisenhower, 7 Sept. 1956, ibid.

contemplated. Such threats of unilateral actions leading to imposed decisions drove Nehru to public criticism of the British government;[44] and he advised Nasser that the time had come to consider a reference to the Security Council, for this would at least delay a crisis.[45] But he had great faith in British common sense and could not believe that any British Prime Minister, let alone Eden, would use force on such an issue;[46] and he again appealed to Eden and to Lloyd not to turn their backs on negotiations. If necessary, an emergency meeting of Commonwealth Prime Ministers should be called.[47] He also requested Dulles to exercise the effective role of the United States.[48] But war had come within the realm of possibility, and he directed the various ministries in Delhi to plan the measures which would be required in the event of hostilities.[49]

Was there anything more that the non-aligned nations could do at this stage? It seemed pointless for the Prime Ministers of the Colombo powers to meet; by now Pakistan was the odd man out, and no purpose would be served by the four others repeating jointly what they had been saying separately. But Nehru continued trying to keep Egypt and the Western powers in touch, at least informally, with each other. The idea of a users' association was a one-sided affair which obviously could not lead to negotiations; but Eden would go no further and ruled out the suggestion of a meeting of Commonwealth Prime Ministers. 'In any event we will maintain close touch with Commonwealth Governments by every means.'[50] The attitude of Dulles was as unhelpful. He recognized Egypt's legal title to the Canal but asserted that an international right of way had been created across her territory. No international regime that did not have the backing of the United Nations would be imposed forcibly on Egypt; but the freedom of navigation had to be protected. The United Nations could deal with overt violations and the users' association with covert ones.[51] Yet, as the days passed, India and Yugoslavia became more optimistic. The threat of war seemed to be receding a little,[52] giving time for fresh efforts by the non-aligned mediators.

The Soviet government made various suggestions: a reference by

[44] Speech in the Lok Sabha, 13 Sept. 1956.

[45] Nehru to Nasser, 13 Sept. 1956, MEA files.

[46] See Krishna Menon's accounts of his discussions with Nehru at this time, M. Brecher, *India and World Politics* (London, 1968), p. 65.

[47] Nehru to Eden and to Lloyd, 14 Sept. 1956, MEA files.

[48] Nehru to Dulles, 14 Sept. 1956, ibid.

[49] Nehru's minute for the Cabinet, 14 Sept. 1956, Nehru Papers.

[50] Eden to Nehru, 16 Sept. 1956, MEA files.

[51] Dulles to Nehru, 16 Sept. 1956, ibid.

[52] Nehru to chief ministers, 20 Sept. 1956, Nehru papers; E. Kardelj in conversation with Indian Ambassador in Belgrade, 22 Sept. 1956, MEA files.

Egypt to the Security Council leading to the setting up of a group of six countries—Egypt, Britain, France, India, the Soviet Union, and the United States—to explore avenues of negotiation; the convening of a conference of the Bandung countries; a major international conference.[53] Nehru was for an immediate reference to the Security Council; the other suggestions could be considered later. But the Egyptian government only informed the Security Council and did not make a complaint before it. Nor was it prepared to formulate any constructive proposal.[54] Perhaps the personal dislike of Menon on the part of Egyptian officials, of which Nehru was unaware, contributed to these reactions; and Nasser and his advisers may also have been disappointed by India's continued lack of enthusiasm for their cause. The latest evidence of this was Nehru's refusal to sanction the supply to Egypt of bren-guns and spare barrels and fuses for mortar bombs: 'For us to supply arms to the Egyptian government at this stage would naturally be greatly resented by the United Kingdom and other Western governments and make them feel that we are supporting Egypt one hundred per cent in peace and war. Our capacity for playing a mediatory role would disappear.'[55] Also, finding that both Nasser and he were due to visit Saudi Arabia, he asked Nasser not to stay on in Riyadh to meet him as this would suggest ganging up.[56]

A new phase of the crisis began on 23 September, with Britain and France asking the Security Council to consider the matter and Egypt filing a counter-complaint the next day. Nehru did not expect the Security Council to achieve positive results but at least it could provide an arena for negotiations. Yugoslavia, which was at this time the only non-aligned country to be an elected member of the Council, helped, at the meeting on 26 September, to secure an adjournment; and Menon was busy again in Cairo and London trying to work out a formula acceptable to both sides. His plan was an amplification of his earlier proposal, with Egypt entering into an agreement for co-operation with a users' association and regular joint sessions of the Egyptian Board and the users' association to discuss all matters in which users were concerned. Egypt would also agree to appoint United Nations advisers in the three main sectors of operations. To make this plan more acceptable to Britain, Menon secured Nasser's assent to permit any question about the 1888 Convention, and particularly the right of Israeli ships to go through the Canal, to be referred to the World Court.[57] Even so, the British government was not satisfied with

---

[53] Nehru to Menon in Cairo, reporting talk with Soviet Ambassador, 17 Sept. 1956, ibid.
[54] Menon to Nehru, 19 Sept. 1956, ibid.
[55] Nehru's note to Foreign Secretary, 17 Sept. 1956, Nehru Papers.
[56] Nehru's telegram to Indian Ambassador in Cairo, 21 Sept. 1956, MEA files.
[57] Brecher, *India and World Politics*, p. 68.

this formula, especially as it lacked any clause providing a means of enforcement.[58] Yet Menon reported to Nehru that he thought he had persuaded Eden and Lloyd to accept these proposals and Nasser should now be pressed to do the same. 'For your information only we have got somewhere. If we can get over one or two smaller hurdles in Cairo, which should be possible with the weight of your backing, we would have turned the corner. Subsequent stages are largely methodological problems.'[59]

Such a misapprehension of the British attitude was soon corrected by Eden himself. He told Nehru that Menon had put some hypothetical questions and the British government could not commit itself by answering these questions. It still stood by its earlier insistence on international control, while Menon's proposals left Egypt in unfettered grasp of the Canal and provided no means of enforcing whatever arrangements might be reached.[60] But as the British government was willing to consider alternatives to the idea of a users' association as the basis of negotiation, Nehru thought there was still room for media-tion.[61] Menon went even further and told Nasser, without showing him the text, that Britain had accepted his proposals with the addition of a provision for arbitration if differences arose over tolls or discrimination against particular countries. Nasser was willing to accept this amend-ment and assumed that the plan which Menon would announce at the United Nations would reflect the Egyptian viewpoint.[62]

Menon's attempts to get his formula through by suggesting, without authority, to each side that the other would accept it might have led to confusion but for the fact that for the first time Egypt and Britain were directly confronting each other at New York under the sponsorship of Hammarskjöld; and one point on which all of them (plus the Soviet representative) seem to have been agreed was a dislike of Menon and his activities. The non-aligned countries were now not at the centre of the picture. Britain, France and Egypt reached an agreement on principles whereby, according to Menon, Egypt had given in far more than she had ever led India to understand she would, and on points which on the face of it were vital to her sovereignty.[63] Dulles thought that this was the best opportunity that they had had or perhaps ever would have for arriving peacefully at a reasonable and honourable

[58] Records of conversations of Lloyd and of Eden (on telephone) with Menon, 28 Sept. 1956, PREM 11/1102.
[59] Menon's telegram from London to Nehru, 29 Sept. 1956, MEA files.
[60] Nehru's note on interview with British High Commissioner, 1 Oct. 1956, ibid.
[61] Nehru to Eden, 4 Oct. 1956, ibid.
[62] Nasser to Fawzi in New York, 7 Oct. 1956, Heikal, *Cutting the Lion's Tail*, p. 165.
[63] Menon's telegram from New York to Nehru, 14 Oct. 1956, MEA files.

solution.[64] Nehru too was confident that the problem had definitely reached a negotiating stage and it would be difficult to go back on this.[65]

Eden, however, was working out other plans. The secret arrangements with Israel necessitated a request for postponement of further exploratory talks with Egypt, scheduled to begin on 29 October. Nehru was as startled as most others by the Israeli attack and the Anglo-French ultimatum. With the invasion of Egypt, a balancing act was no longer possible. Nehru asked Yugoslavia and the Bandung countries to join him in public condemnation of the aggressors, assured Nasser of his full support, called on Hammarskjöld to ensure that the procedures of the United Nations were swifter than those of invasion and aggression, and urged the United States to intervene. 'I cannot imagine a worse case of aggression. . . . The whole future of the relations between Europe and Asia hangs in the balance.'[66] Towards Britain he remained 'not unfriendly and expressed his views more in sorrow than in anger';[67] but he did not conceal the strength of his feelings and his deep regret that Britain, with her record of liberal policies, should now have become again the symbol of colonialism. 'Unless these wrong courses are halted the future appears to me to be dark indeed.'[68]

Nehru's objectives at this point were to help Nasser safeguard the sovereignty of Egypt, obtain a cease-fire and prevent the spread of military action, and save the Commonwealth. He regarded as impractical the proposal first made by the Soviet Union and then supported by Egypt and by China for a reconvening of the Bandung countries;[69] but he was willing to have a meeting of the Colombo powers, as desired by Indonesia, if the other Prime Ministers could come to Delhi. Bandaranaike of Sri Lanka could not come immediately, and the position of Pakistan was ambivalent. She supported Nasser publicly and was concerned about the effect of the aggression on the Baghdad Pact; but her ministers resented Egypt's links with India and agreed privately with Britain that no satisfactory solution of the Suez crisis was possible without the use of force.[70] In the event, the Colombo powers met (without Pakistan) in Delhi on 14 November after the

[64] Dulles to Nehru, 18 Oct. 1956, ibid.
[65] Nehru at a press conference, 25 Oct. 1956, *The Hindu* (Madras), 26 Oct. 1956.
[66] Nehru to Dulles, 31 Oct. 1956, MEA files.
[67] Report of British High Commissioner after interview with Nehru, 31 Oct. 1956, FO 371/121785.
[68] Nehru to Eden, 1 Nov. 1956, MEA files.
[69] Bulganin to Nehru, 2 Nov. 1956, and Nehru's reply of same date; Indian Foreign Secretary to chargé d'affaires in Cairo, 2 Nov. 1956; Zhou Enlai's message to Nehru, 3 Nov. 1956, MEA files.
[70] Feroze Noon, Foreign Minister of Pakistan to British High Commissioner in Karachi, 31 Oct. 1956, FO 371/121788; Heikal, *Cutting the Lion's Tail*, p. 219.

fighting was over and reiterated general principles which they had all
affirmed earlier individually.

Rather than build up an Afro-Asian or even a regional bloc, Nehru
preferred to act through a special session of the General Assembly of
the United Nations. He supported the idea, which was acceptable to
Egypt, of a contingent from the United States to re-establish armistice
lines between Israel and Egypt and of an observer team manned by
Czechoslovakia, Canada, and India. An international police force
would be acceptable on the old Arab–Israeli armistice line for a
temporary period but not in the Suez Canal area or anywhere else in
Egypt. When the United Nations set up an emergency force, he was
prepared for India to participate only if this were desired by the
Egyptian government.[71]

Then came the Soviet proposal for a joint Soviet–American military
effort to stop the fighting, coupled with the threat to use rockets. The
British Ambassador in Moscow, who did not dismiss the threat as an
empty one, advised the Foreign Office to mobilize the United States
and Nehru to warn the Soviet Union of the danger of such action.[72]
But Nehru, even without prompting, appealed to Bulganin not to take
any steps which might lead to a general war but to agree to act through
the United Nations.[73] He also welcomed the Swiss proposal of a
meeting of the heads of government of the United States, the Soviet
Union, Britain, and France, and was prepared to attend if desired.[74]

The need for such a meeting dissolved with the British acceptance of
a cease-fire. Home now requested Nehru to 'come in heavily and assist
in bringing about a speedy settlement'.[75] Nehru's relations with Nasser
at this time were cordial, but this was not reflected in the attitude of the
Egyptian officials; and there was also sniping at India's position by
Iran, Turkey, and Pakistan. Taking the main credit for Britain's
acceptance of a cease-fire, they criticized India for not withdrawing
from the Commonwealth and charged her with weakening Egypt by
standing in the way of military action by the Soviet Union. Ali Sabry
stated Egypt's willingness to accept an international force consisting of
troops from India, Greece, and Colombia—and no one else.[76] But on
12 November Fawzi, the Foreign Minister, suddenly objected to
India's participation on the ground that neither close friends nor
declared foes of Egypt should be represented. The Indian Ambassador

[71] S. Gopal, *Jawaharlal Nehru*, vol. ii: *1947–1956* (London, 1979), pp. 286–7.

[72] Sir W. Hayter, *The Kremlin and the Embassy* (London, 1966), pp. 147–8.

[73] Nehru to Bulganin, 6 Nov. 1956, MEA files.

[74] Nehru to the President of the Swiss Confederation, 6 Nov. 1956, ibid.

[75] Home to Indian Deputy High Commissioner in London, reported in telegram to Foreign
Secretary, 6 Nov. 1956, ibid.

[76] Telegram from Indian Embassy in Cairo, 9 Nov. 1956, ibid.

attributed this unexpected cooling off towards India to either suspicion of the Commonwealth or the objection raised by the United States, at the instance of the British, to the inclusion of India and the exclusion of Pakistan, Canada, and New Zealand. But Nasser within hours over-ruled his Foreign Minister and explained away Fawzi's attitude as born of fears that India's presence in what many Egyptians would regard as an occupation force might damage India's popularity.[77]

Egypt now agreed to a force drawn from eight nations—India, Indonesia, Colombia, Yugoslavia, and the four Scandinavian countries. But Canada was keen to be included and sought Nehru's help in overcoming Nasser's objections.[78] Nehru argued Canada's case strongly. Despite her close links with Britain and France, she had, from the start, opposed their Suez policy and had cancelled the contract with Israel for the supply of aircraft. With Egypt's acceptance of Norway and Denmark, Canada's membership of NATO could not be held against her and insistence on her exclusion would harm Egypt's interests.[79] It was added that India would have no objection to Pakistan's participation as well. Nasser agreed at first to a Canadian ambulance corps and air supplies and Hammarskjöld was satisfied with this; but Nehru pressed for a Canadian contingent, and Nasser finally gave way. But Nehru was less successful in persuading Nasser not to deport British and French nationals and persons of Jewish origin who had not taken part in anti-Egyptian activities. 'True wisdom', remarked a disappointed Nehru,[80] 'consists in knowing how far we can go, to profit by the circumstances and to create a feeling of generosity which again results in a change in one's own favour.'

So, throughout the crisis, India, while keeping the other major non-aligned nations informed, acted mostly on her own, upholding Egypt's right to nationalize but regretting the manner in which it was done and striving to get Britain out of her predicament. The Egyptian government, especially the officials, were not always happy with India's approach; and this feeling was sometimes accentuated by Krishna Menon's personality and methods. But once Britain decided to employ force, India supported Egypt unreservedly, until Britain and France withdrew their troops without demanding any assurance regarding the Canal. 'All they want now appears to be to avoid humiliation.'[81]

---

[77] Indian Ambassador's telegram to Foreign Secretary, 12 Nov. 1956, ibid.

[78] Pearson's message to Nehru, 15 Nov. 1956, ibid.

[79] Nehru's telegram to Indian Ambassador in Cairo, 15 Nov. 1956, ibid.

[80] Nehru to Indian Ambassador in Cairo, 26 Dec. 1956, ibid.

[81] Nehru to Tito, 2 Dec. 1956, Nehru Papers.

10

Eisenhower, Dulles, and the Suez Crisis

ROBERT R. BOWIE

IN analysing the US course in the Suez Crisis in 1956, it is essential to understand the roles of Eisenhower and Dulles. The President was in full charge throughout, making the decisions on policy and its implementation. The Secretary of State, whom he greatly respected and trusted, was his principal adviser and carried out the policy. Eisenhower also drew on the advice of other members of the Cabinet, the Central Intelligence Agency (CIA) and experts, both through the National Security Council (NSC) process and smaller meetings in the Oval Office.[1]

This was the regular procedure in the whole field of foreign affairs, but Eisenhower's role was manifest in the Suez crisis. Following the nationalization of the Suez Canal Company on 26 July, Eisenhower set the initial US course while Dulles was absent for several days in Latin America (though in touch by cable and telephone); and five days after the Israeli attack on 29 October, Dulles was incapacitated by an emergency operation, with the consequence that Eisenhower took direct charge through the critical days at the United Nations. Moreover, from the outset of the crisis Eisenhower set out his views and analyses in a series of personal letters to Eden.

Of course Dulles also played a critical role. He handled the consultations, negotiations, and conferences where the various proposals and positions were discussed and worked out with the British, the French, and others. Thus he negotiated the specific form of the proposed International Board to run the Suez Canal, and developed the idea for the users' association. But at all times, even when abroad, he kept Eisenhower fully informed and obtained his approval on the significant issues.

This chapter will examine the assessments, purposes, and priorities that governed US policy-making, how they appeared to differ from

Since this chapter was first published, much of the relevant documentary material has been made available in the *Foreign Relations* series. See addendum to bibliography, p. 416.

[1] See Richard H. Immerman, 'Eisenhower and Dulles: Who Made The Decisions?', *Political Psychology*, 1: 2 (autumn 1979); and Fred I. Greenstein, *The Hidden-Hand Presidency: Eisenhower as Leader* (New York, 1982).

those of Britain (and France), and the consequences of these divergences. Since its focus is mainly on the approach and actions of Eisenhower and Dulles, it is based primarily on US documents and materials.

Given the limited space, the discussion will concentrate on decision-making on three critical issues:

1. the withdrawal of the Aswan Dam offer;
2. the response to nationalization; and
3. reaction to the attack on Egypt.

THE EVOLVING POLICY TOWARDS NASSER

Between the making of the offer to help Egypt finance the Aswan Dam on 16 December 1955 and its withdrawal on 19 July 1956 there was a general shift in policy toward Nasser by both the United States and Britain. During the year before the offer, their efforts to bolster stability and security in the Middle East had been disappointing. Their secret plan for Arab–Israeli peace (code-named Alpha) had attracted neither Israel nor Egypt. During 1955, Nasser had carried on a steady campaign to discredit the Baghdad Pact and to expand his influence in the region. And in September he had unveiled the Czech (Soviet) deal to supply Egypt arms withheld by the West. Yet in December, after reports of a Soviet offer, the United States and Britain had made the Aswan Dam proposal jointly with the International Bank for Reconstruction and Development (IBRD), which had been studying its feasibility for several years.[2] Obviously, their hope had been to induce Nasser to co-operate in settling the Arab–Israeli conflict and to moderate his efforts to undermine the Baghdad Pact and Western positions in the region.

By March 1956 these hopes were dashed. Early in March Robert Anderson, who had been in the Middle East in January and February as the President's special emissary seeking to mediate between Israel and Egypt, reported to the President that he had made no progress despite tenders of aid, guarantees, and other incentives. And on 1 March, while Selwyn Lloyd was visiting Nasser, King Hussein of Jordan abruptly dismissed General Glubb, who had headed the Arab Legion for some 25 years. The British attributed the dismissal, mistakenly, to Nasser's influence. For the British, and especially for Eden, this

---

[2] The Dam was a huge undertaking, expected to require 12 years to build, and cost some $1.3 billion, of which $900 million in local currency was to be provided by Egypt and $400 million was to be in foreign exchange. The IBRD was to lend $200 million and the US and Britain were to put up $70 million for the first phase and (tentatively) another $130 million for later phases.

was the last straw: from then on Nasser was the hated enemy (who was compared to Mussolini and even Hitler).[3]

During March, both the United States and Britain decided to revise their policies toward Nasser, and consulted intensively. Their analyses and ultimate aims, however, differed significantly. The British concluded that Nasser was now a virtual Soviet tool, seeking to dominate the region and its vital oil, and to undermine all Western influence and alliances. From then on, Eden's explicit goal was to get rid of Nasser.[4] Eisenhower and Dulles adopted a less extreme analysis and objective in a policy paper approved by the President on 28 March. While concerned about Nasser's ambition and links with the Soviet Union, they affirmed:

The primary purpose would be to let Colonel Nasser realize that he cannot cooperate as he is doing with the Soviet Union and at the same time enjoy most-favored-nation treatment by the US. We would want for the time being to avoid any open break which would throw Nasser irrevocably into a Soviet satellite status and we would want to leave Nasser a bridge back to good relations with the West if he so desires.[5]

Besides these differences in ultimate aims, the United States and Britain also differed on other issues. Some related to the Baghdad Pact, which the United States still refused to join. It had objected to including Iran and pressing Jordan to join, and it regretted involving the pact in Iraqi–Egyptian rivalry. The United States also saw the British position on Burami as impeding efforts to lure Saudi Arabia away from Egypt and build up the Saudis as regional leaders.

Despite these divergences, however, the United States and Britain could co-operate on an immediate programme of seeking to put pressure on Nasser and weaken his influence. Their measures included continuing to deny arms, to delay responses to requests for grains and oil under PL 480 and for aid under the Care programme; and 'to delay the conclusion of current negotiations on the Aswan Dam'. Various steps were to be taken to bolster other states in the region such as Libya, Jordan, Ethiopia, Yemen and Lebanon, and also the US position in Saudi Arabia. It was also decided that the United States would increase support of the Baghdad Pact without actually becoming a member.

[3] Sir Anthony Nutting, *No End of a Lesson: The Story of Suez* (London, 1967), pp. 31, 34, 35; and Robert Rhodes James, *Anthony Eden* (New York, 1987), pp. 431–3.

[4] Nutting, *No End of a Lesson*; Selwyn Lloyd, *Suez 1956* (London, 1978), pp. 59–61.

[5] *The Eisenhower Diaries*, ed. R. H. Ferrell (New York, 1981), pp. 318, 319, 323; Memo for Pres. 'Near Eastern Policies', 28 Mar. 1956, Eisenhower Library, Ann Whitman File (hereafter AW), Dulles–Herter Series, Box 5; Memcon, Pres., 28 Mar. 1956, AW, DDE Diary, Box 13; Memcon. Sen. George. 30 Mar. 1956, Dulles Papers (Princeton Library) (hereafter Dulles Papers), Subject Series, Middle East, Box 10.

To undermine Nasser's influence, a campaign by press, radio, and other means was mounted to convince other Arab states of his ambitions for hegemony, the risks from his links with the Soviet Union, and his threat to traditional regimes. The United States was to try to dissuade Israel from provocative actions, and, while continuing to withhold major arms from Israel (or adjoining Arab states except Saudi Arabia and Iraq), it would not object to sales by others of limited amounts of defensive arms to Israel. Planning would begin for more drastic measures, if these did not work, though there was no commitment to pursue them.[6]

US Embassy officials in Cairo were critical. In their view, Nasser was firmly in power, widely supported by moderate Arab nationalism, and determined to keep independent of Soviet or other foreign influence. Pinpricks and dragging one's feet would only anger and antagonize him and most other Arab leaders. Rather than induce moderation, such measures could drive them closer to the Soviet Union. Nevertheless the revised policy was pursued from April on.

THE WITHDRAWAL OF THE ASWAN DAM OFFER

During the spring of 1956, the United States and Britain from time to time discussed the Aswan Dam offer and the Egyptian counter-proposals to make it more favourable, but kept it in suspense. Some, like Treasury Secretary Humphrey in the United States and Sir Ivone Kirkpatrick of the Foreign Office, strongly urged that it be cancelled, and the top leaders were growing steadily less inclined to proceed, though still undecided. In early May, Dulles and Lloyd agreed to let the Aswan offer 'languish'. Nasser was becoming sceptical about US–British intentions.[7]

In mid-May Dulles told the Egyptian Ambassador that the fiscal year 1956 funds set aside for the Dam had been transferred to other uses in view of the absence of a firm deal, so that funding would now depend on future appropriations, which Dulles doubted Congress would approve unless relations improved. And a few days later, Ambassador Byroade in Cairo was instructed to raise the issue of agreement with the Sudan regarding the Nile waters, and advert to the funding uncertainties, but without suggesting US withdrawal (despite grave doubts) in order not to give Egypt grounds for accepting Soviet financing. In early June, Dulles had a draft statement prepared for use

---

[6] Ibid.

[7] Rhodes James, *Eden*, pp. 447–8; Dwight D. Eisenhower, *Waging Peace, 1956–1961* (New York, 1965), pp. 30–2; Memo for Pres., 'Status of U.S. Offer on High Aswan Dam', 3 May 1956, AW, International Series, Box 8.

in case it was decided not to go ahead with the offer, and Britain told the United States that they must decide soon and that Britain was not likely to support it now. The US and British Ambassadors in Cairo, and Eugene Black of the IBRD, strongly favoured going ahead with the Dam project.

Matters were brought to a head on 10 July when word came that Nasser had told Hussein, his Ambassador to the United States, then back in Cairo, to return to Washington and accept the Anglo-American Aswan offer without conditions. According to Heikal, Nasser made it clear to Hussein that he expected that the Western offer would be withdrawn, though Byroade reported Nasser eager to go ahead.[8]

An appointment for the Ambassador to see Dulles was set for the afternoon of 19 July. This prospect led to a flurry of discussions in Washington and between the United States and Britain. A Foreign Office memorandum sent to Dulles on 11 July discussed the pros and cons of going ahead, and as a delaying tactic, proposed the new approach of a Nile Development Board serving the Sudan and other riparian states, as well as Egypt. On 13 July, Dulles told the President that 'we were not in a position now to deal with this matter' because of the legislative uncertainty; moreover 'our views on the merits of this matter had somewhat altered'. Dulles stated that he would consult the President later after further consideration. That same day, Dulles and the British Ambassador reviewed together most of the reasons for not proceeding. Stressing that no final decision had been reached, and recognizing that refusal would no doubt turn Nasser to the Soviets, Dulles tended towards telling him that the offer was withdrawn. The Ambassador indicated that Britain concurred in the analysis and was also uncertain how to respond.[9]

The discussion in this period and earlier in Washington and with the British had crystallized the reasons for not going ahead. In addition to the growing disenchantment with Nasser's course, they were as follows.[10]

1. There was real doubt about Egypt's ability to devote to the Dam the domestic resources needed to complete it, since its cotton exports were heavily mortgaged to pay for the arms deal and other Soviet loans for industrial projects. In late June, however, Eugene Black of the

---

[8] Mohamed H. Heikal, *Cutting the Lion's Tail: Suez Through Egyptian Eyes* (London, 1986), pp. 110, 113–14.

[9] Rhodes James, *Eden*, pp. 448–50, describes the detailed Anglo-American exchanges, correcting the version of Eden and Lloyd; Memcon, Pres. 13 July 1956, Dulles Papers, White House Memo Series: Meetings, file 1.

[10] The grounds for the withdrawal of the Dam offer were reviewed and criticized in an extended speech by Sen. Fulbright (*Cong. Record*, 14 Aug. 1957, pp. 14701–10) and defended by Sen. Knowland (*Cong. Rec.*, 21 Aug. 1957, pp. 15434–9).

Bank, just back from extended discussions about the Dam with Nasser, told Dulles that he thought that the Egyptian economy was no worse off than in December 1955. Egypt therefore could still support the Dam, which was popular and to which Nasser was firmly committed for both economic and political reasons.

2. As Dulles said in the NSC as well as in meetings with the President, the Dam project could well prove a political liability for foreigners involved in carrying it through. The building of the Dam was bound to place a heavy burden on the Egyptian economy and standard of living and the Egyptians would blame the hardships they suffered on the foreign nations supporting this great project. Moreover, the Egyptians would continuously ask for further financial assistance. Foreigners could thus easily become scapegoats for any necessary belt-tightening. (Some months earlier, Nasser had heatedly likened Black to de Lesseps, when he proposed certain restrictions on the Egyptian economy to safeguard an IBRD loan, and he repeated the analogy in his speech nationalizing the Canal Company on 26 July.) Hence it might be better for the long term to let the Soviets undertake it, despite the short-term costs and risks of Soviet influence. That would also leave the United States and Britain freer to provide future aid for smaller projects with higher political pay-offs.

3. Congress might well block support for the Dam. In mid-January, when Hoover appeared before the Senate Foreign Relations Committee regarding support for the Dam, cotton growers were already objecting to the potential competition, although he said that Egypt planned to use the added land for more profitable fruits and vegetables. Wider opposition gradually built up. In late April Senator George, Chairman of the Senate Foreign Relations Committee, had said he adamantly opposed the dam. Various pressure groups were coalescing, including cotton farmers, supporters of Israel, the China lobby angered by Nasser's recognition of Communist China in May, and anti-Communist groups. To placate the Senate Appropriations Committee, Dulles, on 26 June, had agreed not to commit any funds for the fiscal year 1957 for the Aswan Dam without *consulting* the committee. But the Committee Report went further and forbade the use of any 1957 aid funds for the Dam, or any earlier funds, without the prior *approval* of the committee. On 17 July, Dulles wrote to the committee, saying that the Administration would not be bound by the Report. He expected, however, that the Senate might include in the aid legislation itself, which it was taking up on 20 July, a provision forbidding use of any funds for the Dam.[11]

[11] 'Report on the Aswan Dam', 17 Jan. 1956, *Senate Committee on Foreign Relations* (Exec. Sess. of Sen.), vol. viii, 1956, pp. 43–66; *New York Times*, 28 Apr. 1956, p. 1; and n. 10 above.

4. Other friendly countries were suggesting that Egypt was getting more assistance by blackmail than they were by co-operation. Would going ahead with the Dam reinforce this view and alienate other friendly states?

5. The necessary agreement on the Nile waters had not been reached with the Sudan, but this was almost surely solvable.

On 18 July, a Foreign Office message indicated that in their opinion, some of the same considerations made it inexpedient to proceed with the Dam. Not until the morning of the 19th, however, was it finally decided, with Eisenhower's approval, to tell Hussein explicitly that the offer was withdrawn and to issue the communiqué explaining the reasons. Dulles at once told Ambassador Makins, who undertook to telephone London. While another exchange would have been welcome, the decision was in line with the British conclusions, though not finally approved by the Cabinet.[12]

Contrary to some versions (including Rhodes James's), the talk with Hussein, for an hour that afternoon, was calm and good-tempered. Heikal says: 'Dulles was polite but explicit.'[13] Dulles reviewed at length the reasons for not going ahead with support for the project, covering much of the ground outlined above, and affirmed the continued desire for good relations with Egypt as well as the readiness to consider less ambitious proposals for assistance. He also expressed appreciation for the efforts of the Ambassador to improve relations. The Ambassador, accepting the rejection as final, gave a lengthy defence of Nasser's policies: (1) Nasser was eager to build the Dam as the only solution to Egypt's population problem, and was confident of popular acceptance of the necessary austerity; (2) the amount of Soviet arms, less than many reports, was necessary for Egypt's security against Israel, and would not impede the Dam; (3) Nasser was not seeking regional domination or working to damage US interests in Saudi Arabia or Libya; (4) Nasser had wanted US support in order to avoid undue reliance on the Soviet Union, but the pressures to accept its assistance would now be strong. The Secretary reiterated the American acceptance of Egyptian leadership in the Arab world, and stressed that the withdrawal was not in retaliation, or intended to impair Egyptian prestige. The press statement, which Dulles had shown to Hussein, was released after the meeting. It briefly restated the grounds given to him, as well as the desire for good relations and the readiness for other

---

[12] See Rhodes James, *Eden*; Heikal says Dulles, in talking to Fawzi on 6 Oct., stressed the second reason (above) for the refusal, *Cutting the Lion's Tail*, pp. 164–5.

[13] Heikal, *Cutting the Lion's Tail*, p. 115.

assistance in the future.[14] Dulles commented to his brother that Hussein 'had handled himself surprisingly well and with dignity'. The next day, Britain also rescinded its offer on the same grounds as the United States.[15]

Nasser insisted he was not surprised, but resented what he considered to be slurs on the Egyptian economy.[16] (To counter this claim, Byroade later read to Nasser the official US record of the conversation.)

Was the rejection curt, brusque, or abrupt, as has been asserted? Later Eisenhower himself twice raised the question with Dulles. In responding, Dulles stressed the threat of a Congressional prohibition.[17] While that threat was probably not decisive for the withdrawal, it was a major factor in prompting a flat cancellation rather than temporizing. Since the Administration was not going ahead, why not get the benefit in defusing the argument with Congress? Moreover, Nasser had intentionally posed the issue in a form virtually excluding an ambiguous reply.

In the period from March to July, the United States and Britain had managed to work together to a large extent on an immediate policy toward Nasser. Yet the divergence in their assessment of Nasser, and their aims in dealing with him, still remained, and would influence their handling of the Suez crisis. Eden's view of Nasser as a Soviet tool, and a deadly menace to British interests and position in the whole region (and even further afield), called for extreme measures to remove the threat one way or another. For Eisenhower, this view of Nasser and his potential was exaggerated. Nasser was seen as an Egyptian and Arab nationalist who was seeking to combat or undermine what he perceived as foreign domination. He wished to enhance the independence of Egypt and the region, and was prepared to use Soviet assistance to advance his own ends. Since his activities often damaged Western interests and facilitated Soviet entry into the region, the United States wished to modify them or reduce his influence, isolate him, and bolster more co-operative regimes.

THE RESPONSE TO NATIONALIZATION

Nasser's decision on 26 July to nationalize the Suez Canal Company and take over operation of the Canal had not been foreseen by any of the interested States. But their reactions were extremely rapid. Within a few days, Britain, France, and the United States had adopted the

---

[14] The press statement is reprinted in Eisenhower, *Waging Peace*, p. 663.
[15] Rhodes James, *Eden*, pp. 450–1.
[16] Heikal, *Cutting the Lion's Tail*, pp. 115–16.
[17] Eisenhower, *Waging Peace*, pp. 33–4.

basic policies which were to guide each of them through the following months.

The British position emerged with stark clarity over the next few days. And the French attitude, inflamed by Nasser's links with Algeria, was just as vehement, or more so. US policy was shaped by the urgent necessity to respond to Nasser's action, and the effort to influence British and French reactions. Eisenhower was faced with both aspects immediately.

At 8.30 a.m. on 27 July, Hoover, who was Acting Secretary while Dulles was in Latin America, brought Eisenhower a message from the US Embassy in London, reporting on a meeting of Eden with key Cabinet members, the Chiefs of Staff, the French Ambassador, and the US chargé which had started at 11 p.m. on 26 July. It made clear how seriously Britain took the issue. Nasser's action was a grave challenge to Western interests—economic, political and military. He must not be allowed to get away with it. The Joint Chiefs were to produce promptly a study of forces needed to seize the Canal, if military action became necessary. How far would the United States support economic and military measures?[18]

That same day, Eisenhower received an urgent cable from Eden making many of the same points even more strongly and explicitly. Besides the threat to Canal usage, he stressed that if Britain and the United States did not take a firm stand now, 'our influence and yours throughout the Middle East will, we are convinced, be finally destroyed'. Since economic pressures alone were unlikely to attain the desired objective, 'My colleagues and I are convinced that we must be ready, in the last resort, to use force to bring Nasser to his senses. For our part we are prepared to do so.' The Chiefs of Staff had been instructed to prepare a military plan. The United States, Britain and France must exchange views and align their policies for maximum pressure on Egypt.[19]

After discussing the implications of the British position with Acting Secretary Hoover and Deputy Under-Secretary Robert Murphy, Eisenhower sent Murphy to London for tripartite consultations in order to discourage precipitate action. On 30 July, after meeting Eden privately and dining with Macmillan, Murphy cabled that they had urgently asked him to send the following message to the President:

The British government has decided to drive Nasser out of Egypt. They are convinced that military action is necessary and inevitable. They wish the President to understand clearly that the decision is firm, and made calmly and

[18] Donald Neff, *Warriors at Suez* (New York, 1981), p. 276.

[19] Rhodes James, *Eden*, pp. 462–3. See Memcons, Pres. 27 July 1956, and 28 July 1956, AW, DDE Diary Series, Box 16.

without emotion. They see no alternative. (Both stressed these points repeatedly.) Preparations would require six weeks. While flexible as to the procedures leading up to a showdown, at the end they were determined to use force.[20]

In Washington, the President and his advisers were jolted by Murphy's report and the other messages, which they took to be an accurate reflection of British policy. As the British documents now show, they were justified in doing so. On 27 July the Cabinet had decided that HMG should seek, by the use of force if necessary, the reversal of the Egyptian nationalization of the Suez Canal Company. It also appointed the Egypt Committee (Eden, Salisbury, Macmillan, Lloyd, Home and Monckton) to formulate further plans for putting this policy into effect.[21]

On 30 July, the Egypt Committee took action regarding Egyptian sterling, payment of Canal dues, and military preparations. If a conference were held (as the United States urged), Britain would try to obtain a declaration amounting to an ultimatum as a basis for military action if rejected. Most importantly, the committee clearly defined the British objectives: 'While our ultimate purpose was to place the Canal under international control, our immediate [purpose] was to bring about the downfall of the present Egyptian Government.'[22]

The next morning (31 July), Eisenhower held a key meeting with his chief advisers, Dulles, Hoover, Herman Phleger, the Deputy Secretary of Defense, George Humphrey (Treasury), Admiral A. Burke, and several others, to discuss US policy in the light of the Murphy cable, Eden's letter, and other messages. The President said that the British decision was 'very unwise'; their thinking was 'out of date'. Its consequences could jeopardize the supply of oil, and Western influence, as well as 'array the world from Dakar to the Philippine Islands against us'. Dulles warned that resort to force would require stationing large forces in the Canal Zone, which would be vulnerable to terrorist attacks. He thought 'we could make Nasser disgorge what he has seized and agree to internationalize the Canal'—by means other than force. 'After such a try, if it is then necessary to act, world opinion would give greater support.' While Dulles understood why the British and French might want bolder action, that was not necessarily in the US interest. Only Admiral Burke, speaking for the JCS, expressed the view that Nasser was such a growing menace to broader Western interests that he 'must be broken'—by economic and political means, if

---

[20] Robert Murphy, *Diplomat Among Warriors* (New York, 1964), pp. 462–4; Harold Macmillan, *Riding the Storm* (London, 1971), pp. 104–5; see Rhodes James, *Eden*, p. 471.

[21] Rhodes James, *Eden*, pp. 459–61.

[22] Ibid., p. 469.

possible, but if not, by British military force, which the United States should support, though not take part in. 'The President felt it was wrong to give undue stress to Nasser himself. He felt Nasser embodies the emotional demands of the people of the area for independence and for "slapping the white man down".' As the meeting ended, Dulles 'said he thought there is a chance—just a chance—that he can dissuade them, perhaps a bit at a time, gradually deflecting their course of action'.

The President decided to send Dulles to London at once (in three hours) 'to let the British know how gravely we view this matter, what an error we think their decision is, and how this course of action would antagonize the American people'. He then wrote a personal response to Eden's message for Dulles to deliver to him. While recognizing the 'possibility that eventually the use of force might become necessary', he stressed specifically that force should not even be contemplated until 'every peaceful means of resolving the difficulty had previously been exhausted', restating the various reasons discussed at the meeting with his advisers. In urging a conference of maritime nations to put pressure on Nasser, the aim was 'that the efficient operation of the Canal could be assured in the future'.[23]

In London, Dulles found the attitude of the British ministers to be as Murphy had reported, with the French concurring. Nevertheless, he persuaded them to join in calling the conference of 24 maritime nations for 16 August. In doing so, he reiterated that Nasser must be made to 'disgorge' (as Eden never forgot), and joined in espousing an international agency to take over and operate the Canal. But Dulles insisted on retaining US freedom of action if the conference failed. He felt, however, that he had introduced a valuable stopgap and gained time for diplomacy in a setting favourable to moderation and a peaceful solution.[24] In his briefings on the London meeting to the National Security Council on 9 August, and to Congressional leaders on 12 August, Dulles showed considerable sympathy with British antipathy toward Nasser and concern about his ambitions and influence.[25]

Eden was satisfied with the results of the London meeting. In a letter to Eisenhower of 5 August, he reiterated the British objectives: 'to undo what Nasser has done and set up an international regime for the Canal', and 'the removal of Nasser'. He hoped that the plan for

---

[23] Memcon, Pres., 31 July 1956, AW, DDE Diary Series, Box 16, Diary Staff Memos, July 1956; Letter to Eden, Eisenhower, *Waging Peace*, pp. 664–5.

[24] The Tripartite Meetings in London (29 July–2 Aug.) are discussed in Murphy, *Diplomat Among Warriors*, pp. 462–70; Anthony Eden, *Full Circle* (London, 1960), pp. 484–90; Macmillan, *Riding the Storm*, pp. 104–7.

[25] Memo of discussion, NSC meeting, 10 Aug. 1956, AW, NSC Series, Box 8; Legislative Leaders meeting, 12 Aug. 1956, AW, Legislative Meeting Series, Box 2.

international operation would achieve both objectives since 'if Nasser is compelled to disgorge his spoils, it is improbable that he will be able to maintain his internal position'. But Nasser's refusal would require resort to force, since the consequences would otherwise be 'catastrophic' for the whole position in the Middle East.[26]

By mid-August or earlier, Eisenhower had settled on a definite and coherent position sharply differing from that of the British and French. Its main elements were as follows.[27]

1. The objective should be to assure the efficient and reliable operation of the Canal, not the discrediting or unseating of Nasser. That was implicit in his letter of 31 July to Eden, and explicit when he wrote to Eden on 2 September:

We have two problems, the first of which is the assurance of permanent and efficient operation of the Suez Canal with justice to all concerned. The second is to see that Nasser shall not grow as a menace to peace and vital interests of the West. ... The first is the most important for the moment and must be solved in such a way as not to make the second more difficult ... Suez is not the issue on which to attempt to [deflate Nasser] by force.[28]

Besides, Eisenhower believed that the British and French were greatly exaggerating the potential threat of Nasser, as when Eden compared the situation to Hitler in the 1930s and the Soviets in the late 1940s. Their reaction, he felt, was influenced by concern over the loss of prestige and standing in the region and beyond, and was reminiscent of 'imperial' attitudes toward weaker states. Both he and Dulles wished to distance the United States from the taint of 'colonialism'.[29]

Still, Eisenhower had observed to Dulles a few days earlier that he 'realized how tough it was for the British and French but that this was not the issue upon which to try to downgrade Nasser. ... [Getting] an acceptable practical solution of the Suez dispute ... and the question of Nasser and prestige in the Middle East and North Africa could not wisely be confused.'[30]

2. An international agency to operate the Canal might be the ideal way to insulate its operation from politics. But Nasser would certainly not accept that solution even under pressure, since the reversal of his action would totally discredit him (as Eden understood). Nor was this

[26] Rhodes James, *Eden*, p. 483.

[27] See Eisenhower, *Waging Peace*, pp. 39–41.

[28] Letter to Eden (2 Sept. 1956), Eisenhower, *Waging Peace*, pp. 666–8.

[29] Eden to Eisenhower (6 Sept. 1956), Eden, *Full Circle*, pp. 518–21; Eisenhower to Eden (8 Sept. 1956), Eisenhower, *Waging Peace*, pp. 669–71; Dulles Press Conference, 2 Oct. 1956, *Middle East* (State Dept.), p. 103; NSC Discussion, 1 Nov. 1956, AW, NSC file, Box 8; Eisenhower, *Diaries*, pp. 222–4; Letter to Hazlett, 3 Aug. 1956, AW, Name Series.

[30] Memcon, Pres., 30 Aug. 1956, Dulles Papers, WH Memo Series, Box 4, Meetings, file 6.

necessary in Eisenhower's view. Some form of international supervision should provide sufficient protection, as he suggested on 14 August when Dulles was leaving for the London Conference. As recorded by Dulles:

I indicated that I felt it essential that there be an international voice in these matters [Canal employees and tolls] and that they should not be wholly under Egypt's political control. The President said he was disposed to agree. . . . The President suggested there should be some kind of a supervisory Board of say five persons . . . who would have a voice in the selection of a general manager who would be in charge of Canal operations. Also there should be some right of arbitration on the question of tolls. I said this was in line with my thinking. . . . I hoped that we could get the problem onto [such] a practical basis. . . . Then . . . there was a good chance of an acceptable solution.[31]

In his talks with Dulles, Eisenhower repeatedly returned to this concept. But the British and French clung adamantly to the 18-power proposal for international operation. In trying to keep them on board, Dulles's formulations often seemed to commit him to international *operation* as essential.[32]

3. The dispute must be resolved by peaceful means. Nationalization of the Canal was not illegal—it was within Egypt's sovereign rights. Use of force could not be justified, legally or morally, as long as Nasser (1) was operating the Canal efficiently, and (2) was complying with the provisions of the 1888 Convention. From the start, Eisenhower insisted that using force before exhausting all peaceful possibilities and without extreme provocation, would violate the UN Charter, gravely damage Western interests, and probably not assure Canal operation. Later he virtually ruled out force altogether.

Dulles returned to this issue in a talk with the President on 30 August:

I said I wanted to be sure that my mind was working along with that of the President on the basic issues of the Suez matter. I said I had come to the conclusion that, regrettable as it might be to see Nasser's prestige enhanced even temporarily, I did not believe the situation was one which should be resolved by force. I could not see any end to the situation that might be created if the British and the French occupied the Canal and parts of Egypt. They would make bitter enemies of the entire population of the Middle East and much of Africa. Everywhere they would be compelled to maintain themselves by force and in the end their own economy would be weakened virtually beyond repair. . . . The Soviet Union would reap the benefit of a

[31] Memcon, Pres., 14 Aug. 1956, Dulles Papers, WH Memo Series, Box 5, Meetings, file 8.

[32] Memcon, Pres., 6 Sept. 1956, Dulles Papers, WH Memo Series, Box 4, Meetings, file 6; n. 34 below; Memcon Pres., 2 Oct. 1956, Dulles Papers, WH Memo Series, Box 4, Meetings, file 5; see Dulles, Press Conference, 28 Aug. 1956, *Suez Canal Problem* (State Dept., 1956), pp. 295–7.

greatly weakened Western Europe and would move into a position of predominant influence in the Middle East and Africa. No doubt it was for this reason that the Soviets were seeking to prevent a peaceful adjustment of the Suez problem. The President said he entirely agreed with me in this basic analysis.[33]

The joint aims of Britain and France obviously diverged radically from those of the United States. Thus for three months the two sides, though collaborating, were engaged in a struggle regarding both ends and means. Dulles had the difficult task of trying to mobilize pressure on Nasser to achieve adequate safeguards for the Canal operation by peaceful negotiation while restraining the British and French from military action. His leverage on them was mainly their desire for US moral and possibly economic support, oil, and deterrence of Soviet intervention, if they resorted to force. The British and French objective was either to undermine Nasser by forcing reversal of his nationalization or to provoke him into some action which would provide a pretext for resort to force, or at least to lay the basis for force by showing that peaceful methods were ineffective. Their leverage on the United States was the threat of using force on their own.

This conflict in aims was bound to generate frustration and tension, as Dulles tried to keep the negotiations going, and they sought to bring things to a head. The British and French hope for a change in US policy also produced a tendency to 'selective' hearing of what Dulles said. He sometimes fed this tendency by making strong statements in trying to persuade them.

The initial tripartite proposals, which were the basis for the first London Conference in mid-August, reflected the inherent dilemmas and tensions. They called for an International Board to take over the Canal and operate, maintain, and develop it. Though Egypt would be represented on it, control would really rest with the users. This regime would have reversed the nationalization and created another 'foreign' Canal Authority in Egypt in perpetuity (whereas the former Company concession was to expire in twelve years). When Dulles cabled the draft text to him, Eisenhower replied that an *operating* Board would be hard for Nasser to 'swallow', that 'a Board with supervisory rather than operating authority, ... with operating responsibility residing in someone appointed by Nasser, subject to Board approval' should be adequate and acceptable. He hoped rigidity on this point would not wreck the results of the conference. Dulles responded that many thought supervision inadequate and that it would be 'very difficult and perhaps impossible' to persuade the British and French to make this

---

[33] Memcon, 30 Aug. 1956, see n. 30.

change. It was unwise to make concessions in advance 'which we might be willing to make as a matter of last resort in order to obtain Egypt's concurrence. . . . Perhaps something along the lines you suggest may have to be accepted ultimately, and may become acceptable, but neither is clear today.' Despite his concern, Eisenhower, recognizing how boxed in Dulles was, approved whatever decision on the text he felt necessary.[34]

Dulles may have hoped that the proposal, even if not acceptable to Nasser, would evoke a counter-proposal from him and get negotiations started. The British and French, however, sought to forestall this by the mandate to the Menzies Commission to submit the eighteen-power proposal to Nasser but not to negotiate. They wanted the proposal presented as a virtual ultimatum with no opportunity for changes.

Divergent purposes also created friction in the next phase. While the Menzies mission was still in Cairo, Lloyd proposed to Dulles that the Canal dispute be taken directly to the UN Security Council after the expected failure of the Menzies mission. Before doing so, he asked that the United States agree to support the Eighteen Power proposal for international Canal operation and to reject any watering down at the United Nations. While agreeing to support the Eighteen Power proposal, Dulles refused to commit the United States not to consider alternatives. In addition he would not agree to vote against a resolution opposing resort to force that might be offered in the debate. Under these conditions Lloyd preferred to postpone UN action, though bringing the dispute to Security Council attention on 12 September. As Dulles saw it, the Anglo-French appeal to the United Nations at that point and on their terms would be merely a prelude to resort to force.

Instead, on 4 September Dulles submitted to the British and French his idea for a Suez Canal Users' Association (SCUA). This new initiative, admittedly provisional, was another effort by Dulles to find a way to get negotiations started and to gain time. While ingenious, the concept was doubtful as to its workability, as Eisenhower suggested and Dulles agreed. Its premiss was that the users of the Canal were entitled to exercise their rights to transit under the 1888 Convention by creating an association to provide pilots, schedule transit, and collect tolls to be used for expenses and to pay compensation to Egypt. SCUA (as later named) was to co-operate on a practical level with Egypt to assure the efficient and reliable functioning of the Canal. Eisenhower and Dulles hoped it might develop into a mechanism for negotiation by the users with Egypt to reinforce their rights.[35]

[34] Cables to London TEDUL 13, 19 Aug. 1956, and TEDUL 15, 20 Aug. 1956, AW, Dulles–Herter Series, Box 5.

[35] Eisenhower discusses the purposes and brief history of SCUA in Appendix E of *Waging Peace*, pp. 672–5; Memcon, Pres., 8 Sept. 1956, Dulles Papers, WH Memo Series, Box 4, file 5.

The SCUA proposal was developed over the next few days in talks between Dulles and Makins and Alphand, the British and French Ambassadors.[36] SCUA would perform the functions visualized by Dulles, and the members would pay the tolls to SCUA, which would make 'appropriate payment to Egypt for the facilities provided by her'. While British and French shippers were still paying tolls into the old Suez Company account (apparently Nasser intended to treat such payments as a credit toward the compensation for the nationalization), US and other shipowners were paying directly to the Egyptian Authority at the Canal, about thirty per cent of the tolls. This plan would shift all such payments to SCUA. SCUA would seek to co-operate with the Egyptian Canal Authority. If Egypt interfered or refused transit, it was agreed that the members 'would be free to take steps to assure their rights through the United Nations or through other actions appropriate to the circumstances'.[37]

In agreeing to this language, however, Dulles explicitly emphasized to Makins and Alphand several times that SCUA was based on the premiss that if Nasser did refuse transit then ships would be diverted around the Cape. The refusal thus would *not* be a pretext to force passage through the Canal. Indeed, Dulles had stressed to them that for Britain and France the decision to pursue SCUA involved facing the possible economic consequences of having to re-route ships around the Cape.

In embracing SCUA Eden surely knew of this US condition, but he may have believed that it could be used by Britain and France as a means for coercing or humiliating Nasser.

Inevitably SCUA became a source of acrimony. Apparently Eden had visualized that since SCUA would divert most of the tolls from Egypt, Nasser might be provoked into refusing passage, thereby creating grounds for using force, especially if the 'appropriate payment to Egypt' by SCUA was small or delayed.

The most bitter controversy arose about the consequences if Nasser impeded transit. In his speech to Parliament on 12 September Eden made small changes in the agreed language so it sounded threatening, especially in the total context, and was so heard by many Members. This was undoubtedly Eden's intent. He also asked Parliament for freedom to use all necessary means 'to restore' the Suez Canal, and he rejected 'abject appeasement' of Nasser.[38]

---

[36] 'Outline of Proposal for a Voluntary Association of Suez Canal Users', given to Makins, 9 Sept. 1956, and to French, 10 Sept. 1956, Dulles Papers, Subject Series, Suez Problem, Box 7.

[37] Ibid., marked 'Shown to President, Given to Makins (11 Sept. 1956)'.

[38] See Rhodes James, *Eden*, pp. 510–16. He and other critics seem unaware of the Dulles condition regarding the language, referred to in text.

Eden presented SCUA to Parliament in a far more 'bellicose' manner than the Secretary had ever intended. Accordingly, the day after Eden's speech, Dulles held a press conference to give SCUA 'quite a different emphasis', without watering down the original proposal.[39] He endorsed SCUA and said the United States would join, though it was not a permanent solution. Answering questions, he said:

... If physical force should be used to prevent passage, then obviously, as far as the United States was concerned, the alternative for us at least would be to send our vessels around the Cape. ... The President has authoritatively said that, in his opinion, force, if justifiable at all, is only justifiable as a last resort. So, if there are alternatives to the use of force, we believe that they should be fully explored and exhausted. ... I think under those conditions each country would have to decide for itself what it wanted its vessels to do.

And later he said that if force were interposed by Egypt, 'the United States did not intend itself to try to shoot its way through' the Canal.[40] Eden felt he had been betrayed and humiliated: SCUA offered neither coercion nor pretext.

The next day another potential basis for justifying intervention was removed: when the Western pilots left their Canal post on 14 September, the Canal Authority, which had been operating the Canal efficiently since 26 July, continued to do so without delays or difficulties, mainly with Egyptian and Greek pilots plus other recruits. Nasser denounced SCUA the following day.

While SCUA was created at the Second London Conference 19–21 September, it played no real part in resolving the crisis. Instead it kept alive the ongoing dispute about payment of tolls to SCUA and what, if anything, SCUA should pay Egypt.

Finally, on 23 September Britain and France, without the concurrence of the United States, asked for UN action on the Canal issue. The proposed Anglo-French resolution essentially endorsed the Eighteen Power proposal and called on Egypt to negotiate on that basis. Dulles was perplexed as to the real purpose of the British and French action, as he told the President and NSC. He thought the British were divided, and perhaps seeking a negotiated solution, but he was more doubtful about the French. On 5 October, at the United Nations, Dulles had an extended 'heart-to-heart' talk with Lloyd and Pineau to clarify their positions. All three expounded their concerns and positions at length. Dulles reported to the President that he did not think either

---

[39] Memcon, Briefing of Senators, 27 Sept. 1956, Dulles Papers, Subject Series, Suez Problem, Box 7.

[40] *Suez Canal Problem* (State Dept., 1956), pp. 335–45. Here Dulles quotes the precise language agreed to regarding denial of transit (in the middle of p. 339).

side had convinced the other but that the British promised to make an honest effort to settle peacefully and 'Pineau grudgingly went along'.[41]

The proceedings in the Security Council (5–14 October), however, seemed to make a start toward a negotiated solution. The public debate mainly followed predictable lines, but Dulles and Fawzi, the Egyptian Foreign Minister, added something new.

Dulles set out explicitly the view held by the President almost from the start: that a solution based on less than international operation could be acceptable. In his speech in the general debate on 9 October, he endorsed the Eighteen Power proposal, but said, 'There exists, of course, a great variety of means whereby the four basic principles stated by the eighteen nations could be carried out.' The specific Eighteen Power mechanism was not 'sacrosanct'. The 'Council ought not to close its mind to any alternative suggestions.'[42]

Fawzi, speaking for Egypt, was more flexible than in the past.[43] Nasser was under growing pressure to negotiate as a result of the financial squeeze, the loss of tolls on two-thirds of the Canal traffic, and pressure from some of the Arab oil exporters, the Soviet Union, and India and Tito. In concluding his statement to the Council, Fawzi suggested setting up a small negotiating body, and laying down for its guidance a set of principles and objectives, on which he thought there was unanimous agreement. These included: (1) guarantees of unimpeded transit; (2) co-operation between the Canal Authority and users; (3) a fair system of fixing tolls; and (4) allocating adequate revenues for development.

From 9 to 12 October, under Hammarskjöld's auspices, Lloyd, Pineau, and Fawzi had a series of private meetings to discuss possible ways to deal with specific issues. Real progress seemed to be made on some major points that might lay a basis for a negotiated solution. Fawzi showed flexibility regarding safeguards within the context of Egyptian operation. Lloyd seemed co-operative and serious; Pineau, who knew of the Franco-Israeli plans for invasion, was not. Dulles said that the interchanges 'had already yielded important positive results' and urged their continuation. Later Lloyd publicly played down the talks, but Hammarskjöld's memorandum of the discussions seems to refute Lloyd's interpretation, though much remained to be worked out.[44] It was agreed at the time that the talks should be continued in Geneva on 29 October.

---

[41] Memcon Pres., 2 Oct. 1956, Dulles Papers, WH Memo Series, Box 4, Meetings, file 5; Memo, NSC discussion, 4 Oct. 1956, AW, NSC file, Box 8; Memcon Pres., 6 Oct. 1956, AW, DDE Diary Series, Box 19.

[42] *U.S. Policy in the Middle East* (State Dept., 1957), p. 113.

[43] An Egyptian version of the UN proceedings is in Heikal, *Cutting the Lion's Tail*, pp. 160–75.

[44] Letter from UN Sec.-Gen. to Egyptian FM, *U.S. Policy in the Middle East*, pp. 127–33.

On 12 October, Six Principles to govern a settlement were distilled from the main points of agreement and became the first part of a revised Anglo-French resolution. Of the six, the most significant was '(3) the operation of the Canal shall be insulated from the politics of any country.' Item (4) called for fixing tolls 'by agreement between Egypt and the users', and (5) for a fair share of tolls for development. These principles were approved unanimously by the Security Council on 13 October.[45]

But a compromise solution was clearly at odds with concerted resort to force, which the French and Israelis, at least, had virtually agreed on by then. The risk of achieving a peaceful settlement may have helped goad Eden into joining the conspiracy. Accordingly, on 13 October Pineau and Lloyd, at Eden's direction, insisted on adding to their revised resolution approving the Six Principles a second part designed to offend Egypt by disregarding the Egyptian concessions in the private talks. This amendment once more espoused the Eighteen Power proposal and called on Egypt to make 'precise proposals' promptly. This section was approved 9 to 2 but vetoed by the Soviet Union. In his final speech, Dulles tried to take some of the edge off of this section. As he understood the revised Anglo-French resolution, he said, it did not establish the Eighteen Power proposals as the only means for complying with the agreed Principles. The resolution made it quite clear 'that alternative proposals submitted by Egypt, which would also meet those requirements, would be equally acceptable'. On 15 October Lloyd was called back to London by Eden to take part in arranging for the collusion with the French and Israelis.

During the next two weeks, the United States was kept in the dark about British and French plans. Indeed it became aware of the blackout only four or five days before the invasion.

REACTION TO THE ATTACK ON EGYPT

The United States was alerted to the danger of hostilities a few days before the attack, but not to what was actually impending. By 26 October, US intelligence noticed the early stages of the Israeli mobilization, and watched its steady buildup until it was completed on 28 October. In response to queries, including two letters from Eisenhower to Ben-Gurion, the Israelis insisted their action was defensive. Britain implied that Jordan might well be the target. On 28 October, in a long dinner talk with Ambassador Winthrop Aldrich, Lloyd denied having any information suggesting any possibility of a large-scale Israeli

---

[45] See Eisenhower, *Waging Peace*, pp. 54–5; UNSC Resolution, 13 Oct. 1956, *U.S. Policy in the Middle East*, p. 120.

attack on Egypt, or any French involvement in such a venture. An attack on Jordan or Egypt, he said, would put Britain in an 'impossible position' in view of the Tripartite Declaration and Jordon Treaty.[46]

On the morning of 29 October, however, Dulles, after talking to Allen Dulles, cabled Dillon, the US Ambassador in Paris, that bits of intelligence were beginning to indicate that the French, perhaps with British knowledge, might be concerting closely with Israel for an Israeli war against Egypt with probable participation by France and Britain. Dulles laid out his 'profound conviction', and that of the President, as to the dire consequences this would entail, and he warned that the US election would not affect the US reaction. Presciently, he said the die might be cast in a matter of hours.[47] News of the Israeli attack was received about four hours later (3.30 p.m., DC time).

At 7.00 p.m. the President had a long meeting with his chief advisers (Dulles, Hoover, Wilson, Radford, Allen Dulles, and others) to review the situation and decide what to do. Dulles suggested that the British and French would probably intervene, and might indeed have concerted with Israel on the assumption that the United States would have to acquiesce. The President insisted that, however unhappy about helping Egypt, the United States must fulfil its pledge under the Tripartite Declaration to aid the victim of aggression, regardless of the effect on the election. All agreed that the United States, with the French and British if possible, but alone if necessary, should take the initiative in the UN Security Council promptly the next morning to forestall a Soviet move.[48]

The White House issued a press release that evening stating that 'we shall honor our pledge' to assist the victim of any aggression in the Middle East; that the United States was consulting the British and French, as parties to the Tripartite Declaration; and that the matter would be taken to the UN Security Council the following morning. Meanwhile the President stated his position to the British chargé, who was apparently uninformed of the British involvement. Later that evening, at the United Nations, when Cabot Lodge, US representative, approached the British and French representatives, both said flatly that their countries would never join in a resolution against Israel. They brushed aside the Tripartite Declaration as a dead letter. This prompted Eisenhower to cable Eden the next morning (30 October) to ask for full clarification.[49]

[46] Neff, *Warriors at Suez*, pp. 354–60; Memcon, President, 27 Oct. 1956, AW, DDE Diary Series, Staff Memos.

[47] See Memcon, Dulles with Sen. Fulbright, Langer, and George, 29 Oct. 1956, Dulles Papers, Subject Series, Box 7, Suez Problem File.

[48] Memcon, Pres., 29 Oct. 1956, AW, DDE Diary Series, Box 19, Staff Memos.

[49] *Middle East* (State Dept.), p. 137; Memcon, President with Coulson and Dulles, 29 Oct. 1956,

When the President and his advisers met at ten o'clock that morning, the situation was still somewhat confused, especially as to the roles of Britain and France, although their support for Israel's action was now clear. After various possibilities had been explored, Eisenhower reaffirmed strongly his conviction that force was not justified in this situation. He remained determined to go promptly to the UN Security Council for a resolution to end hostilities.[50]

Just after the meeting ended (at about 11.30 a.m., DC time), the fact and nature of the collusion became apparent with Eden's announcement of the Anglo-French ultimatum in the House of Commons. A second cable from Eden to Eisenhower urgently asked for US support because relying on the Security Council would be too slow. A similar message followed from Mollet, the French Prime Minister. To both Eisenhower replied at once expressing his 'very deep concern at the prospect of this drastic action'. At the United Nations that night the British and French vetoed the Security Council resolution calling for a cease-fire and Israeli withdrawal.[51] The matter was then transferred to the General Assembly for a session at 5.00 p.m. on 1 November. That morning in an NSC meeting called to discuss what the US resolution should entail, Dulles described the attack and ultimatum as 'concerted moves among the British, French, and Israelis'. And later that day in Paris, Pineau told Dillon how the collusion had been worked out. At 4.20 a.m. the next morning the General Assembly adopted the US sponsored resolution calling for withdrawal.[52]

Eisenhower had, of course, opposed the Israeli attack from the outset. When the role of Britain and France had been clarified, he applied the basic policy that he had adopted and pressed on them for several months. In his view, resort to force in this situation was unjustified under the UN Charter. Nationalizing the Canal Company was within Egypt's rights and was not adequate grounds for force as long as the Canal was operating efficiently and in conformity with the 1888 Convention. Nor was force justifed by the various other actions of Nasser, harmful though they were.

His reasons for this view had been analysed and set out both in his policy meetings with his advisers and in his series of letters to Eden.

ⵑ. Acquiescing in such a violation of the UN Charter would jeopardize the organization.

2. Using force against Nasser under these conditions would alienate

Dulles Papers, WH Memo Series, Box 4 Meetings, file 3; Eisenhower, *Waging Peace*, pp. 73, and 678-9.

[50] Memcon, Pres., 30 Oct. 1956, Dulles Papers, WH Memo Series, Box 4, Meetings, file 3.
[51] Eisenhower, *Waging Peace*, pp. 76-7.
[52] Discussion at NSC, 1 Nov. 1956, AW, NSC Series, Box 8; Neff, *Warriors at Suez*, pp. 389-92.

not only other Arab and Middle Eastern states, but also other developing countries.

3. This resentment could and would be exploited by the Soviet Union to expand its influence in the Middle East and its potential leverage over oil and the Canal.

4. The hostilities, if not checked, could escalate and spread to become extremely threatening.

5. Any effort to hold the Canal and operate it in a hostile Egypt was bound to fail in the face of determined guerrilla activity or terrorist sabotage.

Until the attack these reasons were essentially estimates of the damaging consequences of resorting to force. Now that the invasion had occurred, they threatened to become real costs except as they could be mitigated. Hence the task, as Eisenhower saw it, was to limit the damage from the attack. But this would involve careful balancing of various objectives. Eisenhower showed his grasp of the problem in a personal memorandum which he sent to Dulles on 1 November after the NSC meeting under a cover note saying: 'Just some simple thoughts that I have jotted down since our meeting this morning.' After stating that the first objective of the United Nations should be to achieve a cease-fire in order to contain hostilities, clarify purposes, and develop considered measures regarding blame and future actions, he continued:

2. The U.S. must take the lead because:

(*a*) While we want to do all the things [just mentioned], we want to prevent immediate issuance by the UN of a harshly worded resolution that would put us in an acutely embarrassing position, either with the French and British, or with all the rest of the world.

(*b*) At all costs the Soviets must be prevented from seizing a mantle of world leadership through a false but misleading exhibition of concern for smaller nations. Since the Africans and Asians almost unanimously hate one of the three nations, Britain, France, and Israel, the Soviets need only propose severe and immediate punishment of these three to have the whole of two continents on their side, unless a good many of the UN nations are already committed to something more moderate that we might immediately formulate. We should act speedily so as to have our forces in good order by 5 p.m. today.

(*c*) We provide the West's only hope that some vestige of real political and economic union can be preserved with the Moslem world, indeed, possibly also with India.

3. Unilateral actions now taken by the US must *not* single out and condemn any one nation—but should serve to emphasize our hope for a quick ceasefire to be followed by sane and deliberate action on the part of the UN, resulting, hopefully in a solution to which all parties would adhere by each conceding something.

4. The US should suspend government shipments now to countries in the battle areas and be prepared to agree with others to take additional action.[53]

Eisenhower was adamant in pursuing his basic policy aim—to reverse the resort to force in vindication of the UN principle. In doing so, he wanted to minimize the harmful consequences outlined above and, while thwarting the 'error' of his allies, to limit the damage to the relationship with them and to future co-operation. He quickly surmounted his anger at his allies 'double-crossing' him, and, though unbending, was not vindictive.

He realized, of course, as Dulles repeatedly stated, that peace involved not only restraint of force but also just solutions of disputes. This applied to the Canal issue as well as to the Arab–Israeli conflict. The United States promptly proposed resolutions addressing both issues. Still, Eisenhower felt it was incompatible with the Charter principles to allow the offending states to make their compliance with the Charter conditional on obtaining solutions of the underlying problems.[54]

These were the guide-lines for his strategy and tactics throughout this phase of the controversy. There is not space to trace in detail how they were applied. For the purpose of this essay, a few examples will suffice.

1. The US resolution, adopted by the General Assembly on 2 November, which called for a cease-fire and withdrawal of forces, and urged others to refrain from bringing in war goods or impeding implementation of the resolution, served several of these purposes. Obviously it gave effect to the UN principle against resort to force to resolve disputes. The US initiative also countered the image of the advanced nations ganging up on the weaker developing countries. In the NSC meeting on 1 November, Eisenhower had wanted 'to do what was decent and right, but still not condemn more furiously than we had to'. By taking the lead the United States headed off a Soviet resolution which would surely have been much harsher but hard to oppose. Moreover, the clause against bringing in military goods or impeding implementation could be used to block any entry of Soviet volunteers, which was a matter of major US concern.

2. The proposal of Lester Pearson, the Canadian Foreign Minister, to create the UN Force, which the United States encouraged and

---

[53] Memo. from President to Dulles, 1 Nov. 1956, Dulles Papers, WH Memo Series (1956), Box 3, file 1.

[54] On 3 Nov. the US submitted to the General Assembly draft resolutions to create a committee to prepare recommendations for an Arab–Israel settlement (UN Document A/3272) and one to prepare a plan for the Suez Canal operation (UN Document A/3273), but subordinated them to the handling of the immediate crisis.

backed, was in part a way of saving face for the British and French. But Eisenhower would not let it be used to delay withdrawal unduly or to coerce concessions from Egypt. He insisted that permanent members of the Security Council should not provide troops for the UN Force in order to exclude Soviet contingents as well as those from Britain and France.

3. Eisenhower was strict in dissociating the United States from the British and French until they complied with the UN resolution. He wished to avoid giving any impression to the Arabs or others that the United States was concerting with the aggressors. He would not permit the Middle East Emergency Committee (charged with planning oil supplies) to take any steps to meet the oil shortage or the Treasury to assist with support for the pound until the Anglo–French commitment to leave Egypt was firm.[55] When Eden telephoned on 7 November about coming with Mollet to Washington, Eisenhower first agreed, but quickly postponed any such visit once its implications were pointed out to him by Goodpaster, Adams, and the State Department.

4. Eisenhower carefully managed the UN resolutions to avoid formal sanctions against Britain, France, and Israel. Quite early in the crisis, however, he knew from Arthur Flemming, head of the Office of Defense Mobilization, and George Humphrey, Treasury Secretary, that Britain would be squeezed by an oil shortage and loss of monetary reserves. He explicitly withheld any help until compliance with the UN resolution was assured, making clear that thereafter it would be promptly and generously provided. In the case of Israel, when Ben-Gurion prolonged withdrawal to obtain further concessions regarding Gaza and Aqaba, Eisenhower finally obtained compliance by a radio–TV address implying readiness to join in imposing sanctions (despite strong objection by Israel's American supporters).[56]

5. Repeatedly in his private meetings and in his public statements, Eisenhower stressed that Britain and France were essential allies, and that this relation must be rebuilt as soon as possible when the Suez crisis was over.[57] When Bulganin sent (and published) threatening letters to Eden, Mollet, and Ben-Gurion, on 5 November, and proposed that joint US–Soviet forces move into Egypt to end the fighting, Eisenhower publicly called the proposal 'unthinkable' and warned that entry of new troops into the Middle East would require all UN

---

[55] See the chapter by Diane B. Kunz.

[56] Ibid.; Address by President Eisenhower, 20 Feb. 1957, *State Dept. Bulletin*, 11 Mar. 1957, pp. 387–91.

[57] NSC meeting, see n. 52; Memcon, President with British Ambassador, Harold Caccia, 9 Nov. 1956, AW, Diary Series, Nov. 1956 Staff Memos; letter to Churchill, 27 Nov. 1956, Eisenhower, *Waging Peace*, pp. 680–1.

members, including the United States, to take effective counter-measures.[58]

CONCLUSION

The review of the record suggests three brief concluding comments.

First, the charge of Eden and others that they were misled by Dulles about the American position seems to me unsupported. Within days after the Canal Company take-over, Eden knew that Eisenhower strongly opposed the course Britain had adopted, and that there was a deep split both in their appraisal of the situation and in their purposes. Their exchanges of letters thereafter only sharpened and clarified this cleavage. And surely they permitted no idea that Eisenhower was uninvolved, or passive, or ambiguous regarding the crisis or US policy.

From late July until the invasion occurred, each side fully under-stood that it was engaged in a struggle to make its own objectives prevail. No doubt Eden hoped that the United States would be boxed into acquiescing in the use of force by the Eighteen Power proposal, by his version of SCUA, and by the UN proceedings in October. He was clearly frustrated each time Dulles (and Eisenhower) escaped from the box and prevented matters coming to a head. The secrecy of their collusion was the clearest evidence that both the British and French fully understood the American position—as Eden and Pineau them-selves later acknowledged.

Since Eden was dealing directly with Dulles, his frustration tended to focus on him. Moreover, Dulles was very much the advocate, and, when seeking to persuade, he instinctively shaped his arguments to appeal to the other party. When Eden was striving to push the United States into supporting his course, he would latch on to formulations or phrases which gave him comfort and hope (such as the famous 'disgorge'). But, as said above, it seems inconceivable that Eden thought Dulles's statements countermanded the clear message of the letters from Eisenhower, and the actual course followed by the United States.

In the end Eden was the victim of self-deception. He, Macmillan, and others simply misjudged Eisenhower: they thought that sentiment, indecision, and the election would cause him to acquiesce in a *fait accompli*. But this was their wishful thinking—not deception by the United States.

Second, the basic views of Eisenhower and Dulles as to the handling of the crisis were clearly congruent. In the first several weeks there may

---

[58] Neff, *Warriors at Suez*, pp. 403–4.

have been some differences in nuance. Dulles seemed to hope that Nasser might be coerced into accepting international control and operation (thereby solving the Canal problem and discrediting him as well), by means of the London Conference, as well as economic and political pressures. Eisenhower discounted this early on and favoured a solution accepting Egyptian operation with user safeguards. He may also have had a little more sympathy with Nasser's concern about foreign domination (though not necessarily with his actions), while Dulles seemed to focus more on the East–West aspects and felt more antipathy to Nasser. But both saw the British position as partly reflecting outdated 'imperial' or 'colonial' attitudes, which were an encumbrance in dealing with the Third World. Both genuinely wanted to build up the United Nations. And both saw resort to force in this situation as damaging and unjustified. Finally, in practice, Dulles was meticulous in keeping in step with Eisenhower. Once the President had decided on the course, after consulting Dulles and others, Dulles always loyally sought to carry it out and never consciously deviated from it.

Third, what about second thoughts on the crisis by Eisenhower and Dulles? The episode inevitably tempts speculation about the possible results of other courses. What if the Dam had been built by the West? If the United States had backed Britain and France, what would have been the consequences in the region? After the invasion, should the crisis have been used, as Lester Pearson urged, as leverage for solving the underlying conflicts in the region?

Much has been made of the anecdote about Dulles's comment to Lloyd and Caccia, when they visited him in hospital after his November operation. According to Rhodes James, while Dulles said he still did not approve of the British methods in the crisis, 'Even so, he deplored that we had not managed to bring down Nasser.'[59] This is puzzling and ambiguous, but it does not seem to me to show regret at the US course.

Eisenhower, who set that course, apparently had no doubts. In his *Memoirs* he briefly raises and discusses several such 'might have beens'. Yet with the benefit of hindsight and nearly ten years for reflection, he at least had no misgivings about the course he had followed.

---

[59] Rhodes James, *Eden*, p. 577.

The Importance of Having Money: The Economic Diplomacy of the Suez Crisis

DIANE B. KUNZ

> I feel that the situation created by the Egyptian Government imperils the survival of the U.K. and the Commonwealth, and represents a very great danger to sterling.
>
> Sir George Bolton, Executive Director, Bank of England

> The British had no sooner invaded than they recognized immediately that they couldn't carry on a war of any scale without financial help; and in view of the U.S. position, taken promptly at the United Nations, we were not prepared to finance their war effort.[1]
>
> W. Randolph Burgess, Under-Secretary, United States Treasury

IF war is the continuation of politics by other means, it is also true that, in certain circumstances, economic pressure can be the equivalent of war. The Suez crisis provides a striking example of the militant use of financial power. American use of economic artillery to achieve its policy objectives largely determined the course of the crisis from the seizure of the Suez Canal (triggered by the Western refusal to finance the Aswan High Dam) to the Israeli evacuation of the Sinai peninsula under the pressure of economic sanctions. This chapter will focus on one of the most important aspects of this story: Anglo-American economic diplomacy during the Suez crisis.[2]

One of the constants of British twentieth-century history has been the disparity between Great Britain's financial means and its strategic and imperial ends. The Suez crisis clearly illustrated the policy

---

[1] G. Bolton, 'Sterling and the Suez Canal Situation', 1 Aug. 1956, Bank of England (hereafter B/E), G1/124; W. Randolph Burgess interview, Dulles Papers, Princeton University (hereafter DP) Dulles Oral History Collection.

[2] This paper is based on a forthcoming study on the economic diplomacy of the Suez crisis which will encompass financial relations between the United States, Great Britain, France, Egypt, and Israel.

ramifications of this predicament. Britain's financial dependence on the United States first curtailed and then destroyed its ability to take a hard line against Egyptian President Gamal Abdel Nasser. Ironically, one of the motives behind the British government's determination to confront Nasser was the belief that the failure to do so would jeopardize both the sterling exchange rate and the very existence of the sterling area. The British decision to use military force, however, nearly ended the viability of sterling as an international currency. The Eden government's calculations concerning the feasibility of its Suez policy were based on the assumption of either American assistance or neutral assent, not overt US hostility. Once the Suez invasion began, as it became evident that the United States would activate its economic arsenal against its errant ally, the question became not whether, but when, Britain would bow to American imperatives. As Bagehot observed, the purse-strings tie us to our kind.

For both historical and contemporary reasons Britain in 1956 fully maintained its long-standing interest in the Middle East in general and Egypt in particular. American attention to the area was of more recent origin but rapidly intensifying. Minimizing tensions with Egypt's charismatic President Nasser was a high priority for both the British government under the premiership of Anthony Eden and the American government under President Dwight Eisenhower. From 1954 until the spring of 1956 this sentiment found its most concrete expression in the Anglo-American decision to join with the World Bank and finance the Aswan High Dam. However, during March 1956, both Western nations had a change of heart. Secretary of State John Foster Dulles wished to demonstrate to Nasser that 'he cannot cooperate as he is doing with the Soviet Union and at the same time enjoy most favoured nation treatment from the United States'.[3] Eden and his colleagues were equally determined not to fund the Dam. Where the two governments differed was that in London the preference was to 'play it long' rather than to announce immediately and bluntly the withdrawal of the offer. Yet the British acquiesced in Dulles's decision to take the opposite approach.[4] Thus on the afternoon of 19 July 1956 the Secretary of State told Egyptian Ambassador Ahmed Hussein that American participation in the project was 'not feasible'. Discussing the meeting with his brother Allen, Dulles noted that Ambassador Hussein 'had handled himself surprisingly well'. To Senator William Know-

---

[3] Memorandum for the White House, 28 Mar. 1956, Dulles files in Dwight D. Eisenhower Presidential Library (hereafter DP/DDE), Subject Series, Box 5.

[4] Sir Roger Makins (Washington) to Foreign Office, 19 July 1956, FO 371/119056 (Public Record Office, London).

land the Secretary added that it would 'be interesting to see what happens'.[5]

Dulles had not envisioned exactly how 'interesting' the future would be. One week later, on 26 July, to the surprise of the world, Nasser announced the nationalization of the Suez Canal Company (officially the Compagnie Universelle du Canal Maritime Suez). While both the United States and Britain placed financial sanctions on Egypt, the British measures were far more sweeping and were potentially devastating to Egypt. In effect they virtually severed the long-standing financial connections between the two nations.[6] These restrictions were made more effective because they were laid down on 27 July, giving the Egyptians little opportunity to withdraw any funds.

After considerable internal debate, narrower American regulations were implemented on 31 July. They only covered the assets of the Egyptian government, the National Bank of Egypt, and the Suez Canal Company.[7] Yet freezing the accounts of the National Bank at the Federal Reserve Bank of New York was significant because from the time Egypt had left the sterling area in July 1947 it had been increasing its dollar and gold reserves and by 1956 approximately 75 per cent of these reserves were kept at the New York Federal Reserve Bank.

31 July also marked the day Dulles left for London, beginning a three-month period of Middle East shuttle diplomacy. The Secretary's initial task was to clarify the Administration's position, first delineated in a letter from Eisenhower to Eden. The President strongly emphasized that all possible peaceful means of settlement must be attempted before using military force. Otherwise he felt sure that 'the American reaction would be severe and that other areas of the world would share that reaction'.[8] The Administration remained convinced throughout the crisis that force was an unacceptable option; Dulles and Eisenhower believed that this would be the wrong war in the wrong place. Unfortunately the British government never understood that all American statements had to be interpreted against this conviction.

Since the Americans wished to devise a formula 'to assure dependable international operation of that [*sic*] Canal consistent with the

[5] Telephone call to Allen Dulles, 19 July 1956, telephone call from Senator Knowland, 19 July 1956, DP/DDE, Telephone Conversations, Box 5.

[6] The Control of Gold and Securities (Suez Canal Company) Direction, 1956, B/E, EC5/356, 1956, No. 1164, Supplies and Services Finance. The Exchange Control (Payments) (Egyptian Monetary Area) Order, 1956, B/E, EC5/356, 1956, No. 1163, Exchange Control.

[7] Egyptian Assets Control Regulations, 31 July 1956, Federal Reserve Bank of New York (hereafter FRBNY), C260.2; telephone call from Secretary Humphrey, 31 July 1956, DP/DDE, Tel. Convs., Box 5.

[8] Eisenhower to Eden, 31 July 1956, DP/DDE, Subject Series, Box 11.

rights and dignity of Egypt', the Administration was split on the wisdom of blocking Egyptian accounts.[9] The American desire to keep an Egyptian bridge open was shown in more tangible ways. The Treasury regulations on Egyptian payments were relaxed on 3 August when a licence was granted authorizing US shipowners and operators to make payments to the Canal Authority in respect of Suez Canal charges provided that they were accompanied by the statement that such payments are made 'under protest and without prejudice to all rights of recovery or otherwise'.[10] However, American assistance in the British financial quarantine of Egypt was more forthcoming than any European country save France. Further, of the Commonwealth countries, the pre-war dominions offered only limited support and the three Asian countries none.[11]

At this time the British and the Americans were also considering the two overwhelming economic dangers facing Britain: the threat to sterling and the question of oil supplies to western Europe. As Sir Edward Bridges, Permanent Secretary to the Treasury, pointed out to the Chancellor of the Exchequer, Harold Macmillan, on 8 August: 'It is already clear that our balance of payments and therefore our gold and dollar reserves are going to be under considerable strain over the next month or so, even if the [London] Conference reaches a successful conclusion.' Bridges also pointed out that it was difficult to plan:

The trouble here is that the action to be taken is almost totally different according to the situation which we are faced with—a limited war, or a not so limited war—a war in which we go it alone, or a war in which we have the Americans with us from the outset.[12]

Bridges was perfectly correct that the presence or absence of overt American assistance would make a great difference to Britain's financial position. He in no way contemplated the possibility of direct American action against Britain, with its disastrous consequences for the pound. Sterling was dependent on the dollar as Britain was dependent on the United States. Neither the currency nor the country could go it alone.

Indeed the position of sterling had been precarious since the end of the Second World War. It was only the extension of $3.75 billion pursuant to the Anglo-American Loan Agreement of 1945 (the 'US Agreement') which had saved Britain from financial disaster. What

---

[9] Statement by the Secretary of State, 14 Aug. 1956, DP, Personal Papers, Box 110.

[10] License Authorizing Current Transactions, Authorization 8.03—Payment of Suez Canal Charges, FRBNY, C260.2, Treasury License Under Egyptian Assets Control Regulations: Section 510.502.

[11] B/E Memorandum, 'Egypt', 7 Aug. 1956, B/E, EC5/356.

[12] Bridges to Macmillan, 8 Aug. 1956, Treasury (hereafter T), 236/4188 (Public Record Office, London).

followed were a series of economic crises in 1947, 1949, and 1951. Despite British weakness and only limited American support, controls over British financial markets and trading in transferable sterling (sterling held outside the sterling area and North and South America) were lifted in incremental steps, and by February 1955 *de facto* convertibility of transferable sterling had been achieved. The irony is that had Britain not accorded transferable sterling convertibility eighteen months earlier, she would not have faced such a perilous financial predicament during the Suez crisis. However, both the Bank of England and the Treasury believed that convertibility had to be maintained if London were to retain its position as a leading financial centre. This, in turn, was seen to be crucial to Britain's role as the head of the Empire and the Commonwealth and to the existence of the sterling area. But for the pound to continue to be a reserve and trading currency, convertibility had to be retained which, given Britain's limited reserves, put sterling at continual risk, thus tending to undermine the strength of the pound, which convertibility was designed to enhance.

During the Suez crisis two factors further endangered the position of the pound. The largest holders of transferable sterling included Arab countries and various oil companies. Thus the pound presented an obvious target if either or both groups of holders decided to turn against Britain. Exacerbating the situation was the fact that Britain customarily paid for its oil in sterling. However, if normal oil supplies were curtailed, either by the closing of the Canal or the blowing up of pipelines (both of which in fact happened), Britain would have to dip into its dollar reserves or sell sterling to obtain dollars in order to purchase oil and pay for its transportation. This would further weaken the position of sterling and encourage increased speculation against the pound.

Attention had been paid to the oil question as early as 30 July, when Dulles held a meeting on the subject. The Administration believed that interruption of Middle Eastern oil supplies could be catastrophic for NATO security.[13] To this end Dr Arthur Flemming, the Director of the Office of Defense Mobilization, was delegated to study the problem of reallocating and delivering American controlled oil to Western Europe. The next step was the formation of the Middle East Emergency Committee (MEEC). Composed of representatives of the five major American oil companies and their subsidiaries, the committee's job was to develop and carry out a plan for transporting oil supplies to NATO countries.

[13] Telephone call to Senator Mansfield, 30 July 1956, DP/DDE, Tel. Convs., Box 5.

This left the British to consider how they would pay for dollar-priced oil. If the Canal and the pipelines were rendered unusable, estimates of the increased dollar cost of obtaining substitute oil supplies hovered between $500m.–$700m. a year. Therefore Denis Wright of the Foreign Office was not being alarmist when he minuted at the end of August that 'If Middle East oil supplies are cut off altogether, it is difficult to see how we could manage to avoid major economic disaster.'[14]

Indeed, in early August the potentially explosive cost of the Suez crisis together with the already ongoing strain on sterling led the Bank of England, the Treasury, and the Foreign Office to consider possible fiscal and monetary measures. Controls over imports and shipping were discussed and Macmillan proposed at a meeting held on 9 August that Britain purchase gold from Australia and consider drawing dollars from the International Monetary Fund. The Chancellor further believed that 'the events in the Eastern Mediterranean might give us grounds for asking this year for the waiver of interest on the United States Agreement'.[15] (Properly, the Financial Agreement dated 6 December 1945, between the Governments of the United States and the United Kingdom, but thereafter the 'US Agreement'.)

The issue of a waiver under the US Agreement was, in the words of the Foreign Office, 'that hardy annual question'.[16] Britain's payments of principal and interest under the American and companion Canadian agreements had begun in 1951. In that same year, the British, after considering whether to ask for a waiver of interest payments, decided against it. In 1955 the question was raised when British Treasury official Sir Leslie Rowan travelled to Washington in December. But he was not only prepared to present a theoretical case. Britain's currency being under siege in 1955, a waiver of interest payments would have been welcome. The problem was not whether Britain was entitled to a waiver—American officials had no quarrel with the British Treasury's position that the current pressure on the pound was exactly the kind of situation the waiver was designed to handle. Unfortunately the clauses of the US Agreement designed to permit a waiver of an interest payment were so poorly drafted as to be by definition inoperative. Therefore the only way the British could

---

[14] D. Wright, *The Egypt Crisis and British Economy*, 27 Aug. 1956, FO 371/120799. Concerning the cost of oil imports see, e.g. 'Maintenance of Supplies on Present Basis to United Kingdom and via United Kingdom to Europe', 18 Sept. 1956, B/E, OV 31/55, and Rickett to Rowan, 2 Nov. 1956, T 236/4188.

[15] Brook to Bridges, 11 Aug. 1956, T236/4188.

[16] Gore Booth to Wright and Chadwick, 20 Nov. 1956, FO 371/120796.

obtain a waiver was for the Administration to propose and Congress to approve an amendment to the US Agreement.[17]

During Rowan's conversations with the Secretary of the Treasury, George Humphrey, the latter expressed himself in favour of amending the waiver clause and said he would sound out a number of Congressmen on the subject.[18] As the pound remained under pressure during the first part of 1956, the use of the waiver continued to be relevant. However, in April Humphrey warned the British that 'any attempt at legislation this year would be dangerous'.[19] Two factors largely determined Humphrey's stance. First, the US Treasury was very unenthusiastic about foreign loans, particularly if there was a possibility that such credits might make it harder to balance the US budget.[20] Secondly, Congress having already proved restive on the subject of foreign aid, it was obviously a poor time to introduce the waiver question, especially since it might raise the unfortunate spectre of Britain's default on its First World War debts. Given Humphrey's strong feelings, at the end of April Macmillan concurred in the recommendation of Lord Harcourt, Economic Minister in Washington, that 'we should *for the time being* decide not to ask the U.S. Administration to introduce any legislation'.[21] The Suez crisis put this decision in a different light.

The British were still pondering these various problems (Dulles thought their economic thinking 'very muddy') during the mid-August London Conference.[22] These sessions resulted in a decision to send a five-nation delegation to Cairo to discuss internationalization of the Canal with Nasser. Not surprisingly the Egyptian leader summarily rejected the notion. Back in Washington Dulles and his aides now devised the Suez Canal Users' Association (SCUA). Premised on the assumption that the Egyptians could not run the Canal, from beginning to end it made no substantive sense. It did, however, meet two American requirements. The first was that it was consistent with Eisenhower's conviction that 'this was not the issue upon which to try to downgrade Nasser'.[23] The second was that it would keep the British

[17] The text of the relevant provisions of the US Agreement is contained in the appendix to this chapter.

[18] Exter Memorandum dated 13 Dec. 1955, concerning conversation with Sir Leslie Rowan, 12 Dec. 1955, FRBNY, C261 England, 1955–9.

[19] D. S. Laskey, 'Anglo-American Loan Agreement: The Waiver', 19 Apr. 1956, FO 371/120796.

[20] Caccia to Foreign Office, 23 Nov. 1956, B/E, G1/124, No. 2335; W. Randolph Burgess interview, DP, Dulles Oral History Collection.

[21] Macmillan to Harcourt, 23 Apr. 1956, FO 371/120796.

[22] Telephone call from Dr Flemming, 28 Aug. 1956, DP/DDE, Tel. Convs., Box 5.

[23] Memorandum of Conversation with the President, 30 Aug. 1956, DP/DDE, White House Memoranda (hereafter WHM), Box 4.

and French occupied, which was important because the Administration believed that 'the passage of time was working in favour of a compromise'.[24]

Eden reluctantly decided to postpone Operation *Musketeer*, a military assault on Egypt which the British and French had been secretly planning, and play along with the SCUA scheme. His hope was that acquiescence now would bring assistance (both military and financial) later. Even when Dulles, contradicting a very bellicose Prime Ministerial announcement, proclaimed to the world that the United States did not intend to shoot its way through the Canal, the British government, in Macmillan's words, still felt it had no choice but 'to accept a further period of delay, and to trust in our friends'.[25]

As September passed, the Bank of England and the Treasury continued to focus on the financial effects of the crisis. Sir Leslie Rowan suggested a whole new approach to the waiver question. Since the real problem of the British was not finding the money *per se* but the dollars necessary to cover the interest payments—in 1956, $75.4m. under the US Agreement—he suggested that the United States be asked to permit Britain to make sterling payments to third countries designated by the United States in the amount of the dollar debt service due in respect of the US Agreement.[26]

At the same time, the Treasury and the Bank of England discussed the possibility of a loan from the US Export-Import ('Ex-Im') Bank to fund the cost of oil shipments. The British Treasury was ambivalent about this prospect. Rowan believed that: 'The advantage of taking an Ex-Im loan is that we get the Americans tied in, and that world opinion sees that they are behind us in this operation.' The Bank of England felt, however, that to increase dollar borrowing, especially at this juncture, could be seen as a sign of weakness. Thus it was decided that no such step would be taken for the present, the Treasury hoping that the SCUA discussions at the least indicated that there was a possibility of American grant aid instead of loans.[27]

Simultaneously, the Treasury together with the Foreign Office considered anew what steps would be necessitated by war with Egypt. Under examination were ideas such as empowering the Bank of England to make special advances, to call for bank holidays, and to close exchange markets. Officials assumed that either the United States would be an active belligerent or, at worst, 'would not overtly support'

---

[24] Memorandum of Conversation with the President, 6 Sept. 1956, DP/DDE, WHM, Box 4.

[25] Department of State Press Release: Transcript of Secretary Dulles's News Conference, 13 Sept. 1956, DP, Personal Papers, Box 110; H. Macmillan, *Riding the Storm, 1956–1959* (London, 1971), p. 122.

[26] Rowan to Myners, 5 Sept. 1956, Allen to Combs, 14 Sept. 1956, FO 371/120796.

[27] Rowan to Macmillan, 12 Sept. 1956, B/E, OV 31/55.

Britain. The Treasury deliberations, according to Bridges, showed 'the vital necessity from the point of view of our currency and our economy of ensuring that we do not go it alone, and that we have the maximum U.S. support'. Reading Bridges' memorandum, Macmillan minuted: 'This is just the trouble. U.S. are being very difficult.'[28] He was right.

Nasser having summarily rejected the SCUA scheme, on 23 September Britain and France signalled their intention to go to the United Nations. Dulles was unhappy because he felt that he had not been sufficiently consulted. While the American delegation co-operated with their British and French counterparts, the Secretary of State encouraged Bernard Baruch, who was conducting secret negotiations with Nasser through an intermediary. At the same time, during Macmillan's late September visit to Washington, Dulles told him that if the British wished, the United States was prepared to tighten the Treasury licence to make it impossible for American flag vessels to pay tolls to Egypt.[29] Dulles went along with this British action although he thought it was foolish because 'primarily it is their funeral and not ours'.[30] Indeed according to Macmillan's own contemporary account of his encounter with Dulles, the Secretary of State reiterated the consistent American opposition towards using force against the Egyptians. Not only were suggestions of American aid very limited and not to be proposed until after the presidential election (6 November), but the Secretary of State specifically asked Macmillan, whatever else happened, to 'try and hold things off until after November 6th'.[31] In light of this and other explicit American cautionary statements, the Eden government's decision to go ahead with *Musketeer* despite Britain's financial dependence on the United States must remain one of the most puzzling facets of the Suez crisis. A mutual failure of perception played a part but, more importantly, it would seem that the British sensing, even if they did not face, American resistance to *Musketeer*, and resenting their dependence on the United States, hoped to box the Administration into a corner where it had no alternative but to support its usually loyal ally. The Eden government would shortly learn that it had made a monumental miscalculation.

By the beginning of October, according to Dulles, the British and

---

[28] Bridges to Macmillan, 7 Sept. 1956, T 236/4188.

[29] Telephone call from Bernard Baruch, 24 Sept. 1956, telephone call to Baruch, 25 Sept. 1956, DP/DDE, Tel. Convs., Box 5; 'Points to be Raised with Harold Macmillan and Roger Makins', 25 Sept. 1956, DP/DDE, Subject Series, Box 7.

[30] Telephone call from Secretary Humphrey, 24 Sept. 1956, DP/DDE, Tel. Convs., Box 5.

[31] Macmillan, 26 Sept. 1956, Note of a Private Talk with Mr Dulles, 25 Sept. 1956, Prime Minister's Office (hereafter PREM), 11/1102 (Public Record Office, London). This should be contrasted with Macmillan's account in *Riding the Storm*, pp. 135–7.

French 'did not feel we were backing them sufficiently and the governments were blaming their failure to get results on the fact that we were holding them back'. This was not surprising since the President's policy was to maintain an independent stance until it was clear what the British and French were planning to do.[32] Reiterating his views on 8 October, Eisenhower suggested that if matters did not go well he was prepared to issue a White House statement stressing that negotiations must be carried on until a peaceful solution was reached and might include a blunt warning that 'the United States would support neither a war nor warlike moves in the Suez area'.[33] Thus it is clear that the Americans were still trying to carve out a middle position between their NATO allies, on the one hand, and Nasser, on the other, but always holding to the basic principle that military force was not acceptable.

The Administration at this time was still using financial diplomacy to help keep the lines of communication with Egypt open. Evidently the Treasury and State Department were aware that the Egyptians were apparently using money from the International Cooperation Administration in order to establish alternative central banking relations in Switzerland.[34] As the ICA was the government agency in charge of distributing foreign aid, this would appear to be another example of the Administration's determination not to push Nasser too far. Furthermore, immediately prior to the Suez invasion, the US Treasury again eased restrictions on Egyptian transactions by allowing payments from blocked accounts 'in appropriate cases involving hardship where shipments of goods have been completed or other services have already been rendered to partnerships or firms in Egypt'.[35] If loosely applied, this determination could render the American blocking regulations virtually meaningless.

Negotiations continued at the United Nations, focusing on the so-called 'Six Principles'. Simultaneously, Britain and France together with Israel prepared to go to war. While the Americans were aware of a continuing Anglo-French military build-up on Cyprus, they were taken by surprise when on 29 October Israel launched its invasion of the Sinai.[36] That night at a White House meeting the basic American policy was formulated. Accepting that there was at least some degree

---

[32] Memorandum of Conversation with the President, 2 Oct. 1956, DP/DDE, WHM, Box 4.

[33] Eisenhower to Hoover, 8 Oct. 1956, DP/DDE, WHM, Box 3.

[34] Davis Memorandum to the Files concerning conversation with Elting Arnold, Acting Director, Foreign Assets Control, US Treasury, 17 Oct. 1956, FRBNY, 260.2.

[35] E. Arnold to J. C. R. Atkins, Chairman, Foreign Exchange Committee, 29 Oct. 1956, B/E, OV 31/55.

[36] Dulles even noted: 'On the whole we have been working comfortably with Israel lately', telephone call to Senator Bridges, 15 Oct. 1956, DP/DDE, Tel. Convs., Box 5.

of British and French involvement, an angry Eisenhower stated that the US commitment under the Tripartite Declaration of 1950 to come to the aid of a victim of aggression in the Middle East, in this case Egypt, now meant that 'we cannot be bound by our traditional alliance'. Therefore the decision was made that the United States would go to the United Nations with or without the British and French.[37]

Throughout the crisis the United States had tried to steer a middle course between the demands of its Western European allies, on the one hand, and the sensibilities of the Arab Middle East, on the other. Now the news of the Anglo-French ultimatum of 30 October caused Under-Secretary of State Herbert Hoover to observe that 'the British and French may feel that they have forced us to a choice—between themselves and the Arabs'. To this the President said 'he did not see much value in an unworthy and unreliable ally and that the necessity to support them might not be as great as they believed'.[38]

Contributing to the Administration's anti-invasion stance were several other factors. Eisenhower and his colleagues, realizing that they had been backed into a corner, were understandably resentful especially as it was a week before election day. There was great concern about the possibility of major erosion of Western influence over the Arabs arising out of anachronistic gunboat diplomacy. Finally the coinciding of the Suez crisis with the Hungarian confrontation had a major effect on the President's tough stand towards the British and French.

Thus it was clear that, as matters stood, the United States was not going to provide assistance to Britain. This was most unfortunate for the British because their financial position already needed buttressing. Problems arising out of the Suez situation superimposed upon the annual summer seasonal strains had put the pound under pressure since August. Further, during October, usually a time of strength for sterling, the Bank of England had lost $84m., further weakening the reserves.[39]

The initial Bank reaction had not been alarmist, but this changed completely when the news of the Anglo-French ultimatum and the corresponding American response made it clear that instead of either American assistance or benign neutrality, the United States would actively oppose British actions. Unclear to what extent a genuine war had started, a concerned Governor, C. F. Cobbold, said on 31 October:

[37] Memorandum of Conference with the President, 29 Oct. 1956, DP/DDE, WHM, Box 4.

[38] Memorandum of Conference with the President, 30 Oct. 1956, DP/DDE, WHM, Box 4.

[39] 'Statement by the Rt. Hon. Harold Macmillan, Chancellor of the Exchequer', 4 Dec. 1956, B/E, G1/124.

'At the moment we can only dig in our toes on the whole exchange front.'[40]

That this was going to be difficult was soon obvious when in the first two days of November the Bank of England lost $50m. Concern over the dollar drain was compounded by worries over oil as the closing of the Canal and the loss of pipelines changed from hypothetical problems to harsh reality. The Bank and the Treasury, believing that the exchange rate of transferable sterling should be maintained within its customary range of one per cent of parity ($2.80), took as their first task the augmenting of the British gold and dollar reserves which on 31 October stood at $2,244m. This meant that after deducting the $50m. loss and the required December debt service payments of $180m., even if the Bank lost no more dollars until year-end, a highly unlikely scenario, the reserves would be close to $2,000m., which had long been regarded by both British and American authorities and by financial markets as the danger point for sterling reserves. Thus the Bank and the Treasury considered such possible steps as an IMF drawing, the US Agreement waiver, the sale of British government-owned US securities, and a possible American loan. When these actions were first mooted in September, they had been rejected, because the British feared that by advertising the pound's predicament these moves could make matters worse. Now the strain on sterling made such reservations an unaffordable luxury.[41]

These discussions were carried on against a backdrop of American-sponsored debate at the United Nations. The Administration continued to distance itself from the British and French. Dulles viewed the American initiative, among other things, as a declaration of independence from obsolete Anglo-French imperial policies.[42]

On 5 November European airborne forces reached Port Said and on the same day the Russians delivered their famous threat. The Soviet intervention concerned the President, who worried 'that the Soviets, seeing their position and their policy failing so badly in the satellites, are ready to take any wild adventure'.[43] Thus the Americans were even more determined to control the British and French who, Dulles told UN Ambassador Henry Cabot Lodge, had perhaps committed a worse crime in Egypt than the Russians had in Hungary. However, Dulles was confident that the recalcitrant allies would soon bow to American wishes because 'there would be a strain on the British and French and it

---

[40] Governor's Note, 31 Oct. 1956, B/E, G1/124.
[41] Rickett, 'Emergency Action', 2 Nov. 1956, B/E, G1/124.
[42] Telephone call from the Vice-President, 31 Oct. 1956, DP/DDE, Tel. Convs., Box 5.
[43] Memorandum of Conversation with the President, 7 Nov. 1956, DP/DDE, WHM, Box 4.

will be economic and quickly [*sic*]'.[44] Indeed the Americans were well informed about the state of British oil and sterling reserves. Not surprisingly, the New York Federal Reserve Bank had been keeping careful tabs on the currency position for years. Furthermore, the MEEC (whose meetings from 30 October were suddenly suspended[45]) had formulated careful statistics on British oil reserves. Therefore the Administration drew the same conclusion as had the British: with reserves of both petroleum and pounds fast dwindling, and no American help in sight, the British must soon accept the United Nations cease-fire.

This was done by an unhappy British government on 6 November— which also happened to be the American election day. Eisenhower, as was predicted, won a landslide victory, doubling his 1952 majority. The British now prepared to go to the United States for massive assistance. In the meantime, on the assumption that American aid was in the offing, the British decided to ignore the crucial $2,000m. number and continue to make propping up the exchange rate the first priority. The Bank of England and the Treasury took this approach for two reasons. The first was that fiscal and monetary measures taken earlier in the year had been very successful; thus a devaluation appeared to have no financial justification. Further, it was believed that a second devaluation, coming so soon after the 1949 devaluation, would destroy the sterling area.[46] Of course the basic underlying premiss was that American assistance would soon be forthcoming.

But the British faith in the imminent arrival of American aid was misplaced. To the contrary, the period after 6 November marked the high point of American use of economic pressure on Britain. The Administration believed that 'it was extremely important to get the British and French troops out of Egypt as soon as possible'.[47] In Humphrey's words, as long as troops were left in Egypt, 'the U.S. Government did not consider [the British] had yet given sufficient evidence of their readiness to carry through the United Nations Resolutions'.[48] Thus as dollars rapidly drained from the Bank of England the British envoys in Washington, newly arrived Ambassador Sir Harold Caccia and Lord Harcourt, found in the latter's words that

[44] Telephone call to Henry Cabot Lodge, 2 Nov. 1956, DP/DDE, Tel. Convs., Box 5; telephone call to Allen Dulles, 1 Nov. 1956, Tel. Convs., Box 5.

[45] Eisenhower was determined not to discuss the question of oil supplies until the British and French withdrawal had begun. See e.g. Memorandum of Conference with the President, 21 Nov. 1956, DP/DDE, WHM, Box 4.

[46] Memorandum of a meeting of the Staff Group on Foreign Interests, 5 Oct. 1956, FRBNY, 0961; Bolton, 'The Foreign Exchange Market', 7 Nov. 1956, B/E, G1/124.

[47] Memorandum of Conversation between the President, the Secretary of State, and Mr. Hoover, Jr., 7 Nov. 1956, DP/DDE, WHM, Box 4.

[48] Caccia to FO, 27 Nov. 1956, B/E, G1/124, No. 2356.

'we meet a brick wall at every turn with the Administration'. A former partner in the merchant bank of Morgan Grenfell and the great grandson of Junius Spencer Morgan, Harcourt shrewdly analysed Humphrey and the other US Treasury representatives he was dealing with:

My own view is that the feeling within the Administration is considerably more hostile than it is amongst the general public. They are hurt and piqued at our action which they look on as a blunder and they seem determined to treat us as naughty boys who have got to be taught that they cannot go off and act on their own without asking Nanny's permission first.[49]

Thus the British attempt to place conditions on their withdrawal was totally unavailing as the double-barrelled pressure of no aid for the pound and no oil for western Europe forced them inexorably into surrender. Furthermore, there were no alternatives to American assistance. Although only thirty years distant, the Suez crisis occurred in a different monetary world from that of the present day. By today's standards, the international financial system was in its infancy, and the US government not only presided over the main capital markets but funded and controlled international institutions such as the IMF and the World Bank.[50] Indeed it was because the United States had a monopoly on the world's dominant currency that its use of financial weapons against Britain was so strikingly successful. Such a policy could not be accomplished today, when not only are international institutions far more independent of the United States but privately held dollars (and other, stronger currencies) within and without the United States far exceed American or other governmental holdings. The British considered going to the New York market for a private loan but not only did US Treasury officials discourage them from taking such a step but the amount which could be raised, around $200m., would not have been sufficient given the catastrophic drain.[51] Not surprisingly then, the Bank and the Treasury urged the government to 'do all in our power to accelerate the return of conditions in which the U.S. Administration is likely to be well disposed towards us', and to authorize J. P. Morgan & Company to sell around $55m. of US Treasury bills.[52]

[49] Harcourt to Rowan, 19 Nov. 1956, B/E, G1/124.

[50] The American attitude to the IMF, which was appreciated completely by the British, is best summed up by Humphrey's comment to Dulles that an IMF loan amounted to the same thing as an American loan; telephone conversation with Humphrey, 5 Dec. 1956, DP/DDE, Tel. Convs., Box 5.

[51] F. J. Portsmore, 'Possible Sources of Dollar Borrowing', 16 Nov. 1956; G. H. Tansley, 'Possibility of Raising a Dollar Loan in New York', 23 Nov. 1956, B/E, OV 31/55.

[52] A. M. Stamp to Bolton, 13 Nov. 1956; Harcourt to Sir Roger Makins, 19 Nov. 1956, B/E, G1/124.

The composition of the Eisenhower Administration was such as to ensure maximum use of the financial power at its disposal. Lawyers, bankers, and businessmen who are conversant with international finance are traditionally Republican and this was never more true than during the Eisenhower era. They were well represented in Washington. John Foster Dulles and Allen Dulles were former partners of Sullivan & Cromwell, a major international law firm; trouble-shooter Robert Anderson was a Texas oil man; and industrialist George Humphrey served as Secretary of the Treasury. Furthermore, men like John J. McCloy, Chief Executive Officer of the Chase Manhattan Bank, served as advisers and were always available to take on special missions. Indeed the mid-century decade was the apogee of influence for what might be termed an American financial–industrial complex that drew its strength from the exercise of America's overwhelming economic and military power by the newly interventionist Republican ascendancy.

Time is always of the essence in financial crises and in this instance both the Americans and the British realized that the latter were working under a 3 December deadline. On that day the November reserve figures were scheduled to be released. Either a delay in announcing them or the revelation that British reserves were below $2,000m. would very likely bring down sterling. Thus Britain's incentive to come to terms with the Americans was great indeed, and the Administration had no reason to modifty its stance on Anglo-French withdrawal.[53]

By 22 November the Bank of England decided that its only course was to sell $100m. gold to the New York Federal Reserve Bank.[54] Yet Caccia and Harcourt as late as 26 November found that the Treasury was not yet ready to discuss specifics of a currency support operation.[55] The British were having meetings with Humphrey and his staff rather than with the State Department, in part because Dulles was still recuperating from his early November operation and in part because Humphrey was determined not to be bulldozed by the State Department. Caccia found this unfortunate because Humphrey struck him as the most anti-British of the Americans.[56]

The support scheme for sterling envisioned by the British was elaborate. It had long been a central tenet of such operations that credits designed to increase the reserves behind a beleaguered currency should be in the largest amount possible. Therefore the British sought

[53] Memorandum of Conference with the President, 21 Nov. 1956, DP/DDE, WHM, Box 4.
[54] Exter Memorandum dated 23 Nov. 1956, concerning telephone conversation with Bolton, 22 Nov. 1956, FRBNY, C261, Bank of England, 1956.
[55] Caccia to FO, 26 Nov. 1956, B/E, G1/124, No. 2347.
[56] Caccia to FO, 23 Nov. 1956, B/E, G1/124, No. 2335.

an IMF drawing of $561m. together with a stand-by arrangement of $739m. in tandem with an Ex-Im Bank loan of $700m. By mid-November it was clear that the month's losses would exceed $200m.; in the event the actual figure was $279m.[57]

The US Treasury was willing to discuss details on 27 November. Humphrey told Caccia that, 'if and when overt cooperation by the U.S. became possible', the IMF drawing would also be possible as would an Ex-Im loan. While the question of a further IMF stand-by was problematic, perhaps because it had been previously and thoroughly discussed, Humphrey was amenable to a British approach on the waiver question.[58]

Negotiations with the Americans on the terms of an Ex-Im loan continued as the Treasury worked on the Chancellor's statement explaining the reserve figures which was scheduled to be delivered to the House of Commons on 3 December. The Foreign Office cabled Caccia a draft in order to get American clearance on what would largely be a summary of US-generated support measures.[59] As late as 1 December the situation was not yet clear; Caccia told the Foreign Office that 'The definitive U.S. Treasury attitude to the statement will, of course, depend on general political developments over the weekend and the receipt of the green light from the President or State Department.'[60]

Indeed matters were unchanged the next day when Humphrey called Harcourt and 'again emphasized that any financial support was subject to agreement on the political front'. The sticking point was American insistence, particularly on Dulles's part, that the British name a precise date and timetable for withdrawal. Thus on 3 December there was neither a Chancellor's speech in the Commons nor a release of reserve figures. Instead the British envoys spent the day with Humphrey and Robert Murphy at the State Department, negotiating over what British action would satisfy the Americans. The issue was decided at the highest levels. Caccia saw Murphy and explained that, while the British felt it was impossible to set a definitive date, in the words of the Foreign Office, 'the plain facts of the case ... are that we have decided to go without delay and we intend to go without delay'.[61] Dulles then called Eisenhower, who was in Augusta, Georgia, and together they agreed that the British 'had gone adequately to meet the

[57] 'First Draft of Cable to Commonwealth Governments', 13 Nov. 1956; 'Statement in the House of Commons by the Rt. Hon. Harold Macmillan, Chancellor of the Exchequer', 4 Dec. 1956, B/E, G1/124.

[58] Caccia to FO, 27 Nov. 1956, B/E, G1/124, No. 2355.

[59] FO to Caccia, 22 Nov. 1956, B/E, G1/124, Nos. 5488 and 5491.

[60] Caccia to FO, 1 Dec. 1956, B/E, G1/124, No. 2393.

[61] Caccia to FO, 2 Dec. 1956, B/E, G1/124, No. 2396.

requirements'. Thus, finally, late in the afternoon Caccia could tell the Foreign Office that the British would now have full US support.[62] The Administration could rest secure in its belief that it had taken the correct stand against its allies who, in Humphrey's words, had 'violated the basic principles in which we believe'.[63] His erstwhile allies might be forgiven if they took a different view of the situation.

POSTSCRIPT

Humphrey had all along said that if the green light was given, the British would get massive US support.[64] In this he was true to his word and in a most expeditious fashion. An IMF loan for $561,470,000 and a further stand-by credit for $738,530,000 was approved by the IMF Executive Board on 10 December. On 12 December the British received $250m.; the remainder of the loan was made available the following week.[65] The commitment for a $500m. line of credit from the Ex-Im Bank was announced on 21 December (the Agreement itself was signed on 25 February 1957). In December the British placed the interest portion of the US Agreement annual debt service in an escrow account with the New York Federal Reserve Bank. An amending Agreement was signed by the two governments on 6 March 1957. It eliminated the waiver formula in favour of granting the British the unconditional right to defer interest and principal payments a total of seven times.[66] After Congressional ratification, the escrowed amounts were released to the Bank of England.

Appendix

The language of the waiver clause of the US Agreement (Section 5) provided that Britain would be eligible for a waiver of interest if:

(A) The government of the United Kingdom finds a waiver is necessary in view of the present and prospective conditions of international exchange and level of its gold and foreign exchange reserves and,

[62] Telephone conversation with the President, 3 Dec. 1956, telephone call to Lodge, 3 Dec. 1956, DP/DDE, Tel. Convs., Box 5; Caccia to FO, Nos. 2401 and 2405, 3 Dec. 1956, FO to Caccia, No. 5681, 3 Dec. 1956, B/E, G1/124.

[63] W. Randolph Burgess to Dulles, 7 Dec. 1956, enclosing draft of speech to be delivered by Humphrey to a dinner of the Pennsylvania Society in New York on 8 Dec. 1956, DP, Personal Papers, Box 104.

[64] See e.g. Caccia to FO, No. 2352, 27 Nov. 1956, No. 2396, 2 Dec. 1956, B/E, G1/124.

[65] 'Memorandum to the Files: United Kingdom: Use of [IMF] Fund's Resources', 11 Dec. 1956, FRBNY, 798.3.

[66] Caccia to FO, 20 Dec. 1956, B/E, OV 31/55, No. 26, Remac; F. J. Portsmore, 'Present Position on Exim Loan and Waiver', 19 Mar. 1957, OV 31/57.

(B) The International Monetary Fund certifies that the income of the United Kingdom from home-produced exports plus its net income from invisible current transactions in its balance of payments was on the average over the five preceding calendar years less than the average annual amount of United Kingdom imports during 1936–8, fixed at £866M, as such figure may be adjusted for changes in the price level of these imports.

For the years 1951–5 average income was to be computed for the calendar years from 1950 until the year preceding that in which the request was made.

However, the United States was also concerned to ensure that Britain did not prefer other obligations over the US debt. Thus Section 6 (iii) of the US Agreement stated that no waiver of interest will be allowed or requested unless

the aggregate of the releases or payments in that year of sterling balances accumulated to the credit of overseas governments, monetary authorities and banks (except in the case of colonial dependencies) before the effective date of the Agreement is reduced proportionately.

The problem was that while the intent of the clause was apparent, i.e., to ensure that payments on sterling balances were correspondingly reduced in any year when interest payments were waived, the language was unworkable. For one thing, it was not clear what 'year' was referred to. Practically speaking, the year referred to would have to be the next succeeding year so that after a waiver was received the British government would reduce sterling payments proportionately. Instead the US Agreement appeared to call for simultaneous proportionate reductions of payments in respect of the sterling balances and of interest payments, which was not feasible because sterling balances were reduced throughout the year as opposed to interest payments which were made at the end of the year.

Further, by 1955 most of the sterling balances were no longer blocked, making it very difficult to reduce withdrawals. In fact, the only country with major blocked accounts, that is to say sterling accounts at the Bank of England which the holder could not draw against at will, was Egypt. However, the British government was loath to enter into negotiations with Nasser in the autumn of 1955 to reduce the amount of free sterling he would receive during 1956.

12

The Soviet Union, the United States, and the Twin Crises of Hungary and Suez

JOHN C. CAMPBELL

IN a brief two-week period in October–November 1956 eruptions of violence in central Europe and in the Middle East shook the foundations of the two major alliance systems and of such stability as the international order had at that time. This was a period of still intense Cold War despite significant measures of *détente* taken in the previous year. Thus, any crisis, even one arising within one coalition, inevitably raised questions about the superpower relationship, the balance of power, and the maintenance of peace between the two blocs. Simultaneous crises increased the complications and the dangers.

Although the two situations were not parallel, let us for purposes of analysis see whether they conformed to any common pattern. The discipline of both blocs seemed to be breaking down. In each case the superpower directly involved had to cope with a challenge which, although not created by the other, might be turned, perhaps disastrously, to the other's advantage. Each superpower, in making its own decisions on intervention or other action, had to consider the possible reaction of the other. Each, in weighing the words and acts of the other and the risks of war, had to judge what was bluff and what was real. Unacknowledged but central to all these calculations was the question: Was there a mutual recognition of spheres of influence to the extent that neither power would mount a military challenge in the sphere of the other, even though such action might seem justified by ideological imperatives, local invitation, or local circumstance?

How far did the two powers count on such a proposition in deciding on their conduct in Hungary and at Suez? How did the Soviets view the American factor in their decisions on Hungary, and how did the Americans view the Soviet factor in dealing with the Suez crisis? How did developments in one theatre affect policies adopted by the two powers in the other?

It may be useful, before drawing the comparison too finely, to point out the significant differences between the two situations. The Soviet bloc in 1956, obviously, was not comparable to the Western alliance, and certainly not to any alignment in the Middle East. Its East European members, nominal allies in the Warsaw Pact and through bilateral treaties, did not have any real independence in matters of foreign policy. After the loss of Yugoslavia in 1948 Stalin had made sure, through purges and tightened control, that no others would follow Tito's separate road. His successors were just as determined to keep the bloc intact. However, as the winds of change began to blow after his death, they were not always in agreement on how to do it. The struggle for power in the Kremlin, the 'new course' in some of the satellites, the riots in east Berlin and elsewhere, the cultural thaw, the reconciliation with Tito, and above all the 20th Party Congress and Khrushchev's speech there introduced large areas of uncertainty into Soviet–satellite relations. How far would de-Stalinization go? If Yugoslavia was to be accepted on Tito's terms—and that was the purport of the Soviet–Yugoslav declarations agreed in Belgrade in 1955 and Moscow in 1956—might Titoism make its influence felt within the bloc, perhaps with Moscow's consent?

The events of the Polish October did not dispel impressions of uncertainty and of Soviet indecision. The Polish Communists, in a dramatic confrontation and hard bargaining with the Soviet leaders, won a significant although still undefined autonomy for a Polish road in domestic affairs. In turn, the new Gomulka regime remained loyal to Soviet international policy and to the Warsaw Pact and accepted the continued presence of Soviet troops on Polish territory. The Soviet choice, taken after disagreement and debate among the top leaders, was for political compromise rather than forceful suppression of the Polish challenge.

The Polish October had a bearing on the immediately following events in Hungary. Not only did it provide encouragement to those Hungarians eager for and demanding change, but the Polish model in one guise or another was in the minds of those reaching decisions in Moscow and Washington, as well as in Budapest, as the crisis in Hungary unfolded.

In the Middle East, by way of contrast, there was no hegemonic power. NATO's commitments and treaty structure did not extend to the region, and the Tripartite Declaration of 1950 was but a limited and often ignored instrument. The Western powers had been trying, with indifferent success, to organize a security system against potential Soviet aggression and expansion. The British imperial position was fading, but not the desire to continue in the role of a major power with vital interests to protect, especially access to Middle East oil, as Eden made clear to Bulganin and Khrushchev early in 1956. France, pushed out of Indo-China and embattled in Algeria, was more determined than ever to remain a major Mediterranean power.

The United States had the resources to supplant Britain as leader of the Western allies in the region but made no claim to that role, had no agreed assignment of responsibilities with the British, and continued to differ with them on many issues even as the two powers sought to serve common interests in working together to contain and resolve the Arab–Israeli conflict and to keep the Russians out of the region. The most serious difference was rooted in their approaches to the Egypt of Abdel Nasser. Where London, especially after Eden became Prime Minister, was increasingly intolerant of Nasser's posturing and saw him as a mortal threat to British interests, Washington still sought his co-operation, or at least his neutralization, rather than his destruction. The issue of 'colonialism', especially in Secretary Dulles's interpretation of British policy, did not die.

The row with Egypt over the High Dam and subsequent nationalization of the Suez Canal Company, in which the United States and Britain at first acted together, did not close the gap but widened it, as the British and French moved toward war with Egypt, concerted their plans with Israel, and kept America in the dark. With the triple attack on Egypt and the sharp American reaction of condemnation and opposition, the Western alliance stood revealed as broken in the Middle East and possibly severely injured where it counted most, in Europe.

What did this mean for the Russians? They had already gained a measure of influence in the Middle East through their arms deliveries to Egypt and Syria following the breakthrough in 1955. Their friend Nasser was under attack and their newly won position in jeopardy. Could they do anything to help him and, more important, to exploit the disarray in Western ranks? In the perspective of the global relationship with America and the West, and taking account of the demands of the situation in eastern Europe, what could be done?

Each superpower entered the period of double crisis sure of its bedrock purposes but unsure of its own course, of the reactions of the other, and of where events might lead.

HUNGARY

When violence broke out in Budapest on 23 October and following days, the men in the Kremlin had to deal with a fluid situation, to decide what changes were tolerable, and to weight the need for the use of force. Doubtless their preference was to handle matters directly with the Hungarians without interference from anywhere: from inside the bloc, from Yugoslavia, or from the West. But if it came to the use of force, could they act without regard to reactions from the West?

In the first days of the revolt the East–West dimension did not loom large in the calculations of authorities either in Budapest or in Moscow. Imre Nagy, who became Prime Minister on 23 October with Soviet consent, did not place himself at the head of the popular revolt or challenge Soviet primacy. He sought to maintain order, as Moscow wished; he promised reforms as a means of ending the uprising; he hoped to negotiate the withdrawal of Soviet forces from Budapest but did not endorse the popular cry of 'Russians, go home!' On the positive side he wanted greater autonomy in domestic affairs, and no reversion to Stalinism. He took this view on the basis of advice he got from the Soviet Ambassador (Andropov) and from Anastas Mikoyan and Mikhail Suslov, two members of the Soviet Presidium who were in Budapest on several occasions and notably from 24 to 26 October.[1]

It appeared, up to 28 October at least, that the outcome would be on the Polish model, with the Soviets accepting greater Hungarian autonomy in domestic policies and practices but with the Communist system intact and the security interests of the Soviet Union fully safeguarded. Khrushchev, as far as we know, would have settled for that result, although the fact that he did not have a united presidium behind him left some doubt as to what the final decisions would be.[2]

In Washington the assessment of Hungarian events was not so very different. The high officials of the Eisenhower Administration were impressed by what had happened in Poland and saw the same thing happening in Hungary. They appraised these developments as proving the rightness and effectiveness of their own declared policy of 'liberation': the subject peoples of the Soviet empire, encouraged by the message of freedom coming from the West, were winning greater independence for themselves, and Moscow was apparently accepting it for lack of a better alternative. Secretary Dulles saw the 'great monolith of Communism' crumbling under the pressure of the East European peoples' conviction that genuine independence was attainable.[3]

---

[1] Indirect evidence indicates that their respective views and counsels did not always coincide. Suslov had gone to Hungary in July 1956 and reported on his return to Moscow that Mátyás Rákosi, the Stalinist leader, should stay in charge. Mikoyan went to Hungary a few days later and reported that the Hungarian comrades, presumably with his advice, had thought it better to replace Rákosi; the Presidium of the Soviet Communist Party agreed. See Veljko Mičunović, *Moscow Diary* (Garden City, NY, 1980), pp. 87–91; Sir William Hayter, *The Kremlin and the Embassy* (New York, 1966), p. 152.

[2] Jiri Valenta, 'Soviet Policy toward Hungary and Czechoslovakia', in *Soviet Policy in Eastern Europe*, ed. Sarah M. Terry (New Haven, 1984), pp. 99–101.

[3] Quoted in Herman Finer, *Dulles over Suez* (Chicago, 1964), p. 343.

Eisenhower was aware of the critical importance of the role of Soviet troops, those already stationed in Hungary and involved in the fighting and those which might be brought in from outside. In a public statement on 25 October he deplored the prior intervention by Soviet forces and noted that their presence, 'as is now demonstrated, is not to protect Hungary against armed aggression from without, but rather to continue an occupation of Hungary by the forces of an alien government for its own purposes'.[4] He foresaw the possibility that the Soviet Union for reasons of its own security would move in with strong new forces to suppress the Hungarian revolt. To help deter that eventuality the American tactic was to reassure rather than to warn or to threaten. The President, who thought the Soviets might be tempted to take extreme measures, 'even to start a world war', was very cautious about raising the temperature.[5]

Washington wished to see the situation in Hungary stabilized so as to lessen the chances of Soviet intervention. The initial US objective for eastern Europe, in the words of a policy paper prepared for the consideration of the National Security Council, was 'the emergence of "national" communist governments, which might still be in a close military alliance with the Soviet Union', as in Poland, for example.[6] But how the situation could be stabilized if what was really happening was the crumbling of Communism and the assertion of genuine Hungarian independence was not clear.

American policy was unveiled to the world in Dulles's speech in Dallas on 27 October. The speech had been in preparation for several days and reflected the thinking of both Dulles and Eisenhower. 'Let me make this clear, beyond a possibility of doubt', said Dulles, 'the United States has no ulterior purpose in desiring the independence of the satellite countries. ... We do not look upon these people as potential military allies'. He offered economic aid as they sought 'to rededicate their productive efforts to the service of their own people, rather than of exploiting masters'. But such aid was not conditioned upon the adoption by these countries 'of any particular form of society'.[7]

How should these declarations be interpreted? Dulles meant them seriously and hoped that the Soviet leaders might be influenced in the direction of moderation. He instructed Ambassador Bohlen in Moscow to draw the attention of the top Soviet leaders to the paragraph about not seeking military allies in eastern Europe—which Bohlen did, but

---

[4] *Department of State Bulletin*, 5 Nov. 1956, p. 700.

[5] Dwight D. Eisenhower, *Waging Peace, 1956–1961* (Garden City, NY, 1965), p. 67. See also Donald Neff, *Warriors at Suez* (New York, 1981), p. 352; Bennett Kovrig, *The Myth of Liberation* (Baltimore, 1973), p. 181.

[6] NSC 5616, 31 Oct. 1956 (prepared by the Planning Board for meeting of 1 Nov. 1956).

[7] *Department of State Bulletin*, 5 Nov. 1956, pp. 695–9.

they evinced little interest.[8] The signals that Khrushchev, who was already convinced that US policy was to break off individual Communist States from the bloc, got from the Dulles speech were surely (*a*) that the protestations of moderation were false, (*b*) that America had encouraged the Hungarian revolt, but (*c*) that the Soviet Union had a free hand if it wished to use force to put it down.

From that point on the decisive actors in the developing situation were the popular forces in Hungary, with their rising demands directed against both Soviet overlordship and the Communist system, and the Soviet Union, trying to hold the line on both those points without resorting to naked intervention with forces from outside Hungary, but not excluding that alternative. In the middle was the Nagy government, pushed forward on the wave of revolution but trying to control it, impressing on the Russians the need for change but wary of provoking them.

The issues had sharpened considerably by 29 October. There was momentary calm as most of the fighting had stopped, but the popular pressure for political change and for ending the Russian presence was increasing; the Communist party had virtually dissolved and was incapable of running the country. Nagy reorganized the party leadership, brought some non-Communists into the government, and abolished the hated security police. It looked as if he still had Soviet support. Mikoyan and Suslov came back to Budapest on 30 October and talked with Hungarian leaders. No minutes of their conversations are available, but the testimony of some Hungarian participants indicates that the Russians agreed to the measures which Nagy announced publicly that same day putting an end to the one-party system and placing the government on a basis of 'democratic co-operation' among the four coalition parties of the 1945–7 period. They also agreed, it appears, to the withdrawal of Soviet troops and to negotiations on Hungary's withdrawal from the Warsaw Pact.[9]

As if in co-ordination with these agreements and pronouncements in Budapest the Soviet government on the same day, 30 October, issued a declaration (carried in *Pravda* on the 31st) on the relations among socialist nations, stressing the principles of sovereignty and equality (along with proletarian internationalism) and making conciliatory statements about the withdrawal of troops from Budapest and from all of Hungary. The fact that the declaration made no mention of

---

[8] Telegram, Dulles to Bohlen, No. 510, 29 Oct. 1956; Bohlen to Dulles, Nos. 993, 1005, 30 Oct. 1956, Declassified Documents, 1984, 2612, 2613, 2614; Charles E. Bohlen, *Witness to History* (New York, 1973), pp. 412–14. (Declassified Documents are on microfiche, catalogue published by Research Publications, Woodbridge, Conn., and Reading, England.)

[9] Charles Gati, *Hungary and the Soviet Bloc* (Durham, NC, 1986), pp. 145–6: Kovrig, *Myth*, p. 185; Paul E. Zinner, *Revolution in Hungary* (New York, 1962), pp. 316–20.

Hungary's abandonment of one-party government or negotiations on the Warsaw Pact and contained ominous references to 'forces of black reaction and counter-revolution' should have raised a warning flag, but did not detract substantially from the general impression of Soviet accommodation to and agreement with the positions the Nagy government had taken.[10]

The very next day (31 October), however, appears to have been the day of the Soviet decision to dispose of the Nagy government and suppress the revolution. Was the declaration of the day before a final effort to reach a settlement without intervention, or was it mere deception, covering a decision to intervene already taken or about to be taken? Ambassador Bohlen, who had previously leaned to the view that the Soviets had decided to cut their losses and pull out, noted on the 30th that they were 'more glum than yesterday', but could only speculate on whether they had reached a decision and what it might be.[11] The available evidence suggests that the crucial political decision was in fact made on the morning of the 31st, just as *Pravda* was spreading the word of a new era in Soviet–satellite relations.[12] It was taken in the absence of Mikoyan and Suslov, who were still in Budapest, either unaware of the deception (which seems unlikely) or active agents of it. In any case, the decision represented a victory for those who had previously argued for the hard line. Khrushchev's taking their side may have been the decisive shift.[13]

By the early morning of 1 November Soviet troops were pouring into Hungary. Nagy got no satisfaction from his inquiries to Andropov (Mikoyan and Suslov had left for home), and so, convinced he had been totally deceived and having the support of the leaders of party and government, declared Hungary's neutrality, withdrew from the Warsaw Pact, appealed to the United Nations, and urged his people to defend 'free, independent, democratic, and neutral Hungary'. The blow did not fall immediately. There was a show of negotiation for a couple of days. Then on 4 November the Soviet army took control of Budapest and the country.

The statements by which Nagy finally made common cause with the desires of the Hungarian people would surely have provoked Soviet

---

[10] Paul E. Zinner (ed.), *National Communism and Popular Revolt in Eastern Europe* (New York, 1956), pp. 485–9.

[11] Telegram, Bohlen to Department of State, No. 1003, 30 Oct. 1956, Declassified Documents, 1983, 952. See also Bohlen, *Witness*, p. 412.

[12] Gati, *Hungary*, p. 148.

[13] Strobe Talbott (ed.), *Khrushchev Remembers* (Boston, 1970), pp. 417–19. Cf. Bohlen, *Witness*, p. 411; Robert Murphy, *Diplomat among Warriors* (New York, 1965), p. 479; Michael C. Fry and Condoleezza Rice, 'The Hungarian Crisis of 1956: The Soviet Decision', *Studies in Comparative Communism* (spring-summer, 1983), 85–98.

intervention if made earlier. Coming after the intervention was already under way, they were merely the last desperate assertion of national will and a vain cry for help. The Soviet attack was not an answer to Nagy's dramatic declarations. They were an answer to an attack already in progress.

One can speculate on what particular events triggered the decision. It may have been the virtual disappearance of the Communist party, the formation of a government likely to be run by non-Communists, the decision to build a new Hungarian army outside Soviet control, the signs that Nagy and others wished to cut loose from the Warsaw Pact, or simply the momentum of a revolution that neither Nagy nor a Soviet policy of concessions and conciliation seemed able to stop. By 31 October a Polish-type solution to the crisis must have seemed no longer attainable. Khrushchev made an interesting point in his explanation to Tito on 2–3 November on the island of Brioni. If he had failed to act, he said, the Stalinist die-hards and especially the military would have held the new Soviet leadership responsible for 'the loss of Hungary'.[14]

What about the international aspects? The US government, having stated its case in Dulles's speech on 27 October, points repeated by Eisenhower in a broadcast address on the 31st, including specific renunciation of resort to force,[15] did not engage in any direct diplomacy with Moscow with a view to seeking solutions by superpower agreement and was not even well informed as to what was happening in Hungary.[16] Bohlen did the rounds of diplomatic receptions in Moscow, which many of the top Soviet leaders, surprisingly, took the time to attend. Marshal Zhukov, in a conversation with him on 29 October, took a hard line against 'counter-revolutionary' elements in Hungary and said that if the Hungarian government asked for help the Soviet Union would give it, as the Warsaw Pact provided (Bohlen reminded him that it did not) for support of the socialist camp and the protection of socialist governments against any threat.[17] It was an early statement of the Brezhnev Doctrine.

[14] Mičunović, *Moscow Diary*, p. 134.

[15] Paul E. Zinner (ed.), *Documents on American Foreign Relations, 1956* (Harper, for the Council on Foreign Relations, 1957), pp. 49–55.

[16] Several observers, in retrospect, have faulted the United States for not trying a diplomatic approach to offer the Soviet Union something in return for withdrawal of its forces from Hungary, e.g. Fred C. Iklé, *How Nations Negotiate* (New York, 1964), pp. 155–6; Escott Reid, *Hungary and Suez 1956: A view from New Delhi* (Oakville, Ont., 1986), pp. 146–8. Only one US official at the time (the President's Special Assistant on Disarmament) proposed such an approach, suggesting that the US government indicate willingness to consult with NATO allies on the possible withdrawal of some US forces from Europe if the Soviet Union would withdraw all its forces from Hungary (see NSC 5616, 31 Oct. 1956). The proposal was not accepted by the National Security Council.

[17] Telegram, Bohlen to Department of State, No. 992, 30 Oct. 1965, Declassified Documents, 1983, 953.

At 4.40 in the morning of 1 November, Secretary Dulles telephoned the President to report on recent developments in the Suez affair. He also mentioned an NSC meeting to be held that day, at which policy for the East European satellites was on the agenda. That subject, he thought, was academic, 'as the situation has pretty much taken care of it'.[18] Allen Dulles, in giving his intelligence briefing at that meeting, rejoiced in the Hungarian 'miracle', which disproved that a popular revolt cannot occur in the face of modern weapons.[19] On the very day that Imre Nagy declared Hungary's neutrality and appealed to the United Nations for help (1 November) the NSC had before it a draft policy paper stating that the events in Poland and Hungary represented 'a serious defeat for Soviet policy', and that the United States, 'in pursuing its immediate objectives of discouraging and, if possible, preventing further Soviet armed intervention in Hungary as well as harsh measures of repression or retaliation', should 'mobilize all appropriate pressures, including U.N. action, on the USSR against such measures, while reassuring the USSR that we do not look on Hungary or other satellites as potential military allies'.[20]

The yawning gap between hopes and actuality received scant notice at that meeting on 1 November. The subject was 'academic', whether Hungary was to win a measure of freedom or to be crushed. The miraculous revolt had occurred, as Allen Dulles said, but by that time its doom was already sealed. When the full force of Soviet might struck Budapest on 4 November, Washington naturally reacted with outraged protest, but the President's letter that day to Bulganin expressing shock and anger[21] and the ensuing votes and resolutions at the United Nations had no effect on the ultimate outcome.

Were the nature and timing of the Soviet decision to intervene, or the nature of the American reaction or absence of reaction, affected by the contemporaneous crisis over Suez? The correspondence of critical dates was indeed striking. Israel mobilized on 28 October and moved into Sinai the next day. On those two days Nagy was making his decisions to broaden the government and to press for the withdrawal of Soviet troops. On the 30th Britain and France issued their ultimatum, a prelude to certain invasion of Egypt. On that day Nagy announced the end of Communist party rule and the decision to form a new

---

[18] Telephone call, Dulles to Eisenhower, 1 Nov. 1956, Declassified Documents, 1984, 629.

[19] Eisenhower, *Waging Peace*, p. 82.

[20] US Policy toward Developments in Poland and Hungary, 31 Oct. 1956, NSC 5616. This document was not adopted at the meeting of 1 Nov., but a later version, NSC 5616/2, taking account of the Soviet take-over but restating the same policies, was approved by the President, 19 Nov. 1956.

[21] Zinner, *Documents on American Foreign Relations*, pp. 257–8.

national army, and on the following day, at the latest, the Soviets took their decision to intervene.

Scholars attempting to probe into the question of the influence of the Middle East crisis on the Soviet decision to move against Hungary generally believe that it had some influence, at least on the timing, but the reasoning is no more than informed guesswork. One Hungarian historian takes the view that the triple attack on Egypt tipped the balance in Moscow in favour of action.[22] At the time Bohlen reported that the attack on Egypt seemed to divert attention from Hungary, where the revolution was at its peak, and 'may have convinced the Kremlin it had a freer hand to destroy the rebels'.[23] The British Ambassador in Moscow, Sir William Hayter, noted that Suez gave the hard-liners in the Kremlin three good arguments: it would divert Third World criticism away from Russia; Britain and France had set an example of taking the law into their own hands; and the Soviet Union could not afford to take two simultaneous defeats in Egypt and in Hungary.[24] This was his reasoning, not necessarily theirs, but it makes sense. Statements by Khrushchev himself, in the Yugoslav account of his explanations to Tito, give some confirmation. He listed as one of several reasons for the Soviet decision the Anglo-French intervention at Suez, which would direct the world's attention away from the Soviet Union's 'assistance' to Hungary.[25]

It is hard to point to any one critical event in Hungary or in the Soviet–Hungarian relationship which was responsible for the swift transition from the conciliatory Soviet positions and pronouncements of 28–30 October to the military invasion of the next few days, but the combination of events noted above was developing up to and beyond the limits of Soviet tolerance, regardless of other international developments. Khrushchev and his colleagues became increasingly convinced, by 31 October wholly convinced, that Nagy could not play a Gomulka-like role; that he did not have the personal strength or the institutional structure and military means to do it.

In this they were undoubtedly right. The revolutionary tide probably would have rolled on, with or without Nagy and in the absence of intervention, to the same positions Nagy declared on 1 November—

---

[22] Miklos Molnár, *De Bela Kun à János Kádár: Soixante-dix ans de communisme hongrois* (Paris, 1987), p. 237. I have found no evidence to support the view of Escott Reid, then Canada's High Commissioner to India, that if the British and their co-conspirators had been willing to call off their planned attack some time between 23 and 30 October because of the revolt in Hungary, they might have strengthened the soft-liners in the Kremlin and saved Hungary, especially if the West had opened negotiations and offered something in return. See Reid, *Hungary and Suez*, pp. 140–1.

[23] Bohlen, *Witness*, p. 432.

[24] Hayter, *The Kremlin and the Embassy*, pp. 153–4.

[25] Mičunović, *Moscow Diary*, p. 134.

independence, neutrality, democracy—in reply to the intervention. None of those positions was acceptable to Moscow. Neutrality, in Khrushchev's view, could not have lasted; the Soviet Union would eventually be faced with a hostile Hungary on its border.[26] Moscow might have made its decision when it did, or a day or two earlier or later, but was bound to make it as the only means of preserving 'socialism' in Hungary, of keeping Hungary in the Soviet camp, and of preventing a devastating example for the entire bloc.[27]

No challenge came from the West. Geography, in Eisenhower's view, would have ruled out any US or NATO action in Hungary by ground or air forces; Czechoslovakia and neutral Austria were in the way, NATO commitments did not extend that far, and the European allies would not have joined in such an adventure even if not preoccupied with Nasser. Soviet forces had every advantage.[28] The United States would certainly not have resorted to nuclear war over Hungary—'madness' in Dulles's view[29]—and had been careful not to threaten it as a deterrent to Soviet action. The only danger of nuclear war that Eisenhower saw lay in the possibility that, in panic or as an irrational response to events, the Soviets themselves might initiate a global war. They, as prudent as he, did not.

SUEZ

Egypt was not a mirror image of Hungary. As the latter was being reduced to the status of satellite in the years following World War II, Egypt was going through the reverse process, so that by the mid-1950s, after the Anglo-Egyptian agreement providing for British military withdrawal from the Suez area, it was able to take on a fully independent role in regional and world politics. Nasser was able to play off Britain and America against each other and, after the Czech arms deal of 1955, to play off the Soviet Union against them both. When 1956 brought a test of force in which he was up against Israel and two European powers determined to overthrow him because they saw their vital interests at stake, he was able to survive and win a political victory

[26] Remarks to the Swedish Ambassador, reported in Bohlen's telegram to Department of State, No. 1164, 11 Nov. 1956, Declassified Documents, 1987, 310.

[27] Anatoly Dobrynin, in a conversation with Canadian delegate John Holmes at the United Nations, said that the Soviet Union was prepared at an earlier stage to withdraw its forces from Hungary, but when developments took place which threatened its vital interests not only in Hungary but in all eastern Europe, it had to take the necessary steps to protect them; see John W. Holmes, *The Shaping of Peace: Canada and the search for world order, 1943–1957*, vol. ii (Toronto, 1982), p. 387. Cf. Talbott (ed.), *Khrushchev Remembers*, pp. 417–19; Mičunović, *Moscow Diary*, pp. 132–3; Murphy, *Diplomat among Warriors*, p. 479.

[28] Eisenhower, *Waging Peace*, pp. 88–9.

[29] Andrew H. Berding, *Dulles on Diplomacy* (Princeton, 1965), pp. 115–16.

because the two superpowers, each for its own reasons, rallied to his side.

It was a bizarre scenario from the standpoint of the East–West Cold War currently sharpened by events in Hungary. The Western powers, by their mishandling of relations with Egypt in 1955–6 and the breakdown of their co-operation on the question of the Suez Canal, furnished the Soviet Union with unexpected opportunities to expand its power in the Arab world and perhaps in Europe as well. America, Britain, France, and Israel were all aware of Soviet expansionist designs, and each attempted to justify its conduct as contributing to defence against them. Eden took the line after Egypt's nationalization of the Canal Company on 26 July that Nasser was not only a menace to Britain's vital interests but a tool of the Soviets, while Eisenhower, in his letter to Eden arguing against the use of force, stated that it would alienate the Middle East peoples and open the way for Soviet penetration.[30] It is not always easy to separate rationalization and propaganda from true conviction. In any event, while the eyes of Britain, France, and Israel were focused primarily on the Egyptian enemy, those of the superpowers, even as they voted together in the United Nations, were fixed on each other.

A first question is whether the Hungarian revolt affected the decisions on Suez. It is not apparent that it did in any substantial way. Britain, France, and Israel made their decisions for military action in mid-October, well before the Hungarian revolt broke out. They chose not to change them on that account, apparently never even considering it at any time between 23 and 29 October. They held to their agreed plan and put it into effect on the agreed dates. The Hungarian affair was seen as, if anything, a windfall in that preoccupation with Hungary would reduce Soviet ability to take action in opposition to them.[31] In any case, Hungary or no Hungary, they counted on achieving rapid military success before the Soviet Union could do anything effective in support of Egypt. President Eisenhower, in addition to being angry at Britain and France for their deception, was more concerned about the combined effect of two major crises on America's world position and on the UN system and world peace.

From the start of the Suez war, US policy was dominated by the perceived need (*a*) to take a stand on the issue of principle—to oppose aggression and support its victim by UN action, and thus 'to redeem our word', pledged both in the Charter and in the Tripartite Declara-

---

[30] Eisenhower's letter of 31 July 1956 to Eden, *Waging Peace*, pp. 664–5 (see above, p. 199).

[31] Ben-Gurion, in informing the Cabinet of his plans on 28 October, mentioned that the Soviet Union had enough power to crush the revolt in Hungary and also to intervene in the Middle East, but said he felt Israel had to take that risk and go ahead with the attack on Egypt (see Yaacov Bar-Siman-Tov, *Israel, the Superpowers, and the War in the Middle East* (New York, 1987), p. 45.

tion of 1950; (*b*) to gain, maintain, or regain prestige and influence in the Arab world and the Third World generally; and (*c*) to compete successfully with the Russians and keep them out of the Middle East. Let us follow the thread of the third factor. Eisenhower's reaction to the news of the Israeli invasion on 29 October (compounded the next day by word of the Anglo-French ultimatum) was that 'if we do not now fulfil our word, Russia is likely to enter the situation in the Middle East', and that the United States, accordingly, should go immediately to the United Nations 'before the USSR gets there'.[32] Dulles, a couple of days later, found it 'nothing less than tragic that at this very time when we are on the point of winning an immense and long-hoped-for victory over Soviet colonialism in eastern Europe [*!*], we should be forced to choose between following in the footsteps of Anglo-French colonialism in Asia and Africa, or splitting our course away from their course'.[33]

What were the Russians doing in the opening days of the Suez war? Earlier, in August, Khrushchev had stated in the presence of many diplomats that if the colonial powers made war on Egypt, Egypt would not be left alone in an armed battle against the West; and that if his son decided to go as a volunteer, he (Khrushchev) would give him his blessing.[34] In letters to Eden and Mollet in September and October Bulganin had warned against military action in the Middle East since aggression there 'touches on the security of the Soviet Union'.[35] From 28 October to the final assault on Budapest on 4 November, however, they were less assertive. At that time they were making their basic decisions on Hungary, carrying through their reconquest, and establishing a puppet regime. Those concerns must have reduced the attention and resources they could devote to the Suez crisis, although one cannot measure it.

In those first days the Soviets confined their action largely to public denunciation of Britain, France, and Israel and to taking positions against them at the United Nations, where they proposed resolutions of their own and eventually voted in favour of the American resolutions (one of which, incidentally, called on member states to refrain from sending arms into the area of hostilities). They offered no military aid to Nasser, who already had a goodly supply of Soviet equipment. According to an interview given much later by Nasser, he requested American help on 1 November but neither wanted nor asked for the

[32] Memorandum of conversation, Eisenhower and Dulles, 29 Oct. 1956, *Declassified Documents*, 1985, 1373.

[33] Eisenhower, *Waging Peace*, p. 83.

[34] Mičunović, *Moscow Diary*, pp. 103–4.

[35] Oles M. Smolansky, 'Moscow and the Suez Crisis, 1956: A Reappraisal', *Political Science Quarterly* (Dec. 1965), 581–605.

help of Soviet military forces, chiefly because he knew that Soviet military intervention would have meant world war.[36] For obvious geographic reasons the Soviet Union could not furnish Egypt with effective military support, and Khrushchev told Shukri el-Quwatly, the Syrian President then visiting Moscow, and the Egyptian Ambassador there not to expect it.[37] It was parallel to America's position with respect to Hungary.

A central reason for Soviet reticence may well have been uncertainty as to where America really stood. If Washington was secretly in league with the British and French—the Soviets may have believed their own propaganda on that point—a commitment to Egypt carried the danger of a military conflict with America.[38] Back in August Dulles had told them, through Bohlen, that if it came to the crunch the United States would support its allies.[39]

In any event, Soviet diplomacy became much more aggressive after 4 November when the Hungarian crisis as a threat to Soviet security was laid to rest and when America's stand in the Middle East was absolutely clear even to Moscow. At that time the British and French were still resisting US and UN pressure and trying to get on with their military campaign. Moscow's propaganda indicated that the Soviet government felt able to flex its muscles and to set alarm bells ringing that it might inject itself more directly into the Suez affair by actions of a military character. Then, in the evening of 5 November, just as Eden was trying to decide whether to yield to pressures from the United States, the Commonwealth, and a sizeable section of the British public and call off the military campaign, Bulganin dispatched his threatening letters to Eden, Mollet, and Ben-Gurion.

Those messages, broadcast by Moscow radio almost at the time of delivery, could be taken as threats of direct Soviet missile attack, although their wording did not go quite that far. 'In what situation would Britain find herself,' read the letter to Eden, 'if she were attacked by a stronger power possessing all types of modern weapons of destruction? Indeed, such countries, instead of sending to the shores of Britain their naval or air forces, could use other means, for instance rocket equipment. ... We are fully determined to use force to smash

[36] Kennett Love, *Suez: The Twice-Fought War* (New York, 1969), p. 557.

[37] Mohamed Heikal, *The Cairo Documents* (Garden City, NY, 1973), pp. 111–12; id., *The Sphinx and the Commissar* (New York, 1978), pp. 70–1. According to Heikal, a few days later Khrushchev told the Ambassador that he did not really mean his first refusal and that, with the sending of the Bulganin letters of 5 Nov., 'we shall stand beside you to defeat aggression'.

[38] Smolansky, 'Moscow and the Suez Crisis, 1956', p. 593; id., *The Soviet Union and the Arab East under Khrushchev* (Lewisburg, Pa, 1974), pp. 47–8. Cf. E. M. Primakov, *Anatomiia Blizhnevostochnogo Konflikta* (Moscow, 1978), pp. 216–20.

[39] Bohlen, *Witness*, pp. 428–9.

the aggressors and restore peace . . .'[40] The Soviet messages set no time limit, but a Soviet draft resolution just submitted at the United Nations proposed that if British, French, and Israeli forces were not withdrawn in three days, the members of the United Nations, especially the United States and the Soviet Union, should aid Egypt with military forces.[41]

How seriously were the references to rockets falling on Britain and France to be taken? They had to be a bluff unless the Soviet leaders really did possess the necessary weapons and had made a decision for global nuclear war, for they knew that would be the result of such an attack. Eden later wrote in his memoirs that the Russians, knowing that the United States was taking the lead against Britain and France at the United Nations, felt they could snarl with the pack and then claim credit for stopping the war. His decision to give up and accept a cease-fire, made in the early hours of 6 November, probably was, as he said, due not to fear of Soviet missiles but to all the other pressures on him.[42] But the atmosphere that night was not one of complacency in London and Paris, or in Washington for that matter. The tough Russian talk could be translated as nuclear blackmail.

The following morning (6 November) the British government anxiously awaited an intelligence report from the American Embassy, receiving with obvious relief Washington's conclusion that the Soviet threat was a bluff, as it was very doubtful that the Soviets had the missile capability or the nuclear warheads.[43] That evening Eden told the House of Commons of his firm rejection of the Soviet threat and added some sharp comments on Soviet conduct in Hungary. At the same time he announced Britain's acceptance of the United Nations demand for a cease-fire.

How did the Americans assess this episode? Bohlen, though not ruling out Soviet military action of some kind (including a move into Iran, submarine action in the Mediterranean, air attacks from bases in Syria, or even the sending of 'volunteers' to Egypt), had judged the primary Soviet aim to be the cessation of hostilities, not the broadening of the war. After the sending of Bulganin's messages he found the situation 'more ominous' and thought that, if the war continued, it would be increasingly difficult for the Soviet government to maintain inaction in view of its own statements. Soviet moves in the Suez crisis, in Bohlen's view, had gone well beyond being simply a cover for the

---

[40] Yaacov Ro'i (ed.), *From Encroachment to Involvement: A Documentary Study of Soviet Policy in the Middle East* (New York and Toronto, 1974), pp. 188–9.

[41] UN Document No. S/3736, 5 Nov. 1956.

[42] Robert Rhodes James, *Anthony Eden* (New York, 1987), pp. 572–4.

[43] Chester L. Cooper, *The Lion's Last Roar: Suez, 1956* (New York, 1978), pp. 199–200.

action against Hungary.[44] Khrushchev at a later date stated that at no time had the Soviet Union contemplated unilateral military action in the Middle East,[45] but if so, neither Bohlen nor his government could know it on 5 November.

The US government, on 5 and 6 November, was trying to deal simultaneously with several related aspects of the crisis and to fit them into an acceptable solution. In all of them, keeping the Soviets out of the game was a leading theme. Eisenhower and his advisers (Foster Dulles now being in the hospital) were trying to put the final pressure on Eden and Mollet to stop the fighting; they were urging Hammarsk-jöld, Pearson, and others to get the UN force organized as quickly as possible; and they were coping with the barrage of threats that came out of Moscow on 5 November. The Soviet proposal made directly to Eisenhower was that unless the aggressors stopped the war, the two superpowers should act together to apply force and make them do so.[46]

Prominent among America's reasons for pressing for an early cease-fire was the desire to forestall any Soviet intervention, especially after Moscow's bellicose messages on the 5th. Ending the war would presumably end the temptation and the excuse for Soviet military action and also reduce potential Soviet political gains in the Arab world. As for the UN force in the process of formation, Eisenhower insisted that the major powers not contribute forces to it. In a telephone call on the 6 November he urged Eden to accept the cease-fire without conditions and give up the idea of British participation in the United Nations Emergency Force (UNEF), so that they could keep out 'the Red boy', who would likely demand the lion's share.[47]

In dealing with the Soviet threats and proposals Eisenhower felt that he had to make it clear to the Soviet leaders that the United States would stand by Britain and France if they were attacked either on their home territory or in the Middle East. Although he believed that the Soviets wished to avoid global war and were not likely to provoke it in the face of unambiguous US warnings, he thought them capable, in view of the failure of their policies in eastern Europe, of 'any wild adventure'.[48] He did not give an immediate and specific response to the veiled threats to rain missiles on London and Paris. America's allies could reject those threats in the knowledge of NATO commitments

---

[44] Telegrams, Bohlen to Department of State, Nos. 1091, 1093, 6 Nov. 1956, Declassified Documents, 1987, 268, 269; Bohlen, *Witness*, pp. 432–3.

[45] Conversation with Swedish Ambassador (see n. 26 above).

[46] Ro'i (ed.), *From Encroachment to Involvement*, pp. 187–8.

[47] Telephone call, Eisenhower to Eden, 6 Nov. 1956, Declassified Documents, 1983, 1430.

[48] Eisenhower, *Waging Peace*, pp. 89–90; Neff, *Warriors at Suez*, p. 403.

and of the declared US policy of 'massive retaliation', of which the Russians were also well aware.[49]

As for the Soviet proposal, preposterous in Eisenhower's eyes, for joint military action to put an end to the aggression in Egypt, the White House issued a statement on 6 November that neither Soviet nor any other forces should enter the Middle East except under the UN mandate, and that it would be the duty of all UN members, including the United States, to oppose such a move. That was a clear message both to the Kremlin and to the European allies. The most important thing the Soviet Union could do for world peace, the statement added pointedly, would be to stop its repression of the Hungarian people and withdraw its troops from Hungary.[50]

The White House statement, on the face of it, covered any Soviet military action against Israel. Israel, however, had not yet agreed to a cease-fire, which Washington was pressing her in the strongest terms to accept. The Israelis took the American position to be that, without such acceptance, the United States would not protect Israel against a Soviet attack. After Ben-Gurion, seeing no alternative, gave in on 8 November, American officials assured Ambassador Eban that in the new situation 'the Soviet attitude would become irrelevant, for the United States would deter the fulfilment or even the reiteration of Soviet threats'.[51]

The worst of the crisis was over with the acceptance of the cease-fire by the warring parties and the constitution of UNEF. But the Soviet Union, trumpeting its decisive role as saviour of the peace and friend and protector of the Arabs, continued to be troublesome, taking exception to delays in the evacuation of forces from Egyptian territory, threatening to send volunteers to take part in 'the struggle of the Egyptian people for their independence' (a threat not made before the cease-fire), and talking about the danger of world war. If nothing else, these moves reminded the Western powers that the Russians were not going to co-operate in cleaning up the mess and in reaching political settlements in the area, but would exploit the effects of the Suez affair

---

[49] In an interview with Kennett Love some years later Eisenhower said that 'we just told them, really, it would be global war if they started it, that's all.' The point was made in those terms a week later in a speech by General Alfred Gruenther, NATO Supreme Commander: 'If Russia attacked the West with its missiles, the Soviet Union and the Soviet bloc would be destroyed . . . as sure as day follows night'. See Love, *Suez*, pp. 614–16.

[50] Zinner (ed.), *Documents on American Foreign Relations*, pp. 357–8.

[51] Abba Eban, *An Autobiography* (New York, 1977), p. 232. See also Bar-Siman-Tov, *Israel*, pp. 61–5, arguing that the US government took the Soviet threat to Israel seriously and was unwilling to act to deter it.

and the split among the Western powers to the best of their ability. In later years Soviet writers developed an elaborate argument to the effect that Soviet intervention in the crisis was decisive in thwarting the imperialists (including the United States) and defending Arab rights and interests.[52]

Eisenhower assured both Eden and Mollet, when he was urging them to stop the Suez war, that he wished to repair the Western alliance as soon as possible in order to block the Russians. Eden and Mollet, for their part, were deploring American policies which had frustrated their efforts to dispose of Russia's chief ally in the area, Nasser, thus indirectly helping Russian expansionism. These disagreements continued into the post-crisis period, as British and French resentment and American self-righteousness still poisoned their relations. In opposing a 'Big Three' summit meeting in the aftermath of the crisis, Dulles drafted some 'thoughts' in his room in the Walter Reed Hospital. As basic differences were not likely to be settled, he believed that a conference could only try to cover them up, and that would 'greatly prejudice our own position in the world, tie us to policies doomed to failure, and expose the Middle East and Africa to almost certain Soviet penetration and dominance'. The only chance of saving those areas from such a fate lay 'in adhering to and developing the recent policies of the United States'.[53]

It was a high point of American optimism. Power and morality would go hand in hand. However, as the United States set about the task of developing those recent policies amid the complexities of the Middle East—trying to draw on its moral capital, to repair relations with European allies on its own terms, to reknit close ties with Israel, to come to terms with Arab nationalism but somehow find and support alternative leadership (e.g. King Saud) more trustworthy than Nasser (still considered a dangerous antagonist and *de facto* ally of the Soviet Union),[54] to fill the 'vacuum' in the Middle East perceived to have been created by the British and French débâcle, and to rally Third World nations to co-operate with America against Soviet imperialism—things did not work out in quite that way.

[52] See Smolansky, 'Moscow and the Suez Crisis, 1956', pp. 594–5.

[53] 'Thoughts on a Big Three Meeting', Dulles draft No. 3, 11 Nov. 1956, Declassified Documents, 1987, 301.

[54] See, e.g. the memorandum from Allen Dulles to Acting Secretary of State Hoover, 10 Nov. 1956, Declassified Documents, 1984, 1840; Henry William Brands, Jr., 'What Eisenhower and Dulles saw in Nasser: Personalities and Interests in U.S.–Egyptian Relations', *American–Arab Affairs* (summer, 1986), 44–54.

SUMMARY AND CONCLUSIONS

The surprising feature of the double crisis was that the two sets of events proceeded as independently of each other as they did.

It has often been said that the outbreak of war in the Middle East made it possible, or easier, for the Soviets to crack down on Hungary, because the West's attention was diverted, because the West had destroyed its moral stand on Hungary by itself resorting to aggression, or because the divisions and disarray of the Western powers made them less inclined or able to negotiate with the Soviets and thus deflect or prevent the assault on Hungary. There is no evidence that such considerations affected, or would have affected, Soviet decisions. The Western powers had already dealt themselves out, by 28 October, as a military factor. The Soviets were not disturbed by moral judgements. The diversion of Western attention may have affected the timing of Soviet moves slightly, but nothing more. In the last analysis it came down to a choice by the Soviet Union on how to protect its own interests. There were no real deterrents outside the bloc to the use of force. The West European powers (Britain and France) were not advocates of 'liberation'; they did not condone Soviet repression of East European nations but they believed in the relative stability of the status quo. The American role in the Hungarian affair, already decided before the attack on Egypt, was assertive in words but not in deeds.

In the Suez affair the West European powers were not influenced in their decisions by what was going on in Hungary, although they were glad to know the Soviets were preoccupied. Their attack on Egypt, in collusion with Israel, was planned in advance of the Hungarian revolt and took place on schedule when that revolt was reaching its climax. They berated the Soviet Union for its barbarism in Hungary in reply to Soviet accusations of imperialism and aggression in Egypt, but this was just the propaganda war on both sides.

The United States was not deterred from breaking with its allies and Israel by the requirements, such as they were, of its policy in Hungary, although bemoaning the fact of the West's discord at a time when the Soviet bloc was in trouble. As for the Soviets, since the Suez war began at a time of critical decisions on Hungary, they kept their statements relatively moderate for the first few days before opening up with full bombast after matters in Hungary were in hand. But Khrushchev and his colleagues still lacked the capacity and the intent to take military action in the Middle East.

The Soviet role in the Suez crisis, words and not deeds, was like the American role with respect to Hungary. But other aspects were not at all parallel. In Hungary the Soviet Union imposed its will, breaking the challenge of local nationalism and leaving the West out of the game. In the Middle East, where the crisis arose over the question of how to cope with Arab nationalism, personified by Nasser, the United States imposed its will on its allies without resolving that question; and the Soviets, having the advantage of a previously won influential position in Egypt and exploiting the rift in the Western camp, were in the game much more actively than the West was in Hungary, and stayed in it when the crisis was over. Nevertheless, their threats and their self-congratulation to the contrary notwithstanding, they had no determining voice in the outcome of the crisis itself.

From the standpoint of the Cold War between the two superpowers, both sides pointed to political and moral victory on both fronts. The Americans said that the Soviet Union had shown its true colours in smashing the hopes and rights of the Hungarian people, while America had stood on firm moral ground both in speaking up for Hungary and in defending principle at Suez, even against its friends and allies, and that the entire world would absorb those two lessons. The Soviets said that they had saved Hungary from fascist reaction supported by the West, and that their strong and principled stand had stopped the imperialist aggressors, saved Egypt's independence, and demonstrated their support of the Arabs and other peoples emerging from colonialism. One can evaluate these moral claims as one will. Judging from the record of succeeding years, they were perhaps more significant as setting the opposing themes of the continuing war of propaganda than in reflecting political realities.

What of the more substantial question of the effects of the twin crises on the global balance of power? There was no sea change. It could be said that a tacit mutual recognition of spheres of influence existed and helped keep the peace, for the moment anyway, in that neither superpower found it militarily feasible or politically advisable to risk global war by intervening in the area of the other's declared vital interest and security system, while each was quite prepared to accept that risk in opposing such intervention in its own area. Both blocs were placed by the events of October–November 1956 under sudden and unprecedented strain not anticipated even a few weeks before. Each recovered, after a fashion. The solidarity of the Eastern bloc was exposed as based on force alone, and Moscow had demonstrated that when it came to the crunch force would be used. The West was still faced by the same Soviet bloc, more questionable as to its bonds of loyalty but still intact. The Western alliance, for its part, survived the shocks of Suez and continued to maintain the East–West balance in Europe.

In the Middle East, however, the outcome was anything but clear-cut. Many observers, at the time and later, came to the conclusion that the Soviet Union was the principal beneficiary, gaining much credit with the Arabs which it could translate into military positions and political influence; but, as Nasser pointed out to US Ambassador Raymond Hare in the aftermath of the crisis, Egypt did not propose to exchange one form of major-power domination for another. If the balance was not tipped in favour of the Soviet Union, the trend was definitely against the West, as the vacuum left by fading European power was being filled by newly assertive local forces.

As for the United States, it welcomed the role of leadership it had helped to take away from Britain and France, and with its professions of anti-colonialism and willingness to provide aid to support the independence of local states, envisaged the building of barriers to Soviet expansion based on co-operation with them and with a chastened Britain. But the events of 1956, if they seemed to Washington to hold out that vista, had surely not created the conditions for it. Simple and easy assumptions soon proved illusory as the Middle East became nobody's bloc but a shifting field of local and regional alignments and conflicts in which the United States and the Soviet Union, with no sure guide-lines, contended for power and position. The crisis of 1956 was no striking turn in the Cold War but, rather, part of a learning process for both powers, and both had much learning still to do.

COMMONWEALTH AND UNITED NATIONS

13

The Commonwealth and the Suez Crisis

PETER LYON

> Suez presented the biggest challenge to Britain's leadership of the Commonwealth since the American War of Independence and saw the Commonwealth in greater disarray than ever before. The hostility of the USA and the USSR was so extreme that the opposition in Commonwealth countries became overlooked and apologists for Suez have needed to play down the weight of Commonwealth objections—the unfavourable Commonwealth reactions were a major factor in the eventual decision to withdraw.
>
> Joe Garner, *Commonwealth Office* (1978)

THE Suez crisis took the Commonwealth by surprise, and threw it briefly into shock, threatened dissolution, and paralytic inactivity. As the crisis unfolded and then moved to its short-lived climax, none of the Commonwealth Prime Ministers—except possibly Menzies on most aspects until mid-September 1956—was kept fully and frankly informed from London beforehand as to Eden's real intentions and moves, though they certainly were not alone in being denied such information. As the crisis abated, rather strenuous efforts were mounted from London, and not least by the Commonwealth Relations Office (CRO), to recompose the Commonwealth. This was an exercise which was well under way and apparently meeting with some success by mid-1957.

Given the tremendous amount of secondary literature of varying quality already extant—and there are four good items already in print on the Commonwealth and Suez[1]—the main aims of this chapter are

---

[1] These four published assessments of the Commonwealth and Suez are notable: (i) The fullest published treatment of the Commonwealth dimension of the Suez crisis is James Eayrs (ed.), *The Commonwealth and Suez: A Documentary Survey* (London, 1964); (ii) ch. 4, 'The Commonwealth and Suez', in J. D. B. Miller's *Survey of Commonwealth Affairs: Problems of Expansion and Attrition, 1953–1969* (London, 1974); (iii) N. Mansergh, *The Commonwealth Experience* (London, 1969); (iv) Joe Garner, *The Commonwealth Office, 1925–68* (London, 1978). The author was a former Permanent Under-Secretary of the CRO and the first head of the combined Foreign and Commonwealth Office (FCO). The primary sources for this paper comprise recently released British official papers for 1956–7, available at the Public Record Office (PRO) in London, in particular from the Commonwealth Relations Office (DO) and the Prime Minister's Office (PREM).

threefold: (1) to give a sketch of what the Commonwealth in the mid-1950s was in actuality, trying to distinguish the current and plausible myths of the day from the more prosaic reality; (2) to focus on the Commonwealth Relations Office and in particular the role of the Secretary of State for Commonwealth Relations, as revealed in the newly opened British records, in order to look at the Suez misadventure through this particular prism, noting what contrasts it affords to hitherto published accounts from around the Commonwealth; and (3) to ask, from the perspective of the present day, how significant and lasting were the consequences of the Suez episode for the Commonwealth. The Commonwealth as a collectivity, of nine member-countries in 1955–7,[2] never cohered as one during 1956. Hence assessments have to be of the individual members and their varying degrees of activity and impact at particular times.

It is neither possible nor necessary in this brief essay-length exposition to try to recount what part each member government of the Commonwealth played at each phase and critical conjuncture—Eayrs' compilation, with lively commentaries by him, published in 1964, is still a generally reliable guide even though based entirely on the sources publicly available at that time. It is suggested in this chapter that there were four phases in the Commonwealth mini-dimensions of this story.

BRITAIN AND THE COMMONWEALTH IN THE MID-1950S

Active interest in and support for the Commonwealth was an unmistakable, if somewhat diffused, part of the prevailing mental orthodoxies of the British Establishment. This was much more pronounced in the mid-1950s than twenty or thirty years later. Within Buckingham Palace, No. 10 Downing Street, the senior ranks of the armed forces, in journalism and broadcasting, in many big merchant houses and banks, as well as in such places as the headquarters of the Royal Empire Society, the Royal Overseas League, and other specifically Commonwealth support groups, there were always to be found people of some influence who were enthusiasts for the Commonwealth. To accord some significance to the Commonwealth as a prominent aspect of Britain's values and role in the world still seemed to many to be an intrinsic and indelible part of the British ethos, and there was still in being a special department, the Commonwealth Relations Office

---

[2] Britain, Canada, Australia, New Zealand, South Africa, India, Pakistan, Ceylon, and, by convention, the Prime Minister of the Federation of Rhodesia and Nyasaland. The latter requested the British government in 1956 for quasi-Dominion status for his country but was refused.

(CRO), primarily charged with attending to Britain's Commonwealth interests.

In diplomatic terms, however, the Commonwealth in 1956 was a small club of only nine members. And even within this small Britain-centric Commonwealth association of the mid-1950s there was an unmistakable kaleidoscopic quality. Not all members agreed on all major matters of policy, though the patterns of their agreements and disagreements differed with particular issues. By mid-1956 there was some mounting evidence that Britain's leadership and assumptions of a general, workable consensus for most major matters were being quietly questioned. Ironically enough, most member governments in 1956 were inclined to think that Britain had handled its recent relations with Egypt rather well but were quite critical of aspects of Britain's policy regarding Cyprus.

Relationships were not, of course, even and equally cordial right across the Commonwealth—a point which was to be unmistakably illustrated many times during the Suez misadventure. To start with, the patterns of diplomatic representation, which serve in part as indicators of interest and mutual responsiveness, were uneven. Britain had High Commissioners in all independent Commonwealth countries and each of them had High Commissions in London; but not all other members were fully represented in every one of each other's capitals. There was, then, neither in 1956 nor at any other time, a complete lattice-work of mutual bilateral diplomatic representation evenly spread from capital to capital right across the Commonwealth. There was, however, in effect, in the mid-1950s, a kind of *de facto* Common-wealth inner circle comprising Ottawa, London, and New Delhi. Most of the senior officials in the CRO had served in either Ottawa or New Delhi, or in both, and sometimes nowhere else.

In the inter-war period, and indeed until 1947, the Dominions Office and the Colonial Office had shared the same building, some common facilities, sometimes the same Secretary of State, and some similarity of outlook. After 1947 the new-fangled Commonwealth Relations Office, made up mostly from the Dominions Office and the former India Office, deliberately sought to differentiate itself from the Colonial Office (now moved to Smith Square), whilst working as closely with the Foreign Office as it was thought the continuance and prosecution of its own distinctive Commonwealth diplomacy allowed. Even so, the CRO never became more than a minor Ministry in Whitehall's implicit hierarchy, and, after a rather unwelcome merger with the Colonial Office, was absorbed into the Foreign Office in 1968. Thus the Foreign Office (FO) became the Foreign and Commonwealth Office (FCO).

In their more optimistic moments, senior CRO officials were prone to regard the Commonwealth and the United States as complementary 'special relationships' for Britain. With suitable adaptation and updating, they could invest such comforting claims with a pedigree going back at least to Winston Churchill's Fulton speech of 5 March 1946,[3] and perhaps even further back to the writings of Lionel Curtis and some of the early Round Tablers.

Then, as now, the Commonwealth in its collectively most self-consciously important moments operated at the Prime Ministerial level. Commonwealth Prime Ministers' conferences were occasions when No. 10 Downing Street and the Cabinet Office (and especially the Secretary to the Cabinet, in 1956 Norman Brook[4]) took an active part with the CRO in planning, conducting, and then assessing and reporting on its outcome to the Commonwealth at large.

As a relatively young man seeking and expecting junior ministerial office in Ramsay MacDonald's National government in 1931, Anthony Eden was worried, unnecessarily as it turned out, that he might be shunted into the relatively lowly Dominions Office (precursor of the CRO, and 'lowly' in Whitehall's tacit pecking order), while the Prime Minister's son obtained preferment in the Foreign Office. In the event, Malcolm MacDonald went to the Dominions Office, understudying for that notoriously indolent brick-dropper, Jimmy Thomas, whilst Eden was happily inducted into the Foreign Office, which was his favourite official base for the rest of his life.

It would be wrong to accuse Eden of having any profound or deeply consistent view on Commonwealth affairs. At heart, in his early years, he was deeply committed to the cause of the British Empire (proud of his family's earlier connections with India) and he was at least as much, and perhaps rather more than many conventional Conservative MPs in the 1920s, a self-professed pro-Empire man. As late as 1947 he seems to have been even less resigned than was Churchill to India's independence, albeit within the Commonwealth. But, as Foreign Secretary in 1954, and in the face of Churchill's strong, privately expressed misgivings, he had negotiated the Anglo-Egyptian agreement providing for the withdrawal of British troops from the Suez Canal Zone within two years, with only the ambiguous proviso that

    [3] 'Political Relations between the US and the Commonwealth', DO 35/7026, 1955–8; also, Wm. Roger Louis and Hedley Bull (eds.), *The Special Relationship: Anglo-American Relations Since 1945* (Oxford, 1986), esp. A. P. Thornton's chapter, 'The Transformation of the Commonwealth and the "Special Relationship" ', pp. 365–78.

    [4] The role of the Cabinet Secretary in Commonwealth Relations is a theme surprisingly neglected by scholars. Lord Trend, Brook's Deputy as Cabinet Secretary and then his successor, wrote in the *Dictionary of National Biography, 1961–70* of Brook's devotion to the Commonwealth in terms which could also be applied to Trend's own stewardship.

maybe they could come back in an as yet undefined 'emergency'—an ironical proposition, as it turned out. All in all, then, by the mid-1950s, on Commonwealth as on other matters, Hugh Thomas's judgement in his book *The Suez Affair* seems just, when he writes that Eden's 'real nature was . . . hidden from the public by well bred though successful platitudes'.

Of the officials who were the dramatis personae in London regularly concerned with Commonwealth relations in 1956, only two top men, the Secretary of State for Commonwealth Relations, Lord Home,[5] and his Permanent Under-Secretary, Sir Gilbert Laithwaite,[6] were made privy to Eden's policy on Suez, and these two were virtually unknown to the public. This virtual anonymity was more surprising in the case of the Secretary of State than of his Under-Secretary, for Sir Gilbert was no different from his predecessors in being an inconspicuous senior mandarin in so far as the British public at large was concerned. Lord Home had by 1956 been in Parliament, with some breaks, for over twenty years, but in so far as he had attracted public attention hitherto it was as Neville Chamberlain's Parliamentary Private Secretary accompanying his Prime Minister to Munich in 1938. The new Secretary of State for Commonwealth Relations, in office since Eden became Prime Minister, had not previously visited a single Commonwealth country. Indeed, he had seldom travelled abroad, as his family tended to congregate together for their holidays either on their estates or elsewhere in Scotland. His first Commonwealth tour as Secretary of State, in a deliberate act of familiarization, took him to Australia and India. It is politically and psychologically interesting to note that he appears to have got on well with Menzies but not with Nehru.[7]

THE MIDDLE EAST: A GAP IN THE COMMONWEALTH?

The Middle East fitted very awkwardly, if at all, into British imperial–Commonwealth arrangements and ideas.

The notion that Britain's colonies were on a transmission belt, and were part of a process whereby nearly all of them eventually would become independent states and voluntarily opt to be members of the

[5] See John Dickie, *The Uncommon Commoner: A Study of Sir Alec Douglas-Home* (London, 1964), and Kenneth Young, *Sir Alec Douglas-Home* (London, 1970). Home's own amiably laconic memoirs, *The Way the Wind Blows*, were published in 1976.

[6] Laithwaite was to Home (his Minister) what Kirkpatrick (head of the FO) was to Eden. He had specialized for most of his career on India (he was Private Secretary to the Viceroy, Linlithgow, from 1936 to 1943) and on Burma, and then joined the CRO in Jan. 1948, becoming Permanent Under-Secretary (PUS) of State for Commonwealth Relations in 1955. See also Garner, *The Commonwealth Office*, pp. 294–6 and 327, and *The Times* obituary, 24 Dec. 1986.

[7] See Dickie, *The Uncommon Commoner*, pp. 98–100, and Home's speech giving impressions of his tour to the House of Lords on 30 Nov. 1955.

Commonwealth, was tried and found wanting in the Middle East. If 'colonies into Commonwealth' prescribed Britain's ideal, there was never any comprehensive, overall metropolitan plan with an accompanying precise timetable for decolonization. What there was in fact was much improvisation, reaction to local events and local nationalisms, and much changing of particular timetables. The Middle East proved to be a region where the Commonwealth idea never took hold. It was as if pan-Arabism, even different local versions of Arab nationalism, had proved to be inimical to the idea and practice of the Commonwealth.

By 1956, for several years there had been much discussion and debate, especially in Britain[8] but also sporadically in some Commonwealth meetings,[9] about the desirability and the feasibility of a Middle East defence pact, MEDO, which in its most ambitious, putative forms was seen as a Middle Eastern equivalent and complement to NATO. What had actually come about, somewhat adventitiously in 1955, was the Baghdad Pact, with the so-called northern tier states— Turkey, Iraq, Iran, and Pakistan—as members, with Britain as the principal progenitor from outside the area and with the United States adopting a somewhat equivocally semi-detached posture towards the alliance, its commitments, and capabilities.

Pakistan was then the only Commonwealth country other than Britain which was a party to the attempt to fabricate a 'Western' or 'free world' (to employ two of the slippery, chameleon-like labels of the day) alliance system in the Middle East. Throughout the Suez crisis the Pakistan government[10] played a carefully considered and quietly efficient specific role (in marked contrast to the emotional outbursts by an attentive Pakistani public in favour of Egypt and critical of Britain)—as is in general accurately traced by both Eayrs and S. M. Burke. It is notable from the British records that Eden appreciated Pakistan's role and difficulties,[11] and much preferred what was said and practised by Karachi (where the government was still based) than

---

[8] See, e.g. F. S. Northedge, *Descent From Power: British foreign policy, 1945–71* (London, 1974).

[9] See, e.g. W. C. B. Tunstall, *The Commonwealth and Regional Defence* (London, 1959). Also, *The Commonwealth at the Summit: Communiqués of Commonwealth Heads of Government Meetings, 1944–1986* (Commonwealth Secretariat, London, 1986).

[10] The Prime Minister and the head of the Muslim League, Chaudri Mohamad Ali, resigned on 8 Sept. The President, Iskander Mirza, called upon the leader of the Awami League, H. S. Suhrawardy, to succeed him. Elements in the Awami League had been critical of an alliance policy for Pakistan, though Suhrawardy had remained uncommitted on this issue heretofore. On 12 September he replaced Hamidul Huq Choudhury by Firoz Khan Noor as Pakistan's Foreign Minister. The latter was a very experienced politician who had, *inter alia*, earlier served as High Commissioner in London.

[11] See e.g. PREM 11/1095.

the moralizings and pro-Nasser positions adopted, as he saw it, by India generally, and by Krishna Menon in particular.[12]

Because of the traumatic circumstances of its origins in the partitions of 1947, its Islamic identity, and its multifaceted difficulties with India, Pakistan's leaders had considered the pros and cons of an alliance policy more fully and carefully perhaps than any Commonwealth country. Given the failure of its attempts between 1949 and 1953 to form an Islamic bloc and links with the Arab states (India had been more successful than Pakistan in this latter respect), Pakistan had rather deliberately plumped for formal treaty ties with Western allies, notably with both Britain and the United States. However, these were governmental calculations, not responses to domestic public mood.

COMMONWEALTH PRIME MINISTERS CONVENE

It is a further irony that, in what might be regarded as a curtain-raiser to the Suez affair, the Commonwealth Prime Ministers met in London in late June and early July 1956 and discussed Middle Eastern matters rather generally but, according to one of their number's public testimony to his Parliament a month later, did not even discuss the Suez Canal.

On 13 June the last British troops had been evacuated from the Suez Canal base complex, ahead of the time fixed by treaty engagement, and to the accompaniment of boastful and rancorous Egyptian pan-Arab propaganda. By this time Egypt was receiving arms from the Soviet-led Warsaw Pact on a substantial scale. A spiralling arms race between the Arab states and Israel was threatening, despite the earlier efforts of the Western powers to dampen down the likelihood of this and their wish to maintain so far as possible a low-level regional military equilibrium. Such was the general Middle Eastern scene as it presented itself to the Commonwealth Prime Ministers when they met in London in the summer of 1956.

Thus the seventh post-war conference of Commonwealth Prime Ministers was held in London from 28 June to 6 July 1956. Eden was in the chair for this rather lengthy gathering of what was still essentially a small, British-run, international club. The Commonwealth was the soft and spongy centre of a now diminishing British world-system. There was no attempt at co-ordination of policies, as even the bland words of the final communiqué, the only press release from this gathering, made

---

[12] There is still no full and authoritative account of Menon's role during the months June–Dec. 1956 based on full access to British and Indian records. The best available accounts to date are in S. Gopal's biography of Nehru, and M. Brecher, *India and World Politics: Krishna Menon's View of the World* (London, 1968). See also DO 35/6319 and 6320.

clear: 'The Prime Ministers considered the situation in the Middle East. They reaffirmed their interest in the peace and stability of this area. They welcomed the efforts of the Secretary-General of the United Nations to ensure observance of the terms of the armistice agreements between Israel and neighbouring Arab States. They agreed that all practicable steps should be urgently taken to consolidate the progress thus made and to seek a lasting settlement of this dispute.'[13] No wonder S. G. Holland, New Zealand's Prime Minister, told his Parliament on 7 August that Suez 'was not even a prospective problem when I was in London ... There was no thought of this crisis developing.'

Another paragraph in the communiqué issued from this Meeting of Commonwealth Prime Ministers is worth quoting, not only because it repeats a standard orthodoxy of the day but, even more, because events were soon to provide an ironical commentary on how fully and decisively its pieties could be ignored by a British government:

Informal Discussions. Apart from the consideration of matters which are of common interest to all Commonwealth countries, these meetings also afford opportunities for discussion outside the formal sessions. Advantage has been taken of these opportunities on this occasion. The continuing exchange of views on matters of common concern is an important element in the relationship between the member countries of the Commonwealth. It is of the utmost value that this should be supplemented at intervals by personal contacts between the political leaders of the Commonwealth countries, and in a rapidly changing world the need for these direct consultations has assumed a new importance.[14]

Henceforth, the CRO, the central London main motor for the regular transaction of official Commonwealth business, became a somewhat erratic and unreliable purveyor of information. It was more starkly than ever before subordinated to the wishes and whims of a British Prime Minister acting out his own sense of crisis at a time when he could not realistically assume, nor apparently did he much try to coax into being, a genuine Commonwealth consensus in support of his policies. Complaints in different tones of regret and irritation, slightly querulous enquiries, or plain requests for more information, recur throughout the official British files and confidential dispatches of the day. Requests that an emergency meeting of Commonwealth Prime Ministers should be convened, threats that some members would leave the Commonwealth, or the belief that the whole association was on the verge of dissolution—these were some of the emotional currents,

[13] See, *The Commonwealth at the Summit*, cited at n. 9 above, p. 50.
[14] Ibid., p. 51.

hitherto unprecedented in their intensity in Commonwealth history, which surfaced during the crisis.

SOME SPECIFIC COMMONWEALTH INVOLVEMENTS: FOUR PHASES

Given that each member of the Commonwealth acted quite independently with not much sustained liaison with any other (New Zealand with Australia slightly, and Ceylon with India to some extent, being the only notable exceptions), it is convenient to depict the varying depth of involvement of individual Commonwealth members in terms of four phases:

1. the Commonwealth differentiates itself;
2. the Commonwealth 'wobbly' and in limbo;
3. the Commonwealth ignored and annoyed;
4. the Commonwealth is recomposed.

The first phase runs from Nasser's announcement of the nationalization of the Suez Canal Company on 26 July until the end of the first London conference of 16–23 August. During this period of about a month it became clear that Rhodesia would play no part and that the South African government was determined to keep its head 'out of the beehive', to cite the words of Johannes Strijdom of 27 July 1956. Menzies, Prime Minister of Australia,[15] was in Washington on 26–7 July, and Holland, Prime Minister of New Zealand,[16] in San Francisco; but both returned to London and both thereafter supported Eden, staying closely identified with British policy: these two antipodean Prime Ministers personally decided their country's policy and in effect ignored whatever domestic misgivings or dissent reached their ears. Canada,[17] as a country which was not a significant user of the Canal, was not a party to the London conference; but its efficient network of missions and men, from Washington to Cairo (where Herbert Norman was head of mission) to Norman Robertson in London,[18] was very actively at work in the wings, though Eden evidently became increasingly irritated by what he regarded as Canada's semi-detachment and mild didacticism.

The positions taken by India, Ceylon, and Pakistan were complex

[15] There is no single authoritative account of all aspects of Australia and Suez—but see J. D. B. Miller's chapter in this book. W. J. Hudson, *Casey* (Canberra, 1987) has a good chapter on Suez, showing how much Casey, rather impotently, disagreed with Menzies.

[16] There is still no authoritative New Zealand account. Professor David McIntyre of the University of Canterbury, Christchurch, New Zealand, has told the present writer that there is some interesting material in the McIntosh papers in Wellington, N.Z.

[17] See, further, Michael Fry's chapter in this book.

[18] See J. L. Granatstein, *A Man of Influence: Norman A. Robertson and Canadian Statecraft 1929–68* (Ottawa, 1981).

but have been ably and fairly fully analysed elsewhere.[19] What the CRO files abundantly reveal is the deep and increasing distrust of Krishna Menon generally held in Whitehall, and by Eden and Home in particular, which neither Nehru's reputation nor Malcolm Mac-Donald's skilful explanations (as Britain's High Commissioner in New Delhi) did much to reduce.

The second phase, which saw the failure of the five-man Menzies group mission to Cairo and the abortive second London conference, to deal with Dulles's idea of a so-called Suez Canal Users' Association (SCUA), from 19 to 22 September, was a time of increasing disarray in Commonwealth consultation. The British government, and Eden in particular, refused to countenance suggestions that there should be much more frank exchanges and perhaps an emergency meeting of Commonwealth Prime Ministers. It was at this time that Brook, Secretary to the British Cabinet, privately characterized the Commonwealth as 'wobbly'—that conveniently euphemistic term from the lexicon of Whitehallese.[20] During this time Pakistan eventually withdrew from the lists of those who initially were ready to explore the idea of a SCUA. India and Ceylon had already refused to do so, and Canada had never been a potential candidate.

The third phase was a time of unprecedented acrimony and lasted from the failure of the second London conference until the 25 October, when the British Cabinet, with varying degrees of knowledge and enthusiasm, endorsed Eden's plan to invade Egypt—keeping the arrangements so secret that no British Ambassadors or High Commissioners were told, and American enquiries were fobbed off with evasions and lies. It was also the time of the actual invasion of Egypt—by Israel on 29 October and then by Anglo-French forces on 5 November. In the face of crescendos of criticism at the United Nations and elsewhere, Britain found very few supporters in the Commonwealth—in fact only the Australian and New Zealand Prime Ministers. Britain and France twice used their vetoes at the United Nations. On 6 November Egypt and Israel both accepted the call for a

---

[19] On India and Suez there is still no full-length authoritative account, but see the chapter by S. Gopal in this book; nor is there (other than the treatments in the general surveys mentioned at n. 1 above) of Ceylon and Suez; on Pakistan, the best available single account is by S. M. Burke, *Pakistan's Foreign Policy: An Historical Analysis* (London, 1973). S. W. R. D. Bandaranaike felt unable to leave Sri Lanka in June 1957 to attend the Commonwealth Prime Ministers' meeting because he feared communal trouble with the Tamils, but sent his urbane Justice Minister, M. W. H. de Silva, to London in his place. Aspects of Bandaranaike's policy are discussed in chapter 8 of James Manor's *The Expedient Utopian: Bandaranaike and Ceylon* (Cambridge, 1989).

[20] Confided to William Clark, Eden's press secretary, in a private conversation at Norman Brook's house on 12 Aug. 1956, William Clark, *From Three Worlds* (London, 1986).

cease-fire and Eden ordered British troops on the Canal to do likewise at midnight that same day.

There were, during this frenzied time, loud cries, becoming more and more pronounced, especially from the Asian capitals, either for withdrawals from the Commonwealth or else for an emergency plenary meeting of Commonwealth leaders with the British government—in practice by this time only Eden's few colleagues on the 'Egypt Committee'.[21]

The fourth phase was the time of repair and recomposition of Commonwealth ties, strained and suspended or rendered inactive during the war and the period immediately preceding it. In this process the illness, political eclipse, and then retirement of Eden enabled Butler and then Macmillan to undertake this task energetically, whilst Home remained at first rather quietly and discreetly in the wings. But, on the wider world stage, there is no doubt that Canada's initiatives in helping decisively to coax the United Nations Emergency Force (UNEF) into being facilitated the process of Commonwealth assuagement.

THE COMMONWEALTH IN SHOCK, JULY–NOVEMBER

Although the Suez affair sent shock waves right around the Commonwealth, these were received with different intensities and degrees of concern in various capitals, as James Eayrs' survey of responses shows with admirable clarity. Each of the Commonwealth members responded individually to the Suez affair. There was no general consultation at a pan-Commonwealth level between July 1956 and July 1957, and little evidence of much general, mutual Commonwealth consultation without Britain—though, doubtless, some informal, bilateral discussion took place, often by telephone. That there were no specially convened meetings of all Commonwealth representatives with or without Britain, either in London or at the United Nations in New York, is an indirect comment on how dominant generally Britain still was in Commonwealth counsels. The CRO tended, throughout the Suez affair, to prefer meetings with individual High Commissioners, or small groups (e.g. Australia and New Zealand), or with the envoys of the 'old' Dominions rather than with all the Commonwealth Heads of Mission in London together.

Within a few days of Nasser's nationalization of the Suez Canal Company, the CRO was complaining that the Foreign Office was telling the press more than it was first divulging to the CRO for transmission to fellow Commonwealth governments. Commenting on

---

[21] For 'Egypt Committee', see Robert Rhodes James, *Anthony Eden* (London, 1986).

an article in *The Times* 'from official sources' that day, Laithwaite wrote to his Secretary of State that not only was the newspaper remarkably 'well informed' but that:

It is far from satisfactory that the Foreign Office's Press department should be handing out to correspondents information which is not really immediately available to [those] who are responsible for dealing with the Commonwealth High Commissioners and with their frequent enquiries as to the state of things; nor, of course, do we in the office know what has been said.[22]

Laithwaite confessed that he was 'a bit uneasy that nothing should be said to the High Commissioners (however negative it might be)' before the debate in the House of Commons. He added that they kept ringing up and asking the position (Laithwaite specifically mentions calls from Norman Robertson, Canada's High Commissioner in London) and that their position *vis-à-vis* their governments was very awkward. He concluded that those 'governments are bound to take the view either that we don't attach much importance to them or else there is a major division of view which our secrecy reflects'. On this occasion the Secretary of State agreed to see the High Commissioners, with his Permanent Under-Secretary, for half an hour before the debate.

Nehru sent a message to Eden on 15 September saying that 'if there is no amelioration in the situation in the coming days we would have to consider requesting you to call an emergency meeting of Commonwealth Prime Ministers before steps that lead on to conflict or war are taken'. There is no evidence available in the British files that this speculative venture by Nehru was answered directly at the time. But Home's note to Eden[23] the same day, 15 September, clearly indicates his attitude to Nehru and India's policy at that time. He wrote that Eden will have seen the series of telegrams from Malcolm MacDonald reporting on his recent conversations with Nehru. 'I am afraid that it is true that the role which India has played in the Suez trouble has until now been helpful to Egypt.' He added: 'I am anxious that we should not break with India so long as we can avoid it, and it may well be that the more they fear war the more inclined they will be to turn their pressure on to Nasser'—a hope which remained unfulfilled and which doubtless exaggerated the degree of influence India would have been able to wield anyway.

A new nadir was reached in Commonwealth 'consultation' at the end of October when Eden expressly ordered that no information about Suez was to be conveyed to the Commonwealth—secrecy was paramount. For a few days the flow of vital information stopped entirely. It was at this point that belief that the Commonwealth was on

[22] DO 35/6317.   [23] PREM 11/1094.

the verge of dissolution became plausible. It was during this time that at least one High Commissioner, Malcolm MacDonald, drafted his resignation and another senior CRO official, Joe Garner, Britain's High Commissioner-designate to Canada, 'offered to stand down since he could not conscientiously defend the policy; but the offer was brushed aside by Home who insisted that Ministers were counting on his help, and he proceeded to his post'.[24] He eventually became Permanent Under-Secretary of the newly amalgamated Foreign and Commonwealth Office.

On 7 November the Opposition put down an emergency motion in both Houses of Parliament, for debate the following day, urging that the government immediately summon a conference of Commonwealth Prime Ministers 'in order to arrive at an agreed policy in support of the UN'. Home immediately discussed with Eden the desirability of sending a telegram from the CRO to all Commonwealth governments on this matter.[25] Eden demurred and did not like the CRO's draft telegram. The Prime Minister concentrated, instead, on how to handle Parliament the next day and advised that the disarming line to be taken was that it is always open to Commonwealth Prime Ministers to propose a meeting but that in any case a full meeting of the United Nations General Assembly, with Foreign Ministers present, was to take place soon. That would provide an opportunity for an interchange of views. A special meeting of Commonwealth Prime Ministers would take about a week to assemble and some days to reach conclusions—no opinion was offered as to whether satisfactory conclusions might be reached at all. Meanwhile, he advised that official spokesmen continue to say that the British government attached the utmost importance to Commonwealth consultations. After a brief period of enforced silence, the familiar runes were being repeated.[26]

During the Suez crisis a file was made up within the CRO which, though it was generally entitled 'Commonwealth Consultation and Co-operation', was more accurately and specifically labelled 'Complaints From Commonwealth Governments About Lack of Prior Consultation'.[27] It is doubtful if it proved to be of much use to the officials, as the comments and possible precedents mostly referred to complaints by Australia in 1954–5 about inadequate or too tardy consultation, with a few complaints also from New Zealand. These were hardly the two most dissentient friends of the British government in 1956.[28] But the

[24] Garner, *The Commonwealth Office*, p. 328.
[25] PREM 11/1097.
[26] See A. P. Thornton's chapter in Louis and Bull, *The Special Relationship*.
[27] DO 35/6992.
[28] But see PREM 11/1095, 12 Oct. 1956, regarding Menzies' questioning the wisdom of taking the Suez issue to the UN Security Council.

comments inscribed on the file are interesting, if not necessarily to be taken as *ex cathedra* pronouncements. One CRO official merely noted that the whole file 'is useful ammunition to discharge against an obdurate Foreign Office'. Another commented that the 'theory of consultation is, I suppose, a subject for bright thoughts by the Constitutional Department and they might like to see our papers'. A third added: 'The theory is always to consult; it is not always possible to observe it fully in practice, though we don't, I suppose, do too badly.' Laithwaite, ever the practical man, commented:

Though of course the ideal would be to consult all Commonwealth countries concerned in any problem fully before deciding on UK action, it is obvious that individual circumstances will dictate our course of action in each case. Moreover, time and policies sometimes prevent us from sticking to our ideal of advance consultation.

RECOMPOSING THE COMMONWEALTH

Some of the familiar political alchemy for composing Commonwealth Relations was soon being tried again and, necessarily, rather energetically: renewing and repairing personal contacts, promoting cordial exchanges, changing personnel, sponsoring goodwill tours, and stressing non-political and functional co-operation, and the like. And such bridge-mending and rebuilding did not await on Eden's resignation from the office of Prime Minister but began purposefully as soon as Butler took over as acting Prime Minister. Later, Harold Macmillan was to become the first serving British Prime Minister to make an extensive Commonwealth tour, as well as to voice authoritatively the claim that British membership of the European Economic Community and participation in the Commonwealth were complementary and not inherently antithetical. This soon became the new official and dominant—if never unchallenged—British orthodoxy, as it still is today.

Prince Philip, Duke of Edinburgh, went off on an extensive overseas tour which included visiting several Commonwealth countries. The Queen did not fail to comment on the Commonwealth dimension of this tour in her Christmas Day message to the Commonwealth while her consort was still abroad.

A few more examples of these processes at work must suffice. Louis St Laurent, Canada's Prime Minister, after a short holiday in Florida, went to play golf with President Eisenhower and commended the wisdom of Nehru and the importance of good Indo-American relations. Nehru and Indira Gandhi travelled to Ottawa just before Christmas. This was immediately after visiting Washington, where they had met Eisenhower, and Nehru had enjoyed a more successful visit to the United States than his rather stilted first official one in 1949. *En route* home, Nehru went with his sister Mrs Pandit (India's High Commissioner in Britain), to see Eden at Chequers on Christmas Eve, where they had a restrained but mutually courteous meeting.[29]

The first post-Suez stage of recomposing the Commonwealth was completed by the Commonwealth Prime Ministers' Conference held in London from 26 June to 5 July 1957. The notion that this was not a time for further recrimination but for a fresh start was aided by the number of newcomers present at that gathering: Diefenbaker for Canada, H. S. Suhrawardy for Pakistan, Kwame Nkrumah for the brand-new country Ghana (the first new member since 1948), and Sir Roy Welensky speaking for the Rhodesian federation. The new chairman, Harold Macmillan (helped by Lord Home, who made a point of meeting and greeting each of the delegates individually outside the conference room and by making full use of Dorneywood),[30] was determined to encourage a fruitful cross-fertilization of ideas through genuine discussion and to avoid the formalism of set speeches.

Thus, within a year, it seemed as if the Commonwealth had lurched to the brink of dissolution, survived the apparent prospect that two or three of its members would leave in protest against the behaviour of the senior member of the club, and had rather swiftly recomposed itself. Was Suez, then, only a marginal matter for the Commonwealth (rhetoric and surface appearances notwithstanding) or was it, perhaps, that the Commonwealth itself already was only of marginal importance in the mainstreams of international politics?

SIGNIFICANCE?

There is, of course, a continuing controversy as to the significance of the Suez misadventure—and this certainly includes raising the question whether Britain's set-backs at Suez hastened British decolonization and the transformation of the Commonwealth into its post-1965 condition of being a peculiar post-imperial form of international organization.

On the surface, what had happened was a series of Commonwealth non-events: no emergency meeting of Commonwealth Prime Ministers was convened, though the notion that one should be assembled had been scouted in private or in public several times; no member of the Commonwealth actually left the association, or suspended its member-

---

[29] Visit to Chequers by India's Prime Minister, PREM 11/1394, 1956.

[30] See Dickie, *The Uncommon Commoner*, pp. 100–1. Dorneywood was the newly available official country residence of the Secretary of State for Commonwealth Relations.

ship, or even broke off diplomatic relations with Britain (as Tanzania and Zambia were later to do in 1965 over Rhodesia). True, there had been a short-lived, massive breakdown in the transmission of information, though in practice this had never been as full and as comprehensively distributed as some naïve enthusiasts for the Commonwealth had hitherto believed. Many of the routines, including Prime Ministers' meetings, with their wellnigh predictable pieties and officialese, soon seemed to be restored.

None the less, Suez did mark a major psychological watershed. It led to a hastening of the removal of vestiges of Britain's imperial statehood, a diminishing proprietorial pride in the Commonwealth amongst Britain's relevant 'attentive publics', and a willingness to reduce or shed the role of principal in Commonwealth affairs—especially if this would facilitate membership in the European Economic Community. Maybe the Suez episode principally showed that the Commonwealth as a whole was a craft only for collective fair-weather sailing, with little or no capacity to deal decisively with sudden storms and foul weather. Maybe Professor Thornton's aphorism applies with particular aptness to the Commonwealth at the time of the Suez crisis: 'The Commonwealth deals less in power than in hope and does not seem to be directed towards anything more concrete than its own continuation.'[31] As has been indicated earlier, Eden's own views on the Commonwealth seem to have been the standard fare of the 1920s and 1930s, rather superficial and not by personal choice at all subject to, or ripe for, agonizing reappraisals. Whatever revisions in his mind the events of 1956 may have prompted, and the evidence available does not suggest that genuine reconsiderations seriously competed with exculpatory self-justifications, it does not seem that he committed to paper or confided to friends for them later to divulge to posterity any significant signs of having new, subsequent thoughts about the Commonwealth, which certainly only features occasionally in the margins of the analyses in his three main volumes of memoirs. Avon, even more than Eden, remained imaginatively locked up with the 'lessons' of the 1930s rather than with the realities of the mid-1950s and after.

The Suez misadventure demonstrated unmistakably that Britain, by the mid-1950s, lacked sufficient financial and military strength and will to maintain a masterful policy. Amidst the volatilities of the Middle East and with the Americans nibbling or gnawing away at their erstwhile local monopolies more and more, the one-time familiar British benefits of great-power privileges on the cheap could no longer be secured. After all, informal empire was the penumbra of actual or

---

[31] Louis and Bull, *The Special Relationship*, p. 365.

formal empire; the maintenance of the simulacra had depended, more than most of the British had seemed to have appreciated, on there being some substance to imperial claims and pretensions. The Suez misadventure hastened and advertised the wellnigh inevitable end of Britain's imperial statehood. In the Middle East, after 1956, there was to be no post-imperial Commonwealth camouflage to provide some semblance of posthumous vindication for empire or to ease the transition to an era when some local leaders would be able to assume active world roles regardless of whether Britain wished to act as their patron or guardian.

14

Australia and the Crisis

J. D. B. MILLER

THIS discussion of Australia and the Suez crisis begins with a brief account of Australia's involvement, goes on to consider why Australia acted as it did, and ends with some consideration of whether the crisis had any major effect on Australians' perception of the international scene and on Australian foreign policy.[1]

When President Nasser announced his decision to nationalize the Suez Canal on 26 July 1956, the Australian Prime Minister, R. G. (later Sir Robert) Menzies was in North America. He had been abroad since May, attending a Commonwealth Prime Ministers' Conference and having talks in Washington. He asked his Cabinet in Canberra whether he should go on to the proposed London conference of user states or come home; the Cabinet told him to proceed to London. Meanwhile he heard from John Foster Dulles of the possibility that Britain and France might use force against Egypt. His own view was that such a possibility should be held in reserve and not actively canvassed at the time, though he was not against it in principle if other ways of persuading Nasser could not be found.

In London, Menzies made it clear on television on 13 August that he did not believe that Nasser's action was legally valid (though it is clear in retrospect that the consensus of international legal opinion held the opposite). He was a prominent figure in the conference; as the only head of government present he had a certain standing. Then, asleep in his hotel, he was awakened at 2 a.m. by a telephone call from the US Ambassador, Winthrop Aldrich, saying that he was needed in a hurry. At the Ambassador's residence he was informed by Dulles, Eden, and

---

[1] Secondary sources used for this paper include W. Macmahon Ball, 'Problems of Australian Foreign Policy, July–December 1956: The Suez Crisis', *Australian Journal of Politics and History*, 2:2 (May 1957), 129–50; James Eayrs (ed.), *The Commonwealth and Suez: A Documentary Survey* (London, 1964); Norman Harper and David Sissons, *Australia and the United Nations* (New York, 1959), pp. 126–34; Norman Harper, 'Australia and Suez', in Gordon Greenwood and Norman Harper (eds.), *Australia in World Affairs, 1950–55* (Melbourne, 1957), pp. 341–56; W. J. Hudson, *Casey* (Melbourne, 1986); Sir Robert Menzies, *Afternoon Light* (London, 1967). Primary sources, noted in footnotes, were kindly provided by Professor Wm. Roger Louis.

Selwyn Lloyd that he was wanted as chairman of a group of five from the conference who would present the majority states' views to Nasser. He demurred but was soon persuaded.

Menzies' approach to his mission was to present the eighteen nations' proposals as fairly and moderately as he could, but not to forget that force was still a possibility. With this in mind, he arrived in Cairo on 2 September along with his four colleagues from the United States, Sweden, Ethiopia, and Iran. There has been some difference of view about whether the Egyptians took the delegation seriously, and whether Menzies behaved well in his treatment of Nasser; but Menzies' own account in his memoirs suggests that he was very much in earnest, that he tried to be diplomatic while not leaving out of account the ultimate possibility, and that Nasser, while over-ideological from Menzies' standpoint, was someone to respect and, if possible, persuade. At the time, however, Menzies was sterner in his judgement of his adversary. Writing to Eden from Cairo on 9 September he described Egypt as a police state and went on:

I was told that Nasser was a man of great personal charm which might beguile me into believing something foreign to my own thought. This is not so. He is in some ways quite a likeable fellow but so far from being charming he is rather gauche, with some irritating mannerisms ... I would say that he was a man of considerable but immature intelligence. He lacks training or experience in many of the things he is dealing with and is, therefore, awkward with them. He will occasionally use rather blustering expressions, but drops them very quickly if he finds them challenged in a good-humoured way. Like many of these people in the Middle East (or even in India) whom I have met, he will produce a perfectly accurate major premiss and sometimes an accurate minor premiss, but his deduction will be astonishing.

In the same letter Menzies described the crux of his visit to Cairo, the fact that President Eisenhower, at a press conference, had destroyed what he regarded as the ultimate weapon in the Western powers' armoury, the use of force. Eisenhower had said 'we are determined to exhaust every possible, every feasible method of peaceful settlement. ... We are committed to a peaceful settlement of this dispute, nothing else.'[2] Menzies reported to Eden:

As you know, I was never optimistic about our prospects but whatever sketchy chances we ever had were, I think, fatally injured by the astonishing intervention of President Eisenhower, whose statements during our confer-

---

[2] Menzies quotes this in *Afternoon Light*, p. 165. After Cairo he went to Washington and confronted Eisenhower on 14 September, to be told that 'when a press conference is held, the democratic process requires that questions should be answered'. Menzies had to be content with this repeated reply (p. 168).

ence were received with glee by the Egyptians and were undoubtedly treated by Nasser as indicating that he could safely reject our proposals.[3]

Menzies returned to Australia, to leave in abeyance a proposal from Eden that 'The Admiralty would welcome the advent say of an Australian frigate or destroyer at Aden or in the Persian Gulf, where the Royal Navy would obviously be preoccupied in any emergency with problems of security and relief apart from active naval operations.'[4] His main task, after such a long absence and such prominence in the newspapers, was to report to Parliament, which he did on 25 September. His speech was a long and powerful one, in which he emphasized his belief that the Egyptian action had been illegal, that the United Nations could provide no solution, that the matter was one which affected Australia's vital interests, and that the British and French were entitled to act as they saw fit. He did not mention the United States. His conclusion was:

[Are we] to be helpless in the presence of an accomplished threat to our industrial and economic future? I believe not. Is our task to 'patch up' peace and no more? Surely our task is not merely to prevent hostilities but to build up a firm order of law and decency, in which 'smash and grab' tactics do not pay. We must avoid the use of force if we can. But we should not, by theoretical reasoning in advance of the facts and circumstances, contract ourselves out of its use whatever those facts and circumstances may be.[5]

The Prime Minister's attitude was strongly attacked by the Leader of the Opposition, Dr H. V. Evatt, who maintained (as he had done since the dispute began) that the matter should be left to the United Nations, and that Australia should abide by its decision. A former High Court judge and President of the UN General Assembly, Evatt presented a characteristically legalistic argument to the effect that war had been outlawed except in defence of one's own territory or in accordance with a UN decision to use military force. Menzies, in contrast, had used a power politics, *raison d'état* approach to justify the possible use of force by Britain and France; in the state of Australian public opinion at the time, his attitude was more acceptable than Evatt's, especially when Egypt's connection with the Soviet Union was stressed, as it frequently was.

Australia was a member of the Security Council when the Anglo-French attack on Egypt came before the United Nations. Its representatives' behaviour was somewhat erratic at first, because of difficulties

[3] Copy of a private letter dated 9 Sept., 1956 from the Prime Minister of Australia to the Prime Minister of the United Kingdom (no identification other than folio nos. 641–6).

[4] Prime Minister's Personal Telegram, serial no. T.404/56, dated 21 Sept. 1956.

[5] Menzies deals with this speech in *Afternoon Light*, pp. 173–6. It is the subject of a hostile analysis in Macmahon Ball's article.

of communication with Canberra, but the general thrust of Australian policy was clear. Along with Britain, France, Israel, and New Zealand, Australia voted against resolutions which condemned the Anglo-French action. The United States and the Soviet Union were, for once, in line with each other; Australia formed part of a very small minority of states which approved what the British and French had done. Menzies was in no sense repentant. He thought that the attack had been justified, and he was distressed when British and French troops were not permitted to form the basis of the UN Emergency Force.

Once that force was established, Australia ceased to be actively involved in the Suez affair. Unlike New Zealand, it did not offer troops, and so did not receive any rebuff. The affair soon ceased to be a matter of public argument, though it continued, as in Britain, to be discussed by intellectuals (almost entirely in terms of condemnation of the British and French action) and to be used by them as a symbol of policy which they disliked.

Why did Australia, alone amongst the Commonwealth countries, behave so aggressively in support of Britain? Even New Zealand, its partner in votes at the United Nations, was more moderate: the prime New Zealand concern when the Anglo-French attack began was that its cruiser RNZS *Royalist*, which was in the Mediterranean, should not be involved in active operations.[6] It welcomed the UN outcome of the affair with much more warmth than Australia.

The explanation of the Australian approach lies partly in the nature of public opinion, partly in the character of Menzies' Cabinet, and partly in Menzies himself. These formed something of an indissoluble whole, apart from the objections which, as we shall see, were raised by the Minister for External Affairs, R. G. (later Lord) Casey.

In 1956 Australian public opinion was still heavily anti-Communist, strongly pro-British because of wartime associations and profitable trade, traditionally anti-Egyptian since the experiences of World War I, and very much pro-American in terms of security, though inclined to be critical of American culture and institutions. The shift from British to other kinds of immigration had not yet affected public life: the people who mattered were overwhelmingly British in origin and pro-British by education and experience. Men in their fifties had grown up during or just after World War I, and had experienced two world wars in which Australia had gladly committed itself to the British side. Australia's trade was largely a matter of trade with Britain: the shift to Japan was only just beginning, and the basis for it—the Japan–

[6] Message from S. G. Holland, New Zealand Prime Minister, to Eden, dated 1 Nov. 1956 (ADM 114/6097).

Australia trade treaty—was not yet in sight. Instead, Australia was about to negotiate a new version of its preferential trading agreement with Britain. Such future developments as Britain's entry into the European Community and its restriction of Commonwealth immigration were not foreseen. Australians passed freely in and out of Britain, took jobs there, renewed family connections, and still thought of themselves as a special sort of British. All these circumstances contributed to a situation in which, if Britain wanted support, the public mind in Australia was largely prepared to provide it without asking too many questions.

In World War I, and to a lesser extent in World War II, Australian troops in the Middle East had developed a particularly unfavourable view of Egyptians. It had become part of Australian folklore. 'The Battle of the Wasser', a series of riots by Australians in the red-light district of Cairo in 1915, had been fought again and again in retrospect, acquiring new detail with the passing of the years.[7] 'Gyppos' were dirty, they told lies, they cheated you; you would be stupid to trust them. It was no surprise, though it was a source of indignation to ex-servicemen, when in 1956, after the Anglo-French attack, a mob in Port Said tore the Anzac memorial from its granite base and damaged the figures. This memorial, conceived in 1916 to commemorate the Australian and New Zealand Mounted Division, had been erected in 1932. It would have been a brave and foolhardy Australian who ventured to suggest that the desecration of it in 1956 was a legitimate demonstration of Egyptian nationalism.

Anti-Egyptian sentiment in Australia was reinforced by ideas about the Suez Canal. Generations of Australians had been taught that it was Australia's lifeline to Britain, and that it was 'our' Canal, having been acquired by Disraeli in a smart move against the French. Little was known about the Canal Company, or about the French interest in its operation; the Canal was something that passenger ships from Australia passed through, the passengers having either triumphed over or been bilked by the traders of Port Said. Since most overseas trade was still with Britain, and the Canal was the fastest route, the notion of it as a 'lifeline' still had some substance. (The Cape route was more expensive, but not so much so as to make it impossible. There was, however, an argument for the Canal in terms of oil supplies.)

The fact that Egypt under Nasser had been getting arms supplies from Communist sources was, as suggested earlier, sufficient to damn him in the minds of conservative Australians. The country was strongly anti-Communist, its sentiments having been fed especially by the

[7] The most recent reliable account is in Bill Gammage, *The Broken Years: Australian Soldiers in the Great War* (Canberra, 1974), pp. 36–40.

Korean war. Throughout the post-war period the Communist party of Australia had been influential in a number of key trade unions and been stigmatized for its activities by parties of all political colours. The Soviet Union's activities in Europe and the efforts of Communist parties in Asia had been highly publicized; the Australian government had refused to recognize the new regime in Peking, and was to continue to ignore it for another seventeen years. It is true that the Menzies government's 1951 attempt to ban the Communist party had been a failure; but the defeat owed more to Australians' concern about their civil liberties than to any sympathy with Communism. If any state could be shown to be associated with the Soviet Union and opposed to the United States and Britain, as was the case with Egypt, it could hardly hope for public sympathy.

Menzies' ministry was composed of a few able men and a majority of nonentities who have now been forgotten. The inner Cabinet of twelve contained a higher proportion of men of substance than the ministry as a whole, but their interests were primarily domestic, and their attitudes towards the outside world those of traditional Australian conservatives. There was an exception in R. G. Casey; but the tone of the ministry was hostile to new departures and new concepts, including the United Nations, which was still regarded with suspicion on account of Evatt's enthusiastic championship of it and his role at the San Francisco conference of 1945. Menzies' lead in foreign affairs was sufficient for the ministry as a whole: American strength and British steadfastness would save the world from disaster, and it was Australia's place to follow on, though not necessarily with arms. As Menzies' lack of positive response to Eden's suggestion about a warship indicated, the Australian government was more inclined to words than deeds.

Casey had been trying to widen the Cabinet's horizons since he became Minister for External Affairs in 1951. He had had little success. His own background was very much that of a seasoned diplomat and associate of world leaders: he had been Australia's representative at the Foreign Office in London during the 1920s, had been its first Ambassador to Washington, had served in wartime as a British Minister in the Middle East and as Governor of Bengal, and had behind him a department which was still in its early state of euphoria and hard work. Yet, as his biographer says,

Casey could not cope with Cabinet. He expected a Cabinet of ministers concerned mainly with domestic matters and largely ignorant of foreign policy and diplomacy to defer to his experience and specialist expertise, and they did not defer. Casey was not personally impressive in Cabinet. Impromptu argument was not his forte, at times he spoke at inordinate length, he was unable to focus on his colleagues' earthier concerns, he gave other ministers the impression that he was too swayed by foreigners' manners and style, and on his own admission he was occasionally embarrassed by inadequate mastery of his department's briefs. Worse for a politician, he did not lobby. He tried to keep the Minister for Defence, Philip McBride, on side, and often they were a minority of two in Cabinet, but even here his aim was less to enlist a vote than to link defence policy and foreign policy as a good in itself. In Casey's papers for the period there are many complaints of hard handling in Cabinet, but very little to suggest that he ever tried to orchestrate support in advance or to hedge his bets if support was not forthcoming. This meant that his relatively sophisticated approach to foreign policy was little reflected in his Government's policies and that a department of increasingly skilled professionals enjoyed less impact on government than it would have liked, or deserved.[8]

From the beginning of the Suez affair, Casey was against the use of force. His position can be summed up in what he said to Menzies on 27 September. In Hudson's words:

he sought out Menzies to warn him again that war over Suez would split the Commonwealth, alienate the USA, destroy British influence in the Middle East and damage Australia in Asian eyes. He proclaimed his devotion still to Britain: 'it was inevitable that Britain would lose face . . . My concern was that she should lose as little'.[9]

Casey had been saying this from the start, and was to keep on saying it, but it did him no good. There is no indication that it affected the thinking of Cabinet, or that it had any influence upon Menzies, once he had decided, early in August, that force might be necessary. The fact that Casey cabled Menzies on 9 August, urging him to ask the British government how, if Nasser refused to accept an international regime for the Canal, force could be so applied as to keep the Canal open,[10] probably hardened Menzies' attitude. During their joint careers, from the 1930s to the 1960s, he had little time for Casey.

Throughout the crisis, Menzies was the central figure in the Australian approach to Suez. His attitude is easy to explain in superficial terms—he was well known for proclaiming that he was 'British to the bootheels'—but harder to follow if one thinks of some of the other occasions in his career. He did not automatically agree with everything a British government said or did: he had been critical of Churchill's strategy in the Mediterranean in 1941, when he was Prime Minister for the first time, and he was disinclined to follow Britain in 1949–50, when the question of recognition of Communist China came up. Similarly, he was careful about Quemoy and Matsu when an American administration seemed likely to be bellicose about them, thus showing that he

[8] Hudson, *Casey*, pp. 234–5.   [9] Ibid., p. 276.   [10] Ibid., p. 272.

could be prudent in respect of Australia's other great and powerful friend. In many respects, he was a judicious policy-maker, one whose political antennae made him aware of a variety of forces, interests, and attitudes.

In this case those antennae failed him, or he refused to heed them. The explanation, I think, lies in his pre-war and wartime experiences with British governments. Unlike Casey, who had studied at Cambridge and spent a decade in London at the level of Foreign Office staff (albeit with access to various fashionable assemblies), Menzies had been introduced to Britain as an Australian Minister in the 1930s, and had been involved in high politics from the beginning. In 1937 and 1938, crucial years in the formation of British policy, he had been an enthusiastic follower of Chamberlain's policy of appeasement. Churchill had been something of a *bête noire*, a freebooter who might upset the carefully constructed policy of Chamberlain. In 1940 and afterwards, Menzies had to deal with a Churchill who held all the cards, and who knew where Menzies' sympathies had lain. It was not an easy situation for either of them. My impression is that Menzies spent the next twenty-five years in erasing his Chamberlain connection and replacing it by the appearance of constant agreement with Churchill.[11]

I think this attitude was transferred to Eden, another figure noted in the 1930s for his opposition to appeasement, and Churchill's chosen successor. In 1956 there were, in Menzies' rhetoric, the clearest echoes of anti-appeasement, along with that figurative identification of Nasser with Hitler or Mussolini which seems to have possessed Eden too. Perhaps it is fanciful to see Menzies as subconsciously determined to set right his errant record in the 1930s by showing himself *plus royaliste que le roi*; but I find it difficult to resist. There was no solid reason of national interest why he should have taken the line which he took, and which was so much at variance with the Canadian. Adopting the Canadian line throughout the affair would have meant avoiding the perils which Casey listed for Menzies; it would also have meant preserving good relations with the United States, and perhaps not quite so good, but still quite viable, relations with Britain. It was not a choice which Menzies showed any sign of accepting.

When these three factors—public opinion, the Cabinet, and Menzies himself—are put together, it is not difficult to explain why Australia acted as it did. The fact that the Australian Labor party, which constituted the Opposition, was tying itself in knots because of internal struggles meant that there was little effective leadership for any sentiment opposed to the government.

[11] His treatment of the two men in ch. 5 of *Afternoon Light* is instructive. The frontispiece is a photograph of himself and Churchill 'on the terrace at 10 Downing Street'.

What was the effect of Suez on Australia? I am tempted to say none, since the Menzies government was returned with a slightly increased majority in 1958, and in 1965 a government still under Menzies enthusiastically sent troops to Vietnam to support Australia's other great ally, the United States. Having accepted without question the British assessment of Nasser, the government saw no reason to be critical of the US assessment of Ho Chi Minh and Mao Tse-tung. Public opinion, while no longer so pro-British as it had been in 1956, had transferred its uncritical faculty to the United States by 1965—or so it seemed at the time.

It is better, perhaps, to view Suez as the end of an era in Australian thinking about the world, and as having had something to do (the causal element defies analysis) with that end. The fact that the Suez Canal was blocked meant that Australian goods had to find another route to Britain; within a few years, the need for it became less apparent. In the British governmental structure many forces were tending towards Western Europe and away from trading partners like Australia. With the independence of Ghana in 1957, a new era began in the evolution of the Commonwealth of Nations, one which proved highly unpalatable to Menzies and those who thought like him. The discovery of vast iron-ore deposits in Australia's north-west, and Japan's growing demand for the ore, meant a change in Australia's exports, soon to be accompanied by a change in imports which caused Japan and the United States to bulk larger in Australian calculations. Immigrants from Greece, Italy, Yugoslavia, and later from the Middle East and Asia began to outnumber those from Britain; by the 1980s their characteristic names were appearing amongst those of Australia's leaders in politics, business, and the professions. Foreign policy soon became closely identified with policy towards Asian countries such as Indonesia, China, Japan, and Malaysia; Egypt dropped out of consideration, and the Middle East was seen as primarily an area of conflict between Israel and the Arabs, secondarily a source of oil, and thirdly a possible basis for superpower conflict. The liners no longer sailed to Britain; if they had, there would have been no difficulty in getting through the Suez Canal.

All these changes made Suez seem a very long way off, and the crisis in 1956 an episode in history, almost in ancient history. If it had an effect, this was probably to speed up in public consciousness, and in governmental policy, the growth of an awareness of what came to be called the Third World. Casey, as External Affairs Minister from 1951 to 1960, laboured to develop such awareness. When it came, it was much more directed towards South-East Asia than the Third World as a whole. It had little to do with the Middle East.

15

Canada, the North Atlantic Triangle, and the United Nations

MICHAEL G. FRY

The opportunity for Britain is clear. She must ceaselessly work for peace, basing her policy on a long-term view of the major issues. British prestige in Europe and in the Near East will not depend on power-political maneuvering, for only with American aid can she afford such playing with fire, but in the deeply profound wisdom of her policy. The old imperialist may turn saint because he can no longer do anything else.

Pearson to Robertson, 4 Aug. 1956, citing Lancelot White's 'wise little book' *Everyman Looks Forward.*

CANADIAN policy during the Suez crisis was developed and implemented, essentially, by the Department of External Affairs led by the Secretary of State, Lester B. Pearson. He enjoyed the confidence of the Prime Minister, a former Secretary of State, Louis St Laurent, who was informed, sympathetic to many Afro-Asian aspirations, but conscious of Canada's Atlantic heritage, and by no means unimportant in foreign policy. Canada's behaviour might well have been different had MacKenzie King still been Prime Minister.[1] St Laurent and Pearson were close; there was respect and a convergence of views. St Laurent gave Pearson wide latitude; Pearson could count on St Laurent's support. Within the department, Jules Leger, Under-Secretary of State, John Holmes, Assistant Under-Secretary, and Marcel Cadieux, head of the UN division, carried weight. Abroad, Pearson was served by a galaxy of trusted friends; Arnold Heeney in Washington, Norman Robertson in London, Escott Reid in New Delhi, Dana Wilgress at NATO, the still controversial Herbert Norman in Cairo and Beirut from August 1956, and R. A. MacKay at the United Nations. General

---

[1] D. C. Thomson, *Louis St. Laurent: Canadian* (Toronto, 1967), pp. 452–90, and John W. Holmes, *The Shaping of Peace: Canada and the Search for World Order, 1943–1957*, vol. ii (Toronto, 1979), pp. 348–93.

E. L. M. Burns commanded the UN Truce Supervision Organization in the Middle East.[2]

Pearson was generally liked and respected abroad.[3] He was a pragmatist on Middle East affairs but with a marked preference for Israel, a proclivity which set 'Rabbi' Pearson apart from opinion in the Defense Department. He had found President Nasser, in November 1955, 'impressive and attractive ... plain and blunt ... friendly and modest', a man of 'sincerity and strength and without any trace of arrogance or self-assertion', but had left the Middle East less than optimistic about the prospects for peace.[4]

Canada did not have an elaborate Middle East policy. A deep concern over refugee and relief matters, involvement in the mainten- ance of the armistice agreements, and a willingness to play a modest, stabilizing role in arms transfers, complemented a mistaken belief that incremental, confidence-building measures, both political and eco- nomic, could help bring about a comprehensive settlement of the Arab–Israeli dispute. That settlement must involve both the United States and the Soviet Union. The St Laurent government accepted the fact that the West faced a new phase of Soviet activism in the Third World generally and in the Middle East in particular. It seemed futile to ignore Soviet influence with the Arab states, secured by arms and economic assistance, and exercised reasonably in 1956, yet irrespon- sible to allow her to manœuvre freely and unchecked.[5] Specifically, the West should secure Soviet agreement to an arms control policy for the Palestine region, which neither undermined the Baghdad Pact and weakened Iraq's ties to the West nor left Israel vulnerable to Egyptian air power. Canadian officials doubted that the Baghdad Pact consti- tuted a barrier against Communism. It could even have prompted increased Soviet penetration of the Middle East. Nasser remained a critical but inscrutable factor, 'one of the most enigmatic personalities of our time'.

The United Nations organization was pivotal in Canadian thinking. The incremental steps to promote a comprehensive Middle East settlement and an agreement itself should be pursued under UN

---

[2] Geoffrey Murray assisted MacKay at the United Nations. G. P. Kidd was *chargé d'affaires* in Tel Aviv. D. M. Johnson, the Ambassador in Moscow, wrote lengthy, indecisive, and not very helpful reports. The Paris Embassy reported admirably what it knew. G. C. McInnis and P. G. R. Campbell gave the views of the Commonwealth and Middle Eastern Division.

[3] Dulles to Eisenhower, 23 Oct. 1956, John Foster Dulles Papers (Princeton University Library), Eisenhower Library files, Chronological Series, Aug. 1956–June 1957, Box 14, file 2. Dulles liked and admired Pearson but felt he was torn between loyalty to NATO and the United States and his desire to be the West's problem solver.

[4] Lester B. Pearson, *Mike*, vol. ii: *1948–57* (Toronto, 1973), pp. 220–3.

[5] Commonwealth and Middle Eastern Division memorandum, 1 June 1956, Department of External Affairs papers (Ottawa) (hereafter cited as DEA), file 50085-40, vol. 2.

auspices. Should a crisis result in a war in the Middle East, UN action, as in Korea, would halt it more effectively than seeking to implement the Tripartite Declaration of 1950. Much would depend on the policies of Britain and the United States and the extent of their co-operation. Thus the acid tests for Canada in a Middle East crisis would be whether it was handled through UN procedures and whether it damaged the Atlantic alliance. The preservation of Commonwealth and NATO unity provided the other measures of significance. Properly managed, a Middle East crisis should not result in a regional or global war.

Anthony Eden and his Foreign Minister, Selwyn Lloyd, had visited Ottawa in early February 1956 after a reasonably satisfactory set of meetings in Washington on Middle Eastern and other issues.[6] Pearson and his colleagues welcomed the evidence of Anglo-American accord, but were concerned that Eden and President Eisenhower had agreed, according to Livingston Merchant, the US Ambassador to Canada, that to put the Arab-Israeli dispute to the United Nations held more risks than advantages. They feared either a Soviet veto of, or, worse still, Soviet participation in, a settlement. At least, however, they had decided to explore the applicability of the 1950 UN resolution, identifying aggressors, to the Middle East. Eden and Lloyd were also too critical of Israel for Pearson's taste.[7] At the Commonwealth conference in late June, however, they were more willing to involve both the United Nations and the Soviet Union in Middle East affairs.[8] The British government, though more sympathetic towards the Arab states than towards Israel, seemed committed to generally sensible, reasonable, and cautious policies, and to the Atlantic alliance. It had handled Cyprus badly but Egypt well. Its subsequent behaviour seemed, therefore, all the more incomprehensible and unjustifiable.

The Commonwealth leaders agreed that, despite Egypt's recent arms acquisitions, the military balance still favoured Israel though she lacked modern aircraft to counter Egypt's bombers. Egypt's acquisition of jet fighters, however, would be destabilizing. In early May, Foster Dulles, seeking to arm Israel with jet fighters but able to make them available only if she were the victim of aggression, had asked Canada to sell the 24 F-86s requested by Israel so that she could train

---

[6] Robertson to Pearson, 21 Jan., Heeney to Pearson, 25 and 27 Jan. and 2 and 4 Feb., DEA, file 50359-40, vol. 1, and Eden to Commonwealth High Commissioners, 11 Feb. 1956, PREM 11/1545 (Prime Minister's files, Public Record Office, London).

[7] Leger to St Laurent, 2 Feb. 1956, DEA, file 50359-40, vol. 1; Eden speech to Parliament, 6 Feb., Eden–Lloyd briefing of the Cabinet, 6 Feb., Pearson to Heeney, 7 and 9 Feb. and Holmes memorandum on conversations between St Laurent, Pearson, Eden, and Lloyd, 7 Feb. 1956, ibid., vol. 2.

[8] Minutes of the meeting on 29 June 1956, DEA, file 50085-F-40, vol. 2.

her pilots. Canada, while recognizing Israel's needs, wanted a settlement not an arms race. The Cabinet decided on 12 July not to release
the F-86s to Israel.[9]

Immediately after Nasser's dramatic, unilateral act of nationalization on 26 July, Britain's consultation with Canada was prompt and
frank.[10] It demonstrated, however, that sharp differences with Britain
and France were probable. They were of substance, method, and
timing. They sprang from two interdependent sources—the nature of
the problem and Canada's relationship to it, and from differing
assumptions and preferences which stemmed largely from propositions
about the relationship between diplomacy and the use of force.

Canada's national interests were not affected directly and seriously
by Nasser's action. The volume and value of Canadian trade passing
through the Canal was not significant. Canadian ships were not among
the principal carriers. Canadians had no stake in the Suez Canal
Company. The St Laurent government did not seriously expect to, and
did not, participate in the first London Conference of August, for
Canada was neither a significant user state nor a signatory of the 1888
Convention. The government did no more than inform Canadian
banks of the legal issues involved in response to Britain's request that
Canada join in economic sanctions against Egypt.[11]

The Canadian government appreciated the explosive nature of the
situation, the propensity for escalation, and the larger issues at stake
for Britain, France, and Egypt—oil with its 'jugular vein' metaphor,
trade, communications, prestige and status, and the conduct of effective policies in the Middle East and North Africa, with a domino
theory prominent and the dominoes being the Canal Zone, Glubb
Pasha, Suez, Aden, and the Gulf. They understood the domestic
political considerations and the personal, psychological factors
involved. Eden had pressured a reluctant Cabinet and caucus to
evacuate from the Canal Zone, assuming that it would preface a new,
co-operative phase in Anglo-Egyptian relations. His critics in the
Conservative party would hold him accountable and warn of negative
consequences for Cyprus and the Baghdad Pact. He needed United
States support but Labour would condemn subservience. Expropria-

[9] Pearson, *Mike*, ii. 223–5, Eban statement, Oral Histories, Dulles Papers, and A. H. Dean to
Dulles, 7 June and 11 July 1956, Dulles Papers, Eisenhower Library files, General Correspondence and Memoranda, Box 2.

[10] Minutes of meeting between Eden, Lloyd, Home, and the Commonwealth High Commissioners, 27 July, PREM 11/1094; Home to Nye, 28 July, Eden to St Laurent, 28 July, St Laurent
to Eden, 31 July, ibid.; CRO to Prime Minister's secretary, 12 Oct., PREM 11/1095, and
Robertson to Pearson, 27 and 28 July 1956, DEA, file 50372-40, vol. 1.

[11] Leger to St Laurent, 30 July, Robertson to Pearson, 1 and 2 Aug., Home to Nye, 2 Aug., and
memorandum on Pearson–Nye conversation of 1 Aug. 1956, DEA, file 50372-40, vol. 1.

tion of the Canal within six weeks of the final act of the British evacuation was very hard to take. Some challenge to Nasser would have to be made.

But Nasser was within his rights and the law to nationalize or expropriate the Canal, with due compensation. Surely Anglo-French assertions that Egypt would not pay compensation and could not operate the Canal efficiently were at least premature, and then disproved. Nasser, justifiably, resented such slurs. Pearson, in any case, made less of strictly legal issues and more of the provocative manner and implications of Nasser's *coup de main*. He condemned publicly Egypt's unilateral, abrupt action as a violation of diplomatic convention. The Canal must be operated in an effective and non-discriminatory way, free of arbitrary and unnecessary interference with the rights of the users, for it had been constructed, maintained, and operated through international co-operation. Thus Canada supported the principle of international involvement in the operation of the Canal, preferably now under the aegis of the United Nations. This view was not judged to be, however, necessarily inconsistent with the act of nationalization. Should Egypt set fair rates, compensate the Company, and co-operate with the users in the efficient operation, maintenance, and improvement of the Canal, and accept processes for the fair resolution of disputes, she would neither be in technical violation of the 1888 Convention nor beyond the pale of international law. Eden's unyielding view that nationalization was incompatible with international involvement was excessive and unproven. Previously condoned discrimination against Israel's shipping was regrettable but was not a basis for militant action at this time.[12]

Pearson and his advisers took a less extreme view of Nasser, thought briefly of a direct approach to him, and never doubted that Egypt would have to be party to a negotiated settlement. They understood the stress, anger, and disillusionment in London, but wondered why Eden, by deliberate calculation not panic, publicly attacked Nasser, indulged in extravagant rhetoric, and seemed set on a dangerous course of escalation. Perhaps the Foreign Office, with Ivone Kirkpatrick prominent and driven by analogical reasoning, was in part to blame.[13] Impressed by Henry Byroade, the US Ambassador, by Nasser, and

[12] Nye to CRO, 27, 28, and 30 July, PREM 11/1094; Robertson to Pearson, 28 and 30 July, Pearson to Robertson, 28 July, Legal Division memorandum, 2 Aug., and Coté (Cairo Embassy) to Pearson, 31 July 1956, DEA, file 50372-40, vol. 1.

[13] Home to Lloyd, 1 Aug., Nye to Home, 1 and 2 Aug., Home to Nye, 2 Aug., Eden to St Laurent, 2 and 3 Aug., and St Laurent to Eden, 3 Aug., PREM 11/1094; Pearson to Robertson, 3 and 7 Aug., Robertson to Pearson, 8 Aug., and Pearson to MacKay, 7 Aug. 1956, DEA, file 50372-40, vol. 2. Robertson did not have a high opinion of Kirkpatrick, Robertson to Pearson, 21 Aug. 1956, ibid., vol. 3.

their rapport, Norman reported that Nasser, though affected by the widespread and profound antagonism in the West to his act of nationalization, was reflective, calm, and composed, speaking with a 'quiet dignity and soft manner'. He was both unmoved by threats of force and resolute to the point of fatalism, willing to risk all and go down fighting. He was gaining prestige at home and in the Arab world, and confident of the disastrous consequences of Anglo-French policy for the Baghdad Pact. Nasser understood that the United Nations would be a friendly forum in which to present Egypt's case and thus he could evade the first London Conference, indict it as a Western fraud, rally Russian and Afro-Asian support against it, and undermine its work. He would argue that nationalization was compatible with the effective operation and improvement of the Canal and that international control meant a return to colonialism. He was confident that a large majority of UN members would applaud his refusal to negotiate under the threat of force, not countenance intimidation, and condemn aggression. After all, the Aswan High Dam decision had demonstrated Western deception and lack of concern for economic development in the Third World. Nasser was well aware of the dangers of being identified with the Soviet bloc but saw ways to evade Soviet control. He knew that the West would not want to push him into Communist arms, that United States support for Britain and France was less than complete, and he spoke of securing a position of prominence, independent of either the West or the Soviet bloc. Anglo-French policy could lead to an 'Algerian' situation from the Atlantic to the Gulf. Some of this posturing could be discounted but so could the deterministically terminal advice from Israeli sources; the reckless despot, Nasser, would be dangerous if he won and desperate if he lost. Israel must rearm; the West must dispose of Nasser.[14]

Canada did not find Anglo-French diplomacy particularly promising, let alone impressive. The faint signs of moderation, prompt consultation with the United States, the search for a multilateral agreement to provide for an international regime for the Canal, and the apparent commitment to the success of the first London Conference were all welcome. But Britain and France were unwilling either to negotiate with Egypt, to submit the dispute to the International Court or to the United Nations, or to involve the Secretary-General in the search for a solution. This was the critical error. It seemed to signal, in Canadian eyes, selective distrust of the United Nations when colonial

[14] Michael Comay (Israeli Ambassador) to Pearson, 27 July and Norman to Pearson, 6 Aug., ibid., vol. 1; Mackay to Pearson, 7 Aug.; and Leger to St Laurent, 15 Aug., ibid., vol. 2; Norman to Pearson, 22 Aug. and 3 Sept., ibid., vols. 3 and 4; Heeney to Pearson, 6 Sept., ibid., vol. 5; and Kidd to Pearson, 2 Oct. 1956, ibid., vol. 7.

issues were involved, a refusal to recognize the significance of the United Nations to the small and middle powers, and a cavalier belief that great power diplomacy still ruled. Britain's preference for negotiations *à trois* with France and the United States had permitted Dulles to exercise influence directly, but it circumvented UN procedures. It kept the Soviet Union at arms length and increased the probability that Egypt would take the initiative at the United Nations, alleging that Anglo-French military preparations threatened the peace. Britain and France might then be the defendants not the aggrieved parties in the dispute. Indeed, the Soviet Union could bring the issue before the Security Council, if only to emphasize that there could be no settlements made in the Middle East without her. Thus, Britain and France, if indicted in the United Nations, stood to lose a measure of international support. As Robertson told Lord Home on 27 July, Britain should work with the international community and not 'gather too many spears to its own bosom'.

Pearson and his colleagues were not naïve; the UN option had many pitfalls. They knew that the Security Council could do little to help member states whose rights had been violated but without the use of force. The Soviet Union would veto an anti-Egyptian strategy or measures to implement it. If Britain and France forced the dispute on to the agenda of the General Assembly, they would face Afro-Asian and Communist bloc votes, much mischief, and more propaganda. It was not at all certain that the General Assembly would adopt a satisfactory resolution, and, if it did, Nasser could ignore it, run the Canal, and risk the low probability of effective economic or political sanctions. A resolution that secured a majority would probably be so broad and general as to be of little use to Britain and France. It would neither condemn nor threaten Egypt. United States anxiety over the Panama Canal was obvious; international control could not be confined to Suez. But Britain and France, their case damaged by exaggerated public statements and labouring under the threat of force, must recognize, according to Pearson's advisers, that

the contradictions between extreme nationalism and international law and order are much more likely to be resolved in the U.N. than in any other forum and the sooner the Western powers adjust their attitudes to that view the more likely the balance in international relations between the old states of Europe and the new states of Asia is to be achieved.[15]

Thus, Canadian officials argued, the Security Council could be used to make a moderate, well-documented, and legitimate case for an inter-

[15] Home to Nye, 27 July, Robertson to Pearson, 27 July, and Pearson to Robertson, 28 July, DEA, file 50372-40, vol. 1; UN division memorandum, 10 Aug., MacKay to Pearson, 10 Aug., and Robertson to Pearson, 10 Aug. 1956, ibid., vol. 2.

national regime for the operation of the Canal, which would carry the day against Egypt's 'unrestricted national claims' and provocative, unilateral behaviour. The Anglo-French case, forestalling an Egyptian or Russian initiative, must avoid condemning Egypt, confirm their devotion to seeking a settlement by peaceful means, and thus recover some of the moral high ground lost by the threat of force. Nasser, in turn, could then compromise with little loss of face, accepting from the United Nations much of what he would find intolerable from the first London Conference. Should that conference fail, Canadian officials argued, a submission to the Security Council rather than the General Assembly was imperative. Finally and ultimately, if Britain and France genuinely exhausted all UN avenues and Egypt proved obdurate, the case for the use of force would be strengthened if not made legal, and the extent of international disapproval reduced. Should Egypt commit an act of aggression in the Canal Zone, force could be applied as an exercise in collective security under the Charter. In both scenarios, economic and diplomatic sanctions would first be applied. The British government disagreed; the UN option would enable Egypt to drag out the dispute indefinitely.

At the heart of this disagreement lay widely different reasoning about the relationship between diplomacy and the threat of force, and ultimately about the use of force in the international system. Canada understood that the Anglo-French strategy was to assert the maximum diplomatic pressure on Nasser, to reverse his success, to cut him down to size, and force him to disgorge his loot. Britain and France assumed that diplomacy alone, and economic measures, would not succeed without an accompanying, credible threat of force. Military preparations assisted diplomacy by demonstrating clear resolve and unswerving determination, and brought antagonists to heel. That is why Anglo-French military moves in the Mediterranean were concerted and open; that is why Ambassador Sir Humphrey Trevelyan and Robert Menzies, during his mission to Cairo, emphasized to Nasser that the military moves were not a bluff but were in earnest, and that the first London Conference had not ruled out a resort to force. Military preparations thus guarded against the danger that Nasser might reject or evade the proposals of the first London Conference. French officials told the Canadian Ambassador that the British, extreme in their hostility to Nasser, were forcing the pace of military preparations. Gladwyn Jebb, the British Ambassador in Paris, reported the reverse.[16]

[16] Home to Nye, 28, 30, and 31 July and 2 Aug., Prime Minister's secretary to CRO, 30 July, and minutes of the Egypt Committee, 28 July, PREM 11/1094; Pearson to Robertson, 28 July, Paris Embassy to Pearson, 2 and 14 Aug., and Robertson to Pearson, 31 July and 1 Aug. 1956, DEA, file 50372-40, vol. 1.

British authorities also reasoned that negotiations sapped the ability to use force and thus must be ended, if they were proving fruitless, at some well-chosen point before they had resulted in military impotence. The decision to end negotiations should be made when the record demonstrated that Britain had acted reasonably and in good faith, and, putting Egypt in the worst possible light, made her responsible for the lack of progress. Eden did not want to see the timetable of military preparations force political decisions, but speed was part of the essence. In sum, military preparedness would reinforce diplomacy and the diplomatic record should, if necessary, provide a basis for the use of force. If Nasser did not capitulate promptly and accept international control of the Canal, then force, portrayed as the regrettable but unavoidable last resort, would be used. There was a vital corollary; Nasser would not be brought to heel, he would be brought down, and neither Syria and Jordan nor the Soviet Union would act to save him. There would be no Middle East war.

The Canadian government did not find these propositions compelling. The plan might pander to a jingoistic press, ingratiate a Prime Minister with his belligerent supporters, and even let the unknown Foreign Secretary become the hero of the Tory party, but it seemed dangerously flawed. It assumed that imperialist behaviour was still possible, that world opinion would condone intimidation, that Nasser could be ostracized and threatened, and that the policy could be presented as anti-Nasser but not anti-Egypt and anti-Arab. It would foster obduracy not compliance for it would stiffen Nasser's resolve, hand him invaluable propaganda and diplomatic weapons, and strengthen his position at home and in the Arab world. He would not cave in. The strategy sought to speed up the pace of events rather than allow a patient search for compromise. It fed the impression that the British were negotiating in bad faith, invited escalation not conciliation, and would make the Anglo-French diplomatic position flawed not impeccable, disingenuous not honest, condemnable not defensible. It would not gain the support of the Commonwealth; a formidable and prestigious Nehru would lead the challenge.

Yet Eden seemed committed to the strategy, and imposed the tightest possible security on military planning to dry up the channels of communication to friends and allies. Defence Ministry officials leaked information, and their counterparts in Ottawa knew early in August, according to General Charles Foulkes, Chairman of the Chiefs of Staff, that:

it would take six weeks before the British were in a position to take military action—the plan for military action was approved by the Chiefs of Staff yesterday and was going to Ministers last night. The general gist of the plan is to form a screen around Egypt from which threats of force can be made. If it comes to active operations, they will quite likely commence with aerial bombing accompanied by ground operations. A temporary headquarters is being set up in London, a commander of the force has been appointed, the armored division in Libya is to be strengthened, and it is likely that some forces will be withdrawn from Germany to make up the necessary ground forces.

It appears to me that if the U.K. decide to take military action against Egypt this would provide a great temptation to the Israelites to strike at the same time and might really start a flare up in the Middle East.[17]

Heeney reported Dulles as saying that Britain and France were 'prepared to act' on 15 September. Robertson and Heeney debated the meaning of the phrase, with Heeney remaining convinced that Dulles meant that 15 September was the day chosen actually to launch an attack on Egypt.

Furthermore, St Laurent and Pearson concluded that military operations would not be confined to the Canal Zone. They saw them for what they were, a move to destroy Nasser. Pearson told Robertson on 28 July, 'There remains the resort to force which they visualize as a last resort. But is it not clear that, to be effective, force would have to be used to destroy the Nasser government and take over Egypt?' He told Sir Archibald Nye, the British High Commissioner, on 1 August, that 'Mr. St. Laurent felt very strongly that the use of force could only be effective if the whole of Egypt and not merely the Canal were occupied and that these measures offered no hope of a solution.'[18] In fact, R. A. Butler, Harold Macmillan, and Selwyn Lloyd admitted to Pearson in December 1956 that they had had no clear idea as to who would have replaced Nasser had they brought him down. Finally, St Laurent and Pearson were convinced that a resort to force could result in a Middle East War.

In the first weeks of the Suez affair Canada was undoubtedly well informed of Anglo-French policy. The St Laurent government did not like what it heard. London knew where Ottawa stood. Canada, according to the Commonwealth Relations Office,

is unlikely to move sympathetically in advance of the United States. If the U.S. fights, Canada may be prepared to do so. But the issue would be likely to give rise to internal dissention in Canada. The best hope of securing her military cooperation would be to secure a decision that NATO, as such, were

[17] Chief of Naval Staff to Chiefs of Staff (Ottawa), July 1956, and Foulkes (Chairman, Chiefs of Staff) to Leger, 3 Aug., DEA, file 50372-40, vol. 1; Robertson to Pearson, 20 Sept., ibid., vol. 6, and Heeney to Pearson, 9 Oct. 1956, ibid., vol. 8.

[18] Pearson to Robertson 28 and 31 July, DEA, file 50372-40, vol. 1; Nye to Home, 1 Aug. 1956, PREM, 11/1094. Canadian fears were fully justified, Lloyd memorandum, 20 Aug. 1956, PREM 11/1100.

involved over Suez, and then it might be possible for the Canadian Government to make a contribution under the NATO umbrella. But these prospects are slender. The Canadian Government is also likely to attach importance to the U.N. being brought in before any military action is engaged.

The probability is that if the U.S. neither contributed nor wholeheartedly endorses military action, Canada will not do so either. Indeed, depending on the U.S. reaction, it is possible that Canada would endeavor to restrain us from resorting to force, and refrain from public support for our action if we nevertheless went ahead.[19]

Robertson was very frank in his conversation with Home on 15 August. The damage done by the use of force would far outweigh the inconvenience that all states would experience from Egypt's incompetent operation of the Canal. Canada would not support military action, even in the most extenuating circumstances. Unless Nasser committed an act of aggression, Britain would be indicted at the United Nations. Robertson doubted that either the Commonwealth or the United Nations could survive that confrontation. Eden noted, 'It's far worse than anything the U.S. government has ever said.' Perhaps, as Home suggested, Robertson, not in good health, depressed, and strongly pro-United Nations, ran ahead of his government. Perhaps Pearson could be persuaded that the use of force with an international mandate, after Nasser had, for example, prevented ships using the Canal, was justifiable if the case were skilfully presented and it were impressed upon him 'how robust is the attitude of the USA'. Home had second thoughts about a direct approach to Ottawa. Eden concurred, 'But I see no advantage in asking Robertson his opinion anymore'[20]— this about the most influential Commonwealth High Commissioner in London who enjoyed Pearson's confidence and respect.

Robertson's sources of information, public and private, official and informal, from the Foreign and Commonwealth Relations Offices and the Joint Intelligence Committee, did not dry up. Pearson, in Ottawa and at NATO meetings, had access to many points of view. The Canadian government understood the broad issues. But it was shut out effectively from the intricacies of Anglo-French relations, their military planning, and ultimately from the collusion with Israel. So were many of Eden's colleagues. At the same time, St Laurent and Pearson had every reason to believe that the Eisenhower Administration shared many of their views, for reasons that went beyond the political

[19] CRO to FO, 9 Aug. 1956, PREM 11/1094.

[20] Robertson to Pearson, 7, 9, and 10 Aug., DEA, file 50372-40, vol. 2; DEA to Robertson, 20 Aug., ibid., vol. 3; record of Robertson–Home conversation, 15 Aug., Home to Nye, n.d., Eden secretary to CRO, 17 Aug. and Home to Eden, 17 Aug. 1956, PREM 11/1094, and J. L. Granatstein, *A Man of Influence: Norman A. Robertson and Canadian Statecraft 1929-1968* (Ottawa, 1981), pp. 296-315.

calculations of an election year. Eisenhower and Dulles were opposed to the use of force but recognized that Eden and Mollet were deadly serious about its use unless Nasser capitulated. They had no doubts about the impact on Atlantic and Commonwealth unity if force were used, and felt that a real threat to Middle Eastern and world peace existed. Dulles also, like Pearson, looked to the NATO allies to restrain Britain and France and to promote a negotiated settlement. The NATO discussions on 6 August were, in that sense, entirely positive.[21] But neither Dulles nor Eisenhower had ruled out force irrevocably. According to P. G. R. Campbell of the Department of External Affairs, 'the depth of United States reservations on this point should not be exaggerated', and their sympathy for Britain and antipathy toward Nasser were well known.[22] The record of Dulles's dealings with Britain, from July to October, demonstrates how Eden, with some wishful thinking, could find more than ambiguity in America's posture. But Pearson's sense that he was very much in step with Dulles was justified. Furthermore, the economic and financial dependence of Britain on the United States evoked a reassuring axiom; sanctions are more effective against economic partners than enemies. Eden, meanwhile, hoped that Canadian opinion, led by the opposition Conservative party, would keep St Laurent straight. Nye concluded, however, that the St Laurent government, while not indifferent to public sentiment, would 'act with typical Canadian caution'.[23]

Caution certainly marked Canada's response to Israel on arms sales.[24] Michael Comay, the Israeli Ambassador, asked Pearson immediately to assist Israel to create an effective deterrent against air strikes by providing jet fighters. On 27 July Robertson asked Home whether, as an interim measure, they might release arms to Israel. Home demurred; if Britain and France launched military operations against Egypt, a rearmed Israel might attack Jordan and thus bring Iraq in on Egypt's side. Pearson confirmed that Home's analysis was 'shared, according to Merchant, in Washington'. There seemed little reason to doubt that Israel, confident both in her military superiority and in the belief that the West would not see her defeated, would explore ways to exploit the situation and seize an opportunity to

---

[21] ·Wilgress to Pearson, 6 and 8 Aug. 1956, DEA, file 50372-40, vol. 1. Pearson recalled that Britain, citing Nehru's opposition to military pacts and their influence, opposed bringing the issue to NATO, Pearson, *Mike*, ii. 229.

[22] Pearson to Robertson, 31 July, Robertson to Pearson, 1 and 2 Aug., Menzies to Acting PM, 29 July, Heeney to Pearson, 2, 4, 7, and 8 Aug., and Campbell memorandum, 10 Aug. 1956, DEA, File 50372-40, vols. 1 and 2.

[23] Nye to Home, 30 July, Home to Nye, 1 Aug. 1956 and Eden minute, PREM 11/1094.

[24] Robertson to Pearson, 27 and 28 July, Pearson to Robertson, 28 July and Comay to Pearson, 27 July, DEA, file 50372-40, vol. 1, and Kidd to Pearson, 8 Aug. 1956, ibid., vol. 2.

improve her national security. Robertson drew a predictably sobering conclusion; an Anglo-French use of force would touch off an Arab–Israeli war, exacerbate the situation in North Africa, and benefit only the Soviet Union.

The Canadian government decided, in the circumstances, to stay in step with the United States. On 28 July, Ambassador Merchant informed St Laurent that the United States had decided not to release helicopters and half-tracks to Israel, and recommended that Canada not deliver F-86s at that time. The Cabinet, on 31 July, agreed to defer action and to wait on further consultations with the United States. Yet, before the first London Conference opened, the United States approved the Israeli purchase of 5 helicopters, 50 half-tracks, and 200 machine-guns. Israel was to keep the sale secret, and neither Canada nor France could use the information to justify the sale of jet fighters to Israel. In view of the plank adopted on 15 August at the Democratic Party's National Convention in Chicago, Canadian officials did not rule out the possibility that political considerations were involved.[25]

The St Laurent government looked to the first London Conference, which convened on 16 August, to provide a basis for a negotiated settlement. Pearson hoped that the users would accept the act of nationalization and that Nasser would agree to a 'continuing committee' of the conference, perhaps a council of the Ambassadors of the user states in Cairo, to restore a degree of international authority to the operation of the Canal and to ensure that Egypt's management of it conformed to the principles of the 1888 Convention. Robertson found Home and his officials unenthusiastic about the idea of a 'continuing committee'. Pearson accepted Robertson's recommendation not to press Britain further while the conference was at work and concluded that 'we have no desire to be critical unless we have constructive suggestions of our own'.[26] With that, Pearson went on leave until 27 August.

The first London Conference ended on 23 August. A five-power commission, chaired by Menzies, would seek Nasser's acceptance of the Eighteen Power proposals as a basis for negotiation. This plan was based on the Suez Canal Conventions of 1888 and proposed that the Canal be maintained as a secure international waterway, open to all nations with major maritime interests. The operation of the Canal would be isolated from the politics of any one nation. Although it asked that compensation be paid to the expropriated Suez Canal

[25] Minutes of meeting between Lloyd, Pineau, and Murphy, 30 July, Home to Nye, 30 and 31 July, and Nye to Home, 1 Aug., PREM 11/1094; Leger to St Laurent 27 July, and Heeney to Pearson, 4 Aug., DEA, file 50372-40, vol. 1, and Leger to St Laurent, 24 Aug. 1956, ibid., vol. 3.
[26] Robertson to Pearson, 8 Aug., and Pearson to Robertson, 9 Aug. 1956, ibid., vol. 2.

Company, the plan also respected the sovereignty of Egypt, and suggested that an increase in the share of Canal tolls be given to Egypt. A supervisory board, composed of members from user nations, would see to the operation, maintenance, and development of the Canal. The Canadian government endorsed the scheme on 29 August but assumed that it would not be imposed on Nasser. Pearson told the press on 30 August that the proposals 'respect not only the sovereignty, the interests and susceptibilities of Egypt, but they make adequate provision for safeguarding through cooperative international arrangements with which the U.N. would be associated in an appropriate way, the international character, use and maintenance of the canal'. He regretted the damage done to Anglo-Indian relations and the excoriation of Krishna Menon, and worried about French intransigence.[27]

On 24 August Canada learned that the United States would issue licences for the export of arms to Israel. Officials in the Department of External Affairs assumed that the decision could not long remain secret, and deplored the likely results. They recommended delaying a decision on the sale of F-86s to Israel pending the outcome of the Menzies mission.[28] Pearson, in part, thought otherwise. He told the French Ambassador, M. Lacoste, on 28 August, that he would recommend to the Cabinet that day that 'the Israeli request be met in full', but that the decision would remain secret until the results of the Menzies mission were known. In Pearson's words, 'If the deal were announced now, the Egyptians would spring to the conclusion that Canada was acting as the agent of the Western powers in building up Israel at the expense of Egypt'. When Parliament was informed, as it ultimately must be, the government would make no mention of 'the French Deal' and not seek to justify its actions on the basis of the French and American decisions. Pearson had given a similar assurance to Ambassador Merchant. Should the French and American decisions leak out, however, as they probably would, then the Canadian government would, justifiably, acknowledge its consultation with France and the United States.[29]

Norman's reports from Cairo and other sources showed that the Menzies mission was not going well. That news, the landing of French troops in Cyprus without notification to NATO, the impenetrable

[27] Pearson, *Mike*, ii. 231. Robertson to Pearson, 18, 21, 25, 27, and 28 Aug., Johnson to Pearson, 24 Aug., Paris Embassy to Pearson, 25 Aug., and Heeney to Pearson, 24 Aug. 1956, DEA, file 50372-40, vol. 3.

[28] Leger to St Laurent, 24 Aug. 1956, ibid., vol. 3.

[29] DEA memorandum, 28 Aug. 1956, ibid., vol. 4. Lacoste called to inform Pearson of a change in French policy and to urge Canada to sell jets to Israel. France 'hoped to supply a few additional jet planes to Israel', but did not want a Canadian decision justified on the basis of French policy.

security in London, and Dulles's 15 September action date reactivated Canadian fears of a resort to force. Pearson, in Paris for NATO meetings in early September, took up the matter in a very forthright manner with a worried, defensive, but unrepentant Selwyn Lloyd, seemingly confident of United States support.[30] He refused to accept Lloyd's description of the military steps as 'purely preparatory and precautionary'. He rejected, as feeble reasoning and dangerous tactics, the use of the threat of force to compel Nasser to capitulate. He welcomed Lloyd's assurance that if Nasser rejected the Eighteen Power proposals Britain would go immediately to the Security Council to seek a majority vote for economic sanctions. He worried that Nasser might in effect simply ignore Menzies and that Britain and France, if Egypt proved unable to operate the Canal efficiently or if their ships were damaged or their citizens injured, would intervene militarily despite US opposition. Pearson knew how easily a pretext for military action could be engineered.[31] He warned Lloyd that a Middle East war would be disastrous and deplored the possibility of Israeli action against Egypt, for it would rally the Arabs behind Nasser. Perhaps he knew that Egypt was already moving forces from Sinai to the Canal Zone and was thus increasingly vulnerable to an Israeli attack.

Two days later Pearson addressed the NATO meeting.[32] He welcomed both the Eighteen Power proposals, which did not constitute an ultimatum to Egypt, and Nasser's apparent willingness to negotiate. Should the Menzies mission fail or be inconclusive, however:

We must rule out force. I say that not without qualification because we would not be spending between 40% and 50% of our budgets on defense. But we must rule out force except as a last resort and use it only in accordance with the principles we have accepted in the NATO Pact and the U.N. Charter.

In other words, the only acceptable use of force would be as an international police action, under the UN Charter, presumably after Egypt had egregiously violated international law.

The failure of the Menzies mission left Britain and France with four

[30] Home to Nye, 1 Sept., McInnis memorandum, 3 Sept., Norman to Pearson, 3 and 4 Sept., and Pearson to St Laurent, 3 Sept. 1956, DEA, file 50372-40, vol. 4, and Pearson, *Mike*, ii. 232.

[31] Canadian information indicated that Egypt was operating the Canal efficiently, Leger to St Laurent, 29 Aug. 1956, DEA, file 50372-40, vol. 4.

[32] Pearson to DEA, 7 Sept., ibid., vol. 5, Pearson to St Laurent, 5 Sept., PREM 11/1094, and Jebb to FO, 5 Sept., PREM 11/1100. Jebb reported that Pearson and Paul-Henri Spaak, representing Belgium, had, without prior notice, raised the UN option; the Greeks would leak this to Nasser who might rush to the Security Council himself to pre-empt Britain and France. Lloyd reported that Pearson 'though averse to military sanctions, took the line that the use of force could not be excluded in the last resort', Cabinet meeting, 6 Sept. 1956, PREM 11/1100.

options[33]—the United Nations,[34] negotiations with Nasser perhaps with the assistance of India, the Dulles plan to craft an international regime for the Canal,[35] and force. Canada disliked what became identified as the SCUA plan, and the fact that it took precedence over the UN option. It was difficult to dismiss Dag Hammarskjöld's view that acts of aggression were likely.[36] With Pearson in Paris and many ministers absent, the Cabinet decided, on 13 September, to postpone a response and to seek further clarification.[37] Robertson, pointing out that the planned conference of users excluded India, Egypt, and Russia, condemned it as 'another stupid step'. He forecast that the conference would collapse and result in Anglo-American discord on the responsibility for its failure and on whether force could be used. Pearson shared his assessment; he stayed in Paris, kept Canada out of the conference, which met from 19 to 21 September, and let it be known that Canada disapproved.[38]

At the same time, Canada found little of merit in Egypt's conciliatory but vague proposal to the Secretary-General of 10 September for a 'negotiating body', presumably another conference, to seek a settlement acceptable to Egypt and the users. Canada, along with the Eighteen Power group, ignored it.[39] Whether the perambulations of Krishna Menon, the Indian Foreign Minister, between Delhi, Cairo, and London would produce a more attractive proposal remained to be seen. Certainly, Pearson did not want Nehru's views shunted aside, but he avoided public identification with the Menon plan.[40]

---

[33] Heeney to Pearson, 15 Sept. 1956, DEA, file 50372-40, vol. 5.

[34] DEA memorandum, 12 Sept., DEA, file 50372-40, vol. 5; Eisenhower to Eden, 3 and 9 Sept., Lloyd to Makins (Ambassador, Washington), 28 and 30 Aug. and 6 Sept., Jebb to FO, 9 Sept., Lloyd to Jebb, 10 Sept., Cabinet meetings, 23 and 24 Aug. and 6 Sept., Egypt Committee, 27, 30 and 31 Aug. and 4 Sept., record of Lloyd–Pineau conversation, 24 Aug., Makins to FO, 7, 8, 9, 11, and 15 Sept., Dixon (Ambassador, UN) to Lloyd, 7 and 8 Sept., Lloyd to Makins, 8 Sept., and Menzies to Eden, 9 Sept., PREM 11/1100 and 1101; Robertson to Pearson, 10 and 11 Sept. 1956, DEA, file 50372-40, vol. 5.

[35] FO to Makins, 11 Sept. and Makins to FO, 9, 11, and 12 Sept., Egypt Committee, 17 Sept., and Trevelyan to FO, 12 Sept., PREM 11/1101; Jebb to FO, 17 Sept., ibid. 11/1102; Paris Embassy to Pearson, 11 Sept., Robertson to Pearson, 12 Sept., and Heeney to Pearson, 15 Sept., DEA, file 50372-40, vol. 5, and Wilgress to Pearson, 16 Sept., 1956 ibid., vol. 6.

[36] MacKay to Pearson, 13 Sept., and Kidd to Pearson, 10 Sept., DEA file 50372-40, vol. 5; Pearson, *Mike*, ii. 235; Nye to CRO, 12 and 13 Sept., PREM 11/1094, and Dixon to FO, 14 Sept. 1956, ibid., 11/1101.

[37] DEA to Pearson, 13 Sept., Pearson to DEA, 14 Sept., and Robertson to DEA, 14 Sept. 1956, DEA, file 50372-40, vol. 5.

[38] Pearson to DEA, 17 Sept., and Heeney to DEA, 18 Sept. 1956, ibid., vol. 6.

[39] Norman to Pearson, 17 Sept. 1956, ibid.

[40] Norman to Pearson, 22 Sept., Reid to Pearson, 3 Oct., and MacKay to Pearson, 26 Sept. and 5 Oct., ibid., vols. 7 and 8; Home to High Commissioner (Delhi), 2 and 3 Oct., FO to Lloyd, 8 Oct., Eden to Nehru, 9 Oct., Eden to Lloyd, 9 Oct., and Dixon to FO, 15 Oct., 1956, PREM 11/1095.

That made it all the more important to explore ways to get the dispute to the United Nations. Robertson told Home that despite the uncertainty of outcome and the danger of losing her freedom of action, Britain should go to the Security Council because 'the Charter of the U.N. prevails over any rights in earlier treaties that may conflict with it, and therefore one can never rely on the 1888 Convention to use force'. More specifically, he proposed that the users submit the Canal question to the United Nations as a technical problem in the management of international traffic. A UN team could then step in, help run the Canal efficiently, demonstrate the merits of co-operation, and buy time to seek a political solution.[41] Marcel Cadieux recommended that the Security Council mediate between Egypt and the Eighteen Power group.[42]

But it was not as simple as that. The Canadian assumption that using the United Nations to solve the dispute and maintaining Anglo-American co-operation were mutually consistent policy goals was unfounded. And when Eden decided to put the dispute to the Security Council on Britain's terms, to serve Anglo-French purposes, despite United States reservations and with the threat of force in place, Canadian officials were pessimistic. They concluded that the Anglo-French case would not now carry the day at the United Nations. The threat of force had begun to alienate the Latin American states; they distrusted the coercive element in Anglo-French policy. The Afro-Asian states were finding Nasser ever more attractive; the heroic underdog was flexible and honourable in negotiation, standing up to the white imperialists and deriding Dulles's scheme, as Egypt operated the Canal successfully. In that climate, it would be easy for the Soviet Union and Yugoslavia to ensure that the Security Council did not attempt to impose the Eighteen Power proposals on Egypt. Any attempt to force Nasser to negotiate under the threat of force or sanctions, to seek to overturn the act of nationalization, and to impose international control over the Canal would fail, despite the West's seven votes in the Security Council, and would never pass in the General Assembly.[43]

Yet MacKay recommended that the Western case be put to the Security Council, to seek a reconciliation of Egypt's right of ownership with the users' rights in the operation of the Canal, to the benefit of the

[41] Home to Lloyd, 11 Sept. 1956, PREM 11/1094.

[42] Cadieux memoranda, 12 and 19 Sept., Robertson to Pearson, 15 Sept., and Leger to St Laurent, 28 Sept. 1956, DEA, file 50372-40, vols. 5 and 7.

[43] Cadieux memoranda, 19, 20, and 25 Sept., McInnis memorandum, 21 Sept., Robertson to Pearson 19, 21, and 27 Sept., and MacKay to Pearson, 24 Sept. 1956, ibid., vol. 6; and personal interview with Geoffrey Murray, July 1987. Robertson described the decision-making process in a divided British government as deeply flawed.

international trading community. As a first step, the Security Council should seek a report from a commission and plan to provide technical assistance to Egypt, or to Egypt and a users' association if they were co-operating. An International Board would set dues, meet current expenses, and place the balance of the revenues in escrow. This policy, MacKay argued, would reduce support for Nasser, give him an opportunity to rethink his options, and help restore Western prestige in the Arab world, for it undeniably sought a negotiated settlement consistent with international law. The Canadian government, for its part, would preserve its independence between Egypt and the users so as to be able to play a mediating role at the United Nations, should the Security Council not produce a settlement and the dispute end up in the General Assembly. It is unclear how the Canadian independent position would be served by the announcement on 21 September that twenty-four F-86 fighters would be delivered to Israel at the rate of four per month, with a review of the policy to be made if the political situation changed. Pearson's subsequent defence, that they did not know of the Anglo-French-Israeli collusion, was singularly unconvincing.[44]

On 23 September Britain and France asked that the issue be put on the agenda of the Security Council. On the next day Egypt filed a counter item with the Security Council. Clearly, Eden was still attempting to secure the essence of the Eighteen Power proposals formulated at the first London Conference. He was trying to exert further pressure on Nasser, reportedly growing in prestige and confidence.[45] The Security Council was not expected to endorse the Anglo-French case unanimously and without reservations, but Eden was determined to avoid the General Assembly or any other negotiating body if the Security Council failed them.

The Anglo-French initiative angered Dulles. Thus Canadian officials faced a situation in which an approach to the United Nations produced an irritating contretemps between Dulles and Eden, and the probability that the United States would not support Britain and France in the Security Council and would vote for an amendment opposing the use of force. They found the Anglo-French case hastily prepared, not thought through, tainted, and unlikely to succeed.[46] This

[44] Leger to Pearson, 27 Sept., DEA, file 50372-40, vol. 7, and Pearson, *Mike*, ii. 236. Egyptian protests were muted and made more in sorrow than anger, Norman to Pearson, 6 Oct. 1956, DEA, file 50372-40, vol. 8. No doubt the modest size of the sale and the protracted schedule of delivery made the decision less significant and damaging.

[45] Trevelyan to FO, 17 and 25 Sept., and Eden to Lloyd, 21 Sept., PREM 11/1102, and DEA, file 50372-40, vol. 7; Paris Embassy to Pearson, 24 Sept. and 3 Oct., CRO to Nye, 25 Sept. and Robertson to Pearson, 27 Sept. 1956, ibid., vols. 6 and 7.

[46] MacKay to Pearson, 24 Sept. 1956, DEA, file 50372-40, vol. 6.

situation and the intense diplomatic activity of late September and early October seemed to reaffirm the differences between Britain and the United States, though without revealing the nuances of their relationship, and thus deepened Canadian concern.[47] Pearson cannot have welcomed Eden's attempts to impress on Eisenhower that Soviet policy was the real danger, that Nasser was in Soviet hands, just as Mussolini had been in Hitler's, and that it would be an error to appease him. The most recent Canadian assessment of Soviet policy confirmed that Moscow was encouraging Cairo and working to keep the dispute alive, but did not want a Middle East war and hoped to deter Britain and France from military intervention. The Soviets would settle for the current strain within NATO and the Commonwealth, and in the West's relations with the Arab and Asian states.[48] The information Pearson had from Paris identified Christian Pineau, the Foreign Minister, as the source of irresponsibility. Eden must convince the French that negotiation not force was the only sound policy. To the extent that Eden was successful, Dulles would be appeased.

Lloyd presented an Anglo-French draft resolution to the Security Council on 5 October after agreeing with Dulles and Pineau that 'Our objective is ... to get maximum endorsement in the Security Council for a settlement by negotiation on the basis of the principles underlying the Eighteen-Power proposals'. The resolution called on Egypt to join in negotiations and, in the meantime, to co-operate with the users in the operation of the Canal.[49]

The Canadian delegation, without a seat on the Security Council and not privy to many private conversations, pieced together a reasonably accurate and detailed record of the main developments from 5 to 9 October in the Security Council.[50] On the evening of 9 October, Lloyd, Pineau, and M. Fawzi, the Egyptian Foreign Minister, began their private discussions, under the eye of the Secretary-General. They were to clarify Egypt's position and find a basis for

[47] Lloyd–Dulles conversation, 21 Sept., FO to Makins, 22 Sept., Makins to FO, 22 and 26 Sept., Eden to Macmillan, 23 Sept., Macmillan to Eden, 25 and 26 Sept., Eden to Lord Privy Seal, 27 Sept., Eden to Makins, 1 Oct., Makins to Eden, 2 Oct., Cabinet meetings, 25 Sept., and 3 Oct., Egypt Committee, 1 Oct., and Eden to Eisenhower, 1 Oct., PREM 11/1102; Leger to St Laurent, 28 Sept., Heeney to Pearson, 25 and 27 Sept., Paris Embassy memoranda, 27 Sept., Wilgress to Pearson, 26 Sept., Davis to Pearson, 3 Oct., Home to Nye, 26 Sept., Robertson to Pearson, 2 Oct., and Kidd to Pearson, 2 Oct. 1956, DEA, file 50372-40, vol. 7.

[48] Johnson to Pearson, 28 Sept. 1956, ibid., vol. 7. No initiatives should be expected in September; the Politburo was on vacation.

[49] Lloyd to Eden, 3 Oct. and conversation between Dulles, Lloyd, and Pineau, 5 Oct. 1956, PREM 11/1102. Robertson reported that Britain had revised downward the estimate of possible economic damage, that the pound was firm, and that confidence had grown, Robertson to Pearson, 3 Oct. 1956, DEA, file 50372-40, vol. 8.

[50] Norman to Pearson, 10 Oct., Australian delegation to Foreign Ministry, 5 Oct., and MacKay to Pearson, 8, 9, and 10 Oct. 1956, DEA, file 50372-40, vol. 8.

negotiation by agreeing on principles that would underpin a settlement. They were not expected to produce the settlement itself; that
would require lengthy and complex negotiations at a later date.
MacKay felt that 'the possibility of a breakdown is becoming more
remote'. The ability to organize either a users' convoy to force the
Canal or a boycott of it was dwindling; the possibility that Dulles
would relinquish his watching brief for one of active intervention to
facilitate a solution was growing. Furthermore, MacKay reported,
Britain and France might, according to Cabot Lodge, the US Ambassador to the United Nations, muster only a slim majority in the
Security Council and face a Soviet veto if they were unyielding. The
private discussions, therefore, MacKay felt, might provide the basis for
a settlement. All seemed relieved to have evaded Menon.[51]

Fawzi, Lloyd, and Pineau bargained from 9 to 12 October. Again
the Canadian delegation was able to report in some detail on the
concessions made by Fawzi, on those issues which continued to worry
Lloyd, and on Pineau's scepticism. MacKay concluded that progress
was being made. He welcomed the Six Principles which Hammarskjöld
gave to the press and the Security Council on the evening of 12 October, though they were not comprehensive. They provided for free and
open passage of the Canal, insulated from the politics of any one
nation, and respected Egyptian sovereignty. They also allowed for the
fixing of tolls based on an agreement between Egypt and the user
nations, determined that a significant share of the revenues would be
allotted for development of the Canal, and maintained that any
disagreements between Egypt and the users would be resolved through
arbitration. However, Hammarskjöld's version of interim measures
and of how the Principles would be implemented did not satisfy Lloyd
and Pineau.[52] They adhered to the Eighteen Power proposals as the
basis for further negotiations, and called on Fawzi to propose precise
ways to apply the Six Principles and thus to bridge their differences.
Lloyd, ominously, denied that the Six Principles were a great victory
for the United Nations.

At the Security Council on 13 October, that part of a revised Anglo-

---

[51] MacKay to Pearson, 11, 12, 13, 15, and 25 Oct., ibid.; Eden to Lloyd, 7, 8, and 9 Oct. and
Lloyd to Eden, 8 and 10 Oct. 1956, PREM 11/1102. Hammarskjöld would be present at the
meetings but initially was acting neither as a mediator nor offering his good offices.

[52] MacKay to Pearson, 12 and 13 Oct., and Home to Pritchard, 12 Oct., Eden to Menzies,
11 Oct., DEA, file 50372-40, vol. 8 and PREM 11/1095; Eden to Lloyd, 10, 11, 12, and 14 Oct.,
Lloyd to Eden, 12, 13, 14, and 15 Oct., Lloyd to FO, 12 Oct., and FO to Lloyd 12 Oct., PREM
11/1102. MacKay felt that the *New York Times* had learned much of the story. The fact that
Menon and D. T. Shepilov, Soviet Foreign Minister, were less than pleased indicated that
progress had been made, Reid to Pearson, 18 Oct. 1956, DEA, file 50372-40, vol. 8.

French resolution embodying the Six Principles was adopted unanimously. But Egypt objected to, and the Soviet Union vetoed, the section which identified the Six Principles with the Eighteen Power proposals and described the latter, therefore, as a suitable basis for further negotiations. A further section of the resolution invited Egypt to propose how the Six Principles might be implemented, and provided for the SCUA and the Egyptian Board to co-operate in the interim on the operation of the Canal. This section was endorsed, however, by a 9 to 2 vote. The next step, therefore, was for Fawzi to work with the Secretary-General to produce proposals which would permit a resumption of negotiations, reportedly in a European capital. This was the closest the Suez affair came to a negotiated settlement, but guarded optimism at the time was wrapped in understandable uncertainty and new threats emerged rapidly.

Norman reported from Cairo that Fawzi might not have had Nasser's full support and that the latter interpreted point 3 of the Six Principles to mean that the Canal would be insulated from the politics of all nations, not just from Egyptian politics. He would not accept international control.[53] From Tel Aviv, Kidd and Burns reported increased border incidents between Jordan and Israel, Israel's truculent attitude, and her intent to attack Jordan. Iraqi troops might enter Jordan to stave off disintegration brought about by pro-Egyptian factions. Britain would support Jordan and Iraq, possibly even to the point of joining in military operations against Israel in order to defend Jordan.[54]

The Embassy in Paris learned from Gladwyn Jebb on 17 October that Eden, Lloyd, Mollet, and Pineau had decided to give Israel assurances on Iraqi troop movements into Jordan so as to prevent an Israeli military response. They had agreed to co-ordinate their policies on Suez, wait for Egyptian proposals for further negotiations, and to urge the United States to ensure that American ships paid tolls to the SCUA and not to Egypt. The Embassy reported on 22 October that there were no plans to meet Egyptian representatives in Geneva on 29 October, because the conditions required for further negotiations had not been met. But Britain and France were still ready to negotiate on the basis of the Eighteen Power proposals.[55] Robertson reported that Foreign Office officials felt that the UN venture had gone well. Nasser was exposed and embarrassed; the next move was his in New

---

[53] Norman to Pearson, 17 Oct. 1956, DEA, file 50372-40, vol. 8.

[54] Kidd to Pearson, 10, 12, and 13 Oct., Beirut Embassy to Pearson, 15 Oct., and MacKay to Pearson, 15 Oct. 1956, ibid. Lloyd told MacKay in New York that Israeli policy was foolish; Iraqi aid was surely preferable to Egyptian control of Jordan.

[55] Embassy (Paris) to Pearson, 17 and 22 Oct. 1956, ibid., vol. 8.

York. If Egypt did not come through, and promptly, Britain and France were free to act. They had evaded a commitment not to use force, and the case had been strengthened for its use as a last resort.[56]

Heeney reported from Washington that State Department officials were pleasantly surprised by the outcome at the United Nations: 'the explosive elements in the Suez situation had now been pretty well removed'. Unfortunately, there was little evidence that negotiations *à trois* would resume. On 23 October Dulles told Lodge that 'the British and French are acting badly'; on 25 October he asked Merchant to 'see Mike [Pearson] and see if they are in touch and if Mike can get the feel of it'.[57] Pearson was monitoring the exchanges between Fawzi and Hammarskjöld, and the Secretary-General's attempts to secure a resumption of the discussions in Geneva on 29 October. By 23 October, as a result of further conversations with Fawzi and the receipt of written, comprehensive proposals from him, he felt able to call the three powers to Geneva on 29 October. Pearson learned, however, on 26 October from Neil Pritchard, the Acting British High Commissioner, that 'nothing will come of the Secretary General's proposals for renewed, direct talks in Geneva'; they are 'water under the bridge'.[58] There was in fact no formal response to Hammarskjöld's call for further negotiations. The act of collusion between Britain, France, and Israel had begun at Sèvres on 22 October. The Canadian government knew nothing of it; the situation between Israel and Jordan seemed to be the more dangerous. On 29 October Israel attacked in the Sinai. On the following day Britain and France issued their discriminatory ultimatum to Egypt and Israel, and on 1 November began bombing Egyptian airfields.

All that Canada feared had come to pass—aggression against Egypt, Anglo-American relations in disarray, the unity of the Commonwealth in jeopardy, loyalties and friendships strained by anger, moral outrage, confusion, and disillusionment, the United Nations flouted and even abused, and an opportunity handed to the Soviet Union. Anglo-Canadian relations were in an abject state. Pearson had entirely failed to influence British policy, though to be sure Eden's conduct represented the triumph of an *idée fixe* over the evidence. St Laurent heard of the ultimatum on the wire service; Robertson was informed one hour before it was issued. Eden's justification lacked credibility; Home's

---

[56] Eden to Lloyd, 13 and 14 Oct., and Lloyd to Eden, 15 Oct., PREM 11/1102; Robertson to Pearson, 17 Oct. and Home to Pritchard, 18 Oct. 1956, DEA, file 50372-40, vol. 8.

[57] Heeney to Pearson, 19 Oct., ibid.; Dulles–Lodge conversations, 23 and 26 Oct., and Dulles–Merchant conversation, 25 Oct. 1956, Dulles Papers, Eisenhower Library files, Box 5, file 3.

[58] Home to Pritchard, 19 and 23 Oct., MacKay to Pearson, 25 Oct., Pearson to MacKay, 26 Oct., Leger to Pearson, 27 Oct., and Commonwealth and Middle Eastern division memorandum, 23 Oct. 1956, DEA, file 50372-40, vol. 8.

explanation was worse. Labour's reaction seemed entirely justified. St Laurent's reply of 31 October to Eden's request for support was firm, civil, and barely balanced; he rejected Eden's explanation, pointed to the damage done, and made it plain that Canada would retain her freedom of action.[59] The embarrassment of British officials, press speculation, and barely credible justifications fed both the conclusion that Britain and France had negotiated in bad faith, snatching aggression out of negotiation, and that collusion had occurred. And collusion required further deception; the front of innocence and justification had to be maintained.

The United States activated UN procedures deliberately and immediately as the best option, but the Security Council, handcuffed by British and French vetoes on 30 and 31 October, put the matter to the General Assembly. Canada deplored British and French actions in the Security Council. But an opportunity was created for Pearson, a former chairman of the General Assembly, to trade on his reputation and his rapport with Hammarskjöld and his aides, Ralph Bunche and Andrew Cordier, and to play a major role in New York from 1 November. He was well served by MacKay, Murray, and Holmes.

There were several Canadian objectives. First, to encourage Hammarskjöld not to resign, to bolster his morale, to inspire him to act decisively, and to assist him fully. Pearson would also remind Hammarskjöld, 'that the Communists have many times broken the Charter without the Secretary-General thinking it necessary to resign'.[60] Second, to ensure that the procedures of the General Assembly were used effectively and responsibly to contain the crisis and to bring about a settlement, and that anti-Western measures, invective, and propaganda were kept to a minimum. To achieve this objective while extricating Britain and France, Pearson must retain his influence with the Afro-Asian delegates. If he were successful, he would help preserve Commonwealth unity. He paid particular attention to Menon in order to curb his excesses, with little success, because of India's standing in the non-aligned movement and the Commonwealth, and her influence at the United Nations and with Egypt.[61] Meanwhile, Escott Reid worked vigorously in New Delhi to persuade a stubborn and reluctant

[59] Pritchard to CRO, 31 Oct. and 1, 9, and 10 Nov., PREM 11/1096, Home to Eden, 1 Nov., PREM 11/1220; St Laurent to Eden, 1 Nov., Pearson, *Mike*, ii. 238–9; Garner to CRO, 14 Dec. 1956, PREM 11/1097; and Merchant and Heeney statements, Oral Histories, Dulles Papers.

[60] Pritchard to CRO, 31 Oct. and 1 Nov., PREM 11/1096; and MacKay to Pearson, 31 Oct. 1956, DEA, file 50372-40, vol. 8. See also B. Urquhart, *Dag Hammarskjöld* (New York, 1972), pp. 159–230; G. Murray, 'Glimpses of Suez, 1956', *International Journal*, 29: 1 (Winter 1973–4), pp. 46–66; Pearson, *Mike*, ii. 237–78, and T. Robertson, *Crisis* (New York, 1965), pp. 165–336.

[61] Pearson to DEA, 6 and 8 Nov., MacKay to DEA, 10, 25, 26, and 27 Nov., and DEA memorandum, 10 Dec., DEA, file 50372-40, vols. 9 and 10; and Garner to CRO, 28 Nov. and 14 Dec. 1956, PREM 11/1097.

Nehru to help convince Nasser to accept the United Nations Emergency Force (UNEF) and a Canadian contingent, to make a more
responsible response to the Hungarian crisis, to continue to walk in step
with Canada, and to rebuild Commonwealth rapport.[62]

Third, to work not merely to help bring about a cease-fire but to
implement effective, emergency peace-keeping as the decisive step
toward settling the crisis and securing a Middle East settlement. A UN
emergency force might serve several purposes, but the idea was novel
and its success would depend on four factors: its composition, the speed
with which it could be assembled, whether Egypt would accept it, and
whether it could force its way between the belligerents. Initially, as
Pearson floated the idea in Ottawa and with Robertson and Heeney on
31 October, he was seeking ways to halt the Israeli advance, and to
make the proposed Anglo-French military operation unnecessary. A
small UN force could perhaps be activated within a week or so; it
should be acceptable to Egypt. Neither the United States nor Britain,
for different reasons, was particularly enthused.

At the 1–2 November session of the General Assembly Pearson
endorsed the use of the 'Uniting for Peace' procedures, but abstained
on the US resolution (A/3256) calling for a cease-fire, an end to
military operations, the withdrawal of forces to the armistice lines, and
the reopening of the Canal. Pearson did so because he regarded the
resolution as a hurried and in some ways inadequate response that did
not propose UN police action and did not strike the right balance
between Afro-Asian expectations and Anglo-French requirements.
The act of abstention was controversial, particularly because of the
Anglo-French air strikes. But there was tactical value in it if Pearson
could mollify Dulles, reduce his scepticism about the practicability of
rapidly constructing a UN force, convert a pessimistic and cool
Hammarskjöld to the idea, and influence British thinking, while the
Canadian delegation worked the corridors to muster support. In his
speech on 2 November he recommended the creation of 'a truly
international peace and police force', and promised Canadian participation. Dulles approved the idea in principle and invited Pearson to
take the initiative.[63]

Pearson returned to Ottawa on 2 November to clarify the concept
and to secure Cabinet support for whatever seemed feasible. Politi-

[62] Escott Reid, *Envoy to Nehru* (Oxford, 1981), pp. 144–90 and *Hungary and Suez* (Oakville,
1986); Merchant to Dulles, 7 Dec., Dulles Papers, Eisenhower Library files, Correspondence and
Memoranda, Box 5; and Garner to CRO, 24 Nov. 1956, PREM 11/1097.

[63] Heeney to DEA, 1 Nov., DEA, file 50372, vol. 9; Home to Lloyd, 2 Nov. 1956, PREM 11/
1096; and Pearson, *Mike*, ii. 244–8. The US resolution passed by 65 votes to 5 with 6 abstentions.
Dulles concluded that 'Canada is unhappy and wants to be mediator', Dulles–Allen Dulles and
Dulles–Lodge conversations, 2 Nov. 1956, Dulles Papers, Eisenhower Library files, Box 5, file 1.

cally, it was desirable neither to condone nor condemn Anglo-French actions. Canada must work through the United Nations but one could not forecast how the General Assembly would vote. Certain considerations took shape. The NATO allies endorsed the idea of a UN emergency force on 2 November. Dulles went over two working papers with Heeney, drafted to settle the Canal and Palestine questions and to be introduced in the General Assembly later as corollaries to the first US resolution. They were welcomed for several reasons, not the least of which was that Robertson could use them in London as evidence that there was no intention of returning to the intolerable status quo ante. Eden, dismayed by the extent of criticism at home and hostility abroad, endorsed on 3 November the idea of a UN police force which he saw as being composed largely of contingents from the Anglo-French force lumbering toward Egypt. Token UN forces could be attached to legitimate the operation; it could be wrapped in the UN flag. Perhaps Eden thought also of a UN force taking over from an Anglo-French force installed in the Canal Zone. These ideas supposedly took Pearson by surprise, but Pritchard reported that 'Pearson said that his immediate personal reaction was one of intense satisfaction'. He would tell the United States

that this is a most important development and that they should give it prior consideration over other ideas they are working on. He thought the main difficulty with the U.N. would be U.K.–French token force ... Would it be possible to devise some U.N. cover for it very quickly—e.g., placing it formally under U.N. command (possibly General Burns), securing small units at once from forces of other U.N. nations (U.S. have forces close at hand). He feared that unless something could be done to cover this point resistance might build up in the U.N.

Pearson and St Laurent adopted the suggestion as a necessary if temporary way of launching a police action to secure the goals of the Dulles resolution, and as a way to extricate Britain and France from a damaging situation until a UN force could be dispatched. There must be, however, no Anglo-French landings on Egyptian soil before the General Assembly had approved of a police action. The scheme would collapse without a positive vote. At some point the Anglo-French contingent presumably would hand over responsibility to a fully constituted UN force, although when, how, and to what extent this would occur was not yet clear. Pearson and his colleagues then drafted a resolution to create and legitimate an emergency force; a General Assembly committee would report within forty-eight hours on its feasibility. The draft was sent to Washington. Pearson returned to New York in the early evening of 3 November. He knew, from Robertson, that he had time to act in the General Assembly; the Anglo-French military operation would not be launched until late on 4 November. He explained to Lodge:

the resolution would provide a basis for an emergency force which could supervise the cease-fire and withdrawal . . . be emergency action, and we had in mind the establishment of a U.N. force of longer service which would maintain peace and order during the period of negotiating settlement of the two main issues, Suez and Palestine—Another aim was to persuade the United Kingdom and France not to land troops in Egypt . . . We were anxious to demonstrate to Israel that its invasion of Egyptian territory could not be condoned. We also hoped to head off any condemnatory resolution proposed by the Afro-Asians—and were anxious to have a text which the United Kingdom and France would not oppose.[64]

By then, however, predictable reservations had surfaced. Eisenhower, Dulles, and Herbert Hoover, Jr., supported the idea of UN emergency police action but objected to using Anglo-French forces. It made little sense to do so in view of the European situation. Egypt and the Arab world would object. Surely it was necessary to secure Egypt's consent and avoid a situation in which a police action, identified with the United Nations, actually forced its way into Egypt. In other words, what had attracted Eden to the scheme repelled Eisenhower. Herman Phleger of the State Department told him that 'there is now a danger that Pearson will propose as the "second action" of which he spoke in the U.N. meeting that a U.N. force simply take over from the British, French and Israeli forces in the Suez and Sinai areas. This is exactly what Eden is now suggesting in order to get himself off the hook'. The State Department, therefore, sent Lodge a draft resolution which called on the Secretary-General, not a committee of five, to report within forty-eight hours to the Assembly on the creation of a UN force, with the consent of all the nations concerned. Lodge apparently assured Pearson that Britain, France, and Egypt would accept the resolution, though, in fact, the situation was less sure than that. There were more discussions with Hammarskjöld, and Pearson agreed to sponsor the US draft resolution. Thus a Canadian concept and draft

---

[64] Pearson, *Mike*, ii. pp. 246–53; Wilgress to Pearson, 2 Nov., and MacKay to Pearson, 4 Nov., DEA, file 50372-40, vol. 9; Pritchard to CRO, 2 and 3 Nov. and CRO to Pritchard, 3 Nov., PREM 11/1096; and personal interview with Geoffrey Murray, July 1987. The Canadian resolution passed by 57 votes to 0 with 19 abstentions. See also Heeney to Mrs Dulles, 4 Nov., Dulles Papers, Box 103, Heeney file, Heeney statement, Oral Histories, Dulles Papers; and Conference with the President, 3 Nov., Eisenhower Papers, Diary Series, Box 19. Phleger told Eisenhower that the US resolution 'had been presented, but not pressed to a vote, in order to enable action to be taken on resolutions submitted by Canada and India', Conference with the President, 4 Nov. 1956, ibid.

proposal had produced an American draft resolution which became the 'Canadian' resolution (A/3276) that Pearson skilfully introduced and linked to the Afro-Asian resolution proposed by India. Both were adopted by the General Assembly in the early hours of 4 November.

Pearson and the Canadian delegation began to work immediately with Hammarskjöld and his staff on two critical acts of implementation. First, from 4 to 6 November an informal planning committee helped produce the Secretary-General's report to the Assembly on the establishment of an emergency force, seeking language acceptable to a majority and extracting the most from that language. The Assembly endorsed on 4 November the resolution (A/3290) sponsored by Canada, Colombia, and Norway creating a UN command structure for the proposed force under General Burns. St Laurent announced that Canada would make a significant contribution and pressed Eden to call off the attack. The General Assembly adopted Hammarskjöld's second report on 7 November providing for an independent UNEF, answerable only to the United Nations, and an Advisory Committee chaired by the Secretary-General to assist him with related political questions. A further resolution (A/3309) was passed, calling on Britain, France, and Israel to withdraw immediately from Egyptian territory; there would be no Anglo-French participation in the UNEF.[65] Second, they helped address the problems associated with making the UNEF effectively and rapidly operational. The force's size, composition (permanent members of the Security Council could not contribute), financial support, deployment, role and function, legal status, and relationship to the government of Egypt required resolution. These problems were both technical and political, they were novel and difficult, requiring improvisation and compromise, and they could set Egypt against the United Nations. Pearson, serving on the Advisory Committee, acquiesced in Hammarskjöld's dubious compromise with Nasser on the UNEF's sovereignty. He defended Hammarskjöld against British complaints about that compromise and that he was dilatory, weak, and ineffective over the Anglo-French withdrawal and the clearing of the Canal. In turn, Pearson attempted to moderate Hammarskjöld's attitude toward Britain and France. His confidence in Hammarskjöld proved well founded. The Secretary-General showed a remarkable capacity for hard work, judgement, pioneering skills, and clear thinking. Pearson told a colleague, 'Thank God we have Dag

---

[65] In the brief period before the Anglo-French attack, both Pearson and Hammarskjöld raised the possibility of using British and French troops. The resolution sponsored by Canada, Columbia, and Norway passed by 57 votes to 0 with 19 abstentions. Hammarskjöld's second report was adopted 64 to 0, with 12 abstentions.

Hammarskjöld as Secretary-General. He has really done magnificent work under conditions of almost unbelievable pressure.'[66]

Pearson also tried to ensure that Anglo-American estrangement, deep, personal, and bitter as it was, should be as temporary and benign as possible. It was a difficult task, particularly because of the hostility in Whitehall toward Robertson personally and Canada. Arnold Smith, then a member of Robertson's staff, was told 'that the bitterness about the Canadian attitude on Suez was as great as that against the Americans . . . For years the Americans and you have been urging us to follow a more European type of policy . . . now you have got it'. Britain, the Foreign Office official said, had acted 'on the rebound . . . foiled in her desire to marry the woman she loved . . . [Britain] found the only thing left was to visit the whore-house. The United States was the woman she loved and France the brothel'. Yet Pearson, advised by Robertson, made the case for seeing British and French policy in the context of Egyptian provocations, American inconsistency, and UN inadequacies. He never indicted Britain and France publicly for violating the Chapter. The UNEF scheme and Canadian support for the two proposed US resolutions on the Canal and the Palestine question were seen in part as ways to offset the Anglo-American confrontation.[67]

After the Anglo-French attack on the Canal Zone, the Canadian delegation at the United Nations functioned as a messenger and interpreter as Lodge generally carried out his instructions to avoid dealings with the British delegation. Heeney provided a similar service in Washington. As Lloyd reported from New York on 20 November, 'We are still being cold shouldered by the U.S. and cannot expect Canada, despite Pearson's helpful attitude, to carry the whole burden of protecting our interests. Pearson had tried to arrange a meeting with

---

[66] Lloyd to FO, 12, 14, 20, and 21 Nov. and Dixon to FO, 12 Nov., PREM 11/1106; Eden to Menzies, 13 and 15 Nov., PREM 11/1097; Heeney to DEA, 7 Nov., MacKay to DEA, 6, 8, and 9 Nov. and 13, 14, 15, 18, 26, and 29 Dec., and Robertson to Pearson, 29 Dec. 1956, DEA, file 50372-40, vols. 9, 10, and 11; Pearson, *Mike* ii. 251–73, Urquhart, *Hammarskjöld*, pp. 186–216, and E. L. M. Burns, 'Pearson and the Gaza Strip, 1957', in Michael G. Fry (ed.), *Freedom and Change: Essays in Honor of Lester B. Pearson* (Toronto, 1975), pp. 26–42.

[67] Robertson to DEA, 1 Nov., Heeney to DEA, 1, 2, and 3 Nov., and DEA memorandum, 10 Nov., DEA, file 50372-40, vol. 9; Eden to St Laurent, 5 and 6 Nov., and St Laurent to Eden, 5 Nov. 1956, PREM 11/1096; and Granatstein, *A Man of Influence*, p. 303. Dulles wanted Pearson as a member of the proposed 3 person commission to help create the Canal regime, and explored the possibility of Canadian co-sponsorship of both draft resolutions. Pearson knew that Dulles thought that Nasser might fall and that a new Egyptian government might be willing to negotiate on the Canal. Perhaps such expectations were one of the bases for subsequent regrets that the Anglo-French military operation had not been more efficient and decisive, though Dulles continued to insist that the Canal issue was not the one over which to bring Nasser down, Emmet Hughes, Heeney, and Alsop brothers's statements, Oral Histories, Dulles Papers, and Lloyd to Eden, 18 Nov. 1956, PREM 11/1106.

Lodge and myself but latter had excused himself on grounds of pressure of work (he is clearly not prepared to work with us on Middle East)'. Pearson and a very angry St Laurent did what they could to convince Eden to accept and observe the cease-fire, to withdraw British forces promptly from Egypt, and to accept US–UN preferences on the clearing of the Canal. Anglo-French compliance on all three issues was essential to the restoration of Atlantic co-operation. Their evasiveness on the second and third issues undermined the impact of their acceptance of the cease-fire, and eliminated the possibility of prompt negotiations to establish a regime for the Canal. This bargaining also damaged further their reputation in the United Nations, where so much authority temporarily resided. The British government was angry at US insistence that it prove itself to be a loyal UN member, and saw the placing of so much responsibility in the hands of the Secretary-General and the General Assembly as an act of faith and a leap in the dark. Pearson did not like this US needling of the British, and searched for formulae to soften the confrontation, but, essentially, he stood with the United States on the three critical questions. Joe Garner, the new British High Commissioner, reported on 14 December that, 'I fear that we are bound to find the Canadian Government will never again accept our judgment so readily as they have been prepared to do so in the past'.

At the same time, Pearson attempted, unsuccessfully, to restrain Lodge from running with Menon and the Afro-Asian delegates at the United Nations in ways that perpetuated Anglo-American discord. But then, Eisenhower met Nehru in December and refused to receive Eden, Lloyd, or Mollet. Lodge's conduct prompted a further initiative by Pearson to link the appearance of the UNEF in Egypt, an Anglo-French promise to withdraw by 14 December, and an Egyptian undertaking to co-operate on the Canal clearing to the resumption of something like normalized Anglo-American relations. Distinct progress seemed to have been made by 29 November, but Britain and France failed to meet the 14 December deadline and continued to haggle on their role in clearing the Canal. Yet there were broader considerations. US concern to counter Soviet influence in the Middle East and to fill the vacuum left by British and French disarray was understandable. But to court the Afro-Asian states to the extent, for example, of possibly adopting their views on Algeria and Cyprus was to risk alienating her NATO allies and proven friends. Pearson told Garner on 28 November that 'His main concern was with the present attitude of the U.S. Government. They pretended that they wanted to retain their alliance with their oldest and best friends but they were certainly doing nothing to help matters over the Middle East. Sooner or later they would have to make a choice between their alliance with the nations of Western Europe and their support for the Arab States.'[68] No doubt such sentiments went down well in London. Pearson's efforts were well motivated and not without effect, but one should neither exaggerate the Canadian role nor ignore the irritation it caused. Canada tried to serve many causes and mend several fences; her officials seemed to see all sides of every issue. They were not always applauded for doing so.

Pearson attempted to use whatever influence he had with Israel to secure her compliance with the cease-fire and withdrawal of forces resolutions, while attempting to ensure that Israel was not pilloried out of hand and that her legitimate security needs were not ignored. Israel bargained rather than complied, and seemed bent on using the situation to secure new boundaries. Eban objected to UN interference with her sovereign rights in territories under Israeli jurisdiction, that is, recently conquered, and regretted that Pearson had switched his attention from efforts to secure a lasting Middle East settlement to the temporary matter of creating a UN police force. Pearson was irritated and dismayed. The security of the state of Israel was not negotiable, but Israeli behaviour was often exasperating to its friends.[69]

From the very outset Pearson saw the Suez crisis, if it were contained and handled imaginatively, as an opportunity to turn to the settlement of urgent and long-standing Middle East problems, with the United States in the lead and without excluding the Soviet Union.[70] Urgent relief and refugee problems could be tackled in Egypt and Gaza, and perhaps the flow of arms could be regulated. There were pressing humanitarian reasons for such steps, and distinct political and psychological advantages to be gained by the West from practical, functional efforts that could preface programmes of economic development and technical assistance, and the convening either of a Middle East

---

[68] Heeney to Pearson, 1, 2, 3, 7, 8, 9, and 14 Nov., Robertson to Pearson, 1 and 23 Nov. and 14 Dec., Home to Pritchard, 12 Nov., Home to Garner, 26 Nov., MacKay to Pearson, 15, 22, 24, 25, 27, and 29 Nov. and 3, 4, 13, and 14 Dec., and Leger to MacKay, 17 Nov., DEA, file 50372-40, vols. 9, 10, and 11; Aldrich and Heeney statements, Oral Histories, Dulles Papers; Eisenhower–Hoover meeting, 19 Nov., Eisenhower Papers, Diary and Memoranda, Box 19, file Nov.; Eisenhower–Humphrey telephone conversation, 26 Nov. and Eisenhower–Dulles telephone conversation, 27 Nov., ibid.; St Laurent to Eden, 7, 8, and 9 Nov., PREM 11/1096; Pritchard to CRO, 5 and 8 Nov., Garner to CRO, 24 and 28 Nov. and 2 Dec. 1956 and 8 Jan. 1957, and CRO to Garner, 2 and 28 Dec., PREM 11/1096 and 1097; Lloyd to FO, 14, 20, 21, 24, 25, 26, and 28 Nov., Caccia (Ambassador, Washington) to FO, 9, 22, and 23 Nov., Dixon to FO, 10, 11, 21, 22, and 28 Nov., and FO to Dixon, 22 and 29 Nov. 1956, PREM 11/1106.

[69] Pearson to DEA, 5 and 8 Nov., Embassy (Paris) to Pearson, 7 Nov., and Heeney to Pearson, 9 Nov. 1956, DEA, file 50372-40, vol. 9; Eban statement, Oral Histories, Dulles Papers.

[70] Heeney to Pearson, 2, 3, 9, and 23 Nov. and 7 Dec., Wilgress to Pearson, 6 Nov., Johnson to Pearson, 6 and 12 Nov., MacKay to Pearson, 6, 12, and 27 Nov., and 4 and 29 Dec. 1956, DEA, file 50372, vols. 9, 10, and 11.

conference or the creation of a committee of the General Assembly to begin the peace process. That is why he encouraged Dulles's proposed draft resolution on Palestine. The obstacles were formidable. Dulles was sceptical about a conference, he had firmer views on how to solve the Canal than the Palestine problem, he gave priority to clearing and developing a regime to operate the Canal, and to reopening the oil pipelines. The estrangement from Britain and France persisted.

But these obstacles surely were temporary; they merely underscored the wisdom of Canadian policy. And thus Pearson came full circle. Anglo-American co-operation, a functioning Commonwealth, a united NATO, and an effective United Nations were the pillars of peace, freedom, and change. He felt that the United Nations could secure a central role in the international system. Eisenhower and Dulles seemed to have come to similar conclusions, if their actions with regard to the Middle East in late 1956 and in the first months of 1957 were any test.[71] Pro-UN policies were certainly good politics. Whether the United States would judge accurately what was best done in the United Nations and what should be handled elsewhere was another matter. In any event, Pearson felt that the powers must be true to the Charter, strengthen the organization, and use its procedures, while at the same time not overburdening the United Nations by expecting it to achieve the improbable. The United Nations, with its rules of the game and powers of adaptation, was not a substitute for normal diplomacy, but it could contribute to the peaceful conduct of international relations in a complementary and even decisive way. During the crisis the United Nations had arranged the cease-fire and established the UNEF, an act of improvisation creating a new form of peacemaking. The crisis had been contained. Then, backed by the United States and the Soviet Union, the United Nations brought about an Anglo-French and then an Israeli withdrawal from Egyptian territory, restored the armistice lines in the Middle East, sponsored the clearing of the Canal, and helped construct a regime for the Canal's operation. UN procedures had helped ensure that no single power had been able to exploit the crisis with any great degree of success. Hammarskjöld's performance, while flawed, had been remarkable; his enhanced stature was a key to the prospects of the organization. He must neither be ignored, for that would be folly, nor overburdened, for that would be irresponsible. To the extent that Britain, France, and Israel were uncomfortable with these conclusions, they were out of step, though their discomfort was not without justification. The Security Council was a flawed instru-

[71] Evidence in the Eisenhower and Dulles papers demonstrates their determination to handle Middle Eastern problems via the United Nations, as a preface to a major initiative in the Middle East in 1957.

ment and had lost influence to the General Assembly, which tended to serve the interests of the Afro-Asian states and the purposes of the Soviet bloc more than the interests of the West. Nevertheless, to argue that the United Nations was virtually impotent because of its record over Hungary and Kashmir, and that Hammarskjöld was irresolute and even devious in dealing with the Suez crisis seemed self-serving and regrettable. To deny that the United Nations helped Britain and France to escape from a damaging predicament was to ignore the evidence. To lament the fact that the United States was beginning to treat the United Nations as a substitute for foreign policy cut little ice. To threaten a boycott of the General Assembly or actually to leave the United Nations, that 'institution for the organization of collective chaos', was short-sighted and even irresponsible. To be willing still to use force to safeguard oil supplies and serve other security needs was to fly in the face of vital trends in a post-imperial world. Such preferences were anachronistic and futile; they were irrational. Thus the St Laurent government, confident of its policies, did not find MacKay's conclusion disturbing. 'Whether we like it or not our role in the Middle East crisis has come to be regarded as a stabilizing element and people here have come to regard Canada as a leading force in the important and difficult tasks facing the U.N. and the world in the Middle East.'[72]

Middle powers harbour such views before they become middle-aged.

[72] MacKay to Pearson, 29 Dec. 1956, DEA, file 50372, vol. 11.

CONSEQUENCES AND
AFTERMATH

16

The Crisis and its Consequences for the British Conservative Party

LORD BELOFF

THE key figure in the Suez crisis around whom all the action revolved
was the British Prime Minister, Anthony Eden. Subsequent historical
writing has not been kind to his memory.[1] Yet both his detractors and
his less numerous defenders would agree that to him, if to anyone in
our time, the phrase *capax imperii nisi imperasset* should apply. Even
though he had never held any of the great domestic offices, and had
from very early on in his political career specialized in external affairs,
he had for a long time been the unchallenged heir for when Churchill
should eventually give up the premiership and the leadership of the
Conservative party.

It is generally agreed that the failures of judgement which marked
his tenure of the highest office were at any rate in part the result of the
long wait which Churchill's unwillingness to leave the scene imposed
upon him. It also made him determined to exert his unchallenged
authority in the field he believed he knew best and to view with
unconcealed hostility any possible threat to his monopoly in foreign
affairs. Hence what Harold Macmillan regarded as his demotion from
the post of Foreign Secretary to that of Chancellor of the Exchequer,
and the choice in his place of Selwyn Lloyd who had none of
Macmillan's independent authority in the party and in the country
and could therefore be relied upon to follow Eden's lead.

It is also the case that Eden's illness in 1955 left him prone to
excessive excitability, the result of persistent ill health of an enervating
kind. Although there are differences of opinion as to how far his
judgement was affected by this fact, no one would exclude it alto-

---

[1] Eden has been the subject of three major studies as well as of many smaller ones. The
biography by David Carlton, *Anthony Eden* (London, 1981) is very unsympathetic to its subject.
That by Robert Rhodes James, *Anthony Eden* (London, 1986), provides the best all-round portrait
of the man and the best attempt to defend his record over Suez. Richard Lamb's *The Failure of the
Eden Government* (London, 1987) is described in its title. While bringing some new material into
consideration, it is idiosyncratic in its judgements and is marred by the author's obvious lack of
acquaintance with important aspects of the period, particularly the nature and functioning of the
US government.

gether. It may have contributed also in some way to the pressing need for reassurance as to the rightness of his conduct, which has been remarked upon by many who were in close contact with him at the crucial time. Press criticism of his alleged indecisiveness tended to make Eden more determined to show himself as tough.

On the other hand, Eden, both during the crisis and subsequently, received the support and admiration of many colleagues who were well placed to judge his contribution to nation and party. Nor must one overlook the fact that what we now know about the course of events in 1956 only gradually percolated into the public mind, so that by the time they did so, the Suez storm had abated and Conservatives at any rate were free to take into account Eden's long and distinguished record in pre-Suez days. It was perhaps unfortunate for his reputation that he insisted on bringing out his own version of the crisis so soon after the events it chronicles, and to have given in this way unnecessary hostages to fortune.[2] It could be said that the most obvious example of Eden's basic lack of judgement at that time was his belief that the 'collusion' with Israel could be kept secret for ever. Neither the French nor the Israeli leaders were under the same pressures for secrecy; but the accusation of deceiving the country and the world about the origins of the Suez expedition came to be the main charge laid against Eden.[3] The graver error, that of falsely estimating the likely reactions of the United States, is easier to explain, and one which Eden shared with his colleagues. Finally, even the critics of his memoirs have to admit that none of his colleagues who gave their own account of the events in print were wholly candid with their readers.

When we confine ourselves to the domestic consequences of the crisis and in particular to its impact upon the Conservative party, Eden's own role is only one factor that needs to be taken into account.[4] It is a subject that from very early on attracted political scientists with an interest in British party politics.[5]

One reason for this interest was the degree of passion aroused in Parliament and the press. Those who had passed through this experience were bound to see it bulk large in their own memory. When he came to set down his own version over ten years afterwards, Harold Macmillan pointed out that, while in times past issues that divided the nation had been mainly of a domestic nature,

---

[2] The Earl of Avon, *Full Circle* (London, 1960).

[3] See Lamb, *Failure of the Eden Government*, pp. 241–2.

[4] For the present purpose, I take the crisis to have lasted from 26 July 1956 when Nasser announced the nationalization of the Suez Canal Company to 16 May 1957 when the House of Commons divided over the government's advice to British shipowners to use the Canal now under Egyptian management.

[5] See in particular Leon D. Epstein, *British Politics in the Suez Crisis* (London and Urbana, 1964).

in recent years the occasions when the whole nation is plunged into bitter controversy, when whole households have been torn apart and long friendships broken, have been upon matters of foreign policy. From time to time there arises a dispute on matters so fundamental and involving such deep feelings as to cause temporary and even permanent rifts between old friends, divisions in families, heavy stresses on the Party organizations, and implicating not merely those affected by political controversy but the whole mass of the population. Such emotions were caused by Munich and nearly twenty years later by Suez.[6]

Macmillan's eloquent passage is, however, misleading in two ways. It is not the case that political opinion has only recently become divided over issues in foreign policy; to go no further back one has only to think of the Crimean War, the 'Bulgarian Atrocities', the Boer War, and the Spanish Civil War. In the second place, it was true of Suez as of other occasions of the kind that the main line of division ran between the main political parties, not within them. Of course many Conservatives were ready to voice in private their doubts about the wisdom of the government's course of action; but there is no convincing evidence that the mass of the party in the country were unwilling to follow their leaders; the cases where the local organization was seriously damaged are hard to find. One would expect a division so fundamental as to cause the kind of impact Macmillan describes to have had more permanent results. It can hardly be compared with the impact in the nineteenth century of the repeal of the Corn Laws upon the Conservative party or of Irish Home Rule upon the Liberal party.

During the Suez Crisis the line of division ran as is usual along the boundary between the parties not inside them. The Labour party did initially share the general reaction in British opinion against Nasser and his doings; but it rapidly shifted its ground to one of outright opposition to the government's policy; it had fewer overt dissidents from the party line than the Conservatives.[7] The Liberal party found itself divided on this as on so much else but, with a bare half a dozen members in the House of Commons, this was not of much importance.[8] Nor is there much evidence to suggest that either Opposition party was much affected by the crisis or its outcome. At the time many government supporters held that a large proportion of working-class voters did not sympathize with the anti-Suez stance largely voiced by the middle-class intellectuals in the leadership. The evidence for this is

[6] Harold Macmillan, *Memoirs*, vol. iv: *Riding the Storm, 1956–1959* (London, 1971).

[7] A weakness of Professor Epstein's book is that he tends, like most Americans, to see foreign policy as 'bipartisan', which it has rarely been in Britain.

[8] Professor Epstein calls attention to the pro-Suez views of Professor Gilbert Murray, a leading figure in the League of Nations Union and its successor the United Nations Association, and of the present writer, then also a Liberal. Epstein, *British Politics*, p. 168.

mainly anecdotal though polling evidence suggests that support for armed action against Egypt was supported by between a third and a fifth of Labour voters at different junctures during the crisis. But neither the polls nor by-elections show that this had much, if any, effect upon voting intentions.[9] By the time Labour got back into power in 1964 the issues with which it was identified had little to do with Suez or its consequences.

The impact of the crisis upon the Conservative party is at once more complex and more important. It had been in power for almost five years before the crisis and was to retain power for another seven years after it was over. While Macmillan may have exaggerated the impact of the affair upon personal relationships, it is true that there was throughout a threefold division within the ranks of the Conservative party. There were those who supported the government both in advance and in retreat; there were those who pressed originally for more rapid and decisive action and who deplored the ultimate retreat; finally there were those who felt the force of at least some of the case presented by the Opposition and to a greater or lesser degree expressed their concern over the resort to arms. All three were visibly present in the Parliamentary party; the activists in the country were prone either to sympathize with the government or with its critics on the right, while in the Cabinet, where serious doubts did exist these were largely concealed at the time, with, in the end, only two junior ministers (Edward Boyle and Anthony Nutting) resigning.[10] To consider the nature of these divisions, it is necessary to take into account the answers to two further questions. Why did policy towards Egypt and the Canal come to divide the party even before the summer of 1956, and what relationship did the divisions that manifested themselves have to earlier issues of controversy within the party?

The two main recent occasions of deep division within the Conservative party had been Churchill's long-drawn-out battle against the 1935 India Act and what Macmillan refers to as 'Munich' or more generally, 'appeasement'. It might be thought that since India was now an independent Republic, even if within the Commonwealth, Egypt was a rather poor substitute as a focus for imperialist sentiment. Yet as Suez showed, it still counted for a great deal.

It was a Conservative Prime Minister, Disraeli, whose purchase of the Khedive's shares in the Suez Canal in 1875 first asserted Britain's intention of playing a primary role in the country through which now passed a principal lifeline of the Empire. And although it was Gladstone's Liberal government that in 1882 took the decisive step of

---

[9] See the tables in Epstein, *British Politics*, pp. 142–51.
[10] Sir Anthony Nutting, *No End of a Lesson* (London, 1967), p. 137.

military intervention, his intention had been to act on behalf of the European powers in general. The failure of Gordon's mission to extricate British forces from the Sudan, and of the relief expedition to reach Khartoum in time to save him from death at the hands of the Mahdi's followers, made the Egyptian involvement deeply unpopular among Liberals. It was under another Conservative Prime Minister, Salisbury, that Kitchener avenged Gordon, established British authority in the Sudan under nominal Egyptian sovereignty, and in the confrontation with France at Fashoda made clear Britain's determination to remain in control of the entire Nile valley. It was exponents of imperialism, on the Tory model of Milner and Cromer, who had created modern Egypt, and it was in the Sudan that there was to be found an early example of constructive colonial rule.

The future of Egypt was an important issue in the debates on British policy after the First World War which had added a new dimension to Britain's imperial role. The subject was again not one on which the Conservative party was united. The debate within the party was similar to that about India. How far was it possible to meet nationalist demands for an increasing measure of self-government leading to independence without sacrificing the essentials of the imperial position?[11] Expense was an additional factor. Egypt, it was argued, was a drain on British manpower and financial resources which could not be justified. This argument was particularly powerful in the mid-1930s, when the increasing threat to the home islands from a resurgent Germany made the 'recall of the legions' seem only sensible. But at the same time, the revelation of Mussolini's Mediterranean ambitions made the safety of the Canal base an equally urgent concern of Britain's military planners.[12]

The Treaty of Alliance between Great Britain and Egypt of August 1936 was held to have provided a way by which the desiderata of both sides were met.[13] Egypt became an independent power and would qualify as a member of the League of Nations. In the event of war or an apprehended national emergency, Egypt would provide Britain

[11] There were personal links between the Indian Empire and the rulers of Egypt. Lord Lloyd, the High Commissioner in Egypt who thought of himself as being in the Milner–Cromer tradition and was out of harmony with Baldwin's 1924–9 government, which he thought of as appeasing Egyptian nationalism, was forced to resign by the 1929 Labour government. He had come to Egypt from the governorship of the Bombay Presidency, where the barrage across the Indus, which he had initiated, irrigated a larger area than the entire cultivable land of Egypt. On Lloyd see John Charmley, *Lord Lloyd and the Decline of the British Empire* (London, 1987).

[12] The course of relations between Britain and Egypt in the inter-war period is put in its imperial context in Max Beloff, *Imperial Sunset*, vol. ii: *Dream of Commonwealth* (London, 1989).

[13] The text of the Treaty is in Royal Institute of International Affairs (RIIA), *Documents on International Affairs, 1936* (London, 1937), pp. 476 ff.

with full facilities on her territory until Egyptian forces were able to take charge of the defence of the Suez Canal, recognized as 'a universal means of communication and also an essential means of communication between the different parts of the British Empire'. Britain was to maintain limited forces of her own in the 'Canal Zone'.

The experience of the early part of the Second World War showed that the Treaty had in fact satisfied neither Egyptian claims to full independence nor British security requirements. The Egyptian government appeared all too willing to give free play to Axis propaganda, a matter of increasing importance after Italy's entry into the war put hostile forces along Egypt's western frontier. The result in February 1942 was a reassertion of British political control when the Ambassador, Sir Miles Lampson (later Lord Killearn) forced the King to appoint as Prime Minister a man of his own choosing. The Middle East was the one theatre of the war in which Britain was not overshadowed by her major allies and in which the victories achieved could be put to the credit of British and imperial forces. Wartime Cairo became a principal centre of the British war effort.[14]

No post-war upholder of the role of the Empire Commonwealth in world affairs could deny the importance of a British foothold in Egypt. Although as Ernest Bevin's tenure of the Foreign Office had shown, this view was not confined to the Conservative party, that party could certainly not easily abandon its commitment to retaining a direct military capacity in the Canal Zone. The instability of Egyptian politics after the war gave no confidence that Egypt could provide a substitute for the British presence, and it was clear that if the occasion arose, Egyptian nationalism could once again be aroused to Britain's detriment. Members of Parliament would also have been well aware that the experience of British servicemen in Egypt had given them no love for its inhabitants, a fact which was to colour their views at the time of the Suez crisis. It was, however, the understandable desire of British statesmen, military men, and diplomats to work with whatever might be the Egyptian government of the day. And when, even before the defeat of the Axis, the old rivalry with Russia in the Middle East was caught up in the new Cold War, this was the view that prevailed.

For many in the British ruling élite, the best way to entrench Britain's position in the Middle East against both the Soviet Union and the United States seemed to be the espousal of the Arab national movement and its inchoate strivings for Arab unity.[15] A majority of

---

[14] The atmosphere of wartime Cairo is brilliantly evoked by the late Olivia Manning in her three novels republished as *The Levant Trilogy* (London, 1982).

[15] See Yehoshua Porath, *In Search of Arab Unity, 1930–1945* (London, 1986).

British Conservatives found themselves committed to going along with Eden's support of the British Labour government in its commitment to the only issue upon which the Arabs were united—opposition to the Jewish claims in Palestine. Sympathy for Zionism as a natural ally for the British in the Middle East, which had been entertained by an earlier generation of Conservative imperialists—Balfour, Churchill, Amery—was now felt only by a minority.[16]

The Arab governments with whom the British felt most at home were those where the British had formed close connections with the ruling élites—Iraq, and what had become in 1948 the Hashemite Kingdom of Jordan. With the Egyptians, whose connection with Britain had not dissipated their cultural preferences for France, relations were less intimate and were further aggravated by the continued Egyptian claims to the Sudan.

The British thus saw the Egyptian revolution of 1952 as an opportunity to resolve outstanding issues between the two governments—the British presence on the Canal, which was still much in excess of that provided for in the 1936 Treaty, and the question of the Sudan—as well as to bring Egypt into the wider plans for Middle Eastern defence.

The question of the Sudan was the first to be dealt with. Churchill, now again Prime Minister, was opposed to giving it independence on the grounds that this would encourage Egypt to reassert its claim; and back-bench sentiment was also mobilized against such a step. Indeed, the group which became known as the 'Suez group' through its opposition to Eden over the Canal Zone, first came together over the fate of the Sudan.[17] Eden was, however, convinced that an agreement over the Sudan was central to his hopes of agreement with Egypt and to his wider hopes in regard to the Arab world. He succeeded in winning over Churchill, and an agreement on independence for the Sudan was announced on 12 February 1953.[18]

The Canal issue took longer to resolve. But on 27 July 1954 the heads of agreement were announced. British troops would all be withdrawn from the Canal Zone, but some of the installations would be maintained by Egyptian contractors and Egypt undertook to allow the British to put the base on a war footing and to operate it should there be an attack from outside the area on Egypt, other members of the Arab League, or Turkey. Egypt also undertook to uphold the 1888 Convention on freedom of navigation in the Canal though she continued to deny it to Israel on the ground that the two countries were

---

[16] See Wm. R. Louis, *The British Empire in the Middle East, 1945–1951* (Oxford, 1984).

[17] Anthony Seldon, *Churchill's Indian Summer* (London, 1981), pp. 622 ff.

[18] RIIA, *Documents on International Affairs, 1953* (London, 1956), pp. 315–18.

at war.[19] Churchill, who had again been opposed to this policy, had been won over by Eden.

The announcement of this agreement led to the first open back-bench Conservative revolt. Churchill, defending the government's policy, argued that the whole strategic picture had been altered by the advent of the hydrogen bomb. In that case, asked Captain Charles Waterhouse, the spokesman of the critics, what was the point of moving the troops to Cyprus which was no less vulnerable. He also queried the value of the Egyptian government's undertaking to uphold free navigation and to allow Britain back into the base in the event of hostilities. In the upshot, one Conservative MP, Major E. A. H. Legge-Bourke, resigned the whip and twenty-seven Conservatives voted against the Government.[20] The Suez group, described by one of their bitterest critics as a 'hotch-potch collection of embittered ex-Ministers and young newly elected members anxious to cut a figure in Parliament by attacking the Government for selling out British imperial interests',[21] was now a recognizable political entity. In a sense, of course, the adjective hotch-potch was correct in that the Suez group's membership could not have been predicted from the previous positions of its members on other issues. It contained for instance both men like Legge-Bourke and Hinchingbrooke, who were notable for anti-Zionist pro-Arab sentiments, and on the other hand Julian Amery, who inherited his father's pro-Zionist leanings.

In any event, the opposition in the party was not such as to put the government off its stride, and after further negotiations a new treaty was signed on 19 October 1954 and ratified on 6 December.[22]

The dismissal of General Glubb by King Hussein of Jordan on 1 March 1956 was not only a blow to Eden, now Prime Minister, but also to the Suez group, a confirmation of their view that his policy had led to a decline in Britain's Middle Eastern position. It did not prevent the government from pulling out the last British troops in mid-June. When in the following month Nasser nationalized the Canal, the views of the pessimists appeared to have been justified, and their position within the party correspondingly strengthened. The Cabinet had therefore no reason to doubt that they would receive party support when at Cabinet

[19] RIIA, *Documents on International Affairs, 1954* (London, 1957), pp. 245–7. The 1954 Treaty is dealt with in Roger Louis's chapter in this volume.

[20] *Parliamentary Debates* (Commons), 29 July 1954. The tellers against the Government were Sir H. Grimston and Sir Patrick Dormer—those voting against were Julian Amery, Ralph Assheton, R. F. Crouch, Sir William Darling, Capt. J. A. L. Duncan, A. Fell, Sir Fergus Graham, Viscount Hinchingbrooke, C. J. Holland-Martin, I. M. Horobin, H. M. Hyde, H. B. Kerby, H. W. Kerr, Sir Guy Lloyd, Patrick Maitland, Angus Maude, Sir John Mellor, G. N. Nabarro, I. J. Pitman, J. Enoch Powell, W. R. Rees Davies, W. Teeling, Charles Waterhouse, C. Williams, P. Williams.

[21] Nutting, *No End of a Lesson*, p. 22.

[22] *Documents on International Affairs, 1954*, pp. 248–55.

meetings on 26 and 27 July a decision was taken to use force as a last resort.[23]

Another factor of importance must be considered in dealing with the impact of the crisis upon the Conservative party, and that perhaps the most important of all. British relations with the United States over the future of the Empire had been uneasy ever since the promulgation of the Atlantic Charter in 1941. In matters of commercial and financial policy, a victory for the United States was implicit in the terms of the US loan negotiated in 1946 and approved by Congress in the following year. The agreement came in for strong criticism in the House of Commons on 5 and 6 December 1946; in the ensuing division a number of right-wing Conservatives went into the lobby with left-wing socialists, while the party officially abstained. No future member of the Suez group was among those who voted against the agreement though Leo Amery, the principal protagonist of imperial preference in the inter-war period, was highly critical from outside Parliament.[24]

But the anti-Americanism which was so obvious an element in the attitudes of the Suez group was not based upon such considerations, which had been rendered largely irrelevant with the new intimacy brought into Anglo-American relations by the Marshall Plan and the setting up of NATO. It was the conduct of the United States in the Middle East itself, particularly as exemplified in the Abadan affair, that now aroused suspicion. It was felt that the objectives of the United States were both to supplant British influence in the region and at the same time to leave Britain with the responsibility of defending it against Soviet encroachments. Britain, it was argued, and not by the Suez group alone, had been pushed by Dulles into making the Baghdad Pact the centre-piece of her Middle East diplomacy with no guarantee that the United States would come to her aid if she were forced to activate its provisions.[25] It is not surprising that Macmillan was later to accuse Dulles of practising 'vicarious brinkmanship'.[26]

The conduct of the United States in the Suez crisis was seen from the beginning as completely unhelpful both by ministers, and by the vast

---

[23] After that debate the development of policy was in the hands of the Egypt Committee of Eden, Macmillan, Salisbury, Selwyn Lloyd, and Monckton. Among these, Monckton was from the beginning doubtful as to the need for military action, and on 18 October gave up his post as Minister of Defence, in which he was succeeded by Anthony Head. He remained in the Cabinet as Paymaster-General rather than create a political storm by resigning, having previously informed Eden that he would not in the last resort rule out the use of force. The Earl of Birkenhead, *Walter Monckton* (London, 1969), pp. 308–9. The ups and downs of Cabinet opinion are traced in Lamb, *The Failure of the Eden Government*.

[24] Julian Amery did not enter the House of Commons until 1950.

[25] See RIIA, *Survey of International Affairs, 1955–1956* (London, 1960), pp. 25–32; *Documents on International Affairs, 1955* (London, 1958), ch. VII.

[26] Macmillan, *Riding the Storm*, p. 91.

majority of Conservatives in and out of Parliament.[27] Each time there seemed to be the prospect of enough pressure to force Nasser into an acceptable settlement, the United States intervened to thwart it. And this was not only the view of those who supported Eden.[28]

The almost venomous hostility shown at the time of the Suez expedition itself by the President and the Secretary of State, and the use by the American Secretary of the Treasury of the financial weapon to force Britain into successive surrenders, was not known in detail at the time to most back-bench MPs. But enough was apparent for opinion to veer sharply in an anti-American direction. To complaints that the British government had erred in not keeping the Americans better informed, it was possible to reply that Dulles did not have the backing of all US experts in the field of foreign policy.[29] Even so harsh a critic of Eden's conduct as Evelyn Shuckburgh found it hard to take American 'anti-colonialism' seriously when it was combined with constant pressure in favour of the Americans' own Arab client, Saudi Arabia.[30] The view that Soviet penetration into the Middle East could best be thwarted by winning the sympathies of ex-colonial peoples at the expense of the United States' European allies held little appeal.[31] An 'early day motion' strongly critical of the United States was signed by over 120 Conservative MPs, while a counter-motion favouring the Americans found only 26 signatories.[32]

The crisis thus brought into play feelings by no means confined to the Suez Group that Britain's retreat from her place in world affairs had been largely due to American pressure. But the Suez action was not simply an effort at national self-assertion. It was in large part the result of calculations about Britain's national interests, with the security of her oil supplies taking an important place among them. But

---

[27] A junior minister of the time was to write later on: 'I still think he [Eden] was right about Suez and his reaction was correct. Unfortunately Suez did not succeed, partly because of the Americans', Reginald Maudling, *Memoirs* (London, 1978), p. 63.

[28] See for instance the diaries of Britain's representative at the United Nations, Sir Pierson Dixon, quoted in Piers Dixon, *Double Diploma: The Life of Sir Pierson Dixon* (London, 1968), ch. XV.

[29] Dean Acheson wrote in the *Sunday Times* on 6 Jan. 1957: 'It is not Machiavellian depravity on the part of the British and French which made them unwilling to trust us with their plan of desperation but a belief that we had not only been disregardful of their vital interests but had deviously led them to frustration'. Quoted by Sir R. Grimston, *Parliamentary Debates* (Commons), 15 May 1957, Col. 466–7.

[30] Diary entry, 14 Dec. 1955, in Evelyn Shuckburgh, *Descent to Suez: Diaries, 1951–1956* (London, 1986), p. 311.

[31] On the United States, and the British Empire in general see Lord Beloff, 'The End of the British Empire and the Assumption of World-wide Commitments by the United States', in Wm. Roger Louis and Hedley Bull (eds.), *The Special Relationship: Anglo-American Relations since 1945* (Oxford, 1986).

[32] Epstein, *British Politics*, p. 57.

it was also, as Macmillan's memoirs make clear, the result of the permanent impact of 'Munich' upon the Conservative party, the feeling that resistance to any challenge rather than renewed appeasement was what the country would rightly demand. Demands for tough action came to a head at the party conference at Llandudno on 11 October 1956 when Nutting himself was put up to make a robust speech in answer to the bellicose resolutions coming from the constituencies.[33]

It would therefore be wrong to think of Eden as isolated from the bulk of his party in advocating resistance, as he had been when opposing appeasement in 1937-9.[34] His critics have made much of his error in equating the threat from Nasser with that from Hitler and Mussolini in the 1930s but he was not alone in making this juxtaposition.[35] Macmillan certainly took the view at the time that those Conservatives who had qualms about going it alone if necessary were in a literal sense scions of the Munichites.[36] Nor were his views to change after the event:

The bulk of the Conservative Party which had supported Chamberlain at Munich were partisans of Eden. There were of course varying degrees of enthusiasm; I noticed that those Conservatives who had been the most violent opponents of the Munich policy were the keenest partisans of the Government's policy, while those who had been *Munichois* tended logically enough to be waverers or opponents. This was not true merely of those in active politics but of private individuals. Those especially who had been depreciators and detractors of Churchill in the years 1935 to 1939 were now equally sneering about Eden.[37]

Macmillan's point here is hard to substantiate where Parliament is concerned. Many of the Conservatives elected in 1955 had not served before the war. It is, however, interesting to note that Sir Horace Wilson, who had, as a civil servant, played a key role in Chamberlain's policies, came out of deep retirement to support the anti-Suez dissi-

---

[33] Nigel Nicolson, *People and Parliament* (London, 1958), p. 116.

[34] As a leading historian of the party has written, 'Eden was surely right on one point, his assurance that popular opinion was with him and that the British people as a whole would accept military action if necessary in defence of national interests.' John Ramsden in Lord Butler (ed.), *The Conservatives* (London, 1977), p. 441.

[35] Sir Ivone Kirkpatrick, an anti-appeaser in the 1930s and one who felt he had been taken in by Hitler and was determined not to be by Nasser, was now Permanent Under-Secretary in the Foreign Office and, unlike many of his colleagues, a supporter of Eden's line. His *DNB* biographer, Sir Con O'Neill, takes him to task for it, *Dictionary of National Biography, 1961–1970*, pp. 616–17.

[36] Macmillan, *Riding the Storm*, p. 124.

[37] Ibid., p. 155. For the divisions in the pre-war Conservative party over appeasement see Neville Thompson, *The Anti-Appeasers* (Oxford, 1971).

dent, Nigel Nicolson, against his constituency party's attack upon him.[38]

Macmillan noted on 20 September that the Chief Whip (Edward Heath) had reported a good deal of trouble in the party from some members opposed to the use of force even in the last resort.[39] But rank and file disquiet would only have been significant if a senior member of the Cabinet opposed to Eden's policy could take advantage of it. Neither Monckton nor another sceptic, Heathcoat Amory, nor Salisbury, who was doubtful on United Nations grounds, could give such leadership even if they had wished to. The only person who could have acted in this sense was R. A. Butler, himself the principal survivor of pre-war appeasement. That he had doubts and did not conceal them is well known.[40] But they were not made public. His official biographer does not accept his own claim never to have wavered in his support for the government: 'The truth probably was that having—as he believed—held back Eden, Salisbury and Macmillan from precipitate military action in both August and September, Rab had convinced himself that he could do the same if need be in October'.[41] Nevertheless, he went along with the plan to intervene, so casting his lot in with an enterprise in which he did not believe.[42]

Butler's own subsequent version of his role is of more interest for his analysis of the divergent interests at work than for its contribution to reconstituting the actual course of events. He did not accept Eden's view that Nasser was the incarnation of evil or a megalomaniac. Yet what Nasser had done was incompatible with British interests and probably with international law as well. Resistance to Nasser was called for by 'deep-seated emotions affecting liberal-minded people, but they coalesced only too easily with less generous sentiments, the residues of illiberal resentment at the loss of Empire, the rise of coloured nationalism, the transfer of world leadership to the United States. It was these sentiments that made the Suez venture so popular, not least among the supporters of the embarrassed Labour Party.'[43]

Butler did not accept much of the anti-colonial case which was part of the staple of the Opposition's criticism of the government, as he had made clear in an address two days before the Llandudno debate on

---

[38] Nicolson, *People and Parliament*, p. 139.

[39] Macmillan, *Riding the Storm*, p. 128.

[40] Macmillan noted them on 13 Sept., *Riding the Storm*, p. 125.

[41] A. Howard, *RAB: The Life of R. A. Butler* (London, 1987), p. 233.

[42] The most significant vote in the full Cabinet was taken on 4 November, the day before the landings. Twelve members voted for going ahead, six against—Butler, Kilmuir, Heathcoat Amory, Salisbury, Buchan-Hepburn, and Monckton. But with no one being willing to come forward with a resignation, which would have brought down the Government, nothing came of the opposition. Lamb, *The Failure of the Eden Government*, pp. 259–60.

[43] Lord Butler, *The Art of the Possible* (London, 1971), pp. 188–9.

Suez.[44] But his hesitations were bound to become known and he added to his difficulties by revealing at a dinner with influential Conservatives on 14 November the extent of the sterling losses that were weakening Britain's position: 'whenever I moved in the weeks that followed, I felt the party knives sticking in my innocent back.'[45] But these hesitations did not prevent him from being the acting Prime Minister when Eden's breakdown forced him into his temporary retreat to Jamaica. In that capacity he was present with Macmillan at a meeting of the 1922 Committee on 22 November, and there made the admission that there was no alternative to a British withdrawal despite the existence of a strong sentiment in the party (largely unaware of the financial pressure being exercised by the United States) that a mistake had been made in the premature cease-fire, and that the expedition should have been carried through to its projected conclusion.[46]

If one accepts the view that it was Suez that ended Butler's hopes of succeeding Eden (and if one believes that the Conservative party would have followed a different course had Butler rather than Macmillan been Prime Minister in the late 1950s and early 1960s), one would have to regard the rejection of Butler as a principal consequence of Suez for the Conservative party. And for this view there is good authority.[47] Yet it could be argued that it was the surviving bitterness over Munich that was the more important and that Butler's hesitations over Suez merely reinforced the party's determination not to have him as its leader. Nor indeed, given the constraints on any British government at the time, is it easy to see how the choice of Butler would have made much difference.

The lack of any alternative leadership may explain why the political fall-out from Suez was so easily contained. As already noted, only two junior ministers, Nutting and Edward Boyle, resigned.[48] Nutting was repudiated by his constituency and disappeared from political life;

[44] Howard, *RAB*, pp. 239–44.

[45] Butler, *The Art of the Possible*, p. 194.

[46] Howard, *RAB*, pp. 240–1.

[47] 'Suez destroyed Rab's chance of ever becoming Prime Minister. At the time he gave the impression that he was lifting his skirt to avoid the dirt. The feeling in the Party was that if he could not take responsibility we would not have him as leader', Maudling, *Memoirs*, p. 64. According to the Lord Chancellor at the time, the Parliamentary party would have disintegrated if Butler had been chosen. The party had found unacceptable 'his habit of publicly hedging his political bets', *Political Adventure: The Memoirs of the Earl of Kilmuir* (London, 1964), p. 286.

[48] According to Nutting, the Marquess of Reading, the Minister of State at the Foreign Office, and the two Under-Secretaries Lord John Hope and Col. A. Dodds-Parker, also considered resigning but did not wish to rock the government further, *No End of a Lesson*, pp. 137–8. The inclusion of Hope seems rather doubtful as he was one of a number of ministers who wrote to Eden in early November expressing their support (Lamb, *The Failure of the Eden Government*, pp. 250–1.) Neither Reading nor Dodds-Parker were included in the Macmillan government. Hope was transferred from the Foreign Office to the Colonial Office.

Boyle, who was not repudiated, was brought back into the government by Macmillan. Of back-benchers with similar anti-Suez sentiments, one, Cyril Banks, resigned the government whip and, in a vote on 8 November after the cease-fire, there were six abstentions on the government benches, Boyle, Nutting, J. J. Astor, Robert Boothby (whose attitude was as unclear as it had been over Munich), Sir Frank Medlicott, and Nigel Nicolson. The last two lost the confidence of their constituency parties and did not contest the general election in 1959.

Dissidence on the Right had a longer run, though the Suez group did not retain all its original support. The inclusion of Julian Amery in Macmillan's government removed one of its principal figures. In May 1957 there was renewed criticism when the government indicated that it could no longer advise British shipping not to use the Canal. Eight members of the group resigned the whip and Lord Lambton also resigned his post as Parliamentary Private Secretary to Selwyn Lloyd.[49] The government's critics were now reinforced by Lord Salisbury, who had left the Macmillan government in March over its policy in Cyprus. In the House of Commons on 16 May, those who had resigned the whip were joined by six others in abstaining.[50] On the other hand, former members of the Suez group, including Legge-Bourke, Ian Horobin, and Enoch Powell, went into the government lobby.

But such matters were for the professionals of politics. In the country, the party's standing seemed unimpaired: 'Suez did us no harm politically, either in the short or in the long view.'[51]

The fact that in the Conservative party the dissidents were stronger on the right than on the left may partially explain the failure of the Opposition to exploit the Suez issue to its advantage. Initially in August it had seemed willing to contemplate strong action. But subsequently it changed its stance completely and indulged in violent denunciation of the Prime Minister. Hugh Gaitskell handled the issue somewhat ineptly.[52] In particular there were objections to his broadcast of 4 November in which he appealed (as he had done in the House of Commons on the previous day) to dissident Conservatives to overthrow Eden and install a new Prime Minister who would get the

[49] The eight members were Lambton, Victor Raikes, Patrick Maitland, Angus Maude, John Biggs-Davidson, Laurence Turner, Anthony Fell, and Paul Williams. Maude left the House of Commons in 1958 but returned to it in 1963, becoming a deputy-chairman of the party in 1975 and a member of the 1979 government.

[50] They were Lambton, Fitzroy Maclean, John Eden, Montgomery Hyde, Norman Pannell, and Greville Howard.

[51] Kilmuir, *Political Adventure*, p. 276.

[52] His biographer does his best to give consistency to Gaitskell's role in the crisis, Philip M. Williams, *Hugh Gaitskell* (London, 1979), pp. 434-5. See also Robert Rhodes James, *Anthony Eden*, pp. 492-3. Gaitskell's rival Aneurin Bevan was more cautious in his criticisms, a fact that the Conservatives did their best to exploit. See John Campbell, *Nye Bevan and the Mirage of British Socialism* (London, 1987), pp. 318-26.

support of the Opposition in halting the invasion, ordering a cease-fire, and complying with the decisions of the United Nations. Even opponents of Eden objected to this attempt to dictate to the Conservatives their choice of leader.[53]

The final proof that the party had not lost its support in the country came with the general election of 1959, which saw the Conservatives returned with an increased majority. But Suez had scarcely figured at all in the campaign on either side. It was naturally not given much place in Conservative election addresses. Only one per cent of them mentioned it. 27 per cent of Liberal addresses and 67 per cent of Labour addresses did refer to Suez but little was made of it. 'The Conservatives', it was commented, 'ignored it because it caused internal party strife; Labour was hesitant to stir the issue for fear that its criticism made it seem unpatriotic.'[54] In fact on all sides in politics there was a new agenda—Suez was history.

It is of course still possible to argue that in the longer view, the episode was not without its effects. A distinguished historian of the party has suggested, on the testimony of Iain McLeod, that Suez was responsible for the Conservatives losing the 'intellectual' vote in the 1960s.[55] Yet so much happened between 1959 and 1964, when Labour at last recovered power, that it is hard to see how such a claim could be documented.

But there are two consequences of the crisis that are easier to demonstrate. The first was the general acceptance in the Conservative party of the fact that the dominance of the United States in world affairs could not be challenged and that the path of safety was at almost any cost to align British policy with that of the United States. Macmillan himself was the conscious agent of this revolution. He blamed himself for failing to grasp the degree to which the Americans would prove hostile to Eden's Suez policy, and for having assured Eden that the Americans would not oppose it. This feeling gave added weight to his determination to use his premiership to put things right.[56]

---

[53] Nigel Nicolson was so horrified and so fearful that people might think his withdrawal of support from the government was due to Gaitskell's appeal that he was for the only time tempted not to go through with his decision, Nicolson, *People and Parliament*, p. 143.

[54] D. E. Butler and R. Rose, *The British General Election of 1959* (London, 1960), p. 64 n.

[55] Robert Blake, *The Conservative Party from Peel to Thatcher* (London, 1985), p. 379. McLeod had been Minister of Health in the Churchill government (outside the Cabinet). He retained the office under Eden but entered the Cabinet in Dec. 1955 as Minister of Labour. He is said to have had misgivings over Suez but to have been insufficiently involved to consider resignation, Ian Gilmour, *Dictionary of National Biography, 1961–1970*, p. 702.

[56] See the interview with Macmillan's authorized biographer, Alistair Horne, *Sunday Times*, 4 Jan. 1987. It has been suggested that Eisenhower and the State Department through the US Ambassador in London actively sponsored a movement to get rid of Eden and to encourage the assumption of the premiership by Macmillan (or possibly Butler). Not all the documentation on the US side needed to substantiate this claim is as yet in the public domain and the evidence that is so available does not support it. No evidence on the British side appears to exist, W. Scott Lucas, 'Suez, the Americans and the Overthrow of Anthony Eden', *LSE Quarterly*, 1:3 (1987).

The other consequence was the abandonment by the Conservatives of their role as the imperial party. Until Suez many Conservatives had cherished the idea that even with its new 'non-British' members the Commonwealth might still form a viable international system on its own. But the utter identification by Nehru of India's cause with that of Nasser destroyed that vision for good. Free of the bonds of 'Commonwealth *d'abord*', Britain, and British Conservatives in particular, could now adopt the ideal of European unity, hitherto of interest only to a minority. In this rather negative or roundabout way, Suez can be seen as a proximate cause of Britain's application to join the Common Market. And this also fell to Macmillan to put forward, though on this first occasion without success.

Anthony Eden thus takes on a new image—that of the last British Prime Minister who believed in common with the majority of the citizens of the country that Britain was still a world power, only temporarily weakened by the impact of the war years. His diplomacy in the Middle East, whether attempting in Project Alpha to design a settlement of the Palestine problem or, as at Suez, colluding with Israel and France to bring down Nasser as an obstacle to his designs, reflects the illusions of a passing age. In that sense his tragic fall was more significant than some of its chroniclers would have us believe.

17

Post-Suez France

MAURICE VAISSE

AFTER Suez, France was never the same again. If one considers the period extending from Suez to Evian, the 1958 cleavage is not as clear-cut as it may appear at first. Gaullist France was already on the horizon in 1956. The origins of the 1960s must be sought, in part, in the results of the Suez crisis. Developments long since begun were suddenly accelerated and ended in favour of Gaullism.[1]

At the foreign policy level the consequences were both direct and indirect, and all of them were serious. The Suez crisis bluntly revealed what the post-World War II situation, General de Gaulle's struggle for power, and the possession of a colonial empire had concealed: France was no longer a great power. Certainly, she still possessed a reliable military machine but, without a genuine expeditionary force and financial independence, she no longer had the ability to impose her will. Her impotence was obvious—not, of course, *vis-à-vis* Egypt, but *vis-à-vis* international pressure.

France, birthplace of the Rights of Man, the champion of the Kellogg–Briand Pact, had irrecoverably damaged her reputation. The Security Council member had broken the rule against resort to armed force. France's position, already a difficult one because of the Tunisian affair in the United Nations, was shaken. With the Afro-Asian tide submerging the United Nations, the organization turned hostile to France at the moment when she faced debates over Algeria. The planning of the Franco-British-Israeli operation had led, it seemed, to collusion with Israel, duplicity in international relations, and aggression against Egypt.

French influence in the Arab world was in ruins.[2] France had had important cultural, financial, and economic interests in Egypt. Nearly 60,000 pupils and students were henceforth deprived of a French education. Industrial and commercial enterprises were sequestered, and later liquidated in disadvantageous conditions. France thus lost

---

[1] For more extended discussions, see J. Doise and M. Vaïsse, *Diplomatie et outil militaire, 1871–1969* (Paris, 1987).

[2] See Marc Ferro, *Suez* (Brussels, 1982).

nearly 400 billion francs in investments; banks, insurance companies, and the Alsthom and Air Liquide firms were hard hit. Nearly 6,000 Frenchmen—teachers, engineers, staff personnel, businessmen—were forced to leave Egypt in distressing circumstances. Furthermore, the Suez Canal was closed, unusable for months. In a few days the work of Ferdinand de Lesseps was undermined. For a few years France cut herself off from part of the Third World, whose emerging role in international relations was rapidly expanding. In 1956 France experienced a crisis of confidence in the Atlantic alliance and in her American ally, whose attitude in Indo-China after the cease-fire, and ambiguous position respecting North Africa, raised doubts as to its friendship. As for the Suez affair, the Americans, responsible for the outbreak of the crisis by the withdrawal of their offer to finance the Aswan Dam, then abandoned their allies engaged in the common combat against the Egyptian dictator. The lack of solidarity evident during the diplomatic phase of the crisis became an out-and-out 'abandonment' when it became open and warlike. Some reports refer to strange 'exercises' and 'drunken' manœuvres by the American Sixth Fleet (which placed the French and British ships in an uncomfortable and rather demoralized position). This was resented by the French military as an 'humiliation, rancour over which will not soon subside'.[3] American financial pressure against the pound sterling and refusal to use the American atomic umbrella in face of the Soviet threat demonstrated a lack of solidarity in the Atlantic alliance, in which the preponderant role of the United States was placed in question. 'During this crisis they chose to ensure our defeat.'[4]

Two major foreign policy reorientations in the years 1956–8 stemmed from this reconsideration of the Atlantic alliance; in the structure of Europe on the one hand, and in military policy on the other. These years were in fact marked by a remarkable advance in the European field. The conferences at Messina (June 1955) and Venice (May 1956) culminated in the signing of the Treaties of Rome in March 1957.[5] The Suez crisis served as an accelerating factor since international tension, interruption of the supply of petroleum from the Middle East, and the weakness of the European countries relative to the superpowers clearly demonstrated the necessity for greater European solidarity. 'Europe will be your revenge', Konrad Adenauer is supposed to have said to Guy Mollet the very day the Suez operation was halted. According to Robert Marjolin, 'Guy Mollet . . . felt that

---

[3] Philippe Masson, 'Origines et bilan d'une défaite', in *Revue Historique des Armées*, No. 4 (1986), pp. 42–8.

[4] Note by E. de Croüy-Chauvel for the Secretary-General, 10 Nov. 1956, Diplomatic Archives.

[5] Cf. Pierre Gerbet, *La Naissance du Marché Commun* (Paris, 1987).

the only way to erase, or at least to attenuate, the humiliation France had just undergone was the rapid conclusion of a European treaty. He threw his full weight into the balance, and it tipped to his side.'[6] Incidentally, the Europe in the making was more than ever built around a Franco-German axis, whereas the Anglophile Guy Mollet had previously seemed anxious to restore a preferred Paris–London axis. The crisis demonstrated that France and Great Britain no longer carried enough weight to influence world affairs effectively. Franco-British relations did not survive the failure of the operation they conducted together.

The effects in the military field were both numerous and important. They should be considered from two points of view: that of the army, and that of defence policy. From the military standpoint the failure of the Suez operation widened the gulf between the army and the Republic. Settlement of the Indo-China affair had left deep scars in the army. Its commitment in North Africa, particularly in Algeria, made it the object of increasing solicitude by the governments of the Fourth Republic. The army, convinced that the key to the Algerian war lay in Egypt, accepted with enthusiasm the opportunity to settle accounts with Nasser. After successive retreats by the Fourth Republic in Indo-China and North Africa the army still believed the regime was capable of rising to the occasion. The military therefore acted in perfect harmony with the political leaders in preparing for the Suez operation. However, the political secrecy surrounding the operation eventually caused the military hierarchies to lose credibility, and this in turn undermined discipline, the traditional strength of armies.[7] And the military operation, hampered by political and diplomatic interference, thus collapsed. Contradictory orders were issued; the cease-fire order was given even as the soldiers were discreetly informed that they were free to advance as far as Suez. The reproach was made, after the event, that they should have known enough to disobey the order to cease fire. The precedent proved to be a dangerous one, for the soldiers who returned to Algeria, crowned with an ambiguous glory, were to remember the lesson. The crisis of morale worsened, as Colonel Godard explains: 'Early in this month of January we have no wounds to bind up, but we have a morale to resuscitate. It has been weakened by two months' unemployment on the banks of the Canal.'[8]

The attempt to seek solutions of political problems by military means failed, but left its traces: the army was called upon to find

[6] Robert Marjolin, *Mémoires* (Paris, 1986).

[7] Cf. on this point the interesting discussion of General Robineau, 'Les Porte-à-faux de l'affaire de Suez', *Revue Historique des Armées*, No. 4 (1986), p. 43.

[8] Cited by Paul Gaujac, *Suez* (Paris, 1986), p. 292.

political solutions, but the government did not let it go all the way. Conspiracies began to develop, for example the attack on General Salan. General staffs drafted reports justifying their actions during the Suez operation and directly indicting the political authorities. The great 'silent' service expressed itself in the events of 13 May 1958, and later in the generals' *putsch* of April 1961.

From the defence policy point of view, the failure of the Suez operation also meant the failure of Franco-British military co-operation and, oddly enough, of the integration already accomplished. As is known, the British assumed leadership of the operation and the French accepted the principle of an integrated command in order to avoid any possible mishaps due to overlapping responsibilities. Each French commander was assigned a British superior. The joint-command system placed the French troops under the close control of a British officer, as in the case of the AMX Squadron of the 10th Parachute Division, which General Stockwell requisitioned on 6 November, at a time when General Beaufre wished to use it. In the worst cases during the Suez operation, integration deprived each partner of any initiative. The operation's failure called in question the principle of integration, which was the basis of the Atlantic alliance's military organization. Thus re-examination of military integration was added to the crisis of confidence in the NATO framework. 'It has now become clear as a self-evident truth that France's security depends entirely on the American alliance', one diplomat penetratingly observed.[9] Here also the Suez crisis served to reveal the obvious: French independence at the defence level did not exist. The door was nearly closed: France could not aspire to anything beyond influencing her greatest ally. No independence, no power, only influence: that was all France had left.

The decisions taken leading toward the creation of French atomic weapons revealed a new orientation in the defence effort. Some component elements already existed, both civilian and military: the Atomic Energy Commission (CEA) and the office headed by Colonel Ailleret within the General Staff of the Armies were already working to produce a French bomb, and in 1956 the process was accelerated. On 10 November the CEA was ordered to supply the plutonium. Ailleret (now General) drew up the manufacturing programme, and soon selected Reggane as the production site.

At the level of domestic politics, the consequences of Suez in France were of slight importance compared with what happened in Britain. Not only did Guy Mollet, the Prime Minister, remain in power—in contrast to Anthony Eden, who was obliged to resign—his position was even strengthened. On 20 December 1956 the government won a

---

[9] Note by E. de Croüy-Chauvel, 10 Nov. 1956, Diplomatic Archives.

vote of confidence in the National Assembly by 325 to 210. Public opinion did not disapprove of the military intervention in Egypt, as polls in November 1956 and March 1957 confirmed. Although the number of 'undecided' rose, the majority of those polled (respectively, 44 per cent and 43 per cent) approved, while the number who disapproved diminished. The phrase 'national-Molletism' was coined. It was, in fact, a resentful nationalism that led the country to an ever deeper involvement in the Algerian war.[10]

Nevertheless, taking a closer look, Suez aggravated the political crisis. The Fourth Republic suffered another defeat. The budget deficit increased because of imports of expensive oil. Inflation rose at a higher rate, and the franc weakened. The Section Française de l'Internationale Ouvrière, exercising power through Guy Mollet, passed through a severe crisis: on 24 November prominent socialist figures publicly criticized the policy, followed by their comrades in power, from the time of the dispatch of troops from Algeria to Suez, to the time of the interception of Ben Bella's plane. This was the prelude to the fragmentation of the socialist party. But the other political forces were hardly in a better position. The *Mouvement républicain populaire* was disunited. The Poujadist star was setting. The Communists were discredited by the Soviet intervention in Hungary. In *Le Monde* on 20 November Maurice Duverger summed up the atmosphere: 'Disheartened, disoriented, uneasy...'[11]

More than ever, de Gaulle appeared to be the remedy. He was believed to have discreetly approved the idea of intervention at Suez, but condemned its having been carried out under British command with the French towed along behind.[12] The seeds of General de Gaulle's return were sown in the failure of the Suez operation.

Finally, the consequences of the Suez affair demonstrate that the 1958 watershed was less of a divide than it might appear. Many characteristics of Gaullist France had already appeared in 1956-7, in particular the reconsideration of the Atlantic alliance, the nationalist resurgence asserting French independence and French autonomy in decision-making, the European option, and defence policy based on an independent nuclear force.

The Algerian war was itself a unifying force throughout the period. It was the principal explanation of the Suez operation from the French

[10] J. P. Rioux, *La France de la IVᵐᵉ République* (Paris, 1983), p. 114 and *l'Histoire*, No. 38 (Oct. 1981), pp. 35-7.

[11] Michel Winock, *La République se meurt: Chronique 1956-1958* (Paris, 1978).

[12] On 29 Dec. 1956 he wrote to General Jacques Massu: 'As for the Canal affair, there is no fault to be found with the French forces. But in order to succeed in an enterprise of this nature, you have to have a government', *Revue Historique des Armées*, No. 4 (1986), p. 36.

point of view. And the gamble of invading Egypt nearly succeeded, at least momentarily. Observers noted in Algeria a marked slow-down in the Army of National Liberation's activity, and a more docile population, which was impressed by the French military deployment. But this situation rapidly deteriorated. France's prestige among the masses was severely damaged, and the Egyptian victory was duly exploited by the National Liberation Front (FLN), now moving toward extremism. Failure of the intervention did not mean the end of the conflict in Algeria, quite the contrary. With the armed contingent sent to Algeria and the Battle of Algiers in 1957, France was deeply involved in war. Meanwhile, since the FLN forces proved unable to win the war themselves, the conflict was internationalized. Not only did the Algerian war weigh upon internal politics, it encumbered French foreign policy increasingly, day by day. With the end of the Algerian war ended an era for France.

18

The Aftermath of Suez: Consequences for French Decolonization:

ADAM WATSON

IN 1956 I was the Head of the African Department of the Foreign Office, which dealt with Egypt and therefore the Suez affair. I was at the centre of things so far as Britain was concerned, but several layers below the Cabinet ministers who took the decisions.

During that summer British ministers did not communicate to officials like myself the details of their mysterious negotiations with the French government, and even more obscure ones with the Israelis. But it was my strong impression that the French government played the leading role in the decision to intervene. The impression strengthened as the story unfolded. It seemed to me that the French government was leading our Francophile Prime Minister by the nose. There were of course a number of the Prime Minister's advisers, both politicians and senior military and civil servants, who advocated the same course. But without the active persuasion from Paris, I did not think he would take action alone.

As I and some others in the Foreign Office saw it, the central concern of the French government, and also of the armed services, was Algeria. The disaster of Dien Bien Phou, which had cost France Indo-China, had occurred two years before, in May 1954. There was considerable frustration in the French armed services, who felt that they had not had adequate backing from the government. Both the army and public opinion were becoming increasingly concerned that there would be a similar failure to suppress the rebellion in Algeria, which unlike remote Indo-China included three departments of metropolitan France with a European French population of a million. Nasser was supporting and arming the rebels, but this was difficult to prove. The French government's decision in the spring of 1956 to restore independence to Algeria's two neighbours, Morocco and Tunisia, heightened the concern. The *Loi Cadre* or basic law of that spring, granting greater self-government to France's black African colonies, also seemed to many to confirm a policy of 'scuttle'. A strike against Nasser, especially in association with Israel and Great Britain, would show that the French government meant business, would restore the morale of the armed services by a successful demonstration of strength, and would capture the evidence which the government needed of Nasser's interference in French Algeria as well as put an end to it. The idea of a multilateral military operation in Egypt seemed to me made in Paris.

When the military operations began, the evidence I saw suggested to me that there was more determination on the French side than on ours. Just before the decision to stop the advance along the Canal, my long-time personal friend Georges Gorse, a junior French minister whom Mollet had sent to London to help co-ordinate the operation, said to me that what the French wanted from us was '*de la tenue*', a greater resolve. Some French military officers were even more critical of British hesitancy.

The failure of the Suez adventure taught both British and French policy-makers some severe lessons. The effect on French external policies over the following few years was more radical than on the British.

First, the French learnt how closely Britain was tied to the United States. The British government was visibly unable to quarrel with America, for the economic reasons set out in Diane Kunz's chapter. But there was a degree of mutuality as well, almost a sense of kinship in which the French felt they did not share. They were impressed by the speed with which the American Administration, and the new half-American British Prime Minister, Macmillan, moved after Suez to restore cordial relations. 'Les Anglo-Saxons' seemed less interested in France than in each other.

The Suez adventure was not unpopular in France. The collapse of the Fourth Republic eighteen months later was precipitated by the failure of the French government to put an end to the rebellion in Algeria, although the army was able to dominate the territory militarily with a force of some 400,000 men. The failure of Suez, and the resulting increased hostility of the Arab world to France, contributed to the public conviction in France that the army, and the national interest in general, had been let down by the ineptitude of the régime and by France's Anglo-Saxon allies. A quarrel between France and Tunisia about Tunisian interference in Algeria led not only to vociferous championship of the newly independent Arab country by Nasser and all those states which had opposed Suez, but also to the American–British attempt at mediation or 'good offices' between France and her former protectorate. That a Conservative British government should put its former partner on a par with an Arab state in this way increased French distrust.

General de Gaulle became Prime Minister of France on 1 June 1958; in September nearly 80 per cent of the French electorate voted for a new constitution, the Fifth Republic, with greatly increased powers for the President; and in December de Gaulle assumed that office. From the beginning he applied the military realism which was his chief asset to France's foreign and colonial policies.

One lesson of Indo-China and Suez for de Gaulle was that the price of holding on to the French African empire was now higher than its value to France. He gradually decided to renounce the use of coercion anywhere on that continent, except by the invitation of a local government. It seemed to me that he also reckoned that, if he ended formal colonization quickly enough south of the Sahara, and turned the government of the territories over to French-educated élites, France could retain a large degree of economic, political, and moral influence in the newly sovereign states, which would be too weak to stand alone. His new constitution, accepting the implications of the *Loi Cadre* of 1956 and of Britain's grant of independence to Ghana in 1957, gave France's African colonies a choice between autonomy in a *Communauté Française* or independence. Only Guinea chose independence, and turned to the Soviet Union for help. To the autonomous states that remained in association with France, de Gaulle offered substantial carrots, in the form of financial and administrative aid. On Guinea he used the stick, not of coercion but of deprivation: '*il faut que la Guinée souffre*' was his formula, to encourage the others to remain '*ensemble*' with France. Within two years he interpreted that term as covering the formal independence which the ruling élites in all colonies coveted: and in 1960 eleven former French colonies joined the United Nations, the symbolic legitimation of independence. (In 1959 I was appointed Minister for African Affairs attached to the British Embassy in Paris, and became the first British Ambassador to several of the new French African states on independence.) Both de Gaulle's carrot and his stick, and the speed with which he granted wholesale political independence to African colonies, were greater than Macmillan's more piecemeal and more absolute decolonization. Pierre Messmer, the last French Governor-General of French West Africa and later Defence Minister, observed to me in 1960 that political independence was the decisive step on the road to complete independence, but certainly not the last. In black Africa, de Gaulle substantially achieved his realistic aims.

Algeria was such a burning issue in France, and the commitment of the army to holding it so great, that it took de Gaulle more than three years to reach the drastic conclusion that Algeria was untenable. France could hold the territory militarily; but by 1962 he and most Frenchmen acknowledged that the cost in blood, money, and prestige was not worth it, and that no compromise could be negotiated. France badly needed the oil recently discovered there, but it might still be

obtainable after independence. The army and the European population were ruefully withdrawn to European France. The retreat from
Algeria was strategic realism, but it was a defeat for de Gaulle.

In the Western world generally, de Gaulle wanted to overcome the
disastrous breach which Suez and its aftermath had caused to French
relations with America and Britain, and to establish a tripartite
directorate in which France would be regarded as juridically equal to
her partners—as she already was in Germany and Austria—though the
French contribution would be economically and strategically less than
that of Britain and much less than that of the United States. When the
Americans turned down this rather unrealistic concept, and the British
opted for a subordinate special relationship with the United States, de
Gaulle threw his energies into forging a closer west European Community, to be based on a special relationship with West Germany, the
'Paris–Bonn axis'. By concentrating on Europe, an impoverished and
resentful France could recover its prosperity and self-confidence.
Unlike his European partners, de Gaulle was determined to keep his
Carolingian community free from Anglo-Saxon influence, and to
exclude Britain, which had shown its unreliability at Suez and would
be an American Trojan horse. I considered, and still do, that the
French army's distrust of military integration and especially of subor-
dination to a British command, which de Gaulle shared, led in due
course to French withdrawal from the integrated organization of the
North Atlantic Alliance (while remaining formally an ally), to the
eviction of NATO headquarters from Paris, and to the development of
an independent nuclear deterrent. In order to lessen France's dependence on America, de Gaulle also worked to improve relations with the
Soviet Union, and spoke of *détente* leading to *entente*. The emotional
disappointment of Suez helped to shape French policies in Europe.

If we place the Suez crisis in its wider historical context, we can see
that it was part of the great tide of political revolt and cultural
rejection of alien dominance that, in the middle of the twentieth
century, swept over what came to be called the Third World. The
assertion of independence was directed against the Soviet Union as
well as against the West. Two of the four main founding fathers of the
non-aligned grouping of states struggling for freedom from imperial
control, Zhou Enlai and Tito, were determined to emancipate their
countries from Russian dominance. The other two, Nasser and Nehru,
wanted to free themselves from Britain and not be dominated by the
United States; and for them and for the other leaders of the revolt
against the West, the Soviet Union seemed a plausible source of
support.

The dual nature of the rejection of white imperialism by Asia and Africa was not yet clearly perceived by Western statesmen. But the Soviet leaders who in 1956 were struggling against each other for power, following Stalin's death three years before, were more keenly aware of it. They inherited and continued Stalin's quarrels with the Chinese and Yugoslav Communists; and they understood that the anti-imperial movement threatened their imperial positions outside the Soviet borders, and even the Asian republics of the Soviet Union. During the crucial summer of 1956 they were engaged in a brutal repression of the Hungarian uprising for independence from them. But they saw that the revolt against the overseas empires of the west Europeans, though part of the general tide, was specifically directed against Britain and France, the enemies of the Soviet Union in the Cold War. At one remove, it was against the United States, the leader of the Western camp and the strategic and economic guarantor of Britain, France, and Israel. The Soviet leaders therefore accepted and acted on the temporary congruence of their interests with Nasser's. At the same time, though the evidence from the Soviet side is still unavailable, it appears in retrospect that some Soviet leaders were already considering whether to substitute non-Communist India for insubordinate and heretical Communist China as their principal ally in Asia. The tenor of Krishna Menon's remarks, at SCUA meetings and in private conversations with British statesmen, suggests that he too sensed that option, perhaps more clearly than Nehru.

The Soviet Union enhanced its position with all anti-Western states and liberation movements by its economic and moral support for Egypt during the Suez crisis. Its *Realpolitik* in the Suez affair benefited its standing in the Third World more than its repression of Hungarian independence damaged that standing. Three years after Suez, Fidel Castro drew the same conclusion in Cuba, and has since argued persuasively that the Soviet Union is the natural ally of the so-called 'non-aligned' and of those opposed to Western imperialism. Britain and France, for their part, were partially but not wholly able to repair the damage done to their reputations in the Third World by the gross ineptitude of Suez.

The statesmanlike decisions of Macmillan and de Gaulle to accept the wind of change implemented the post-imperial mood that took hold of their peoples. They negotiated the wholesale decolonization of their empires, and aided and collaborated with the usually frail successor states. The balance of advantage for the United States is harder to assess. America disillusioned its European allies without winning the support of the newly emancipated ex-colonies. However, the US Administration demonstrated that it could and would make America's client allies conform to its policies; and after the crisis Eisenhower moved quickly and effectively to restore cordial relations with at least Britain and Israel. America's implementation of its anti-colonial principles kept it in line with the tide of history, and earned it a grudging respect in Egypt as well as throughout Asia and Africa.

19

Reflections on the Suez Crisis: Security in the Middle East

HERMANN FREDERICK EILTS

AFTER reading the comprehensive chapters on various aspects of the Suez crisis of 1956, and hearing pertinent discussions during the Wilson Center conference, it occurred to me that a brief supplementary commentary by one who was operationally involved in US policy formulation and implementation toward the Middle East during that period and in the years leading up to it might offer additional perspectives. Some regional legacies of the policies pursued then by the United States persist to this day. In the Middle East, as well as elsewhere, the past is progenitor of the present. The burden of history, ancient and more recent, hangs heavily.

It is now more than thirty years since the Suez crisis erupted. Much has transpired in the Middle East and in the world at large since that time. Britain and France, then still significant external actors on the Middle East scene, have become politically marginal; in their place, the United States, for better or for worse, and judgements vary on this point, has arrogated their once pre-eminent external role in the area. Despite eroded credibility in recent years, it remains the principal external influence in the Middle East because of its comparative power, economic affluence, and its pervasive presence. Granted, the American position is now being challenged by Islamic fundamentalism, whatever that may mean in specific terms, but thus far this remains a manageable threat. Israel has become a major military force of the region and, save for Egypt, is still unacceptable to the Arab, and to much of the Muslim, world. The Soviet Union, whether one likes it or not, is a superpower competitor in the Middle East, as elsewhere, that cannot be sloughed off, as some Americans would like to do. Truly, the socio-political changes of these thirty odd years in the Middle East have been phenomenal.

Inevitably, in the circumstances, it is difficult to recapture today all of the disparate attitudinal and causal elements that went into the making of US policy toward Egypt in 1956, on the one hand, and toward the then prevailing American imperative of forging some kind of Middle East security arrangements, on the other. That the regional political objectives of Egypt under Gamal Abdel Nasser and concurrent Western concerns about a need to contain the Soviet Union in the Middle East (and elsewhere) were in conflict is indisputable. No less so, let it be expressly stated at the outset, was Nasser's personal and political right to react in any way he wished to what he perceived to be Western or other challenges. In the West, including the United States, Nasser came increasingly to be recognized as primarily reactive to what he chose to see as external pressures or slights rather than as a statesmanlike thinker or innovator of ideas. There was a Pavlovian quality about him. Whatever the hubris created by his rhetoric in Egypt and in some parts of the Arab world, or even the sincerity of his avowed purpose of unfettering Egypt from real or imagined foreign domination, one may legitimately question—and could even then—his broader political sagacity in handling Egypt's relations with foreign states. In short-range terms, Nasser's unrestrained public rhetoric and often dramatic reactions to regional and other events undoubtedly enhanced his populist Arab and Third World image; conversely, in longer range terms, it inexorably eroded his initially positive image and his international influence where it potentially still counted most—with the West in general and with the United States in particular. Few objective observers would today dispute that Nasser was a consummate tactician, but a poor strategist.

On another level, whether American efforts during the Eisenhower Administration, largely articulated by the Secretary of State, John Foster Dulles, to bridge the politico-psychological gap between emergent and patently restive Third World nationalisms and very real Western security concerns about suspected Soviet intentions, were optimally conducted is a subject of proper debate. The recent biography of Anthony Eden by Robert Rhodes James attributes considerable, but not total, blame for the Suez crisis of 1956 to irresolution on the part of the Eisenhower Administration and especially to alleged discordant signals to the British leadership on the part of Dulles.[1] This, too, was and remains a matter of individual and, separately, national perception.

Dulles was a controversial figure, and will remain so for historians. One either admired and respected him or deplored his conservative doctrinal rigidity and moralist inability to comprehend why newly independent nations might wish to be neutralist. His action in repudiating an earlier US commitment to help finance a High Dam at

---

[1] Robert Rhodes James, *Anthony Eden: A Biography* (New York, 1987). Chapters 11–13 (pp. 441–562) deal with the Suez Crisis.

Aswan, while perhaps not as felicitously handled as it might have been, was understandable in terms of growing Congressional and Administration debate about Nasser's purposes and reliability. Nasser, through his rhetoric and his actions, had in the United States, no less than in the West in general, managed to transform his initially positive image into one of malevolence.

In fact, Nasser clearly expected the withdrawal of American support and was ready to seize upon it to nationalize the Suez Canal. The American and British rejections afforded the Soviets the opportunity to assist in the High Dam project, which they did with alacrity. The eventual political reward for ten years of effort and substantial financing for the High Dam was humiliating: near-total Egyptian political ingratitude except for a gross commemorative monument in Aswan. Despite their help to Egypt, the Soviets found Nasser and the Egyptians difficult to deal with. Try as they might, they could not forge enduring co-operation and, beginning just over fifteen years later, under Sadat, found themselves progressively eliminated from the Egyptian political, economic, and strategic scene.

The Soviet Union is currently trying to improve its relations with Egypt, but this observer has yet to hear a Soviet official who is not privately critical of Egypt's almost cavalier dismissal of massive Soviet help in that project. Dulles's methodology of rejection aside, he— whether purposefully or not—neatly extracted the US government from involvement in what is still a controversial project. Some Egyptians may challenge this assertion, but they are well aware of the ongoing controversy of whether or not the High Dam, all things considered, has turned out to be a good thing. Here, too, opinions may legitimately vary.

International perceptions of where prime responsibility for the ensuing Suez Crisis lay are understandably diffuse. Certain it is that many Britons, particularly those on the Tory side of the political spectrum, and many official Americans saw Nasser and whether or not he posed a threat to Western interests in the Middle East in diverse ways.

As one who was at the time involved as a middle-grade State Department official, responsible for the preparation of numerous draft papers on US policy toward various aspects of the Middle East scene, particularly the Baghdad Pact, and regional affairs in the Arab world, four spheres of pertinent American thinking deserve brief elaboration: the Baghdad Pact; American official attitudes toward Nasser; prevalent Israeli security concerns; and the US conception of the Palestinian problem that existed at the time. US policy attitudes toward the Middle East were not at the time monolithic, and sharp divergencies often existed and were vigorously argued by area specialists and senior US policy-makers. The former frequently questioned the wisdom of their superiors. This was as natural then as it is now.

THE BAGHDAD PACT

The Baghdad Pact, renamed the Central Treaty Organization (CENTO) after Iraq's defection in 1959, came into being in early 1955. It initially took the form of an Iraqi–Turkish bilateral security agreement, signed on 24 February 1955, to which Britain, Iran, and Pakistan acceded within the year. Each did so for different reasons, but these need not concern us here.[2] The inaugural ministerial meeting of the new security organization took place in Baghdad in November 1955, at which time the pact received its name.

At a time when a Cold War global dichotomy largely dominated US foreign policy thinking, Dulles had been a major proponent of such a Middle East security arrangement. The newly appointed US Ambassador to Iraq, Waldemar J. Gallman, a career diplomat of experience and proven abilities, who was sent to Baghdad in October 1954, had specific instructions from the Secretary of State to persuade the Iraqi leadership to join in some fashion with like-minded 'northern tier' Middle East states in an effort to contain what Washington perceived to be serious Soviet expansionist designs southward.[3] Yet, in view of the earlier failure of a Western attempt to form a Middle East Defense Organization (MEDO), few in the American leadership believed that early realization of such a regional security arrangement was likely. The prevailing wisdom was that any indigenous Middle East appreciation for such a concept would require time to mature.

The Iraqi leadership under the Prime Minister, Nuri al-Said Pasha, who assumed office for the twelfth time on 4 August 1954, was initially prudently cautious about entering into any extra-Arab security arrangement. For their part, the British, still at the time the predominant external influence in Iraq, having been in the earlier abortive effort to achieve MEDO and politically burned by being so, seemed to many in the State Department to be dubious about prospects of persuading Iraq to enter any such organization. Such a regional alliance might be a continuing objective, but it was hardly an early expectation.

To a considerable extent, it was the persuasive, catalytic efforts of

---

[2] For further background of the organization and its structure, see Waldemar J. Gallman, *Iraq under General Nuri: My Recollections of Nuri al-Said, 1954–1958* (Baltimore, 1964), pp. 21–87; and (UK) Reference Division, Central Office of Information, No. R3889, *The Baghdad Pact* (London, June, 1958). For the text of the Iraqi–Turkish agreement, see Baghdad Pact Secretariat, *The Baghdad Pact* (Baghdad, 1957), pp. 72–4.

[3] Gallman, *Iraq under General Nuri*, p. xiii.

Turkish Prime Minister Adnan Menderes, dangling the bait of increased US military assistance to Iraq (but without authorization to do so), that prompted Nuri Pasha to conclude the Iraqi–Turkish agreement. This writer well recalls the surprise both of members of the American Embassy in Baghdad and of their British counterparts, with their special entrée into Iraqi political circles, when hearing the news in January 1955, that a bilateral Iraqi–Turkish pact might soon be concluded. Until it was actually signed, British and American officials in Baghdad alike remained sceptical that such an agreement would in fact materialize. Politically, both agreed, it went against the grain of Iraq's Arab associations.

Dulles had been a prime mover of the concept of a Middle East security pact, and had publicly endorsed it just prior to reports that it would be signed. Yet when the alliance—phoenix-like—suddenly sprang forth, the United States, ironically, was ambivalent. Despite expectations from the regional member states, who had assumed that by joining they were acceding to American desires, Washington had belated second thoughts about the political desirability of US membership in the new Baghdad Pact organization. All of the forces in the State Department, and in the US government as a whole, which had earlier questioned the concept of a Middle East security pact, but had muted their doubts in the conviction that nothing of this sort would emerge in the foreseeable future, now actively and openly entered the fray in order to dissuade American accession.

US membership in the Baghdad Pact, one school of thought argued, would offend Nasser and those Arab leaders and polities who took their guidance from him. Pakistan's membership, another contended, would alienate India, a point strongly made by the then American Ambassador to India, Ellsworth Bunker. Because of Turkey's membership, still others pointed out, Greece would be gravely vexed, a contention echoed by the powerful Greek lobby in Congress. Should the United States join the Baghdad Pact, a fourth group of opponents observed, an American security guarantee would have to be given to Israel, which at that time Washington was reluctant to do. State Department liaison officers with the Congress considered it unlikely that requisite Senate 'advice and consent' could be obtained for US accession to the Baghdad Pact treaty without a concurrent, parallel security guarantee for Israel.

In the circumstances, the Eisenhower Administration, to the disappointment of the regional Baghdad Pact signatories, contented itself with observer status in the organization. This meant that the United States could hardly urge others to join. Despite its non-member observer status, however, the United States played a major role in all

Baghdad Pact deliberations, provided economic and military aid to the various regional member states, assigned personnel to the Pact secretariat, and eventually designated an American major-general to head the Combined Military Planning Staff of the organization. As the Pact developed, and in response to regional state pressures, it also joined the Pact's military, economic, and counter-subversion committees, while somewhat incongruously retaining its overall observer status. Moreover, on Dulles's instructions, the United States encouraged close liaison between the Baghdad Pact and NATO and SEATO, but with only marginal success. Dulles's concept was of a global girdle of discrete, but interrelated 'Free World' regional security organizations with the common purpose of containing the Soviet Union. Neither NATO nor SEATO took the Baghdad Pact seriously, especially since the United States refused to join that organization.

In contrast, the British, who had initially—at least on a regional operational level—been sceptical about what became the Baghdad Pact, now suddenly saw accession to the Pact as an ideal opportunity to improve their political position in Iraq, flagging since the 1948 Iraqi repudiation of a treaty with Britain, and in this way to retain access to the important air bases at Shaiba and Habbaniya.[4] It was largely this realization that prompted British membership. From a British point of view, it made eminent political sense, weakened only by US non-adherence.

From the outset, Nasser opposed the Baghdad Pact and unremittingly pilloried the Iraqi government for joining it. In the months before the signing of the Iraqi–Turkish agreement, there had been numerous exchanges at various levels between Baghdad and Cairo about the desirability (or otherwise) of some sort of a Middle East security organization. Major Salah Salem, then Minister of Guidance in the Egyptian government and allegedly a close confidant of Nasser, visited Iraq in August 1954, in order to discuss politico-security issues. At talks held at Sarsank, north of Baghdad, he had agreed with his Iraqi hosts, including Nuri Pasha, that the Arab League Collective Security Pact of 1950 might be broadened to include regional non-Arab and other states, specifically Turkey, Great Britain, and the United States. His negotiations were angrily repudiated by Nasser immediately on his return to Cairo. But how could the Iraqi leadership be expected to know that Salem, sometimes dubbed the 'dancing major', lacked the plenipotentiary authority to speak for his chief? Subsequent talks between Nasser and Nuri Pasha in Cairo caused the

---

[4] For the British accession document, and accompanying exchange of notes with Iraq, see His Majesty's Stationery Office, *Accession of the United Kingdom to the Pact of Mutual Co-operation Between Turkey and Iraq, Signed at Baghdad on February 24, 1955*, Cmd. 9429 (London, 1955).

latter to conclude that Egypt's *rais*, or 'boss', however reluctantly, had recognized that Iraq's more exposed geographic location made its membership in some kind of a 'northern tier' organization necessary and that this would not be incompatible with its Arab ties.

Events were to prove that communications between the two leaders, direct and indirect, were poor or deliberately distorted. In truth, the two men appear to have talked at rather than with one other. The Iraqi leadership, especially Nuri Pasha, always maintained that Nasser had violated his verbal pledge. The point is today unprovable, but there is surely no reason why the late Nuri Pasha's version does not deserve at least the same weight as Nasser's denial. Nuri Pasha's Arab nationalist credentials, though generationally one removed, were no less impressive than those of Nasser. While Egyptians refused to recognize this, and saw Nuri as a British 'stooge', his contribution to the earlier evolution of Arab nationalism had been commendable.

In a clearly justificatory effort to assure its Arab League confrères, the Iraqi leadership, when signing the Iraqi–Turkish agreement, attached a unilateral declaratory letter, affirming its continued strong adherence to the general Arab stance on Palestine. But neither the series of bilateral talks that had taken place between the Egyptian and Iraqi leaderships, nor the aforementioned Iraqi letter, placated Nasser. His denunciations of the Baghdad Pact and of Iraq for having joined reached shrill proportions as 1955 progressed and 1956 came into being.

In retrospect, even accepting Nasser's pan-Arab ambitions, it is difficult to see why he should have made the Baghdad Pact the object of such bitter political recriminations. His own neutralist objectives for Egypt notwithstanding, he could hardly expect to dictate Iraq's security requirements. Egypt had consistently rejected any suggestion of foreign interference, including Arab, in its own sovereign policy decisions. Yet, other Arab states objected that Egypt did not hesitate to violate its own declared precepts by overtly and covertly seeking to interfere in their affairs. Only King Faisal of Saudi Arabia eventually stood up to the prevailing Nasser syndrome in much of the Arab world and did so effectively by calling for Islamic unity as an alternative to Nasser's narrower Arab unity concept.

Politically, from an Arab point of view, the pact at worst abjured involvement in the Arab–Israeli problem, although it gave Israel absolutely no advantages. At best, it offered prospects of eliciting at least regional Muslim member states' sympathy for the Arab position on the Palestinians. It in no way gave the Iraqi leadership an opportunity to try to wrest Arab hegemony from Nasser's hands, although Iraqi support of British efforts in 1956 to bring Jordan and

Syria into the Pact were so interpreted by the Egyptian leadership. But Nasser's attacks on the Pact had begun long before those abortive British efforts were even attempted.

From a military point of view, moreover, the Baghdad Pact never achieved a capability that in any way made it a security threat to Egypt or to any other Arab state. It was certainly not a political threat. The Iraqis made no effort whatsoever to convert it into an anti-Egyptian alliance. From beginning to end, the Pact was physically a toothless tiger. Indeed, its several regional state members, much to US distress, increasingly sought to include area differences—Turkey with Greece over Cyprus and control of the Aegean; Iran with Afghanistan over its Herat River problems; and Pakistan with India over Kashmir. This flailing of pact objectives was surely reported to Nasser by his ubiquitous and efficient intelligence organization. Moreover, the persistent failure of the United States to join, partly in order to avoid offending Nasser's sensibilities, was something of which Nasser was most certainly aware. Indeed, the American Ambassador in Cairo had told him just that.

It is hard to avoid the conclusion that Nasser deliberately chose to make the Baghdad Pact, and Iraq's membership of it, a contrived source of tension and division in the Middle East. He deliberately misrepresented its purposes in order to further his Arab objectives. He saw such attacks as a means of garnering political capital in the Arab world, with minimal risk. Again, while it may have been his right to do so, it was hardly astute politically in terms of Egypt's broader development interests. Nasser may have found doing so was advantageous for his relations with the Soviets, who cast the Pact as a threat to their security. True, the times were right in an emergent nationalist-orientated Middle East for such political charades, and Nasser was himself a believer in conspiracy theories which attributed hidden motives to the former colonial powers and what gradually came to be called the neo-imperialist United States. That Nasser's anti-Pact diatribes had some effect was evidenced in the 1956 Jordanian dismissal of British General Glubb Pasha and, later, on 14 July 1958, in the overthrow of the Hashemite monarchy in Iraq.

All American and British efforts to explain to Nasser that the Baghdad Pact was in no way directed at Egypt were unavailing. Had Nasser given even reasonable consideration to the overriding Western concern at the time of a Soviet threat to the Middle East area, even if he believed that notion was exaggerated, and had he been willing to see the Baghdad Pact in the sharply restrictive context in which it was organized rather than as a competitive political instrument, some of the germinating tensions that ultimately led to the Suez crisis of 1956 might have been avoided. But Nasser was still politically inexperienced and immature; his judgement was short rather than long term. Egypt would for long suffer from that myopia, although this was not immediately apparent.

Nasser's persistent vilification of the Baghdad Pact was one factor, but only one, in increasingly embittering Western and American leaders toward him. Some contend that Nasser's attacks on the Pact were political symbolism and no more. Perhaps so, but they helped alienate even those Americans who were, and wanted to remain, favourably disposed toward the Egyptian leader.

NASSER

In the preceding paragraphs, Nasser's role in seeking to undermine the Baghdad Pact regional security organization has been adumbrated. It should be noted, however, that there were deeply divided views in the US government about Nasser.[5]

To many American diplomatic professionals with experience in the Middle East, Nasser, when he first assumed office, was seen as the embodiment of long suppressed, but deserving Egyptian and Arab nationalism. Anti-colonialism was rampant in post-World War II American official and private thinking. An influential body of Americans initially saw Nasser as the epitome of this legitimate, indigenous revulsion, and applauded him. The American Ambassador in Cairo, Jefferson Caffrey, and his staff had in July 1952, played a minor, but none the less significant role in the Egyptian Revolutionary Command Council's ousting of King Farouk. Not surprisingly, therefore, a widespread American belief existed that Nasser and the military men around him represented a new and refreshing kind of Egyptian leadership, charismatic, middle and lower middle class in provenance, genuinely attuned to the pressing socio-economic needs of Egypt, and, above all, incorruptible.

Nasser soon came to be viewed enthusiastically by many American professionals in the State Department, CIA, and elsewhere, as the indisputable and unchallengeable leader of the Arab world, not only because of Egypt's size and prominence in Arab circles, but because of his forceful personality, his confidence, his leadership aura, and his apparent appeal to Arab peoples everywhere. Radio Cairo assiduously projected that public image. It was also hoped in Washington that

[5] For two variant perceptive views of Nasser as a political leader during the Suez Crisis, see Robert Stephens, *Nasser: A Political Biography* (London, 1971), pp. 140–250, and Najla M. Abu Izzaddin, *Nasser of the Arabs* (London, 1981), pp. 159–76. For a sympathetic evaluation of Nasser by a British minister who resigned in protest over British involvement in the attack on Egypt, see Anthony Nutting, *Nasser* (New York, 1972), pp. 147–95.

Nasser, perceived as a political realist, would lead the Arabs into an Arab–Israeli peace and, equally important, that he could do so if he wished. These were major American delusions.

For years, even as Nasser gave increasing evidence of anti-Western and anti-American attitudes, the Eisenhower Administration sedulously sought to get along with him. Ambassador Henry Byroade, who served as American Ambassador to Egypt from 5 March 1955 to 10 September 1956, sought valiantly—some charged parochially—to influence Nasser and, separately, to advocate the latter's case with Washington. Byroade's frequent nocturnal discussions with Nasser, usually from midnight to the early hours of the morning, seemed always to produce fine words, but little substantive American–Egyptian rapport. In fact, Nasser effectively destroyed the credibility of Byroade, one of Egypt's most favourably disposed American friends, with the Ambassador's superiors at home.

Byroade's successor, the politically astute Raymond Hare, who served as American Ambassador in Cairo from September 1956 to 29 March 1958, managed to retain reasonable dialogue with Nasser. In contrast to Byroade, he was never taken in, and perceptively analysed the Egyptian leader's strengths and his weaknesses. Representing diplomatic professionalism at its best, Hare was American Ambassador to Egypt during the actual Suez crisis and undoubtedly benefited from the Eisenhower Administration's distancing itself from Britain, France, and Israel during that critical period.

To be sure, there was from the outset a small group of professionals in the State Department who entertained doubts about Nasser and his real attitude toward American interests in the Middle East. Some such sceptics saw Nasser as congenitally anti-Israeli, whatever seemingly positive remarks he might on occasion make to special American emissaries, such as Robert Anderson, about wanting peace with Israel. Others, especially those concerned with trying to forge regional security arrangements such as as the Baghdad Pact, were concerned at Nasser's efforts to undermine that organization and the Iraqi regime.

For years, however, such critics were a distinct minority in the US bureaucracy. From 1952 to 1955, the Eisenhower Administration, despite nagging doubts about Nasser, earnestly sought good relations with him, indeed seemed at times even ignobly to propitiate him. One wonders whether Nasser's realization that the Administration, at least in its early days, seemed willing to tolerate his political excesses may have encouraged his increasingly strident challenge to Western interests and his self-assumed impression of political invincibility.

Nasser's reputation in the United States was eroded sharply in late 1955 for a variety of reasons: chief among them, the Czech arms deal;

his attendance at the Bandung conference; his non-alignment posture; his recognition of the People's Republic of China; and, eventually, his nationalization of the Suez Canal. In contrast to British attitudes, his attacks against Iraq and the Baghdad Pact were, from an American point of view, secondary to the aforementioned issues, though passingly annoying. Yet, even with its extensive litany of other complaints against Nasser, the Eisenhower Administration firmly opposed the tripartite Anglo-French-Israeli attack of October 1956 against Egypt and unravelled its military successes. In doing so, it is arguable that the Administration, in what it considered its morally correct and legally rooted position, but which others saw as politically short-sighted and generally irresolute stance at that period, provided Nasser with an opportunity to snatch still another political victory from defeat, as he had managed to do before. One may legitimately speculate that it may have encouraged him to take those subsequent actions which ultimately led to the 1967 Arab–Israeli war and Egypt's resultant total military defeat.

Paradoxically, there is no gainsaying that the residual political mystique of Nasser, even after 1956, and no matter how badly he behaved toward American and general Western interests, remained a strong, if increasingly tenuous element in official American thinking toward the Arab world until the 1967 Arab–Israeli war. Then it suddenly ended with a resounding crash and was never revived. Nasser's almost pleading efforts after the 1967 war to re-establish ties with the United States were rebuffed by the Johnson Administration. Three years later he died, according to his closest associates, a broken man. It required the advent of Anwar Sadat in September 1970, after Nasser's death, before a new US–Egyptian relationship could be developed.

ISRAELI SECURITY CONCERNS

Senior American officials at the time, and some later historians, have been sharply critical of Israel for participating in the tripartite attack on Egypt in September 1956. The Eisenhower Administration was outraged that a country with which the United States had such close relations and which received American economic aid should have acted in this matter, largely at French and British behest, in utter disregard of Washington's unconcealed opposition. The Administration tended to play down Egyptian-inspired *fedayeen* raids from Gaza into Israel as insufficiently serious to warrant an all out Israeli attack on Egypt and had long regularly deplored what it considered disproportionate Israeli military responses to Arab guerrilla incursions into Israel.

Immediately after Israel's invasion of Egypt in October 1956, despite the fact that he was involved in a presidential election, Eisenhower ordered all American economic aid to Israel to be stopped until the Prime Minister, David Ben-Gurion, agreed to withdraw Israeli forces from both Sinai and Gaza. That an Administration which had become increasingly soured by Nasser's international policies should thus have acted on behalf of what even it branded as an errant Egyptian leadership was truly astonishing, a fact forgotten by many Egyptians then and now. The Soviet warning to Israel, Britain, and France of 5 November 1956, which some Egyptians and other Arabs cite today as the major factor forcing Israeli withdrawal, was regarded by the United States and Britain alike as fatuous, except perhaps for the possibility that some Russian 'volunteers' might be deployed to assist in Egypt's defence. Nasser himself could hardly have been unaware of the empty nature of the Soviet threat as a means of providing meaningful succour to Egypt's hard-pressed military position, even though many Egyptians and Arabs may not have realized how substantively void Moscow's bluster was.

The Administration's excoriation of Israel for the latter's Sinai adventure was as strong as its criticisms of its two NATO allies, Britain and France. In a sense, however, it was short-sighted. Whether the Israeli attack on Egypt in 1956 was justified or not will always be debatable. In assessing the action, what should not be forgotten is that Israel at the time had no outside security guarantee whatsoever and felt decidedly vulnerable. Only the French, who had jettisoned the Tripartite Declaration of 1950, seemed sympathetic to Israel's security concerns and were willing to provide some military equipment. The British warned Israel in no uncertain terms that they would support Jordan in the event of an Israeli attack on that country. Israel, perhaps paranoically but understandably so, saw its very survival threatened by hostile Arab states on its borders, led or incited in large part by an implacably hostile Nasser. True, modest American economic aid was being provided to Israel, but regular Israeli efforts to obtain a US security guarantee had consistently been rebuffed.

Not surprisingly, the Israeli Embassy in Washington showed an exceptional interest in the inception and the evolution of the Baghdad Pact. At one point, indeed, the Israeli Ambassador in Washington, Abba Eban, had proposed to Dulles that Israel become a member of the Pact. This was clearly inconceivable since it would have been unacceptable to Iraq. Since that route was closed, there were frequent hints on the part of pro-Israeli elements in the country that if the

United States joined the Baghdad Pact, the price of Senate approval would have to be a parallel bilateral security agreement with Israel. Neither of these options were politically acceptable to the Eisenhower Administration.

It was no lack of basic sympathy for Israel that accounted for the Administration's reluctance, although Ben-Gurion hardly endeared himself to Eisenhower or Dulles. Instead there was realization of the fact that any US security guarantee for Israel would severely damage American relations with the Arab world, where the United States also had interests. There was also concern that a US security guarantee, though it might ease Israeli concerns, might also encourage the Israeli leadership to engage in military ventures against neighbouring Arab states, which could endanger broader American interests in the region. A security guarantee to Israel, if one were to be given, American officials were generally agreed, should only be in the context of a settlement of the Arab–Israeli conflict, but not before.

To be sure, a partial US security guarantee was extended in 1957 in conjunction with Israel's withdrawal from Sinai and Gaza. This was not honoured in May 1967, because of American involvement in the Vietnam war. That American failure, comprehensible though it seemed at the time in US eyes, damaged the future credibility of US security guarantees in subsequent American sponsored Arab–Israeli peace negotiations. To this day, Israel insists it must rely primarily upon its own military capability for its defence; outside guarantees, including those from the United States, while still wanted, are viewed by Israel as at best an uncertain back-up line of defence.

Israel's military actions against Egypt in Gaza and Sinai in 1956, while hard fought, were successful. In contrast, many Israelis are still critical of the failure of the British and French to act more effectively at the time and believe that Nasser could have been toppled had there been more Anglo-French resolve, military and political. The US posture in the affair is equally criticized, and there is almost a kind of Israeli *schadenfreude* about subsequent American problems with Nasser.

THE PALESTINIAN DIMENSION

The role of the Palestinians in the events leading to the Suez crisis is peripheral. Nasser, like other Arab leaders, had frequently publicly supported a Palestinian state in accordance with the UN partition resolution, but there were many who doubted how much he really cared. Palestinian refugees in Gaza, it was clear, were as much pawns of Egyptian foreign policy as their displaced confrères in Jordan, Syria, and Lebanon were for the governments of those states. Gaza Palestinians complained of Egyptian ill-treatment and Unrwa and other observers confirmed Egyptian heavy-handedness in that occupied area. Despite later Egyptian denials, there was ample suspicion that Egyptian intelligence officials in Gaza instigated, at least after February 1955, Palestinian *fedayeen* incursions into Israel. Palestinians took the brunt of Israeli retaliation, but the knowledge of Egyptian instigation certainly heightened Israeli hostility toward Nasser.

Then, and in ensuing years, there seemed to be evidence that Egyptian intelligence officials—with or without Nasser's direct knowledge—had become laws unto themselves. For many years thereafter, they remained unbridled and disruptively active, wherever they were. This writer, for example, when American Ambassador to Saudi Arabia in 1967, had his Embassy and US military mission installations blown up by what the Saudi authorities definitively ascertained were Gaza Palestinians enlisted by local Egyptian intelligence officials to engage in such sabotage. Such external Egyptian subversion did not stop until the Egyptian defeat of 1967.

The United States during the 1950s tended to view the Palestinian issue as one of many global refugee problems. The Palestinian refugees, living largely in squalid camps in Jordan, Lebanon, and to some extent in Syria, required humanitarian assistance. True, the 1947 UN partition resolution had prescribed both an Arab and a Jewish state (along with a *corpus separatum* for Jerusalem), but the United States informally recognized that the 1948 Arab–Israeli war, coupled with Jordan's annexation of the West Bank and East Jerusalem in 1950, negated prospects of any Arab state in the former Palestine mandate. It was noted that the Arab states had unanimously rejected the UN partition resolution of 1947, and their belated efforts in the 1950s to ask for its implementation were seen as trying to turn back the clock after a resounding military defeat. Unrwa, the UN organization charged with providing economic and welfare assistance to the dispersed Palestinian refugees, was generously supported by the United States, which consistently provided one-third of that relief agency's total budget.

The Palestinians, as a political element in their own right, were largely ignored, not only by the United States, but by most Arab states as well. Instead, implementation of the concept of UN resolution 194 of 11 December 1948, calling for repatriation or compensation (precedent to resettlement elsewhere) was the objective of US policy. In this context, there was still the hope that Israel might be persuaded to take back some Palestinians and that the remainder would eventually be resettled either in the Arab countries where they were located or elsewhere. That the Palestinians might have nationalist aspirations of their own was hardly considered. The Suez crisis, when it erupted, once again relegated the Palestinian issue to the sidelines. The conflict was an Israel–Egyptian confrontation in which the Palestinians, especially those in Gaza, were not only ignored by, but indeed once again became the hapless victims of, both antagonists.

It was the increasingly bitter Palestinian realization of overall Arab indifference to their plight—before, during, and after 1956—that was a significant factor in the organization of the Palestine Liberation Organization (PLO) in 1964. To the surprise of many Arabs and Westerners alike, a full-blown Palestinian national mystique suddenly emerged after the disastrous Arab military defeat of June 1967, which, while still unfulfilled in territorial terms, is today a major element in the unresolved Arab–Israeli problem. Myopically, few allegedly well-informed US or foreign observers foresaw any such likelihood in 1956. Nor did most Arab leaders. Yet it was the succession of Egyptian and other Arab military defeats, including that of 1956, that caused Palestinians to conclude that they must take their destiny into their own hands.

20

The Economic Consequences of the
Suez Crisis for Egypt

ROGER OWEN

We proceeded, dear Bretheren, to establish a free economy based on solid grounds. We were not affected by threats, we were not terrorised by aggression, we were determined to put our wishes and desires into execution by making our economy free, sound, nationalist and Arab. We Egyptianised the companies which dominated our economy, we Egyptianised the banks and insurance companies and rebuilt them.

> Speech by President Nasser on the occasion of the laying of the foundation-stone of the Aswan Dam, 9 January 1960[1]

INTRODUCTION

In a paper presented at the Middle East Institute in Washington in April 1961 Charles Issawi noted: 'In the last forty years, and more particularly in the last ten, three main shifts in economic power have taken place in the Middle East; from foreigners to nationals; from the landed interest to the industrial, financial, commercial and managerial interests; and from the private sector to the state.'[2] These words were written with the Suez crisis very much in mind and provide a useful way to consider its effects on Egypt's economy when viewed in a large historical perspective. For Issawi, as for all the writers who have followed him, the nationalization of the Canal, followed by the takeover of British and French shares in a host of major banks and industrial and commercial companies, is seen as a major landmark along the road towards Egyptianization, industrialization, and state control.[3]

---

[1] *President Gamal Abdel-Nasser's Speeches and Press-interviews, January–March 1960* (Egypt, Information Dept., Cairo, n.d.), pp. 358–9.

[2] Extracts from this paper are reprinted in Charles Issawi (ed.), *The Economic History of the Middle East 1800–1914* (Chicago, 1966), pp. 505 ff.

[3] The best treatments of this period of Egyptian economic history are to be found in Bent Hansen and Girgis A. Marzouk, *Development and Economic Policy in the UAR (Egypt)* (Amsterdam, 1965); Robert Mabro, *The Egyptian Economy, 1952–1972* (London, 1974); Robert Mabro and

I too find this a useful starting place. Nevertheless, there is obviously more to the story than that and, to my knowledge, no writer has gone on to examine the economic effects of the crisis in detail, whether in terms of the short-term consequences (which, given the disruption caused by the freezing of Egypt's overseas dollar, franc, and sterling assets, the blocking of the Canal, and the damage caused by the war itself, were bound to be negative) or in terms of the way in which the processes set in train by the nationalization of British and French property actually worked themselves out in practice over the next four to five years. This chapter represents a first effort to try to isolate the major factors vital to an understanding of the economic consequences of Suez from these two perspectives.

THE SHORT-TERM CONSEQUENCES OF THE SUEZ CRISIS ON THE EGYPTIAN ECONOMY

Egypt's nationalization of the Suez Canal had two immediate economic effects. The first was the freezing of the country's foreign currency holdings held in Britain, France, and the United States and the immediate cessation of all American aid. Figures for the value of these assets vary but are generally of the order of some £110m. in the No. 1 and No. 2 accounts in London and perhaps $27m. in the United States.[4] This was at a time when total Egyptian foreign trade amounted to just over £E300m. a year (£E1 = £1. 0s. 6d). Second, from August onwards, there was a virtual trade embargo instituted by Britain, far and away the most important of Egypt's commercial partners, while commercial exchange with France and the United States also fell away rapidly. This was followed, in November 1956, by the blocking of the Canal for six months, leading to some loss of

---

Samir Radwan, *The Industrialization of Egypt, 1939–1973: Policy and Performance* (Oxford, 1976); and Patrick O'Brien, *The Revolution in Egypt's Economic System: From Private Enterprise to Socialism, 1952–1965* (London, 1966). The major Egyptian works in Arabic are: 'Ali Jiritli, *Al–ta'rikh al-iqtisadi lil-thawra, 1952–1966* (Cairo, 1974) and *Khamsa wa 'ishrun 'aman dirasa tahliya lil-siyasat al-iqtisadiya fi Misr, 1952–1977* (Cairo, 1977). See also 'Adil Husain, *Al-iqtisadi al-Misri min al-istiqlal ila-l-taba'iyat, 1974–1979*, vol. i (Cairo, 1981).

   [4] According to the Egyptian National Bank, Egypt's sterling assets stood at £111.5m. on 30 Aug. 1956, quoted in Jean Ducruet, *Les Capitaux européens au Proche-Orient* (Paris, 1964), p. 166; Hansen and Marzouk give a figure of £107 for Dec. 1956, *Development and Economic Policy*, p. 190. The value of Egypt's frozen dollar assets was estimated to be $27.3m. as of 1 May 1958, Federal Reserve Bank of New York, Office Correspondence, Norman P. Davis to Mr Exter, 1 May 1958, file C261-Egypt. However, this figure included the accumulated interest minus the sums which had been deducted under various Treasury regulations allowing payments from blocked accounts, notably those involving hardship 'where shipments of goods [had] been completed or other services [had] already been rendered to partnerships or firms in Egypt', Bank of England, E. Arnold to J. C. R. Atkins, 29 Oct. 1956, file OV 31/55. I am grateful to Ms Diane B. Kunz for these last two references.

revenue and to major difficulties in maintaining Egypt's trade with countries east of Suez and in importing its usual supplies of Middle Eastern oil. To this should be added the costs of military mobilization, the destruction of plant and buildings, and the loss of access to mines and other productive assets as a result of Israel's brief occupation of the Sinai peninsula.[5]

The effect of these losses continued to be felt throughout most of 1957, most obviously in the need to preserve scarce resources of foreign currency. This led to a policy decision to maintain imports of consumer goods at as high a level as possible but to restrict the import of everything else. The resulting reduction in the purchase of raw materials, and of intermediary and capital goods led to a sharp drop in certain types of industrial output in 1957 and to an even sharper drop in capital investment. Nevertheless, the economy was still buoyant enough for national income to continue to grow through 1956 and 1957, helped, among other things, by a large loan of $100m. (in convertible currency) from Saudia Arabia and the fact that the Soviet Union, China, and the rest of the Eastern Bloc countries were only too happy to provide Egypt with wheat and other necessities as well as to expand their market for the cotton which it could no longer sell in Britain and the West.

Even more important, Egypt's problems were enormously reduced by the speed at which the Canal was cleared and reopened and by the fact that negotiations for the restoration of normal economic relations with France, the United States, and Britain were able to proceed at a relatively rapid pace. As is well known, the Canal was officially reopened on 10 April 1957, while the problem of the payment of dues was quickly settled with the decision of the United States government and the Suez Canal Users' Association to instruct ships to pay for their passage direct to the Egyptian government according to the arrangements set out in the Egyptian note to the United Nations of 24 April— with the face-saving formula that this was being done 'under protest'. British ships began to use the Canal in mid-May (92 of them from 13 to 31 May) and French ships in June. As a result, Egypt obtained £E24.5m. in receipts in 1957 as opposed to the £E2.3m. it had received from the Canal Company under the old arrangements in 1955.[6] Meanwhile, there was a continuous increase in Canal traffic, even though it was not until August 1958 that it had been dredged

---

[5] Prior to the start of the financial discussions between Egypt and Britain and France in 1958 the Egyptian delegation claimed that the military intervention had caused £E78m. in damage, Ducruet, *Les Capitaux européens*, p. 168 n.

[6] For 1955, John Waterbury, *The Egypt of Nasser and Sadat: The Political Economy of Two Regimes* (Princeton, 1983), p. 68; for 1957, National Bank of Egypt, *Economic Bulletin*, 11 (1958), 54.

sufficiently to allow the passage of ships of 35ft. draught, the maximum which had been permissible before it had silted up as a result of the 1956 closure.

A second key event on the road back to normalization was the agreement reached with the Suez Canal Company in May 1958 (although not formally signed until July) by which the Egyptian government undertook to pay compensation of £E26.5m. for the nationalization of its Egyptian assets—assets which the Company itself had originally valued at some £E70m.[7] This at once paved the way for the unfreezing of Egypt's American dollar account, the restoration of American aid, and a financial agreement with France signed on 22 August 1958. The only remaining problem was the question of reaching a final settlement with the British, something which was not achieved until February 1959.

From an Egyptian point of view, there is no doubt that the crisis brought on by the withdrawal of the Western offer to finance the Aswan High Dam, the consequent nationalization of the Suez Canal, and then the Anglo-French and Israeli invasion had not only been resolved satisfactorily in financial terms but also in very quick time. The reasons for this are obviously partly political (notably the role of the United States) and partly economic. Given the importance of the Canal to world shipping, the pressure from Western business interests to be allowed to resume trade with Egypt, the fear that Egypt was falling into the Russian economic sphere, and the fact that the Western powers held quite a substantial bargaining counter in the shape of Egypt's blocked foreign assets, there were many good reasons to come to a speedy solution. Nevertheless, in the end, it would seem that the short-term balance sheet was very much to Egypt's advantage: not only had it obtained ownership of the Canal and access to its revenues but it had also obtained an estimated £E45m. worth of British and French assets after all compensation had been paid.[8]

MEDIUM-TERM CONSEQUENCES OF THE CRISIS: 1957–1960

The main medium-term consequences of the Suez crisis for the Egyptian economy stem from a series of measures and policy decisions taken either during the crisis itself or shortly thereafter. I will begin by setting out the most important of these in chronological order.

---

[7] For estimates of the value of the Canal given at the time of the final settlement, see Ducruet, *Les Capitaux européens*, pp. 170–3.

[8] This estimate, based on figures in Ducruet, *Les Capitaux européens*, pp. 318–23, comes from Mourad M. Wahba, *The Role of the State in the Egyptian Economy, 1945–81* (D.Phil., Oxford, 1986), p. 108.

1. July 1956: the nationalization of the Canal.

2. November 1956: the sequestration under Military Law No. 5 (1.11.1956) of all the goods and property belonging to the British and French governments in Egypt as well as British and French companies, institutions, and private persons. These included 9 banks (the largest of which was Barclays) with a capital of £E2m., 64 British, French, and Australian insurance companies (valued by the Egyptian Ministry of Finance at just under £E10m.), and shares in a large number of industrial and commercial companies either wholly or partially owned by British and French interests (e.g. Eastern Tobacco and the Egyptian assets of Shell, Marconi, etc.) the value of which was later calculated at over £E50m.[9]

3. January 1957: the creation of a new government department, the Economic Organization (*a*) to lay down policies for the investment of Egyptian public funds in works of development and (*b*) to take over most of the sequestered British and French companies (but not the major banks which were given—or sold—to Egyptian banks) and most of the sequestered foreign shares.[10]

4. January 1957: the establishment of a National Planning Council to absorb all previous committees and councils connected with planning with control over a National Planning Committee with 200 Egyptian and foreign experts. The latter was set to work to produce an interim investment programme for 1957–8 and to collect the materials necessary to draw up a longer term, Five Year Plan, to begin in 1960.[11]

5. April 1957: the announcement by the Minister of Industry of a Five Year Industrial Plan (discussion of which had begun in October 1956). This consisted of 115 projects (many of which had already been approved and some actually started) with a major emphasis on factories producing intermediate and capital goods like chemicals, rubber, and machines. The programme was later estimated to cost £E114m. of which £E24m. was to be provided by the state and the remainder from private sector savings.[12]

6. June/July 1957: the National Bank (which before November 1956 was controlled largely by British and French capital) was turned into a Central Bank with power to regulate credit and banking policy

---

[9] For information about these companies and their value, see Ducruet, *Les Capitaux européens*, pp. 318–23 and Hossam I. Issa, *Capitalisme et sociétés anonymes en Egypte: Essai sur le rapport entre le structure sociale et droit* (Paris, 1970), pp. 214–21.

[10] The best source on the Economic Organization is Mabro and Radwan, *The Industrialization of Egypt*, pp. 66–8. See also, Issa, *Capitalisme et sociétés anonymes*, pp. 216–18.

[11] The best source for the origins of the Egyptian planning process is O'Brien, *The Revolution in Egypt's Economic System*, particularly chs. 4 and 8. O'Brien lived in Egypt in the early 1960s and got to know most of the leading planners.

[12] Mabro and Radwan, *The Industrialization of Egypt*, pp. 66–7.

in general. This was accompanied by a new Banking and Credit Law which strengthened the power of the state over the Central Bank and the Central Bank over the rest of the banking system.

7. January 1958: final agreement on a Soviet loan of about £E62m. plus Russian assistance towards the implementation of 65 projects including the expansion of electricity generating and the increased production of chemicals, textiles, and medical equipment, most of which were in the Five Year Industrial Plan. As a result, according to the Minister of Industry: 'We have acquired all that we need to develop our industry'.

8. October 1958: Soviet Agreement to help with the construction and finance of the Aswan High Dam.

Taken at face value, such measures certainly testify to the significant impact of the Suez crisis on the management of the Egyptian economy. However, their analysis poses several problems. To begin with, a number of these measures represent no more than a continuation of developments which had already begun some time before the summer of 1956. For example, a Permanent Council for the Development of National Production had been set up by the Revolutionary Command Council (RCC) soon after the military coup of July 1952. And, although it had started off by concentrating mostly on projects aimed at deepening Egypt's economic infrastructure, it had gone on to explore ways of using the resources of the state to develop a capital goods industry, notably with the decision to go ahead with the establishment of the iron and steel complex at Helwan. Again, the switch towards the Eastern Bloc as a major trading partner was well under way before the Suez crisis with the latter's share in Egypt's total exports climbing from 11 per cent in 1954 to 28 per cent in 1956.[13]

Nevertheless, all writers agree that a qualitative change in the regime's economic goals and system of economic management took place in 1956–7, even if there is no general agreement about just what this was, or how to sum it up. Thus for O'Brien the movement was from 'free enterprise' to 'guided capitalism' while, for Mabro, the year 1957 marked the moment when the government really 'meant business' as far as economic planning was concerned.[14] Part of the problem is obviously one of interpretation and definition. But another part stems from the incoherence of the regime's own policies during the late 1950s and the fact that the political realities which underlay this incoherence are extremely difficult to establish. Finally, there is the difficult problem of working out just how the policies of this period led up to the

---

[13] Mabro and Radwan, *The Industrialization of Egypt*, p. 227.
[14] Mabro, *The Egyptian Economy*, pp. 113–14; O'Brien, *The Revolution in Egypt's Economic System*, titles of chs. 3 and 4.

introduction of Egypt's one and only Five Year Plan in 1960 and to the wave of nationalizations which followed. For the remainder of this chapter I will offer a few observations of my own on this complex subject.

Probably the best place to start is with the impact of the Suez crisis on President Nasser's own thinking. Even before the crisis his increasing prestige inside Egypt, solidified by his election to the Presidency in 1956, had meant that he was able to rise above his Free Officer colleagues to dominate the Egyptian political scene; after it, his leading role in policy-making and in the setting of regime guide-lines was absolutely assured. In these circumstances he was well placed to act on his belief that events of 1956 represented an economic as well as a political victory and provided the basis for a programme of accelerated development directed, for the first time, by a government able to pay proper attention to Egypt's own national interest. On the one hand, the take-over of companies which were either owned or controlled by British and French nationals put an end to the major source of foreign domination over key sectors of the Egyptian economy, notably banking, insurance, mortgages, and the financing of foreign trade.[15] On the other, possession of these same companies opened up opportunities for the state to play a very much more active role in directing investment towards the expansion of manufacturing industry, which was seen by Nasser as lying at the heart of the drive towards an independent, modern economy. Thus while the sequestration of British and French assets was originally presented as a process of Egyptianization designed to transfer control over the country's financial and commercial resources into Egyptian private hands, the decision to sell off all but a few of these assets was quickly rescinded, probably by the President himself, and they were then transferred to the newly created Economic Organization, to form the basis of what was soon to become Egypt's dominant public sector.[16]

Something of the President's attitude to industry is well captured in speeches he gave at this time, notably the one at the opening of the Helwan Iron and Steel complex in 1958. As he summed up his own beliefs: 'Today our aim is to build as many factories as possible, to employ as great a number of machines as possible and to save as much money as possible in order to place out savings in fresh investments, for the more investments we have, the higher the standard of living is raised'.[17] This is the rhetoric of what Albert Hirschman (writing of

---

[15] Issa, *Capitalisme et sociétés anonymes*, pp. 151–4, 214–15.

[16] O'Brien, *The Revolution in Egypt's Economic System*, p. 95.

[17] *President Gamal Abdel-Nasser's Speeches and Press Interviews, 1958* (Egypt, Information Dept., Cairo n.d.), p. 247.

Latin America) has called the exuberant phase of development by import substitution when all seems possible.[18] In President Nasser's own case the exuberance was further accentuated by his success in obtaining superpower support for his projects, notably the two Soviet agreements of 1958 and the American decision to provide Egypt with large PL 480 wheat shipments beginning in 1959.

However, although Nasser's goals may have been clear enough, there was no general agreement among either the politicians or the planners about how they were to be achieved. For one thing, there was considerable debate inside the RCC itself with the majority of its senior members opposed to further acts of state control. For men like Hassan Ibrahim, the first director of the Economic Organization, or Hussain Shafai and Abd al-Latif Baghdadi, the first and second heads of the planning apparatus, the major priority was simply to rationalize the existing situation and to make sure that the firms already taken into public ownership were made to perform properly.[19] On the other hand, there were more junior colleagues among the Free Officers and their civilian associates who wanted to seize the opportunity to expand state ownership and control still further. As Waterbury correctly notes, they had come to this position not for ideological reasons but because of their concern with technical issues such as a better allocation of resources or the need for proper mechanisms to determine investment priorities.[20] Chief among them was the ambitious technocrat, Aziz Sidqi, who had obtained a doctorate in regional planning in the United States and who had been appointed the first Minister of the newly created Ministry of Industry in 1956.

Apart from these differences, there was also a great deal of incoherence in the system of management, with powers of planning and execution divided between the National Planning Council (transformed into the Higher Council of National Planning in 1958 with President Nasser as Chairman), the Ministry of Industry, the Economic Organization, and the Ministry of Finance. Problems were then exacerbated by the speed at which the Five Year Plan for Industry had been drawn up by Sidqi's Ministry with little thought as to how it was to be properly financed; while the fact that the Economic Organization was put in charge of what was essentially a rag-bag of different types of companies, large and small, meant that it was difficult for it either to devise a coherent strategy or to work out a satisfactory system of co-operation with an increasingly suspicious private sector. Whereas the

[18] Albert O. Hirschman, 'The turn to authoritarianism in Latin America and the search for its economic determination', in David Collier (ed.), *The New Authoritarianism in Latin America* (Princeton, 1979), p. 67.

[19] Waterbury, *The Egypt of Nasser and Sadat*, p. 69.

[20] Ibid.

take-over of British and French assets had paved the way for effective management of the banking system, it had destroyed what seems to have been the logic of the regime's pre-1956 development strategy by which the state had looked after heavy industry while leaving control over light industries like textiles and food-processing to the private sector.[21] In these circumstances there was understandably a great deal of irritation and confusion, as well as an opportunity for the Minister of Industry, generally with Nasser's backing, to attempt an enforced rationalization of the situation by extending his control over the whole machinery of planning, for example, by means of the 1958 Decree which gave his Ministry the sole power to license any new industrial plant.

To speak very generally, there seem to have been two major unresolved problems at this time. The first stemmed from the state's failure to define its relationship with private capital. As O'Brien's characterization suggests, what the regime was trying to do between 1957 and 1961 was to manage what was fundamentally a mixed economy, but without any of the mechanisms for ensuring smooth co-operation between the public and the private sector which had been instituted, for example, in contemporary India. On the one hand, there was a private sector dominated by a few mammoth enterprises like the Bank Misr and the Abboud industrial and commercial empires, which had so little confidence in the regime that they were busily running down their assets by means of huge annual distributions to share-holders out of profits.[22] On the other, there was a government which, while constantly exhorting private capitalists to finance new projects, was both unwilling to replace the pre-1956 institutional mechanisms for regular consultation embodied in the old Permanent Council for the Development of National Product and unable to produce a satisfactory working definition of the role which it thought the private sector should play.[23]

The result was the creation of something of a vicious circle, with the private sector making the bulk of its new investments in those areas like urban property and tourism, which it considered safe, and then, when the government tried to block off these outlets in order to force it into more productive lines, showing considerable ingenuity in evading the new regulations. This in turn led to increasing frustration inside the

[21] O'Brien, *The Revolution in Egypt's Economic System*, pp. 231–2.

[22] See figures in Issa, *Capitalisme et sociétés anonymes*, p. 452.

[23] R. W. Baker, *Egypt's Uncertain Revolution under Nasser and Sadat* (Cambridge, Mass., 1978), p. 62; O'Brien, *The Revolution in Egypt's Economic System*, p. 88. According to Waterbury, Aziz Sidqi did set up an Agency for the Consolidation of Industry with 10 public officials and 5 representatives of private industry in May 1958, but this was not enough to establish 'a good working relationship', *The Egypt of Nasser and Sadat*, pp. 69–70.

regime, exacerbated by the growing evidence provided by the planners that the large private companies were the only really major source of the domestic savings needed to finance the First Five Year Plan which was due to begin so soon.[24] Attacks on the selfish nature of the Egyptian bourgeoisie increased demonstrably from 1959 onwards, while in 1960 it was enough to justify the nationalization of the Bank Misr on the grounds that its own investment programme was not in conformity with that of the government and that it might be in a position to block the state's plans—not that it actually had.[25] If private capital, which was still responsible for at least two-thirds of national production, would neither co-operate with the regime, nor agree to be properly controlled, then there was a growing number of people inside Egypt's small ruling group ready to argue that the only way forward was to take its major enterprises firmly into public ownership.

The second problem concerned the fact that attempts to increase the rate of industrialization and to move decisively into new areas of activity simply did not work as they were supposed to do. This was partly because of divided responsibilities and faulty planning. It was also the result of the shortcomings of the Economic Organization, the main agent entrusted with the task of increasing industrial investment. Not only was it unable to find the right formula for co-operation with private capital but it also failed to develop the types of intermediate and capital goods industries which were required. Detailed evidence concerning its activities is hard to find. However, it would seem that it started few new plants during the three years of its existence, while the areas where it did have some little success in expanding production tended to involve well-tried activities like textiles rather than innovative path-breakers like chemicals or machine tools.[26] It is not clear why this should have been so. But we can guess at a combination of conservative management, the unwieldy nature of the organization itself, and, certainly not least, the fundamental problems which must face any Third World country which tries to deepen its industrial base by moving into lines which require much greater capital, entrepreneurial ability, and technical skills.

If the foregoing argument is largely correct, it would be tempting to conclude with O'Brien that the three or four years after Suez were simply a period of trial and error while the country awaited the inevitable appearance of a comprehensive national development plan which would have the necessary consequence of forcing the regime,

---

[24] O'Brien, *The Revolution in Egypt's Economic System*, p. 88.

[25] Hansen and Marzouk, *Development and Economic Policy*, p. 20; Mabro and Radwan, *The Industrialization of Egypt*, p. 68.

[26] Ibid., p. 68; O'Brien, *The Revolution in Egypt's Economic System*, p. 107.

and its experts, to spell out more clearly what type of economic system they wanted and how it ought properly to be managed.[27] It would then follow that the major economic impact of the 1956 crisis has to be seen in terms of the political decision to take advantage of the opportunities it presented to go full ahead with a state-directed drive to mobilize all of Egypt's national resources.

Nevertheless, this cannot possibly be the whole of the story. For one thing, it does not explain why President Nasser and his regime put so much energy into economic planning after 1956 when they had talked so much about it before that date and achieved so little. The answer must certainly include reference not only to the effects of the crisis on internal Egyptian politics, for example its enhancement of Nasser's own leading role, but also on the way it cemented economic relations with the Eastern Bloc as a whole, and the Soviet Union in particular. Thus, by 1958, Egypt was sending nearly half of its exports to the Soviet Bloc (including China) and receiving almost a third of its imports from there, much of it as a result of barter deals, and all under one type of long-term bilateral arrangement or another.[28] At the same time, the Eastern Bloc was opening up as the most promising market for Egypt's expanding exports of manufactured goods.

A second, and equally important, point concerns the regime's relationship with Egyptian private capital. O'Brien's focus on the drive towards comprehensive planning makes conflict between the two parties almost inevitable. But this is to slide over a number of important issues which have yet to be adequately explored. One is the fillip which the Suez nationalizations gave to native Egyptian capitalists and businessmen by removing almost all of their main, locally based, foreign competitors at one fell swoop. That they took advantage of the situation to move quickly into the vacant positions in the banks and insurance companies and other enterprises is clear. But could this not also have provided the basis for a new partnership between the state and Egyptian private capital? Or was it simply that the new opportunities siphoned off much of the investment and the entrepreneurial energy which the regime was so anxious to see directed towards manufacturing industry? Reading between the lines of much of the Egyptian official literature of this period we can see that questions of this kind were subject to a considerable debate, with no shortage of people to present the private sector's own case.[29] And yet, in the end, it was the advocates of public control which triumphed.

[27] Ibid., p. 100.

[28] Mabro and Radwan, *The Industrialization of Egypt*, p. 227; National Bank of Egypt, *Economic Bulletin*, 12: 2 (1959), 178.

[29] Georges Vaucher, *Gamal Abdel Nasser et son equipe: L'Édification de la République Arabe Unie* (Paris, 1960), pp. 281–2.

Perhaps, once again, the answer lies in an analysis of President Nasser's own leadership. As far as his own speeches and interviews given at this time are concerned, he seems to have had a low opinion of private capitalists, whom on one private occasion in 1957 he described as all 'speculators' (with the exception of Ahmad Abboud), and on another public one as people who needed special guidance if they were to be prevented from 'exploiting both the individual and society'.[30] So long as the state lacked the resources to replace the private sector, such views were balanced by others stressing the need for partnership and co-operation. But they must certainly have provided plenty of comfort to those anxious, for their own reasons, to expand the sphere of technocratic and bureaucratic control.

Probably even more important was the cumulative effect of some of the key decisions which the President was making at this same time. One, already mentioned, was the determination to use the opportunities presented by Suez to accelerate economic development by means of state-directed investment within the framework of a national plan. This led on to the creation of an elaborate organization to draw up the plan itself, something which soon created further necessities in the shape of the need to establish targets and also administrative mechanisms for implementation and control. Just what role Nasser himself played in the detailed formulation of the plan is unclear, but we do know from men who had access to him at this time (for example Ismail Sabri Abdullah) that he used many evenings to become acquainted with the thinking of the leading development economists, either by reading such works as W. W. Rostow's, *The Stages of Economic Growth*, with its attractive notion of the 'take-off', or by using his position as head of state to arrange informal seminars with experts. But in all this there is no doubt that he never lost sight of the political importance of the plan as something which would cement the legitimacy of his regime by providing immediate and tangible examples of economic progress. And it was very much in this light that he overrode the wishes of the planners themselves to insist that its central target should be the doubling of national income in ten years, an intervention he seems to have made without prior discussion with any of his former Free Officer colleagues. References to the new target pepper many of the speeches he made in the summer of 1959, and it inevitably came to be seen as the touchstone of the regime's future performance.[31] While it is true that the slogan of 'socialism' had been added to those of 'democracy' and 'co-operation' in 1957 as one of the defining features of the post-Suez

---

[30] Quoted in Don Peretz, 'In search of a doctrine: A study of the ideology of the Egyptian revolution', *Middle East Forum*, 35: 6 (1959), 17.

[31] E.g., speech of 25 July 1959, *President Gamal Abdel-Nasser's Speeches and Press-Interviews, 1959*, (Egypt, Information Dept., n.d.), p. 300.

regime, it was not ideology which drove President Nasser along at this time but his own intense practical vision of a new, strong, independent, industrial Egypt.

Seen in these terms, 1960 must have seemed something of an *annus mirabilis* to Egypt's President and a wonderful culmination of the whole Suez crisis. Not only was it the year in which work on the High Dam began and in which the comprehensive Five Year Plan was introduced but it was also the one in which, for the first time, both the United States and the Soviet Union seemed firmly united in support of Egypt's economic development, with the added bonus of the imminent release of Egypt's considerable sterling balances, the bulk of which had been accumulated in London during the Second World War. But, as we now know, things were not to remain so hopeful. September 1961 saw the secession of the Syrian region from the United Arab Republic, spurred on in part by Egypt's attempt to submit the Syrian economy to the same processes of planning and control which it had just introduced for its own. These included the wave of nationalizations of July 1961 which brought most of the country's major companies into state ownership, providing the system of economic management with a challenge with which it was never able to come to terms. The result, a huge and badly managed public sector, can be considered to be the major, harmful, economic consequence of the Suez crisis. But we should also remember its other more positive legacy: a High Dam which stored enough water to save Egypt's agriculture from disaster in the years after the Blue Nile flow had begun to decline in 1965, a well-managed, profitable Suez Canal, and a flourishing, if unruly, private sector dominated by the Egyptian businessmen who emerged some-what belatedly after Anwar Sadat's economic 'liberalization' as the major beneficiaries of the 1956 Egyptianizations.

21

Consequences of the Suez Crisis in the Arab World

RASHID KHALIDI

BEYOND its effect on Egypt and the other direct participants, the Suez crisis had a profound impact on the rest of the Arab world. This was illustrated throughout the crisis over Suez from mid-1955 onwards in the powerful wave of Arab support for Egypt. It was particularly striking in view of the initial lukewarm response of many Arabs to the Egyptian military regime which had emerged from the 1952 revolution. Suez changed this, firmly establishing Gamal Abdel Nasser as the pre-eminent Arab leader until the end of his life, and Arab nationalism as the leading Arab ideology for at least that long.

Suez also gave a final push to the tottering hegemony over the Arab world which Britain and France had sometimes shared and sometimes disputed for over a century. It exposed their weaknesses, encouraging Iraqis, Algerians, Adenis, and others to liquidate their last footholds in the region. Arab leaders ceased paying attention to London and Paris, turning instead towards Cairo, Washington, and Moscow. Finally, because it involved Israel in overt collaboration with the old imperial powers, and in an invasion of the territory of an existing Arab state, the Suez crisis established an image of Israel in the Arab world, and a pattern of conflict with it, which had an impact perhaps as important as that of the 1948 war.

In spite of the significant effects of the Suez crisis on the Arab world, relatively little primary material has emerged to illuminate the motivations of different Arab leaders and governments (with the exception of course of Egypt), and to enable researchers to chronicle this aspect of the crisis.[1] Whereas we can now follow the Egyptian, British, French,

---

[1] The limited primary material available dealing with the impact of Suez on the Arab world includes King Hussein, *Uneasy Lies the Head* (London, 1962); Khalid al-'Azm, *Mudhakkirat Khalid al-'Azm* (Memoirs of Khalid al-Azm) (Beirut, 1972); Camille Chamoun, *Crise au Moyen-Orient* (Paris, 1963); Abu Iyad with Eric Rouleau, *My Home, My Land: A Narrative of the Palestinian Struggle* (New York, 1981); and works by Mohamed H. Heikal, notably *Cutting The Lion's Tail: Suez through Egyptian Eyes* (New York, 1987), a translation of *Milaffat al-Suways: harb al-thalathin sana* (The Suez Files: The Thirty Years War) (Cairo, 1986), without the latter's valuable documentary appendices, which include primary materials which shed much light on Arab aspects of the crisis.

Israeli, and American sides of the Suez controversy relatively easily through archival or memoir material, to study the various Arab actors involved we are forced to rely largely on the considerable amount of secondary material which has accumulated since 1956.

For this and other reasons, therefore, this assessment of the consequences of Suez for the Arab world will be strictly thematic and reflective rather than detailed and exhaustive. Although we have fewer first-hand accounts by Arab participants in the events compared with others, much can be said about the impact of the crisis on the Arab world. Among other things, it is clear that this impact was felt on several levels. These were:

1. Arab relations with, and attitudes towards, the great powers;
2. The internal and inter-Arab policies of several Arab polities;
3. The Arab–Israeli conflict.

ARAB RELATIONS WITH THE GREAT POWERS

It is acknowledged by virtually all students of Suez, of the policies of the superpowers in the Middle East, and of the Arab–Israeli conflict, that Suez marked some sort of turning-point. This is true whether we are speaking of the policies of the countries directly involved in the aggression on Egypt, Egypt itself, the superpowers, or other actors. It is perhaps insufficiently appreciated that as far as Arab relations with, and attitudes towards, the great powers were concerned, Suez only confirmed, magnified, and strengthened existing trends.

Thus the United States emerges from the Suez crisis in most accounts as the dominant Western power in the region, having benefited from the disaster of the Anglo-French-Israeli aggression on Egypt, to replace Britain and France, and soon to inherit Israel from Britain and France as a privileged regional client and ally. Looking at the United States from the perspective of the Arab states, including in this case Egypt, it seems that Washington did not get all of the credit it might otherwise have won for its forthright opposition to the tripartite attack and to Israel's later attempts to maintain its occupation of Sinai and the Gaza Strip. The United States was certainly accorded even more importance in the region after Suez than it had been before, and yet the late 1950s and 1960s were a period of Soviet rather than American advances in the region (as witnessed by scholarly titles on the subject such as *Red Star on the Nile* and *Soviet Advances in the Middle East*.[2]

The main reason for America's failure to gain more Arab approval

---

[2] Alvin Rubinstein, *Red Star on the Nile* (Princeton, 1977), and George Lenczowski, *Soviet Advances in the Middle East* (Washington, DC, 1971).

for its resolute stand in 1956 would seem to be simple. Many Arabs perceived that the United States had played a crucial role in precipitating the crisis via Dulles's sudden withdrawal of the US offer of funds to help construct the Aswan Dam. They also resented American hostility, both before and after the Suez war, to the policy of neutralism, which was growing increasingly popular in the Arab world, and to Arab nationalism. All of this undermined the credit the United States might otherwise have expected for the positive diplomatic outcomes it played a major role in achieving in the autumn of 1956 and the spring of 1957.

Although this may seem too simple an answer, it takes into account a factor often ignored by analysts: for the long period in which the crisis was brewing, and until the invasion actually took place, US–Egyptian relations were far from good. Thus what America eventually did during the tripartite attack came against a background of many months of its apparent hostility to Egypt, to Nasser, and to Arab nationalism (following a honeymoon for well over two years after the 1952 revolution in Egypt). It might be added that once the crisis was over, American policy under Dulles, as seen in such initiatives as the Eisenhower Doctrine and the American intervention in Lebanon in 1958, did little to dispel impressions in the Arab world that such hostility was the basis of US policy.[3]

It was perhaps partly in consequence of this situation in US–Egyptian relations that the Soviet Union managed to get as much credit as it did in Arab eyes for its role in the crisis. Egypt, moreover, probably played a determinant role in influencing Arab attitudes towards both the Soviet Union and the United States at this point. This is understandable, for after it had stood up to Britain, France, and Israel in 1956 and survived, the revolutionary regime in Egypt had virtually unlimited legitimacy in the Arab world. Consequently the lead it took was widely followed.

We know from accounts by such Egyptians close to the centre of decision-making as Mohamed Hassanein Heikal and Amin Hewedy that Egyptian leaders knew just how limited the Soviet role was.[4] These leaders seem nevertheless to have consciously stressed publicly the importance of the Soviet contribution to the outcome of the Suez crisis.

---

[3] That this impression was not totally incorrect can be seen from the accounts of two of those charged with the implementation of the policies of John Foster and Allen Dulles during this period: Wilbur Crane Eveland, *Ropes of Sand: America's Failure in the Middle East* (New York, 1980), and Miles Copeland, *The Game of Nations* (New York, 1970). That such an impression was strongly held by Egyptian leaders can be seen, *inter alia*, from documents in Heikal's *Milaffat*.

[4] Notably in Heikal's *The Sphinx and the Commissar* (New York, 1978) and his *Milaffat*, and Amin Hewedy's *Hurub 'Abd al-Nasir* (Nasser's Wars) (Beirut, 1977). More detail can be found in the accounts by Egyptian policy-makers collected in Muhammad 'Awda *et al.* (eds.), *Qissat al-Sawfiyat wa Misr* (The Story of the Soviets and Egypt) (Beirut, 1975).

They apparently did this in the hope of creating a counter-weight to the United States, which now was the dominant Western power in the region, and which seemed to hold little goodwill for Egypt (whose funds for example remained tied up in American banks by government order until the crisis was well over). Egypt's publicly restrained attitude to the United States and its overt praise of its new Soviet friends in the wake of Suez thus sent a clear signal to the rest of the Arab world.

There is much other evidence that Suez simply confirmed existing tendencies in the Arab world. There was already a clear trend away from involvement with great power military blocs, alliances, and pacts, out of a not entirely groundless fear that these were simply a cover for the maintenance of foreign bases and of a continued unequal relationship between the Arab states and their former colonial masters. There was, further, a strong interest in Egypt, Syria, and Jordan in non-alignment, and a growing fascination with the Soviet Union as a possible counter-weight to the Western powers. Suez simply accentuated processes already under way, showing that the Soviet Union was now a factor in the region which could be used to Arab advantage, and that Britain and France were indeed as ill-intentioned and as hostile to Arab nationalist aspirations as most Arabs already knew they were from decades of experience.

Suez destroyed any slim possibility that Britain and France would remain major powers in the Arab world. As damning in Arab eyes as the perceived sin of attacking Egypt and Arab nationalism (Nasser was increasingly representative and symbolic of both) was the fact that the two powers had collaborated with Israel. This collusion confirmed the most extreme Arab nationalist theses, which argued that the great powers' support for the creation of a Jewish state in Palestine had always been motivated by their desire to use it as a pawn against the Arabs.[5] What we now know about the collusion from Israeli, French, and British sources indicates that far from being paranoid fantasies, these suspicions were at least in this case quite close to the mark: Israel played an essential role in both British and French planning to defeat the forces of militant nationalism in the Arab world. Thus, when added to provocations like the Lavon and *Bat-Galim* affairs of 1954,[6] which seemed timed to coincide with crucial moments in Egypt's relations with the Western powers, the long-drawn-out Suez crisis

---

[5] See, e.g. the work of the Arab nationalist historian Amin Saʿid, al-ʿUdwan, 29 October 1956–1 November 1958 (The Aggression) (Cairo, 1959), which strongly argues this view.

[6] Heikal, *Cutting the Lion's Tail*, pp. 47–9. The former involved a plot by Israeli agents to plant explosives in American and British targets in Cairo, discovered by Egyptian security forces, while the latter concerned an attempt to send the Israeli ship *Bat-Galim* through the Suez Canal.

revived Arab fears regarding Israel's role in the region which might otherwise have eased in time.

Suez had one other important consequence as far as the position of the old colonial powers in the Arab world was concerned. This was to tar fatally their local collaborators, clients, and allies with the brush of complicity not only with the colonial powers but also with Israel in a joint effort to destroy a popular Arab symbol. This association contributed to the sequence of events which brought down the Iraqi monarchy and, with it, trusted British collaborators such as Nuri Said. It also briefly threatened the throne of King Hussein in Jordan, strengthened the growing opposition to President Chamoun in Lebanon, and proved the kiss of death for those Syrian leaders and party factions associated with Britain and Iraq who had been persuaded to launch an abortive coup against the pro-Egyptian regime timed to coincide with the Suez attack.[7]

It could be argued that in any case the days of Nuri and the Iraqi monarchy were numbered, and that Hussein, Chamoun, and the Syrian politicians aligned with Britain and Iraq were all on shaky ground. Certainly all were swimming with difficulty against a powerful, growing Arab nationalist tide throughout the region. But Suez did make a difference: now all these men were identified not just with the old colonialism, but with Israel as well, after a direct tripartite assault on Egypt and its head of state, who had developed a considerable Arab popular following. Their domestic opponents capitalized on this association in the popular mind, and within just over two years all but King Hussein were out of office. Indeed, the Jordanian monarch had to resort to extreme measures to wrest back power in April 1957 from the first (and last) freely elected, populist, and pan-Arabist government in Jordanian history, that of Suleiman al-Nabulsi, which had come into office in October 1956 at the height of the Arab nationalist fervour preceding the Suez war.

INTERNAL AND INTER-ARAB POLITICS OF THE ARAB STATES

As we have just seen, the net effect of the Suez crisis on domestic Arab politics, particularly in Syria, Jordan, Lebanon, and Iraq, was a further radicalization of an already unstable situation. Throughout the region, Suez gave a decisive impetus to the growing Arab nationalist trend, led and symbolized by Nasser, whose regime in 1954 had achieved the extraordinary feat of securing a British military with-

---

[7] The Syrian *coup* episode is chronicled by Patrick Seale in *The Struggle for Syria: A Study of Post-War Arab Politics, 1945–1958* (London, 1965), pp. 262–82, and in Eveland, *Ropes of Sand*, pp. 180–230. See also documents in Heikal, *Milaffat*.

drawal from Egypt after seventy-two years of occupation. Such an achievement had a powerful resonance in an Arab world still dotted with French bases in Morocco, Algeria, and Tunisia, British bases in Libya, Jordan, Iraq, Aden, and the Gulf, and American bases in Morocco, Libya, and Saudi Arabia.

This nationalist trend and the accompanying radicalization provided the main impetus for a wave of fundamental regime changes and other upheavals in the Arab world in the middle and late 1950s. The outcome of the Suez war reinforced the power of Nasser's already persuasive rhetoric, to which many Arabs were already listening. The influence exerted in inter-Arab affairs by Nasser, the Ba'th Party in Syria, and other Arab nationalist leaders and formations had been growing markedly even before Suez. It was reinforced by the visible decline in British power, and the weakening of the solidarity and ability to govern by the dominant traditional élites of the Arab world in the face of rising new social forces which identified with radical Arab nationalism. After Suez, however, with their British allies virtually out of the picture, in Syria and Iraq these élites crumbled before the push of parties and cliques of officers drawn largely from the middle and lower middle classes. They only clung to power in Jordan and Lebanon with difficulty, and, in part, thanks to external help.

Clearly, there was no single formula for these changes which resulted from Suez, and which were refracted differently in the specific politics of each state, much as has been the impact of Islamic political activism in recent years. In general, however, what Britain, France, and Israel achieved was diametrically opposed to their original intentions. Far from destroying Nasser and thereby ending Egypt's insidious influence, by targeting him and failing to unseat him, they made the Egyptian leader's position nearly impregnable for many years and increased his country's prestige and influence. All three parties to the collusion simultaneously witnessed a reinforcement of just those forces in the region which they had most wanted to defeat: pan-Arabism and radicalism. Beyond these general results, there were specific consequences of Suez in the politics of several Arab states, most of them the opposite of those intended by its planners.

In Syria, the conflict between different political factions and their various external backers, so arrestingly described by Patrick Seale in *The Struggle for Syria*,[8] had already reached a level of intense bitterness. This was further exacerbated by a plot to overthrow the country's pro-Egyptian government, which had been timed to coincide with the Suez attack, and had been planned by an almost amateurish coalition of the

---

[8] Op. cit. in n. 7.

Iraqi, British, and American intelligence services.[9] Their bungled conspiracy contributed in turn to the sense of insecurity among the radical nationalist Syrian factions then in power, helping to drive them in a little over a year into the embrace of Egypt and the ill-fated United Arab Republic.

The failed plot also played a role in bringing closer to power the politicized military officers who had long been interfering actively in Syrian politics, but who soon afterwards were to take control of the country. In such a national emergency, with Syria under pressure from a formidable array of foes, who could better claim to protect it than the military? The traditional civilian politicians, as well as the social class most of them came from, were already losing their dominant position in politics and society, but Suez gave a major impetus to the young military men who took their places and who have ruled with only a few interruptions ever since the late 1950s.

The impact of Suez was devastating to the Iraqi monarchy. The abortive Syrian *coup* attempt marked one of the last occasions that the Iraqi regime was able to project its power beyond its borders. After Suez it was increasingly on the defensive, the outcome of its struggle with Egypt for leadership of the Arab states a foregone conclusion in the wake of Nasser's triumph. To its traditional sin in nationalist eyes of collaborating with imperialist Britain, the regime had now to bear the burden of accusations of having in effect colluded with Israel via involvement in the plot to overthrow the Syrian regime timed to coincide with the tripartite aggression against Egypt. Following Suez, Patrick Seale writes, throughout the region, 'Nuri became the butt of ever more strident attacks: he was an "ally of the Jews", a "valet of colonialism", a "traitor and tyrant such as the East had never known".'[10]

Certainly the Iraqi monarchy was already tottering before Suez. But one of its few remaining assets, its prestige in the Arab world, was irrevocably shattered by the attack on Egypt of its protector Britain, and by its own apparent complicity via involvement in the anti-Syrian plot. Before Suez, Iraq could presume to act like the major power in the Arab world, even if both Egypt and Saudi Arabia fiercely contested that claim. After Suez, there could be no hope of such a claim being accepted, and this in turn diminished the already declining domestic strength of Nuri's government. For just as the new order in Egypt gained internally from the pan-Arab legitimacy it acquired at Suez, so

---

[9] The almost farcical outcome is best described in the works cited in n. 7, especially that of Eveland, who was instrumental in the plot according to his own account.

[10] Seale, *The Struggle for Syria*, p. 282. Heikal, *Milaffat*, includes a number of fascinating documents on this subject.

did the old order in Iraq lose internally from the pan-Arab obloquy it suffered because of Suez.

In Jordan and Lebanon, the impact of Suez, although less decisive than in Syria and Iraq, was also great. Both were deeply fissured polities in the mid-1950s, with large segments of their populations (possibly a majority in both cases) still reluctant to accord legitimacy to their governments and even to the very existence of Jordan and Lebanon as states. The impact of the Suez crisis added markedly to the pressures both were already facing.

Jordan had been subject to intense political strains from within and without following its incorporation of a new majority of restive, politicized, and educated Palestinians after its annexation of the West Bank in 1950 (an annexation which was recognized by no Arab state). Strongly nationalist, anti-Hashemite, intensely anti-Zionist, and searching for a formula which would help them to regain their lost homeland, most of these Palestinians were strongly attracted to Egypt and to Nasser, as were many Jordanians. This was particularly the case after the British evacuation of the Canal in 1954 was followed by more active Egyptian leadership in the Arab world based on a policy of non-alignment and Arab nationalism. The Egyptian example was already influential before the Suez war: at the height of the crisis, on 21 October, just before the invasion began, a general election in Jordan returned a parliament dominated by an Arab nationalist majority, which soon produced the pro-Egyptian and anti-British government of Suleiman al-Nabulsi.

Although the King eventually overcame this popular current, ending parliamentary government and, during a period of martial law which lasted until 1963, reimposing his personal rule through hand-picked servants of the throne, the Anglo-Egyptian conflict over Suez and the resulting tripartite invasion had an impact on Jordan. They created a favourable regional environment for the Nabulsi government to come to power, terminate the Anglo-Jordanian treaty, and liquidate British bases. They also helped move Hussein away from his family's traditional patron, Great Britain, and eventually towards a new one, the United States, which in 1957 began subventions to Jordan which continue to this day. As for the country's restive population, Suez left most Palestinians and many Jordanians with an allegiance to Arab nationalism and a devotion to Nasser, which frequently focused on the Palestine issue. This powerful current continued to express itself in spite of governmental repression, often exploding and forcing the hand of the King at times of crisis, such as the years preceding and following the 1967 war.

In Lebanon too, the new assertiveness of Egyptian policy before and after Suez struck a responsive chord, particularly among Sunnis, Druze, and many Greek Orthodox Christians who chafed at Maronite domination of the Lebanese system, opposed President Chamoun's strong pro-Western orientation, and were not fully reconciled to the idea of the total separation of Lebanon from its Arab hinterland. Chamoun's blatant rigging of the 1957 parliamentary elections (with funds provided by the American intelligence services, according to the account of the man who personally handed some of the money over to the Lebanese President,[11]) further inflamed passions. The resulting polarization ended in the civil war of the summer of 1958, a conflict which seems almost genteel by comparison with the horrors the country has witnessed since 1975.

The Nasserist current in Lebanon, powerfully reinforced by the effect of Suez, was enshrined in a number of forms. One was the strict observance by Chamoun's successor, President Shihab, of a foreign policy closely aligned with that of Egypt. Thus insulated from the potential wrath of the dominant power in the Arab world, Lebanon was able to escape many of the stresses which affected other regional states in the late 1950s and early 1960s, until the Palestine issue forcefully intruded itself after the 1967 war. Another form taken by the influence of Egypt and its leader in Lebanon following the victory of Suez was the rapid proliferation of Nasserist organizations in the popular quarters of the Sunni cities of the coast. Vestiges of some of these, such as the Nasserist Popular Organization in Sidon and the Arab Socialist Union (which united in 1987) linger on even today.

In the sectarian political environment of Lebanon, as to a lesser extent in Iraq and Syria during the late 1950s, Nasserism was among many other things an ideological and organizational bastion for the Sunni urban populace. It held somewhat less appeal for Christians or Shiites, Kurds, or Alawis in all three countries.[12] Although Nasserism was primarily an expression of pan-Arab sentiment, in the Lebanese, Iraqi, and Syrian contexts it was also (occasionally perhaps even more so) a sectarian expression of identity by urban Sunnis. This factor should not be overemphasized, for the ideological aspects of Nasserism, whether in terms of anti-imperialism, non-alignment, or a striving for social justice, affected most sectors of these societies. This was particularly true after the Suez crisis confirmed the status of Arab nationalism as the primary vehicle of expression for the long-standing Arab desire

[11] This was again Eveland, who tells this story on pp. 248–53 of his book.
[12] For some of these sectarian factors, see Eveland. On Iraq see Hanna Batatu, *The Old Social Classes and the Revolutionary Movements of Iraq* (Princeton, 1978); on Syria, Seale and Nikolaos Van Dam, *The Struggle for Power in Syria: Sectarianism, Religion and Tribalism in Politics, 1961–1980* (2nd ed., London, 1981); and on Lebanon, Michael Hudson, *The Precarious Republic* (New York, 1968).

for national dignity and for the elimination of the last vestiges of foreign domination. Nevertheless, Western efforts to combat Egyptian influence in the mid-1950s, via mobilization of diverse local forces, especially sectarian ones, seem to have spurred the emergence of a largely Sunni Nasserist tendency in certain countries as a response.

Lebanon, where the mainly Christian Phalangist and Syrian Social Nationalist parties (the latter known by the initials PPS for *Parti Populaire Syrien*) backed President Chamoun, and where the opposition was organized largely (but not entirely) along sectarian lines, was the most extreme example in this regard. In Syria as well, the opposition to Arab nationalism and Nasser of the largely Christian PPS, widely suspected of being controlled by the CIA, and the involvement in the 1956 coup plot of a leading Aleppo Christian politician, Mikhail Ilyan, aroused long-standing Syrian fears of minority sectarian forces being used against the nationalist movement by the Western powers. In Iraq after the 1958 revolution, the allegiance of many Shiites and Kurds to Iraqi independence, which they expressed via the Communist party and other vehicles, including support for Nasser's rival, Iraqi leader Abd al-Karim Qasim, was matched by loyalty of urban Sunnis to Nasserism, a contradiction which came to a bloody conclusion in Mosul in 1959 and afterwards.

It might be noted in passing that the prestige which accrued to Egypt in the Arab world as a result of Suez meant that henceforth it would be the Egyptian interpretation of Arab nationalism—in practice that of Nasser and the circle around him—which prevailed, rather than versions that had emerged in the Arab countries to the east, which were the original cradle of Arab nationalism. Thus, when Syria and Egypt united in 1958, it was on the basis of Egypt's preferences and understanding of Arab unity rather than those of the Syrian Ba'th party that the new union was organized. Egypt, which had come relatively recently to Arabism, thus found itself in the lead, rather than Syria, which had prided itself on being 'the beating heart of Arabism' for nearly half a century. In practice, the result was that Arabism took on a more activist and pragmatic form than it would have had the Ba'th party or another such formation continued as its primary protagonist. The story of the role of Arab nationalism in the efforts of Egypt's diplomatic, information, and intelligence services in the Arab world after Suez will perhaps one day be told.

Egypt's ascendancy in the Arab world was probably inevitable even before Suez, and indeed it was perhaps only because it seemed so that Britain, France, and Israel chose to attack Egypt in the first place. But Suez set the seal on this process, giving a powerful impetus to Egyptian influence on the internal politics not only of those Arab countries we have already briefly examined, but others further afield, such as Algeria, Libya, North and South Yemen, Saudi Arabia and other states of the Arabian Peninsula.[13]

Egypt had an impact as well on the Palestinian polity, within Jordan and outside of it. Events before and after Suez played a major role in the revival of the Palestinian nationalist movement, which earlier had been crippled by its defeat in 1947–8 and the resultant expulsion and flight of about 750,000 Palestinians from their homes. While the Palestinian national movement before 1948 had been relatively weak, divided, and disorganized, it expressed faithfully the fierce desire of the Arab population for the independence of their country as well as its freedom from domination by any of the Arab regimes. These trends re-emerged as the Palestinian national movement slowly and clandestinely revived in the 1950s, in large measure under the impetus of Suez, and provided important elements of continuity with the pre-1948 period.

Although Suez and the other triumphs of the Egyptian regime convinced many Palestinians that their salvation lay in alliance with the powerful new force of Arab nationalism, whether in its Nasserist or Ba'thist variety, others, particularly those with experience in the Gaza Strip or inside Egypt itself, drew different conclusions. For them, the lessons of Suez, and of their several years of experience with the new regime in Egypt before the Suez war, were altogether more ambivalent. Unlike Palestinians in Jordan, Lebanon, and Syria, who tended to think of Egypt as a distant and benevolent ally against Israel and their local opponents and oppressors, most Palestinians in the Gaza Strip and Egypt saw things quite differently.[14] They were intimately acquainted with the fact that Egypt's commitment to the Palestine cause was necessarily almost completely subject to sober considerations of *raison d'état*. Many of them had learned these hard lessons inside Egyptian prisons. They had been sent there for launching attacks on Israel which contravened the new regime's desire to avoid tensions with its formidable Israeli neighbour. Some Palestinian nationalists were only released from prison in the period immediately before the Suez war in order to launch such attacks when it suited Egypt's policy of the moment.

The lesson a group of men from this background who secretly formed the nucleus of Fatah in the mid-1950s drew was that the Palestinians must have a status independent of the Arab regimes, even

---

[13] On the considerable impact of Egypt and Nasserism on the Arabian Peninsula, see Fred Halliday, *Arabia without Sultans* (London, 1974).

[14] This is well brought out in Laurie Brand, *Palestinians in the Arab World: Institution Building and the Search for a State* (New York, 1988).

that of Nasser, whom they feared, respected, and at times assiduously courted. Speaking of this period, Salah Khalaf (Abu Iyad), a founder of Fatah, stated: 'We believed that the Palestinians could rely only on themselves'.[15] This current led by Fatah came to be the dominant one in the reborn Palestinian national movement, and its leaders have been the most prominent ones in the PLO in the years since that organization was taken over by independent Palestinian nationalist factions in 1968.

The other major current in Palestinian nationalism, that led by the Arab Nationalist Movement (ANM), founded in the early 1950s by Palestinian graduates of the American University in Beirut like Dr George Habash and Dr Wadi Haddad, soon became almost an auxiliary of Egyptian foreign policy. Unlike the ANM, Fatah from the outset tried to maintain its distance from Egypt, eventually developing relations with the neo-Ba'th regime in Syria and the Algerian revolution, in part to play them off against the powerful centrifugal pull of Egypt. It was significant for the course of Palestinian politics that Fatah, with its nuanced attitude towards Egypt born of events both before and after Suez, and its insistence on 'the independence of the Palestinian decision',[16] came to dominate the Palestinian polity over the three decades after Suez.

THE ARAB–ISRAELI CONFLICT

However important were the changes wrought by Suez on the Arab world's relations with the great powers and on its internal politics, the crisis had perhaps its most lasting impact on the Arab–Israeli conflict. Israel's attack on Egypt—when seen against the background of earlier related incidents between these two countries, such as the *Bat-Galim* and Lavon affairs of 1954, the Israeli attack on Gaza of February 1955, and the Khan Yunis raid of August 1955—can be said to have fundamentally transformed that conflict. After Suez, it changed definitively from a dispute primarily related to the question of the disposition of Palestine, albeit one with important implications for the regional power balance, into an inter-state conflict for regional hegemony. This conflict concerned bilateral issues which were often

---

[15] Abu Iyad, *My Home, My Land*, p. 20.

[16] This has been a favourite slogan of the Fatah leadership for several decades. As a rule, it comes into prominence in moments of tension with a major Arab regime, e.g. during the clashes with Syria in 1976 and again in 1983–7. See the resolutions of the 17th and 18th sessions of the Palestine National Council, in 1984 and 1987, for the prominent use of this term: *Journal of Palestine Studies*, 14: 2 (winter, 1985) 257, and 16: 4 (summer, 1987), 196. In the latter the wording is: 'Adhering to the PLO's independence and rejecting . . . interference in its internal affairs.'

unrelated to Palestine and involved Israel and several Arab countries, foremost among them Egypt.

The potential for such a development had always been there, and indeed was implicit from the very beginning of the Arab states' involvement in the Palestine question in the late 1930s. However, it took Israel's 1956 invasion of Sinai, seen as the culmination of a specific line of policy pursued by Ben-Gurion and his followers from 1954 (and best analysed by Avi Shlaim in an important article,[17]) to make this potential real. With Suez, Israel in a sense succeeded, at least for a number of years, in pushing the conflict into its neighbours' territory, making them fight on its terms, obscuring the Palestinian core of the dispute, and putting the Arab states on the defensive. In a sense this represented a continuation of the last phase of the Palestine war of 1948–9, when Israeli forces triumphed on all fronts and invaded Egyptian territory. Suez, however, took Israel much farther, and much more strongly emphasized all these achievements.

It could be argued that as a result of factors such as this emerging from Suez, the 1947–9 war was the last one fought primarily over the disposition of Palestine until the 1982 Israeli invasion of Lebanon. The fighting from 1967 to 1973 thus followed a pattern set by Suez, in that it involved the balance of power between Israel and the Arab states, the question of regional hegemony, and the interests of the super-powers far more than it did the interests of the Palestinians or the fate of their homeland. A cynic might argue further that, while the interest of most Arab regimes in the Palestine question until 1949 reflected in large measure the genuine sympathy of Arab public opinion for the Palestinians, after that it dwindled into rhetorical decoration for these regimes' *realpolitik* attitudes towards Israel (with a few exceptions such as the Syrian neo-Ba'th regime of 1966–70, or the initial years of Algerian independence).[18] From this perspective, Suez accelerated an existing trend. Even without going quite so far, it is clear that Suez, and the aggressive tendency in Israeli policy towards the Arab states championed by Ben-Gurion and his disciples which it represented, refocused the Palestine conflict into an Arab–Israeli dispute. It furthermore deprived the Arab regimes of the illusion that they could ignore Israel.

[17] Avi Shlaim, 'Conflicting Approaches to Israel's Relations with the Arabs: Ben-Gurion and Sharett, 1953–1956', *The Middle East Journal*, 37: 2 (spring, 1983), 180–201. Some of these issues are dealt with in S. Shamir's and M. Bar-On's chapters in this volume, as well as in works by Egyptian and Israeli authors cited by Shamir.

[18] This argument, influential in the Arab world over more than a decade and seen in the writings of Naji 'Alloush, Sadiq Jalal al-'Azm, and others, is set forth in Ibrahim Barhoum, 'The Arab States' Acceptance of Israel, 1949–1979', MA thesis (Political Studies and Public Administration Department, American University of Beirut, 1981).

In the specific case of Egypt, Suez completed a major, wrenching shift in attitudes which had only begun two years earlier. This involved a reorientation by the new Egyptian regime away from its initial focus on domestic affairs and the issue of British bases on Egyptian soil to a wider arena. Perhaps this shift can be said to have begun when Egypt's leaders came to see that the problems of British bases and relations with Britain were linked to a related struggle with Britain and its clients for regional dominance—a struggle waged in Syria, Jordan, and Lebanon, as well as farther afield. But it had its most long-lasting consequences when Israel added its own unique ingredients to this explosive mix.

There has long been a controversy about the lead-up to the Egyptian–Israeli component of the 1956 war. One school would have it that Egypt in fact provoked Israel over a period of several years.[19] This seems hard to sustain in view of the work done by Shlaim and the revelations in Moshe Sharett's diaries,[20] which not only show that Ben-Gurion and his followers in the Israeli establishment were largely responsible for the war (or at least its Israeli component), but also bear out the long-standing Egyptian contention that until 1955 Egypt would have preferred to avoid a conflict with Israel, and the arms buildup this entailed. In Shlaim's words: 'The 1956 war was not the product of an Arab strategy but of an Israeli strategy which could only be implemented following the triumph of the Ben Gurion faction in the internal power struggle.'[21]

The litmus test of Egyptian intentions towards Israel can be said to be its attitude towards the Palestinians during this period. For before the Israeli challenges of 1954 and 1955 (the *Bat-Galim* affair, the 1954 Israeli sabotage attacks on American and British institutions in Egypt revealed during the Lavon affair, and the Gaza attack of February 1955), Palestinian and Israeli primary sources are unanimous in describing an unyielding Egyptian opposition to any Palestinian attacks on Israel, at a time that secret talks were going on between Nasser and Sharett. Shlaim notes that a study by the Israeli Arabist Ehud Ya'ari, based on

[19] This is the thesis, e.g., of Uri Ra'anan, who goes to great lengths in *The USSR Arms the Third World* (Cambridge, Mass., 1969), to show the Egyptian–Soviet arms deal to have been negotiated before Israel's attack on Gaza in February 1955, thus signifying Egypt's prior aggressive intentions.

[20] Sharett's diaries, published in Hebrew in Tel Aviv in 8 volumes from 1978 until 1980 under the title *Yoman Ishi* (Personal Diary), have proven a fertile source for researchers, and include much material at odds with the received version of Israel's early years. Livia Rokach's study entitled *Israel's Sacred Terrorism* (Belmont, Mass., 1980) includes translations from the diaries bearing on Suez, the Lavon affair, and other related matters.

[21] Shlaim, 'Conflicting Approaches', p. 201. Shlaim's equally radical revisionist conclusions regarding other aspects of the conflict can be found in *Collusion Across the Jordan: King Abdullah, the Zionist Movement and the Partition of Palestine* (New York, 1988).

records of Egyptian military intelligence captured by Israel during the Sinai War confirm[s] that until the Gaza raid the Egyptian authorities had a firm and consistent policy of curbing infiltration by Palestinians from the Gaza Strip into Israel, and that it was only in the aftermath of the Gaza raid that a new policy got underway of organizing the *fedayeen* and turning them into an official instrument of warfare against Israel.[22]

Thus raids launched from Gaza by one of Salah Khalaf's comrades, Khalil al-Wazir (Abu Jihad) in 1954 led to his being 'promptly arrested by Egyptian Security'.[23] Only well *after* the floodgates had been opened by the victory within the Israeli Cabinet of Ben-Gurion's aggressive line, which resulted in the bloody attack on Gaza in February 1955—in 'reprisal' for Palestinian attacks which the Egyptian authorities had done their best to prevent—did Egypt change its policy and begin to sponsor *fedayeen* attacks.

The rest is well known: Palestinian attacks later in 1955, acquiesced in or instigated by Egyptian intelligence, led to even bloodier Israeli reprisal raids in August 1955 at Khan Yunis and in November 1955 at el-Auja, as the Ben-Gurion line gained strength. In the interim the Soviet arms deal was announced, and soon war was inevitable. It had not been inevitable in 1954, any more than was the resulting resurgence of Palestinian nationalism, which was inflamed by the events of 1954–6 and the subsequent harsh Israeli occupation of the Gaza Strip. Although the effect of this resurgence did not appear immediately (Fatah was founded in 1959, and only revealed itself in 1965), it is not a coincidence that almost without exception the men who have played the most central leadership roles in the Palestinian national movement since then—Arafat, Khalaf, al-Wazir, and others—were in Egypt and the Gaza Strip at this time, were deeply involved in these events, and all describe them in retrospect as formative ones for them.[24]

The Suez war, its antecedents, and its aftermath thus not only contributed to a transformation of the conflict between Israel and the Arabs, inaugurating or accentuating crucial inter-state dynamics, unrelated to the question of Palestine *per se*, which proved long-lasting. It also played a role in sparking off the modern resurgence of Palestinian nationalism, thus ultimately reviving an older aspect of the conflict which many Israeli leaders had hoped they had permanently buried: the Palestinian–Israeli one. Today the inter-state conflict

[22] See Shlaim, 'Conflicting Approaches', p. 188, also Abu Iyad, *My Home, My Land*, p. 22, and Alan Hart, *Arafat: Terrorist or Peacemaker?* (London, 1984), which is based on interviews with Khalil al-Wazir and Arafat, pp. 98–110. Both books, and all other Palestinian accounts of the period, confirm Shlaim and Ya'ari's assessments.

[23] Abu Iyad, *My Home, My Land*, p. 24. The same events are described in Hart, *Arafat*, pp. 100–103.

[24] See the works cited in the preceding note for the testimony of all three.

between Israel and the Arabs has been settled in the case of Egypt, is virtually dormant in the case of Jordan, and has been quiet between Israel and Syria since 1974 except for their potentially explosive proxy wars in Lebanon. One of the most enduring legacies of Suez may thus prove to be its contribution to the reactivation of the conflict's Palestinian–Israeli aspect.

22

Conclusion

ALBERT HOURANI

THE events which we call 'the Suez crisis' seemed at the time—and perhaps still seem in retrospect—to be more than ordinary happenings: one of those moments when

> ... graves have yawn'd, and yielded up their dead;
> Fierce fiery Warriours fight upon the Clouds
> In Rankes and Squadrons, and right forme of Warre
> Which drizel'd blood upon the Capitoll:
> The noise of Battell hurtled in the Ayre ...
> And Ghosts did shrieke and squeale about the Streets.[1]

Some of those who were actively involved in the crisis seemed to be moved to action by the sight of ghosts from the past. For Eden and those who thought like him in Britain, 1956 was a repetition of 1938, but one which should have a different ending: Nasser was throwing down a challenge to the order of the world, but this time the challenge should be met. Some of his supporters saw this as the moment to halt or reverse that retreat from power and responsibility which had begun with the withdrawal from India in 1947. The men who controlled the French government were engaged, Vaïsse tells us, in 'a veritable contest of collective memory'; they were moved by recollections of Munich and the Resistance, the withdrawal from the Levant, imposed upon France in its weakness by its allies, and the defeat in Indo-China. When Nasser spoke in Alexandria, announcing the nationalization of the Suez Canal Company, he called up in the minds of his listeners the collective memory of what the building of the Canal had meant to the Egyptian peasants forced to work on it; when he rallied the nation at the moment of the attack, he went to the Azhar mosque, the central point of the moral universe of Egypt for many centuries. When Israeli soldiers reached Mount Sinai in their advance, Ben-Gurion hailed it as a return 'to the place where the Law was given, and where we were commanded to be a Chosen People'.[2] In the mind of Eisenhower, did

---

[1] Shakespeare, *Julius Caesar*, Act II, Scene ii.
[2] Quoted in E. B. Childers, *The Road to Suez* (London, 1962), p. 176.

memories of the alliance of two world wars clash with thoughts of the
revolt against colonial rule?

It would be wrong, however, to think of the protagonists simply as
actors in a drama, moving in a formal dance, even if this may have
been how they appeared to some observers and opponents: Eden
vanishing into clouds of unreality under the stress of illness, or Nasser
as an Othello rolling his eyes to heaven in the throes of a megalomaniac
passion. While the ghosts of the past did come to the surface under the
pressure of crisis, they did so because they were consonant with, and
gave strength to, the national interests which each of the protagonists
thought he was pursuing. They can be seen as symbolic ways of
expressing those interests, but also as having their own force, tending to
distort the ways in which interests were pursued, and tempt politicians
to carry their actions beyond the bounds of reason. Fully to understand
what happened, it is necessary to look beyond the myths to what
Shamir calls the 'inner logic' of the various attitudes and policies.

At bottom, the crisis was one which arose out of the relations of
Britain with Egypt and with the United States, and most of the
problems which the chapters in this book try to resolve—and some
which may still perplex the historian—are problems about the logic of
British policies.

There is no mystery about the essence of those policies. To put it
briefly, the aim of the Eden government, as it had been that of the
Attlee and Churchill governments which preceded it, was to preserve
the Middle East (or at least the Arab parts of it) as a region in which
Britain could still act independently as a great power, and indeed as the
dominant power. This was, with one significant difference, a continuation of Bevin's policy of preserving British power in the age of
independent nation-states. The policy had been shaken by what was
generally regarded as a British defeat during the Palestine crisis of
1948, but had not been destroyed. The United States was willing to
leave to Britain the major part in the defence of Western interests;
Britain continued to have a special position in Iraq, Jordan, Libya, and
parts of the Arabian Peninsula, relations with Syria and Lebanon were
good, those with Israel had improved, and those with Egypt seemed
likely to be strengthened by the agreement of 1954; the British share in
the oil industry was important, and sterling was still a major international currency.

For such a policy to succeed, the 'pro-Western' regimes, and that of
Iraq in particular, had to be supported; strongly 'anti-Western'
regimes should be checked or even destroyed, if necessary by covert
action or force (here lay the difference from Bevin's policy).[3] European

---

[3] See W. R. Louis, *The British Empire in the Middle East, 1945–1951* (Oxford, 1984), *passim*.

access to the oil supplies of Iraq, Saudi Arabia, and the Gulf had to be maintained, at prices fixed by the cartel of great oil companies. This was important not only because the oil was essential for the recovery of the British and European economies after the war, but also for financial reasons: the companies in which British investments were large were highly profitable, and the oil could be paid for in sterling.

Such a policy, in the circumstances of the world at that time, presupposed a special relationship with the United States: the US government would be willing to accept Britain's position as the main guardian of western interests in the region, and use its power to support British actions. Until the summer of 1956, this condition was fulfilled. The two governments worked together to overturn the regime of Musaddiq in Iran and make a new arrangement for the control of the export and sale of Iranian oil. They supported the creation of a defensive alliance of countries lying round the southern rim of the Soviet Union. Although there was some suspicion on the British side that the Americans had shown too much sympathy towards Egypt during the difficult period of tension and negotiation which led to the agreement of 1954, once that agreement was made it met with American approval. Both powers believed that good relations with Egypt were necessary, not only in the hope that Egypt's neutralist policy could be inclined in favour of the West, but also, and more urgently, because Egypt was seen to hold the key to the resolution of the problem of Arab–Israeli relations. They were in general agreement on this, and the discussions they held with each other, with Israel, and with Egypt were, as Shamir shows, pursued with great determination and a certain optimism, although the minimal demands of the two sides were too far apart to make agreement possible at that time.

The attitude of the two governments towards Egypt and its leader changed in March 1956, but it was a change which involved both of them and caused no breach between them. It may partly have been that the failure of the attempt to resolve the Arab–Israeli problem by means of the Alpha plan weakened their interest in Nasser, but there were also more positive reasons for the change of attitude. Egyptian neutralism seemed to be inclining more in the Russian direction; Kyle refers to reports from M.I.6 (for what they may be worth) claiming that Nasser had become a 'Ṣoviet instrument', and the United States was alarmed by the Egyptian purchase of arms from the Soviet bloc and recognition of Communist China. More important, at least in British eyes, was the growing breach between Egypt and the 'pro-Western' Arab states, and Iraq in particular. Here too there may have been an irrational element of misunderstanding and dislike between Nasser and the leading Iraqi politician, Nuri Said; not only was there a gap between the generations, there was also a distance between a child of the Egyptian peasantry, with its long hostility to Turkish rule, and a former officer of the Ottoman army who, for all his Arab nationalist sentiments, still had something of the acquired attitudes of the Ottoman ruling élite in its last age. This too should not be exaggerated, however; at the root of the disagreement lay two different national interests, and two opposed views about the place of the Middle East in world affairs. What added to the tension, and to British distrust of Nasser, was his fateful decision to appeal over the heads of Arab governments to their peoples, in the name of a real or supposed common nationality, in particular by means of the radio station called, significantly, *The Voice of the Arabs.*

The decision to withdraw the offer of British and American aid for the building of the High Dam was a joint decision: an official of the Foreign Office, according to Kyle, said there was 'no more than a nuance' of difference between the points of view of the two governments. Dulles recorded that the interview at which he conveyed this decision to the Egyptian emissary was polite and reasonable. This may have been because the government of Egypt had already come to the conclusion that the United States was not going to provide aid, and was therefore prepared for the decision; but the way in which the emissary appeared to receive it may have given the United States government cause to hope that Egypt would not react with undue heat, and friendly relations would continue to exist. The nationalization of the Suez Canal Company came as a surprise, and it ended the harmony of British and American policies.

It is clear from what Kyle and other writers say—if indeed it was not clear before—that from the moment of nationalization Eden's government was determined to get rid of the Nasser regime, by force if necessary. The plan to assassinate Nasser, to which Peter Wright refers in his book *Spycatcher*,[4] may have been no more than a fantasy hatched in the underworld of M.I.6, but the plans of military action, in their successive stages, were intended to be carried out. There was no wish for a negotiated settlement; the attack was finally agreed upon, and put into action, at a time when discussions at the United Nations seemed to bring closer the prospect of a peaceful resolution of the crisis.

It is at this point that a certain irrational element comes to the surface in British thoughts and statements. Nasser becomes a new Mussolini, if not quite a Hitler: his book, *The Philosophy of the Revolution*, had at first been quite well received, but now became a new version of *Mein Kampf*. In the tormented mind of Eden, there may have been some loss of judgement, due perhaps to ill health: of that judgement

[4] Peter Wright, *Spycatcher* (New York, 1987), pp. 160–1.

and skill which he had shown as recently as 1954, his *annus mirabilis*, the year of the agreements about Trieste and Indo-China, the Anglo-Egyptian agreement, and the resolution of the problem of Iranian oil. The hostility towards Nasser was not confined to Eden, however. British politicians and officials delivered apocalyptic statements and prophecies of doom: 'I remain firmly convinced', wrote the Colonial Secretary, Lennox-Boyd, 'that if Nasser wins or even appears to win we might as well as a government (and indeed as a country) go out of business'; the Commonwealth Secretary, Lord Home, said, 'I am convinced that we are finished if the Middle East goes'; Kirkpatrick, Permanent Under-Secretary at the Foreign Office, spelled it out in detail (as quoted in Kyle's chapter):

If we sit back while Nasser consolidates his position and gradually acquires control of the oil-bearing countries, he can, and is, according to our information, resolved to wreck us. . . . I doubt whether we shall be able to pay for the bare minimum necessary for our defence. And a country that cannot provide for its defence is finished.

Behind such extreme statements, however, there lay some rational calculations. Nasser's action could reasonably be seen as posing a threat to certain British interests. It could be regarded as a sign of his determination to dominate the Arab countries and ensure that the outside world should deal with them by way of Cairo; this might at least bring about a change in the favourable position which Western oil companies held in Arabia and the Gulf, and at worst it might weaken the position of Arab regimes at present linked with Britain or the United States, and lead to their replacement by neutralist governments more inclined towards the Soviet Union. One feature of the crisis which may need more explanation than it has received in these chapters is the influence exercised upon the British government by Iraq and other countries in a similar position. The King of Iraq, accompanied by Nuri Said, was dining at 10 Downing Street on the evening when news of the nationalization of the Suez Canal Company was received, and Nuri urged Selwyn Lloyd to 'hit Nasser hard and quickly'.[5] (Here too, there may have been an element of irrational feeling: Eden may have shared the belief of many British Arabists of his generation that somehow the Egyptians were not true Arabs, but a mongrel race who had no right to claim the leadership of the Arab world.)

To take military action, however, posed political problems, as well as

---

[5] Robert Rhodes James, *Anthony Eden* (London, 1986), p. 453. See also minute by Michael Wright on conversation with Nuri Said and the Crown Prince, 30 July 1956: Public Record Office, FO371/121662. (I owe this reference to Keith Kyle.)

the strategic problems of timing, place, and method. One of them was that of making a military assault upon Egypt acceptable to the British public, to world opinion, and to the opinion of those Arab countries which had close links with Britain. It would not have been enough, once the first flush of indignation was over, to say that Nasser's action was contrary to international law; apart from the Lord Chancellor, the government's advisers on law did not believe it to be illegal. The argument that Egypt was not able to keep the Canal open to shipping was soon proved to be false; the British government tried its best to show it to be true, by arranging for an exceptionally large number of ships to approach the Canal at the same time, but the pilots employed by Egypt were able to cope with them.

It was in this context that the French plan for an Israeli attack upon Egypt, followed by British and French intervention, ostensibly to restore peace, seemed attractive to Eden. The operation would be a 'peace-keeping' one; the British public, the Commonwealth, the United States, and the United Nations might be persuaded to accept it as such. There was one difficulty, however: those whom Eden thought of as real or good Arabs, and Iraq in particular, would not look kindly upon a British attack arranged in advance with Israel; when, that evening in Downing Street, Nuri had told Eden to act now, he had said that it should be done without the Israelis. It was for this reason, among others, that the agreement with France and Israel had to be secret and deniable, and that Eden was so angry when told that it had been embodied in a written document. To think that it could be kept secret was childish, however, and perhaps the best sign that Eden by this time had lost his judgement. The Foreign Office, British Ambassadors, and Commonwealth governments could be kept in the dark, and the House of Commons could be misled by official denials, which it accepted with surprising meekness, but neither the French nor the Israelis had any reason to keep the agreement secret, and they had some reason indeed for making it public, in order to oblige the British government to carry out the pledge which it had shown itself somewhat reluctant to give. The French Foreign Minister, Christian Pineau, told the US Ambassador in Paris about the agreement on the very day the Anglo-French ultimatum was published.

So much is clear from the chapters in this volume. There are at least two problems, however, on which further light is needed. First, what was the regime which the British government thought would replace that of Nasser if the military action was successful? This is a question which it is still difficult to answer. It is not easy to believe that there had been no soundings of Egyptian politicians in advance, but there is no clear evidence of it, and Kyle states that the relevant documents in the

Public Record Office are not accessible. No doubt, during the years of Nasser's rule, members of the opposition had expressed the hope to British officials or ministers that he would be overthrown, by overt action or in other ways, and had indicated that they would be more friendly to British interests. It may be that this was all the British government was relying on; if so, this too would have been an error of judgement, for politicians who would have been willing to take power after a *coup d'état* similar to that which had overturned Musaddiq in Iran, might well have hesitated to do so after a foreign invasion; even if they had agreed, they could not easily have remained in office unless the British occupation were to be a permanent one.

It may be that political thinking did not keep pace with the military planning. The early military plan had provided for little more than bombardment from the air, a landing by limited forces, and psychological warfare; the assumption was that this would precipitate some kind of internal movement which would lead to the overthrow of Nasser. If it was assumed that this would be sufficient, then there would be no problem about finding an alternative government which would not need British military support. It was only gradually that the military planners came to the belief that there would be serious resistance from Egyptian forces, and the attack would be a real operation with many Egyptian civilian casualties, but perhaps the politicians did not draw the political implications of this. Unless there was to be a more or less permanent British occupation, would any Egyptian politician have been willing to take responsibility under the shadow of British and French forces, and after Cairo and Alexandria had been bombed and occupied? The only alternative authority which did not need to look for public support, the monarchy, no longer existed, as it had existed during the British occupation of 1882: when the British refused to intervene at the time when King Farouk was deposed, he is said to have warned them that they would regret it.

There is another problem about which more perhaps needs to be said. Since World War II a major aim of British policy, in the Miidle East as elsewhere, had been to make sure that Britain acted with American agreement or at least friendly acquiescence. Why then did it act at Suez in a way which incurred direct and effective American opposition? In spite of British accusations that the government was misled, the attitude of the United States government was clear from the beginning of the crisis, and it had been explained to the British and French throughout the long weeks of negotiation. The United States did not want to see the Canal fall under the total control of Egypt, and wished for an arrangement by which there could be some kind of international supervision (but not for the return of the Suez Canal

Company). It did not believe, however, that this was an issue which could or should be decided by war. It wished to limit the growing power of Nasser, and in certain circumstances might be willing to contemplate overturning him by covert action, as it had done to Musaddiq, but it did not think that this was 'the issue on which to bring Nasser down'.

There may have been some ambiguities in Dulles's ways of expressing himself; Nasser, he said, must be made to 'disgorge'. It is impossible, however, to believe that Eden and his associates misunderstood what the Americans were telling them. Why did they think that, in spite of what he told them, Eisenhower would accept their action: at worst he would not oppose it, and at best might even give some degree of diplomatic or financial support? The answer to the question seems to lie in the belief that, when it came to the point, the United States could do nothing. This calculation may have been based partly on the imminence of the presidential election in the United States, partly on a misreading of Eisenhower's character, based upon memories of the time when he was Commander-in-Chief of the allied forces in North Africa and then in Europe; but a military commander of mixed armies, responsible to more than one government, was bound to act in quite a different way from the President of the United States. There may also have been a belief that, if its hand was forced, the United States would have no alternative to supporting the British action, and might even secretly approve of it; it would recognize that the British 'understood the Middle East', or that the unity of the Western alliance and the maintenance of the sterling bloc were more important than relations with Egypt. As Chancellor of the Exchequer, Macmillan played a part in encouraging this illusion; he had not raised the matter of Suez during his recent meeting with Eisenhower in Washington, and may have taken it for granted that the United States at the very least would give immediate aid to sterling in the difficulties which would be caused by a temporary interruption of oil supplies from the Middle East to Europe. This was a fatal miscalculation, for—as Kunz makes clear— the United States was only willing to give help after the British withdrew from Egypt.

Compared with the complexities of British aims and calculations, those of the other principal actors seem comparatively simple. Although Nasser was portrayed by his enemies as a crazed megalomaniac, there was a logical pattern in his intentions and actions. Coming to power without much knowledge of the outside world, he was gradually moving towards a certain conception of world politics, and of Egypt's role in it. He wished Egypt and other countries of the Middle East to be really independent, and in his view this implied that they should not be too closely linked with either of the power blocs, but should keep a careful distance from both of them. He believed too that the Arab countries should be united in their actions, and that Egypt should be their leader. This implied, in his view, that Arab countries should not pursue policies which were incompatible with Egyptian interests. The Baghdad Pact appeared to him to pose a triple danger: it bound an important Arab country to one of the power blocs, and threatened to bring other countries in; it breached the unity of the Arab states; and it set up Baghdad as an alternative centre of leadership, decision, and negotiation with the great powers. Although the logic of the Egyptian position would in due course lead to Nasser adopting the Palestinian cause as an Egyptian cause, there is no clear evidence that he wished at this time to support it in any way except that of negotiation. In spite of what the Israeli government believed, it is unlikely that he was planning an attack upon Israel; Egypt was just beginning a process of rearming its forces, and at the best of times it could only hope to challenge Israel in armed conflict if it had the kind of external support which it did not then possess. The purchase of arms from Czechoslovakia was a response to Israel's purchase of arms from France; support for the Palestinian *fedayeen* in the Gaza Strip was a riposte to the Israeli raid on Egyptian soldiers in the Strip, and was withdrawn during the period of delicate negotiation after the nationalization of the Suez Canal Company.

There is, however, a question to raise about one aspect of Egyptian policy. Was the nationalization of the Company simply a response to the withdrawal of the offer of aid for building the High Dam, or was it planned and premeditated in advance? No clear answer can be given. The idea that Egypt should take control of its canal was one which had been in the minds of Egyptian nationalists at least since the conflict over the renewal of the concession in 1909, but it is unlikely that Nasser would have done it without being given the opportunity presented by what appeared to Egyptians as a public humiliation by the United States and Britain. He showed the tactical sense which had been displayed throughout his political career. Once the act was done, he seems to have used all his efforts to bring about a peaceful solution, but one which would leave Egypt in control of the Canal. His policy was one of going as far as he could without losing his hold on the situation, in the hope that, at the brink, the United States or United Nations would pull his enemies back.

There is little that is obscure about the aims of Israel too, or at least of its Prime Minister, Ben-Gurion, once he had re-established his ascendancy after a moment when he seemed to have lost it. According to Bar-On, he believed that Egypt was preparing to attack Israel, but it is difficult to understand why he thought so; he must have been aware of the conditions on which either Egypt or Israel would be able to mount an attack upon the other. The Arab guerrilla attacks also were no more than a pinprick, a minor irritant. His basic reason is to be found in a certain view of Arab–Israeli relations to which he had come as early as the 1930s: that, while temporary accommodations might be possible, real peace would not come until the Arabs were convinced of the insuperable strength of the Jews in Palestine:

> only after total despair on the part of the Arabs, despair that will come not only from the failure of the disturbances and the attempt at rebellion, but also as a consequence of our growth in the country, may the Arabs possibly acquiesce in a Jewish Erez Israel.[6]

Such had been his conclusion in the time of the Mandate, and the creation of the state of Israel had given it added force. So long as there was no formal peace, it was possible to hope for a change of frontiers, and resist pressure to take back Arab refugees; to increase the number of Arabs in the new state, at a time of mass Jewish immigration, would have posed grave problems. It was with such considerations in mind that the Israeli government had taken the decision, at the Lausanne conference in 1949, not to offer to accept a substantial number of refugees, the essential condition of a peace settlement. Seen in this perspective, the rise of a strong leader in an Arab country, and particularly in Egypt, appeared as a danger. The negotiations over the Alpha plan had shown the gulf that existed between the least that Egypt would accept and the most that Israel would offer; it was necessary then to bring Nasser face to face with the reality of Israeli strength.

A demonstration of strength in the face of Egypt lay therefore in the 'inner logic' of Ben-Gurion's policy, but this had implications. He did not have the same need to justify his policy to the opinion of his own country as did Eden, but he needed a certain degree of military support from a greater power, and at least the absence of hostility from others. The military agreement with France provided part of what was needed: arms and the possibility even of direct support (such as was given in fact by the French during the Israeli advance). This was not sufficient by itself, however; Israel needed to be sure that Britain would not be hostile, as it would be if there were an attack upon Jordan, and the United States would at least be acquiescent. The agreement which was reached at Sèvres gave this assurance. There was no reason why Israel should keep it secret after the event, and some reason why it should not: a formal and acknowledged alliance would give Israel a

---

[6] David Ben-Gurion, *My Talks with Arab Leaders*, Eng. trs. (Jerusalem, 1972), pp. 15 f.

kind of legitimacy which it had not previously possessed. As Bar-On shows, it was only a sense of obligation to Eden which held Ben-Gurion back from revealing it.

French policy also showed none of the hesitation of British. As in Britain, there was a tendency to portray the situation in apocalyptic terms. To quote from Vaïsse's chapter (p. 137):

. . . we have only a few weeks in which to save North Africa. Of course, the loss of North Africa would then be followed by that of Black Africa, and the entire territory would rapidly escape European control and influence.

Such statements, however, were only an exaggerated expression of a rational policy. Even if the Algerian war could not be won by striking Nasser down, to weaken Egypt would at least cut down external support for the Algerians and might shake their confidence. A victory over the ruler of Egypt would also reassert France's traditional position as a Middle Eastern power from which, so most Frenchmen thought, it had been dislodged by British intrigue at the moment of France's mortal weakness.

The plan for a joint attack by Israel and France may have been first put forward by the Israelis, but the suggestion that the British should be brought in was made by the French General Challe. While the British needed to keep the agreement secret for their own purposes, the French had something to gain by making it public, once it had been put into practice: this would commit Britain to the plan and make it more difficult for them to withdraw.

The Soviet Union was a minor actor in the crisis. It seems clear that it had no possibility and no intention of intervening actively; apart from being involved in the Hungarian crisis which erupted at the same moment, its policy in the Middle East at the time was cautious and exploratory. Its relations with Egypt and Syria were not yet firm enough to provide a basis for an active policy, and it had no position of strength in the Middle East from which it could intervene. Without doing anything, however, it could only gain from the division which had appeared among the Western powers, and between them and the newly independent states of Asia. The crisis gave it an opportunity to assert the principle that the Middle East was an open region, one which was not the area of exclusive influence of a single power or a group of them, but where the interests of all had to be taken into account. The famous letter threatening that rockets might fall on London and Paris was only sent on 5 November, when it had become clear that the United States was opposed to the Anglo-French attack. It may have alarmed Britain and France, and made the United States more anxious to end the crisis quickly, but it was not a factor which decided the way in which the crisis would end.

It has become a commonplace to speak of the Suez crisis as a turning-point, but to do so is to raise two kinds of question: what exactly was it that turned, and did it turn because of what happened in the Suez crisis, or was the crisis simply a 'moment of truth', the sign of changes which were already taking place, not for one reason but for many?

In Britain, the crisis laid some ghosts to rest. The apocalyptic vision of a return of the 1930s vanished. Although none of those who had held responsibility at the time ever admitted that they had made a mistake, politicians henceforward spoke in different terms; Macmillan's remark about 'the winds of change' was to be the motto of the next decade. The crisis also showed clearly a change which had taken place, but had not yet been fully recognized: not even in the Middle East could Britain act as the dominant power, that is to say, as one which could make its interests prevail over all others. This had been true since 1945, but had not become apparent because of American willingness to acquiesce in Britain's playing the major role in the Arab parts of the Middle East. After 1956, no British government would take this acquiescence for granted, but, provided the ultimate consonance of British and American interests was accepted, the British position still appeared to be strong. By what may seem to be a paradox, the crisis showed the ultimate strength of the Anglo-American alliance. The speed with which good relations were restored owed something to the disappearance of Eden from the scene, and something to the personal link between Macmillan and Eisenhower, and then Macmillan and Kennedy, but it was due more deeply to a shared belief in common interests. British influence in the Middle East therefore remained, in Iraq, Jordan, and parts of Arabia, but it was exercised in implicit or explicit collaboration with the United States. This was shown two years later, when the Iraqi revolution of July 1958 was followed by a concerted intervention of the two powers, the United States in Lebanon and Britain in Jordan. This was a last effort, however; what seemed to be a reassertion of British power was only an echo. The Iraqi revolution destroyed the basis of Britain's position. The last vestiges of it disappeared between then and 1971; by this time the withdrawal from Africa had taken place, and the imperial age had come to an end.

One of the pillars of British policy was restored for the moment, but another was shown to be less solid than had been imagined. The Commonwealth had seemed to many in Britain to be a continuation of empire by other means, offering help and support in times of trouble, and making it possible for Britain still to play a major role in the world. The crisis was, as Lyon says, a 'psychological watershed' in the life of the Commonwealth. It showed that it was not a decision-making body, and could not serve, as it had done in two world wars, to bring together a significant concentration of forces. This was so even though it had not yet become the amorphous body of sovereign states that it is today. It was what Lyon calls 'a small, British-run international club'. At the moment of crisis, however, the members of the club were neither consulted nor informed by the British government, and they reacted to the British action in different ways: Australia supported it wholehear-tedly, New Zealand rather less so; Canada was not in favour of military action, and wished the crisis to be resolved by way of the United Nations. Nehru of India, as Gopal points out, thought that Nasser's decision to nationalize the Suez Canal Company had been taken 'in the wrong spirit', but believed that the crisis it opened could be resolved by negotiation, and was totally opposed to the use of force; Pakistan was less resolutely opposed, because of its membership of the Baghdad Pact. The Commonwealth survived the crisis because its members thought it to be valuable in other ways. Here too, however, the crisis did not change things so much as make clear changes which were already taking place, and were to be carried further in the next few years. Membership of the club grew as more colonial territories became independent; the interests of the members diverged; even Australia was changing, as immigration altered the pattern of its people, and its relations with eastern and south-eastern Asia became more important.

The effects of the crisis on British internal politics were significant but limited. Eden's political life came to an end, and it would be long before those who thought and wrote of it could look back beyond the débâcle to the lengthy and honourable career to which it had put an end; Robert Rhodes James' biography, published thirty years later, devoted a quarter of its pages to an attempt to justify his policy at Suez.[7] The crisis does not appear, however, to have had a deep impact on parties or the electorate. It reunited the Conservative party, by bringing together the 'Suez group', those who accused the government of being too weak in the face of challenges to Britain's imperial position, with most of the other Conservative Members of Parliament; in the general election of 1959 Suez was not a major issue, and the Conservative party retained its majority. One consequence, however, was to be important for the future. The crisis, as Beloff points out, destroyed R. A. Butler's chances of becoming Prime Minister. His

[7] Rhodes James, *Anthony Eden*.

hesitations about the Suez policy revived memories of his support for the policy of appeasement in the 1930s; his skill, as Acting Prime Minister after Eden fell ill, in redeeming something from the disaster did not endear him to the more robust Conservatives. That Butler never became Prime Minister was perhaps to have permanent consequences for the Conservative party and the country.

If the crisis showed Britain that it could not act independently of the United States on major matters in the Middle East, it also drew the United States into the centre of the political process, and made it aware of its final responsibility for Western interests there. It does not appear to have altered the main lines of American policy. As Eisenhower and Dulles had made clear in discussions with Britain during 1955 and 1956, they accepted the independence of the Middle Eastern countries and even a certain degree of neutralism, but wished to incline it in the Western direction, and to hold on to such positions of strength as existed. They desired to limit the influence of Nasser and Egypt over other Arab states, and in some circumstances were prepared to try to overturn him, but at a time and in ways they thought appropriate; they wanted to show that the results which Britain had tried to achieve by force could be achieved in different ways, by a combination of economic aid and covert action. Two events in 1957 were to show this policy in action. The first was the issuing of the 'Eisenhower Doctrine', a pledge of support for Middle Eastern regimes which were threatened by 'subversion' and of economic aid for them. The second was the United States' own exercise in subversion, the attempt to overthrow the Syrian regime by a combination of internal revolt and intervention by neighbours. Neither of these two efforts came to anything, and for the next few years there was a certain ambivalence in United States policy towards the Middle East, and towards Nasser in particular: relations grew warmer and cooler, economic aid was given and withheld, until the next crisis, that of 1967, led to a breakdown in American–Egyptian relations, which was to continue until Sadat's diplomatic revolution.[8]

In France, the consequences went deeper. The Suez adventure marked the end of any serious French attempt to assert an independent power in the Middle East, and virtually destroyed the fabric of French economic and cultural enterprises which had been created in Egypt during the previous century and a half. In Algeria, the failure of the plan not only encouraged the nationalist rebellion, it also showed that the problem could only be resolved in Algeria itself, and with the Algerians; the coalition of 'anti-colonialist' forces which had shown itself at the United Nations during the crisis would be active in support

---

[8] See W. J. Burns, *Economic Aid and American Policy toward Egypt, 1955–1981* (Albany, NY, 1985).

of Algerian independence. What was more important still, the failure showed certain important facts about France's position in the world: its political and military impotence, even in matters where a major national interest was thought to be involved; its alienation from the 'Anglo-Saxon' world, for, when it came to a choice, Britain would always prefer the American to the French alliance; and the weakness of the political structure of the Fourth Republic. As Vaïsse remarks, it was from the débâcle of Suez that a new France, that of de Gaulle, was to emerge, politically strong, with its own independent military power, and with a united Europe built around Franco-German friendship as the basis of its policy: 'Europe will be your revenge', was Adenauer's comment. The France of de Gaulle was even able to recover something of its position in the Middle East, pursuing a new policy, closer to the Arab states, more distant from Israel.

The failure of the Suez expedition did not inaugurate a new Russian policy, but made it possible to pursue one on which it had already embarked, and which an Anglo-French success might have prevented: that of creating relationships with neutralist states which would ensure that Russian interests in the region could not be ignored. The relationships were cautious on both sides, however. Neither Egypt nor Syria, the strong points of Russian influence, had any intention of being drawn too far into the power of the Soviet Union, which for its part did not try to go so far as to provoke a strong American reaction; some other regions were more important for the interests of the Soviet Union than the Middle East.

In Israel, the episode does not appear to have had any direct political repercussions. To Israelis who believed that Nasser had been planning to attack them, the crisis appeared to have removed the danger for a time, and it gave them a sense of security. Ben-Gurion's policy was not rejected by any considerable body of public opinion, and he and his younger collaborators remained at the centre of political life. The crisis did, however, make clear that there was a radical change in the relations between Israel, her Arab neighbours, and the great powers. The Arab–Israeli problem was restated in a new form. It was clear that it was not simply a problem of frontiers or the return of refugees, but a struggle for power between states. The Palestinian Arabs played only a minor part in the crisis; the challenge to Israel came from Egypt under Nasser, and even if he were willing to make peace with Israel, it would be peace on his own terms, which the secret discussions of earlier years had shown to be far apart from Israel's.

From this time, secret Israeli–Egyptian contacts virtually came to an end, and the thought of the Israeli government moved along different lines. Nothing was left of the brief alliance with Britain, except for a vestigial feeling of obligation towards Eden on the part of Ben-Gurion; he would not allow details of the secret agreement to be revealed so long as Eden lived. The French alliance, more solidly based as it was, ceased to exist after de Gaulle came to power. The main necessities of Israeli policy were to build up military power against the strongest potential enemy, Egypt, and to make sure at least of the benevolent neutrality of the United States; the resolution of the Suez crisis gave Israel a breathing space during which to assimilate the lessons of the campaign. The next great crisis, that of 1967, was to show, however, that the lessons which Ben-Gurion had drawn from the Suez episode may have been different from those drawn by his younger followers. His advice to Israel after the 1967 war, to hand back the conquered territories, may have expressed his sense of the limits upon Israeli power even in the most favourable circumstances.

For Egypt, the crisis appeared to end in a kind of triumph. Nasser's gamble had paid off; the intervention of the United States had pulled his enemies back at the brink. The crisis had been, in Egyptian eyes, a kind of declaration of independence. Egypt had shown that it was determined and able to pursue its own interests. The increased revenues derived from the operation of the Suez Canal, the appropriation of foreign private interests which followed the Anglo-French attack, and the provision of support for the High Dam by the Soviet Union all held out the hope of greater freedom of action and greater economic growth. On the other side of the balance, there was cultural loss: the closing of British and French institutions, the dissolution of the cosmopolitan society of Cairo, Alexandria, and the Canal cities, the virtual demise of that Franco-Ottoman civilization which had grown up during the previous century. It may be, however, that this evoked little sorrow in Egypt at the time.

The triumph was Nasser's as well as Egypt's. It gave him a new kind of legitimacy; it brought about that identification of a country with an individual which only a great crisis can create. Later events would tarnish the image, the undercurrent of hostility and scepticism was always there, but the extraordinary demonstrations which took place at the funeral of Nasser in 1970 showed that, in the collective imagination of the Egyptian people, he was no ordinary Pharaoh.

In the Arab world as a whole, the power of Nasser's personality was enhanced, and his view of Arab nationalism endorsed by success. The policy of appealing over the heads of governments to their peoples seemed to have succeeded; in every Arab country there were movements of feeling (whether organized in parties or not) which looked to him and Egypt for leadership. The results were shown in the next few months. In Jordan, a nationalist government headed by Suleiman al-Nabulsi held office for a time. In Syria, the balance of political forces inclined in favour of the populist nationalism of the Ba'th and other parties; in Lebanon, the opposition to President Chamoun, aroused partly by his pro-Western foreign policy, looked for support to the Egyptian Embassy. The surge of Nasserist feeling and opinion reached its height in 1958: Egypt and Syria came together to create the United Arab Republic, an almost unique example of a sovereign state sinking its independence in a larger unity; the revolution in Iraq in July destroyed the regime which had been the firmest Arab opponent of Nasserist nationalism and neutralism, and replaced it by a new government controlled by leaders similar in background to those who ruled Egypt, and with ideas on economic and social reform which seemed much like theirs.

Later events were to show, however, that in some ways the victory was an illusion; Suez created new myths at the same time as it destroyed old ones. Egypt's leadership of the Arab world had its limits; whatever the unity of feeling, there still remained the differing interests of ruling groups and systems of government. Egypt was caught in the tangle of relations between stronger and weaker entities; the weaker would try to use the strength of the larger for their own purposes. The new regime which emerged from the Iraqi revolution soon showed that it had its own interests to pursue, and Baghdad could not be dominated by Cairo; the union between Egypt and Syria collapsed in 1961, for a number of reasons, of which the most fundamental was that Damascus too could not be controlled from Cairo. When negotiations for a new union between Egypt, Syria, and Iraq took place in 1963, Nasser showed he had learnt the lesson, and would not once more go into a closer relationship unless the terms of it were made clear in advance.[9]

The next decade showed the dangers of a position of apparent political strength which was not supported by military strength. Nasser was to become the prisoner of the expectations which he had aroused. The crisis came in 1967 when, under pressure from the Palestinians and the other Arab states to stand up to Israeli challenges, he once more took a gamble: a political act which would arouse Israeli hostility, and from the consequences of which he may have hoped to be saved by American intervention at the last moment. The gamble did not succeed this time; Israel's military effort did not depend upon foreign military support, and the United States was rather more than benevolently neutral towards it.

The Israeli victory of 1967 changed the terms of the Israeli–Arab

---

[9] See M. Kerr, *The Arab Cold War* (London, 1965), pp. 58–101.

confrontation once again, but it did so in more than one way. As Khalidi shows, the Palestinian Arabs too had drawn their conclusions from the events of 1956. They had found themselves caught in the kind of situation where a weaker group looks to a stronger one to solve its problems, but finds its interests subordinate to those of the stronger. A new generation of Palestinians was growing up in exile. Some looked to Nasser to defend their cause; nowhere was Nasserist sentiment stronger than among the Palestinians. Others understood, however, that in a struggle for power in the Middle East, they would be no more than pawns to be used, unless they were able to generate a strength of their own and preserve a certain freedom of action. This path led to the formation of Fatah and other Palestinian movements, and their taking over the Palestinian Liberation Organization after the defeat of 1967. In the next phase, the Palestinians were to be near the centre of the action.

Select Bibliography

HOWARD J. DOOLEY

AMBROSE, STEPHEN, *Eisenhower the President*, ii (New York, 1984).

ARMITAGE, AIR MARSHAL SIR M. J., and MASON, AIR COMMODORE R. A., *Air Power in the Nuclear Age 1945–1984: Theory and Practice* (London, 1985).

ARONSON, GEOFFREY, *From Side Show to Center Stage: U.S. Policy toward Egypt, 1946–1956* (Boulder, 1986).

'AWDA, MUHAMMAD, *et. al.* (eds.), *Qissat al-Sawfiyat wa Misr* (The Story of the Soviets and Egypt) (Beirut, 1975).

AZEAU, HENRI, *Le Piège de Suez (5 novembre 1956)* (Paris, 1964).

BAEYENS, JACQUES, *Un Coup d'épée dans l'eau du canal: La seconde campagne d'égypte* (Paris, 1976).

AL-BAGHDADI, 'ABD AL-LATIF, *Mudhakkirat*, ii (Memoirs) (Cairo, 1977).

BARJOT, ADM. PIERRE, 'Réflexions sur les opérations de Suez 1956', *Revue de défense nationale*, 22 (1966), 1911–24.

BAR-ON, MORDECHAI, 'Ha'iska Hatsekhit-Mitsrit: She'la shel tiarukh' (The Czech-Egyptian Arms Deal: Problems and Periodization), *Ma'arakhot*, 306–307 (Dec. 1986–Jan. 1987).

—— 'Ma'arekhet Sinai 1956: Matarot ve Tsipiot' (The Sinai Campaign: Aims and Expectations), *Zemanim*, 24 (Winter 1987).

BAR-ZOHAR, MICHEL, *Suez: Ultra-Secret* (Paris, 1964).

—— *Ben-Gurion: The Armed Prophet* (Englewood Cliffs, 1968).

—— *Ben-Gurion: A Biography* (New York, 1977).

BEAUFRE, GEN. ANDRÉ, *The Suez Expedition, 1956* (New York, 1969).

BEN-GURION, DAVID, *Ma'arekhet Sinai* (The Sinai Campaign) (Tel Aviv, 1959).

—— *Israel: A Personal History* (New York, 1971).

—— *My Talks with Arab Leaders* (New York, 1973).

BOHLEN, CHARLES, *Witness to History* (New York, 1973).

BOWIE, ROBERT, *Suez 1956: International Crisis and the Role of Law* (London, 1974).

BRADDON, RUSSELL, *Suez: Splitting of a Nation* (London, 1973).

BRECHER, MICHAEL, *India and World Politics: Krishna Menon's View of the World* (London, 1968).

—— *The Foreign Policy System of Israel: Setting, Images, Process* (New Haven, 1972).

—— *Decisions in Israel's Foreign Policy* (New Haven, 1975).

BRIGGS, LORD (ASA), *Governing the BBC* (London, 1979).

BROMBERGER, MERRY and SERGE, *Les Secrets de l'expédition d'égypte* (Paris, 1957); trans. *Secrets of Suez* (London, 1957).

BULL, HEDLEY, 'The Revolt Against the West', in Hedley Bull and Adam Watson (eds.), *The Expansion of International Society* (Oxford, 1984).

BURKE, S. M., *Pakistan's Foreign Policy: An Historical Analysis* (London, 1973).

BURNS, GEN. E. L. M., *Between Arab and Israeli* (London, 1962).

BURNS, WILLIAM J., *Economic Aid and American Policy toward Egypt, 1955–1981* (Albany, 1985).

CALVOCORESSI, PETER, *Suez: Ten Years After* (New York, 1967).

CARLTON, DAVID, *Anthony Eden: A Biography* (London, 1981).

—— *Britain and the Suez Crisis* (Oxford, 1988).

CAROZ, YAACOV, *The Arab Secret Service* (London, 1978).

CHALLE, GEN. MAURICE, *Notre révolte* (Paris, 1968).

CHAMOUN, CAMILLE, *Crise au Moyen-Orient* (Paris, 1963).

CHAUVEL, JEAN, *Commentaire*, iii (Paris, 1973).

CHILDERS, ERSKINE, *The Road to Suez: A Study in Western–Arab Relations* (London, 1962).

CLARK, WILLIAM, *From Three Worlds* (London, 1986).

COOPER, CHESTER L., *The Lion's Last Roar: Suez, 1956* (New York, 1978).

COPELAND, MILES, *The Game of Nations* (London, 1969).

CROSBIE, SYLVIA K., *A Tacit Alliance: France and Israel from Suez to the Six Day War* (Princeton, 1974).

DAYAN, MOSHE, *Diary of the Sinai Campaign, 1956* (New York, 1966).

—— *Story of My Life: An Autobiography* (New York, 1976).

DIVINE, ROBERT, *Eisenhower and the Cold War* (Oxford, 1981).

DOOLEY, HOWARD, 'The Suez Crisis, 1956: A Case Study in Contemporary History', D.Phil. thesis (Notre Dame, 1976).

'Dossier: La Crise de Suez', *L'histoire*, 38 (Oct. 1981), 10–43.

'Dossier: L'Affaire de Suez trente ans après', *Revue Historique des Armées*, 165 (Dec. 1986), 1–58.

DUPUY, TREVOR, N., *Elusive Victory: The Arab–Israeli Wars, 1947–1974* (New York, 1978).

EAYRS, JAMES (ed.), *The Commonwealth and Suez: A Documentary Survey* (London, 1964).

EBAN, ABBA, *An Autobiography* (New York, 1977).

EDEN, ANTHONY, *Full Circle: The Memoirs of Anthony Eden* (London, 1960).

EISENHOWER, DWIGHT D., *The White House Years*, i: *Mandate for Change, 1953–1956* (New York, 1963).

—— *The White House Years*, ii: *Waging Peace, 1956–1961* (Garden City, NY, 1965).

ÉLY, GEN. PAUL, *Mémoires*, ii: *Suez . . . le 13 mai* (Paris, 1969).

ENGLER, ROBERT, *The Politics of Oil* (New York, 1961).

EPSTEIN, LEON D., *British Politics in the Suez Crisis* (London and Urbana, 1964).

EVELAND, WILBUR CRANE, *Ropes of Sand: America's Failure in the Middle East* (New York and London, 1980).

EVRON, YOSEF, *Beyom Sagrir: Su'ets Me'ahorei Haklayim* (In Stormy Days: Suez Behind the Scenes) (Tel Aviv, 1968).

—— *Su'ets 1956: Bemabat Hadash* (Suez 1956: A New View) (Tel Aviv, 1986).

FAHMY-ABDOU, ANTOUN, *La Nazionalizzazione Della Società Del Canale Di Suez* (Cairo, 1962).

FARNIE, DOUGLAS, *East and West of Suez: The Suez Canal in History, 1854–1956* (Oxford, 1969).

FAWZI, MAHMOUD, *Suez 1956: An Egyptian Perspective* (London, 1986).

FERRO, MARC, *Suez: Naissance d'un Tiers-Monde* (Brussels, 1982).

FINER, HERMAN, *Dulles Over Suez: The Theory and Practice of his Diplomacy* (Chicago, 1964).

FITZSIMONS, MATTHEW, *Empire by Treaty: Britain and the Middle East in the Twentieth Century* (Notre Dame, 1964).

FULLICK, ROY, and POWELL, GEOFFREY, *Suez: The Double War* (London, 1980).

GARNER, JOE, *The Commonwealth Office, 1925–1968* (London, 1978).

GAUJAC, PAUL, *Suez 1956* (Paris, 1986).

GEORGES-PICOT, JACQUES, *The Real Suez Crisis* (New York, 1975).

GILBERT, MARTIN, *Winston S. Churchill*, viii: *Never Despair, 1945–1965* (London, 1988).

GOPAL, SARVEPALLI, *Jawaharlal Nehru: A Biography*, ii: *1947–1956* (London, 1979).

GROVE, ERIC, *Vanguard to Trident: British Naval Policy since World War II* (London, 1987).

HEIKAL (Haikal), MOHAMED H., *Nasser: The Cairo Documents* (London, 1972).

—— *The Sphinx and the Commissar: The Rise and Fall of Soviet Influence in the Middle East* (New York, 1978).

—— *Milaffat al-Suways* (The Suez Files) (Cairo, 1986).

—— *Cutting the Lion's Tail: Suez through Egyptian Eyes* (London, 1986).

HENRIQUES, ROBERT, *One Hundred Hours to Suez* (New York and London, 1957).

HERZOG, CHAIM, *The Arab–Israeli Wars* (New York, 1982).

HOOPES, TOWNSEND, *The Devil and John Foster Dulles* (Boston, 1973).

HORNE, ALISTAIR, *Macmillan, 1894–1956: vol. i of the Official Biography* (London, 1988).

HOWARD, ANTHONY, *RAB: The Life of R. A. Butler* (London, 1987).

HUDSON, W. J., *Casey* (Melbourne, 1986).

HUREWITZ, J. C., *The Middle East and North Africa in World Politics*, vols. i and ii (New Haven, 1975 and 1979).

—— *Middle East Politics: The Military Dimension* (New York, 1969; Boulder, 1982).

HUWAIDI (HEWEDY), AMIN, *Hurub 'Abd al-Nasir* (Nasser's Wars) (Beirut, 1977).

ISMA'IL, MUHAMMAD HAFIZ, *Aman Misr al-Qawmi fi 'Asr al-Tahaddiyat* (Egypt's National Security in a Time of Challenges) (Cairo, 1987).

JOHNSON, PAUL, *The Suez War* (London, 1957).

KEIGHTLEY, GEN. CHARLES, 'Operations in Egypt—November to December 1956', *Supplement to London Gazette*, 10 Sept. 1957.

KYLE, KEITH, *The Suez Conflict: Thirty Years After* (London, forthcoming).

LAMB, RICHARD, *The Failure of the Eden Government* (London, 1987).

LLOYD, SELWYN, *Suez 1956: A Personal Account* (London, 1978).

LOUIS, WM. ROGER, *The British Empire in the Middle East, 1945–1951* (Oxford, 1984).

—— and Bull, Hedley (eds.), *The Special Relationship: Anglo-American Relations since 1945* (Oxford, 1986).

LOVE, KENNETT, *Suez: The Twice-Fought War* (New York, 1969).

LUTTWAK, EDWARD, and HOROWITZ, DAN, *The Israeli Army* (London, 1975).

McDERMOTT, GEOFFREY, *The Eden Legacy and the Decline of British Diplomacy* (London, 1969).

McDONALD, IVERACH, *The History of The Times*, v: *Struggles in War and Peace 1939–1966* (London, 1984).

MACKSEY, KENNETH, *The Tanks: The History of the Royal Tank Regiment 1945–1975* (London, 1979).

MACMILLAN, HAROLD, *Riding the Storm, 1956–1959* (London, 1971).

MARSHALL, GEN. S. L. A., *Sinai Victory* (New York, 1959; 2nd edn., 1967).

MASSU, GEN. JACQUES, and LE MIRE, HENRI, *Vérité sur Suez 1956* (Paris, 1978).

MÉNAGER, BERNARD, *et al.*, *Guy Mollet, un camarade en république* (Lille, 1987).

MENZIES, ROBERT, *Afternoon Light* (London, 1967).

MONROE, ELIZABETH, *Britain's Moment in the Middle East* (London, 1963).

MURPHY, ROBERT, *Diplomat Among Warriors* (New York, 1964).

NEFF, DONALD, *Warriors at Suez: Eisenhower Takes America into the Middle East* (New York, 1981).

NUTTING, ANTHONY, *No End of a Lesson: The Story of Suez* (London, 1967).

—— *Nasser* (New York, 1972).

PARMET, HERBERT S., *Eisenhower and the American Crusades* (New York, 1972).

PARTNER, PETER, *Arab Voices: The BBC Arabic Service, 1938–1988* (London, 1988).

PEARSON, LESTER B., *Mike*, vol. ii: *1948–57* (Toronto, 1973).

PERES, SHIMON, *Hashalav Haba* (The Next Stage) (Tel Aviv, 1965).

—— *David's Sling: The Arming of Israel* (London, 1970).

PINEAU, CHRISTIAN, *1956: Suez* (Paris, 1976).

RAʿANAN, URI, *The U.S.S.R. Arms the Third World: Case Studies in Soviet Foreign Policy* (Cambridge, Mass., 1969).

REID, ESCOTT, *Hungary and Suez, 1956: A View from New Delhi* (Oakville, Ont., 1986).

RHODES JAMES, ROBERT, *Anthony Eden: A Biography* (London, 1986).

ROBERTSON, TERENCE, *Crisis: The Inside Story of the Suez Conspiracy* (New York, 1964).

ROʾI, YAACOV (ed.), *From Encroachment to Involvement: A Documentary Study of Soviet Policy in the Middle East* (New York, 1974).

ROKACH, LIVIA, *Israel's Sacred Terrorism* (Belmont, Mass., 1986).

SAʿID, AMIN, *al-ʿUdwan, 29 October 1956–1 November 1958* (The Aggression) (Cairo, 1959).

SEALE, PATRICK, *The Struggle for Syria: A Study in Post-War Arab Politics, 1945–1958* (London, 1965).

SHARETT, MOSHE, *Yoman Ishi* (Personal Diary) (Tel Aviv, 1978).

SHLAIM, AVI, 'Conflicting Approaches to Israel's Relations with the Arabs: Ben-Gurion and Sharett, 1953–1956', *The Middle East Journal*, 37 (1983), 180–201.

SHUCKBURGH, EVELYN, *Descent to Suez: Diaries, 1951–56* (London, 1986).

SMOLANSKY, OLES, *The Soviet Union and the Arab East under Khrushchev* (Lewisburg, Pa., 1974).

SPIEGEL, STEVEN, *The Other Arab–Israeli Conflict: Making America's Middle East Policy, from Truman to Reagan* (Chicago, 1985).

STOCK, ERNEST, *Israel on the Road to Sinai, 1949–1956* (Ithaca, NY, 1967).

STOCKWELL, GEN. HUGH., 'Suez from the Inside', *Sunday Telegraph* (London), 30 Oct., 6 and 13 Nov. 1966.

'Suez, 1956: Air Aspects', *R.A.F. Historical Society Proceedings*, 3 (Jan. 1988).

TAWIL, MUHAMMAD, *Laʿbat al-Umam wa-ʿAbd al-Nasir* (The Game of Nations and Abdel Nasser) (Cairo, 1986).

TEHAN, LT. COL. BEN TZION, 'Maʿarekhet Sinai', *Maʿarakhot*, 103 (May 1958).

TEVETH, SHABTAI, *Moshe Dayan* (London, 1972).

THOMAS, ABEL, *Comment Israël fut sauvé: Les Secrets de l'expédition de Suez* (Paris, 1978).

THOMAS, HUGH, *The Suez Affair* (London, 1967; 2nd edn. rev., 1970).

TOURNOUX, JEAN-RAYMOND, *Secrets d'état* (Paris, 1960).

TREVELYAN, HUMPHREY, *The Middle East in Revolution* (London and Boston, 1970).

TROEN, ILAN, and SHEMESH, MOSHE, *The Suez–Sinai Crisis: Retrospective and Reappraisal* (New York, 1990).

TSUR, JACOB, *Prélude à Suez: journal d'une ambassade, 1953–1956* (Paris, 1968).

URQUHART, BRIAN, *Hammarskjöld* (New York, 1973).

—— *A Life in Peace and War* (London, 1987).

UTLEY, T. E., *Not Guilty (The Conservative Reply)* (London, 1957).

WATT, DONALD CAMERON, *Documents on the Suez Crisis* (London, 1957).

YOUNES, MAHMOUD, 'La Nationalisation du Canal de Suez', *Le Scribe* (Cairo) (May 1963), 68–75.

Addendum, August 1990

'A Canal Too Far', BBC Radio 3, 31 January 1987.

BIALER, URI, *Between East and West: Israel's Foreign Policy Orientation, 1948–1956* (Cambridge, 1990).

BONIN, HUBERT, *Suez: du canal à la finance* (Paris, 1987).

CLOAKE, JOHN, *Templer: Tiger of Malaya, The Life of Field Marshall Sir Gerald Templer* (London, 1985).

COHEN, STUART, 'A Still Stranger Aspect of Suez: British Operational Plans to Attack Israel', *International History Review*, 10 (May 1988), 261–81.

DANN, URIEL, *King Hussein and the Challenge of Arab Radicalism: Jordan, 1955–1967* (Oxford, 1989).

DOOLEY, HOWARD, 'Great Britain's "Last Battle" in the Middle East: Notes on Cabinet Planning during the Suez Crisis of 1956', *International History Review*, 11 (Aug. 1989), 486–517.

FOOT, MICHAEL, and JONES, MERVYN, *Guilty Men, 1957: Suez and Cyprus* (London, 1957).

GOLAN, MATTI, *The Road to Peace: A Biography of Shimon Peres* (New York, 1989).

GORST, ANTHONY, 'Suez 1956: A Consumer's Guide to Papers at the Public Record Office', *Contemporary Record*, 1 (Spring 1987), 9–11.

—— and LUCAS, W. SCOTT, 'The Other Collusion: Operation Straggle and Anglo-American Intervention Against Syria, 1955–1956'. *Intelligence and National Security*, 4 (July 1989), 576–95.

JOHNSON, PAUL, *The Suez War* (London, 1957).

HAKIM, TAWFIQ AL-, *'Awdat al-Wa'i: The Return of Consciousness* (Beirut, 1984; London, 1985).

HENNESSY, PETER, and LAITY, MARK, 'Suez: What the Papers Say', *Contemporary Record*, 1 (Spring 1987), 2–8.

HORNE, ALISTAIR, *Macmillan, 1957–1986: Vol. II of the Official Biography* (London, 1989).

HUDSON, W. J., *Blind Loyalty; Australia and the Suez Crisis, 1956* (Melbourne, 1989).

IMMERMAN, RICHARD (ed.), *John Foster Dulles and the Diplomacy of the Cold War: A Centennial Reappraisal* (Princeton, 1989).

LACOUTURE, JEAN, *Nasser: A Biography* (New York, 1973).

LAPPING, BRIAN, *End of Empire* (New York, 1985).

LITTLE, DOUGLAS, 'Cold War and Covert Action: The United States and Syria, 1945–1958', *Middle East Journal*, 44 (Winter 1990), 51–75.

LODGE, HENRY CABOT, *As It Was: An Inside View of Politics and Power in the 1950's and 1960's* (New York, 1976).

LOGAN, SIR DONALD, 'Collusion at Suez', *Financial Times* (London), 8 Nov. 1986.

LUCAS, W. SCOTT, 'Redefining the Suez "Collusion"', *Middle Eastern Studies*, 26 (Jan. 1990), 88–112.

Ministère des Affaires Etrangères, *Documents diplomatiques français, I: 1 janvier–30 juin 1956* (Paris, 1988).

——, *Documents diplomatiques français, II: 1 juillet–23 octobre 1956* (Paris, 1989).

——, *Documents diplomatiques français, III: 24 octobre–31 decembre 1956* (Paris, 1990).

NASSER, GAMAL ABDEL, 'Nasser Reveals Story of Operations and Secrets Behind the Sinai Attack', *Egyptian Gazette* (Cairo), 6 Dec. 1956.

——, 'My Revolutionary Life: President Nasser's Own Story', *Sunday Times* (London), 17, 24 June, 1 July 1962.

NUTTING, ANTHONY, *Nasser* (New York, 1972).

OREN, MICHAEL, 'Canada, the Great Powers, and the Middle East Arms Race, 1950–1956', *International History Review*, 12 (May 1990), 280–300.

——, 'A Winter of Discontent: Britain's Crisis in Jordan, December 1955–March 1956', *International Journal of Middle East Studies*, 22 (May 1990), 171–84.

ROOSEVELT, ARCHIE, *For Lust of Knowing: Memoirs of an Intelligence Officer* (Boston, 1989).

'The Secrets of Suez', BBC Television, 12 Nov. 1986.

SCHIFF, ZE'EV, *A History of the Israeli Army* (New York, 1985).

STEPHENS, ROBERT, *Nasser: A Political Biography* (London, 1971).

THORPE, D. R., *Selwyn Lloyd* (London, 1989).

US Department of State, *Foreign Relations of the United States, 1955–1957*, vol. xiv, *Arab-Israeli Dispute, 1955* (Washington, DC, 1989).

——, *Foreign Relations of the United States, 1955–1957*, vol. xv, *The Arab-Israeli Dispute, January 1–July 26, 1956* (Washington, DC, 1989).

——, *Foreign Relations of the United States, 1955–1957*, vol. xvi, *Suez Crisis, July 26–December 31, 1956* (Washington, DC, 1990).

——, *Foreign Relations of the United States, 1955–1957*, vol. xvii, *Arab-Israeli Dispute, 1957* (Washington, DC, 1990).

ZAMETICA, JOHN, 'Suez: The Secret Plan', *Spectator* (17 Jan. 1987,) 11–13.

ZIEGLER, PHILIP, *Mountbatten: The Official Biography* (London, 1985).

Index

The British Empire in the Middle East
Arab Nationalism, The United States, and Postwar Imperialism
Wm. Roger Louis
Paperback

'Based on a staggering amount of recently released official and private papers . . . this magnificent and comprehensive book . . . unravels with compelling detail the way in which the British "official mind" engaged in (an) imperial and strategic juggling act, as it sought to preserve national interests in an era of unprecedented global change.'

New York Times Book Review

'may be read with pleasure and profit by students of the Middle East, of British foreign policy and of the imperial saga.'

Times Literary Supplement

Imperialism at Bay
The United States and the Decolonization of the British Empire, 1941–1945
Wm. Roger Louis
Paperback

'Louis's book, as full of wit and insight as it is of information, will instruct every modern historian.' *American Historical Review*

'In putting together this very complicated international jigsaw he always seems able to find the vital bits . . . Here is one historical study that will not need to be done again.' *English Historical Review*